Why WileyPLUS for Computer Science

WileyPLUS for Computer Science is a dynamic online environment that motivates students to spend more time practicing the problems and explore the material they need to master in order to succeed.

"I used the homework problems to practice before quizzes and tests. I re-did the problems on my own and then checked WileyPLUS to compare answers."

— Student Alexandra Leifer, Ithaca College

+ The integrated, online text offers students a low-cost alternative to the printed text, enhanced with direct links to specific portions of the text, plus interactive animations and videos to help students visualize concepts.

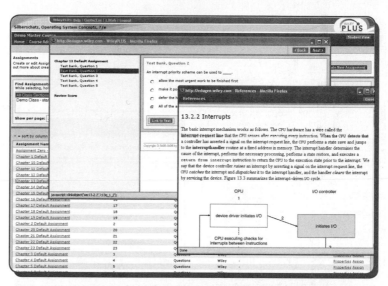

+ Select WileyPLUS courses include LabRat, the programming assignment tool allows you to choose from hundreds of programming exercises to automate the process of assigning, completing, compiling, testing, submitting, and evaluating programming assignments. When students spend more time practicing, they come to class better prepared.

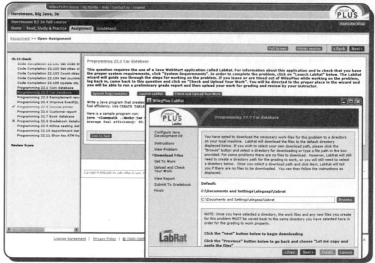

Try WileyPLUS with LabRat:
www.wileyplus.com/tours

See and try WileyPLUS *in action!*
Details and Demo: www.wileyplus.com

www.wileyplus.com

WileyPLUS combines robust course management tools with the complete online text and all of the interactive teaching & learning resources you and your students need in one easy-to-use system.

"Overall the WileyPLUS package made the material more interesting than if it was just a book with no additional material other than what you need to know."
– Edin Alic, North Dakota State University

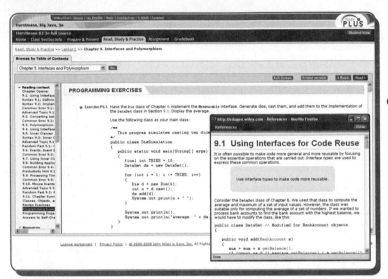

● *Students easily access source code for example problems, as well as self-study materials and all the exercises and readings you assign.*

● *All instructional materials, including PowerPoints, illustrations and visual tools, source code, exercises, solutions and gradebook organized in one easy-to-use system.*

"WileyPLUS made it a lot easier to study. I got an A!"
– Student Jeremiah Ellis Mattson, North Dakota State University

www.wileyplus.com

Big C++

SECOND EDITION

Cay Horstmann
SAN JOSE STATE UNIVERSITY

Timothy A. Budd
OREGON STATE UNIVERSITY

WILEY

John Wiley & Sons, Inc.

EXECUTIVE PUBLISHER:	Don Fowley
ASSOCIATE PUBLISHER:	Dan Sayre
SENIOR EDITORIAL ASSISTANT:	Carolyn Weisman
MEDIA EDITOR:	Lauren Sapira
SENIOR PRODUCTION EDITOR:	Ken Santor
SENIOR DESIGNER:	Madelyn Lesure
TEXT DESIGNER:	Nancy Field
COVER DESIGNER:	Howard Grossman
COVER ILLUSTRATOR:	Susan Cyr
PHOTO EDITOR:	Lisa Gee
PRODUCTION MANAGEMENT:	Cindy Johnson

This book was set in 10.5/12 Stempel Garamond by Publishing Services and printed and bound by R.R. Donnelley – Crawfordsville. The cover was printed by R.R. Donnelley.

This book is printed on acid-free paper ∞

ISBN 978-0-470-38328-5

Printed in the United States of America

10 9 8 7 6 5

Preface

This book provides a traditional introduction to computer science, focusing on program development and effective use of the C++ programming language. It is suitable for motivated beginners as well as students with prior programming experience. The book can be used in a variety of settings, such as an introductory computer science course, a two-semester course sequence that covers data structures and object-oriented design, or an advanced course on C++ and its applications.

When writing the book, we were guided by the following principles:

- **Teach computer science principles and not just C++.** We use the C++ programming language as a vehicle for introducing computer science concepts, and in this "Big" book, we cover a large subset of the C++ language. However, we do not aim to cover all esoteric aspects of C++. This book focuses on the modern features of the C++ standard, such as the string class and the STL containers. By minimizing the use of error-prone and confusing constructs, your students will learn more computer science and become more productive programmers.

- **Use a spiral approach to teach complex topics.** We do not think it is wise to overwhelm students when we introduce new topics. Generally, we start with the essential facts that illustrate a concept, then cover technical details at a later time. Here is an example. For efficiency's sake, large object parameters should be passed by constant reference, not by value. But that consideration obscures more fundamental issues. For that reason, we don't use constant references when we first introduce classes. In the next turn of the spiral, students are comfortable with classes and reference parameters, and a discussion of efficiency is appropriate. We believe this spiral approach is essential when teaching a language as complex as C++.

- **Introduce C++ as an object-oriented language.** Objects are introduced in two stages. From Chapter 2 on, students learn to *use* objects—in particular, strings, streams, instances of the simple Time and Employee classes, and graphical shapes. Students become comfortable with creating objects and calling member functions as the book continues along a traditional path, discussing and providing practice with control structures and functional decomposition. In Chapter 5, students learn how to implement classes and member functions. From then on, objects and classes are used as the natural building blocks of computer programs.

- **Keep the order flexible.** The book is highly modular. Do you prefer to cover arrays before classes? Simply switch the chapters. Do you want to cover streams and files earlier? This is not a problem. We supply a graphics library, but it is entirely optional. We have found that students enjoy programming exercises in which numbers and visual information reinforce each other. But you may not want to spend class time on it. Students can read the material on their own, or you can skip it altogether. (See Figure 1 on page viii for the chapter dependencies.)

- **Offer choices for advanced and applied topics.** This "Big" book contains so much material that it would be difficult to cover every chapter, even in an ambitious two-semester course. The core material (Part A in Figure 1) contains what is typically covered in a one-semester introductory course: control structures, functions, arrays, classes, inheritance, and stream I/O. The advanced material is grouped into four parts to make it easy to choose a focus that fits your course.

New in This Edition

Streamlined Core Chapters

This edition has been reorganized to make it more suitable for a course that aims to cover advanced C++ features, data structures, or object-oriented design. The introductory material has been condensed, and the material on control structures has been consolidated into a single chapter.

Modular Design

The advanced chapters are now grouped into four distinct parts:

- Data structures and algorithms
- Advanced C++ and the STL
- Object-oriented design
- Applications

Part B covers an introduction to data structures and algorithms, suitable for a second-semester programming course. Part C focuses on advanced C++ and covers the STL in detail. Part D covers object-oriented design, UML, and design patterns. Finally, Part E (which is available on the Web) contains applied material on graphical user interface programming, databases, and XML that you may find useful as a capstone. Except as shown in Figure 1, the parts are independent of each other.

➕ The web-only chapters are part of the WileyPLUS eBook and may also be downloaded from the book's web site at www.wiley.com/college/horstmann. If you are interested in adopting a custom print edition that incorporates portions of the online material, please contact your local Wiley representative.

Contemporary C++

This book continues to focus on the modern features of the C++ standard, such as the string class and the STL containers. This edition prepares students for the future with a new Chapter 21 on the features of the upcoming C++0x standard (included in Part C).

A large number of extended examples and 15 case studies show how C++ features are used in complete and useful programs.

Optional Graphics Programming

The graphics programming coverage is provided because many students enjoy writing programs that create drawings, and because graphical shapes are splendid examples of objects. However, this edition makes it easier to skip this focus if desired.

Chapter 2 introduces the simple graphics library provided with this book as another type of object students may program with. Thereafter, exercises that make use of the graphics library are clearly identified at chapter end. An optional Chapter 25 covers graphical user interfaces and the wxWidgets library.

WileyPLUS

The first two pages of this book describe an innovative online tool for teachers and students: WileyPLUS. WileyPLUS can be adopted with the book, or as an alternative to the printed text for about half the cost of print. WileyPLUS integrates all of the instructor and student web resources into an online version of this text. For more information and a demo, please visit the web site listed on pages i–ii, or talk to your Wiley representative. (To locate your local representative, visit www.wiley.com/college and click on "Who's My Rep".)

Student and Instructor Resources in WileyPLUS

This edition offers enhanced electronic supplements. In particular, the test bank has been completely revised to provide a significant number of multiple-choice questions that are suitable for self-check assignments and quizzes.

The following resources for students and instructors can be found in the Wiley-PLUS course for this book. Web chapters and source code are also available on the Web at www.wiley.com/college/horstmann.

- Solutions to all exercises (for instructors only)
- A test bank (for instructors only)
- A laboratory manual
- Lecture slides that summarize each chapter and include code listings and figures
- Source code for all examples in the book, the Employee and Time classes, and the optional graphics library
- The programming style guide (Appendix A) in modifiable electronic form
- Help with common compilers, the graphics library, and wxWidgets.

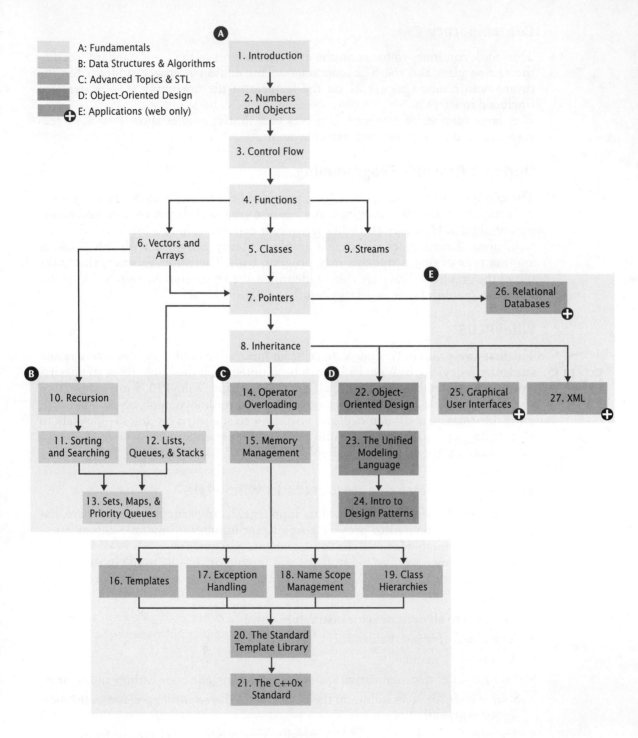

Figure 1   Chapter Dependencies

Pedagogical Structure

This edition builds on the pedagogical elements in the last edition and offers additional aids for the reader. Each chapter begins with the customary overview of chapter objectives and motivational introduction. A listing of the chapter contents then provides a quick reference to the special features in the chapter.

> Margin notes mark and reinforce new concepts and are summarized at chapter end.

Throughout each chapter, margin notes show where new concepts are introduced and provide an outline of key ideas. These notes are summarized at the end of the chapter as a chapter review.

The program listings are carefully designed for easy reading. Comments are typeset in a separate font that is easier to read than the monospaced "computer" font. Functions are set off by a subtle outline. Keywords, strings, and numbers are "color-coded" consistently as they would be in a development environment. (The code for all program listings in the book (plus any additional files needed for each example) is available in the WileyPLUS course for the book.)

Special Features

Throughout the chapters, special features set off topics for added flexibility and easy reference. Syntax boxes highlight new syntactical constructs and their purpose. An alphabetical list of these constructs can be found on page xxii.

Five additional features, entitled "Common Error", "Productivity Hint", "Quality Tip", "Advanced Topic", and "Random Fact", are identified with the icons below and set off so they don't interrupt the flow of the main material. Some of these are quite short; others extend over a page. Each topic is given the space that is needed for a full and convincing explanation—instead of being forced into a one-paragraph "tip". You can use the tables on pages xxiv–xxxi to see the features in each chapter and the page numbers where they can be found.

Here is a list of the special features and their icons.

- **Common Errors** describe the kinds of errors that students often make, with an explanation of why the errors occur, and what to do about them. Most students quickly discover the Common Error sections and read them on their own.

- **Quality Tips** explain good programming practices. Since most of them require an initial investment of effort, these notes carefully motivate the reason behind the advice and explain why the effort will be repaid later.

- **Productivity Hints** teach students how to use their tools more effectively, familiarizing them with tricks of the trade such as keyboard shortcuts, global search and replace, or automation of common tasks with scripts.

- **Advanced Topics** cover nonessential or more difficult material. Some of these topics introduce alternative syntactical constructions that are not necessarily technically advanced. In many cases, the book uses one particular language construct but explains alternatives as Advanced Topics. Instructors and students should feel free to use those constructs in their own programs if they prefer them. It has, however, been our experience that many students are grateful for the "keep it simple" approach, because it greatly reduces the number of gratuitous decisions they have to make.

- **Random Facts** provide historical and social information on computing, as required to fulfill the "historical and social context" requirements of the ACM curriculum guidelines, as well as capsule reviews of advanced computer science topics.

Appendices

- Appendix A contains a style guide for use with this book. We have found it highly beneficial to require a consistent style for all assignments. We realize that our style may be different from yours. If you have strong feelings about a particular issue, or if this style guide conflicts with local customs, feel free to modify it. The style guide is available in electronic form for this purpose.
- Appendices B and C contain summaries of the C++ keywords and operators.
- Appendix D lists character escape sequences and ASCII character code values.
- Appendix E documents all of the library functions and classes used in this book.
- Appendices F and G contain a discussion of binary and hexadecimal numbers, and the C++ bit and shift operations.
- Appendix H contains a summary of the UML features that are used in this book.
- Appendix I compares C++ and Java. This appendix should be helpful to students with a prior background in Java.

Acknowledgments

Many thanks to Dan Sayre, Lauren Sapira, Lisa Gee, and Carolyn Weisman at John Wiley & Sons, and to the team at Publishing Services for their hard work and support for this book project. An especially deep acknowledgment and thanks to Cindy Johnson, who, through enormous patience and attention to detail, made this book a reality.

Several individuals assisted in the creation of the online resources for this edition. We would like to thank Kurt Schmidt, *Drexel University*, and Diya Biswas, Maria Kolakowska, and John O'Meara for a great set of lecture slides. We are grateful to Fred Annexstein, *University of Cincinnati*, Steven Kollmansberger, *South Puget Sound Community College*, and Gwen Walton, *Florida Southern College*, for their contributions to the solutions. And thank you to John Russo, *Wentworth Institute of Technology*, for working with us to prepare the labs that accompany the book.

We are very grateful to the many individuals who reviewed this and the prior edition of the book, made many valuable suggestions, and brought an embarrassingly large number of errors and omissions to our attention. They include:

Charles Allison, *Utah Valley State College*

Vladimir Akis, *California State University, Los Angeles*

Richard Borie, *University of Alabama, Tuscaloosa*

Ramzi Bualuan, *Notre Dame University*

Drew Coles, *Boston University*

Roger DeBry, *Utah Valley State College*

Joseph DeLibero, *Arizona State University*

Martin S. Dulberg, *North Carolina State University*

Jeremy Frens, *Calvin College*

Timothy Henry, *University of Rhode Island*

Robert Jarman, *Augusta State University*

Jerzy Jaromczyk, *University of Kentucky*

Debbie Kaneko, *Old Dominion University*

Vitit Kantabutra, *Idaho State University*

Stan Lippman, *Microsoft Corporation*

Brian Malloy, *Clemson University*

Stephen Murrell, *University of Miami*

Jeffery Popyack, *Drexel University*

John Russo, *Wentworth Institute of Technology*

Kurt Schmidt, *Drexel University*

William Shay, *University of Wisconsin, Green Bay*

Joseph R. Shinnerl, *University of California, Los Angeles*

Deborah Silver, *Rutgers University*

John Sterling, *Polytechnic University*

Gwen Walton, *Florida Southern College*

Joel Weinstein, *New England University*

Lillian Witzke, *Milwaukee School of Engineering*

Our gratitude also to those who took time to tell us about their C++ course and whose advice shaped this new edition:

Fred Annexstein, *University of Cincinnati*

Noah D. Barnette, *Virginia Tech*

Stefano Basagni, *Northeastern University*

Peter Breznay, *University of Wisconsin, Green Bay*
Subramaniam Dharmarajan, *Arizona State University*
Stephen Gilbert, *Orange Coast College*
Barbara Guillott, *Louisiana State University*
Mir Behrad Khamesee, *University of Waterloo*
Sung-Sik Kwon, *North Carolina Central University*
W. James MacLean, *University of Toronto*
Ethan V. Munson, *University of Wisconsin, Milwaukee*
Kurt Schmidt, *Drexel University*
Michele A. Starkey, *Mount Saint Mary College*
William Stockwell, *University of Central Oklahoma*
Jonathan Tolstedt, *North Dakota State University*
David P. Voorhees, *Le Moyne College*
Salih Yurttas, *Texas A&M University*

Contents

Alphabetical List of Syntax Boxes

Chapter	Common Errors	Quality Tips
1 Introduction	Omitting Semicolons 19 Misspelling Words 21	

2 Numbers and Objects	Buffered Input 42
	Failed Input 44
	Roundoff Errors 49
	Integer Division 58
	Unbalanced Parentheses 59
	Forgetting Header Files 60
	Trying to Call a Member Function
	  Without an Object 73
		Initialize Variables When You
		  Define Them 36
		Choose Descriptive Variable
		  Names 37
		Do Not Use Magic Numbers 53
		White Space 61
		Factor Out Common Code 61

3 Control Flow	Confusing = and == 107
	Comparison of Floating-
	  Point Numbers 108
	The Dangling else Problem 112
	Multiple Relational Operators 117
	Confusing && and ||
	  Conditions 118
	Infinite Loops 123
	Off-by-One Errors 124
	Forgetting a Semicolon 129
		Brace Layout 103
		Compile with Zero
		  Warnings 107
		Use for Loops for Their
		  Intended Purpose Only 128
		Don't Use != to Test the End
		  of a Numeric Range 128
		Symmetric and
		  Asymmetric Bounds 130
		Count Iterations 130

4 Functions	Missing Return Value 171 Type Mismatch 173	Use Meaningful Names for Parameters 173 Minimize Global Variables 185 Keep Functions Short 188

5 Classes	Mixing >> and getline Input 230
	Forgetting a Semicolon 234
	const Correctness 240
	Forgetting to Initialize All Fields
	  in a Constructor 246
	Trying to Reset an Object by
	  Calling a Constructor 247
		File Layout 252

6 Vectors and Arrays	Bounds Errors 272
	Omitting the Column Size of
	  a Two-Dimensional Array
	  Parameter 292
		Don't Combine Vector Access
		  and Index Increment 273
		Make Parallel Vectors into
		  Vectors of Objects 279
		Name the Array Size and
		  Capacity Consistently 291

Chapter 1

Introduction

CHAPTER GOALS

- To understand the activity of programming
- To learn about the architecture of computers
- To learn about machine languages and higher-level programming languages
- To become familiar with your compiler
- To compile and run your first C++ program
- To recognize syntax and logic errors
- To understand the notion of an algorithm

This chapter contains a brief introduction to the architecture of computers and an overview of programming languages. You will learn about the activity of programming: how to write and run your first C++ program, how to diagnose and fix programming errors, and how to plan your programming activities.

CHAPTER CONTENTS

1.1 What Is a Computer?

> Computers execute very basic operations in rapid succession.

You have probably used a computer for work or fun. Many people use computers for everyday tasks such as balancing a checkbook or writing a term paper. Computers are good for such tasks. They can handle repetitive chores, such as totaling up numbers or placing words on a page, without getting bored or exhausted.

More importantly, the computer presents the checkbook or the term paper on the screen and lets you fix mistakes easily. Computers make good game machines because they can play sequences of sounds and pictures, involving the human user in the process.

> Different tasks require different programs.

What makes all this possible is not only the computer. The computer must be programmed to perform these tasks. One program balances checkbooks; a different program, probably designed and constructed by a different company, processes words; and a third program plays a game. The computer itself is a machine that stores data (numbers, words, pictures), interacts with devices (the monitor, the sound system, the printer), and executes programs. Programs are sequences of instructions and decisions that the computer carries out to achieve a task.

Today's computer programs are so sophisticated that it is hard to believe that they are composed of extremely primitive operations. A typical operation may be one of the following.

- Put a red dot at this screen position.
- Get a number from this location in memory.

- Add up these two numbers.
- If this value is negative, continue the program at a certain instruction.

The computer user has the illusion of smooth interaction because a program contains a huge number of such operations, and because the computer can execute them at great speed.

The flexibility of a computer is quite an amazing phenomenon. The same machine can balance your checkbook, print your term paper, and play a game. In contrast, other machines carry out a much narrower range of tasks; a car drives and a toaster toasts. Computers can carry out a wide range of tasks because they execute different programs, each of which directs the computer to work on a specific task.

1.2 What Is Programming?

Programmers produce computer programs to make the computer solve new tasks.

A computer program tells a computer, in minute detail, the sequence of steps that are needed to fulfill a task. The act of designing and implementing these programs is called computer programming. In this book, you will learn how to program a computer—that is, how to direct the computer to execute tasks.

To use a computer you do not need to do any programming. When you write a term paper with a word processor, that program has been programmed by the manufacturer and is ready for you to use. That is only to be expected—you can drive a car without being a mechanic and toast bread without being an electrician. Most people who use computers every day never need to do any programming.

Since you are reading this introductory computer science book, it may well be your career goal to become a professional computer scientist or software engineer. Programming is not the only skill required of a computer scientist or software engineer; indeed, programming is not the only skill required to create successful computer programs. Nevertheless, the activity of programming is central to computer science. It is also a fascinating and pleasurable activity that continues to attract and motivate bright students. The discipline of computer science is particularly fortunate that it can make such an interesting activity the foundation of the learning path.

To write a computer game with motion and sound effects or a word processor that supports fancy fonts and pictures is a complex task that requires a team of many highly skilled programmers. Your first programming efforts will be more mundane. The concepts and skills you learn in this book form an important foundation, and you should not be disappointed if your first programs do not rival the sophisticated software that is familiar to you. Actually, you will find that there is an immense thrill even in simple programming tasks. It is an amazing experience to see the computer carry out a task precisely and quickly that would take you hours of drudgery, to make small changes in a program that lead to immediate improvements, and to see the computer become an extension of your mental powers.

1.3 The Anatomy of a Computer

To understand the programming process, you need to have a rudimentary understanding of the building blocks that make up a computer. We will look at a personal computer. Larger computers have faster, larger, or more powerful components, but they have fundamentally the same design.

> The central processing unit (CPU) executes one operation at a time.

At the heart of the computer lies the *central processing unit (CPU)* (see Figure 1). It consists of a single *chip*, or a small number of chips. A computer chip (integrated circuit) is a component with a plastic or metal housing, metal connectors, and inside wiring made principally from silicon. For a CPU chip, the inside wiring is enormously complicated. For example, the Pentium chip (a popular CPU for personal computers at the time of this writing) is composed of several million structural elements, called *transistors*.

> Data values can be brought into the CPU for processing from storage or from input devices such as the keyboard, the mouse, or a communications link.

Figure 2 shows a magnified detail view of a CPU chip. The CPU performs program control, arithmetic, and data movement. That is, the CPU locates and executes the program instructions; it carries out arithmetic operations such as addition, subtraction, multiplication, and division; it fetches data from external memory or devices and stores data back. All data must travel through the CPU whenever it is moved from one location to another. (There are a few technical exceptions to this rule; some devices can interact directly with memory.)

> Storage devices include random-access memory (RAM) and secondary storage.

The computer stores data and programs in *memory*. There are two kinds of memory. *Primary storage* is fast but expensive; it is made from memory chips: so-called *random-access memory (RAM)* and *read-only memory (ROM)*. Read-only memory contains certain programs that must always be present—for example, the code needed to

Figure 1   Central Processing Unit

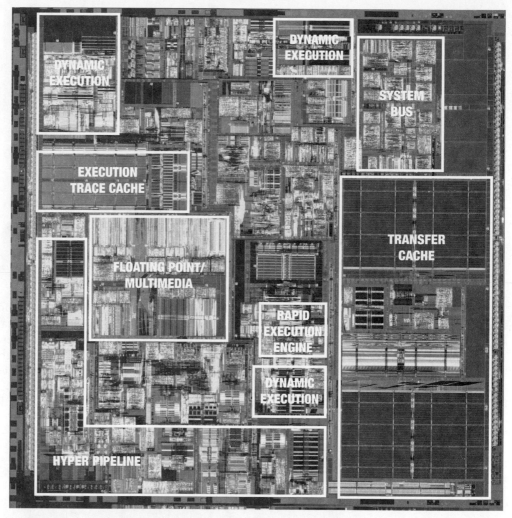

Figure 2 CPU Chip Detail

start the computer. Random-access memory might have been better called "read-write memory", because the CPU can read data from it and write data back to it. That makes RAM suitable to hold changing data and programs that do not have to be available permanently. RAM memory has two disadvantages. It is comparatively expensive, and it loses all its data when the power is turned off. *Secondary storage*, usually a *hard disk* (see Figure 3), provides less expensive storage that persists without electricity. A hard disk consists of rotating platters, which are coated with a magnetic material, and read/write heads, which can detect and change the magnetic flux on the platters. Programs and data are typically stored on the hard disk and loaded into RAM when the program starts. The program then updates the data in RAM and writes the modified data back to the hard disk.

Figure 3 A Hard Disk

The central processing unit, RAM memory, and the electronics controlling the hard disk and other devices are interconnected through a set of electrical lines called a *bus*. Data travels along the bus from the system memory and peripheral devices to the CPU and back. Figure 4 shows a *motherboard*, which contains the CPU, the RAM, and card slots, through which cards that control peripheral devices connect to the bus.

Figure 4 A Motherboard

To interact with a human user, a computer requires peripheral devices. The computer transmits information to the user through a display screen, speakers, and printers. The user can enter information and directions to the computer by using a keyboard or a pointing device such as a mouse.

Some computers are self-contained units, whereas others are interconnected through *networks*. Through the network cabling, the computer can read data and programs from central storage locations or send data to other computers. For the user of a networked computer it may not even be obvious which data reside on the computer itself and which are transmitted through the network.

Figure 5 gives a schematic overview of the architecture of a personal computer. Program instructions and data (such as text, numbers, audio, or video) are stored on the hard disk, on a CD-ROM, or elsewhere on the network. When a program is started, it is brought into RAM memory, from where the CPU can read it. The CPU reads the program one instruction at a time. As directed by these instructions, the CPU reads data, modifies it, and writes it back to RAM memory or the hard disk. Some program instructions will cause the CPU to place dots on the display screen or printer or to vibrate the speaker. As these actions happen many times over and at great speed, the human user will perceive images and sound. Some program instructions read user input from the keyboard or mouse. The program analyzes the nature of these inputs and then executes the next appropriate instructions.

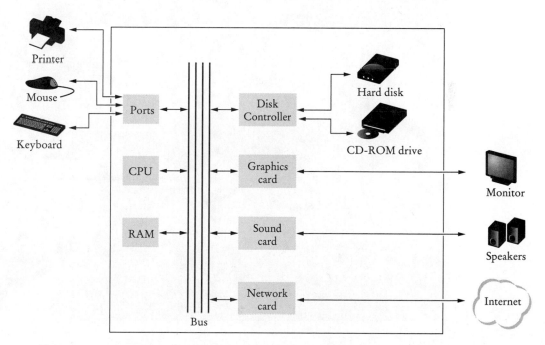

Figure 5   Schematic Design of a Personal Computer

RANDOM FACT 1.1

The ENIAC and the Dawn of Computing

The ENIAC (*electronic numerical integrator and computer*) was the first usable electronic computer. It was designed by J. Presper Eckert and John Mauchly at the University of Pennsylvania and was completed in 1946—two years before transistors were invented. The computer was housed in a large room and consisted of many cabinets containing about 18,000 vacuum tubes (see Figure 6). Vacuum tubes burned out at the rate of several tubes per day. An attendant with a shopping cart full of tubes constantly made the rounds and replaced defective ones. The computer was programmed by connecting wires on panels. Each wiring configuration would set up the computer for a particular problem. To have the computer work on a different problem, the wires had to be replugged.

Work on the ENIAC was supported by the U.S. Navy, which was interested in computations of ballistic tables that would give the trajectory of a projectile, depending on the wind resistance, initial velocity, and atmospheric conditions. To compute the trajectories, one must find the numerical solutions of certain differential equations; hence the name "numerical integrator". Before machines like ENIAC were developed, humans did this kind of work, and until the 1950s the word "computer" referred to these people. The ENIAC was later used for peaceful purposes such as the tabulation of U.S. Census data.

Figure 6   The ENIAC

1.4 Translating Human-Readable Programs to Machine Code

On the most basic level, computer instructions are extremely primitive. The processor executes *machine instructions*. A typical sequence of machine instructions is

1. Move the contents of memory location 40000 into register eax. (A register is a storage location in the CPU.)

2. Subtract the value 100 from register eax.

3. If the result is positive, continue with the instruction that is stored in memory location 11280.

Computer programs are stored as machine instructions in a code that depends on the processor type.

Actually, machine instructions are encoded as numbers so that they can be stored in memory. On a Pentium processor, this sequence of instruction is encoded as the sequence of numbers

161 40000 45 100 127 11280

On a processor from a different manufacturer, the encoding would be quite different. When this kind of processor fetches this sequence of numbers, it decodes them and executes the associated sequence of commands.

How can we communicate the command sequence to the computer? The simplest method is to place the actual numbers into the computer memory. This is, in fact, how the very earliest computers worked. However, a long program is composed of thousands of individual commands, and it is a tedious and error-prone affair to look up the numeric codes for all commands and place the codes manually into memory. As we said before, computers are really good at automating tedious and error-prone activities, and it did not take long for computer programmers to realize that the computers themselves could be harnessed to help in the programming process.

The first step was to assign short names to the commands. For example, mov denotes "move", sub "subtract", and jg "jump if greater than 0". Using these commands, the instruction sequence becomes

```
mov 40000, %eax
sub 100, %eax
jg  11280
```

That is much easier to read for humans. To get the instruction sequences accepted by the computer, though, the names must be translated into the machine codes. This is the task of another computer program: a so-called *assembler*. It takes the sequence of characters "mov %eax", translates it into the command code 161, and carries out similar operations on the other commands. Assemblers have another feature: they can give names to *memory locations* as well as to instructions. Our program sequence might be checking that some interest rate is greater than 100 percent, and the interest rate might be stored in memory location 40000. It is usually not important where a value is stored; any available memory location will do. By using symbolic names instead of memory addresses, the program gets even easier to read:

```
mov int_rate, %eax
sub 100, %eax
jg  int_error
```

It is the job of the assembler program to find suitable numeric values for the symbolic names and to put those values into the generated code sequence.

Assembler instructions were a major advance over programming with raw machine codes, but they suffer from two problems. It still takes a great many instructions to achieve even the simplest goals, and the exact instruction sequence differs from one processor to another. For example, the above sequence of assembly instructions must be rewritten for the Sun SPARC processor, which poses a real problem for people who invest a lot of time and money producing a software package. If a computer becomes obsolete, the program must be completely rewritten to run on the replacement system.

In the mid-1950s, higher-level programming languages began to appear. In these languages, the programmer expresses the idea behind the task that needs to be performed, and a special computer program, a so-called *compiler*, translates the higher-level description into machine instructions for a particular processor.

For example, in C++, the high-level programming language that we will use in this book, you might give the following instruction:

```
if (int_rate > 100) cout << "Interest rate error";
```

This means, "If the interest rate is over 100, display an error message". It is then the job of the compiler program to look at the sequence of characters "if (int_rate > 100)" and translate that into

$$161 \ 40000 \ 45 \ 100 \ 127 \ 11280$$

Compilers are quite sophisticated programs. They have to translate logical statements, such as the if, into sequences of computations, tests, and jumps, and they must find memory locations for variables like int_rate. In this book, we will generally take the existence of a compiler for granted. If you become a professional computer scientist, you may well learn more about compiler-writing techniques later in your studies.

> Higher-level languages are independent of the processor.

Higher-level languages are independent of the underlying hardware. For example, the instruction if (int_rate > 100) does not rely on particular machine instructions. In fact, it will compile to different code on an Intel Pentium and a Sun SPARC processor.

1.5 Programming Languages

> Programming languages are designed by computer scientists for a variety of purposes.

Programming languages are independent of specific computer architecture, but they are human creations. As such, they follow certain conventions. To ease the translation process, those conventions are much stricter than they are for human languages. When you talk to another person, and you scramble or omit a word or two, your conversation partner will usually still understand what you have to say.

Compilers are less forgiving. For example, if you omit the quotation mark close to the end of the instruction,

```
if (int_rate > 100) message_box("Interest rate error);
```

the C++ compiler will get quite confused and complain that it cannot translate an instruction containing this error. This is actually a good thing. If the compiler were to try to guess what you did wrong and try to fix it, it might not guess your intentions correctly. In that case, the resulting program would do the wrong thing—quite possibly with disastrous effects, if that program controlled a device on whose functions someone's well-being depended. When a compiler reads programming instructions in a programming language, it will translate them into machine code only if the input follows the language conventions exactly.

Just as there are many human languages, there are many programming languages. Consider the instruction

```
if (int_rate > 100) cout << "Interest rate error";
```

This is how you must format the instruction in C++. C++ is a very popular programming language, and it is the one we use in this book. But in Visual Basic (a popular programming language for business applications) the same instruction would be written as

```
if int_rate > 100 then System.Console.Write("Interest rate error") end if
```

Compilers are language-specific. The C++ compiler will translate only C++ code, whereas a Visual Basic compiler will reject anything but legal Visual Basic code. For example, if a C++ compiler reads the instruction if int_rate > 100 then ..., it will complain, because the condition of the if statement isn't surrounded by parentheses ( ), and the compiler doesn't expect the word then. The choice of the layout for a language construct such as the if statement is somewhat arbitrary. The designers of different languages make different tradeoffs among readability, easy translation, and consistency with other constructs.

1.6 The Evolution of C++

C++ is built upon the C programming language, which was developed to be translated efficiently into fast machine code, with a minimum of housekeeping overhead. C++ builds on C by adding features for "object-oriented programming", a programming style that enables modeling of real-world objects.

The initial version of the C language was designed about 1972, but features were added to it over the years. Because different compiler writers added different features, the language actually sprouted various dialects. Some programming instructions were understood by one compiler but rejected by another. Such divergence is a major obstacle to a programmer who wants to move code from one computer to another. An effort got underway to iron out the differences and come up with a standard version of C. The design process ended in 1989 with the completion of the ANSI (American National Standards Institute) standard. In the meantime, Bjarne Stroustrup of AT&T added features of the language Simula (an object-oriented language designed for carrying out simulations) to C. The resulting language was called C++. From 1985 until today, C++ has grown by the addition of many features. A standardization process culminated in the publication of the international C++ standard in 1998. A minor update to the standard was issued in 2003, and a major revision is expected to come to fruition around 2009.

C++ is a general-purpose language that is in widespread use for systems and embedded programming.

At this time, C++ is the most commonly used language for developing system software such as databases and operating systems. Just as importantly, C++ is increasingly used for programming "embedded systems", small computers that control devices such as automobile engines or cellular telephones.

RANDOM FACT 1.2

Standards Organizations

Two organizations, the American National Standards Institute (ANSI) and the International Organization for Standardization (ISO), have jointly developed the definitive standard for the C++ language.

Why have standards? You encounter the benefits of standardization every day. When you buy a light bulb, you can be assured that it fits in the socket without having to measure the socket at home and the bulb in the store. In fact, you may have experienced how painful the lack of standards can be if you have ever purchased a flashlight with nonstandard bulbs. Replacement bulbs for such a flashlight can be difficult and expensive to obtain.

The ANSI and ISO standards organizations are associations of industry professionals who develop standards for everything from car tires and credit card shapes to programming languages. Having a standard for a programming language such as C++ means that you can take a program that you developed on one system with one manufacturer's compiler to a different system and be assured that it will continue to work.

To find out more about standards organizations, check out the following Web sites: www.ansi.org and www.iso.ch.

1.7 Becoming Familiar with Your Computer

Set aside some time to become familiar with the computer system and the C++ compiler that you will use for your class work.

As you use this book, you may well be doing your work on an unfamiliar computer system. You should spend some time making yourself familiar with the computer. Because computer systems vary widely, this book can only give an outline of the steps you need to follow. Using a new and unfamiliar computer system can be frustrating. Look for training courses that your campus offers, or just ask a friend to give you a brief tour.

Step 1   Log In

If you use your own home computer, you don't need to worry about logging in. Computers in a lab, however, are usually not open to everyone. Access is usually restricted to those who paid the necessary fees and who can be trusted not to mess up the configuration. You will likely need an account number and a password to gain access to the system.

Step 2   Locate the C++ Compiler

Computer systems differ greatly in this regard. Some systems let you start the compiler by selecting an icon or menu. On other systems you must use the keyboard to type a command to launch the compiler. On many personal computers there is a so-called *integrated environment* in which you can write and test your programs. On other computers you must first launch one program that functions like a word processor, in which you can enter your C++ instructions; then launch another program to translate them to machine code; and then run the resulting machine code.

Step 3   Understand Files and Folders

As a programmer, you will write C++ programs, try them out, and improve them. You will be provided a place on the computer to store them, and you need to find out where that place is. You will store your programs in *files*. A C++ file is a container of C++ instructions. Files have names, and the rules for legal names differ from one system to another. Some systems allow spaces in file names; others don't. Some distinguish between upper- and lowercase letters; others don't. Most C++ compilers require that C++ files end in an *extension* .cpp, .cc, or .C; for example, test.cpp.

Files are stored in *folders* or *directories*. These file containers can be nested. A folder can contain files as well as other folders, which themselves can contain more files and folders (see Figure 7). This hierarchy can be quite large, especially on net-

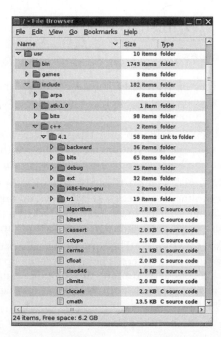

Figure 7
A Directory Hierarchy

worked computers where some of the files may be on your local disk, others elsewhere on the network. While you need not be concerned with every branch of the hierarchy, you should familiarize yourself with your local environment. Different systems have different ways of showing files and directories. Some use a graphical display and let you move around by clicking the mouse on folder icons. In other systems, you must enter commands to visit or inspect different locations.

Step 4   Write a Simple Program

In the next section, we will introduce a very simple program. You will need to learn how to type it in, run it, and fix mistakes.

Step 5   Save Your Work

Develop a strategy for keeping backup copies of your work before disaster strikes.

You will spend many hours typing C++ programs in and improving them. The resulting program files have some value, and you should treat them as you would other important property. A conscientious safety strategy is particularly important for computer files. They are more fragile than paper documents or other more tangible objects.

It is easy to delete a file by accident, and occasionally files are lost because of a computer malfunction. Unless you keep another copy, you must retype the contents. Because you are unlikely to remember the entire file, you will likely find yourself spending almost as much time as you did to enter and improve it in the first place. This lost time may cause you to miss deadlines. It is therefore crucially important that you learn how to safeguard files and get in the habit of doing so *before* disaster strikes. You can make safety or *backup* copies of files by saving copies on a memory stick or on another computer.

PRODUCTIVITY HINT 1.1

Backup Copies

Backing up files on a memory stick is a an easy and convenient storage method for many people. Another increasingly popular form of backup is Internet file storage. Here are a few pointers to keep in mind.

- *Back up often.* Backing up a file takes only a few seconds, and you will hate yourself if you have to spend many hours recreating work that you could have saved easily. I recommend that you back up your work once every thirty minutes.

- *Rotate backups.* Use more than one directory for backups, and rotate them. That is, first back up onto the first directory. Then back up onto the second directory. Then use the third, and then go back to the first. That way you always have three recent backups. If your recent changes made matters worse, you can then go back to the older version.

- *Back up source files only.* The compiler translates the files that you write into files consisting of machine code. There is no need to back up the machine code files, since you can recreate them easily by running the compiler again. Focus your backup activity on those files that represent your effort. That way your backup disks won't fill up with files that you don't need.

- *Pay attention to the backup direction.* Backing up involves copying files from one place to another. It is important that you do this right—that is, copy from your work location to the backup location. If you do it the wrong way, you will overwrite a newer file with an older version.
- *Check your backups once in a while.* Double-check that your backups are where you think they are. There is nothing more frustrating than to find out that the backups are not there when you need them.
- *Relax, then restore.* When you lose a file and need to restore it from backup, you are likely to be in an unhappy, nervous state. Take a deep breath and think through the recovery process before you start. It is not uncommon for an agitated computer user to wipe out the last backup when trying to restore a damaged file.

1.8 Compiling a Simple Program

You are now ready to write and run your first C++ program. The traditional choice for the very first program in a new programming language is a program that displays a simple greeting: "Hello, World!" We follow that tradition. Here is the "Hello, World!" program in C++.

ch01/hello.cpp

```
1  #include <iostream>
2
3  using namespace std;
4
5  int main()
6  {
7     cout << "Hello, World!\n";
8     return 0;
9  }
```

Program Run

```
Hello, World!
```

You can download this program file from the companion web site for this book. The line numbers are not part of the program. They are included so that your instructor can reference them during lectures.

We will explain this program in a minute. For now, you should make a new program file and call it hello.cpp. Enter the program instructions and compile and run the program, following the procedure that is appropriate for your compiler.

By the way, C++ is *case-sensitive*. You must enter upper- and lowercase letters exactly as they appear in the program listing. You cannot type MAIN or Return. On the other hand, C++ has *free-form layout*. Spaces and line breaks are not important.

You can write the entire program on a single line,

```
int main(){cout<<"Hello, World!\n";return 0;}
```

or write every keyword on a separate line,

```
int
main()
{
cout
<<
"Hello, World!\n"
;
return
0;
}
```

However, good taste dictates that you lay out your programs in a readable fashion, so you should follow the layout in the program listing.

When you run the program, the message

```
Hello, World!
```

will appear on the screen. On some systems, you may need to switch to a different window to find the message.

Now that you have seen the program working, it is time to understand its makeup. The basic structure of a C++ program is shown in Syntax 1.1 on page 18.

> Every C++ program contains #include directives, to access necessary features such as input and output, and a function called main.

The first line,

```
#include <iostream>
```

tells the compiler to read the file iostream. That file contains the definition for the *stream input/output* package. Your program performs output onto the screen and therefore requires the services provided in iostream. You must include this file in all programs that read or write text.

By the way, you will see a slightly different syntax, #include <iostream.h>, in many C++ programs.

The next line,

```
using namespace std;
```

tells the compiler to locate names such as cout in the "standard name space". In large programs, it is quite common that different programmers will use the same names to denote different things. They can avoid name conflicts by using separate name spaces. However, for the simple programs that you will be writing in this book, separate name spaces are not necessary. You will always use the standard name space, and you can simply add the directive using namespace std; at the top of every program that you write, just below the #include directives. Name spaces are a relatively recent feature of C++, and your compiler may not yet support them.

The construction

```
int main()
{
    ...
```

```
    return 0;
  }
```

defines a *function* called main. A function is a collection of programming instructions that carry out a particular task. Every C++ program must have a main function. Most C++ programs contain other functions besides main, but it will take us
until Chapter 4 to discuss how to write other functions. The instructions or *statements* in the *body* of the main function—that is, the statements inside the curly
braces {}—are executed one by one. Note that each statement ends in a semicolon.

```
  cout << "Hello, World!\n";
  return 0;
```

A sequence of characters enclosed in quotation marks

```
  "Hello, World!\n"
```

is called a *string*. You must enclose the contents of the string inside quotation marks
so that the compiler knows you literally mean "Hello, World!\n". In this short program, there is actually no possible confusion. Suppose, on the other hand, you
wanted to display the word *main*. By enclosing it in quotation marks, "main", the
compiler knows that you mean the sequence of characters m a i n, not the function
named main. The rule is simply that you must enclose all text strings in quotation
marks, so that the compiler considers them plain text and not program instructions.

The text string "Hello, World!\n" should not be taken *completely* literally. You
do not want the odd-looking \n to appear on the screen. The two-character
sequence \n actually denotes a single, nonprinting character, a so-called *newline*.
When the newline character is sent to the display, the cursor is moved to the first
column in the next screen row. If you don't send a newline character, then the next
displayed item will simply follow the current string on the same line. In this program we only printed one item, but in general we will want to print multiple items,
and it is a good habit to end all lines of output with a newline character.

The backslash \ character is used as a so-called *escape character*. The backslash
does not denote itself; instead, it is used to encode other characters that would otherwise be difficult or impossible to show in program statements. There are a few
other backslash combinations that you will encounter later. Now, what do you do if
you actually want to show a backslash on the display? You must enter two in a row.
For example,

```
  cout << "Hello\\World!\n";
```

would print

```
  Hello\World!
```

Finally, how can you display a string containing quotation marks, such as

```
  Hello, "World"!
```

You can't use

```
  cout << "Hello, "World"!\n";
```

As soon as the compiler reads "Hello, ", it thinks the string is finished, and then it
gets all confused about World followed by a second string "!\n". Compilers have a

one-track mind, and if a simple analysis of the input doesn't make sense to them, they just refuse to go on, and they report an error. In contrast, a human would probably realize that the second and third quotation marks were supposed to be part of the string. Well, how do we then display quotation marks on the screen? The backslash escape character again comes to the rescue. Inside a string the sequence \" denotes a literal quote, not the end of a string. The correct display statement is therefore

```
cout << "Hello, \"World\"!\n";
```

To display values on the screen, you must send them to an entity called cout. The << operator denotes the "send to" command. You can also print numerical values. For example, the statement

```
cout << 3 + 4;
```

displays the number 7.

> In a simple program, main just displays a message on the screen and then returns with a success indicator.

Finally, the return statement denotes the end of the main function. When the main function ends, the program terminates. The zero value is a signal that the program ran successfully. In this small program there was nothing that could have gone wrong during the program run. In other programs there might be problems with the input or with some devices, and you would then have main return a nonzero value to indicate an error. By the way, the int in int main()indicates that main returns an integer value, not a fractional number or string.

SYNTAX 1.1 Simple Program

```
header files
using namespace std;
int main()
{
    statements
    return 0;
}
```

Example:

```
#include <iostream>
using namespace std;
int main()
{
    cout << "Hello, World!\n";
    return 0;
}
```

Purpose:

A simple program, with all program instructions in a main function.

COMMON ERROR 1.1

Omitting Semicolons

In C++ every statement must end in a semicolon. Forgetting to type a semicolon is a common error. It confuses the compiler because the compiler uses the semicolon to find where one statement ends and the next one starts. The compiler does not use line ends or closing braces to recognize the ends of statements. For example, the compiler considers

```
cout << "Hello, World!\n"
return 0;
```

a single statement, as if you had written

```
cout << "Hello, World!" return 0;
```

and then it doesn't understand that statement, because it does not expect the keyword return in the middle of an output command. The remedy is simple. Just scan every statement for a terminating semicolon, just as you would check that every English sentence ends in a period.

1.9 Errors

Experiment a little with the hello program. What happens if you make a typing error such as

```
cot << "Hello, World!\n";
cout << "Hello, World!\";
cout << "Hell, World!\n";
```

Syntax errors are faulty constructs that do not conform to the rules of the programming language.

In the first case, the compiler will complain. It will say that it has no clue what you mean by cot. The exact wording of the error message is dependent on the compiler, but it might be something like "Undefined symbol cot". This is a *compile-time error* or *syntax error*. Something is wrong according to the language rules, and the compiler finds it. When the compiler finds one or more errors, it will not translate the program to machine code, and as a consequence there is no program to run. You must fix the error and compile again. In fact, the compiler is quite picky, and it is common to go through several rounds of fixing compile-time errors before compilation succeeds for the first time.

If the compiler finds an error, it will not simply stop and give up. It will try to report as many errors as it can find, so you can fix them all at once. Sometimes, however, one error throws it off track. This is likely to happen with the error in the second line. The compiler will miss the end of the string because it thinks that the \" is an embedded quote character. In such cases, it is common for the compiler to emit bogus error reports for neighboring lines. You should fix only those error messages that make sense to you and then recompile.

The error in the third line is of a different kind. The program will compile and run, but its output will be wrong. It will print

```
Hell, World!
```

Logic errors are constructs that can be translated into a running program, but the resulting program does not perform the intended action.

This is a *run-time error* or *logic error*. The program is syntactically correct and does something, but it doesn't do what it is supposed to do. The compiler cannot find the error, and it must be flushed out when the program runs, by testing it and carefully looking at its output.

During program development, errors are unavoidable. Once a program is longer than a few lines, it requires superhuman concentration to enter it correctly without slipping up once. You will find yourself omitting semicolons or quotes more often than you would like, but the compiler will track down these problems for you.

Logic errors are more troublesome. The compiler will not find them—in fact, the compiler will cheerfully translate any program as long as its syntax is correct—but the resulting program will do something wrong. It is the responsibility of the program author to test the program and find any logic errors. Testing programs is an important topic that you will encounter many times in this book. Another important aspect of good craftsmanship is *defensive programming*: structuring programs and development processes in such a way that an error in one place in a program does not trigger a disastrous response.

The error examples that you saw so far were not difficult to diagnose or fix, but as you learn more sophisticated programming techniques, there will be much more room for error. It is an uncomfortable fact that locating all errors in a program is very difficult. Even if you can observe that a program exhibits faulty behavior, it may not be obvious what part of the program caused it and how to fix it. There are special software tools, *debuggers*, that let you trace through a program to find *bugs*—that is, logic errors. In this book you will learn how to use a debugger effectively.

Note that all these errors are different from the kind of errors that you are likely to make in calculations. If you total up a column of numbers, you may miss a minus sign or accidentally drop a carry, perhaps because you are bored or tired. Computers do not make these kinds of errors. When a computer adds up numbers, it will get the correct answer. Admittedly, computers can make overflow or roundoff errors, just as pocket calculators do, when you ask them to perform computations whose result falls outside their numeric range. An overflow error occurs if the result of a computation is very large or very small. For example, most computers and pocket calculators overflow when you try to compute 10^{1000}. A roundoff error occurs when a value cannot be represented precisely. For example, $\frac{1}{3}$ may be stored in the computer as 0.3333333, a value that is close to, but not exactly equal to $\frac{1}{3}$. If you compute $1 - 3 \times \frac{1}{3}$, you may obtain 0.0000001, not 0, as a result of the roundoff error. We will consider such errors logic errors, because the programmer should have chosen a more appropriate calculation scheme that handles overflow or roundoff correctly.

The programmer is responsible for inspecting and testing the program to guard against logic errors.

You will learn a three-part error management strategy in this book. First, you will learn about common errors and how to avoid them. Then you will learn defensive programming strategies to minimize the likelihood and impact of errors. Finally, you will learn debugging strategies to flush out those errors that remain.

COMMON ERROR 1.2

Misspelling Words

If you accidentally misspell a word, strange things may happen, and it may not always be completely obvious from the error messages what went wrong. Here is a good example of how simple spelling errors can cause trouble:

```
#include <iostream>

using namespace std;

int Main()
{
    cout << "Hello, World!\n";
    return 0;
}
```

This code defines a function called Main. The compiler will not consider this to be the same as the main function, because Main starts with an uppercase letter and the C++ language is *case-sensitive*. Upper- and lowercase letters are considered to be completely different from each other, and to the compiler Main is no better match for main than rain. The compiler will compile your Main function, but when the linker is ready to build the executable file, it will complain about the missing main function and refuse to link the program. Of course, the message "missing main function" should give you a clue where to look for the error.

If you get an error message that seems to indicate that the compiler is on the wrong track, it is a good idea to check for spelling and capitalization. All C++ keywords, and the names of most functions, use only lowercase letters. If you misspell the name of a symbol (for example out instead of cout), the compiler will complain about an "undefined symbol". This error message is usually a good clue that you made a spelling error.

1.10 The Compilation Process

Some C++ development environments are very convenient to use. You just enter the code in one window, click on a button or menu to compile, and click on another button or menu to run your code. Error messages show up in a second window, and the program runs in a third window. Figure 8 shows the screen layout of a popular C++ compiler with these features. With such an environment you are completely shielded from the details of the compilation process. On other systems you must carry out every step manually.

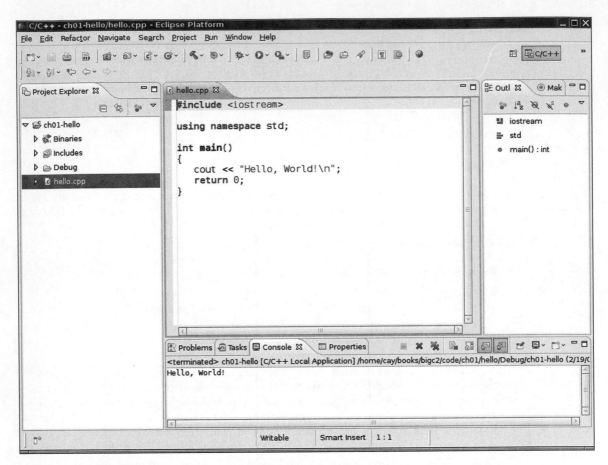

Figure 8   Screen Layout of an Integrated C++ Environment

Even if you use a convenient C++ environment, it is useful to know what goes on behind the scenes, mainly because knowing the process helps you solve problems when something goes wrong.

You first enter the program statements into a text editor. The editor stores the text and gives it a name such as hello.cpp. If the editor window shows a name like noname.cpp, you should change the name. You should *save* the file to disk frequently, because otherwise the editor only stores the text in the computer's RAM memory. If something goes wrong with the computer and you need to restart it, the contents of the RAM (including your program text) are lost, but anything stored on a hard disk is permanent even if you need to restart the computer.

When you compile your program, the compiler translates the C++ *source code* (that is, the statements that you wrote) into *machine code*. The resulting file consists of machine instructions and information on how to load the program into memory prior to execution. Machine code is sometimes called *object code*, but we do not use that terminology to avoid confusion with C++ objects. Machine code

> C++ programs are translated by a program called a compiler into machine code.

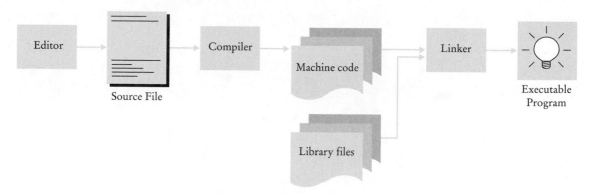

Figure 9   From Source Code to Executable Program

files usually have the extension .obj or .o. For example, the machine code for the hello program might be stored in hello.obj.

> A program called a linker combines machine code with previously translated machine code for input/ output and other services to build your program.

The machine code file contains only the translation of the code that you wrote. That is not enough to actually run the program. To display a string on a window, quite a bit of low-level activity is necessary. The authors of the iostream package (which defines cout and its functionality) have implemented all necessary actions and placed the required machine code into a *library*. A library is a collection of code that has been programmed and translated by someone else, ready for you to use in your program. (More complicated programs are built from more than one machine code file and more than one library.) A special program called the *linker* takes your machine code file and the necessary parts from the iostream library and builds an *executable file*. (Figure 9 gives an overview of these steps.) The executable file is usually called hello.exe or hello, depending on your computer system. It contains all machine code necessary to run the program. You can run the program by typing hello at a command prompt, or by clicking on the file icon, even after you exit the C++ environment. You can e-mail that file to another user who doesn't have a C++ compiler or who may not know that there is such a thing as C++, and that person can run the program in the same way.

Your programming activity centers around these files. You start in the editor, writing the source file. You compile the program and look at the error messages. You go back to the editor and fix the syntax errors. When the compiler succeeds, the linker builds the executable file. You run the executable file. If you find an error, you can run the debugger to execute it one line at a time. Once you find the cause of the error, you go back to the editor and fix it. You compile, link, and run again to see whether the error has gone away. If not, you go back to the editor. This is called the *edit-compile-debug loop* (see Figure 10). You will spend a substantial amount of time in this loop in the months and years to come.

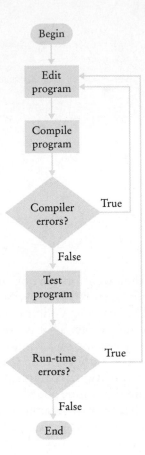

Figure 10
Edit-Compile-Debug Loop

1.11 Algorithms

An algorithm is a description of steps to solve a problem that is unambiguous, executable, and terminating.

You will soon learn how to program calculations and decision making in C++. But before we look at the mechanics of implementing computations in the next chapter, let us consider the planning process that precedes the implementation.

You may have run across advertisements that encourage you to pay for a computerized service that matches you up with a love partner. Let us think how this might work. You fill out a form and send it in. Others do the same. The data are processed by a computer program. Is it reasonable to assume that the computer can perform the task of finding the best match for you? Suppose your younger brother, not the computer, had all the forms on his desk. What instructions could you give him? You can't say, "Find the best-looking person of the opposite sex who likes inline skating and browsing the Internet". There is no objective standard for good looks, and your brother's opinion (or that of a computer program analyzing the digitized photo) will likely be different from yours. If you can't give written instructions for someone to solve the problem, there is no way the computer can magically solve the problem. The computer can only do what you tell it to do. It just does it faster, without getting bored or exhausted.

Now consider the following investment problem:

> You put $10,000 into a bank account that earns 5 percent interest per year. How many years does it take for the account balance to be double the original?

Could you solve this problem by hand? Sure, you could. You figure out the balance as follows:

Year	Balance
0	$10,000.00
1	$10,500.00 = $10,000.00 × 1.05
2	$11,025.00 = $10,500.00 × 1.05
3	$11,576.25 = $11,025.00 × 1.05
4	$12,155.06 = $11,576.25 × 1.05

You keep going until the balance goes over $20,000. Then the last number in the year column is the answer.

Of course, carrying out this computation is intensely boring. You could tell your younger brother to do it. Seriously, the fact that a computation is boring or tedious is irrelevant to the computer. Computers are very good at carrying out repetitive calculations quickly and flawlessly. What is important to the computer (and your younger brother) is the existence of a systematic approach for finding the solution. The answer can be found by following a series of steps that involves no guesswork. Here is such a series of steps:

Step 1   Start with the table

Year	Balance
0	$10,000.00

Step 2   Repeat steps 2a–2c while the balance is less than $20,000.

   Step 2a   Add a new row to the table.

   Step 2b   In column 1 of the new row, put one more than the preceding year's value.

   Step 2c   In column 2 of the new row, place the value of the preceding balance, multiplied by 1.05 (5 percent).

Step 3 Report the last number in the year column as the number of years required to double the investment.

Of course, these steps are not yet in a language that a computer can understand, but you will soon learn how to formulate them in C++. What is important is that the method described be

- Unambiguous
- Executable
- Terminating

The method is *unambiguous* because there are precise instructions for what to do at each step and where to go next. There is no room for guesswork or creativity. The method is *executable* because each step can be carried out in practice. Had we asked to use the actual interest rate that will be charged in years to come, and not a fixed rate of 5 percent per year, our method would not have been executable, because there is no way for anyone to know what that interest rate will be. Finally, the computation will eventually come to an end. With every step, the balance goes up by at least $500, so eventually it must reach $20,000.

A solution technique that is unambiguous, executable, and terminating is called an *algorithm*. We have found an algorithm to solve our investment problem, and thus we can find the solution with the computer. The existence of an algorithm is an essential prerequisite for programming a task. Sometimes finding an algorithm is very simple. At other times it requires ingenuity or planning. If you cannot find an algorithm, you cannot use the computer to solve your problem. You need to satisfy yourself that an algorithm exists, and that you understand its steps, before you start programming.

CHAPTER SUMMARY

1. Computers execute very basic operations in rapid succession.

2. Different tasks require different programs.

3. Programmers produce computer programs to make the computer solve new tasks.

4. The central processing unit (CPU) executes one operation at a time.

5. Data values can be brought into the CPU for processing from storage or from input devices such as the keyboard, the mouse, or a communications link.

6. Storage devices include random-access memory (RAM) and secondary storage.

7. Computer programs are stored as machine instructions in a code that depends on the processor type.

8. Higher-level languages are independent of the processor.

9. Programming languages are designed by computer scientists for a variety of purposes.

10. C++ is a general-purpose language that is in widespread use for systems and embedded programming.

11. Set aside some time to become familiar with the computer system and the C++ compiler that you will use for your class work.

12. Develop a strategy for keeping backup copies of your work before disaster strikes.

13. Every C++ program contains #include directives, to access necessary features such as input and output, and a function called main.

14. In a simple program, main just displays a message on the screen and then returns with a success indicator.

15. Syntax errors are faulty constructs that do not conform to the rules of the programming language.

16. Logic errors are constructs that can be translated into a running program, but the resulting program does not perform the intended action.

17. The programmer is responsible for inspecting and testing the program to guard against logic errors.

18. C++ programs are translated by a program called a compiler into machine code.

19. A program called a linker combines machine code with previously translated machine code for input/output and other services to build your program.

20. An algorithm is a description of steps to solve a problem that is unambiguous, executable, and terminating.

REVIEW EXERCISES

Exercise R1.1. Explain the difference between using a computer program and programming a computer.

Exercise R1.2. Name the various ways in which a computer can be programmed that were discussed in this chapter.

Exercise R1.3. Which parts of a computer can store program code? Which can store user data?

Exercise R1.4. Which parts of a computer serve to give information to the user? Which parts take user input?

Exercise R1.5. A toaster is a single-function device, but a computer can be programmed to carry out different tasks. Is your cell phone a single-function device, or is it a programmable computer? (Your answer will depend on your cell phone model.)

Exercise R1.6. Describe the utility of the computer network in your department computer lab. To what other computers is a lab computer connected?

Exercise R1.7. Assume a computer has the following machine instructions, coded as numbers:

160 n: Move the contents of register A to memory location n.

161 n: Move the contents of memory location n to register A.

44 n: Add the value n to register A.

45 n: Subtract the value n from register A.

50 n: Add the contents of memory location n to register A.

51 n: Subtract the contents of memory location n from register A.

52 n: Multiply register A with the contents of memory location n.

53 n: Divide register A by the contents of memory location n.

127 n: If the result of the last computation is positive, continue with the instruction that is stored in memory location n.

128 n: If the result of the last computation is zero, continue with the instruction that is stored in memory location n.

Assume that each of these instructions and each value of n requires one memory location. Write a program in machine code to solve the investment-doubling problem.

Exercise R1.8. Design mnemonic instructions for the machine codes in Exercise R1.7 and write the investment-doubling program in your "assembler code", using your mnemonics and suitable symbolic names for variables and labels.

Exercise R1.9. Explain two benefits of higher-level programming languages over assembler code.

Exercise R1.10. List the programming languages mentioned in this chapter.

Exercise R1.11. Explain at least two advantages and two disadvantages of C++ over other programming languages.

Exercise R1.12. On your own computer or on your lab computer, find the exact location (folder or directory name) of

a. The sample file `hello.cpp`, which you wrote with the editor

b. The standard header file `iostream`

c. The header file `ccc_time.h`, needed for some of the programs in this book

Exercise R1.13. Explain the special role of the \ escape character in C++ character strings.

Exercise R1.14. Write three versions of the `hello.cpp` program that have different syntax errors. Write a version that has a logic error.

Exercise R1.15. How do you discover syntax errors? How do you discover logic errors?

Exercise R1.16. Write an algorithm to settle the following question: A bank account starts out with $10,000. Interest is compounded monthly at 6 percent per year (0.5 percent per month). Every month, $500 is withdrawn to meet college expenses. After how many years is the account depleted?

Exercise R1.17. Consider the question of Exercise R1.16. Suppose the numbers ($10,000, 6 percent, $500) were user-selectable? Are there values for which the algorithm you developed would not terminate? If so, change the algorithm to make sure it always terminates.

Exercise R1.18. The value of π can be computed according to the following formula:

$$\frac{\pi}{4} = 1 - \frac{1}{3} + \frac{1}{5} - \frac{1}{7} + \frac{1}{9} - \cdots$$

Write an algorithm to compute π. Because the formula is an infinite series and an algorithm must stop after a finite number of steps, you should stop when you have the result determined to six significant digits.

Exercise R1.19. Suppose you put your younger brother in charge of backing up your work. Write a set of detailed instructions for carrying out his task. Explain how often he should do it, and what files he needs to copy from which folder to which location. Explain how he should verify that the backup was carried out correctly.

PROGRAMMING EXERCISES

Exercise P1.1. Write a program that prints the message, "Hello, my name is Hal!" Then, on a new line, the program should print the message "What would you like me to do?" Then it's the user's turn to type in an input. You haven't yet learned how to do it—just use the following lines of code:

```
string user_input;
getline(cin, user_input);
```

Finally, the program should ignore the user input and print the message "I am sorry, I cannot do that."

This program uses the `string` data type. To access this feature, you must place the linc

```
#include <string>
```

before the `main` function.

Here is a typical program run. The user input is printed in boldface.

```
Hello, my name is Hal!
What would you like me to do?
Clean up my room
I am sorry, I cannot do that.
```

When running the program, remember to hit the Enter key after typing the last word of the input line.

Exercise P1.2. Write a program that prints out a message "Hello, my name is Hal!" Then, on a new line, the program should print the message "What is your name?" As in Exercise P1.1, just use the following lines of code:

```
string user_name;
getline(cin, user_name);
```

Finally, the program should print the message "Hello, *user name*. I am glad to meet you!" To print the user name, simply use

```
cout << user_name;
```

As in Exercise P1.1, you must place the line

```
#include <string>
```

before the main function.

Here is a typical program run. The user input is printed in boldface.

```
Hello, my name is Hal!
What is your name?
Dave
Hello, Dave. I am glad to meet you!
```

Exercise P1.3. Write a program that computes the sum of the first ten positive integers, $1 + 2 + \cdots + 10$. *Hint:* Write a program of the form

```
int main()
{
   cout <<
   return 0;
}
```

Exercise P1.4. Write a program that computes the *product* of the first ten positive integers, $1 \times 2 \times \cdots \times 10$, and the sum of the reciprocals $1/1 + 1/2 + \cdots + 1/10$. This is harder than it sounds. First, you need to know that the * symbol, not ×, is used for multiplication in C++. Try writing the program, and check the results against a pocket calculator. The program's results aren't likely to be correct. Then write the numbers as *floating-point* numbers, 1.0, 2.0, . . ., 10.0, and run the program again. Can you explain the difference in the results? We will explain this phenomenon in Chapter 2.

Exercise P1.5. Write a program that displays your name inside a box on the terminal screen, like this:

```
 ------
| Dave |
 ------
```

Do your best to approximate lines with characters such as | - +.

Chapter 2

Numbers and Objects

- To understand the properties and limitations of integer and floating-point numbers

- To write arithmetic expressions and assignment statements in C++

- To appreciate the importance of comments and good code layout

- To be able to define and initialize variables and constants

- To learn how to read user input and display program output

- To use the standard C++ string type to define and manipulate character strings

- To become familiar with using objects and invoking member functions

- To write simple graphics programs (optional)

This chapter teaches you how to manipulate numbers and character strings in C++. You will also learn how to use objects that were designed for use with this textbook. The goal of this chapter is to write simple programs using basic data types.

CHAPTER CONTENTS

2.1 Number Types

Most computer programs process numbers. Typical numeric values include physical quantities, counters, and prices. In this section, you will learn how numbers are represented in a C++ program.

Consider the following simple problem. I have 8 pennies, 4 dimes, and 3 quarters in my purse. What is the total value of the coins?

Here is a C++ program that solves this problem.

ch02/coins1.cpp

```
1   #include <iostream>
2
3   using namespace std;
4
```

```
 5  int main()
 6  {
 7     int pennies = 8;
 8     int dimes = 4;
 9     int quarters = 3;
10
11     double total = pennies * 0.01 + dimes * 0.10
12        + quarters * 0.25; // Total value of the coins
13
14     cout << "Total value = " << total << "\n";
15
16     return 0;
17  }
```

Program Run

```
Total value = 1.23
```

> The most common number types in C++ are double (floating-point number) and int (integer).

This program manipulates two kinds of numbers. The coin counts (8, 4, 3) are *integers*. Integers are whole numbers without a fractional part. (Zero and negative whole numbers are integers.) The numerical values of the coins (0.01, 0.10, and 0.25) are *floating-point numbers*. Floating-point numbers can have decimal points. They are called "floating-point" because of their internal representation in the computer. The numbers 250, 2.5, 0.25, and 0.025 are all represented in a very similar way: namely, as a sequence of the significant digits—2500000—and an indication of the position of the decimal point. When the values are multiplied or divided by 10, only the position of the decimal point changes; it "floats". (Actually, internally the numbers are represented in base 2, but the principle is the same.) You have probably guessed that int is the C++ name for an integer. The name for the floating-point numbers used in this book is double; the reason is discussed in Advanced Topic 2.1 on page 38.

Why have two number types? One could just use

```
double pennies = 8;
```

There are two reasons for having separate types—one philosophical and one pragmatic. By indicating that the number of pennies is an integer, we make explicit an assumption: There can only be a whole number of pennies in the purse. The program would have worked just as well with floating-point numbers to count the coins, but it is generally a good idea to choose programming solutions that document one's intentions. Pragmatically speaking, integers are more efficient than floating-point numbers. They take less storage space and they are processed faster.

In C++, multiplication is denoted by an asterisk *, not a raised dot · or a cross ×. (There are no keys for these symbols on most keyboards.) For example, $d \cdot 10$ is written as d * 10. Do not write commas or spaces in numbers in C++. For example, 10,150.75 must be entered as 10150.75. To write numbers in exponential notation in C++, use an En instead of "× 10^n". For example, 5.0×10^{-3} becomes 5.0E-3.

The output statement

```
cout << "Total value = " << total << "\n";
```

shows a useful feature: *stream* output. You can display as many items as you like (in this case, the string "Total value = ") followed by the value of total and a string containing a newline character, (to move the cursor to the next line). Just separate the items that you want to print by <<. (See Syntax 2.1.) Alternatively, you could write three separate output statements

```
cout << "Total value = ";
cout << total;
cout << "\n";
```

This has exactly the same effect as displaying the three items in one statement.

Note the *comment*

```
// Total value of the coins
```

next to the definition of total. This comment is purely for the benefit of the human reader, to explain in more detail the meaning of total. Anything between // and the end of the line is completely ignored by the compiler. Comments that span multiple lines can be enclosed in /* and */ symbols.

The most important feature of our sample program is the introduction of *symbolic names*. We could have just programmed

```
int main()
{
   cout << "Total value = "
      << 8 * 0.01 + 4 * 0.10 + 3 * 0.25 << "\n";

   return 0;
}
```

This program computes the same answer. Compare it with the first program, though. Which one is easier to read? Which one is easier to update if we need to change the coin counts, such as by adding some nickels? By giving the symbolic names, pennies, dimes, and quarters, to the counts, we made the program more readable and maintainable. This is an important consideration. You introduce symbolic names to explain what a program does, just as you use variable names such as *p*, *d*, and *q* in algebra.

SYNTAX 2.1 Output Statement

cout << *expression*$_1$ << *expression*$_2$ << ... << *expression*$_n$;

Example:

```
cout << pennies;
cout << "Total value = " << total << "\n";
```

Purpose:

Print the values of one or more expressions.

In C++, each variable has a *type*. By defining int pennies, you proclaim that pennies can only hold integer values. If you try to put a floating-point value into the pennies variable, the fractional part will be lost.

You define a variable by first giving its type and then its name, such as int pennies. You may add an *initialization value*, such as = 8. Then you end the definition with a semicolon. See Syntax 2.3. Although the initialization is optional, it is a good idea to always initialize variables with a specific value. See Quality Tip 2.1 on page 36 for the reason.

> A variable is a storage location with a name. In C++, you also specify the type of the values that can be stored.

Variable names in algebra are usually just one letter long, such as p or A, maybe with a subscript such as p_1. In C++, it is common to choose longer and more descriptive names such as price or area. You cannot type subscripts; just tag an index behind the name: price1. You can choose any variable names you like, provided you follow a few simple rules. Names must start with a letter or the underscore (_) character, and the remaining characters must be letters, numbers, or underscores. You cannot use other symbols such as $ or %. Spaces are not permitted inside names either. Furthermore, you cannot use *reserved words* such as double or return as names; these words are reserved exclusively for their special C++ meanings. Variable names are also *case-sensitive*, that is, Area and area are different

---

SYNTAX 2.2 **Comment**

```
/* comment text */
// comment text
```

Example:

```
/* Total value of the coins */
// Total value of the coins
```

Purpose:

Add a comment to help a human reader understand the program.

SYNTAX 2.3 **Variable Definition**

```
type_name variable_name;
type_name variable_name = initial_value;
```

Example:

```
double total;
int pennies = 8;
```

Purpose:

Define a new variable of a particular type, and optionally supply an initial value.

names. It would not be a good idea to mix the two in the same program, because it would make that program very confusing to read. To avoid any possible confusion, we will never use any uppercase letters in variable names in this book. You will find that many programmers use names like `listPrice`; however we will always choose `list_price` instead. (Because spaces are not allowed inside names, `list price` is not permissible.)

QUALITY TIP 2.1

Initialize Variables When You Define Them

You should always initialize a variable at the same time you define it. Let us see what happens if you define a variable but leave it uninitialized.
 If you just define

```
int nickels;
```

the variable `nickels` comes into existence and memory space is found for it. However, it contains some random values since you did not initialize the variable. If you mean to initialize the variable to zero, you must do so explicitly:

```
int nickels = 0;
```

Why does an uninitialized variable contain a random value? It would seem less trouble to just put a 0 into a variable than to come up with a random value. Anyway, where does the random value come from? Does the computer roll electronic dice?
 When you define a variable, sufficient space is set aside in memory to hold values of the type you specify. For example, when you declare `int nickels`, a block of memory big enough to hold integers is reserved. The compiler uses that memory whenever you inquire about the value of `nickels` or when you change it.

> nickels = [   ]

When you initialize the variable, `int nickels = 0`, then a zero is placed into the newly acquired memory location.

> nickels = [0   ]

If you don't specify the initialization, the memory space is found and left as is. There is already *some* value in the memory. After all, you don't get freshly minted transistors—just an area of memory that is currently available and that you give up again when `main` ends. Its uninitialized values are just flotsam left over from prior computations. Thus, it takes no effort at all to give you a random initial value, whereas it does take a tiny effort to initialize a new memory location with zero or another value.
 If you don't specify an initialization, the compiler assumes that you are not quite ready to come up with the value that you want to store in the variable. Maybe the value needs to be computed from other variables, like the `total` in our example, and you haven't defined all components yet. It is quite reasonable not to waste time initializing a variable if that initial value is never used and will be overwritten with the truly intended value momentarily.

However, suppose you have the following sequence of events:

```
int nickels; // I'll get around to setting it presently
int dimes = 3;
double total = nickels * 0.05 + dimes * 0.10; // Error
nickels = 2 * dimes;
// Now I remember—I have twice as many nickels as dimes
```

This is a problem. The value of nickels has been used before it has been set. The value for total is computed as follows: Take a random number and multiply it by 0.05, then add the value of the dimes. Of course, what you get is a totally unpredictable value, which is of no use at all.

There is an additional danger here. Because the value of nickels is random, it may be different every time you run the program. Of course, you would get tipped off pretty soon if you ran the program twice and you got two different answers. However, suppose you ran the program ten times at home or in the lab, and it always came up with one value that looked reasonable. Then you turned the program in to be graded, and it came up with a different and unreasonable answer when the grader ran it. How can this happen? Aren't computer programs supposed to be predictable and deterministic? They are—as long as you initialize all your variables. On the grader's computer, the uninitialized value for nickels might have been 15,054, when on your machine on that particular day it happened to have been 6.

What is the remedy? *Reorder the definitions* so that all of the variables are initialized. This is usually simple to do:

```
int dimes = 3;
int nickels = 2 * dimes; // I have twice as many nickels as dimes
double total = nickels * 0.05 + dimes * 0.10; // OK
```

QUALITY TIP 2.2

Choose Descriptive Variable Names

We could have saved ourselves a lot of typing by using shorter variable names, as in

```
int main()
{
   int p = 8;
   int d = 4;
   int q = 3;

   double t = p * 0.01 + d * 0.10 + q * 0.25;   // Total value of the coins

   cout << "Total value = " << t << "\n";

   return 0;
}
```

Compare this program with the previous one, though. Which one is easier to read? There is no comparison. Just reading pennies is a lot less trouble than reading p and then *figuring out* it must mean "pennies".

In practical programming, this is particularly important when programs are written by more than one person. It may be obvious to *you* that p must stand for pennies and not percentage (or maybe pressure), but is it obvious to the person who needs to update your code years later, long after you were promoted (or laid off)? For that matter, will you remember yourself what p means when you look at the code six months from now?

Of course, you could use comments:

```
int main()
{
   int p = 8; // Pennies
   int d = 4; // Dimes
   int q = 3; // Quarters

   double t = p * 0.01 + d * 0.10 + q * 0.25;   // Total value of the coins

   cout << "Total value = " << t << "\n";

   return 0;
}
```

That makes the definitions pretty clear, but the computation p * 0.01 + d * 0.10 + q * 0.25 is still cryptic.

If you have the choice between comments and self-commenting code, choose the latter. It is better to have clear code with no comments than cryptic code with comments. There is a good reason for this. In actual practice, code is not written once and handed to a grader, to be subsequently forgotten. Programs are modified and enhanced all the time. If the code explains itself, you just have to update it to new code that explains itself. If the code requires explanation, you have to update both the code and the explanation. If you forget to update the explanation, you end up with a comment that is worse than useless because it no longer reflects what is actually going on. The next person reading it must waste time trying to understand whether the code is wrong or the comment.

ADVANCED TOPIC 2.1

Numeric Ranges and Precisions

Unfortunately, int and double values do suffer from one problem. They cannot represent arbitrary integer or floating-point numbers. On some compilers for personal computers, the int type can represent numbers in the range from –2,147,483,648 to 2,147,483,647, or about 2 billion. (These strange-looking limits are the result of the use of binary numbers in computers.) You can use floating-point numbers to represent larger quantities. You should keep in mind that the double type has a precision of about fifteen decimal digits. For example, the number 299,999,999,999,999.95 cannot be represented exactly—it is rounded to 299,999,999,999,999.9375. For most programs, the precision of the double type is sufficient, but read Common Error 2.3 on page 49 for information about a related issue: roundoff errors.

C++ has another floating-point type, called float, which has a much more limited precision—only about seven decimal digits. You should not normally use the float type in your programs. The limited precision can be a problem in some programs, and all mathematical functions return results of type double. If you save those results in a variable of type float, the compiler will warn about possible information loss (see Advanced Topic 2.2 on page 49).

In addition to the int type, C++ has integer types short, long and long long. For each integer type, there is an unsigned equivalent. For example, the short type typically has a range from –32768 to 32767, whereas unsigned short has a range from 0 to 65535. The ranges for integer types are not standardized, and they differ among compilers. Table 1 contains typical values.

Table 1 — Number Types		
Type	**Typical Range**	**Typical Size**
int	−2,147,483,648 . . . 2,147,483,647 (about 2 billion)	4 bytes
unsigned	0 . . . 4,294,967,295	4 bytes
short	−32,768 . . . 32,767	2 bytes
unsigned short	0 . . . 65,535	2 bytes
long long	−9,223,372,036,854,775,808 . . . 9,223,372,036,854,775,807	8 bytes
double	The double-precision floating-point type, with a range of about $\pm 10^{308}$ and about 15 significant decimal digits	8 bytes
float	The single-precision floating-point type, with a range of about $\pm 10^{38}$ and about 7 significant decimal digits	4 bytes

RANDOM FACT 2.1

The Pentium Floating-Point Bug

In 1994, Intel Corporation released what was then its most powerful processor, the Pentium. Unlike previous generations of its processors, it had a very fast floating-point unit. Intel's goal was to compete aggressively with the makers of higher-end processors for engineering workstations. The Pentium was an immediate huge success.

In the summer of 1994, Dr. Thomas Nicely of Lynchburg College in Virginia ran an extensive set of computations to analyze the sums of reciprocals of certain sequences of prime numbers. The results were not always what his theory predicted, even after he took the Pentium in Intel's lineup. This should not have happened. The optimal roundoff behavior of floating-point calculations has been standardized by the Institute for Electrical and Electronic Engineers (IEEE) and Intel claimed to adhere to the IEEE standard in both the 486 and the Pentium processors. Upon further checking, Dr. Nicely discovered that indeed there was a very small set of numbers for which the product of two numbers was computed differently on the two processors. For example,

$$4{,}195{,}835 - \left((4{,}195{,}835 / 3{,}145{,}727) \times 3{,}145{,}727 \right)$$

is mathematically equal to 0, and it did compute as 0 on a 486 processor. On his Pentium processor the result was 256.

As it turned out, Intel had independently discovered the bug in its testing and had started to produce chips that fixed it. The bug was caused by an error in a table that was used to speed up the floating-point multiplication algorithm of the processor. Intel determined that the problem was exceedingly rare. They claimed that under normal use, a typical consumer would only notice the problem once every 27,000 years. Unfortunately for Intel, Dr. Nicely had not been a normal user.

Now Intel had a real problem on its hands. It figured that the cost of replacing all Pentium processors that it had already sold would cost a great deal of money. Intel already had more orders for the chip than it could produce, and it would be particularly galling to have to give out the scarce chips as free replacements instead of selling them. Intel's management decided to punt on the issue and initially offered to replace the processors only for those customers who could prove that their work required absolute precision in mathematical calculations. Naturally, that did not go over well with the hundreds of thousands of customers who had paid retail prices of $700 and more for a Pentium chip and did not want to live with the nagging feeling that perhaps, one day, their income tax program would produce a faulty return.

Ultimately, Intel caved in to public demand and replaced all defective chips, at a cost of about 475 million dollars.

What do you think? Intel claims that the probability of the bug occurring in any calculation is extremely small—smaller than many chances we take every day, such as driving to work in an automobile. Indeed, many users had used their Pentium computer for many months without reporting any ill effects, and the computations that Professor Nicely was doing are hardly examples of typical user needs. As a result of its public relations blunder, Intel ended up paying a large amount of money. Undoubtedly, some of that money was added to chip prices and thus actually paid by Intel's customers. Also, a large number of processors, whose manufacture consumed energy and caused some environmental impact, were destroyed without benefiting anyone. Could Intel have been justified in wanting to replace only the processors of those users who could reasonably be expected to suffer an impact from the problem?

Suppose that, instead of stonewalling, Intel had offered you the choice of a free replacement processor or a $200 rebate. What would you have done? Would you have replaced your faulty chip, or would you have taken your chances and pocketed the money?

2.2 Input

Use the >> operator to read a value from an input stream and place it in a variable.

Most programs ask for input and produce output that depends on the values supplied by the program user. For example, the program of the preceding section can be improved by allowing the user to supply the coin quantities. Here is the improved program.

ch02/coins2.cpp

```
1  #include <iostream>
2
3  using namespace std;
4
5  int main()
6  {
7     cout << "How many pennies do you have? ";
8     int pennies;
```

```
 9      cin >> pennies;
10
11      cout << "How many nickels do you have? ";
12      int nickels;
13      cin >> nickels;
14
15      cout << "How many dimes do you have? ";
16      int dimes;
17      cin >> dimes;
18
19      cout << "How many quarters do you have? ";
20      int quarters;
21      cin >> quarters;
22
23      double total = pennies * 0.01 + nickels * 0.05
24         + dimes * 0.10 + quarters * 0.25;
25            // Total value of the coins
26
27      cout << "Total value = " << total << "\n";
28
29      return 0;
30  }
```

Program Run

```
How many pennies do you have? 3
How many nickels do you have? 2
How many dimes do you have? 1
How many quarters do you have? 4
Total value = 1.23
```

When this program runs, it will ask, or *prompt*, you:

```
How many pennies do you have?
```

The cursor will stay on the same line as the prompt, and you should enter a number, followed by the Enter key. Then there will be three more prompts, and finally the answer is printed and the program terminates.

Reading a number into the variable pennies is achieved by the statement

```
cin >> pennies;
```

When this statement is executed, the program waits for the user to type in a number and press the Enter key. The number is then placed into the variable, and the program executes the next statement.

In this case, we did not initialize the variables that count the coins because the input statements move values into these variables. We moved the variable definitions as close as possible to the input statements to indicate where the values are set.

You can read floating-point values as well:

```
double balance;
cin >> balance;
```

When you specify that an integer is to be read from the keyboard, zero and negative numbers are allowed as inputs but floating-point numbers are not. If the user nevertheless provides a floating-point input, only the integer part is read. See Common Error 2.2 on page 44.

It is possible to read more than one value at a time. For example, the input statement

```
cin >> pennies >> nickels >> dimes >> quarters;
```

reads four values from the keyboard (see Syntax 2.4). The values can be all on one line, such as

```
8 0 4 3
```

or on separate lines, such as

```
8
0
4
3
```

All that matters is that the numbers are separated by *white space*: that is, blank spaces, tabs, or newlines. You enter a blank space by hitting the space bar, a tab by hitting the tab key (often marked with an arrow and vertical bar →|), and a newline by hitting the Enter key. These key strokes are used by the input reader to separate input.

SYNTAX 2.4 Input Statement

cin >> *variable$_1$* >> *variable$_2$* >> ... >> *variable$_n$*;

Example:

```
cin >> pennies;
cin >> first >> middle >> last;
```

Purpose:

Read the value for one or more variables from the input.

COMMON ERROR 2.1

Buffered Input

Keyboard input is *buffered*. All input is placed into a buffer until the user hits the Enter key. At that time, input is read from the buffer. When the buffer is empty, the user can provide more input. This buffering can have surprising effects. For example, suppose the coin calculation program prompts you

```
How many pennies do you have?
```

As a response, you enter

```
8 0 4 3
```

Nothing happens until you hit the Enter key (see Steps 1 and 2 in Figure 1).

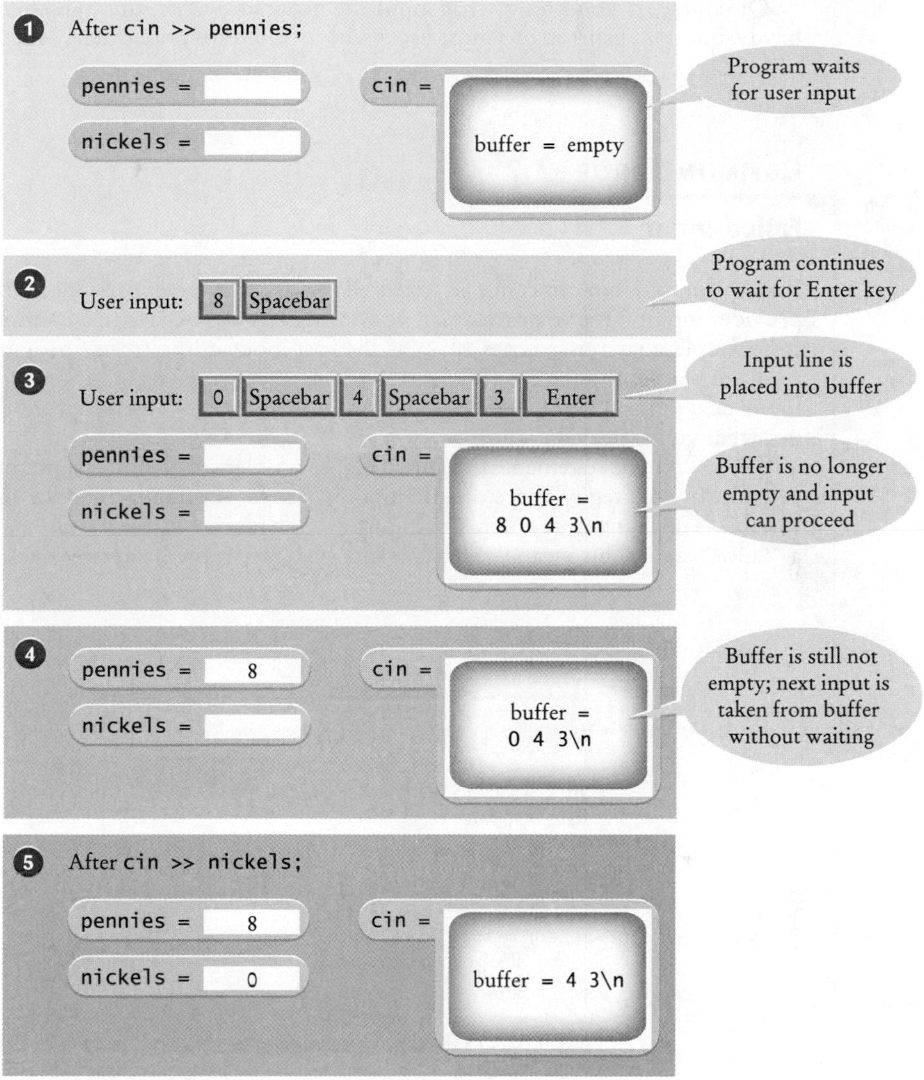

1 After `cin >> pennies;`

pennies = [   ]   cin = [
nickels = [   ]   buffer = empty]

Program waits for user input

2 User input: [8] [Spacebar]

Program continues to wait for Enter key

3 User input: [0] [Spacebar] [4] [Spacebar] [3] [Enter]

Input line is placed into buffer

pennies = [   ]   cin = [
nickels = [   ]   buffer = 8 0 4 3\n]

Buffer is no longer empty and input can proceed

4 pennies = [8]   cin = [
nickels = [   ]   buffer = 0 4 3\n]

Buffer is still not empty; next input is taken from buffer without waiting

5 After `cin >> nickels;`

pennies = [8]   cin = [
nickels = [0]   buffer = 4 3\n]

Figure 1   Separating Input

Suppose you hit it. The line is now sent for processing by `cin`. The first input command reads the 8 and removes it from the input stream buffer (see Steps 3 and 4 in Figure 1). The other three numbers are left in the buffer for subsequent input operations.

Then the prompt

`How many nickels do you have?`

is displayed, and the program *immediately* reads the 0 from the buffer. You don't get a chance to type another number. Then the other two prompts are displayed, and the other two numbers are processed.

Of course, if you know what input the program wants, this type-ahead feature can be handy, but it is surprising to most users who are used to more orderly input processing.

COMMON ERROR 2.2

Failed Input

Frankly, input from `cin` is not all that well suited for interaction with human users. If a user provides input in the wrong format, your programs can behave in a confusing way. Suppose, for example, that a user types 10.75 as the first input in the coins2 program. The 10 will be read and placed into the `pennies` variable. The .75 remains in the buffer. It will be considered in the next input statement. (See Steps 1 and 2 in Figure 2.) This is not intuitive and probably not what you expected.

The next input statement runs into a bigger problem. The buffer contains .75 which is not suitable for an integer. Therefore, no input is carried out (that is, the old value of the `nickels` variable is unchanged, see Step 3 in Figure 2.). What's more, the `cin` input stream sets itself to a "failed" state. This means, `cin` has lost confidence in the data it receives, so all subsequent

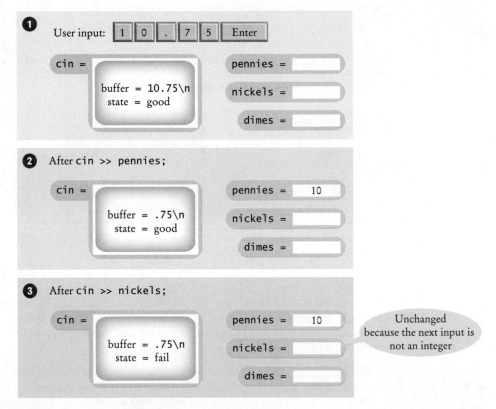

Figure 2   Processing Input

Figure 2 Processing Input, continued

input statements will be ignored. (See Step 4 in Figure 2.) Unfortunately, there is no warning beep or error message that alerts the user to this problem. You will learn in Chapter 3 how to recognize and solve input problems. Of course, that is a necessary skill for building programs that can survive untrained or careless users. At this point we must just ask you to type in the right kind of responses to the input prompts.

2.3 Assignment

> An assignment statement stores a new value in a variable, replacing the previously stored value.

The contents of a variable can vary over time. To change the value of a variable, you use an *assignment statement* (see Syntax 2.5 on page 48). The left hand of an assignment statement consists of a variable. The right hand is an expression that has a value. That value is stored in the variable, overwriting its previous contents.

For example, consider this statement:

```
total = pennies * 0.01;
```

The value of the expression pennies * 0.01 is stored in total, replacing the previous value of total.

The following program demonstrates the use of assignment statements. Let us compute the value of the coins by keeping a *running total*. First, ask for the number of pennies and set the total to the value of the pennies. Then ask for the number of nickels and *add* the value of the nickels to the total. Then do the same for the dimes and quarters. Here is the program.

ch02/coins3.cpp

```
1  #include <iostream>
2
3  using namespace std;
4
5  int main()
6  {
```

```
 7    cout << "How many pennies do you have? ";
 8    int count;
 9    cin >> count;
10    double total = count * 0.01;
11
12    cout << "How many nickels do you have? ";
13    cin >> count;
14    total = count * 0.05 + total;
15
16    cout << "How many dimes do you have? ";
17    cin >> count;
18    total = count * 0.10 + total;
19
20    cout << "How many quarters do you have? ";
21    cin >> count;
22    total = count * 0.25 + total;
23
24    cout << "Total value = " << total << "\n";
25
26    return 0;
27 }
```

In this program, we only need one count variable, because we process the value right away, accumulating it into the total.

The first processing statement, double total = count * 0.01, is straightforward. The second statement is much more interesting:

```
total = count * 0.05 + total;
```

It means, "Compute the value of the nickel contribution (count * 0.05), add to it the value of the running total, *and place the result again into the variable* total" (see Figure 3).

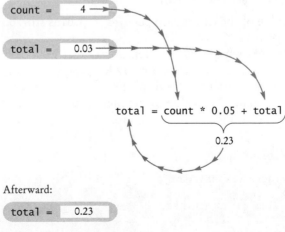

Afterward:

Figure 3   Assignment

When you make an assignment of an expression into a variable, the *types* of the variable and the expression need to match. For example, it is an error to assign

```
total = "a lot";
```

because `total` is a floating-point variable and `"a lot"` is a string. It is, however, legal, to store an integer in a floating-point variable.

```
total = count;
```

If you assign a floating-point expression to an integer, the expression will be truncated to an integer. Unfortunately, that will not necessarily be the closest integer; Common Error 2.3 on page 49 contains a dramatic example. Therefore it is never a good idea to make an assignment from floating-point to integer. In fact, many compilers emit a warning if you do.

There is a subtle difference between the statements

```
double total = count * 0.01;
```

and

```
total = count * 0.05 + total;
```

The first statement is the *definition* of `total`. It is a command to create a new variable of type `double`, to give it the name `total`, and to initialize it with `count * 0.01`. The second statement is an *assignment statement*: an instruction to replace the contents of the existing variable `total` with another value.

It is not possible to have multiple definitions of the same variable. The sequence of statements

```
double total = count * 0.01;
...
double total = count * 0.05 + total; // Error
```

is illegal. The compiler will complain about an attempt to redefine `total`, because it thinks you want to define a new variable in the second statement. On the other hand, it is perfectly legal, and indeed very common, to make multiple assignments to the same variable:

```
total = count * 0.05 + total;
...
total = count * 0.10 + total;
```

The = sign doesn't mean that the left-hand side *is equal* to the right-hand side but that the right-hand side value is copied into the left-hand side variable. You should not confuse this *assignment operation* with the = used in algebra to denote *equality*. The assignment operator is an instruction to do something, namely place a value into a variable. The mathematical equality states the fact that two values are equal. For example, in C++, it is perfectly legal to write

```
month = month + 1;
```

It means to look up the value stored in the variable `month`, to add 1 to it, and to stuff the sum back into `month`. (See Figure 4.) The net effect of executing this statement is to increment `month` by 1. Of course, in mathematics it would make no sense to write that month = month + 1; no value can equal itself plus 1.

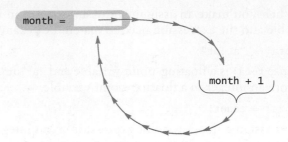

Figure 4   Incrementing a Variable

The concepts of assignment and equality have no relationship with each other, and it is a bit unfortunate that the C++ language uses = to denote assignment. Other programming languages use a symbol such as <- or :=, which avoids the confusion.

> The ++ operator adds 1 to a variable; the -- operator subtracts 1.

Consider once more the statement month = month + 1. This statement increments the month counter. For example, if month was 3 before execution of the statement, it is set to 4 afterwards. This increment operation is so common when writing programs that there is a special shorthand for it, namely

```
month++;
```

This statement has the exact same effect, namely to add 1 to month, but it is easier to type. As you might have guessed, there is also a decrement operator --. The statement

```
month--;
```

subtracts 1 from month.

The ++ increment operator gave the C++ programming language its name. C++ is the incremental improvement of the C language.

SYNTAX 2.5 Assignment

variable = expression;

Example:

```
total = pennies * 0.01;
```

Purpose:

Store the value of an expression in a variable.

COMMON ERROR 2.3

Roundoff Errors

Roundoff errors are a fact of life when calculating with floating-point numbers. You probably have encountered that phenomenon yourself with manual calculations. If you calculate 1/3 to two decimal places, you get 0.33. Multiplying again by 3, you obtain 0.99, not 1.00.

In the processor hardware, numbers are represented in the binary number system, not in decimal. You still get roundoff errors when binary digits are lost. They just may crop up at different places than you might expect. Here is an example.

```cpp
#include <iostream>

using namespace std;

int main()
{
   double x = 4.35;
   int n = x * 100;
   cout << n << "\n"; // Prints 434!
   return 0;
}
```

Of course, one hundred times 4.35 is 435, but the program prints 434.

Most computers represent numbers in the binary system. In the binary system, there is no exact representation for 4.35, just as there is no exact representation for 1/3 in the decimal system. The representation used by the computer is just a little less than 4.35, so 100 times that value is just a little less than 435. When a floating-point value is converted to an integer, the entire fractional part, which is almost 1, is thrown away, and the integer 434 is stored in n.

To avoid this problem, you should always add 0.5 to a positive floating-point value before converting it to an integer:

```cpp
double y = x * 100;
int n = y + 0.5;
```

Adding 0.5 works, because it turns all values above 434.5 into values above 435.

Of course, the compiler will still issue a warning that assigning a floating-point value to an integer variable is unsafe. See Advanced Topic 2.2 on how to avoid this warning.

ADVANCED TOPIC 2.2

Casts

Occasionally, you need to store a value into a variable of a different type. Whenever there is the risk of *information loss*, the compiler issues a warning. For example, if you store a double value into an int variable, you can lose information in two ways:

- The fractional part is lost.
- The magnitude may be too large.

For example,

```cpp
int p = 1.0E100; // NO
```

is not likely to work, because 10^{100} is larger than the largest representable integer.

Nevertheless, sometimes you do want to convert a floating-point value into an integer value. If you are prepared to lose the fractional part and you know that this particular floating-point number is not larger than the largest possible integer, then you can turn off the warning by using a *cast*: a conversion from one type (such as `double`) to another type (such as `int`) that is not safe in general, but that you know to be safe in a particular circumstance. You express this in C++ as follows:

```
int n = static_cast<int>(y + 0.5);
```

Before the `static_cast` notation (see Syntax 2.6) was invented, C++ programmers used a different notation, shown below:

```
int n = (int)(y + 0.5);
```

SYNTAX 2.6 Cast

static_cast<*type_name*>(*expression*)

Example:

static_cast<int>(x + 0.5)

Purpose:

Change an expression to a different type.

ADVANCED TOPIC 2.3

Combining Assignment and Arithmetic

In C++, you can combine arithmetic and assignment. For example, the instruction

```
total += count * 0.05;
```

is a shortcut for

```
total = total + count * 0.05;
```

Similarly,

```
total -= count * 0.05;
```

means the same as

```
total = total - count * 0.05;
```

and

```
total *= 2;
```

is another way of writing

```
total = total * 2;
```

Many programmers find this a convenient shortcut. If you like it, go ahead and use it in your own code. For simplicity, we won't use it in this book, though.

2.4 Constants

> A constant is a named value that cannot be changed.

Using descriptive variable names makes a program easier to read. The same is true for constant values. Using a descriptive name is better than using the value itself.

Consider the following program:

```
int main()
{
   double bottles;
   cout << "How many bottles do you have? ";
   cin >> bottles;

   double cans;
   cout << "How many cans do you have? ";
   cin >> cans;

   double total = bottles * 2 + cans * 0.355;

   cout << "The total volume is " << total << "\n";

   return 0;
}
```

What is going on here? What is the significance of the 0.355?

This formula computes the amount of soda in a refrigerator that is filled with two-liter bottles and 12-oz. cans. (See Table 2 for conversion factors between metric and nonmetric units.) Let us make the computation clearer by using constants (see Syntax 2.7 on page 53).

Table 2 Conversion Between Metric and Nonmetric Units	
English	Metric
1 (fluid) ounce (oz.)	29.586 milliliter (ml)
1 gallon	3.785 liter (l)
1 ounce (oz.)	28.3495 grams (g)
1 pound (lb.)	453.6 grams
1 inch	2.54 centimeter (cm)
1 foot	30.5 centimeter
1 mile	1.609 kilometer (km)

ch02/volume.cpp

```
1   #include <iostream>
2
3   using namespace std;
4
5   int main()
6   {
7      double bottles;
8
9      cout << "How many bottles do you have? ";
10     cin >> bottles;
11
12     double cans;
13     cout << "How many cans do you have? ";
14     cin >> cans;
15
16     const double BOTTLE_VOLUME = 2.0;
17     const double CAN_VOLUME = 0.355;
18     double total = bottles * BOTTLE_VOLUME
19        + cans * CAN_VOLUME;
20
21     cout << "The total volume is " << total << " liter.\n";
22
23     return 0;
24  }
```

Program Run

```
How many bottles do you have? 2
How many cans do you have? 6
The total volume is 6.13 liter.
```

In C++, you use the const keyword to declare a constant:

```
const double CAN_VOLUME = 0.355;
```

Now CAN_VOLUME is a named entity. Unlike total, it is constant. After initialization with 0.355, it never changes.

In fact, you can do even better and explain where the value for the can volume came from.

```
const double LITER_PER_OZ = 0.029586;
const double CAN_VOLUME = 12 * LITER_PER_OZ; // 12-oz. cans
```

Sure, it is more trouble to type the constant definitions and use the constant names in the formulas. But it makes the code much more readable. It also makes the code much easier to change. Suppose the program does computations involving volumes in several different places. And suppose you need to switch from two-liter bottles to half-gallon bottles. If you simply multiply by 2 to get bottle volumes, you must now replace every 2 by 1.893 ... well, not *every* number 2. There may have been other uses of 2 in the program that had nothing to do with bottles. You have to *look* at every number 2 and see if you need to change it. If, on the other hand, the constant BOTTLE_VOLUME is conscientiously used throughout the program, one need only update it in *one location*. Named constants are very important for program maintenance. See Quality Tip 2.3 on page 53 for more information.

Constants are commonly written using capital letters to distinguish them visually from variables.

Syntax 2.7 Constant Definition

```
const type_name constant_name = initial_value;
```

Example:

```
const double LITER_PER_OZ = 0.029586;
```

Purpose:

Define a new constant of a particular type and supply its value.

Quality Tip 2.3

Do Not Use Magic Numbers

A *magic number* is a numeric constant that appears in your code without explanation. For example,

```
if (col >= 66) ...
```

Why 66? Maybe this program prints in a 12-point font on 8.5 × 11-inch paper with a 1-inch margin on the left- and right-hand sides? Indeed, then you can fit 65 characters on a line. Once you reach column 66, you are beyond the right margin and must do something special. However, these are awfully fragile assumptions. To make the program work for a different paper size, one must locate all values of 65 (and 66 and 64) and replace them, taking care not to touch those 65s (and 66s and 64s) that have nothing to do with paper size. In a program that is more than a few pages long, that is incredibly tedious and error-prone.

The remedy is to use a named constant instead:

```
const int RIGHT_MARGIN = 65;

if (col > RIGHT_MARGIN) ...
```

Even the most reasonable cosmic constant is going to change one day. You think there are 365 days per year? Your customers on Mars are going to be pretty unhappy about your silly prejudice. Make a constant

```
const int DAYS_PER_YEAR = 365;
```

By the way, the device

```
const int THREE_HUNDRED_AND_SIXTY_FIVE = 365;
```

is counterproductive and frowned upon.

You should *never* use magic numbers in your code. As a rule of thumb, when you find yourself writing a number other than 0 or 1, consider using a named constant instead.

ADVANCED TOPIC 2.4

Enumerated Types

Sometimes a variable should only take values from a limited set of possibilities. For example, a variable describing a weekday (Monday, Tuesday, ..., Sunday) can have one of seven states.

In C++, we can define such *enumerated types*:

```
enum Weekday { MONDAY, TUESDAY, WEDNESDAY, THURSDAY,
   FRIDAY, SATURDAY, SUNDAY };
```

This makes Weekday a type, similar to int. As with any type, we can declare variables of that type.

```
Weekday homework_due_day = WEDNESDAY;
// Homework due every Wednesday
```

Of course, you could have declared homework_due_day as an integer. Then you would need to encode the weekdays into numbers.

```
int homework_due_day = 2;
```

That violates our rule against "magic numbers". You could go on and define constants

```
const int MONDAY = 0;
const int TUESDAY = 1;
const int WEDNESDAY = 2;
const int THURSDAY = 3;
const int FRIDAY = 4;
const int SATURDAY = 5;
const int SUNDAY = 6;
```

However, the Weekday enumerated type is clearer, and it is a convenience that you need not come up with the integer values yourself. It also allows the compiler to catch programming errors. For example, the following is a compile-time error:

```
Weekday homework_due_day = 10; // Compile-time error
```

In contrast, the following statement will compile without complaint and create a logical problem when the program runs:

```
int homework_due_day = 10; // Logic error
```

It is a good idea to use an enumerated type whenever a variable can have a finite set of values.

2.5 Arithmetic

You already saw how to add and multiply values:

```
double total = bottles * BOTTLE_VOLUME + cans * CAN_VOLUME;
```

> In C++, you use * for multiplication and / for division.

All four basic arithmetic operations—addition, subtraction, multiplication, and division—are supported. You must write a * b to denote multiplication, not ab or a · b. Division is indicated with a /, not a fraction bar.

For example,

$$\frac{a+b}{2}$$

becomes

```
(a + b) / 2
```

Parentheses are used just as in algebra: to indicate in which order the subexpressions should be computed. For example, in the expression (a + b) / 2, the sum a + b is computed first, and then the sum is divided by 2. In contrast, in the expression

```
a + b / 2
```

only b is divided by 2, and then the sum of a and b / 2 is formed. Just as in regular algebraic notation, multiplication and division take precedence over addition and subtraction. For example, in the expression a + b / 2, the / is carried out first, even though the + operation occurs further to the left.

> If both arguments of / are integers, the remainder is discarded. The % operator computes the remainder of an integer division.

Division works as you would expect, as long as at least one of the numbers involved is a floating-point number. That is,

```
7.0 / 4.0
7 / 4.0
7.0 / 4
```

all yield 1.75. However, if *both* numbers are integers, then the result of the division is always an integer, with the remainder discarded. That is,

```
7 / 4
```

evaluates to 1 because 7 divided by 4 is 1 with a remainder of 3 (which is discarded). This can be a source of subtle programming errors; see Common Error 2.4 on page 58.

If you are just interested in the remainder, use the % operator:

```
7 % 4
```

is 3, the remainder of the integer division of 7 by 4. The % operator must be applied to integers only, not to floating-point values. For example, 7.0 % 4 is an error. The % symbol has no analog in algebra. It was chosen because it looks similar to /, and the remainder operation is related to division.

Here is a typical use for the integer / and % operations. Suppose we want to know the value of the coins in a purse in dollar and cents. We can compute the value as an integer, denominated in cents, and then compute the whole dollar amount and the remaining change:

ch02/coins4.cpp

```
1  #include <iostream>
2
3  using namespace std;
4
5  int main()
6  {
```

```
 7    cout << "How many pennies do you have? ";
 8    int pennies;
 9    cin >> pennies;
10
11    cout << "How many nickels do you have? ";
12    int nickels;
13    cin >> nickels;
14
15    cout << "How many dimes do you have? ";
16    int dimes;
17    cin >> dimes;
18
19    cout << "How many quarters do you have? ";
20    int quarters;
21    cin >> quarters;
22
23    const int PENNIES_PER_NICKEL = 5;
24    const int PENNIES_PER_DIME = 10;
25    const int PENNIES_PER_QUARTER = 25;
26    const int PENNIES_PER_DOLLAR = 100;
27
28    int value = pennies + PENNIES_PER_NICKEL * nickels
29       + PENNIES_PER_DIME * dimes + PENNIES_PER_QUARTER * quarters;
30    int dollar = value / PENNIES_PER_DOLLAR;
31    int cents = value % PENNIES_PER_DOLLAR;
32
33    cout << "Total value = " << dollar << " dollars and "
34       << cents << " cents.\n";
35
36    return 0;
37 }
```

Program Run

```
How many pennies do you have? 3
How many nickels do you have? 2
How many dimes do you have? 1
How many quarters do you have? 4
Total value = 1 dollars and 23 cents
```

> The C++ library defines many mathematical functions such as sqrt (square root) and pow (raising to a power).

To take the square root of a number, you use the sqrt function (see Syntax 2.8). For example, $\sqrt{x}$ is written as sqrt(x). To compute x^n, you write pow(x, n). However, to compute x^2, it is significantly more efficient simply to write x * x. To use sqrt and pow, you must place the line #include <cmath> at the top of your program file. The header file cmath is a standard C++ header that is available with all C++ systems, just like iostream.

As you can see, the effect of the /, sqrt, and pow operations is to flatten out mathematical terms. In algebra, you use fractions, exponents, and roots to arrange

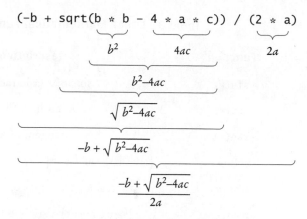

Figure 5 Analyzing an Expression

expressions in a compact two-dimensional form. In C++, you have to write all expressions in a linear arrangement. For example, the subexpression

$$\frac{-b + \sqrt{b^2 - 4ac}}{2a}$$

of the quadratic formula becomes

```
(-b + sqrt(b * b - 4 * a * c)) / (2 * a)
```

Figure 5 shows how to analyze such an expression. With complicated expressions like these, it is not always easy to keep the parentheses matched—see Common Error 2.5 on page 59.

Table 3 on page 58 shows additional functions that are declared in the `cmath` header. Inputs and outputs are floating-point numbers.

SYNTAX 2.8 Function Call

function_name(*expression₁*, *expression₂*, ..., *expressionₙ*)

Example:

```
sqrt(x)
pow(z + y, n)
```

Purpose:

Call a function and supply the values for the function parameters.

Table 3	Other Mathematical Functions
Function	**Description**
sin(x)	sine of x (x in radians)
cos(x)	cosine of x
tan(x)	tangent of x
asin(x)	$\left(\text{arc sine}\right)\ \sin^{-1} x \in \left[-\pi/2,\ \pi/2\right],\ x \in \left[-1,\ 1\right]$
acos(x)	$\left(\text{arc cosine}\right)\ \text{arc}^{-1} x \in \left[0,\ \pi\right],\ x \in \left[-1,\ 1\right]$
atan(x)	$\left(\text{arc tangent}\right)\ \tan^{-1} x \in \left(-\pi/2,\ \pi/2\right)$
atan2(y, x)	$\left(\text{arc tangent}\right)\ \tan^{-1}\left(y/x\right) \in \left[-\pi/2,\ \pi/2\right],\ x$ may be 0
exp(x)	e^x
log(x)	$\left(\text{natural log}\right)\ \log_e\left(x\right),\ x > 0$
log10(x)	$\left(\text{decimal log}\right)\ \log_{10}\left(x\right),\ x > 0$
sinh(x)	hyperbolic sine of x
cosh(x)	hyperbolic cosine of x
tanh(x)	hyperbolic tangent of x
ceil(x)	smallest integer $\geq x$
floor(x)	largest integer $\leq x$
fabs(x)	absolute value $\left|x\right|$

COMMON ERROR 2.4

Integer Division

It is unfortunate that C++ uses the same symbol, namely /, for both integer and floating-point division. These are really quite different operations. It is a common error to use integer division by accident. Consider this program segment that computes the average of three integers.

```
cout << "Please enter your last three test scores: ";
int s1;
int s2;
int s3;
cin >> s1 >> s2 >> s3;
double average = (s1 + s2 + s3) / 3; // Error
cout << "Your average score is " << average << "\n";
```

What could be wrong with that? Of course, the average of s1, s2, and s3 is

$$\frac{s1+s2+s3}{3}$$

Here, however, the / does not mean division in the mathematical sense. It denotes integer division since both s1 + s2 + s3 and 3 are integers. For example, if the scores add up to 14, the average is computed to be 4, the result of the integer division of 14 by 3. That integer 4 is then moved into the floating-point variable average. The remedy is to make the numerator or denominator into a floating-point number:

```
double total = s1 + s2 + s3;
double average = total / 3;
```

or

```
double average = (s1 + s2 + s3) / 3.0;
```

COMMON ERROR 2.5

Unbalanced Parentheses

Consider the expression

```
1.5 * ((-(b - sqrt(b * b - 4 * a * c)) / (2 * a))
```

What is wrong with it? Count the parentheses. There are five (and four). The parentheses are *unbalanced*. This kind of typing error is very common with complicated expressions. Now consider this expression.

```
1.5 * (sqrt(b * b - 4 * a * c))) - ((b / (2 * a))
```

This expression has five (and five), but it still is not correct. In the middle of the expression,

```
1.5 * (sqrt(b * b - 4 * a * c))) - ((b / (2 * a))
                                ↑
```

there are only two (but three), which is an error. In the middle of an expression, the count of (must be greater or equal than the count of), and at the end of the expression the two counts must be the same.

Here is a simple trick to make the counting easier without using pencil and paper. It is difficult for the brain to keep two counts simultaneously. Keep only one count when scanning the expression. Start with 1 at the first opening parenthesis, add 1 whenever you see an opening parenthesis, and subtract one whenever you see a closing parenthesis. Say the numbers aloud as you scan the expression. If the count ever drops below zero, or is not zero at the end, the parentheses are unbalanced. For example, when scanning the previous expression, you would mutter

```
1.5 * (sqrt(b * b - 4 * a * c) ) ) - ((b / (2 * a))
       1    2                  1 0 -1
```

and you would find the error.

COMMON ERROR 2.6

Forgetting Header Files

Every program that you write needs at least one header file, to include facilities for input and output; that file is normally iostream.

If you use mathematical functions such as sqrt, you need to include cmath. If you forget to include the appropriate header file, the compiler will not know symbols such as sqrt or cout. If the compiler complains about an undefined function or symbol, check your header files.

Sometimes you may not know which header file to include. Suppose you want to compute the absolute value of an integer using the abs function. As it happens, abs is not defined in cmath but in cstdlib. How can you find the correct header file? You need to locate the documentation of the abs function, preferably using the online help of your development environment or a reference site on the Internet such as **http://www.cplusplus.com** [1]. The documentation includes a short description of the function and the name of the header file that you must include (see Figure 6).

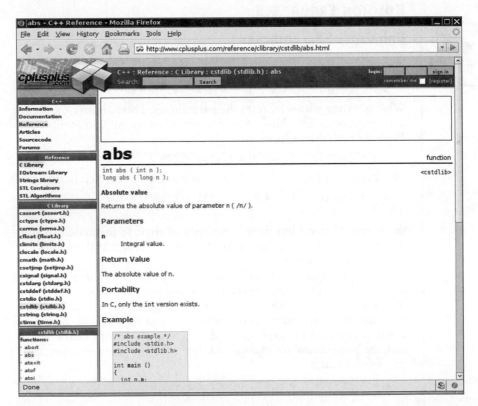

Figure 6   Online Documentation

ADVANCED TOPIC 2.5

Remainder of Negative Integers

You often compute a remainder (a % n) to obtain a number in the range between 0 and n - 1. However, if a is a negative number, the remainder a % n yields a negative number. For example, -7 % 4 is –3. That result is inconvenient, because it does not fall into the range between 0 and 3 and because it is different from the usual mathematical definition; in mathematics, the remainder is the number that you reach by starting with a and adding or subtracting n until you reach a number between 0 and n - 1. For example, the remainder of 11 by 4 is 11 – 4 – 4 = 3. The remainder of –7 by 4 is –7 + 4 + 4 = 1, which is different from -7 % 4. To compute the correct remainder for negative numbers, use the following formula:

```
int rem = n - 1 - (-a - 1) % n; // If a is negative
```

For example, if a is –7 and n is 4, this formula computes $3 - (7 - 1) \% 4 = 3 - 2 = 1$.

QUALITY TIP 2.4

White Space

The compiler does not care whether you write your entire program onto a single line or place every symbol on a separate line. The human reader cares very much. You should use blank lines to group your code visually into sections. For example, you can signal to the reader that an output prompt and the corresponding input statement belong together by inserting a blank line before and after the group. You will find many examples in the source code listings in this book.

White space inside expressions is also important. It is easier to read

```
x1 = (-b + sqrt(b * b - 4 * a * c)) / (2 * a);
```

than

```
x1=(-b+sqrt(b*b-4*a*c))/(2*a);
```

Simply put spaces around all operators + - * / % =. However, don't put a space after a *unary* minus: a – used to negate a single quantity, such as -b. That way, it can be easily distinguished from a *binary* minus, as in a - b. Don't put spaces between a function name and the parentheses, but do put a space after every C++ keyword. That makes it easy to see that the sqrt in sqrt(x) is a function name, whereas the if in if (x > 0) is a keyword.

QUALITY TIP 2.5

Factor Out Common Code

Suppose we want to find both solutions of the quadratic equation $ax^2 + bx + c = 0$. The quadratic formula tells us that the solutions are

$$x_{1,2} = \frac{-b \pm \sqrt{b^2 - 4ac}}{2a}$$

In C++, there is no analog to the ± operation, which indicates how to obtain two solutions simultaneously. Both solutions must be computed separately.

```
x1 = (-b + sqrt(b * b - 4 * a * c)) / (2 * a);
x2 = (-b - sqrt(b * b - 4 * a * c)) / (2 * a);
```

This approach has two problems. The computation of sqrt(b * b - 4 * a * c) is carried out twice, which wastes time. Second, whenever the same code is replicated, the possibility of a typing error increases. The remedy is to *factor* out the common code:

```
double root = sqrt(b * b - 4 * a * c);
x1 = (-b + root) / (2 * a);
x2 = (-b - root) / (2 * a);
```

We could go even further and factor out the computation of 2 * a, but the gain from factoring out very simple computations is small, and the resulting code can be hard to read.

2.6 Strings

2.6.1 String Variables

| Strings are sequences of characters. |

Next to numbers, *strings* are the most important data type that most programs use. A string is a sequence of characters, such as "Hello". In C++, strings are enclosed in quotation marks, which are not themselves part of the string.

You can declare variables that hold strings.

```
string name = "John";
```

The string type is a part of the C++ standard. To use it, simply include the header file, string:

```
#include <string>
```

Use assignment to place a different string into the variable.

```
name = "Carl";
```

You can also read a string from the keyboard:

```
cout << "Please enter your name: ";
cin >> name;
```

When a string is read from an input stream, only one word is placed into the string variable. (Words are separated by white space.) For example, if the user types

```
Harry Hacker
```

as the response to the prompt, then only Harry is placed into name. To read the second string, another input statement must be used. This constraint makes it tricky to write an input statement that deals properly with user responses. Some users might type just their first names, others might type their first and last names, and others might even supply their middle initials.

To handle such a situation, use the getline command. The statement

```
getline(cin, name);
```

reads all keystrokes until the Enter key, makes a string containing all of the keystrokes, and places it into the name variable. With the preceding input example, name is set to the string "Harry Hacker". This is a string containing 12 characters, one of which is a space. You should always use the getline function if you are not sure that the user input consists of a single word.

The number of characters in a string is called the *length* of the string. For example, the length of "Harry Hacker" is 12, and the length of "Hello, World!\n" is 14—the newline character counts as one character only. You can compute the length of a string with the length function. Unlike sqrt or getline, the length function is invoked with the *dot notation*. You write first the variable name of the string whose length you want, then a period, then the name of the function, followed by parentheses:

A member function is invoked on an object, using the dot notation.

```
int n = name.length();
```

Many C++ functions require you to use this dot notation, and you must memorize (or look up) which do and which don't. These functions are called *member functions* (see Syntax 2.9 on page 64). We say that the member function length is *invoked on* the variable name. Member functions are always invoked on objects such as strings or streams, never on numbers.

A string of length zero, containing no characters, is called the *empty string*. It is written as "". Unlike number variables, string variables are guaranteed to be initialized; they are initialized with the empty string.

The length member function yields the number of characters in a string.

```
string response; // Initialized as ""
```

2.6.2 Substrings

Once you have a string, what can you do with it? You can extract substrings, and you can glue smaller strings together to form larger ones. To extract a substring, use the substr member function. The call

```
s.substr(start, length)
```

returns a string that is made from the characters in the string s, starting at character start, and containing length characters. Just like length, substr uses the dot notation. Inside the parentheses, you write the parameters that describe which substring you want. Here is an example:

```
string greeting = "Hello, World!\n";
string sub = greeting.substr(0, 4);
// sub is "Hell"
```

> Use the substr member function to extract a substring of a string.

The substr operation makes a string that consists of four characters taken from the string greeting. Indeed, "Hell" is a string of length 4 that occurs inside greeting. The only curious aspect of the substr operation is the starting position. Starting position 0 means "start at the beginning of the string". For technical reasons that used to be important but are no longer relevant, string position numbers start at 0. The first item in a sequence is labeled 0, the second one 1, and so on. For example, here are the position numbers in the greeting string: The position number of the last character (13) is always one less than the length of the string.

```
H  e  l  l  o  ,     W  o  r  l  d  !  \n
0  1  2  3  4  5  6  7  8  9  10 11 12 13
```

Let us figure out how to extract the substring "World". Count characters starting at 0, not 1. You find that W, the 8th character, has position number 7. The string you want is 5 characters long. Therefore, the appropriate substring command is

```
string w = greeting.substr(7, 5);
```

```
                        5
H  e  l  l  o  ,     W  o  r  l  d  !  \n
0  1  2  3  4  5  6  7  8  9  10 11 12 13
```

The string functions you have seen so far are summarized in Table 4.

Table 4   String Functions

Name	Purpose
s.length()	The length of s
s.substr(i)	The substring of s from index i to the end of the string
s.substr(i, n)	The substring of s of length n starting at index i
getline(f, s)	Read string s from the input stream f

SYNTAX 2.9   Member Function Call

expression.*function_name*(*expression*$_1$, *expression*$_2$, ..., *expression*$_n$)

Example:
```
name.length()
name.substr(0, n - 1)
```

Purpose:
Call a member function and supply the values for the function parameters.

2.6.3 Concatenation

Use the + operator to *concatenate* strings; that is, put them together to yield a longer string.

Now that you know how to take strings apart, let's see how to put them back together. Given two strings, such as "Harry" and "Hacker", we can *concatenate* them to one long string:

```
string fname = "Harry";
string lname = "Hacker";
string name = fname + lname;
```

The + operator concatenates two strings. The resulting string is "HarryHacker". Actually, that isn't really what we are after. We'd like the first and last name separated by a space. No problem:

```
string name = fname + " " + lname;
```

Now we concatenate three strings, "Harry", " ", and "Hacker". The result is

```
"Harry Hacker"
```

You must be careful when using + for strings. One or both of the strings surrounding the + must be a string *object*. The expression fname + " " is OK, but the expression "Harry" + " " is not. This is not a big problem; in the second case, you can just write "Harry ".

Here is a simple program that puts these concepts to work. The program asks for your full name and prints out your initials.

ch02/initials.cpp

```
1   #include <iostream>
2   #include <string>
3
4   using namespace std;
5
6   int main()
7   {
8      cout << "Enter your full name (first middle last): ";
9      string first;
10     string middle;
11     string last;
12     cin >> first >> middle >> last;
13     string initials = first.substr(0, 1)
14        + middle.substr(0, 1) + last.substr(0, 1);
15     cout << "Your initials are " << initials << "\n";
16
17     return 0;
18  }
```

Program Run

```
Enter your full name (first middle last): Harold Joseph Hacker
Your initials are HJH
```

The operation first.substr(0, 1) makes a string consisting of one character, taken from the start of first. The program does the same for the middle and last strings.

first = | H | a | r | o | l | d |
         | 0 | 1 | 2 | 3 | 4 | 5 |

middle = | J | o | s | e | p | h |
         | 0 | 1 | 2 | 3 | 4 | 5 |

last = | H | a | c | k | e | r |
         | 0 | 1 | 2 | 3 | 4 | 5 |

Figure 7   initials = | H | J | H |
Building the `initials` String | 0 | 1 | 2 |

Then it concatenates the three one-character strings to get a string of length 3, the `initials` string. (See Figure 7.)

ADVANCED TOPIC 2.6

Characters and C Strings

C++ has a data type `char` to denote individual characters. In the C language, the precursor to C++, the only way to implement strings was as sequences of individual characters. You can recognize C strings in C or C++ code by looking for types like `char*` or `char[]`. Individual characters are enclosed in single quotes. For example, `'a'` is the character *a*, whereas `"a"` is a string containing the single character *a*.

Using character sequences for strings puts a tremendous burden on the programmer to locate storage space for these sequences manually. In C, a common error is moving a string into a variable that is too small to hold all of its characters. For efficiency's sake, there is no check against this possibility, and it is all too easy for the inexperienced programmer to corrupt adjacent variables.

The standard C++ strings handle all these chores completely automatically. For most programming tasks, you do not need the data type `char` at all. Instead, just use strings of length 1 for individual characters. Chapter 6 contains a brief introduction to C strings.

2.6.4 Formatted Output

When you display several numbers, each of them is printed with the minimum number of digits needed to show the value. This often yields ugly output. Here is an example.

```
cout << pennies << " " << pennies * 0.01 << "\n";
cout << nickels << " " << nickels * 0.05 << "\n";
cout << dimes << " " << dimes * 0.10 << "\n";
cout << quarters << " " << quarters * 0.25 << "\n";
```

A typical output might look like this.

```
1 0.01
12 0.6
4 0.4
120 30
```

What a mess! The columns don't line up, and the money values don't show dollars and cents. We need to *format* the output. Let us make each column eight characters wide, and use two digits of precision for the floating-point numbers.

You use the setw *manipulator* to set the width of the next output field. For example, if you want the next number to be printed in a column that is eight characters wide, you use

```
cout << setw(8);
```

This command does not produce any output; it just manipulates the stream so that it will change the output format for the next value. To use stream manipulators, you must include the iomanip header:

```
#include <iomanip>
```

When the next value is displayed, it is padded with spaces so that the total width is 8. For example,

```
cout << setw(8) << 34.95;
```

yields

```
···34.95
```

(where each · represents a space).

When lining up currency values, you also need to control the number of digits after the decimal point. For example, you want 34.5 to display as 34.50 and 34.249997 as 34.25.

Another pair of manipulators, fixed and setprecision, is used for this purpose. The command

```
cout << fixed << setprecision(2);
```

ensures that subsequent floating-point numbers are printed with two digits after the decimal point.

Combining these three manipulators achieves the desired result:

```
cout << fixed << setprecision(2) << setw(8) << x;
```

Mercifully, the setprecision and fixed manipulators need only to be used once; the stream remembers the formatting directives. However, setw must be specified anew for *every* item.

Here is a sequence of instructions that can be used to beautify the table.

```
cout << fixed << setprecision(2);
cout << setw(8) << pennies << " "
    << setw(8) << pennies * 0.01 << "\n";
cout << setw(8) << nickels << " "
    << setw(8) << nickels * 0.05 << "\n";
cout << setw(8) << dimes << " "
    << setw(8) << dimes * 0.10 << "\n";
cout << setw(8) << quarters << " "
    << setw(8) << quarters * 0.25 << "\n";
```

Now the output is

```
  1    0.01
 12    0.60
  4    0.40
120   30.00
```

2.7 Using Objects

An object is a value that can be manipulated without knowledge of its internal structure.

An *object* is a value that can be manipulated in a computer program without having to know its internal structure. For example, the stream cout is an object. When you use it to produce output, you do not need to know how the output is sent to its destination.

Every object belongs to a class. A class determines the behavior of its objects.

In C++ every object must belong to a *class*. A class is a data type, just like int or double. However, classes are *programmer-defined*, whereas int and double are defined by the designers of the C++ language. At this point, you haven't learned how to define your own classes, so the distinction between the built-in types and programmer-defined class types is not yet important.

In this chapter you will learn to work with the class Time, the class Employee, and four classes that represent graphical shapes. These classes are not part of standard C++; they have been created for use in this book.

2.7.1 Time Objects

Suppose you want to know how many seconds will elapse between now and midnight. This sounds like a pain to compute by hand. However, the Time class makes the job easy. You will see how, in this section and the next.

First, you will learn how to specify an object of type Time. The end of the day is 11:59 P.M. and 59 seconds. Here is a Time object representing that time:

```
Time(23, 59, 59)
```

The act of creating an object is called construction. To specify the initial state of an object, you supply construction parameters.

You specify a Time object by giving three values: hours, minutes, and seconds. The hours are given in "military time": between 0 and 23 hours.

When a Time object is specified from three integer values such as 23, 59, 59, we say that the object is *constructed* from these values, and the values used in the construction are the *construction parameters*. In general, an object value is constructed as shown in Syntax 2.10 on page 69.

You should think of Time(23, 59, 59) as an entity that is very similar to a number such as 7.5 or a string such as "Hello". In particular, when using a Time object you should *not* worry about its internals, just as you probably don't worry about the bits that make up a floating-point number.

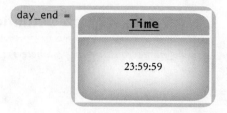

Figure 8   A Time Object and Variable

Just as floating-point values can be stored in double variables, Time objects can be stored in Time variables:

    Time day_end = Time(23, 59, 59);

Think of this as the analog of

    double interest_rate = 7.5;

or

    string greeting = "Hello";

There is a shorthand for this very common situation (See Syntax 2.11 on page 70).

    Time day_end(23, 59, 59);

This defines a variable day_end that is initialized to the Time object Time(23,59,59). (See Figure 8.)

Many classes have more than one construction mechanism. For example, there are two methods for constructing times: by specifying hours, minutes, and seconds, and by specifying no parameters at all.

The expression

    Time()

creates an object representing the current time, that is, the time when the object is constructed. Making an object with no construction parameter is called *default construction*.

> When defining an object with default construction, you do not supply any construction parameters.

SYNTAX 2.10 **Object Construction**

ClassName(*construction parameters*)
ClassName()

Example:

Time(19, 0, 0)
Time()

Purpose:

Construct a new object for use in an expression. The first version uses the given parameters to set the object's initial state. The second version sets the object to a default state.

SYNTAX 2.11 **Object Variable Definition**

ClassName variable_name(*construction parameters*);
ClassName variable_name;

Example:

```
Time homework_due(19, 0, 0);
Time homework_due;
```

Purpose:

Define a new object variable. The first version uses the given parameters to set the object's initial state. The second version sets the object to a default state.

Of course, you can store a default Time object in a variable:

```
Time now = Time();
```

The shorthand notation for using default construction is slightly inconsistent:

```
Time now; // OK. This defines a variable and invokes the default constructor.
```

and not

```
Time now(); // NO! This does not define a variable.
```

If you are unhappy with the current object stored in a variable, you can overwrite it with another one:

```
homework_due = Time(23, 59, 59);
```

Figure 9 shows this replacement.

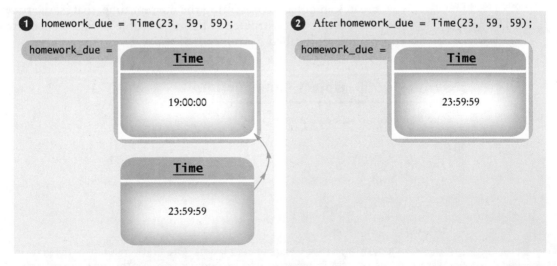

Figure 9   Replacing an Object with Another

Table 5 Member Functions of the Time Class

Name	Purpose
Time()	Constructs the current time
Time(h, m, s)	Constructs the time with hours h, minutes m, and seconds s
t.get_seconds()	Returns the seconds value of t
t.get_minutes()	Returns the minutes value of t
t.get_hours()	Returns the hours value of t
t.add_seconds(n)	Changes t to move by n seconds
t.seconds_from(t2)	Computes the number of seconds between t and t2

What can you do with a Time object after constructing it? The Time class specifies the operations that you can carry out (see Table 5). Here is one of them. You can add a certain number of seconds to the time:

```
wake_up.add_seconds(1000);
```

Afterward, the object in the variable wake_up is changed. It is no longer the time value assigned when the object was constructed, but a time object representing a time that is exactly 1,000 seconds (16 minutes and 40 seconds) from the time previously stored in wake_up. (See Figure 10.)

Whenever you apply a function (such as add_seconds) to an object variable (such as wake_up), you use the same dot notation that we already used for string member functions:

```
int n = greeting.length();
cout << greeting.substr(0, 4);
```

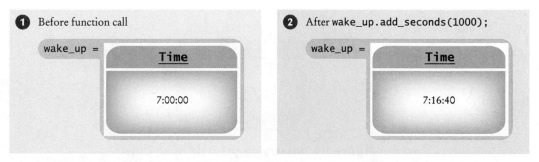

Figure 10 Changing the State of an Object

Now that you've seen how to change the state of a `Time` object, how can you find out the current time stored in the object? You have to ask it. There are three member functions for this purpose, called

```
get_seconds()
get_minutes()
get_hours()
```

They too are applied to objects using the dot notation. (See Figure 11.)

Since you can *get* the hours of a time, it seems natural to suggest that you can *set* it as well:

```
homework_due.set_hours(2); // No! Not a supported member function
```

`Time` objects do not support this member function. There is a good reason, of course. Not all hour values make sense. For example,

```
homework_due.set_hours(9999); // Doesn't make sense
```

Of course, one could try to come up with some meaning for such a call, but the author of the `Time` class decided simply not to supply these member functions. Whenever you use an object, you need to find out which member functions are supplied; other operations, however useful they may be, are simply not possible.

Finally, a `Time` object can figure out the number of seconds between itself and another time. For example, here is how you can compute how many seconds are left before the homework is due:

```
Time now;
int seconds_left = homework_due.seconds_from(now)
```

Note that you pass the `now` object (a value of type `Time`) to the `seconds_from` function. In general, objects behave just like numbers—you can store them, copy them, and pass them to functions, just as you do numbers.

To use objects of the `Time` class, you must include the file `ccc_time.h`. Unlike the `iostream` or `cmath` headers, this file is not part of the standard C++ headers. Instead, the `Time` class is supplied with this book to illustrate simple objects. Because the `ccc_time.h` file is not a system header, you do not use angle brackets `< >` in the `#include` directive; instead, you use quotation marks:

```
#include "ccc_time.h"
```

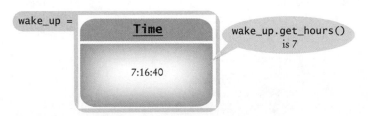

Figure 11   Querying the State of an Object

The online documentation of the code library that accompanies this book gives more instructions on how to compile programs that use the book's class library.

The following program computes the time that is 1,000 seconds after 7 A.M., and the number of seconds between the current time and the last second of the day.

ch02/time.cpp

```
1   #include <iostream>
2
3   using namespace std;
4
5   #include "ccc_time.h"
6
7   int main()
8   {
9      Time wake_up(7, 0, 0);
10     wake_up.add_seconds(1000); // A thousand seconds later
11     cout << wake_up.get_hours()
12        << ":" << wake_up.get_minutes()
13        << ":" << wake_up.get_seconds() << "\n";
14
15     Time now;
16     int seconds_left = Time(23, 59, 59).seconds_from(now);
17
18     cout << "There are "
19        << seconds_left
20        << " seconds left in this day.\n";
21
22     return 0;
23  }
```

Program Run

```
7:16:40
There are 43517 seconds left in this day.
```

COMMON ERROR 2.7

Trying to Call a Member Function Without an Object

Suppose your code contains the instruction

```
add_seconds(30); // Error
```

The compiler will not know which time to advance. You need to supply an object of class Time:

```
Time liftoff(19, 0, 0);
liftoff.add_seconds(30);
```

2.7.2 Employee Objects

One reason for the popularity of object-oriented programming is that it is easy to *model* entities from real life in computer programs, making programs easy to understand and modify. As an example, we provide a simple Employee class, whose member functions are listed in Table 6. Consider the following program that manipulates an object of the Employee class:

ch02/employee.cpp

```
1   #include <iostream>
2
3   using namespace std;
4
5   #include "ccc_empl.h"
6
7   int main()
8   {
9      Employee harry("Hacker, Harry", 45000.00);  ❶
10
11     double new_salary = harry.get_salary() + 3000;  ❷
12     harry.set_salary(new_salary);  ❸
13
14     cout << "Name: " << harry.get_name() << "\n";
15     cout << "Salary: " << harry.get_salary() << "\n";
16
17     return 0;
18  }
```

Program Run

```
Name: Hacker, Harry
Salary: 48000
```

This program creates a variable harry and initializes it with an object of type Employee. There are two construction parameters: the name of the employee and the starting salary.

Table 6   Member Functions of the Employee Class

Name	Purpose
Employee(n, s)	Constructs an employee with name n and salary s
e.get_name()	Returns the name of e
e.get_salary()	Returns the salary of e
e.set_salary(s)	Sets salary of e to s

We then give Harry a $3,000 raise (see Figure 12). We first find his current salary with the get_salary member function. We determine the new salary by adding $3,000 and storing the result in new_salary. We use the set_salary member function to set the new salary.

Finally, we print out the name and salary of the Employee object. We use the get_name and get_salary member functions to get the name and salary.

As you can see, this program is easy to read because it carries out its computations with meaningful entities, namely Employee objects.

Note that you can change the salary of an employee with the set_salary member function. However, you cannot change the name of an Employee object.

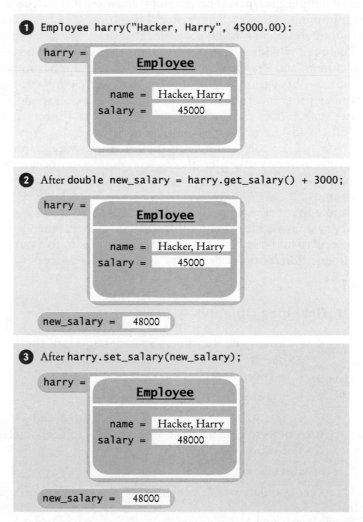

Figure 12 Invoking Member Functions on an Employee Object

This Employee class has been kept as simple as possible. In a real data-processing program, Employee objects would also have ID numbers, addresses, job titles, and so on. As you will see in Chapter 5, it is easy to enhance the Employee class to model these additional attributes.

You need to include the header file ccc_empl.h in all programs that use the Employee class.

2.8 Displaying Graphical Shapes (Optional)

In the following sections you will learn how to use a number of useful classes to render simple graphics. The graphics classes will provide a basis for interesting programming examples. This material is optional, and you can safely skip it if you are not interested in writing programs that draw graphical shapes.

There are two kinds of C++ programs that you will write in this course: *console applications* and *graphics applications*. Console applications read input from the keyboard (through cin) and display text output on the screen (through cout). Graphics programs read keystrokes and mouse clicks, and they display graphical shapes such as lines and circles, through a window object called cwin.

You already know how to write console programs. You include the header file iostream and use the >> and << operators. To activate graphics for your programs, you must include the header file ccc_win.h into your program. Moreover, you need to supply the function ccc_win_main instead of main as the entry point to your program.

Unlike the iostream library, which is available on all C++ systems, this graphics library was created for use in this textbook. As with the Time and Employee classes, you need to add the code for the graphics objects to your programs. The online documentation for the code library describes this process.

2.8.1 Graphics Objects

Points, lines, circles, and messages can be displayed in a window on the computer screen.

Points, circles, lines, and messages are the four types of graphical objects that you will use to create diagrams. A *point* has an x- and a y-coordinate. For example,

```
Point(1, 3)
```

is a Point object with x-coordinate 1 and y-coordinate 3. You frequently use points to construct more complex graphical objects, such as a circle (see Figure 13). The expression

```
Circle(Point(1, 3), 2.5)
```

yields a Circle object whose center is the point with coordinates (1, 3) and whose radius is 2.5.

The following code defines and initializes a Point variable and then displays the point. Then a circle with center p is created and also displayed.

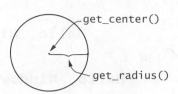

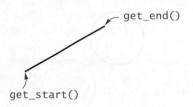

Figure 13   A Circle   **Figure 14**   A Line

ch02/circle.cpp

```
1   #include "ccc_win.h"
2
3   int ccc_win_main()
4   {
5      Point p(1, 3);
6      cwin << p << Circle(p, 2.5);
7
8      return 0;
9   }
```

Two points can be joined by a line (see Figure 14), represented by a Line object that is constructed from two Point objects, its start and end points.

```
Point p(1, 3);
Point q(4, 7);
Line s(p, q);
```

The get_start and get_end member functions return the start and end points from which the line was constructed.

In a graphics window you can display text anywhere you like using the Message class. When constructing a Message object, you need to specify what you want to show and where it should appear (see Figure 15).

```
Point p(1, 3);
Message greeting(p, "Hello, Window!");
```

The point parameter specifies the *upper left corner* of the message. The second parameter can be either a string or a number.

There is one member function that all our graphical classes implement: move. If obj is a Point, Circle, Line, or Message, then

```
obj.move(dx, dy)
```

changes the position of the object, moving the entire object by dx units in the *x*-direction and dy units in the *y*-direction. Either or both of dx and dy can be zero or

get_start()
# Hello, Window!

Figure 15   A Message

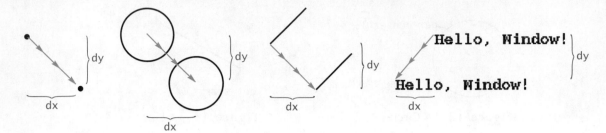

Figure 16   The move Operation

negative (see Figure 16). For example, the following code draws a square (see Figure 17). The program first constructs two Line objects that represent the lines at the top and left. Then the move member function is applied to move the lines to the right and the bottom of the square.

ch02/square.cpp

```
1  #include "ccc_win.h"
2
3  int ccc_win_main()
4  {
5     Point top_left(1, 3);
6     Point top_right(1, 4);
7     Point bottom_left(2, 3);
8
9     Line horizontal(top_left, top_right);
10    Line vertical(top_left, bottom_left);
11
12    cwin << horizontal << vertical;
13
14    horizontal.move(1, 0);
15    vertical.move(0, 1);
16
17    cwin << horizontal << vertical;
18
19    return 0;
20 }
```

After a graphical object has been constructed and perhaps moved, you sometimes want to know where it is currently located. There are two member functions for Point objects: get_x and get_y. They get the x- and y-positions of the point.

The Circle get_center and get_radius member functions return the center and radius of a circle. The Line get_start and get_end member functions return the

Figure 17
Square Drawn by square.cpp

starting point and end point of a line. The `get_start` and `get_text` member functions of a `Message` object return the starting point and the message text. Because `get_center`, `get_start`, and `get_end` return `Point` objects, you may need to apply `get_x` or `get_y` to them to determine their *x*- and *y*-coordinates. For example,

```
Circle c(...);
...
double cx = c.get_center().get_x();
```

You now know how to construct graphical objects, and you have seen all member functions for manipulating and querying them (summarized in Tables 7 through 10). The design of these classes was purposefully kept simple, so some common tasks require a little ingenuity.

Table 7   Member Functions of the Point Class

Name	Purpose
Point(x, y)	Constructs a point at location (x, y)
p.get_x()	Returns the *x*-coordinate of point p
p.get_y()	Returns the *y*-coordinate of point p
p.move(dx, dy)	Moves point p by (dx, dy)

Table 8   Member Functions of the Circle Class

Name	Purpose
Circle(p, r)	Constructs a circle with center p and radius r
c.get_center()	Returns the center point of circle c
c.get_radius()	Returns the radius of circle c
c.move(dx, dy)	Moves circle c by (dx, dy)

Table 9   Member Functions of the Line Class

Name	Purpose
Line(p, q)	Constructs a line joining points p and q
l.get_start()	Returns the starting point of line l
l.get_end()	Returns the ending point of line l
l.move(dx, dy)	Moves line l by (dx, dy)

Table 10	Member Functions of the Message Class
Name	**Purpose**
Message(p, s)	Constructs a message with starting point p and text string s
Message(p, x)	Constructs a message with starting point p and a label equal to the number x
m.get_start()	Returns the starting point of message m
m.get_text()	Gets the text string of message m
m.move(dx, dy)	Moves message m by (dx, dy)

RANDOM FACT 2.2

Computer Graphics

The generation and manipulation of visual images is one of the most exciting applications of the computer. We distinguish between different kinds of graphics.

Diagrams, such as numeric charts or maps, are artifacts that convey information to the viewer (see Figure 18). They do not directly depict anything that occurs in the natural world, but are a tool for visualizing information.

Scenes are computer-generated images that attempt to depict images of the real or an imagined world (see Figure 19). It turns out to be quite a challenge to render light and shadows accurately. Special effort must be taken so that the images do not look too neat and simple; clouds, rocks, leaves, and dust in the real world have a complex and somewhat random appearance. The degree of realism in these images is constantly improving.

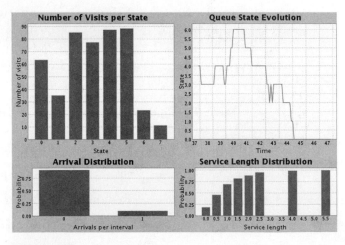

Figure 18   Diagrams

Figure 19 Scene

Figure 20 Manipulated Image

Manipulated images are photographs or film footage of actual events that have been converted to digital form and edited by the computer (see Figure 20). For example, film sequences of the movie *Apollo 13* were produced by starting from actual images and changing the perspective, showing the launch of the rocket from a more dramatic viewpoint.

Computer graphics is one of the most challenging fields in computer science. It requires processing of massive amounts of information at very high speed. New algorithms are constantly invented for this purpose. Viewing overlapping three-dimensional objects with curved boundaries requires advanced mathematical tools. Realistic modeling of textures and biological entities requires extensive knowledge of mathematics, physics, and biology.

2.8.2 Choosing a Coordinate System

When displaying graphical shapes, you need to know how *x*- and *y*-coordinates are mapped to the screen. For example, where is the point with *x*-coordinate 1 and *y*-coordinate 3 located? Some graphics systems use pixels, the individual dots on the display, as coordinates, but different displays have different pixel counts and densities. Using pixels makes it difficult to write programs that look pleasant on every display screen. The library supplied with this book uses a coordinate system that is independent of the display.

Figure 21 shows the default coordinate system used by this book's library. The origin is at the center of the screen, and the *x*-axis and *y*-axis are 10 units long in either direction. The axes do not actually appear (unless you create them yourself by drawing Line objects).

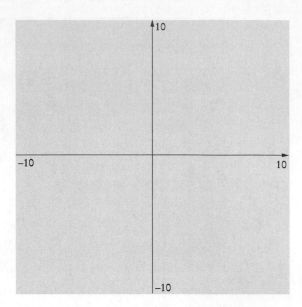

Figure 21
Default Coordinate System
for Graphics Library

> When writing programs
> that display data sets,
> you should select a
> coordinate system that
> fits the data points.

If your data has x- and y-values that don't fall between −10 and 10, you need to change the coordinate system. For example, suppose we want to show a graph plotting the average temperature (degrees Celsius) in Phoenix, Arizona, for every month of the year (see Table 11).

Here, the x-coordinates are the month values, ranging from 1 to 12. The y-coordinates are the temperature values, ranging from 11 (in January) to 33 (in July). Figure 22 shows the coordinate system that we need. As you can see, the top left corner is (1, 33) and the bottom right corner is (12, 11).

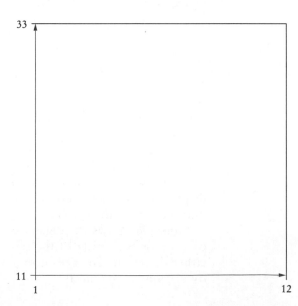

Figure 22
Coordinate System for Temperature

Table 11 Average Temperatures in Phoenix, Arizona

Month	Average Temperature	Month	Average Temperature
January	11°C	July	33°C
February	13°C	August	32°C
March	16°C	September	29°C
April	20°C	October	23°C
May	25°C	November	16°C
June	31°C	December	12°C

To select this coordinate system, use the following instruction:

```
cwin.coord(1, 33, 12, 11);
```

Following a common convention in graphics systems, you must first specify the desired coordinates for the *top left* corner (which has x-coordinate 1 and y-coordinate 33), then the desired coordinates for the bottom right corner ($x = 12, y = 11$) of the graphics window.

After setting the coordinate system, you can plot the points without adjusting the x- and y-values. The graphics window makes the necessary adjustments to ensure that the points are displayed in the correct location.

Here is the complete program:

ch02/phoenix.cpp

```
1   #include "ccc_win.h"
2
3   int ccc_win_main()
4   {
5      cwin.coord(1, 33, 12, 11);
6      cwin << Point(1, 11);
7      cwin << Point(2, 13);
8      cwin << Point(3, 16);
9      cwin << Point(4, 20);
10     cwin << Point(5, 25);
11     cwin << Point(6, 31);
12     cwin << Point(7, 33);
13     cwin << Point(8, 32);
14     cwin << Point(9, 29);
15     cwin << Point(10, 23);
16     cwin << Point(11, 16);
17     cwin << Point(12, 12);
18
19     return 0;
20  }
```

Figure 23   Average Temperatures in Phoenix, Arizona

Figure 23 shows the output of the program.

2.8.3 Getting Input from the Graphics Window

Graphical programs can obtain both text and mouse input from the user.

The graphics library supplies a set of member functions for getting text and mouse input from the user. (In a graphics program, you cannot read the input from cin.) The command for reading string input is

```
string response = cwin.get_string(prompt);
```

This is how you inquire about the user name:

```
string name = cwin.get_string("Please type your name:");
```

The prompt and a field for typing the input are displayed in a special input area. Depending on your computer system, the input area is in a dialog box or at the top or bottom of the graphics window. The user can then type input. After the user hits the Enter key, the user's keystrokes are placed into the name string. The message prompt is then removed from the screen.

The get_string function always returns a string. Use get_int or get_double to read an integer or floating-point number:

```
int age = cwin.get_int("Please enter your age:");
```

The user can specify a point with the mouse. To prompt the user for mouse input, use

```
Point response = cwin.get_mouse(prompt);
```

For example,

```
Point center = cwin.get_mouse("Click center of circle");
```

Table 12 Member Functions of the `GraphicWindow` Class

Name	Purpose
`w.coord(x1, y1, x2, y2)`	Sets the coordinate system for subsequent drawing: (x1, y1) is the top left corner, (x2, y2) the bottom right corner
`w << x`	Displays the object x (a point, circle, line, or message) in window w
`w.clear()`	Clears window w (erases its contents)
`w.get_string(p)`	Displays prompt p in window w and returns the entered string
`w.get_int(p)`	Displays prompt p in window w and returns the entered integer
`w.get_double(p)`	Displays prompt p in window w and returns the entered floating-point value
`w.get_mouse(p)`	Displays prompt p in window w and returns the mouse click point

The user can move the mouse to the desired location. Once the user clicks on the mouse button, the prompt is cleared and the selected point is returned.

Here is a program that puts these functions (summarized in Table 12) to work. It asks the user to enter a name and to try to click inside a circle. Then the program displays the point that the user specified.

ch02/click.cpp

```
1   #include "ccc_win.h"
2
3   int ccc_win_main()
4   {
5      string name = cwin.get_string("Please type your name:");
6      Circle c(Point(0, 0), 1);
7      cwin << c;
8      Point m = cwin.get_mouse("Please click inside the circle.");
9      cwin << m << Message(m, name + ", you clicked here");
10
11     return 0;
12  }
```

CHAPTER SUMMARY

1. The most common number types in C++ are double (floating-point number) and int (integer).

2. A variable is a storage location with a name. In C++, you also specify the type of the values that can be stored.

3. Use the >> operator to read a value from an input stream and place it in a variable.

4. An assignment statement stores a new value in a variable, replacing the previously stored value.

5. The ++ operator adds 1 to a variable; the -- operator subtracts 1.

6. A constant is a named value that cannot be changed.

7. In C++, you use * for multiplication and / for division.

8. If both arguments of / are integers, the remainder is discarded. The % operator computes the remainder of an integer division.

9. The C++ library defines many mathematical functions such as sqrt (square root) and pow (raising to a power).

10. Strings are sequences of characters.

11. A member function is invoked on an object, using the dot notation.

12. The length member function yields the number of characters in a string.

13. Use the substr member function to extract a substring of a string.

14. Use the + operator to *concatenate* strings; that is, put them together to yield a longer string.

15. An object is a value that can be manipulated without knowledge of its internal structure.

16. Every object belongs to a class. A class determines the behavior of its objects.

17. The act of creating an object is called construction. To specify the initial state of an object, you supply construction parameters.

18. When defining an object with default construction, you do not supply any construction parameters.

19. Points, lines, circles, and messages can be displayed in a window on the computer screen.

20. When writing programs that display data sets, you should select a coordinate system that fits the data points.

21. Graphical programs can obtain both text and mouse input from the user.

FURTHER READING

1. http://www.cplusplus.com Online documentation for C++.

REVIEW EXERCISES

Exercise R2.1. Write the following mathematical expressions in C++.

$$s = s_0 + v_0 t + \frac{1}{2} g t^2$$

$$G = 4\pi^2 \frac{a^3}{p^2(m_1 + m_2)}$$

$$FV = PV \cdot \left(1 + \frac{INT}{100}\right)^{YRS}$$

$$c = \sqrt{a^2 + b^2 - 2ab\cos\gamma}$$

Exercise R2.2. Write the following C++ expressions in mathematical notation.

a. `dm = m * (sqrt(1 + v / c) / sqrt(1 - v / c) - 1);`

b. `volume = PI * r * r * h;`

c. `volume = 4 * PI * pow(r, 3) / 3;`

d. `p = atan2(z, sqrt(x * x + y * y));`

Exercise R2.3. What is wrong with this version of the quadratic formula?

```
x1 = (-b - sqrt(b * b - 4 * a * c)) / 2 * a;
x2 = (-b + sqrt(b * b - 4 * a * c)) / 2 * a;
```

Exercise R2.4. What happens when you multiply two integers whose product is larger than the largest int value? Try out an example and report your findings. Give an example of multiplying two floating-point numbers that demonstrates limited precision.

Exercise R2.5. Let n be an integer and x a floating-point number. Explain the difference between

```
n = x;
```

and

```
n = static_cast<int>(x + 0.5);
```

For what values of x do they give the same result? For what values of x do they give different results? What happens if x is negative?

Exercise R2.6. Find at least five *syntax* errors in the following program.

```
#include iostream

int main();
{
    cout << "Please enter two numbers:"
    cin << x, y;
    cout << "The sum of << x << "and" << y
        << "is: " x + y << "\n";
    return;
}
```

Exercise R2.7. Find at least three *logic* errors in the following program.

```
#include <iostream>

using namespace std;

int main()
{
    int total;
    int x1;
    cout << "Please enter a number:";
    cin >> x1;
    total = total + x1;
    cout << "Please enter another number:";
    int x2;
    cin >> x2;
    total = total + x1;
    float average = total / 2;
    cout << "The average of the two numbers is "
        << average << "\n";
    return 0;
}
```

Exercise R2.8. Explain the differences between 2, 2.0, "2", and "2.0".

Exercise R2.9. Explain what each of the following program segments computes:

a. ```
x = 2;
y = x + x;
```
b. ```
s = "2";
t = s + s;
```

Exercise R2.10. How do you get the first character of a string? The last character? How do you *remove* the first character? The last character?

Exercise R2.11. How do you get the last digit of a number? The first digit? That is, if n is 23456, how do you find out 2 and 6? *Hint:* %, log.

Exercise R2.12. Suppose a C++ program contains the two input statements

```
cout << "Please enter your name: ";
string fname, lname;
cin >> fname >> lname;
```

and

```
cout << "Please enter your age: ";
int age;
cin >> age;
```

What is contained in the variables fname, lname, and age if the user enters the following inputs?

a. James Carter
   56

b. Lyndon Johnson
   49

c. Hodding Carter 3rd
   44

d. Richard M. Nixon
   62

Exercise R2.13. What are the values of the following expressions? In each line, assume that

```
double x = 2.5;
double y = -1.5;
int m = 18;
int n = 4;
string s = "Hello";
string t = "World";
```

a. x + n * y - (x + n) * y

b. m / n + m % n

c. 5 * x - n / 5

d. sqrt(sqrt(n));

e. static_cast<int>(x + 0.5)

f. s + t;

g. t + s;

h. 1 - (1 - (1 - (1 - (1 - n))))

i. s.substr(1, 2)

j. s.length() + t.length()

Exercise R2.14. Explain the difference between an object and a class.

Exercise R2.15. Give the C++ code for an *object* of class Time and for an *object variable* of class Time.

Exercise R2.16. Explain the differences between a member function and a nonmember function.

Exercise R2.17. Explain the difference between

```
Point(3, 4);
```

and

```
Point p(3, 4);
```

Exercise R2.18. Give the C++ code to construct the following objects:

a. Lunch time

b. The current time

c. The top right corner of the graphics window in the default coordinate system

d. Your instructor as an employee (make a guess for the salary)

e. A circle filling the entire graphics window in the default coordinate system

f. A line representing the *x*-axis from –10 to 10.

Write the code for objects, not object variables.

Exercise R2.19. Repeat Exercise R2.18, but now define variables that are initialized with the required values.

Exercise R2.20. Find the errors in the following statements:

a. `Time now();`

b. `Point p = (3, 4);`

c. `p.set_x(-1);`

d. `cout << Time`

e. `Time due_date(2004, 4, 15);`

f. `due_date.move(2, 12);`

g. `seconds_from(millennium);`

h. `Employee harry("Hacker", "Harry", 35000);`

i. `harry.set_name("Hacker, Harriet");`

Exercise R2.21. Describe all constructors of the Time class. List all member functions that can be used to change a Time object. List all member functions that don't change the Time object.

Exercise R2.22. What is the value of t after the following operations?

```
Time t;
t = Time(20, 0, 0);
t.add_seconds(1000);
t.add_seconds(-400);
```

G **Exercise R2.23.** What is the value of `c.get_center` and `c.get_radius` after the following operations?

```
Circle c(Point(1, 2), 3);
c.move(4, 5);
```

G **Exercise R2.24.** You want to plot a bar chart showing the grade distribution of all students in your class (where A = 4.0, F = 0). What coordinate system would you choose to make the plotting as simple as possible?

G **Exercise R2.25.** Let c be any circle. Write C++ code to plot the circle c and another circle that touches c. *Hint:* Use move.

G **Exercise R2.26.** Write C++ instructions to display the letters X and T in a graphics window, by plotting line segments.

PROGRAMMING EXERCISES

Exercise P2.1. Write a program that prints the values
1
10
100
1000
10000
100000
1000000
10000000
100000000
1000000000
10000000000
100000000000
as integers and as floating-point numbers. Explain the results.

Exercise P2.2. Write a program that displays the squares, cubes, and fourth powers of the numbers 1 through 5.

Exercise P2.3. Write a program that prompts the user for two integers and then prints
- The sum
- The difference
- The product
- The average
- The distance (absolute value of the difference)
- The maximum (the larger of the two)
- The minimum (the smaller of the two)

Hint: The max and min functions are defined in the algorithm header.

Exercise P2.4. Write a program that prompts the user for a measurement in meters and then converts it to miles, feet, and inches.

Exercise P2.5. Write a program that prompts the user for a radius and then prints
- The area and circumference of a circle with that radius
- The volume and surface area of a sphere with that radius

Exercise P2.6. Write a program that asks the user for the lengths of the sides of a rectangle. Then print
- The area and perimeter of the rectangle
- The length of the diagonal (use the Pythagorean theorem)

Exercise P2.7. Write a program that prompts the user for
- The lengths of two sides of a triangle
- The size of the angle between the two sides (in degrees)

Then the program displays
- The length of the third side
- The sizes of the other two angles

Hint: Use the law of cosines.

Exercise P2.8. Write a program that prompts the user for
- The length of a side of a triangle
- The sizes of the two angles adjacent to that side (in degrees)

Then the program displays
- The lengths of the other two sides
- The size of the third angle

Hint: Use the law of sines.

Exercise P2.9. *Giving change.* Implement a program that directs a cashier how to give change. The program has two inputs: the amount due and the amount received from the customer. It should compute the difference, and compute the dollars, quarters, dimes, nickels, and pennies that the customer should receive in return.

Hint: First transform the difference into an integer balance, denominated in pennies. Then compute the whole dollar amount. Subtract it from the balance. Compute the number of quarters needed. Repeat for dimes and nickels. Display the remaining pennies.

Exercise P2.10. Write a program that asks the user to input
- The number of gallons of gas in the tank
- The fuel efficiency in miles per gallon
- The price of gas per gallon

Then print out how far the car can go with the gas in the tank and print the cost per 100 miles.

Exercise P2.11. *File names and extensions.* Write a program that prompts the user for the drive letter (C), the path (\Windows\System), the file name (Readme), and the extension (TXT). Then print the complete file name C:\Windows\System\Readme.TXT. (If you use UNIX or a Macintosh, use / or : instead of \ to separate directories.)

Exercise P2.12. Write a program that reads a number greater than or equal to 1,000 from the user and prints it *with a comma separating the thousands.* Here is a sample dialog; the user input is in boldface:

```
Please enter an integer >= 1000: 23456
23,456
```

Exercise P2.13. Write a program that reads a number between 1,000 and 999,999 from the user, where the user enters a comma in the input. Then print the number without a comma. Here is a sample dialog; the user input is in boldface:

```
Please enter an integer between 1,000 and 999,999: 23,456
23456
```

Hint: Read the input as a string. Measure the length of the string. Suppose it contains n characters. Then extract substrings consisting of the first $n - 4$ characters and the last three characters.

Exercise P2.14. *Printing a grid.* Write a program that prints the following grid to play tic-tac-toe.

```
+--+--+--+
|  |  |  |
+--+--+--+
|  |  |  |
+--+--+--+
|  |  |  |
+--+--+--+
```

Of course, you could simply write seven statements of the form

```
cout << "+--+--+--+";
```

You should do it the smart way, though. Define string variables to hold two kinds of patterns: a comb-shaped pattern and the bottom line. Print the comb three times and the bottom line once.

Exercise P2.15. Write a program that reads in an integer and breaks it into a sequence of individual digits. For example, the input 16384 is displayed as

```
1 6 3 8 4
```

You may assume that the input has no more than five digits and is not negative.

Exercise P2.16. Write a program that reads two times in military format (0900, 1730) and prints the number of hours and minutes between the two times. Here is a sample run. User input is in boldface.

```
Please enter the first time: 0900
Please enter the second time: 1730
8 hours 30 minutes
```

Extra credit if you can deal with the case that the first time is later than the second time:

```
Please enter the first time: 1730
Please enter the second time: 0900
15 hours 30 minutes
```

Exercise P2.17. Run the following program, and explain the output you get.

```
#include <iostream>

using namespace std;

int main()
{
    int total;
    cout << "Please enter a number: ";
    double x1;
    cin >> x1;
    cout << "total = " << total << "\n";
    total = total + x1;
    cout << "total = " << total << "\n";
    cout << "Please enter a number: ";
    double x2;
    cin >> x2;
    total = total + x2;
    cout << "total = " << total << "\n";
    total = total / 2;
    cout << "total = " << total << "\n";
    cout << "The average is " << total << "\n";
    return 0;
}
```

Note the *trace messages* that are inserted to show the current contents of the total variable. Then fix up the program, run it with the trace messages in place to verify it works correctly, and remove the trace messages.

Exercise P2.18. *Writing large letters.* A large letter H can be produced like this:

```
*   *
*   *
*****
*   *
*   *
```

It can be declared as a string constant like this:

```
const string LETTER_H =
   "*   *\n*   *\n*****\n*   *\n*   *\n";
```

Do the same for the letters E, L, and O. Then write the message

```
H
E
L
L
O
```

in large letters.

Exercise P2.19. Write a program that transforms numbers 1, 2, 3, ..., 12 into the corresponding month names January, February, March, ..., December. *Hint:* Make a very long string "January February March ...", in which you add spaces such that each month name has *the same length*. Then use substr to extract the month you want.

Exercise P2.20. Write a program that asks for the due date of the next assignment (hour, minutes). Then print the number of minutes between the current time and the due date.

Exercise P2.21. Write a program that prompts the user for the first name and last name of an employee and a starting salary. Then give the employee a 5 percent raise, and print out the name and salary information stored in the employee object.

G   Exercise P2.22. Write a program to plot the following face.

G   Exercise P2.23. Write a program to plot the string "HELLO", using just lines and circles. Do not use the Message class, and do not use cout.

G   Exercise P2.24. *Plotting a data set.* Make a bar chart to plot a data set such as this:

Name	Longest Span (ft)
Golden Gate	4,200
Brooklyn	1,595
Delaware Memorial	2,150
Mackinaw	3,800

Prompt the user to type in four names and measurements. Then display a bar graph. Make the bars horizontal for easier labeling.

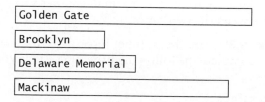

Hint: Set the window coordinates to 5,000 in the *x*-direction and 4 in the *y*-direction.

G **Exercise P2.25.** Write a graphics program that prompts the user to click on three points. Then draw a triangle joining the three points. *Hint:* To give the user feedback about the click, it is a nice touch to draw the point after each click.

```
Point p = cwin.get_mouse("Please click on the first point");
cwin << p; // Feedback for the user
```

G **Exercise P2.26.** Write a program that displays the Olympic rings. *Hint:* Construct and display the first circle, then call move four times.

G **Exercise P2.27.** Write a graphics program that asks the user to enter four data values. Then draw a pie chart showing the data values.

G **Exercise P2.28.** Write a graphics program that draws a clock face with the current time:

Hint: You need to determine the angles of the hour hand and the minute hand. The angle of the minute hand is easy: The minute hand travels 360 degrees in 60 minutes. The angle of the hour hand is harder; it travels 360 degrees in 12 × 60 minutes.

G **Exercise P2.29.** Write a program that tests how fast a user can type. Get the time. Ask the user to type "The quick brown fox jumps over the lazy dog". Read a line of input. Get the current time again in another variable of type Time. Print out the seconds between the two times.

G **Exercise P2.30.** Your boss, Juliet Jones, is getting married and decides to change her name. Complete the following program so that you can type in the new name for the boss:

```
int main()
{
    Employee boss("Jones, Juliet", 45000.00);
    // Your code goes here; leave the code above and below unchanged
```

```
        cout << "Name: " << boss.get_name() << "\n";
        cout << "Salary: " << boss.get_salary() << "\n";

        return 0;
    }
```

The problem is that there is no set_name member function for the Employee class. *Hint:* Make a new object of type Employee with the new name and the same salary. Then assign the new object to boss.

G   **Exercise P2.31.** Write a program that draws the picture of a house. It could be as simple as the figure below, or if you like, make it more elaborate (3-D, skyscraper, marble columns in the entryway, whatever).

Chapter 3

Control Flow

CHAPTER GOALS

- To be able to implement branches and loops
- To learn how to compare integers, floating-point numbers, and strings
- To be able to use the Boolean data type
- To avoid infinite loops and off-by-one errors
- To understand nested branches and loops
- To learn how to process text input
- To implement approximations and simulations

One **of the** essential features of nontrivial computer programs is their ability to make decisions and to carry out different actions, depending on the nature of the inputs. In this chapter, you will learn how to program simple and complex decisions, as well as how to implement instruction sequences that are repeated multiple times.

You will learn to apply these techniques in practical programming situations, for processing text files and for implementing simulations.

CHAPTER CONTENTS

3.1 The if Statement

The if statement is used to implement a decision. It has two parts: a *condition* and a *body* (see Syntax 3.1 on page 102). If the condition is true, the body of the statement is executed.

> The body of an if statement is executed when a condition is true.

The body of the if statement can consist of a single statement:

```
if (area < 0)
    cout << "Error: Negative area\n";
```

This warning message is displayed only when the area is negative (see Figure 1).

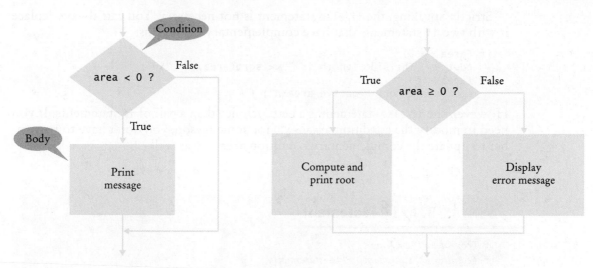

Figure 1 A Decision   **Figure 2** Flowchart for if/else Statement

Quite often, the body of the if statement consists of multiple statements that must be executed in sequence whenever the test is successful. These statements must be grouped together to form a *block statement* by enclosing them in braces { } (see Syntax 3.2 on page 102).

> A block statement contains a sequence of statements, enclosed in braces.

For example,

```
if (area < 0)
{
    cout << "Error: Negative area\n";
    length = 0;
}
```

If the area is negative, then all statements inside the braces are executed: a message is printed, and the variable length is set to 0.

Often, you want to take an action when a condition is fulfilled and a different action in all other cases. In this situation you add else followed by another statement.

> The else part of an if/else statement is executed when a condition is false.

Here is a typical example. When the area of a square is positive or zero, we display its side length. Otherwise, we display an error message.

```
if (area >= 0)
    cout << "The side length is " << sqrt(area) << "\n";
else
    cout << "Error: Negative area\n";
```

The flowchart in Figure 2 gives a graphical representation of the branching behavior.

Strictly speaking, the if/else statement is not necessary. You can always replace it with two if statements that have complementary conditions:

```
if (area >= 0)
    cout << "The side length is " << sqrt(area) << "\n";
if (area < 0)
    cout << "Error: Negative area\n";
```

However, the if/else statement is a better choice than a pair of if statements. If you need to modify the condition area >= 0 for some reason, you don't have to remember to update the complementary condition area < 0 as well.

SYNTAX 3.1 if Statement

if (*condition*) *statement*$_1$
if (*condition*) *statement*$_1$ else *statement*$_2$

Example:

```
if (x >= 0) y = sqrt(x);
if (x >= 0) y = sqrt(x); else { y = 0; cout << "Error"; }
```

Purpose:

Execute a statement if the condition is true. When paired with else, execute the second statement if the condition is false. The statement can be a simple statement (ending in a semicolon) or a block statement.

SYNTAX 3.2 Block Statement

```
{
    statement₁;
    statement₂;
    ...
    statementₙ;
}
```

Example:

```
{
    double length = sqrt(area);
    cout << area << "\n";
}
```

Purpose:

Group several statements into a block that can be controlled by another statement.

QUALITY TIP 3.1

Brace Layout

The compiler doesn't care where you place braces, but we strongly recommend that you follow the simple rule of making { and } line up.

```
int main()
{
   double area;
   cin >> area;
   if (area >= 0)
   {
      double length = sqrt(area);
      ...
   }
   ...
   return 0;
}
```

This scheme makes it easy to spot matching braces. Some programmers put the opening brace on the same line as the if:

```
if (area >= 0) {
   double length = sqrt(area);
   ...
}
```

which makes it harder to match the braces, but it saves a line of code, allowing you to view more code on the screen without scrolling. There are passionate advocates of both styles.

It is important that you pick a layout scheme and stick with it consistently within a given programming project. Which scheme you choose may depend on your personal preference or a coding style guide that you need to follow.

PRODUCTIVITY HINT 3.1

Tabs

Block-structured code has the property that nested statements are indented one or more levels:

```
int main()
{
|  double area;
|  ...
|  if (area >= 0)
|  {
|  |  double length = sqrt(area);
|  |  ...
|  }  |
|  ...
|  return 0;
}  |  |
0  1  2
```
Indentation level

How many spaces should you use per indentation level? Some programmers use eight spaces per level, but that isn't a good choice:

```cpp
int main()
{
        double area;
        ...
        if (area >= 0)
        {
                double length = sqrt(area);
                ...
        }
        ...
        return 0;
}
```

It crowds the code too much to the right side of the screen. As a consequence, long expressions frequently must be broken into separate lines. More common values are 2, 3, or 4 spaces per indentation level.

How do you move the cursor from the leftmost column to the appropriate indentation level? A perfectly reasonable strategy is to hit the space bar a sufficient number of times. However, many programmers use the Tab key instead. A tab moves the cursor to the next tab stop. By default, there are tab stops every 8 columns, but most editors let you change that value; you should find out how to set your editor's tab stops to, say, every 3 columns. (Note that the Tab key does not simply enter three spaces. It moves the cursor to the next tab column.)

Some editors actually help you out with an *autoindent* feature. They automatically insert as many tabs or spaces as the preceding line had, because it is quite likely that the new line is supposed to be on the same indentation level. If it isn't, you must add or remove a tab, but that is still faster than tabbing all the way from the left margin.

As nice as tabs are for data entry, they have one disadvantage: They can mess up printouts. If you send a file with tabs to a printer, the printer may either ignore the tabs altogether or set tab stops every eight columns. It is therefore best to save and print your files with spaces instead of tabs. Most editors have settings to automatically convert tabs to spaces when saving or printing. Look at the documentation of your editor to find out how to activate this useful setting.

ADVANCED TOPIC 3.1

The Selection Operator

C++ has a *selection operator* of the form

   test ? *value1* : *value2*

The value of that expression is either $value_1$ if the test passes or $value_2$ if it fails. For example, we can compute the absolute value as

```cpp
y = x >= 0 ? x : -x;
```

which is a convenient shorthand for

```
if (x >= 0) y = x;
else y = -x;
```

The selection operator is similar to the `if/else` statement, but it works on a different syntactical level. The selection operator combines *expressions* and yields another expression. The `if/else` statement combines statements and yields another statement.

Expressions have values. For example, `-b + sqrt(r)` is an expression, as is `x >= 0 ? x : -x`. Any expression can be made into a statement by adding a semicolon. For example, `y = x` is an expression (with value x), but `y = x;` is a statement. Statements do not have values. Because `if/else` forms a statement and does not have a value, you cannot write

```
y = if (x > 0) x; else -x; // Error
```

We don't use the selection operator in this book, but it is a convenient and legitimate construct that you will find in many C++ programs.

3.2 Relational Operators

Relational operators are used to compare numbers and strings.

Every `if` statement performs a test. In many cases, the test compares two values. For example, in the previous examples we tested `area < 0` and `area >= 0`. The comparisons `<` and `>=` are called *relational operators*. C++ has six relational operators:

C++	Math Notation	Description
>	>	Greater than
>=	≥	Greater than or equal
<	<	Less than
<=	≤	Less than or equal
==	=	Equal
!=	≠	Not equal

As you can see, only two C++ relational operators (`>` and `<`) look as you would expect from the mathematical notation. Computer keyboards do not have keys for ≥, ≤, or ≠, but the `>=`, `<=`, and `!=` operators are easy to remember because they look similar. The `==` operator is initially confusing to most newcomers to C++. In C++, `=` already has a meaning, namely assignment. The `==` operator denotes equality testing:

```
a = 5; // Assign 5 to a
if (a == 5)  // Test whether a equals 5
```

Use == for equality testing, = for assignment.

You must remember to use == inside tests and to use = outside tests. (See Common Error 3.1 on page 107 for more information.)

You can compare strings as well:

```
if (name == "Harry") ...
```

In C++, letter case matters. For example, "Harry" and "HARRY" are not the same string.

The lexicographic or dictionary order is used to compare strings.

If you compare strings using < <= > >=, they are compared in dictionary order. For example, the test

```
string name = "Tom";
if (name < "Dick") ...
```

fails, because in the dictionary Dick comes before Tom. Actually, the dictionary ordering used by C++ is slightly different from that of a normal dictionary. C++ is case-sensitive and sorts characters by listing numbers first, then uppercase characters, then lowercase characters. For example, 1 comes before B, which comes before a. The space character comes before all other characters. Strictly speaking, the character sort order is implementation-dependent, but the majority of systems use the so-called *ASCII code* (American Standard Code for Information Interchange), or one of its extensions, whose characters are sorted as described.

When comparing two strings, corresponding letters are compared until one of the strings ends or the first difference is encountered. If one of the strings ends, the longer string is considered the later one. If a character mismatch is found, compare the characters to determine which string comes later in the dictionary sequence. This process is called *lexicographic comparison*. For example, compare "car" with "cargo". The first three letters match, and we reach the end of the first string. Therefore "car" comes before "cargo" in the lexicographic ordering. Now compare "cathode" with "cargo". The first two letters match. Since t comes after r, the string "cathode" comes after "cargo" in lexicographic ordering. (See Figure 3.)

You can only compare numbers with numbers and strings with strings. The test

```
string name = "Harry";
if (name > 5)    // Error
```

is not valid.

You cannot use relational operators to compare objects of arbitrary classes. For example, if s and t are two objects of the Time class, then the comparison s == t is an error.

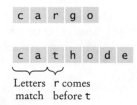

Figure 3   Lexicographic Ordering

COMMON ERROR 3.1

Confusing = and ==

The rule for the correct usage of = and == is very simple: In tests, always use == and never use =. If it is so simple, why can't the compiler be helpful and flag any errors?

Actually, the C++ language allows the use of = inside tests. To understand this, we have to go back in time. For historical reasons, the expression inside an if () need not be a logical condition. Any numeric value can be used inside a condition, with the convention that 0 denotes false and any non-0 value denotes true. Furthermore, in C++ assignments are also expressions and have values. For example, the value of the expression a = 5 is 5. That can be convenient—you can capture the value of an intermediate expression in a variable:

```
x1 = (-b - (r = sqrt(b * b - 4 * a * c))) / (2 * a);
x2 = (- b + r) / (2 * a);
```

The expression r = sqrt(b * b - 4 * a * c) has a value, namely the value that is assigned to r, and thus can be nested inside the larger expression. We don't recommend this style of programming, because it is not much more trouble to set r first and then set x1 and x2, but there are situations in which the construction is useful.

These two features—namely that numbers can be used as truth values and that assignments are expressions with values—conspire to make a horrible pitfall. The test

```
if (x = y) ...
```

is legal C++, but it does not test whether x and y are equal. Instead, the code sets x to y, and if that value is not zero, the body of the if statement is executed.

Fortunately, most compilers issue a warning when they encounter such a statement. You should take such warnings seriously. (See Quality Tip 3.2 for more advice about compiler warnings.)

Some shell-shocked programmers are so nervous about using = that they use == even when they want to make an assignment:

```
x2 == (-b + r) / (2 * a);
```

Again, this is legal C++. This statement tests whether x2 equals the expression of the right-hand side. It doesn't do anything with the outcome of the test, but that is not an error. Some compilers will warn that "the code has no effect", but others will quietly accept the code.

QUALITY TIP 3.2

Compile with Zero Warnings

There are two kinds of messages that the compiler gives you: *errors* and *warnings*. Error messages are fatal; the compiler will not translate a program with one or more errors. Warning messages are advisory; the compiler will translate the program, but there is a good chance that the program will not do what you expect it to do.

You should make an effort to write code that emits no warnings at all. Usually, you can avoid warnings by convincing the compiler that you know what you are doing. For example, many compilers warn of a possible loss of information when you assign a floating-point expression to an integer variable:

```
int pennies = 100 * (amount_due - amount_paid);
```

Use an explicit cast (see Common Error 3.2), and the compiler will stop complaining:

```
int pennies = static_cast<int>(100 * (amount_due - amount_paid));
```

Some compilers emit warnings that can only be turned off with a great deal of skill or trouble. If you run into such a warning, confirm with your instructor that it is indeed unavoidable.

COMMON ERROR 3.2

Comparison of Floating-Point Numbers

Floating-point numbers have only a limited precision, and calculations can introduce round-off errors. For example, the following code multiplies the square root of 2 by itself. We expect to get the answer 2:

```
double r = sqrt(2);
if (r * r == 2) cout << "sqrt(2) squared is 2\n";
else cout << "sqrt(2) squared is not 2 but " << r * r << "\n".
```

Strangely enough, this program displays

```
sqrt(2) squared is not 2 but 2
```

To see what really happens, we need to see the output with higher precision. Then the answer is

```
sqrt(2) squared is not 2 but 2.0000000000000004
```

This explains why r * r didn't compare to be equal to 2. Unfortunately, roundoff errors are unavoidable. It does not make sense in most circumstances to compare floating-point numbers exactly. Instead, we should test whether they are *close* enough. That is, the magnitude of their difference should be less than some threshold. Mathematically, we would write that x and y are close enough if

$$|x - y| \leq \varepsilon$$

for a very small number, ε. ε is the Greek letter epsilon, a letter commonly used to denote a very small quantity. It is common to set ε to 10^{-14} when comparing double numbers.

However, this test is often not quite good enough. Suppose x and y are rather large, say a few million each. Then one could be a roundoff error for the other even if their difference was quite a bit larger than 10^{-14}. To overcome this problem, we really need to test whether

$$\frac{|x - y|}{\max(|x|, |y|)} \leq \varepsilon$$

This formula has one limitation. Suppose either x or y is zero. Then

$$\frac{|x - y|}{\max(|x|, |y|)}$$

has the value 1. Conceptually, there is not enough information to compare the magnitudes in this situation. In that situation, you need to set ε to a value that is appropriate for the problem domain, and check whether $|x - y| \leq \varepsilon$.

3.3 Multiple Alternatives

Multiple if/else
statements can be
combined to evaluate
complex decisions.

Up to this point, you saw how to program a two-way branch with an
if/else statement. In many situations, there are more than two cases.

Consider the task of translating a value on the Richter scale, a
measurement of the strength of an earthquake, into a description the
likely impact. You use a sequence of if/else statements, like this:

```cpp
if (richter >= 8.0)
   cout << "Most structures fall";
else if (richter >= 7.0)
   cout << "Many buildings destroyed";
else if (richter >= 6.0)
   cout << "Many buildings considerably damaged, some collapse";
else if (richter >= 4.5)
   cout << "Damage to poorly constructed buildings";
else
   cout << "Generally no damage";
```

As soon as one of the tests succeeds, a description is displayed, and no further tests
are attempted. If none of the four cases applies, an error message is printed. Figure 4
shows the flowchart for this multiple-branch statement. (See ch03/richter.cpp for
the complete program.)

When using multiple
if/else statements,
pay attention to the
order of the conditions.

Note that the order of the tests is important. Suppose we reverse
the order:

```cpp
if (richter >= 4.5)
   cout << "Damage to poorly constructed buildings";
else if (richter >= 6.0)
   cout << "Many buildings considerably damaged,"
      << "some collapse";
else if (richter >= 7.0)
   cout << "Many buildings destroyed";
else if (richter >= 8.0)
   cout << "Most structures fall";
```

This does not work. Suppose richter has the value 7.1. That value matches the first
condition, and a wrong description is displayed.

In this example, it is also important that we use an if/else/else test, not just
multiple independent if statements. Consider this sequence of independent tests:

```cpp
if (richter >= 8.0) // Didn't use else
   cout << "Most structures fall";
if (richter >= 7.0)
   cout << "Many buildings destroyed";
if (richter >= 6.0)
   cout << "Many buildings considerably damaged, some collapse";
if (richter >= 4.5)
   cout << "Damage to poorly constructed buildings";
```

Now the alternatives are no longer exclusive. If richter is 7.1, then the last *three*
tests all match, and three messages are printed.

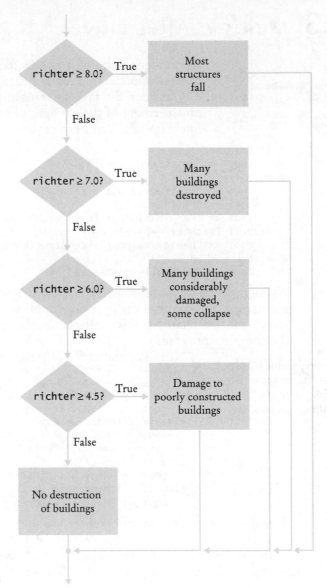

Figure 4
Multiple Alternatives

ADVANCED TOPIC 3.2

The switch Statement

A sequence of if/else/else that compares a *single integer value* against several *constant* alternatives can be implemented as a switch statement. For example,

```
int digit;
...
```

```
switch(digit)
{
    case 1: digit_name = "one"; break;
    case 2: digit_name = "two"; break;
    case 3: digit_name = "three"; break;
    case 4: digit_name = "four"; break;
    case 5: digit_name = "five"; break;
    case 6: digit_name = "six"; break;
    case 7: digit_name = "seven"; break;
    case 8: digit_name = "eight"; break;
    case 9: digit_name = "nine"; break;
    default: digit_name = ""; break;
}
```

This is a shortcut for

```
int digit;
if (digit == 1) digit_name = "one";
else if (digit == 2) digit_name = "two";
else if (digit == 3) digit_name = "three";
else if (digit == 4) digit_name = "four";
else if (digit == 5) digit_name = "five";
else if (digit == 6) digit_name = "six";
else if (digit == 7) digit_name = "seven";
else if (digit == 8) digit_name = "eight";
else if (digit == 9) digit_name = "nine";
else digit_name = "";
```

Well, it isn't much of a shortcut. It has one advantage—it is obvious that all branches test the *same* value, namely `digit`—but the switch statement can be applied only in narrow circumstances. The test cases must be constants, and they must be integers. You cannot use

```
switch(name)
{
    case "penny": value = 0.01; break; // Error
    ...
}
```

There is a reason for these limitations. The compiler can generate efficient test code (using so-called jump tables or binary searches) only in the situation that is permitted in a switch statement. Of course, modern compilers will be happy to perform the same optimization for a sequence of alternatives in an if/else/else statement, so the need for the switch has largely gone away.

We forgo the switch statement in this book for a different reason. Every branch of the switch must be terminated by a break instruction. If the break is missing, execution *falls through* to the next branch, and so on, until finally a break or the end of the switch is reached. There are a few cases in which this is actually useful, but they are very rare. Peter van der Linden [1, p. 38] describes an analysis of the switch statements in the Sun C compiler front end. Of the 244 switch statements, each of which had an average of 7 cases, only 3 percent used the fall-through behavior. That is, the default—falling through to the next case unless stopped by a break—is *wrong 97 percent of the time*. Forgetting to type the break is an exceedingly common error, yielding wrong code.

We leave it to you to use the switch statement for your own code or not. At any rate, you need to have a reading knowledge of switch in case you find it in the code of other programmers.

The Dangling else Problem

When an if statement is nested inside another if statement, the following error may occur.

```
double shipping_charge = 5.00; // $5 inside continental U.S.

if (country == "USA")
   if (state == "HI")
      shipping_charge = 10.00; // Hawaii is more expensive
else // Pitfall!
   shipping_charge = 20.00; // as are foreign shipments
```

The indentation level seems to suggest that the else is grouped with the test country == "USA". Unfortunately, that is not the case. The compiler ignores all indentation and follows the rule that an else always belongs to the closest if. That is, the code is actually

```
double shipping_charge = 5.00; // $5 inside continental U.S.
if (country == "USA")
   if (state == "HI")
      shipping_charge = 10.00; // Hawaii is more expensive
   else // Pitfall!
      shipping_charge = 20.00;
```

That isn't what you want. You want to group the else with the first if. This problem is called a *dangling* else. To resolve it, you must use braces.

```
double shipping_charge = 5.00; // $5 inside continental U.S.
if (country == "USA")
{
   if (state == "HI")
      shipping_charge = 10.00; // Hawaii is more expensive
}
else
   shipping_charge = 20.00; // as are foreign shipments
```

To avoid having to think about the pairing of the else, we recommend that you *always* use a set of braces when the body of an if contains another if.

3.4 Nested Branches

It is often necessary to include an if/else statement inside another. Such an arrangement is called a *nested* set of statements. Here is a typical example.

In the United States different tax rates are used depending on the taxpayer's marital status. There are two main tax schedules, for single and for married taxpayers. Married taxpayers add their income together and pay taxes on the total. (In fact, there are two other schedules, "head of household" and "married filing separately", which we will ignore for simplicity.) Table 1 gives the tax rate computations for each of the filing categories, using the values for the 1992 federal tax return (which had a particularly simple structure).

Table 1 Federal Tax Rate Schedule

If your status is Single and if the taxable income is over	but not over	the tax is	of the amount over
$0	$21,450	15%	$0
$21,450	$51,900	$3,217.50 + 28%	$21,450
$51,900		$11,743.50 + 31%	$51,900

If your status is Married and if the taxable income is over	but not over	the tax is	of the amount over
$0	$35,800	15%	$0
$35,800	$86,500	$5,370.00 + 28%	$35,800
$86,500		$19,566.00 + 31%	$86,500

Now compute the taxes due, given a filing status and an income figure. The key point is that there are two *levels* of decision making. First, you must branch on the filing status. Then, for each filing status, you must have another branch on income level. (See Figure 5 for a flowchart.)

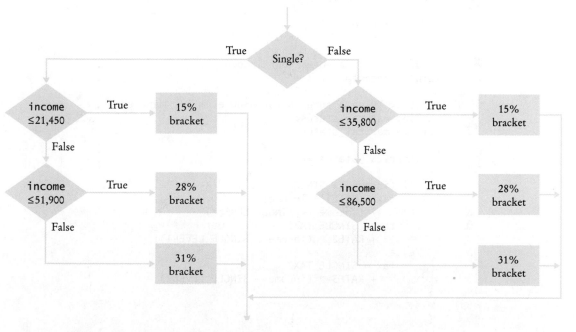

Figure 5 Income Tax Computation

The two-level decision process is reflected in two levels of `if` statements in the program at the end of this section. In theory, nesting can go deeper than two levels. A three-level decision process (first by state, then by status, then by income level) requires three nesting levels.

ch03/tax.cpp

```cpp
1    #include <iostream>
2    #include <string>
3
4    using namespace std;
5
6    int main()
7    {
8       const double SINGLE_LEVEL1 = 21450.00;
9       const double SINGLE_LEVEL2 = 51900.00;
10
11      const double SINGLE_TAX1 = 3217.50;
12      const double SINGLE_TAX2 = 11743.50;
13
14      const double MARRIED_LEVEL1 = 35800.00;
15      const double MARRIED_LEVEL2 = 86500.00;
16
17      const double MARRIED_TAX1 = 5370.00;
18      const double MARRIED_TAX2 = 19566.00;
19
20      const double RATE1 = 0.15;
21      const double RATE2 = 0.28;
22      const double RATE3 = 0.31;
23
24      double income;
25      double tax;
26
27      cout << "Please enter your income: ";
28      cin >> income;
29
30      cout << "Please enter s for single, m for married: ";
31      string marital_status;
32      cin >> marital_status;
33
34      if (marital_status == "s")
35      {
36         if (income <= SINGLE_LEVEL1)
37            tax = RATE1 * income;
38         else if (income <= SINGLE_LEVEL2)
39            tax = SINGLE_TAX1
40               + RATE2 * (income - SINGLE_LEVEL1);
41         else
42            tax = SINGLE_TAX2
43               + RATE3 * (income - SINGLE_LEVEL2);
44      }
45      else
46      {
```

```
47        if (income <= MARRIED_LEVEL1)
48           tax = RATE1 * income;
49        else if (income <= MARRIED_LEVEL2)
50           tax = MARRIED_TAX1
51              + RATE2 * (income - MARRIED_LEVEL1);
52        else
53           tax = MARRIED_TAX2
54              + RATE3 * (income - MARRIED_LEVEL2);
55     }
56     cout << "The tax is $" << tax << "\n";
57     return 0;
58 }
```

3.5 Boolean Operations

When you make complex decisions, you often need to combine conditions that can be true or false. An operator that combines conditions is called a *Boolean* operator, named after the mathematician George Boole (1815–1864), a pioneer in the study of logic.

BOOLE ORDERS LUNCH

C++ has two boolean operators that combine conditions: && (and) and || (or).

In C++, you use the && operator to combines several tests into a new test that passes only when all conditions are true. The || logical operator also combines two or more conditions. The resulting test succeeds if at least one of the conditions is true.

Suppose that a discount shipping rate applies to packages inside the U.S. that weigh at most one pound. The test for the discount passes only if both conditions are true. You use the && operator to join the conditions. (This operator is pronounced *and*.)

```
if (country == "USA" && weight <= 1)
   shipping_charge = 2.50;
```

If either one of the conditions is false, then the test fails.

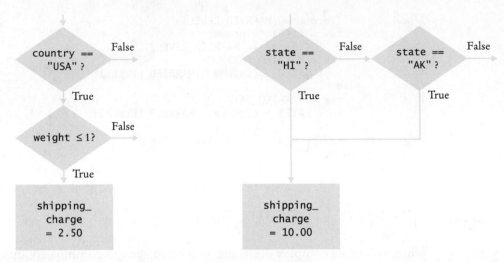

Figure 6   Flowcharts for and and or Combinations

To test whether at least one condition is true, use the || operator (pronounced *or*). For example, in the following test we test whether an order is shipped to Alaska or Hawaii.

```
if (state == "HI" || state == "AK")
    shipping_charge = 10.00;
```

Figure 6 shows flowcharts for these examples.

> The && and || operators are computed *lazily:* As soon as the truth value is determined, no further conditions are evaluated.

The && and || operators are computed using *lazy evaluation.* In other words, logical expressions are evaluated from left to right, and evaluation stops as soon as the truth value is determined. When an *or* is evaluated and the first condition is true, the second condition is not evaluated, because it does not matter what the outcome of the second test is. Here is an example:

```
if (r >= 0 && -b / 2 + sqrt(r) >= 0) ...
```

If r is negative, then the first condition is false, and thus the combined statement is false, no matter what the outcome of the second test is. The second test is never evaluated for negative r, and there is no danger of computing the square root of a negative number.

> The Boolean type bool has two values, false and true.

Sometimes, you need to evaluate a logical condition in one part of a program and use it elsewhere. To store a condition that can be true or false, you use a variable of a special data type bool. That type has exactly two values, denoted false and true. These values are not strings or integers; they are special values, just for Boolean operations.

For example, you may want to remember whether a shipment gets a discount:

```
bool discounted = country == "USA" && weight <= 1;
```

The variable is set to the value of the Boolean expression on the right, that is, true if both conditions are true and false otherwise.

To invert a Boolean value, use the ! (not) operator.

The ! operator (pronounced *not*) inverts a Boolean value. For example,

    !discounted

is true if discounted is false.

Here is a summary of the three logical operations:

A	B	A && B
true	true	true
true	false	false
false	Any	false

A	B	A || B
true	Any	true
false	true	true
false	false	false

A	!A
true	false
false	true

COMMON ERROR 3.4

Multiple Relational Operators

Consider the expression

    if (-0.5 <= x <= 0.5) // Error

This looks just like the mathematical test $-0.5 \le x \le 0.5$. Unfortunately, it is not.

Let us dissect the expression -0.5 <= x <= 0.5. The first half, -0.5 <= x, is a test with outcome true or false, depending on the value of x. The outcome of that test (true or false) is then compared against 0.5. This seems to make no sense. Can one compare truth values and floating-point numbers? Is true larger than 0.5 or not? Unfortunately, to stay compatible with the C language, C++ converts false to 0 and true to 1.

You therefore must be careful not to mix logical and arithmetic expressions in your programs. Instead, use *and* to combine two separate tests:

    if (-0.5 <= x && x <= 0.5) ...

Another common error, along the same lines, is to write

```
if (x && y > 0) ... // Error
```

instead of

```
if (x > 0 && y > 0) ...
```

Unfortunately, the compiler will not issue an error message. Instead, it does the opposite conversion, converting x to true or false. Zero is converted to false, and any nonzero value is converted to true. If x is not zero, then it tests whether y is greater than 0, and finally it computes the and of these two truth values. Naturally, that computation makes no sense.

COMMON ERROR 3.5

Confusing && and || Conditions

It is a surprisingly common error to confuse *and* and *or* conditions. A value lies between 0 and 100 if it is at least 0 *and* at most 100. It lies outside that range if it is less than 0 *or* greater than 100. There is no golden rule; you just have to think carefully.

Often the *and* or *or* is clearly stated, and then it isn't too hard to implement it. But sometimes the wording isn't as explicit. It is quite common that the individual conditions are nicely set apart in a bulleted list, but with little indication of how they should be combined. The instructions for the 1992 tax return say that you can claim single filing status if any one of the following is true:

- You were never married.
- You were legally separated or divorced on December 31, 1992.
- You were widowed before January 1, 1992, and did not remarry in 1992.

Since the test passes if *any one* of the conditions is true, you must combine the conditions with *or*. Elsewhere, the same instructions state that you may use the more advantageous status of married filing jointly if all five of the following conditions are true:

- Your spouse died in 1990 or 1991 and you did not remarry in 1992.
- You have a child whom you can claim as dependent.
- That child lived in your home for all of 1992.
- You paid over half the cost of keeping up your home for this child.
- You filed (or could have filed) a joint return with your spouse the year he or she died.

Because *all* of the conditions must be true for the test to pass, you must combine them with an *and*.

ADVANCED TOPIC 3.3

De Morgan's Law

> De Morgan's law tells you how to negate an &&/|| condition: Reverse the operator and move the ! inward.

Humans generally have a hard time comprehending logical conditions with *not* operators applied to *and/or* expressions. De Morgan's Law, named after the logician Augustus De Morgan, can be used to simplify these Boolean expressions.

Suppose we want to charge a higher shipping rate if we don't ship within the continental United States.

```
if (!(country == "USA"
        && state != "AK"
        && state != "HI"))
    shipping_charge = 20.00;
```

This test is a little bit complicated, and you have to think carefully through the logic. When it is *not* true that the country is USA *and* the state is not Alaska *and* the state is not Hawaii, then charge $20.00. Huh? It is not true that some people won't be confused by this code.

The computer doesn't care, but it takes human programmers to write and maintain the code. Therefore, it is useful to know how to simplify such a condition.

De Morgan's Law has two forms: one for the negation of an *and* expression and one for the negation of an *or* expression:

`!(A && B)`	is the same as	`!A || !B`
`!(A || B)`	is the same as	`!A && !B`

Pay particular attention to the fact that the *and* and *or* operators are *reversed* by moving the *not* inward. For example, the negation of "the state is Alaska *or* it is Hawaii",

```
!(state == "AK" || state == "HI")
```

is "the state is not Alaska *and* it is not Hawaii":

```
!(state == "AK") && !(state == "HI")
```

That is, of course, the same as

```
state != "AK" && state != "HI"
```

Now apply the law to our shipping charge computation:

```
!(country == "USA"
    && state != "AK"
    && state != "HI")
```

is equivalent to

```
!(country == "USA")
    || !(state != "AK")
    || !(state != "HI")
```

That yields the simpler test

```
country != "USA"
    || state == "AK"
    || state == "HI"
```

To simplify conditions with negations of *and* or *or* expressions, it is usually a good idea to apply De Morgan's Law to move the negations to the innermost level.

RANDOM FACT 3.1

Artificial Intelligence

When one uses a sophisticated computer program such as a tax preparation package, one is bound to attribute some intelligence to the computer. The computer asks sensible questions and makes computations that we find a mental challenge. After all, if doing one's taxes were easy, we wouldn't need a computer to do it for us.

As programmers, however, we know that all this apparent intelligence is an illusion. Human programmers have carefully "coached" the software in all possible scenarios, and it simply replays the actions and decisions that were programmed into it.

Would it be possible to write computer programs that are genuinely intelligent in some sense? From the earliest days of computing, there was a sense that the human brain might be nothing but an immense computer, and that it might well be feasible to program computers to imitate some processes of human thought. Serious research into *artificial intelligence* began in the mid-1950s, and the first twenty years brought some impressive successes. Programs that play chess—surely an activity that appears to require remarkable intellectual powers—have become so good that they now routinely beat all but the best human players. As far back as 1975, an expert-system program called Mycin gained fame for being better in diagnosing meningitis in patients than the average physician.

However, there were serious setbacks as well. From 1982 to 1992, the Japanese government embarked on a massive research project, funded at over 40 billion Japanese yen. It was known as the *Fifth-Generation Project*. Its goal was to develop new hardware and software to improve the performance of expert system software greatly. At its outset, the project created great fear in other countries that the Japanese computer industry was about to become the undisputed leader in the field. However, the end results were disappointing and did little to bring artificial intelligence applications to market.

From the very outset, one of the stated goals of the AI community was to produce software that could translate text from one language to another, for example from English to Russian. That undertaking proved to be enormously complicated. Human language appears to be much more subtle and interwoven with the human experience than had originally been thought. Even the grammar-checking tools that come with word-processing programs today are more of a gimmick than a useful tool, and analyzing grammar is just the first step in translating sentences.

The CYC (from encyclopedia) project, started by Douglas Lenat in 1984, tries to codify the implicit assumptions that underlie human speech and writing. The team members started out analyzing news articles and asked themselves what unmentioned facts are necessary to actually understand the sentences. For example, consider the sentence "Last fall she enrolled in Michigan State". The reader automatically realizes that "fall" is not related to falling down in this context, but refers to the season. While there is a state of Michigan, here Michigan State denotes the university. A priori, a computer program has none of this knowledge. The goal of the CYC project is to extract and store the requisite facts—that is, (1) people enroll in universities; (2) Michigan is a state; (3) many states have universities named X State University, often abbreviated as X State; (4) most people enroll in a university in the fall. By 1995, the project had codified about 100,000 common-sense concepts and about a million facts of knowledge relating them. Even this massive amount of data has not proven sufficient for useful applications.

In recent years, artificial intelligence technology has seen substantial advances. One of the most astounding examples is the outcome of a series of "grand challenges" for autonomous vehicles by the Defense Advanced Research Projects Agency (DARPA). Competitors were

Figure 7   The Winner of the 2007 DARPA Urban Challenge

invited to submit computer-controlled vehicles which had to complete obstacle courses, without a human driver or remote control. The first event, in 2004, was a disappointment, with none of the entrants finishing the route. In 2005, five vehicles completed a grueling 212 km course in the Mojave desert. Stanford's Stanley came in first, with an average speed of 30 km/h. In 2007, DARPA moved the competition to an "urban" environment, an abandoned air force base. Vehicles had to be able to interact with each other, following California traffic laws. As Stanford's Sebastian Thrun explained: "In the last Grand Challenge, it didn't really matter whether an obstacle was a rock or a bush, because either way you'd just drive around it. The current challenge is to move from just sensing the environment to understanding the environment."

3.6 The while Loop

In an `if` statement, a condition is evaluated and an action is taken. However, this process only happens once. In many situations, you want to repeat an action multiple times, depending on a condition. In this section, you will see how to use the `while` statement for repeating an action.

Recall the investment problem from Chapter 1. You put $10,000 into a bank account that earns 5 percent interest per year. How many years does it take for the account balance to be double the original investment?

In Chapter 1 we developed an algorithm for this problem, but we didn't present enough C++ syntax to implement it. Here is the algorithm.

Step 1 Start with the table.

Year	Balance
0	$10,000.00

Step 2   Repeat steps 2a ... 2c while the balance is less than $20,000.

Step 2a   Add a new row to the table.

Step 2b   In column 1 of the new row, put one more than the preceding year's value.

Step 2c   In column 2 of the new row, place the value of the preceding balance, multiplied by 1.05 (5 percent).

Step 3   Report the last number in the year column as the answer.

You now know that each column in that table corresponds to a C++ variable, and you know how to update and print the variables. What you don't yet know is how to carry out "Repeat steps 2a ... 2c while the balance is less than $20,000".

In C++, the `while` statement (see Syntax 3.3 on page 123) implements such a repetition. The code

> A while loop executes a block of code repeatedly, while a condition remains true.

```
while (condition)
    statement
```

keeps executing the statement while the condition is true. The statement can be a block statement if you need to carry out multiple actions in the loop.

A `while` statement is often called a *loop*. If you draw a flowchart, the control loops backwards to the test after every iteration (see Figure 8).

Here is the program that solves the investment problem:

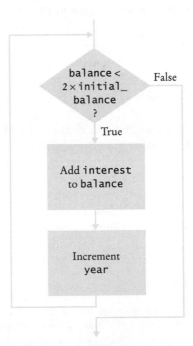

Figure 8   Flowchart of a `while` Loop

ch03/doublinv.cpp

```cpp
1   #include <iostream>
2
3   using namespace std;
4
5   int main()
6   {
7      double rate = 5;
8      double initial_balance = 10000;
9      double balance = initial_balance;
10     int year = 0;
11
12     while (balance < 2 * initial_balance)
13     {
14        double interest = balance * rate / 100;
15        balance = balance + interest;
16        year++;
17     }
18
19     cout << "The investment doubled after "
20        << year << " years.\n";
21
22     return 0;
23  }
```

Program Run

```
The investment doubled after 15 years.
```

SYNTAX 3.3 while Statement

while (*condition*) *statement*

Example:

while (x >= 10) x = sqrt(x);

Purpose:

Execute the statement while the condition remains true.

COMMON ERROR 3.6

Infinite Loops

The most annoying loop error is an infinite loop: a loop that runs forever and can be stopped only by killing the program or restarting the computer. If there are output statements in the loop, then reams and reams of output flash by on the screen. Otherwise, the program just sits there and *hangs*, seeming to do nothing. On some systems, you can kill a hanging program by hitting Ctrl + Break or Ctrl + C. On others, you can close the window in which the program runs.

A common reason for infinite loops is forgetting to update the variable that controls the loop:

```
year = 1;
while (year <= 20)
{
   double interest = balance * rate / 100;
   balance = balance + interest;
}
```

> An infinite loop keeps running until the program is forcibly terminated.

Here the programmer forgot to add a year++ command in the loop. As a result, the year always stays at 1, and the loop never comes to an end.

Another common reason for an infinite loop is accidentally incrementing a counter that should be decremented (or vice versa). Consider this example:

```
year = 20;
while (year > 0)
{
   double interest = balance * rate / 100;
   balance = balance + interest;
   year++;
}
```

The year variable really should have been decremented, not incremented. This is a common error because incrementing counters is so much more common than decrementing that your fingers may type the ++ on autopilot. As a consequence, year is always larger than 0, and the loop never terminates. (Actually, eventually year may exceed the largest representable positive integer and *wrap around* to a negative number. Then the loop exits—of course, with a completely wrong result.)

COMMON ERROR 3.7

Off-by-One Errors

Consider our computation of the number of years that are required to double an investment:

```
int year = 0;
while (balance < 2 * initial_balance)
{
   double interest = balance * rate / 100;
   balance = balance + interest;
   year++;
}
cout << "The investment doubled after "
   << year << " years.\n";
```

Should year start at 0 or at 1? Should you test for balance < 2 * initial_balance or for balance <= 2 * initial_balance? It is easy to be *off by one* in these expressions.

An off-by-one error occurs when a programmer mistakenly uses a value that is one more or less than the correct value.

Some people try to solve off-by-one errors by randomly inserting +1 or -1 until the program seems to work—a terrible strategy. It can take a long time to compile and test all the various possibilities. Expending a small amount of mental effort is a real time saver.

Fortunately, off-by-one errors are easy to avoid, simply by thinking through a couple of test cases and using the information from the test cases to come up with a rationale for your decisions.

Should year start at 0 or at 1? Look at a scenario with simple values: an initial balance of $100 and an interest rate of 50 percent. After year 1, the balance is $150, and after year 2 it is $225, or over $200. So the investment doubled after 2 years. The loop executed two times, incrementing years each time. Hence years must start at 0, not at 1.

In other words, the balance variable denotes the balance after the end of the year. At the outset, the balance variable contains the balance after year 0 and not after year 1.

Next, should you use a < or <= comparison in the test? This is harder to figure out, because it is rare for the balance to be exactly twice the initial balance. There is one case when this happens, namely when the interest is 100 percent. The loop executes once. Now year is 1, and balance is exactly equal to 2 * initial_balance. Has the investment doubled after one year? It has. Therefore, the loop should not execute again. If the test condition is balance < 2 * initial_balance, the loop stops, as it should. If the test condition had been balance <= 2 * initial_balance, the loop would have executed once more.

In other words, you keep adding interest while the balance *has not yet doubled*.

3.7 The for Loop

The for loop is used when a value runs from a starting point to an ending point with a constant increment or decrement.

Far and away the most common loop has the form

```
i = start;
while (i <= end)
{
    . . .
    i++;
}
```

Because this loop is so common, there is a special form for it (see Syntax 3.4 on page 127) that amplifies the pattern:

```
for (i = start; i <= end; i++)
{
    . . .
}
```

You can optionally define the loop variable in the loop. It then persists until the loop exits.

```
for (int i = 1; i <= 10; i++)
{
    . . .
} // i no longer defined here
```

The three slots in the for header can contain any three expressions. We can count down instead of up:

```
for (int i = 10; i >= 0; i--)
{
    ...
}
```

The increment or decrement need not be in steps of 1:

```
for (int i = 0; i <= 10; i = i + 2) ...
```

It is possible—but a sign of unbelievably bad taste—to put unrelated conditions into the loop:

```
for (rate = 6; month--; cout >> balance) ... // Bad taste
```

We won't even begin to decipher what that might mean. You should stick with for loops that initialize, test, and update a single variable.

The following program uses a for loop to print a table of values. Figure 9 shows the corresponding flowchart.

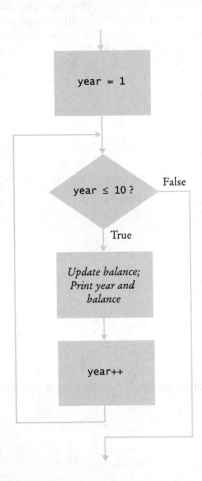

Figure 9
Flowchart of a for Loop

ch03/baltable.cpp

```cpp
1   #include <iostream>
2   #include <iomanip>
3
4   using namespace std;
5
6   int main()
7   {
8      double rate = 5;
9      double balance = 10000;
10
11     for (int year = 1; year <= 10; year++)
12     {
13        double interest = balance * rate / 100;
14        balance = balance + interest;
15        cout << setw(2) << year << ": "
16           << fixed << setprecision(2) << balance << "\n";
17     }
18     return 0;
19  }
```

Program Run

```
 1: 10500.00
 2: 11025.00
 3: 11576.25
 4: 12155.06
 5: 12762.82
 6: 13400.96
 7: 14071.00
 8: 14774.55
 9: 15513.28
10: 16288.95
```

SYNTAX 3.4 **for Statement**

for (*initialization_statement*; *condition*; *update_expression*) *statement*

Example:

for (int i = 1; i <= 10; i++) sum = sum + i;

Purpose:

Repeatedly execute a statement, typically while updating a variable in regular increments. The initialization statement is executed once. While the condition remains true, the statement and the update expression are executed.

QUALITY TIP 3.3

Use for Loops for Their Intended Purpose Only

A for loop is an *idiom* for a while loop of a particular form. A counter runs from the start to the end, with a constant increment:

```
for (i = start; i < (or <=) end; i = i + increment)
{
   ...
   // i, start, end, increment not changed here
}
```

If your loop doesn't match this pattern, don't use the for construction. The compiler won't prevent you from writing idiotic for loops:

```
// Bad style—unrelated header expressions
for (cout << "Inputs: "; cin >> x; sum = sum + x)
   count++;

for (i = 0; i < s.length(); i++)
{
   // Bad style—modifies counter inside loop
   if (s.substr(i, 1) == ".") i++;
   count++;
}
```

These loops will work, but they are plainly bad style. Use a while loop for iterations that do not fit into the for pattern.

QUALITY TIP 3.4

Don't Use != to Test the End of a Numeric Range

Here is a loop with a hidden danger:

```
for (i = 1; i != nyear; i++)
{
   ...
}
```

The test i != nyear is a poor idea. What would happen if nyear happened to be negative? Of course, nyear should never be negative, because it makes no sense to have a negative number of years—but the impossible and unthinkable do happen with distressing regularity. If nyear is negative, the test i != nyear is never true, because i starts at 1 and increases with every step. The program dies in an infinite loop.

The remedy is simple. Test

```
for (i = 0; i < nyear; i++) ...
```

For floating-point values there is another reason not to use the != operator: Because of roundoff errors, the exact termination point may never be reached.

Of course, you would never write

```
for (rate = 5; rate != 10; rate = rate + 0.3333333) ...
```

because it looks highly unlikely that rate would match 10 exactly after 15 steps. But the same problem may happen for the harmless-looking

```
for (rate = 5; rate != 10; rate = rate + 0.1) ...
```

The number 0.1 is exactly representable in the decimal system, but the computer represents floating-point numbers in binary. There is a slight error in any finite binary representation of 1/10, just as there is a slight error in a decimal representation 0.3333333 of 1/3. Maybe rate is exactly 10 after 50 steps; maybe it is off by a tiny amount. There is no point in taking chances. Just use < instead of !=:

```
for (rate = 5; rate < 10; rate = rate + 0.1) ...
```

COMMON ERROR 3.8

Forgetting a Semicolon

It occasionally happens that all the work of a loop is already done in the loop header. This code looks for the position of the first period in a filename:

```
string filename; // e.g., hello.cpp
string name;
...
for (i = 0; filename.substr(i, 1) != "."; i++)
    ;

name = filename.substr(0, i); // e.g., hello
```

The body of the for loop is completely empty, containing just one empty statement terminated by a semicolon.

We are not advocating this strategy. This loop doesn't work correctly if filename doesn't happen to contain a period. Such an anemic loop is often a sign of poor error handling.

If you do run into a loop without a body, it is important that you really make sure the semicolon is not forgotten. If the semicolon is accidentally omitted, then the code

```
for (i = 0; filename.substr(i, 1) != "."; i++)

name = filename.substr(0, i); // e.g., hello
```

repeats the statement name = filename.substr(0, i) until a period is found, and then it doesn't execute it again. (If filename is "hello.cpp", the last assignment into name is "hell".)

You can avoid this error by using an empty block {} instead of an empty statement:

```
for (i = 0; filename.substr(i, 1) != "."; i++)
{}
```

Or, even better, follow Quality Tip 3.3 on page 128, and rewrite the loop as a while loop:

```
int i = 0;
while (filename.substr(i, 1) != ".")
    i++;
```

QUALITY TIP 3.5

Symmetric and Asymmetric Bounds

It is easy to write a loop with i going from 1 to n.

```
for (i = 1; i <= n; i++) ...
```

The values for i are bounded by the relation $1 \leq i \leq n$. Because there are $\leq$ on both bounds, the bounds are called *symmetric*.

When traversing the characters in a string, the bounds are *asymmetric*.

```
for (i = 0; i < s.length(); i++) ...
```

The values for i are bounded by $0 \leq i < s.length()$, with a $\leq$ to the left and a $<$ to the right. That is appropriate, because s.length() is not a valid position.

It is not a good idea to force symmetry artificially:

```
for (i = 0; i <= s.length() - 1; i++) ...
```

That is more difficult to read and understand.

For every loop, consider which form is most natural according to the needs of the problem and use that.

QUALITY TIP 3.6

Count Iterations

Finding the correct lower and upper bounds for an iteration can be confusing. Should you start at 0? Should you use <= b or < b as a termination condition?

Counting the number of iterations is a very useful device for better understanding a loop. Counting is easier for loops with asymmetric bounds. The loop

```
for (i = a; i < b; i++) ...
```

is executed b - a times. For example, the loop traversing the characters in a string,

```
for (i = 0; i < s.length(); i++) ...
```

runs s.length() times. That makes perfect sense, as there are s.length() characters in a string.

The loop with symmetric bounds,

```
for (i = a; i <= b; i++)
```

is executed b - a + 1 times. That "+1" is the source of many programming errors. For example,

```
for (x = 0; x <= 10; x++)
```

runs 11 times. Maybe that is what you want; if not, start at 1 or use < 10.

One way to visualize this "+1" error is by looking at a fence. A fence with ten sections (=) has eleven fence posts (|).

$$|=|=|=|=|=|=|=|=|=|=|$$

Each section has one fence post to the left, and there is a final post on the right of the last section. Forgetting to count the last value is often called a "fence post error".

If the increment is a value c other than 1, then the counts are

```
(b - a)/c        for the asymmetric loop
(b - a)/c + 1    for the symmetric loop
```

For example, consider the loop

```
for (i = 10; i <= 40; i = i + 5)
```

Here, a is 10, b is 40, and c is 5. Therefore, the loop executes $(40 - 10)/5 + 1 = 7$ times.

3.8 The do Loop

The do loop is appropriate when the loop body must be executed at least once.

Sometimes you want to execute the body of a loop at least once and perform the loop test after the body is executed. The do loop (see Syntax 3.5 on page 132) serves that purpose:

```
do
{
    statements
}
while (condition);
```

A typical example of such a loop is ensuring that a user supplies a correct input (see Figure 10).

```
do
{
    cout << "Please enter a positive number;
    cin >> x;
} while (x <= 0);
```

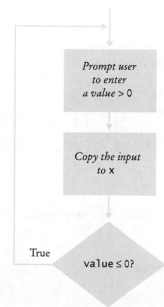

Figure 10
Flowchart of a do Loop

The do loop is the right choice for this situation. We must first read the input before we can decide whether it passes the test.

SYNTAX 3.5 do Statement

do *statement* while (*condition*);

Example:

do x = sqrt(x); while (x >= 10);

Purpose:

Execute the statement, then test the condition, and repeat the statement while the condition remains true.

3.9 Nested Loops

In Section 3.4, you saw how to nest two if statements. Similarly, complex iterations sometimes require nested loops: a loop inside another loop statement. As an example, consider the task of printing a triangle shape such as this one:

```
[]
[][]
[][][]
[][][][]
```

The first row contains one box, the second row contains two boxes, and so on.

To print a triangle consisting of n rows, we use a loop:

```
for (int i = 1; i <= n; i++)
{
    print triangle row
}
```

Each row contains i boxes. To print a triangle row, a second loop is required.

```
for (int j = 1; j <= i; j++)
    cout << "[]";
cout << "\n";
```

That loop is nested inside the outer loop, as shown in the following program.

ch03/triangle.cpp

```
1  #include <iostream>
2
3  using namespace std;
4
5  int main()
6  {
```

```
7        cout << "Enter number of rows: ";
8        int n;
9        cin >> n;
10
11       for (int i = 1; i <= n; i++)
12       {
13          for (int j = 1; j <= i; j++)
14             cout << "[]";
15          cout << "\n";
16       }
17
18       return 0;
19  }
```

3.10 Processing Inputs

When processing a sequence of inputs, you need to have a way of knowing when you have reached the end of the sequence.

A sentinel value denotes the end of a sequence of values, without being a part of the sequence.

Sometimes you are lucky and no input value can be zero. Then you can prompt the user to keep entering numbers, or 0 to finish that data set. If zero is allowed but negative numbers are not, you can use –1 to indicate termination. Such a value, which is not an actual input, but serves as a signal for termination, is called a *sentinel*.

The following program computes the average of a sequence of values, using –1 as a sentinel.

ch03/average.cpp

```
1   #include <iostream>
2
3   using namespace std;
4
5   int main()
6   {
7      double sum = 0;
8      int count = 0;
9      bool more = true;
10
11     while (more)
12     {
13        double input;
14        cout << "Enter a value, -1 to finish: ";
15        cin >> input;
16
17        if (input == -1)
18           more = false;
19        else
20        {
21           sum = sum + input;
22           count++;
23        }
```

```
24      }
25
26      if (count > 0)
27         cout << "Average: " << sum / count << "\n";
28
29      return 0;
30  }
```

Program Run

```
Enter a value, -1 to finish: 10
Enter a value, -1 to finish: 30
Enter a value, -1 to finish: 5
Enter a value, -1 to finish: -1
Average: 15
```

Sentinels only work if there is some restriction on the input. In many cases, though, there isn't. Suppose you want to compute the average of a data set that may contain 0 or negative values. Then you cannot use 0 or −1 to indicate the end of the input. One option is to use a sentinel that is not a number.

> When an input stream senses an input error, it enters the failed state. You can test for failure with the fail function.

Consider a program processing the statement cin >> value. If the user types an input that is not a number then the variable value is not set. Instead, the stream is set to a "failed" state. You can test for that special state by calling the fail member function:

```
if (cin.fail())
{
   cout << "End of input.\n";
   more = false;
}
```

Because testing for input failure is so common, there is a shortcut. You can simply use a stream variable as a condition:

```
if (cin)
{
   // The stream did not fail
   ...
}
else
{
   // The stream failed
   ...
}
```

That is, the test

```
if (cin)
```

is exactly the same as the test

```
if (!cin.fail()).
```

It tests whether cin is still in a good state. Many people find this a bit confusing, and we recommend that you explicitly query cin.fail().

There is, however, one popular idiom that relies on treating a stream as a condition. The expression cin >> x has a value, namely cin. (That is what makes it possible to chain the >> operators: cin >> x >> y first executes cin >> x, which reads input into x and again yields cin, which is combined with y. The operation cin >> y then reads y.)

Because the expression cin >> x has cin as its value, and you can use a stream as the condition of an if statement, you can use the following test:

```
if (cin >> x) ...
```

This means "Read x, and if that didn't make cin fail, then continue". That idiom is compelling for loops:

```
cout << "Enter values, Q to quit.\n";
while (cin >> values)
{
   sum = sum + input;
   count++;
}
```

The loop is executed while the input succeeds.

Advanced Topic 3.4

The Loop-and-a-Half Problem

Some programmers dislike loops that are controlled by a Boolean variable, such as:

```
bool more = true;
while (more)
{
   cin >> input;
   if (cin.fail())
      more = false;
   else
   {
      process input
   }
}
```

The true test for loop termination is in the middle of the loop, not at the top. This is called a *loop and a half* because one must go halfway into the loop before knowing whether one needs to terminate.

As an alternative, you can use the break keyword.

```
while (true)
{
   cin >> input;
   if (cin.fail()) break;
   process input
}
```

The break statement breaks out of the enclosing loop, independent of the loop condition.

In the loop-and-a-half case, `break` statements can be beneficial. But in other situations, the `break` statement can lead to code that is confusing or plainly wrong. We do not use the `break` statement in this book.

PRODUCTIVITY HINT 3.2

Redirection of Input and Output

> Use input redirection to read input from a file. Use output redirection to capture program output in a file.

Consider the program that computes the average value of an input sequence. If you use such a program, then it is quite likely that you already have the values in a file, and it seems a shame that you have to type them all in again. The command line interface of your operating system provides a way to link a file to the input of a program, as if all the characters in the file had actually been typed by a user. If you type

```
average < numbers.txt
```

the program is executed. Its input instructions no longer expect input from the keyboard. All input commands get their input from the file `numbers.txt`. This process is called *input redirection*.

Input redirection is an excellent tool for testing programs. When you develop a program and fix its bugs, it is boring to keep entering the same input every time you run the program. Spend a few minutes putting the inputs into a file, and use redirection.

You can also redirect output. In this program, that is not terribly useful. If you run

```
average < numbers.txt > output.txt
```

the file `output.txt` contains a single line such as "Average: 15". However, redirecting output is obviously useful for programs that produce lots of output. You can print the file containing the output or edit it before you turn it in for grading.

ADVANCED TOPIC 3.5

End-of-File Detection

When reading input from a file, it is not common to use a sentinel value. Instead, simply detect the end of the file. When the end of the file has been reached, the next input will fail. Simply place all your data into a file, use input redirection, and read the data with a loop

```
while (cin >> input)
{
    process input
}
```

This mechanism works equally well for reading numbers and strings. However, there is one trick you need to know if you process strings and occasionally supply input from the keyboard. When reading input from the console, you indicate the end of input with a special character, Ctrl + Z on a Windows system or Ctrl + D on UNIX, after you have entered all values. That value signals to `cin` that the end of the console "file" has been reached.

Sometimes, you may want to know whether input has failed because the end of the file has been reached or because one of the input values was bad. After determining that the stream has failed, call the `eof` function:

```
if (cin.fail())
{
    if (cin.eof())
    {
        // End of file has been reached
    }
    else
    {
        // Bad input
    }
}
```

Be careful that you call `eof` only *after the input stream has failed.* The following loop does not work:

```
while (more)
{
    cin >> value;
    if (cin.eof()) // Don't!
    {
        more = false;
    }
    else
    {
        sum = sum + value;
    }
}
```

If the stream input fails for another reason (usually because a non-number was encountered in the input), then all further input operations fail, and the end of the file is never reached. The loop then becomes an infinite loop. For example, consider the input

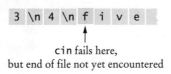

cin fails here,
but end of file not yet encountered

ADVANCED TOPIC 3.6

Clearing the Failure State of a Stream

Once a stream fails, all further input operations also fail. If you want to read two number sequences and use a letter as a sentinel, you need to clear the failure state after reading the first sentinel. Call the `clear` method:

```
cout << "Enter values, Q to quit.\n";
while (cin >> values)
{
   process input
}
cin.clear();
```

Suppose the user has entered 30 10 5 Q. The input of Q has caused the failure. Because only successfully processed characters are removed from the input, the Q character is still present. Read it into a dummy variable:

```
string sentinel;
cin >> sentinel;
```

Now you can go on and read more inputs.

RANDOM FACT 3.2

The Denver Airport Luggage Handling System

Making decisions is an essential part of any computer program. Nowhere can this be seen more than with a computer system that helps sort luggage at an airport. After scanning the luggage identification codes, the system sorts the items and routes them to different conveyor belts. Human operators then place the items onto trucks. When the city of Denver

Figure 11
The Denver airport originally had a fully automatic system for moving luggage, replacing human operators with robotic carts. Unfortunately, the system never worked and was dismantled before the airport was opened.

built a huge airport to replace an outdated and congested facility, the luggage system contractor went a step further. The new system was designed to replace the human operators with robotic carts. Unfortunately, the system plainly did not work. It was plagued by mechanical problems, such as luggage falling onto the tracks and jamming carts. Just as frustrating were the software glitches. Carts would uselessly accumulate at some locations when they were needed elsewhere.

The airport had been scheduled for opening in 1993, but without a functioning luggage system, the opening was delayed for over a year while the contractor tried to fix the problems. The contractor never succeeded, and ultimately a manual system was installed. The delay cost the city and airlines close to a billion dollars, and the contractor, once the leading luggage systems vendor in the United States, went bankrupt.

Clearly, it is very risky to build a large system based on a technology that has never been tried on a smaller scale. As robots and the software that controls them will get better over time, they will take on a larger share of luggage handling in the future. But it is likely that this will happen in an incremental fashion.

3.11 Simulations

In a simulation program, you use the computer to simulate an activity. You can introduce randomness by calling the random number generator.

In a simulation we generate random events and evaluate their outcomes. Here is a typical problem that can be decided by running a simulation, the *Buffon needle experiment*, devised by Comte Georges-Louis Leclerc de Buffon (1707–1788), a French naturalist. A needle of length 1 inch is dropped onto paper that is ruled with lines 2 inches apart. If the needle drops onto a line, we count it as a *hit*. Buffon conjectured that the quotient *tries/hits* approximates π. (See Figure 12.)

Now, how can you run this experiment in the computer? You don't actually want to build a robot that drops needles on paper. The C++ library has a *random number generator*, which produces numbers that appear to be completely random. Calling rand() yields a random integer between 0 and RAND_MAX (which is an implementation-dependent constant, typically 32767 or 2147483647). The rand function is defined in the cstdlib header. The following program calls the rand function ten times.

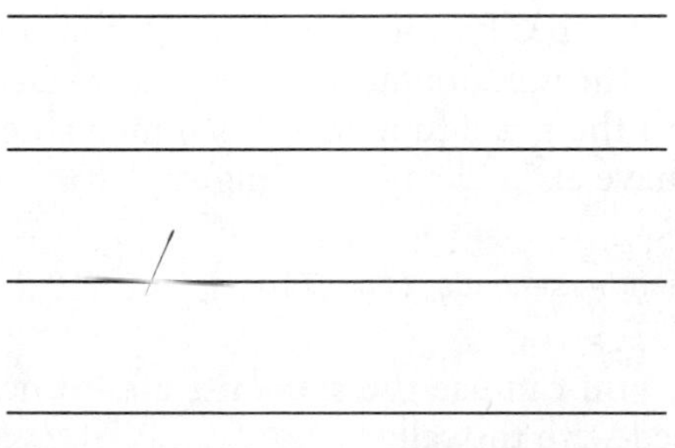

Figure 12   The Buffon Needle Experiment

ch03/random.cpp

```cpp
1   #include <iostream>
2   #include <cstdlib>
3
4   using namespace std;
5
6   int main()
7   {
8      int i;
9      for (i = 1; i <= 10; i++)
10     {
11        int r = rand();
12        cout << r << "\n";
13     }
14     return 0;
15  }
```

Program Run

```
41
18467
6334
26500
19169
15724
11478
29358
26962
24464
```

Actually, the numbers are not completely random. They are drawn from very long sequences of numbers that don't repeat for a long time. These sequences are actually computed from fairly simple formulas; they just behave like random numbers. For that reason, they are often called *pseudorandom* numbers. How to generate good sequences of numbers that behave like truly random sequences is an important and well-studied problem in computer science. We won't investigate this issue further. Just use the random numbers produced by rand.

Try running the program again. You will get the *exact same output!* This confirms that the random numbers are generated by formulas. However, when running simulations, you don't always want to get the same results. To overcome this problem, you need to specify a *seed* for the random number sequence. Every time you use a new seed, the random number generator starts generating a new sequence. The seed is set with the srand function. A simple value to use as a seed is the number of seconds that have elapsed since midnight:

```cpp
Time now;
int seed = now.seconds_from(Time(0, 0, 0));
srand(seed);
```

Alternatively, you can use the standard time function defined in the ctime header, and set the seed with the call:

```cpp
srand(time(0));
```

Simply place these instructions at the beginning of your program, before generating any random numbers. Then the random numbers will be different in every program run.

Of course, in actual applications, you want to generate random numbers in different ranges. For example, to simulate the throw of a die, you need random numbers between 1 and 6. In general, consider the problem of generating random integers between two bounds a and b. As you know from Quality Tip 3.6 on page 130, there are b - a + 1 values between a and b, including the bounds themselves. First compute rand() % (b - a + 1) to obtain a random value between 0 and b - a, then add that to a, yielding a random value between a and b:

```
int r = a + rand() % (b - a + 1);
```

For example, here is a program that simulates the throw of a pair of dice.

ch03/dice.cpp

```
1   #include <iostream>
2   #include <string>
3   #include <cstdlib>
4   #include <ctime>
5
6   using namespace std;
7
8   int main()
9   {
10      // Sets the seed of the random number generator.
11      srand(time(0));
12
13      for (int i = 1; i <= 10; i++)
14      {
15          int d1 = 1 + rand() % 6;
16          int d2 = 1 + rand() % 6;
17          cout << d1 << " " << d2 << "\n";
18      }
19      cout << "\n";
20      return 0;
21  }
```

Program Run

```
5 1
2 1
1 2
5 1
1 2
6 4
4 4
6 1
6 3
5 2
```

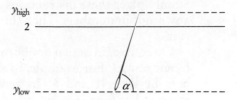

Figure 13
A Hit in the Buffon Needle Experiment

To run the Buffon needle experiment you have to work a little harder. When you throw a die, it has to come up with one of six faces. When throwing a needle, however, there are many possible outcomes.

You must generate a random *floating-point number*. First, note that the quantity `rand() * 1.0 / RAND_MAX` is a random floating-point value between 0 and 1. (You have to multiply by `1.0` to ensure that one of the operands of the `/` operator is a floating-point value. The division `rand() / RAND_MAX` would be an integer division— see Common Error 2.2.) To generate a random value ranging between a and b, you have to make a simple transformation:

```
double r = a + (b - a) * (rand() * 1.0 / RAND_MAX);
```

For the Buffon needle experiment, you must generate two random numbers: one to describe the starting position and one to describe the angle of the needle with the *x*-axis. Then test whether the needle touches a grid line. Stop after 10,000 tries.

Generate the *lower* point of the needle. Its *x*-coordinate is irrelevant, and you may assume its *y*-coordinate y_{low} to be any random number between 0 and 2. The angle α between the needle and the *x*-axis can be any value between 0 and 180 degrees. The upper end of the needle has *y*-coordinate

$$y_{high} = y_{low} + \sin \alpha$$

The needle is a hit if y_{high} is at least 2, as shown in Figure 13.

Here is the program that carries out the simulation of the needle experiment.

ch03/buffon.cpp

```
1  #include <iostream>
2  #include <cstdlib>
3  #include <cmath>
4  #include <ctime>
5
6  using namespace std;
7
8  int main()
9  {
```

```
10      // Sets the seed of the random number generator.
11      srand(time(0));
12
13      const int NTRIES = 10000;
14      const double PI = 3.141592653589793;
15
16      int hits = 0;
17      for (int i = 1; i <= NTRIES; i++)
18      {
19         double ylow = 2 * (rand() * 1.0 / RAND_MAX);
20         double angle = 180 * (rand() * 1.0 / RAND_MAX);
21         double yhigh = ylow + sin(angle * PI / 180);
22         if (yhigh >= 2) hits++;
23      }
24      cout << "Tries / Hits = "
25         << NTRIES * (1.0 / hits) << "\n";
26      return 0;
27   }
```

Program Run

```
Tries / Hits = 3.16256
```

The point of this program is *not* to compute π (after all, we needed the value of π when converting degrees to radians). Rather, the point is to show how a physical experiment can be simulated on the computer. Buffon had to drop the needle physically thousands of times and record the results, which must have been a rather dull activity. We can have the computer execute the experiment quickly and accurately.

Simulations are very common computer applications. Many simulations use essentially the same pattern as the code of this example: In a loop, a large number of sample values are generated. The values of certain observations are recorded for each sample. Finally, when the simulation is completed, the averages of the observed values are printed out.

A typical example of a simulation is the modeling of customer queues at a bank or a supermarket. Rather than observing real customers, one simulates their arrival and their transactions at the teller window or checkout stand in the computer. One can try out different staffing or building layout patterns in the computer simply by making changes in the program. In the real world, making many such changes and measuring their effect would be impossible, or at least very expensive.

CHAPTER SUMMARY

1. The body of an if statement is executed when a condition is true.

2. A block statement contains a sequence of statements, enclosed in braces.

3. The else part of an if/else statement is executed when a condition is false.

4. Relational operators are used to compare numbers and strings.

5. Use == for equality testing, = for assignment.

6. The lexicographic or dictionary order is used to compare strings.

7. Multiple if/else statements can be combined to evaluate complex decisions.

8. When using multiple if/else statements, pay attention to the order of the conditions.

9. C++ has two boolean operators that combine conditions: && (*and*) and || (*or*).

10. The && and || operators are computed *lazily:* As soon as the truth value is determined, no further conditions are evaluated.

11. The Boolean type bool has two values, false and true.

12. To invert a Boolean value, use the ! (*not*) operator.

13. De Morgan's law tells you how to negate an &&/|| condition: Reverse the operator and move the ! inward.

14. A while loops executes a block of code repeatedly, while a condition remains true.

15. An infinite loop keeps running until the program is forcibly terminated.

16. An off-by-one error occurs when a programmer mistakenly uses a value that is one more or less than the correct value.

17. The for loop is used when a value runs from a starting point to an ending point with a constant increment or decrement.

18. The do loop is appropriate when the loop body must be executed at least once.

19. A sentinel value denotes the end of a sequence of values, without being a part of the sequence.

20. When an input stream senses an input error, it enters the failed state. You can test for failure with the fail function.

21. Use input redirection to read input from a file. Use output redirection to capture program output in a file.

22. In a simulation program, you use the computer to simulate an activity. You can introduce randomness by calling the random number generator.

FURTHER READING

1. Peter van der Linden, *Expert C Programming*, Prentice-Hall, 1994.

2. Rudolf Flesch, *How to Write Plain English*, Barnes & Noble Books, 1979.

REVIEW EXERCISES

Exercise R3.1. Find the errors in the following if statements.

    a. `if quarters > 0 then cout << quarters << " quarters";`

    b. `if (1 + x > pow(x, sqrt(2)) y = y + x;`

    c. `if (x = 1) y++; else if (x = 2) y = y + 2;`

    d. `if (x && y == 0) cwin << Point(0, 0);`

    e. `if (1 <= x <= 10) cout << "Enter y: "; cin >> y;`

    f. `if (s != "nick" || s != "penn"`
        `|| s != "dime" || s != "quar")`
        `cout << "Input error!";`

    g. `if (input == "N" || "NO")`
        `return 0;`

    h. `cin >> x; if (cin.fail()) y = y + x;`

    i. `language = "English";`
      `if (country == "USA")`
        `if (state == "PR") language = "Spanish";`
    `else if (country = "China")`
        `language = "Chinese";`

Exercise R3.2. Explain why it is more difficult to compare floating-point numbers than integers. Write C++ code to test whether an integer n equals 10 and whether a floating-point number x equals 10.

Exercise R3.3. Of the following pairs of strings, which comes first in lexicographic order?

    a. `"Tom", "Dick"`

    b. `"Tom", "Tomato"`

    c. `"church", "Churchill"`

    d. `"car manufacturer", "carburetor"`

    e. `"Harry", "hairy"`

    f. `"C++", " Car"`

    g. `"Tom", "Tom"`

    h. `"Car", "Carl"`

    i. `"car", "bar"`

Exercise R3.4. When reading a number in, there are two possible ways for a stream to be set to the "failed" state. Give examples for both. How is the situation different when reading a string?

Exercise R3.5. What is wrong with the following program?

```
cout << "Enter the number of quarters: ";
cin >> quarters;
total = total + quarters * 0.25;
if (cin.fail()) cout << "Input error.";
```

Exercise R3.6. Reading numbers is surprisingly difficult, because a C++ input stream looks at the input one character at a time. First, white space is skipped. Then the stream consumes those input characters that can be a part of a number. Once the stream has recognized a number, it stops reading if it finds a character that cannot be a part of a number. However, if the first non-white space character is not a digit or a sign, or if the first character is a sign and the second one is not a digit, then the stream fails.

Consider a program reading an integer:

```
cout << "Enter the number of quarters: ";
int quarters;
cin >> quarters;
```

For each of the following user inputs, circle how many characters have been read and whether the stream is in the failed state or not.

a. 15.9

b. 15 9

c. +159

d. -15A9

e. Fifteen

f. -Fifteen

g. + 15

h. 1.5E3

i. +1+5

Exercise R3.7. Explain the difference between an if/else/else statement and nested if statements. Give an example for each.

Exercise R3.8. Give an example for an if/else/else statement where the order of the tests does not matter. Give an example where the order of the tests matters.

Exercise R3.9. Before implementing any complex algorithm, it is a good idea to understand and analyze it. The purpose of this exercise is to gain a better understanding of the tax computation algorithm.

Some people object to the fact that the tax rates increase with higher incomes, claiming that certain taxpayers are then better off *not* to work hard and get a raise, since they would then have to pay a higher tax rate and actually end up with less money after taxes. Can you find such an income level? If not, why?

Another feature of the tax code is the *marriage penalty.* Under certain circumstances, a married couple pays higher taxes than the sum of what the two partners would pay if they both were single. Find examples for such income levels.

Exercise R3.10. True or false? *A* && *B* is the same as *B* && *A* for any Boolean conditions *A* and *B*.

Exercise R3.11. Complete the following truth table by finding the truth values of the Boolean expressions for all combinations of the Boolean inputs p, q, and r.

p	q	r	(p && q) || !r	!(p && (q || !r))
false	false	false		
false	false	true		
false	true	false		
...				
5 more combinations				
...				

Exercise R3.12. Explain the difference between

```
s = 0;
if (x > 0) s++;
if (y > 0) s++;
```

and

```
s = 0;
if (x > 0) s++;
else if (y > 0) s++;
```

Exercise R3.13. Use De Morgan's Law to simplify the following Boolean expressions.

a. !(x > 0 && y > 0)

b. !(x != 0 || y != 0)

c. !(country == "USA" && state != "HI" && state != "AK")

d. !(x % 4 != 0 || !(x % 100 == 0 && x % 400 != 0))

Exercise R3.14. Make up another C++ code example that shows the dangling else problem using the following statement: A student with a GPA of at least 1.5, but less than 2, is on probation. With a GPA of less than 1.5, the student is failing.

Exercise R3.15. What is an infinite loop? On your computer, how can you terminate a program that executes an infinite loop?

Exercise R3.16. What is an "off-by-one" error? Give an example from your own programming experience.

Exercise R3.17. What is a sentinel value? Give simple rules when it is better to use a sentinel value and when it is better to use the end of the input file to denote the end of a data sequence.

Exercise R3.18. What is a "loop and a half"? Give two strategies to implement the following loop and a half:

loop
    read employee name
    if not OK, exit loop
    read employee salary
    if not OK, exit loop
    give employee 5 percent raise
    print employee data

Use a Boolean variable and a break statement. Which of these approaches do you find clearer?

Exercise R3.19. Give a set of test cases for the tax program in Section 3.4. Manually compute the expected results.

Exercise R3.20. Which loop statements does C++ support? Give simple rules when to use each loop type.

Exercise R3.21. How often do the following loops execute? Assume that i is not changed in the loop body.

  a. `for (int i = 1; i <= 10; i++)` ...

  b. `for (int i = 0; i < 10; i++)` ...

  c. `for (int i = 10; i > 0; i--)` ...

  d. `for (int i = -10; i <= 10; i++)` ...

  e. `for (int i = 10; i >= 0; i++)` ...

  f. `for (int i = -10; i <= 10; i = i + 2)` ...

  g. `for (int i = -10; i <= 10; i = i + 3)` ...

Exercise R3.22. Rewrite the following for loop into a while loop.

```
int i;
int s = 0;
for (i = 1; i <= 10; i++) s = s + i;
```

Exercise R3.23. Rewrite the following do/while loop into a while loop.

```
int n;
cin >> n;
double x = 0;
double s;
do
{
   s = 1.0 / (1 + n * n);
   n++;
   x = x + s;
}
while (s > 0.01);
```

Exercise R3.24. What are the values of s and n after the following loops?

```
a. int s = 1;
   int n = 1;
   while (s < 10) s = s + n;
   n++;
b. int s = 1;
   int n;
   for (n = 1; n < 5; n++) s = s + n;
c. int s = 1;
   int n = 1;
   do
   {
      s = s + n;
      n++;
   }
   while (s < 10 * n);
```

Exercise R3.25. What do the following loops print? Work out the answer without using the computer.

```
a. int s = 1;
   int n;
   for (n = 1; n <= 5; n++)
   {
      s = s + n;
      cout << s;
   }
b. int s = 1;
   int n;
   for (n = 1; n <= 5; cout << s)
   {
      n = n + 2;
      s = s + n;
   }
c. int s = 1;
   int n;
   for (n = 1; n <= 5; n++)
   {
      s = s + n;
      n++;
   }
   cout << s << " " << n;
```

Exercise R3.26. What do the following program segments print? Find the answers by hand, not by using the computer.

```
a. int i;
   int n = 1;
   for (i = 2; i < 5; i++) n = n + i;
   cout << n;
   int i;
   double n = 1 / 2;
   for (i = 2; i <= 5; i++) n = n + 1.0 / i;
   cout << i;
```

```
b. double x = 1;
   double y = 1;
   int i = 0;
   do
   {
      y = y / 2;
      x = x + y;
      i++;
   }
   while (x < 1.8);
   cout << i;

c. double x = 1;
   double y = 1;
   int i = 0;
   while (y >= 1.5)
   {
      x = x / 2;
      y = x + y;
      i++;
   }
   cout << i;
```

Exercise R3.27. Give an example of a for loop where symmetric bounds are more natural. Give an example of a for loop where asymmetric bounds are more natural.

PROGRAMMING EXERCISES

Exercise P3.1. Write a program that prints all solutions to the quadratic equation $ax^2 + bx + c = 0$. Read in a, b, c and use the quadratic formula. If the discriminant $b^2 - 4ac$ is negative, display a message stating that there are no solutions.

Exercise P3.2. Write a program that takes user input describing a playing card in the following shorthand notation:

A	Ace
2 ... 10	Card values
J	Jack
Q	Queen
K	King
D	Diamonds
H	Hearts
S	Spades
C	Clubs

Your program should print the full description of the card. For example,

```
Enter the card notation: QS
Queen of spades
```

Exercise P3.3. Write a program that reads in three floating-point numbers and prints the largest of the three inputs. For example:

```
Please enter three numbers: 4 9 2.5
The largest number is 9.
```

Exercise P3.4. Write a program that translates a letter grade into a number grade. Letter grades are A, B, C, D, and F, possibly followed by + or –. Their numeric values are 4, 3, 2, 1, and 0. There is no F+ or F–. A + increases the numeric value by 0.3, a – decreases it by 0.3. However, an A+ has value 4.0.

```
Enter a letter grade: B-
The numeric value is 2.7.
```

Exercise P3.5. Write a program that translates a number between 0 and 4 into the closest letter grade. For example, the number 2.8 (which might have been the average of several grades) would be converted to B–. Break ties in favor of the better grade; for example 2.85 should be a B.

Exercise P3.6. *Roman numbers.* Write a program that converts a positive integer into the Roman number system. The Roman number system has digits

I	1
V	5
X	10
L	50
C	100
D	500
M	1,000

Numbers are formed according to the following rules. (1) Only numbers up to 3,999 are represented. (2) As in the decimal system, the thousands, hundreds, tens, and ones are expressed separately. (3) The numbers 1 to 9 are expressed as

I	1
II	2
III	3
IV	4
V	5
VI	6
VII	7
VIII	8
IX	9

As you can see, a I preceding a V or X is subtracted from the value, and you can never have more than three I's in a row. (4) Tens and hundreds are done the same way, except that the letters X, L, C and C, D, M are used instead of I and V, X, respectively.

Your program should take an input, such as 1978, and convert it to Roman numerals, MCMLXXVIII.

Exercise P3.7. Write a program that reads in three strings and sorts them lexicographically.

```
Enter three strings: Charlie Able Baker
Able
Baker
Charlie
```

Exercise P3.8. Write a program that reads in two floating-point numbers and tests whether they are the same up to two decimal places. Here are two sample runs.

```
Enter two floating-point numbers: 2.0 1.99998
They are the same up to two decimal places.
Enter two floating-point numbers: 2.0 1.98999
They are different.
```

Exercise P3.9. Write a program that reads in the name and salary of an employee object. Here the salary will denote an *hourly* wage, such as $9.25. Then ask how many hours the employee worked in the past week. Be sure to accept fractional hours. Compute the pay. Any overtime work (over 40 hours per week) is paid at 150 percent of the regular wage. Print a paycheck for the employee.

Exercise P3.10. Write a unit conversion program using the conversion factors of Table 2 in Chapter 2. Ask the users from which unit they want to convert (fl. oz, gal, oz, lb, in, ft, mi) and which unit they want to convert to (ml, l, g, kg, mm, cm, m, km). Reject incompatible conversions (such as gal → km). Ask for the value to be converted; then display the result:

```
Convert from? gal
Convert to? ml
Value? 2.5
2.5 gal = 9462.5 ml
```

Exercise P3.11. If you look at the tax tables in Section 3.4, you will note that the percentages 15%, 28%, and 31% are identical for both single and married taxpayers, but the cutoffs for the tax brackets are different. Married people get to pay 15% on their first $35,800, then pay 28% on the next $50,700, and 31% on the remainder. Single people pay 15% on their first $21,450, then pay 28% on the next $30,450, and 31% on the remainder. Write a tax program with the following logic: Set variables cutoff15 and cutoff28 that depend on marital status. Then have a single formula that computes the tax, depending on the incomes and the cutoffs. Verify that your results are identical to that of the tax.cpp program.

Exercise P3.12. A year with 366 days is called a leap year. A year is a leap year if it is divisible by four (for example, 1980), except that it is not a leap year if it is divisible by 100 (for example, 1900); however, it is a leap year if it is divisible by 400 (for example, 2000). There were no exceptions before the introduction of the Gregorian calendar on October 15, 1582 (1500 was a leap year). Write a program that asks the user for a year and computes whether that year is a leap year. Your program should contain a single if statement.

Exercise P3.13. Write a program that asks the user to enter a month (1 for January, 2 for February, and so on) and then prints the number of days in the month. For February, print "28 or 29 days".

```
Enter a month: 5
30 days
```

Exercise P3.14. *Projectile flight.* Suppose a cannonball is propelled straight into the air with a starting velocity v_0. Any calculus book will state that the position of the ball after t seconds is $s(t) = -\frac{1}{2}gt^2 + v_0 t$, where $g = 9.81 \text{ m}/\text{sec}^2$ is the gravitational force of the earth. No calculus book ever mentions why someone would want to carry out such an obviously dangerous experiment, so we will do it in the safety of the computer.

In fact, we will confirm the theorem from calculus by a simulation. In our simulation, we will consider how the ball moves in very short time intervals Δt. In a short time interval the velocity v is nearly constant, and we can compute the distance the ball moves as $\Delta s = v\Delta t$. In our program, we will simply set

```
const double delta_t = 0.01;
```

and update the position by

```
s = s + v * delta_t;
```

The velocity changes constantly—in fact, it is reduced by the gravitational force of the earth. In a short time interval, $\Delta v = -g\Delta t$, we must keep the velocity updated as

```
v = v - g * delta_t;
```

In the next iteration the new velocity is used to update the distance.

Now run the simulation until the cannonball falls back to the earth. Get the initial velocity as an input (100 m/sec is a good value). Update the position and velocity 100 times per second, but print out the position only every full second. Also print out the values from the exact formula $s(t) = -\frac{1}{2}gt^2 + v_0 t$ for comparison.

What is the benefit of this kind of simulation when an exact formula is available? Well, the formula from the calculus book is *not* exact. Actually, the gravitational force diminishes the farther the cannonball is away from the surface of the earth. This complicates the algebra sufficiently that it is not possible to give an exact formula for the actual motion, but the computer simulation can simply be extended to apply a variable gravitational force. For cannonballs, the calculus-book formula is actually good enough, but computers are necessary to compute accurate trajectories for higher-flying objects such as ballistic missiles.

Exercise P3.15. *Currency conversion.* Write a program that first asks the user to type today's exchange rate between U.S. dollars and Japanese yen, then reads U.S. dollar values and converts each to yen. Use 0 or a negative input as a sentinel.

Exercise P3.16. Write a program that first asks the user to type in today's exchange rate between U.S. dollars and Japanese yen, then reads U.S. dollar values and converts each to Japanese yen. Use 0 as the sentinel value to denote the end of dollar inputs. Then the program reads a sequence of yen amounts and converts them to dollars. The second sequence is terminated by the end of the input file.

Exercise P3.17. *Mean and standard deviation.* Write a program that reads a set of floating-point data values from the input. When the end of file is reached, print out the count of the values, the average, and the standard deviation. The average of a data set $\{x_1, ..., x_n\}$ is $\bar{x} = \sum x_i / n$, where $\sum x_i = x_1 + ... + x_n$ is the sum of the input values. The standard deviation is

$$s = \sqrt{\frac{\sum (x_i - \bar{x})^2}{n-1}}$$

However, this formula is not suitable for the task. By the time the program has computed $\bar{x}$, the individual x_i are long gone. Until you know how to save these values, use the numerically less stable formula

$$s = \sqrt{\frac{\sum x_i^2 - \frac{1}{n}\left(\sum x_i\right)^2}{n-1}}$$

You can compute this quantity by keeping track of the count, the sum, and the sum of squares as you process the input values.

Exercise P3.18. The *Fibonacci numbers* are defined by the sequence

$$f_1 = 1$$
$$f_2 = 1$$
$$f_n = f_{n-1} + f_{n-2}$$

As in the algorithm to compute the square root of a number, reformulate that as

```
fold1 = 1;
fold2 = 1;
fnew = fold1 + fold2;
```

After that, the value of fold2 is no longer needed. Set fold2 to fold1 and fold1 to fnew. Repeat fnew for an appropriate number of times.

Implement a program that computes the Fibonacci numbers in that way.

Exercise P3.19. *Flesch Readability Index.* The following index [2] was invented by Flesch as a simple tool to gauge the legibility of a document without linguistic analysis.

1. Count all words in the file. A *word* is any sequence of characters delimited by white space, whether or not it is an actual English word.

2. Count all syllables in each word. To make this simple, use the following rules: Each *group* of adjacent vowels (a, e, i, o, u, y) counts as one syllable (for example, the "ea" in "real" contributes one syllable, but the "e ... a" in "regal" counts as two syllables). However, an "e" at the end of a word doesn't count

as a syllable. Also each word has at least one syllable, even if the previous rules give a count of 0.

3. Count all sentences. A sentence is ended by a period, colon, semicolon, question mark, or exclamation mark.

4. The index is computed by

$$\text{Index} = 206.835 - 84.6 \times \frac{\text{Number of syllables}}{\text{Number of words}} - 1.015 \times \frac{\text{Number of words}}{\text{Number of sentences}}$$

rounded to the nearest integer.

This index is a number, usually between 0 and 100, indicating how difficult the text is to read. Some examples of random material from various publications are

Comics	95
Consumer ads	82
Sports Illustrated	65
Time	57
New York Times	39
Auto insurance policy	10
Internal Revenue Code	−6

Translated into educational levels, the indices are

91–100	5th grader
81–90	6th grader
71–80	7th grader
66–70	8th grader
61–65	9th grader
51–60	High school student
31–50	College student
0–30	College graduate
Less than 0	Law school graduate

The purpose of the index is to force authors to rewrite their text until the index is high enough. This is achieved by reducing the length of sentences and by removing long words. For example, the sentence

> The following index was invented by Flesch as a simple tool to estimate the legibility of a document without linguistic analysis.

can be rewritten as

> Flesch invented an index to check whether a document is easy to read. To compute the index, you need not look at the meaning of the words.

His book [2] contains delightful examples of translating government regulations into "plain English".

Your program should read in a text file, one word at a time, and compute the legibility index.

Exercise P3.20. *Factoring of integers.* Write a program that asks the user for an integer and then prints out all its factors. For example, when the user enters 150, the program should print

    2
    3
    5
    5

Exercise P3.21. *Prime numbers.* Write a program that prompts the user for an integer and then prints out all prime numbers up to that integer. For example, when the user enters 20, the program should print

    2
    3
    5
    7
    11
    13
    17
    19

Recall that a number is a prime number if it is not divisible by any number except 1 and itself.

Exercise P3.22. *The game of Nim.* This is a well-known game with a number of variants. The following variant has an interesting winning strategy. Two players alternately take marbles from a pile. In each move, a player chooses how many marbles to take. The player must take at least one but at most half of the marbles. Then the other player takes a turn. The player who takes the last marble loses.

You will write a program in which the computer plays against a human opponent. Generate a random integer between 10 and 100 to denote the initial size of the pile. Generate a random integer between 0 and 1 to decide whether the computer or the human takes the first turn. Generate a random integer between 0 and 1 to decide whether the computer plays *smart* or *stupid*. In stupid mode the computer simply takes a random legal value (between 1 and $n/2$) from the pile whenever it has a turn. In smart mode the computer takes off enough marbles to make the size of the pile a power of two minus 1—that is, 3, 7, 15, 31, or 63. That is always a legal move, except if the size of the pile is currently one less than a power of two. In that case, the computer makes a random legal move.

You will note that the computer cannot be beaten in smart mode when it has the first move, unless the pile size happens to be 15, 31, or 63. Of course, a human player who has the first turn and knows the winning strategy can win against the computer.

Exercise P3.23. Program the following simulation: Darts are thrown at random points onto a square with corners (1, 1) and (−1, −1). If the dart lands inside the unit circle (that is, the circle with center (0, 0) and radius 1), it is a hit. Otherwise it is a miss. Run this simulation and use it to determine an approximate value for π. Explain why this is a better method for estimating π than the Buffon needle program.

G **Exercise P3.24.** Write a program that draws a square with corner points (0, 0) and (1, 1). Prompt the user for a mouse click. If the user clicked inside the square, then show a message "Congratulations". Otherwise, show a message "You missed".

G **Exercise P3.25.** Write a graphics program that asks the user to specify two circles. Each circle is input by clicking on the center and typing in the radius. Draw the circles. If they intersect, then display the message "Circles intersect". Otherwise, display "Circles don't intersect". *Hint:* Compute the distance between the centers and compare it to the radii. Your program should terminate if the user enters a negative radius.

G **Exercise P3.26.** *Random walk.* Simulate the walk of a drunkard in a square street grid. Draw a grid of 10 streets horizontally and 10 streets vertically. Place a simulated inebriated person in the middle of the grid, denoted by a point. For 100 times, have the simulated person randomly pick a direction (east, west, north, south), move one block in the chosen direction, and redraw the dot. After the iterations, display the distance that the drunkard has covered. (One might expect that on average the person might not get anywhere because the moves in different directions cancel each other out in the long run, but in fact it can be shown that with probability 1 the person eventually moves outside any finite region.)

G **Exercise P3.27.** Most cannonballs are not shot upright but at an angle. If the starting velocity has magnitude v and the starting angle is α, then the velocity is actually a vector with components $v_x = v\cos\alpha$, $v_y = v\sin\alpha$. In the x-direction the velocity does not change. In the y-direction the gravitational force takes its toll. Repeat the simulation from Exercise P3.14, but store the position of the cannonball as a Point variable. Update the x- and y-positions separately, and also update the x- and y-components of the velocity separately. Every full second, plot the location of the cannonball on the graphics display. Repeat until the cannonball has reached the earth again.

This kind of problem is of historical interest. The first computers were designed to carry out just such ballistic calculations, taking into account the diminishing gravity for high-flying projectiles and wind speeds.

G **Exercise P3.28.** Write a program that plots a *regression line:* that is, the line with the best fit through a collection of points. First ask the user to specify the data points by clicking on them in the graphics window. To find the end of the input, place a small rectangle labeled "Stop" at the bottom of the screen; when the user clicks inside that rectangle, then stop gathering input. The regression line is the line with equation

$$y = \bar{y} + m(x - \bar{x}), \quad \text{where } m = \frac{\sum x_i y_i - n\bar{x}\,\bar{y}}{\sum x_i^2 - n\bar{x}^2}$$

$\bar{x}$ is the mean of the x-values and $\bar{y}$ is the mean of the y-values.

As in the preceding exercise, you need to keep track of
- the count of input values
- the sum of x, y, x^2, and xy values

To draw the regression line, compute its endpoints at the left and right edges of the screen, and draw a segment.

G **Exercise P3.29.** It is easy and fun to draw graphs of curves with the C++ graphics library. Simply draw 100 line segments joining the points $(x, f(x))$ and $(x + d, f(x + d))$, where x ranges from x_{min} to x_{max} and $d = (x_{max} - x_{min})/100$. Draw the curve $f(x) = x^3/100 - x + 10$, where x ranges from -10 to 10 in this fashion.

G **Exercise P3.30.** Draw a picture of the "four-leaved rose" whose equation in polar coordinates is $r = \cos 2\theta$, $0 \le \theta \le 2\pi$. Let θ go from 0 to 2π in 100 steps. Each time, compute r and then compute the (x, y) coordinates from the polar coordinates by using the formula

$$x = r\cos\theta$$
$$y = r\sin\theta$$

You will get extra credit if you can vary the number of petals.

Functions

CHAPTER GOALS

- To be able to program functions and procedures

- To become familiar with the concept of parameter passing

- To recognize when to use value and reference parameters

- To appreciate the importance of function comments

- To be able to determine the scope of variables

- To minimize the use of side effects and global variables

- To develop strategies for decomposing complex tasks into simpler ones

- To document the responsibilities of functions and their callers with preconditions

- To learn the fundamental principles of testing and debugging

Functions are a fundamental building block of C++ programs. A function packages a computation in a form that can be easily understood and reused. In this chapter, you will learn how to design and implement your own functions, and how to break up complex tasks into sets of cooperating functions.

CHAPTER CONTENTS

4.1 Functions as Black Boxes

> A function receives input parameters and computes a result that depends on those inputs.

You have used a number of functions that were provided with the C++ system library. Examples are

sqrt   Computes the square root of a floating-point number
getline Reads a line from a stream

You probably don't know how these functions perform their jobs. For example, how does sqrt compute square roots? By looking up values in a table? By repeated guessing of the answer? As it happens, computing square roots requires only a simple loop and basic arithmetic, but you don't need to know the details of the computation to use the square root function. You can think of sqrt as a *black box*, as shown in Figure 1.

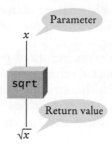

Figure 1
The sqrt Function as a Black Box

> Parameter values are supplied in the function call. The return value is the result that the function computes.

When you use sqrt(x) inside main, the input or *parameter value* x is transferred, or *passed*, to the sqrt function. The execution of the main function is temporarily suspended. The sqrt function becomes active and computes the output or *return value*—the square root of the input value—using some method that (we trust) will yield the correct result. That return value is transferred back to main, which resumes the computation using the return value. The input value to a function need not be a single variable; it can be any expression, as in sqrt(b * b - 4 * a * c). Figure 2 shows the flow of execution when a function is called.

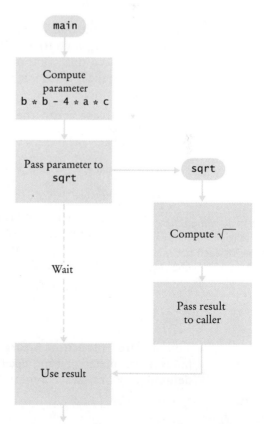

Figure 2
Execution Flow During a Function Call

Some functions have more than one input. For example, the pow function has two parameters: pow(x, y) computes x^y. Functions can have multiple inputs, but they only have one output.

Each function takes inputs of particular types. For example, sqrt receives only numbers as parameter values, whereas getline expects a stream and a string. It is an error to call sqrt with a string input.

Each function returns a value of a particular type: sqrt returns a floating-point number, substr returns a string, and main returns an integer.

4.2 Implementing Functions

In this section, you will learn how to implement a function from a given specification. Consider this example. Our task is compute the value of a savings account with an initial balance of $1,000 after 10 years. If the interest rate is p percent, then the balance after 10 years is

$$b = 1000 \times \left(1 + p/100\right)^{10}$$

For example, if the interest rate is 5 percent per year, then the initial investment of $1,000 will have grown to $1,628.94 after 10 years.

We will place this computation inside a function called future_value. Before implementing the function, it is a good idea to think about how we will use it. Here is a typical example:

```
cout << "Please enter the interest rate in percent: ";
double rate;
cin >> rate;

double balance = future_value(rate);
cout << "After 10 years, the balance is "
    << balance << "\n";
```

> When defining a function, you provide a name and type for each parameter and a type for the result.

Now write the function. The function receives a floating-point input and returns a floating-point value. You must give a *name* to the input value so you can use it in the computation. Let us call it p, just like in the formula.

```
double future_value(double p)
{
    ...
}
```

This declares a function future_value that returns a value of type double and that takes a parameter of type double. Just as with main, the body of the function is delimited by braces; see Syntax 4.1 on page 165.

Next you need to compute the function result:

```
double future_value(double p)
{
    double b = 1000 * pow(1 + p / 100, 10);
    ...
}
```

Finally, you need to return that result to the caller of the function:

```
double future_value(double p)
{
    double b = 1000 * pow(1 + p / 100, 10);
    return b;
}
```

This completes the definition of the future_value function. Figure 3 shows the flow of data into and out of the function.

The program is now composed of two functions: future_value and main. Both function definitions must be placed into the program file. Because main calls future_value, the future_value function must be known before the main function executes. The easiest way to achieve this is to place future_value first and main last in the source file. (See Advanced Topic 4.1 on page 173 for an alternative.)

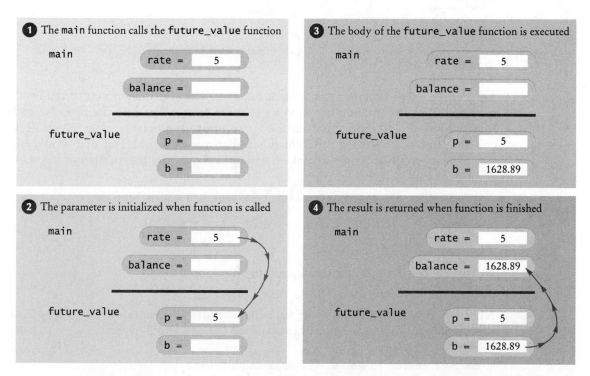

Figure 3 A Function Receiving a Parameter Value and Returning a Result

ch04/futval.cpp

```
1  #include <iostream>
2  #include <cmath>
3
4  using namespace std;
5
6  double future_value(double p)
7  {
8     double b = 1000 * pow(1 + p / 100, 10);
9     return b;
10 }
11
12 int main()
13 {
14    cout << "Please enter the interest rate in percent: ";
15    double rate;
16    cin >> rate;
17
18    double balance = future_value(rate);
19    cout << "After 10 years, the balance is "
20       << balance << "\n";
21
22    return 0;
23 }
```

Program Run

```
Please enter the interest rate in percent: 5
After 10 years, the balance is 1628.89
```

The future_value function has a major blemish: The starting amount of the investment ($1,000) and the number of years (10) are *hard-wired* into the function code.
It is not possible to use this function to compute the balance after 20 years. Of
course, you could write a different function future_value20, but that would be a
very clumsy solution. Instead, make the initial balance and the number of years into
additional parameters:

```
double future_value(double initial_balance, double p, int n)
{
   double b = initial_balance * pow(1 + p / 100, n);
   return b;
}
```

We now need to supply those values in the function call:

```
double b = future_value(1000, rate, 10);
```

Now our function is much more valuable, because it is *reusable*. For example, we
can trivially modify main to print the balance after 10 and 20 years.

```
double b = future_value(1000, rate, 10);
cout << "After 10 years, the balance is " << b << "\n";

b = future_value(1000, rate, 20);
cout << "After 20 years, the balance is " << b << "\n";
```

SYNTAX 4.1 Function Definition

return_type function_name(*parameter₁, parameter₂, ..., parameterₙ*)
{
    statements
}

Example:

```
double abs(double x)
{
    if (x >= 0) return x;
    else return -x;
}
```

Purpose:

Define a function and supply its implementation.

Why are we using a function in the first place? We could have made the computations directly, without a function call.

```
double b = 1000 * pow(1 + p / 100, 10);
cout << "After 10 years, the balance is " << b << "\n";

b = 1000 * pow(1 + p / 100, 20);
cout << "After 20 years, the balance is " << b << "\n";
```

If you look at these two solutions in comparison, it should be quite apparent why functions are valuable. The function allows you to abstract an *idea*—namely, the computation of compound interest. Once you understand the idea, it is clear what the change from 10 to 20 means in the two function calls. Now compare the two expressions that compute the balances directly. To understand them, you have to look closely to find that they differ only in the last number, and then you have to remember the significance of that number.

> Turn computations that can be reused into functions.

When you find yourself coding the same computation more than once, or coding a computation that is likely to be useful in other programs, you should make it into a function.

PRODUCTIVITY HINT 4.1

Write Functions with Reuse in Mind

Functions are fundamental building blocks of C++ programs. When properly written, they can be reused from one project to the next. As you design the interface and implementation of a function, you should keep reuse in mind.

Keep the focus of the function specific enough that it performs only one task, and solve that task completely. For example, when computing the future value of an investment, just compute the value; don't display it. Another programmer may need the computation, but might not want to display the result on the terminal.

Take the time to handle even those inputs that you may not need immediately. Now you understand the problem, and it will be easy for you to do this. If you or another programmer needs an extended version of the function later, that person must rethink the problem. This takes time, and misunderstandings can cause errors. For this reason, we turned the initial balance and interest rate into parameters of the `future_value` function.

Then you need to check for the legal range of all inputs. Does it make sense to allow negative percentages? Negative investment amounts? Fractional years? Generalizations with clear benefits should be implemented.

4.3 Function Comments

> Function comments explain the purpose of the function and the meaning of the parameters and return value, as well as any special requirements.

There is one final important enhancement that we need to make to the `future_value` function. We must *comment* its behavior. Comments are for human readers, not compilers, and there is no universal standard for the layout of a function comment. In this book, we will always use the following layout:

```
/**
    Computes the value of an investment with compound interest.
    @param initial_balance the initial value of the investment
    @param p the interest rate per period in percent
    @param n the number of periods the investment is held
    @return the balance after n periods
*/
double future_value(double initial_balance, double p, int n)
{
    double b = initial_balance * pow(1 + p / 100, n);
    return b;
}
```

Whoa; the comment is longer than the function! Indeed it is, but that is irrelevant. We were just lucky that this particular function was easy to compute. The function comment does not document the implementation but the idea—ultimately a more valuable property.

According to the documentation style used in this book, every function (except `main`) must have a comment. The first part of the comment is a brief explanation of the function. Then supply an `@param` entry for each parameter, and an `@return` entry to describe the return value. As you will see later, some functions have no parameters or return values. For those functions, `@param` or `@return` can be omitted.

This particular documentation style is borrowed from the Java programming language—it is often called the *javadoc* style. There are a number of tools available that process C++ files and extract HTML pages containing a hyperlinked set of comments—see Figure 4. The companion web site for this book contains instructions for downloading and using such a tool.

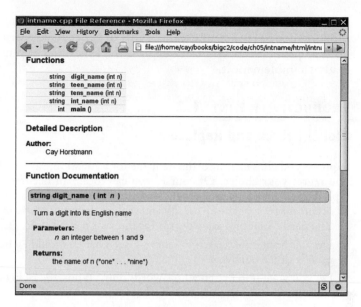

Figure 4 HTML Documentation of a Function

Occasionally, you will find that the documentation comments are silly to write. That is particularly true for general-purpose functions:

```
/**
    Computes the maximum of two integers.
    @param x  an integer
    @param y  another integer
    @return  the larger of the two inputs
*/
int max(int x, int y)
{
    if (x > y)
        return x;
    else
        return y;
}
```

It should be pretty clear that max computes the maximum, and it is obvious that the function receives two integers x and y. Indeed, in this case, the comment is somewhat overblown. We nevertheless strongly recommend writing the comment for every function. It is easy to spend more time pondering whether the comment is too trivial to write than it takes just to write it. In practical programming, very simple functions are rare. It is harmless to have a trivial function overcommented, whereas a complicated function without any comment can cause real grief to future maintenance programmers.

Practical experience has shown that comments for individual variables are rarely useful, provided the variable names are chosen to be self-documenting. Functions make up a very important logical division of a C++ program, and a large part of the documentation effort should be concentrated on explaining their black-box behavior.

It is always a good idea to write the function comment *first*, before writing the function code. This is an excellent test to see that you firmly understand what you need to program. If you can't explain the function's inputs and outputs, you aren't ready to implement it.

PRODUCTIVITY HINT 4.2

Global Search and Replace

Suppose you chose an unfortunate name for a function, say `fv` instead of `future_value`, and you regret your choice. Of course, you can locate all occurrences of `fv` in your code and replace them manually. However, most programming editors have a command to search for all occurrences of `fv` automatically and replace them with `future_value`.

You need to specify some details for the search.

- Do you want your search to ignore case? That is, should `FV` be a match? In C++ you usually don't want that.

- Do you want it to match whole words only? If not, the `fv` in `Golfville` is also a match. In C++ you usually want to match whole words.

- Is this a regular expression search? No, but regular expressions can make searches even more powerful—see Productivity Hint 4.3.

- Do you want to confirm each replace or simply go ahead and replace all matches? Confirm the first three or four matches, and when you see that it works as expected, give the go-ahead to replace the rest. (By the way, a *global* replace means to replace all occurrences in the document.) Good text editors can undo a global replace that has gone awry. Find out whether or not yours will.

- Do you want the search to go from the cursor through the rest of the program file, or should it search the currently selected text? Restricting replacement to a portion of the file can be very useful, but in this example you would want to move the cursor to the top of the file and then replace until the end of the file.

Not every editor has all these options. You should investigate what your editor offers.

PRODUCTIVITY HINT 4.3

Regular Expressions

Regular expressions describe character patterns. For example, numbers have a simple form. They contain one or more digits. The regular expression describing numbers is `[0-9]+`. The set `[0-9]` denotes any digit between 0 and 9, and the `+` means "one or more".

What good is it? A number of utility programs use regular expressions to locate matching text. Also, the search commands of some programming editors understand regular expressions. The most popular program that uses regular expressions is `grep` (which stands for "global regular expression print"). You can run `grep` from a command prompt or from inside some compilation environments. It needs a regular expression and one or more files to search. When `grep` runs, it displays a set of lines that match the regular expression.

Suppose you want to find all magic numbers (see Quality Tip 2.3) in a file. The command

```
grep [0-9]+ homework.cpp
```

lists all lines in the file homework.cpp that contain sequences of digits. This isn't terribly useful; lines with variable names x1 will be listed. You want sequences of digits that do *not* immediately follow letters:

```
grep [^A-Za-z][0-9]+ homework.cpp
```

The set [^A-Za-z] denotes any characters that are *not* between A and Z or between a and z. This works much better, and it shows only lines that contain actual numbers.

There are a bewildering number of symbols (sometimes called *wildcards*) with special meanings in the regular expression syntax, and unfortunately, different programs use different styles of regular expressions. It is best to consult the program documentation for details.

4.4 Return Values

> The return statement terminates a function call and yields the function result.

You use the return statement to specify the result of a function. When the return statement is processed, the function exits *immediately*. This is convenient for handling exceptional cases at the beginning:

```cpp
double future_value(double initial_balance, double p, int n)
{
   if (n < 0) return 0;
   if (p < 0) return 0;
   double b = initial_balance * pow(1 + p / 100, n);
   return b;
}
```

If the function is called with a negative value for p or n, then the function returns 0 and the remainder of the function is not executed. (See Figure 5.)

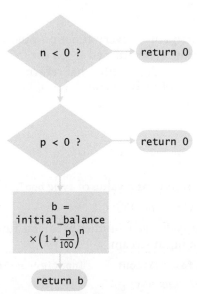

Figure 5
return Statements Exit
a Function Immediately

In the preceding example, each `return` statement returned a constant or a variable. Actually, the `return` statement can return the value of any expression, as shown in Syntax 4.2 on page 171. Instead of saving the return value in a variable and returning the variable, it is often possible to eliminate the variable and return a more complex expression:

```
double future_value(double initial_balance, double p, int n)
{
    return initial_balance * pow(1 + p / 100, n);
}
```

This is commonly done for very simple functions.

It is important that every branch of a function return a value. Consider the following incorrect version of the `future_value` function:

```
double future_value(double initial_balance, double p, int n)
{
    if (p >= 0)
        return initial_balance * pow(1 + p / 100, n);
    // Error
}
```

Suppose you call `future_value` with a negative value for the interest rate. Of course, you aren't supposed to call that, but it might happen as the result of a coding error. Because the `if` condition is not true, the `return` statement is not executed. However, the function must return *something*. Depending on circumstances, the compiler might flag this as an error, or a random value might be returned. This is always bad news, and you must protect against this by returning some safe value.

```
double future_value(double initial_balance, double p, int n)
{
    if (p >= 0)
        return initial_balance * pow(1 + p / 100, n);
    return 0;
}
```

The last statement of every function ought to be a `return` statement. This ensures that *some* value gets returned when the function reaches the end.

> A predicate function returns a Boolean value.

A function that returns a truth value is called a *predicate function*. Here is a typical example, a function that tests whether a value is an even number:

```
bool is_even(int n)
{
    return n % 2 == 0;
}
```

The function returns a value of type `bool`, which can be used inside a test.

```
if (is_even(input)) ...
```

You have already seen another predicate function: the `fail` function that checks for failure of an input stream.

```
if (cin.fail()) cout << "Input error!\n";
```

> ### SYNTAX 4.2 return Statement
>
> return *expression*;
>
> **Example:**
>
> return pow(1 + p / 100, n);
>
> **Purpose:**
>
> Exit a function, returning the value of the expression as the function result.

COMMON ERROR 4.1

Missing Return Value

A function always needs to return something. If the code of the function contains several if/
else branches, make sure that each one of them returns a value:

```
int sign(double x)
{
   if (x < 0) return -1;
   if (x > 0) return +1;
   // Error: missing return value if x equals 0
}
```

This function computes the sign of a number: –1 for negative numbers and +1 for positive
numbers. If the parameter x is zero, however, no value is returned. Most compilers will issue
a warning in this situation, but if you ignore the warning and the function is ever called with
a parameter value of 0, a random quantity will be returned.

4.5 Parameters

When you implement a function, you define variables that hold the parameter values. We call such a variable a *parameter variable*, or, if there is no ambiguity, simply
parameter. Another commonly used term is *formal parameter*. When you call a
function, you supply expressions for each parameter. We call the value of such an
expression a *parameter value*. Other commonly used terms are *actual parameter*
and *argument*.

> Parameter variables hold
> the parameter values
> supplied in the
> function call.

When a function starts, its parameter variables are initialized with
the expressions in the function call. Suppose you call

```
b = future_value(total / 2, rate, year2 - year1)
```

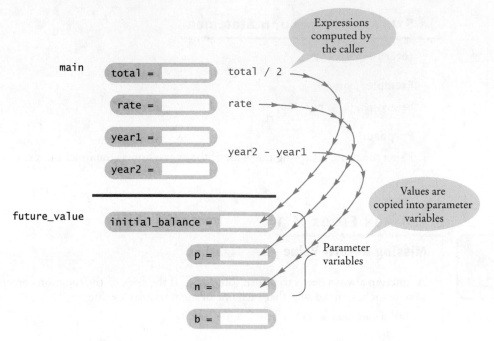

Figure 6   Parameter Passing

The future_value function has three parameter variables: initial_balance, p, and n. Before the function starts, the values of the expressions total / 2 and year2 - year1 are computed. Each parameter variable is initialized with the corresponding parameter value. Thus, initial_balance becomes total / 2, p becomes rate, and n becomes year2 - year1. Figure 6 shows the parameter-passing process.

The term *parameter variable* is appropriate in C++. It is entirely legal to modify the values of the parameter variables later. Here is an example, using p as a variable:

```
double future_value(double initial_balance, double p, int n)
{
   p = 1 + p / 100;
   double b = initial_balance * pow(p, n);
   return b;
}
```

Actually, many programmers consider this practice bad style. It is best not to mix the concept of a parameter (input to the function) with that of a variable (local storage needed for computing the function result).

In this book we will always treat parameter variables as constants and never modify them. However, in Section 4.8 you will encounter reference parameters that refer to variables outside the function, not to local variables. Modifying a reference parameter is useful—it changes the parameter value not just inside the function, but outside it as well.

QUALITY TIP 4.1

Use Meaningful Names for Parameters

You can give any name you like to function parameters. Choose explicit names for parameters that have specific roles; choose simple names for those that are completely generic. The goal is to make the reader understand the purpose of the parameter without having to read the description.

double sin(double x) is not as good as double sin(double radian). Naming the parameter radian gives additional information: namely, that the angle cannot be given in degrees.

The C++ standard library contains a function that is declared as

```
double atan2(double y, double x)
```

I can never remember whether it computes $\tan^{-1}(x/y)$ or $\tan^{-1}(y/x)$. I wish they had named the parameters more sensibly:

```
double atan2(double numerator, double denominator)
```

If a function is designed to take *any* parameter of a given type, then simple parameter names are appropriate.

```
bool is_even(double n)
```

COMMON ERROR 4.2

Type Mismatch

The compiler takes the function parameter and return types very seriously. It is an error to call a function with a value of an incompatible type. The compiler converts between integers and floating-point numbers, but it does not convert between numbers and strings or objects. For this reason, C++ is called a *strongly typed* language. This is a useful feature, because it lets the compiler find programming errors before they create havoc when the program runs.

For example, you cannot give a string to a numerical function, even if the string contains only digits:

```
string num = "1024";
double x = sqrt(num); // Error
```

You cannot store a numerical return value in a string variable:

```
string root = sqrt(2); // Error
```

ADVANCED TOPIC 4.1

Function Declarations

Functions need to be known before they can be used. This can be achieved easily if you first define lower-level helper functions, then the midlevel workhorse functions, and finally main in your program. Sometimes that ordering does not work. Suppose function f calls function g, and g calls f again. That setup is not common, but it does happen. Another situation is much more common. The function f may use a function such as sqrt that is defined in a separate file. To make f compile, it suffices to *declare* the functions g and sqrt. A declaration of a function lists the return value, function name, and parameters, but it contains no body:

```
int g(int n);
double sqrt(double x);
```

These are advertisements that promise that the function is implemented elsewhere, either later in the current file or in a separate file. It is easy to distinguish declarations from definitions: Declarations end in a semicolon, whereas definitions are followed by a {...} block (see Syntax 4.3 on page 174). Declarations are also called *prototypes*.

The declarations of common functions such as sqrt are contained in header files. If you have a look inside cmath, you will find the declaration of sqrt and the other math functions.

Some programmers like to list all function declarations at the top of the file and then write main and then the other functions. For example, the futval.cpp file can be organized as follows:

```
#include <iostream>
#include <cmath>

using namespace std;

// Declaration of future_value
double future_value(double initial_balance, double p, int n);

int main()
{
   ...
   // Use of future_value
   double balance = future_value(1000, rate, 5);
   ...
}

// Definition of future_value
double future_value(double initial_balance, double p, int n)
{
   double b = initial_balance * pow(1 + p / 100, n);
   return b;
}
```

SYNTAX 4.3 Function Declaration (or Prototype)

return_type function_name(parameter$_1$, parameter$_2$, ..., parameter$_n$);

Example:

```
double abs(double x);
```

Purpose:

Declare a function so that it can be called before it is defined.

This arrangement has one advantage: It makes the code easier to read. You first read the top-level function main, then the helper functions such as future_value. There is, however, a drawback. Whenever you change the name of a function or one of the parameter types, you need to fix it in both places: in the declaration and in the definition.

For short programs, such as the ones in this book, this is a minor issue, and you can safely choose either approach. For longer programs, it is useful to separate declarations from definitions. Chapter 5 contains more information on how to break up larger programs into multiple files and how to place declarations into header files. As you will see in Chapter 5, member functions of classes are first declared in the class definition and then defined elsewhere.

4.6 Side Effects

> A side effect is an externally observable effect caused by a function call, other than the returning of a result.

Consider the future_value function, which *returns* a number. Why didn't we have the function *print* the value at the same time?

```
double future_value(double initial_balance, double p, int n)
{
    double b = initial_balance * pow(1 + p / 100, n);
    cout << "The balance is now " << b << "\n";
    return b;
}
```

It is a general design principle that a function had best leave no trace of its existence except for returning a value. If a function prints out a message, it will be worthless in an environment that has no output stream, such as a graphics program or the controller of a bank teller machine.

One particularly reprehensible practice is printing error messages inside functions. You should never do that:

```
double future_value(double initial_balance, double p, int n)
{
    if (p < 0)
    {
        cout << "Bad value of p."; // Bad style
        return 0;
    }

    double b = initial_balance * pow(1 + p / 100, n);
    return b;
}
```

Printing an error message severely limits the reusability of the future_value function. It can be used only in programs that can print to cout, eliminating graphics programs. It can be used only in applications in which a user actually reads the output, eliminating background processing. Also, it can be used only in applications where the user can understand an error message in the English language, eliminating the majority of your potential customers. Of course, your programs must contain some messages, but you should group all the input and output activity together—

for example, in main if your program is short. Let the functions do the computation, not the error report to the user.

An externally observable effect of a function is called a *side effect*. Displaying characters on the screen, updating variables outside the function, and terminating the program are examples of side effects.

In particular, a function that has no side effects can be run over and over with no surprises. Whenever it is given the same inputs, it will faithfully produce the same outputs. This is a desirable property for functions, and indeed most functions have no side effects.

4.7 Procedures

> A procedure is a sequence of actions that depends on parameters and does not yield a result.

Sometimes, you need to carry out similar action sequences, but the actions do not yield a value. You can place the actions into a *procedure*. Like a function, a procedure can have parameters, but it returns no value.

Here is a typical example. Suppose you need to print an object of type Time:

```
Time now;
cout << now.get_hours() << ":"
    << setw(2) << setfill('0') << now.get_minutes() << ":"
    << setw(2) << now.get_seconds() << setfill(' ');
```

An example printout is 9:05:30. The setw and setfill manipulators serve to supply a leading zero if the minutes or seconds are single digits.

Of course, this is a pretty common task that may well occur again:

```
cout << liftoff.get_hours() << ":"
    << setw(2) << setfill('0') << liftoff.get_minutes() << ":"
    << setw(2) << liftoff.get_seconds() << setfill(' ');
```

The solution is to define a procedure for printing a Time value:

```
void print_time(Time t)
{
    cout << t.get_hours() << ":"
        << setw(2) << setfill('0') << t.get_minutes() << ":"
        << setw(2) << t.get_seconds() << setfill(' ');
}
```

> Use a return type of void to indicate that a function does not return a value.

Note that this code doesn't compute any value. It performs some actions and then returns to the caller. The missing return value is indicated by the keyword void.

Procedures are called just as functions are, but there is no return value to use in an expression:

```
print_time(now);
```

Because a procedure does not return a value, it must have some other side effect; otherwise it would not be worth calling. This procedure has the side effect of printing the time.

Ideally, a function computes a single value and has no other observable effect. Calling the function multiple times with the same parameter values returns the same value every time and leaves no other trace. Ideally, a procedure has only a side effect, such as setting variables or performing output, and returns no value.

Sometimes these ideals get muddied by the necessities of reality. Commonly, procedures return a status value. For example, a procedure print_paycheck might return a bool to indicate successful printing without a paper jam. However, computing that return value is not the principal purpose of calling the operation—you wouldn't print a check just to find out whether there is still paper in the printer. Hence, we would still call print_paycheck a procedure, not a function, even though it returns a value.

ch04/printtime.cpp

```
1   #include <iostream>
2   #include <iomanip>
3
4   using namespace std;
5
6   #include "ccc_time.h"
7
8   /**
9       Prints a time in the format h:mm:ss.
10      @param t the time to print
11  */
12  void print_time(Time t)
13  {
14      cout << t.get_hours() << ":"
15          << setw(2) << setfill('0') << t.get_minutes() << ":"
16          << setw(2) << t.get_seconds() << setfill(' ');
17  }
18
19  int main()
20  {
21      Time liftoff(7, 0, 15);
22      Time now;
23      cout << "Liftoff: ";
24      print_time(liftoff);
25      cout << "\n";
26
27      cout << "Now: ";
28      print_time(now);
29      cout << "\n";
30
31      return 0;
32  }
```

Program Run

```
Liftoff: 7:00:15
Now: 12:14:57
```

4.8 Reference Parameters

If you want to write a function or procedure that changes the values of a parameter, you must use a *reference parameter* in order to allow the change. We first explain why a different parameter type is necessary, and then we show you the syntax for reference parameters.

Consider a procedure that raises the salary of an employee by a given percentage. We want to call the procedure in the following way:

```
Employee harry;
...
raise_salary(harry, 5); // Now Harry earns 5 percent more
```

Here is a first attempt:

```
void raise_salary(Employee e, double by) // Does not work
{
    double new_salary = e.get_salary() * (1 + by / 100);
    e.set_salary(new_salary);
}
```

But this doesn't work. Let's walk through the procedure. As the procedure starts, the parameter variable e is set to the same value as harry, and by is set to 5. Then e is modified, but that modification had no effect on harry, because e is a separate variable. When the procedure exits, e is forgotten, and harry didn't get a raise.

A parameter such as e or by is called a *value parameter*, because it is a variable that is initialized with a value supplied by the caller. All parameters in the functions and procedures that we have written so far have been value parameters. In this situation, though, we don't just want e to have the same value as harry. We want e to refer to the actual variable harry (or joe or whatever employee is supplied in the call). The salary of *that* variable should be updated.

> A reference parameter denotes a reference to a variable that is supplied in a function call.

You use a reference parameter when you want to update a variable that was supplied in the method call. When we make e into a reference parameter, then e is not a new variable but a reference to an existing variable, and any change in e is actually a change in the variable to which e refers in that particular call. Figure 7 shows the difference between value and reference parameters.

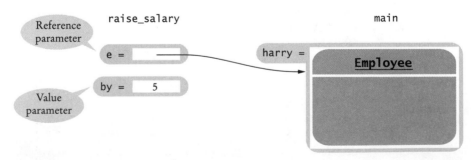

Figure 7   Reference and Value Parameters

The syntax for a reference parameter is cryptic, as shown in Syntax 4.4. You place an & after the type name to denote a reference parameter. Employee& is read "employee reference" or, more briefly, "employee ref".

```
void raise_salary(Employee& e, double by)
{
    double new_salary = e.get_salary() * (1 + by / 100);
    e.set_salary(new_salary);
}
```

The raise_salary procedure has two parameters: one of type "employee ref" and the other a floating-point number.

The raise_salary procedure clearly has an observable side effect: It modifies the variable supplied in the call. Apart from producing output, reference parameters are the most common mechanism for achieving a side effect.

Note that the parameter e refers to different variables in different procedure calls. If raise_salary is called twice,

```
raise_salary(harry, 5 + bonus);
raise_salary(charley, 1.5);
```

then e refers to harry in the first call, raising his salary by 5 percent plus the amount bonus. In the second call, e refers to charley, raising his salary by just 1.5 percent.

Should the second parameter be a reference?

```
void raise_salary(Employee& e, double& by)
```

That is not desirable. The parameter by is never modified in the procedure; hence, we gain nothing from making it a reference parameter. All we accomplish is to restrict the call pattern. A reference parameter must be bound to a *variable* in the call, whereas a value parameter can be bound to any *expression*. With by a reference parameter, the call

```
raise_salary(harry, 5 + bonus)
```

becomes illegal, because you cannot have a reference to the expression 5 + bonus. It makes no sense to change the value of an expression.

ch04/raisesal.cpp

```
1   #include <iostream>
2
3   using namespace std;
4
5   #include "ccc_empl.h"
6
7   /**
8       Raises an employee salary.
9       @param e  employee receiving raise
10      @param by  the percentage of the raise
11  */
12  void raise_salary(Employee& e, double by)
13  {
14      double new_salary = e.get_salary() * (1 + by / 100);
15      e.set_salary(new_salary);
```

```
16  }
17
18  int main()
19  {
20     Employee harry("Hacker, Harry", 45000.00);
21     raise_salary(harry, 5);
22     cout << "New salary: " << harry.get_salary() << "\n";
23     return 0;
24  }
```

Program Run

```
New salary: 47250
```

SYNTAX 4.4 Reference Parameter

type_name& parameter_name

Example:

```
Employee& e
int& result
```

Purpose:

Define a parameter that is bound to a variable in the function call, to allow the function to modify that variable.

ADVANCED TOPIC 4.2

Constant References

It is not very efficient to pass variables of type Employee to a function by value. An employee record contains several data items, and all of them must be copied into the parameter variable. Reference parameters are more efficient. Only the location of the variable, not its value, needs to be communicated to the function.

You can instruct the compiler to give you the efficiency of call by reference and the meaning of call by value, by using a *constant reference* as shown in Syntax 4.5. The procedure

```
void print_employee(const Employee& e)
{
   cout << "Name: " << e.get_name()
      << " Salary: " << e.get_salary() << "\n";
}
```

works exactly the same as the procedure

```
void print_employee(Employee e)
{
   cout << "Name: " << e.get_name()
      << " Salary: " << e.get_salary() << "\n";
}
```

There is just one difference: Calls to the first procedure execute faster.

Adding const& to value parameters is generally worthwhile for objects but not for numbers. Using a constant reference for an integer or floating-point number is actually slower than using a value parameter. It would be nice if the compiler could perform this optimization on its own initiative, but there are unfortunate technical reasons why it cannot.

Adding const& to speed up the passing of objects works only if the function or procedure never modifies its value parameters. While it is legal to modify a value parameter, changing a constant reference is an error. In Section 4.5 it was recommended to treat value parameters as constants. If you follow that recommendation, you can apply the const& speedup.

For simplicity, const& is rarely used in this book, but you will always find it in production code.

SYNTAX 4.5 Constant Reference Parameter

const *type_name*& *parameter_name*

Example:

const Employee& e

Purpose:

Define a parameter that is bound to a variable in the function call, to avoid the cost of copying that variable into a parameter variable.

RANDOM FACT 4.1

The Explosive Growth of Personal Computers

In 1971, Marcian E. "Ted" Hoff, an engineer at Intel Corporation was working on a chip for a manufacturer of electronic calculators. He realized that it would be a better idea to develop a *general-purpose* chip that could be *programmed* to interface with the keys and display of a calculator, rather than to do yet another custom design. Thus, the *microprocessor* was born. At the time, its primary application was as a controller for calculators, washing machines, and the like. It took years for the computer industry to notice that a genuine central processing unit was now available as a single chip.

Hobbyists were the first to catch on. In 1974 the first computer *kit*, the Altair 8800, was available from MITS Electronics for about $350. The kit consisted of the microprocessor, a circuit board, a very small amount of memory, toggle switches, and a row of display lights. Purchasers had to solder and assemble it, then program it in machine language through the toggle switches. It was not a big hit.

The first big hit was the Apple II. It was a real computer with a keyboard, a monitor, and a floppy disk drive. When it was first released, users had a $3,000 machine that could play Space Invaders, run a primitive bookkeeping program, or let users program it in BASIC. The original Apple II did not even support lowercase letters, making it worthless for word processing. The breakthrough came in 1979, with a new *spreadsheet* program, VisiCalc (see Figure 8). In a spreadsheet, you enter financial data and their relationships into a grid of rows and columns. Then you modify some of the data and watch in real time how the others

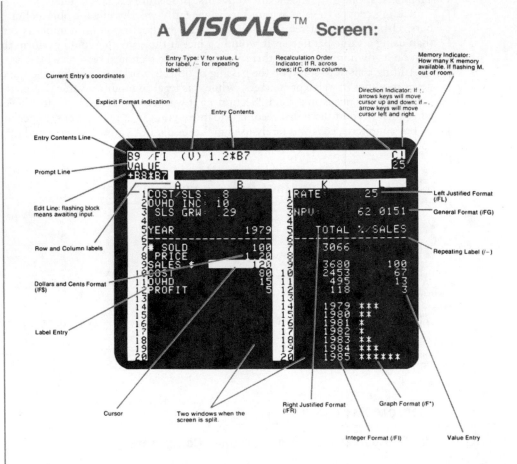

Figure 8   The Visicalc Spreadsheet Running on an Apple II

change. For example, you can see how changing the mix of widgets in a manufacturing plant might affect estimated costs and profits. Middle managers in companies, who understood computers and were fed up with having to wait for hours or days to retrieve their data runs from the computing center, snapped up VisiCalc and the computer that was needed to run it. For them, the computer was a spreadsheet machine.

The next big hit was the IBM Personal Computer, ever after known as the PC. It was the first widely available personal computer that used Intel's 16-bit processor, the 8086, whose successors are still being used in personal computers today. The success of the PC was based not on any engineering breakthroughs, but on the fact that it was easy to *clone*. IBM published specifications for plug-in cards, and it went one step further. It published the exact source code of the so-called BIOS (Basic Input/Output System), which controls the keyboard, monitor, ports, and disk drives and must be installed in ROM form in every PC. This allowed third-party vendors of plug-in cards to ensure that the BIOS code, and third-party extensions of it, interacted correctly with the equipment. Of course, the code itself was the property of IBM and could not be copied legally. Perhaps IBM did not foresee that functionally equivalent versions of the BIOS nevertheless could be recreated by others. Compaq, one of the first clone vendors, had fifteen engineers, who certified that they had never seen the original IBM code, write a new version that conformed precisely to the IBM specifications. Other companies did the same, and soon there were a number of vendors selling computers that ran the same software as IBM's PC but distinguished themselves by a lower price, increased portability, or better performance. In time, IBM lost its dominant position in the PC market. It is now one of many companies producing IBM PC-compatible computers.

IBM never produced an operating system for its PCs. An operating system organizes the interaction between the user and the computer, starts application programs, and manages disk storage and other resources. Instead, IBM offered customers the option of three separate operating systems. Most customers couldn't care less about the operating system. They chose the system that was able to launch most of the few applications that existed at the time. It happened to be DOS (Disk Operating System) by Microsoft. Microsoft cheerfully licensed the same operating system to other hardware vendors and encouraged software companies to write DOS applications. A huge number of useful application programs for PC-compatible machines was the result.

PC applications were certainly useful, but they were not easy to learn. Every vendor developed a different *user interface*: the collection of keystrokes, menu options, and settings that a user needed to master to use a software package effectively. Data exchange between applications was difficult, because each program used a different data format. The Apple Macintosh changed all that in 1984. The designers of the Macintosh had the vision to supply an intuitive user interface with the computer and to force software developers to adhere to it. It took Microsoft and PC-compatible manufacturers years to catch up.

At the time of this writing, most personal computers are used for accessing information from online sources, entertainment, word processing, and home finance. Some analysts predict that the personal computer will merge with the television set and cable network into an entertainment and information appliance.

4.9 Variable Scope and Global Variables

It is sometimes possible to define the same variable name more than once in a program. When the variable name is used, you need to know to which definition it belongs. In this section, we discuss the rules for dealing with multiple definitions of the same name.

Consider the variable r in the following example:

```
double future_value(double initial_balance, double p, int n)
{
   double r = initial_balance * pow(1 + p / 100, n);
   return r;
}

int main()
{
   cout << "Please enter the interest rate in percent: ";
   double r;
   cin >> r;
```

```
        double balance = future_value(10000, r, 10);
        cout << "After 10 years, the balance is "
            << balance << "\n";

        return 0;
    }
```

Perhaps the programmer chose r to denote the *return value* in the future_value function, and independently chose r to denote the *rate* in the main function. These variables are independent of each other. You can have variables with the same name *r* in different functions, just as you can have different motels with the same name "Bates' Motel" in different cities.

> The scope of a variable is the part of the program in which it is visible.

In a program, the part within which a variable is visible is known as the *scope* of the variable. The scope of a variable that is defined in a function extends from its definition to the end of the block in which it was defined. The scopes of the variables r are indicated with color.

```
double future_value(double initial_balance, double p, int n)
{
    double r = initial_balance * pow(1 + p / 100, n);
    return r;
}
```

```
int main()
{
    cout << "Please enter the interest rate in percent: ";
    double r;
    cin >> r;

    double balance = future_value(10000, r, 10);
    cout << "After 10 years, the balance is "
        << balance << "\n";

    return 0;
}
```

> A local variable is defined inside a function. A global variable is defined outside a function.

Variables that are defined inside functions are sometimes called *local variables*. C++ also supports *global variables*: variables that are defined outside functions. A global variable is visible to all functions that are defined after it.

In the following code, balance is a global variable. Note how it is set in main and read in future_value.

ch04/global.cpp

```
1   #include <iostream>
2   #include <cmath>
3
4   using namespace std;
5
6   double balance;
7
```

```
 8   /**
 9       Accumulates interest in the global variable balance.
10       @param p the interest rate in percent
11       @param n the number of periods the investment is held
12   */
13   void future_value(double p, int n)
14   {
15       balance = balance * pow(1 + p / 100, n);
16   }
17
18   int main()
19   {
20       balance = 10000;
21       future_value(5, 10);
22       cout << "After ten years, the balance is "
23          << balance << "\n";
24       return 0;
25   }
```

Program Run

```
After ten years, the balance is 16288.9
```

Of course, this is not considered a good way of transmitting data from one function to another. For example, suppose a programmer accidentally calls future_value before balance is set. Then the function computes the wrong investment result. Especially as a program gets long, these kinds of errors are extremely difficult to find. Of course, there is a simple remedy: Rewrite future_value and add a parameter for the initial balance.

Sometimes global variables cannot be avoided (for example, cin, cout, and cwin are global variables), but you should make every effort to avoid global variables in your programs.

QUALITY TIP 4.2

Minimize Global Variables

There are a few cases where global variables are required, but they are quite rare. If you find yourself using many global variables, you are probably writing code that will be difficult to maintain and extend. As a rule of thumb, you should have no more than two global variables for every thousand lines of code.

How can you avoid global variables? Use *parameters* and use *classes*. You can always use function parameters to transfer information from one part of a program to another. If your program manipulates many variables, that can get tedious. In this case, you need to design classes that cluster related variables together. You will learn more about this process in Chapter 5.

4.10 Stepwise Refinement

> Use the process of stepwise refinement to decompose complex tasks into simpler ones.

One of the most powerful strategies for problem solving is the process of *stepwise* refinement. To solve a difficult task, break it down into simpler tasks. Then keep breaking down the simpler tasks into even simpler ones, until you are left with tasks that you know how to solve.

Now apply this process to a problem of everyday life. You get up in the morning and simply must *get coffee*. How do you get coffee? You see whether you can get

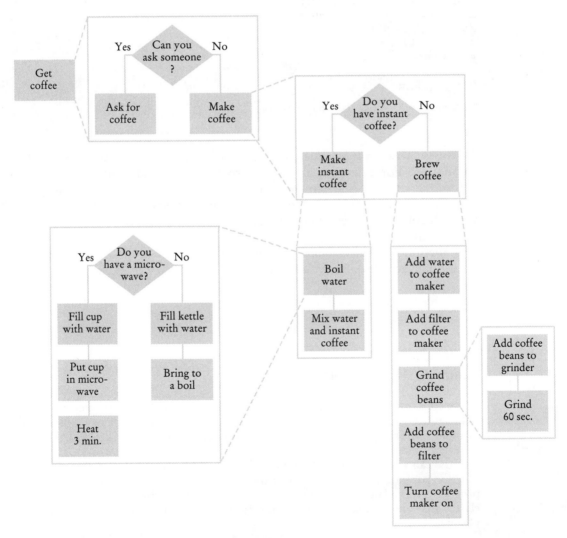

Figure 9　Flowchart of Coffee-Making Solution

someone else, such as your mother or mate, to bring you some. If that fails, you must *make coffee*. How do you make coffee? If there is instant coffee available, you can *make instant coffee*. How do you make instant coffee? Simply *boil water* and mix the boiling water with the instant coffee. How do you boil water? If there is a microwave, then you fill a cup with water, place it in the microwave and heat it for three minutes. Otherwise, you fill a kettle with water and heat it on the stove until the water comes to a boil. On the other hand, if you don't have instant coffee, you must *brew coffee*. How do you brew coffee? You add water to the coffee maker, put in a filter, *grind coffee*, put the coffee in the filter, and turn the coffee maker on. How do you grind coffee? You add coffee beans to the coffee grinder and push the button for 60 seconds.

The solution to the coffee problem breaks down tasks in two ways: with *decisions* and with *refinements*. We are already familiar with decisions: "If there is a microwave, use it, *else* use a kettle." *Decisions* are implemented as `if/else` in C++. A refinement gives a name to a composite task and later breaks that task down further: "… put in a filter, *grind coffee*, put the coffee in the filter …. To grind coffee, add coffee beans to the coffee grinder … ." Refinements are implemented as functions in C++. Figure 9 shows a flowchart view of the coffee-making solution. Decisions are shown as branches, refinements as expanding boxes. Figure 10 shows a second view: a *call tree* of the tasks. The call tree shows which tasks are subdivided into which other tasks. It does not show decisions or loops, though. The name "call tree" is simple to explain: When you program each task as a C++ function, the call tree shows which functions call each other.

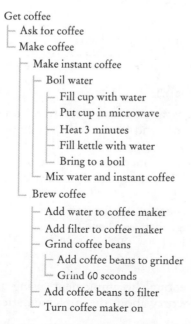

Figure 10   Call Tree of Coffee-Making Process

QUALITY TIP 4.3

Keep Functions Short

There is a certain cost for writing a function. The function needs to be documented; parameter values need to be passed; the function must be tested. Some effort should be made to find whether the function can be made reusable rather than tied to a specific context. To avoid this cost, it is always tempting just to stuff more and more code in one place rather than going through the trouble of breaking up the code into separate functions. It is quite common to see inexperienced programmers produce functions that are several hundred lines long.

Ideally, each function should contain no more than one screenful of text, making it easy to read the code in the text editor. Of course, this is not always possible. As a rule of thumb, a function that is longer than 50 lines is usually suspect and should probably be broken up.

4.11 Case Study: From Pseudocode to Code

When printing a check, it is customary to write the check amount both as a number ("$274.15") and as a text string ("two hundred seventy four dollars and 15 cents"). Doing so reduces the recipient's temptation to add a few digits in front of the amount (see Figure 11). For a human, this isn't particularly difficult, but how can a computer do this? There is no built-in function that turns 274 into "two hundred seventy four". We need to program this function. Here is the description of the function we want to write:

```
/**
    Turns a number into its English name.
    @param n  a positive integer < 1,000,000
    @return  the name of n (e.g., "two hundred seventy four")
*/
string int_name(int n)
```

Before starting the programming, we need to have a plan. Consider a simple case. If the number is between 1 and 9, we need to compute "one" ... "nine". In fact, we need the same computation *again* for the hundreds (two hundred). Any time you need something more than once, it is a good idea to turn that into a function. Rather than writing the entire function, write only the comment:

```
/**
    Turns a digit into its English name.
    @param n  an integer between 1 and 9
    @return  the name of n ("one" ... "nine")
*/
string digit_name(int n)
```

This sounds simple enough to implement, using an if/else statement with nine branches, so we will worry about the implementation later.

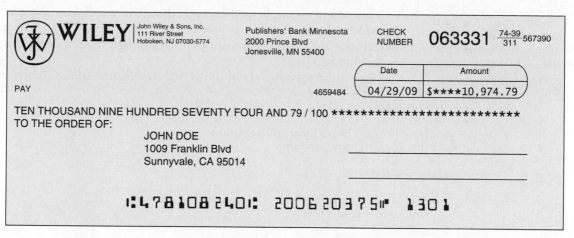

Figure 11 Check Showing the Amount as Both a Number and a String

Numbers between 10 and 19 are special cases. Let us have a separate function `teen_name` that converts them into strings `"eleven"`, `"twelve"`, `"thirteen"`, and so forth:

```
/**
    Turns a number between 10 and 19 into its English name.
    @param n an integer between 10 and 19
    @return the name of n ("ten" ... "nineteen")
*/
string teen_name(int n)
```

Next, suppose that the number is between 20 and 99. Then we show the tens as `"twenty"`, `"thirty"`, ..., `"ninety"`. For simplicity and consistency, put that computation into a separate function:

```
/**
    Gives the English name of a multiple of 10.
    @param n an integer between 2 and 9
    @return the name of 10 * n ("twenty" ... "ninety")
*/
string tens_name(int n)
```

Now suppose the number is at least 20 and at most 99. If the number is evenly divisible by 10, we use `tens_name`, and we are done. Otherwise, we print the tens with `tens_name` and the ones with `digit_name`. If the number is between 100 and 999, then we show a digit, the word `"hundred"`, and the remainder as described previously.

If the number is 1,000 or larger, then we convert the multiples of a thousand, in the same format, followed by the word `"thousand"`, then the remainder. For example, to convert 23,416, we first make 23 into a string `"twenty three"`, follow that with `"thousand"`, and then convert 416.

Pseudocode is a mixture of English and source code that is used in the early stages of implementing complex code.

This sounds complicated enough that it is worth turning it into *pseudocode*. Pseudocode is code that looks like C++, but the descriptions it contains are not explicit enough for the compiler to understand.

Here is the pseudocode of the verbal description of the algorithm.

```
string int_name(int n)
{
    int c = n; // The part that still needs to be converted
    string r; // The return value

    if (c >= 1000)
    {
        r = name of thousands in c + "thousand";
        remove thousands from c;
    }

    if (c >= 100)
    {
        r = r + name of hundreds in c + "hundred";
        remove hundreds from c;
    }

    if (c >= 20)
    {
        r = r + name of tens in c;
        remove tens from c;
    }

    if (c >= 10)
    {
        r = r + name of c;
        c = 0;
    }

    if (c > 0)
        r = r + name of c;

    return r;
}
```

This pseudocode has a number of important improvements over the verbal description. It shows how to arrange the tests, starting with the comparisons against the larger numbers, and it shows how the smaller number is subsequently processed in further if statements.

On the other hand, this pseudocode is vague about the actual conversion of the pieces, just referring to "name of tens" and the like. Furthermore, we lied about spaces. As it stands, the code would produce strings with no spaces, twohundredseventyfour, for example. Compared to the complexity of the main problem, one would hope that spaces are a minor issue. It is best not to muddy the pseudocode with minor details.

Some people like to write pseudocode on paper and use it as a guide for the actual coding. Others type the pseudocode into an editor and then transform it into the final code. You may want to try out both methods and see which one works better for you.

Now turn the pseudocode into real code. The last three cases are easy, because helper functions are already developed for them:

```
if (c >= 20)
{
   r = r + " " + tens_name(c / 10);
   c = c % 10;
}

if (c >= 10)
{
   r = r + " " + teen_name(c);
   c = 0;
}

if (c > 0)
   r = r + " " + digit_name(c);
```

The case of numbers between 100 and 999 is also easy, because you know that c / 100 is a single digit:

```
if (c >= 100)
{
   r = r + " " + digit_name(c / 100) + " hundred";
   c = c % 100;
}
```

Only the case of numbers larger than 1,000 is somewhat vexing, because the number c / 1000 is not necessarily a digit. If c is 23,416, then c / 1000 is 23, and how are we going to obtain the name of *that*? We have helper functions for the ones, teens, and tens, but not for a value like 23. However, we know that c / 1000 is less than 1,000, because we assume that c is less than one million. We also have a perfectly good function that can convert any number <1,000 into a string—namely the function int_name itself.

```
if (c >= 1000)
{
   r = int_name(c / 1000) + " thousand";
   c = c % 1000;
}
```

Here is the function in its entirety:

```
/**
   Turns a number into its English name.
   @param n  a positive integer < 1,000,000
   @return the name of n (e.g., "two hundred seventy four")
*/

string int_name(int n)
{
```

```
int c = n; // The part that still needs to be converted
string r; // The return value

if (c >= 1000)
{
   r = int_name(c / 1000) + " thousand";
   c = c % 1000;
}

if (c >= 100)
{
   r = r + " " + digit_name(c / 100) + " hundred";
   c = c % 100;
}

if (c >= 20)
{
   r = r + " " + tens_name(c / 10);
   c = c % 10;
}

if (c >= 10)
{
   r = r + " " + teen_name(c);
   c = 0;
}

if (c > 0)
   r = r + " " + digit_name(c);

   return r;
}
```

You may find it odd that a function can call itself, not just other functions. This is actually not as far-fetched as it sounds at first. Here is an example from basic algebra. You probably learned in your algebra class how to compute a square of a number such as 25.4 without the benefit of a calculator. This is a handy trick if you are stuck on a desert island and need to find out how many square millimeters are in a square inch. (There are 25.4 millimeters in an inch.) Here is how you do it. You use the binomial formula

$$(a + b)^2 = a^2 + 2ab + b^2$$

with $a = 25$ and $b = 0.4$. To compute 25.4^2, you first compute the simpler squares 25^2 and 0.4^2: $25^2 = 625$ and $0.4^2 = 0.16$. Then you put everything together: $25.4^2 = 625 + 2 \times 25 \times 0.4 + 0.16 = 645.16$.

The same phenomenon happens with the int_name function. It receives a number like 23,456. It is stuck on the 23, so it suspends itself and calls a function to solve that task. It happens to be another copy of the same function. That function returns "twenty three". The original function resumes, threads together "twenty three thousand", and works on the remainder, 456.

There is one important caveat. When a function invokes itself, it must give a *simpler* assignment to the second copy of itself. For example, int_name couldn't just call itself with the value that it received or with 10 times that value; then the calls would never stop. That is, of course, a general truth for solving problems by a series of functions. Each function must work on a simpler part of the whole. In Chapter 10, we will examine functions that call themselves in greater detail.

Now you have seen all the important building blocks for the int_name function. As mentioned previously, the helper functions must be declared or defined *before* the int_name function. Here is the complete program.

ch04/intname.cpp

```
1   #include <iostream>
2   #include <string>
3
4   using namespace std;
5
6   /**
7       Turns a digit into its English name.
8       @param n  an integer between 1 and 9
9       @return  the name of n ("one" ... "nine")
10  */
11  string digit_name(int n)
12  {
13      if (n == 1) return "one";
14      if (n == 2) return "two";
15      if (n == 3) return "three";
16      if (n == 4) return "four";
17      if (n == 5) return "five";
18      if (n == 6) return "six";
19      if (n == 7) return "seven";
20      if (n == 8) return "eight";
21      if (n == 9) return "nine";
22      return "";
23  }
24
25  /**
26      Turns a number between 10 and 19 into its English name.
27      @param n  an integer between 10 and 19
28      @return  the name of n ("ten" ... "nineteen")
29  */
30  string teen_name(int n)
31  {
32      if (n == 10) return "ten";
33      if (n == 11) return "eleven";
34      if (n == 12) return "twelve";
35      if (n == 13) return "thirteen";
36      if (n == 14) return "fourteen";
37      if (n == 15) return "fifteen";
38      if (n == 16) return "sixteen";
39      if (n == 17) return "seventeen";
40      if (n == 18) return "eighteen";
41      if (n == 19) return "nineteen";
```

```
42      return "";
43  }
44
45  /**
46      Gives the English name of a multiple of 10.
47      @param  n  an integer between 2 and 9
48      @return  the name of 10 * n ("twenty" ... "ninety")
49  */
50  string tens_name(int n)
51  {
52      if (n == 2) return "twenty";
53      if (n == 3) return "thirty";
54      if (n == 4) return "forty";
55      if (n == 5) return "fifty";
56      if (n == 6) return "sixty";
57      if (n == 7) return "seventy";
58      if (n == 8) return "eighty";
59      if (n == 9) return "ninety";
60      return "";
61  }
62
63  /**
64      Turns a number into its English name.
65      @param  n  a positive integer < 1,000,000
66      @return  the name of n (e.g. "two hundred seventy four")
67  */
68  string int_name(int n)
69  {
70      int c = n; // The part that still needs to be converted
71      string r; // The return value
72
73      if (c >= 1000)
74      {
75          r = int_name(c / 1000) + " thousand";
76          c = c % 1000;
77      }
78
79      if (c >= 100)
80      {
81          r = r + " " + digit_name(c / 100) + " hundred";
82          c = c % 100;
83      }
84
85      if (c >= 20)
86      {
87          r = r + " " + tens_name(c / 10);
88          c = c % 10;
89      }
90
91      if (c >= 10)
92      {
93          r = r + " " + teen_name(c);
94          c = 0;
95      }
```

```
96
97      if (c > 0)
98         r = r + " " + digit_name(c);
99
100     return r;
101   }
102
103   int main()
104   {
105      int n;
106      cout << "Please enter a positive integer: ";
107      cin >> n;
108      cout << int_name(n);
109      return 0;
110   }
```

Program Run

```
Please enter a positive integer: 1729
one thousand seven hundred twenty nine
```

4.12 Walkthroughs

A walkthrough is a manual simulation of program code.

When you implement a complex set of functions, it is a good idea to carry out a manual *walkthrough* before entrusting it to the computer. In this section, you will see how to carry out a walkthrough. All you need is a stack of index cards.

Consider the int_name function of the preceding section. There are a number of other subtleties that are worth analyzing. For example, consider

```
if (c >= 20)
{
   r = r + " " + tens_name(c);
   c = c % 10;
}

if (c >= 10)
{
   r = r + " " + teen_name(c);
   c = 0;
}
```

Why does the first branch set c = c % 10, whereas the second branch sets c = 0? Actually, when I first wrote the code, both branches set c = c % 10, and then I realized my error when testing the code in my mind with a few examples. A walkthrough is simply a systematic mental test of a piece of code.

Take an index card, or some other piece of paper; write down the function call that you want to study.

```
                    int_name(n = 416)
```

Then write the names of the function variables. Write them in a table, since you will update them as you walk through the code.

int_name(n = 416)	
c	r
416	""

Skip past the test c >= 1000 and enter the test c >= 100. c / 100 is 4 and c % 100 is 16. digit_name(4) is easily seen to be "four".

Write the value that you expect at the top of a separate index card.

```
                    digit_name(n = 4)
```

digit_name(n = 4)
Returns "four"?

Had digit_name been complicated, you would have started another index card to figure out that function call. This could get out of hand if that function calls a third function. Computers have no trouble suspending one task, working on a second one, and coming back to the first, but people lose concentration when they have to switch their mental focus too often. So, instead of walking through subordinate function calls, you can just assume that they return the correct value, as you did with `digit_name`.

Set this card aside and walk through it later. You may accumulate numerous cards in this way. In practice, this procedure is necessary only for complex function calls, not simple ones like `digit_name`.

Now you are ready to update the variables. r has changed to r + " " + digit_name(c / 100) + " hundred", that is "four hundred", and c has changed to c % 100, or 16. You can cross out the old values and write the new ones under them.

```
          int_name(n = 416)

  c          r
  416        ""
  16         "four hundred"



```

Now you enter the branch c >= 10. `teens_name(16)` is `sixteen`, so the variables now have the values

```
          int_name(n = 416)

  c          r
  416        ""
  16         "four hundred"
  0          "four hundred sixteen"



```

Now it becomes clear why you need to set c to 0, not to c % 10. You don't want to get into the c > 0 branch. If you did, the result would be "four hundred sixteen six". However, if c is 36, you want to produce "thirty" first and then send the leftover 6 to the c > 0 branch.

In this case the walkthrough was successful. However, you will very commonly find errors during walkthroughs. Then you fix the code and try the walkthrough again. In a team with many programmers, regular walkthroughs are a useful method of improving code quality and understanding.

PRODUCTIVITY HINT 4.4

Commenting Out a Section of Code

Sometimes you are running tests on a long program, and a part of the program is incomplete or hopelessly messed up. You may want to ignore that part for some time and focus on getting the remainder of the code to work. Of course, you can cut out that text, paste it into another file, and paste it back later, but that is a hassle. Alternatively, you could just enclose the code to be ignored in comments.

The obvious method is to place a /* at the beginning of the offending code and a */ at the end. Unfortunately, that does not work in C++, because comments do not *nest*. That is, the /* and */ do not pair up as parentheses or braces do:

```
/*

/**
    Turns a number between 10 and 19 into its English name.
    @param n an integer between 10 and 19
    @return the name of n ("ten" ... "nineteen")
*/
string teen_name(int n)
{
    if (n == 11) return "eleven";
    else ...
}

*/
```

The */ closing delimiter after the @return comment matches up with the /* opening delimiter at the top. All remaining code is compiled, and the */ at the end of the function causes an error message. This isn't very smart, of course. Some compilers do let you nest comments, but others don't. Some people recommend that you use only // comments. If you do, you can comment out a block of code with the /* ... */ comments—well, kind of: If you first comment out a small block and then a larger one, you run into the same problem.

There is another way of masking out a block of code: by using so-called *preprocessor directives*.

```
#if 0

/**
    Turns a number between 10 and 19 into its English name.
    @param n an integer between 10 and 19
    @return the name of n ("ten" ... "nineteen")
*/
string teen_name(int n)
{
    if (n == 11) return "eleven";
    else ...
}

#endif
```

Preprocessing is the phase before compilation, in which #include files are included, macros are expanded, and portions of code are conditionally included or excluded. All lines starting with a # are instructions to the preprocessor. Selective inclusion of code with #if ... #endif is useful if you need to write a program that has slight variations to run on different platforms. Here we use the feature to exclude the code. If you want to include it temporarily, change the `#if 0` to `#if 1`. Of course, once you have completed testing, you must clean it up and remove all `#if 0` directives and any unused code. *Unlike* `/* ... */` comments, the `#if ... #endif` directives can be nested.

PRODUCTIVITY HINT 4.5

Stubs

Some people first write all code and then start compiling and testing. Others prefer to see some results quickly. If you are among the impatient, you will like the technique of *stubs*.

A stub is a function that is completely empty and returns a trivial value. The stub can be used to test that the code compiles and to debug the logic of other parts of the program.

```
/**
    Turns a digit into its English name.
    @param n an integer between 1 and 9
    @return the name of n ("one" ... "nine")
*/
string digit_name(int n)
{
    return "mumble";
}

/**
    Turns a number between 10 and 19 into its English name.
    @param n an integer between 10 and 19
    @return the name of n ("ten" ... "nineteen")
*/
string teen_name(int n)
{
    return "mumbleteen";
}

/**
    Gives the English name of a multiple of 10.
    @param n an integer between 2 and 9
    @return the name of 10 * n ("twenty" ... "ninety")
*/
string tens_name(int n)
{
    return "mumblety";
}
```

If you combine these stubs with the `int_name` function and test it with an input of 274, you will get an output of `"mumble hundred mumblety mumble"`, which shows you that you are on the right track. You can then flesh out one stub at a time.

This method is particularly helpful if you like composing your programs directly on the computer. Of course, the initial planning requires thought, not typing, and is best done at a desk. Once you know what functions you need, however, you can enter their interface descriptions and stubs, compile, implement one function, compile and test, implement the next function, compile and test, until you are done.

4.13 Preconditions

What should a function do when it is called with inappropriate inputs? For example, how should sqrt(-1) react? What should digit_name(-1) do? There are two choices.

- A function can choose to accept all inputs and return default values when the inputs are inappropriate. For example, the digit_name function simply returns an empty string when it is called with an unexpected input.

- A function can choose to notify programmers which inputs it will accept. Such a notification is called a *precondition*. If an inappropriate input is provided despite the notification, the function may do anything it chooses, perhaps computing a wrong result or even terminating the program.

> Preconditions are documented restrictions on the function parameters.

Perhaps surprisingly, the "nice" approach—always returning a default value—is not such a good idea. Consider a square root function. It would be an easy matter to return 0 for negative inputs and the actual square root for positive inputs. Suppose you use that function to compute the intersection points of a circle and a line. Suppose they don't intersect, but you forgot to take that possibility into account. Now the square root of a negative number will return a wrong value, namely 0, and you will obtain bogus intersection points. You may miss that during testing, and the faulty program may make it into production. This isn't a big deal for a student program, but suppose the program directs a dental drill robot. It would start drilling somewhere outside the tooth.

It would be much better if the function complained loudly during testing, by printing an error message that clearly indicates the problem with the parameter value.

The assert macro, shown in Syntax 4.6 on page 201, was designed for this purpose. (A *macro* is a special instruction to the compiler that inserts code into the program text.) If the condition inside the assert macro is false, then the program aborts with an error message that shows the line number and file name. If the condition inside the macro is true when the macro is encountered, then nothing happens. For example, the macro

```
assert(x >= 0);
```

can be used to protect against negative values of x.

For efficiency, it is possible to change the behavior of assert when a program has been fully tested. After a certain switch has been set in the compiler, assert statements are simply ignored. No time-consuming test takes place, no error message is generated, and the program never aborts.

Here is what you should do when writing a function:

1. Establish clear *preconditions* for all inputs. Write in the @param comment what values you are not willing to handle for each parameter.

2. Write assert statements that enforce the preconditions.

3. Be sure to supply correct results for all inputs that fulfill the precondition.

Let's apply this strategy to the future_value function:

```
/**
    Computes the value of an investment with compound interest.
    @param initial_balance the initial value of the investment
    @param p the interest rate in percent; must be ≥ 0
    @param n the number of periods the investment is held;  must be ≥ 0
    @return the balance after n periods
*/
double future_value(double initial_balance, double p, int n)
{
    assert(p >= 0);
    assert(n >= 0);

    return initial_balance * pow(1 + p / 100, n);
}
```

We advertised that p and n must be ≥ 0. These are the preconditions of our future_value function. The function is responsible only for handling inputs that conform to the precondition. Calling the function with bad inputs causes the program to terminate. That may not be "nice", but it is legal. Remember that the function can do anything if the precondition is not fulfilled.

Bertrand Meyer [1] compares preconditions to contracts. The function promises to compute the correct answer for all inputs that fulfill the precondition. The caller promises never to call the function with illegal inputs. If the caller fulfills its promise and gets a wrong answer, it can take the function to programmer's court. If the caller doesn't fulfill its promise and something terrible happens as a consequence, it has no recourse.

SYNTAX 4.6 Assertion

assert(*expression*);

Example:

assert(x >= 0);

Purpose:

If the expression is true, do nothing. If it is false, terminate the program, displaying an error message with the file name, line number, and expression.

RANDOM FACT 4.2

The Therac-25 Incidents

The Therac-25 is a computerized device that delivers radiation treatment to cancer patients (see Figure 12). Between June 1985 and January 1987, several of these machines delivered serious overdoses to at least six patients, killing some of them and seriously maiming the others.

The machines were controlled by a computer program. Bugs in the program were directly responsible for the overdoses. According to [1], the program was written by a single programmer, who had since left the manufacturing company producing the device and could not be located. None of the company employees interviewed could say anything about the educational level or qualifications of the programmer.

The investigation by the federal Food and Drug Administration (FDA) found that the program was poorly documented and that there was neither a specification document nor a formal test plan. (This should make you think. Do you have a formal test plan for your programs?)

The overdoses were caused by an amateurish design of the software that controlled different devices concurrently, namely the keyboard, the display, the printer, and the radiation device itself. Synchronization and data sharing between the tasks were done in an ad hoc way, even though safe multitasking techniques were known at the time. Had the programmer enjoyed a formal education that involved these techniques or taken the effort to study the literature, a safer machine could have been built. Such a machine would have probably involved a commercial multitasking system, which might have required a more expensive computer.

The same flaws were present in the software controlling the predecessor model, the Therac-20, but that machine had hardware interlocks that mechanically prevented overdoses.

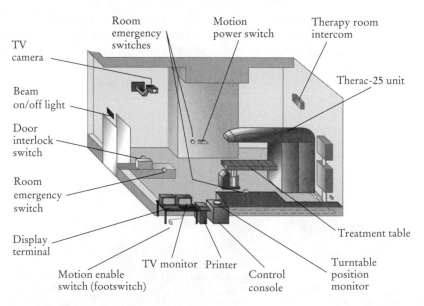

Figure 12   Typical Therac-25 Facility

The hardware safety devices were removed in the Therac-25 and replaced by checks in the software, presumably to save cost.

Frank Houston of the FDA wrote in 1985 [1]: "A significant amount of software for life-critical systems comes from small firms, especially in the medical device industry; firms that fit the profile of those resistant to or uninformed of the principles of either system safety or software engineering".

Who is to blame? The programmer? The manager who not only failed to ensure that the programmer was up to the task but also didn't insist on comprehensive testing? The hospitals that installed the device, or the FDA, for not reviewing the design process? Unfortunately, even today there are no firm standards of what constitutes a safe software design process.

4.14 Unit Testing

A black-box test does not consider the internal structure of a program; a white-box test does.

Testing the functionality of a computer program without consideration of its internal structure is called *black-box testing*. You probably performed some black-box testing when you provided inputs to your homework programs and checked the results.

However, it is impossible to ensure absolutely that a program will work correctly on all inputs, just by supplying a finite number of test cases. As the famous computer scientist Edsger Dijkstra pointed out, testing can only show the presence of bugs—not their absence. To gain more confidence in the correctness of a program, it is useful to consider its internal structure. Testing strategies that look inside a program are called *white-box testing*.

A unit test checks a function in isolation.

One important part of white-box testing is to test functions of a program in isolation. You write a short program, called a *test harness*, that calls the function to be tested and verifies that the results are correct. This process is called *unit testing*.

For example, a unit test for the int_name function might look like this:

```
int main()
{
    assert(int_name(19) == "nineteen");
    assert(int_name(29) == "twenty nine");
    assert(int_name(1093) == "one thousand ninety three");
    assert(int_name(30000) == "thirty thousand");
}
```

A unit test framework allows you to organize your unit tests.

When the program completes without an error message, then all the tests have passed. If a test fails, then you get an error message, telling you which line failed. This approach works fine for a small set of test cases. Various *unit test frameworks* have been developed for C++ to make it easier to organize unit tests (see [2] and[3]). These testing frameworks are excellent for testing larger programs, providing good error reporting and the ability to keep going when some test cases fail or crash.

> A boundary case is a test case that is at the boundary of valid inputs.

Selecting test cases is an important skill. Of course, you want to test your program with inputs that a typical user might supply.

Next, you should include *boundary cases*. Boundary cases are still legitimate inputs, and you expect that the function that is being tested will handle them correctly. Boundary cases for the int_name function are 1 and 999999, the smallest and largest valid input.

> To ensure good test coverage, select test cases that cover each branch of the function.

You want to make sure that each part of your code is exercised at least once by one of your test cases. This is called *test coverage*. If some code is never executed by any of your test cases, you have no way of knowing whether that code would perform correctly if it ever were executed by user input. That means that you need to look at every if/else branch to see that each of them is reached by some test case. Many conditional branches are in the code only to take care of strange and abnormal inputs, but they still do something. It is a common phenomenon that they end up doing something incorrect but that those faults are never discovered during testing because nobody supplied the strange and abnormal inputs. Of course, these flaws become immediately apparent when the program is released and the first user types in a bad input and is incensed when the program crashes. Your test cases should ensure that each part of the code is covered by some input.

For example, in testing the int_name function, you want to make sure that every if statement is entered for at least one test case and that it is skipped for another test case. For example, you might test the inputs 1234 and 1034 to see what happens if the test if (c >= 100) is entered and what happens if it is skipped.

It is a good idea to write the first test cases *before* the program is written completely. Designing a few test cases can give you insight into what the program should do, which is valuable for implementing it. You will also have something to throw at the program when it compiles for the first time.

It is a common and useful practice to make a new test case whenever you find a program bug. You can use that test case to verify that your bug fix really works. Don't throw it away; feed it to the next version after that and all subsequent versions. Such a collection of test cases is called a *test suite*.

> In regression testing, you test new versions of a program against past failures.

You will be surprised how often a bug that you fixed will reappear in a future version. This is a phenomenon known as *cycling*. Sometimes you don't quite understand the reason for a bug and apply a quick fix that appears to work. Later, you apply a different quick fix that solves a second problem but makes the first problem reappear. Of course, it is always best to really think through what causes a bug and fix the root cause instead of doing a sequence of "Band-Aid" solutions. If you don't succeed in doing that, however, at least you want to have an honest appraisal of how well the program works. By keeping all old test cases and testing them all against every new version, you get that feedback. The process of testing against a set of past failures is called *regression testing*.

In summary, the most important principles of testing are to aim for complete coverage (executing all code at least once), and to use regression testing (never throwing a test case away). Organize your test cases in one or more test harnesses, and run them whenever you fix a bug. Use a test framework when simple test harnesses become unwieldy.

4.15 The Debugger

> With a debugger, you can control the execution of a program and observe the contents of program variables.

Modern development environments contain special programs, so-called *debuggers*, that help you locate bugs by letting you follow the execution of a program. You can stop and restart your program and see the contents of variables whenever your program is temporarily stopped. At each stop, you have the choice of what variables to inspect and how many program steps to run until the next stop.

Some people don't want to learn a new tool and try to get by with inserting trace statements. However, for larger programs, that approach becomes quite unproductive. You will find that the time invested in learning about the debugger is amply repaid in your programming career.

Some people feel that debuggers are just a tool to make programmers lazy. Admittedly some people write sloppy programs and fix them up with the debugger, but that is not smart. It takes time to set up and carry out an effective debugging session. Effective programmers design their programs carefully and use a debugger only when necessary.

RANDOM FACT 4.3

The First Bug

According to legend, the first bug was found in the Mark II, a huge electromechanical computer at Harvard University. It really was caused by a bug—a moth was trapped in a relay switch.

Actually, from the note that the operator left in the log book next to the moth (see Figure 13), it appears as if the term "bug" had already been in active use at the time.

The pioneering computer scientist Maurice Wilkes wrote: "Somehow, at the Moore School and afterwards, one had always assumed there would be no particular difficulty in

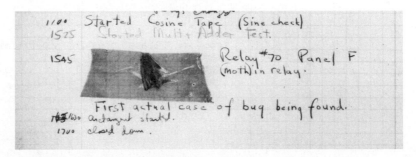

Figure 13 The First Bug

getting programs right. I can remember the exact instant in time at which it dawned on me that a great part of my future life would be spent finding mistakes in my own programs."

4.15.1 Using a Debugger

> You can make effective use of the debugger by mastering just three commands: "run until this line", "step to next line", and "inspect variable".

Like compilers, debuggers vary widely from one system to another. On some systems they are quite primitive and require you to memorize a small set of arcane commands; on others they have an intuitive window interface.

You will have to find out how to prepare a program for debugging and how to start the debugger on your system. If you use an integrated development environment, which contains an editor, compiler, and debugger, this step is usually very easy. You just build the program in the usual way and pick a menu command to start debugging. On many UNIX systems, you must manually build a debug version of your program and invoke the debugger.

Once you have started the debugger, you can go a long way with just three debugging commands: "run until this line", "step to next line", and "inspect variable". The names and keystrokes or mouse clicks for these commands differ widely between debuggers, but all debuggers support these basic commands. You can find out how either from the documentation or a lab manual, or by asking someone who has used the debugger before.

The "run until this line" command is the most important. Many debuggers show you the source code of the current program in a window. Select a line with the mouse or cursor keys. Then hit a key or select a menu command to run the program to the selected line. On other debuggers, you have to type in a command or a line number. In either case, the program starts execution and stops as soon as it reaches the line you selected (see Figure 14). Of course, you may have selected a line that will not be reached at all during a particular program run. Then the program terminates in the normal way. The very fact that the program has or has not reached a particular line can be valuable information.

```
primebug.cpp ⊠
/* 24 */ {
/* 25 */     int n;
/* 26 */     cout << "Please enter the upper limit: ";
/* 27 */     cin >> n;
/* 28 */     int i;
/* 29 */     for (i = 1; i <= n; i = i + 2)
/* 30 */     {
/* 31 */         if (isprime(i))
/* 32 */         cout << i << "\n";
/* 33 */     }
```

Figure 14   Debugger Stopped at Selected Line

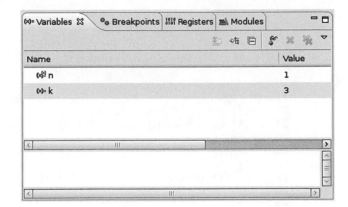

Figure 15
Inspecting Variables
in the Debugger

The "step to next line" command executes the current line and stops at the next program line.

Once the program has stopped, you can look at the current values of variables. Again, the method for selecting the variables differs among debuggers. On some debuggers you select the variable name with the mouse or cursor keys and then issue a menu command such as "inspect variable". In other debuggers you must type the name of the variable into a dialog box. Some debuggers automatically show the values of all local variables of a function.

The debugger displays the name and contents of the inspected variable (Figure 15). If all variables contain what you expected, you can run the program until the next point where you want to stop.

The program also stops to read data, just as it does when you run it without the debugger. Just enter the inputs in the normal way, and the program will continue running.

Finally, when the program has completed running, the debug session is also finished. You can no longer inspect variables. To run the program again, you may be able to reset the debugger, or you may need to exit the debugging program and start over. Details depend on the particular debugger.

4.15.2 A Sample Debugging Session

Consider the following program, whose purpose is to compute all prime numbers up to a number n. An integer is defined to be prime if it is not evenly divisible by any number except by 1 and itself. Also, mathematicians find it convenient not to call 1 a prime. Thus, the first few prime numbers are 2, 3, 5, 7, 11, 13, 17, 19.

ch04/primebug.cpp

```
1   #include <iostream>
2
3   using namespace std;
4
```

```
 5  /**
 6      Tests if an integer is a prime.
 7      @param n  any positive integer
 8      @return  true if n  is a prime
 9  */
10  bool isprime(int n)
11  {
12      if (n == 2) return true;
13      if (n % 2 == 0) return false;
14      int k = 3;
15      while (k * k < n)
16      {
17          if (n % k == 0) return false;
18          k = k + 2;
19      }
20      return true;
21  }
22
23  int main()
24  {
25      int n;
26      cout << "Please enter the upper limit: ";
27      cin >> n;
28      int i;
29      for (i = 1; i <= n; i = i + 2)
30      {
31          if (isprime(i))
32          cout << i << "\n";
33      }
34      return 0;
35  }
```

Program Run

```
Please enter the upper limit: 10
1
3
5
7
9
```

Have a close look at the program output. This is not very promising; it looks as if the program just prints all odd numbers. Let us find out what it does wrong by using the debugger. Actually, for such a simple program, it is easy to correct mistakes simply by looking at the faulty output and the program code. However, we want to learn to use the debugger.

Let us first go to line 31. On the way, the program will stop to read the input into n. Supply the input value 10.

```
23  int main()
24  {
```

```
25      int n;
26      cout << "Please enter the upper limit: ";
27      cin >> n;
28      int i;
29      for (i = 1; i <= n; i = i + 2)
30      {
31          if (isprime(i))
32          cout << i << "\n";
33      }
34      return 0;
35  }
```

Start by investigating why the program treats 1 as a prime. Go to line 12.

```
10  bool isprime(int n)
11  {
12      if (n == 2) return true;
13      if (n % 2 == 0) return false;
14      int k = 3;
15      while (k * k < n)
16      {
17          if (n % k == 0) return false;
18          k = k + 2;
19      }
20      return true;
21  }
```

Convince yourself that the argument of isprime is currently 1 by inspecting n. Then execute the "run to next line" command. You will notice that the program goes to lines 13, 14, and 15, and then directly to line 20.

Inspect the value of k. It is 3, and therefore the while loop was never entered. It looks like the isprime function needs to be rewritten to treat 1 as a special case.

Next, we would like to know why the program doesn't print 2 as a prime even though the isprime function does recognize that 2 is a prime, whereas all other even numbers are not. Go again to line 10, the next call of isprime. Inspect n; you will note that n is 3. Now it becomes clear: The for loop in main tests only odd numbers. The main function should either test both odd and even numbers or, better, just handle 2 as a special case.

Finally, we would like to find out why the program believes 9 is a prime. Go again to line 10 and inspect n; it should be 5. Repeat that step twice until n is 9. (With some debuggers, you may need to go from line 10 to line 11 before you can go back to line 10.) Now use the "run to next line" command repeatedly. You will notice that the program again skips past the while loop; inspect k to find out why. You will find that k is 3. Look at the condition in the while loop. It tests whether k * k < n. Now k * k is 9 and n is also 9, so the test fails. Actually, it does make sense to test divisors only up to $\sqrt{n}$; if n has any divisors except 1 and itself, at least one of them must be less than $\sqrt{n}$. However, that isn't quite true; if n is a perfect square of a prime, then its sole nontrivial divisor is *equal* to $\sqrt{n}$. That is exactly the case for $9 = 3^2$.

By running the debugger, we have now discovered three bugs in the program:

- isprime falsely claims 1 to be a prime.
- main doesn't handle 2.
- The test in isprime should be while (k * k <= n).

Here is the improved program:

ch04/goodprime.cpp

```
1   #include <iostream>
2
3   using namespace std;
4
5   /**
6       Tests if an integer is a prime.
7       @param n  any positive integer
8       @return true if n is a prime
9   */
10  bool isprime(int n)
11  {
12     if (n == 1) return false; // Fixed
13     if (n == 2) return true;
14     if (n % 2 == 0) return false;
15     int k = 3;
16     while (k * k <= n)   // Fixed
17     {
18        if (n % k == 0) return false;
19        k = k + 2;
20     }
21     return true;
22  }
23
24  int main()
25  {
26     int n;
27     cout << "Please enter the upper limit: ";
28     cin >> n;
29     int i;
30     if (n >= 2) cout << "2\n";   // Fixed
31     for (i = 3; i <= n; i = i + 2)
32     {
33        if (isprime(i))
34           cout << i << "\n";
35     }
36     return 0;
37  }
```

Program Run

```
Please enter the upper limit: 10
2
3
5
7
```

The debugger can be used to analyze the presence of bugs, but not to show that a program is bug-free.

Is the program now free from bugs? That is not a question the debugger can answer. Remember: Testing can show only the presence of bugs, not their absence.

4.15.3 Stepping Through a Program

You have learned how to run a program until it reaches a particular line. Variations of this strategy are often useful.

There are two methods of running the program in the debugger. You can tell it to run to a particular line; then it gets speedily to that line, but you don't know how it got there. You can also *single-step* with the "run to next line" command. Then you know how the program flows, but it can take a long time to step through it.

Actually, there are two kinds of single-stepping commands, often called "step over" and "step into". The "step over" command always goes to the next program line. The "step into" command steps into function calls. For example, suppose the current line is

```
r = future_value(balance, p, n);
cout << setw(10) << r;
```

When you "step over" function calls, you get to the next line:

```
r = future_value(balance, p, n);
cout << setw(10) << r;
```

However, if you "step into" function calls, you enter the first line of the future_value function.

```
double future_value(double initial_balance,
    double p, int n)
{
    double b = initial_balance * pow(1 + p / 100), n);
    return b;
}
```

You should step into a function to check whether it carries out its job correctly. You should step over a function if you know it works correctly.

If you single-step past the last line of a function, either with the "step over" or the "step into" command, you return to the line in which the function was called.

You should not step into system functions like setw. It is easy to get lost in them, and there is no benefit in stepping through system code. If you do get lost, there are three ways out. You can just choose "step over" until you are finally again in familiar territory. Many debuggers have a command "run until function return" that executes to the end of the current function, and then you can select "step over" to get out of the function.

The techniques you've seen so far let you trace through the code in various increments. All debuggers support a second navigational approach: You can set so-called *breakpoints* in the code. Breakpoints are set at specific code lines, with a command "add breakpoint here"; again, the exact command depends on the debugger. You can set as many breakpoints as you like. When the program reaches any one of them, execution stops and the breakpoint that causes the stop is displayed.

Breakpoints are particularly useful when you know at which point your program starts doing the wrong thing. You can set a breakpoint, have the program run at full speed to the breakpoint, and then start tracing slowly to observe the program's behavior.

Some debuggers let you set *conditional breakpoints*. A conditional breakpoint stops the program only when a certain condition is met. You could stop at a particular line only if a variable n has reached 0, or if that line has been executed for the twentieth time. Conditional breakpoints are an advanced feature that can be indispensable in knotty debugging problems.

4.15.4 Inspecting Objects

You have learned how to inspect variables in the debugger with the "inspect" command. The "inspect" command works well to show numeric values. When inspecting an object variable, all fields are displayed (see Figure 16). With some debuggers, you must "open up" the object, usually by clicking on an icon in the variable display.

To inspect a string object, you need to select the variable that contains the actual character sequence in memory. That variable is called _Ptr, _str, _M_p or a similarly obscure name, depending on the library implementation. With some debuggers, you may need to select that variable to view its contents. The debugger may also show other values, such as npos or allocator, which you should ignore.

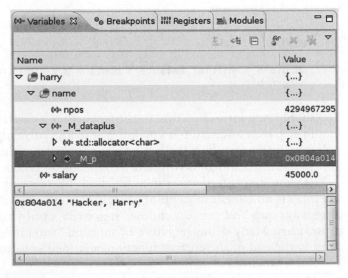

Figure 16 Inspecting an Object

4.15.5 Debugging Strategies

Now you know about the mechanics of debugging, but all that knowledge may still leave you helpless when you fire up the debugger to look at a sick program. There are a number of strategies that you can use to recognize bugs and their causes.

> For effective debugging, you need to be able to reproduce the buggy behavior.

As you test your program, you notice that your program sometimes does something wrong. It gives the wrong output, it seems to print something completely random, it runs in an infinite loop, or it crashes. Find out exactly how to *reproduce the behavior*. What inputs did you provide? If you run the program again with the same inputs, does it exhibit the same behavior? If so, then you are ready to fire up the debugger to study this particular problem. Debuggers are good for analyzing particular failures. They aren't terribly useful for studying a program in general.

> Use the "divide-and-conquer" technique to locate the point of failure of a program.

Once you have a particular failure, you want to get as close to it as possible. Use a technique of *divide and conquer*. Step over the functions in main, but don't step inside them. Eventually, the failure will happen again.

Now you know which function contains the bug: It is the last function that was called from main before the error manifested itself. Restart the debugger and go back to that line in main, then step inside that function. Repeat the process. Eventually, you will have pinpointed the line that contains the error.

> You must know what a program should do in order to debug it.

Always keep in mind that the debugger shows you what the program *does* do. You must know what the program *should* do, or you will not be able to find bugs. Before you trace through a loop, ask yourself how many iterations you *expect* the program to make. Before you inspect a variable, ask yourself what you expect to see. If you have no clue, set aside some time and think first. Have a calculator handy to make independent computations. When you know what the value should be, inspect the variable. This is the moment of truth. If the program is still on the right track, then that value is what you expected, and you must look further for the bug. If the value is different, you may be on to something.

> When fixing an error, understand the cause and the fix.

Once you find that a loop makes too many iterations, or a variable has the wrong content, it is very tempting to apply a "Band-Aid" solution. Such a quick fix has an overwhelming probability of creating trouble elsewhere. You really need to have a thorough understanding of how the program should be written before you apply a fix.

It does occasionally happen that you find bug after bug and apply fix after fix, and the problem just moves around. That usually is a symptom of a larger problem with the program logic. There is little you can do with the debugger. You must rethink the program design and reorganize it.

CHAPTER SUMMARY

1. A function receives input parameters and computes a result that depends on those inputs.

2. Parameter values are supplied in the function call. The return value is the result that the function computes.

3. When defining a function, you provide a name and type for each parameter and a type for the result.

4. Turn computations that can be reused into functions.

5. Function comments explain the purpose of the function and the meaning of the parameters and return value, as well as any special requirements.

6. The return statement terminates a function call and yields the function result.

7. A predicate function returns a Boolean value.

8. Parameter variables hold the parameter values supplied in the function call.

9. A side effect is an externally observable effect caused by a function call, other than the returning of a result.

10. A procedure is a sequence of actions that depends on parameters and does not yield a result.

11. Use a return type of void to indicate that a function does not return a value.

12. A reference parameter denotes a reference to a variable that is supplied in a function call.

13. The scope of a variable is the part of the program in which it is visible.

14. A local variable is defined inside a function. A global variable is defined outside a function.

15. Use the process of stepwise refinement to decompose complex tasks into simpler ones.

16. Pseudocode is a mixture of English and source code that is used in the early stages of implementing complex code.

17. A walkthrough is a manual simulation of program code.

18. Preconditions are documented restrictions on the function parameters.

19. A black-box test does not consider the internal structure of a program; a white-box test does.

20. A unit test checks a function in isolation.

21. A unit test framework allows you to organize your unit tests.

22. A boundary case is a test case that is at the boundary of valid inputs.

23. To ensure good test coverage, select test cases that cover each branch of the function.

24. In regression testing, you test new versions of a program against past failures.

25. With a debugger, you can control the execution of a program and observe the contents of program variables.

26. You can make effective use of the debugger by mastering just three commands: "run until this line", "step to next line", and "inspect variable".

27. The debugger can be used to analyze the presence of bugs, but not to show that a program is bug-free.

28. For effective debugging, you need to be able to reproduce the buggy behavior.

29. Use the "divide-and-conquer" technique to locate the point of failure of a program.

30. You must know what a program should do in order to debug it.

31. When fixing an error, understand the cause and the fix.

FURTHER READING

1. Bertrand Meyer, *Object-Oriented Software Construction*, Prentice-Hall, 1989, Chapter 7.
2. `cppunit.sourceforge.net/` The CppUnit testing framework.
3. `boost.org/libs/test/doc/index.html` The Boost.Test framework.

REVIEW EXERCISES

Exercise R4.1. Give realistic examples of the following:

   a. A function with a `double` parameter and a `double` return value
   b. A function with an `int` parameter and a `double` return value
   c. A function with an `int` parameter and a `string` return value
   d. A function with two `double` parameters and a `bool` return value
   e. A procedure with two `int&` parameters and no return value
   f. A function with no parameter and an `int` return value

G   g. A function with a `Circle` parameter and a `double` return value

G   h. A function with a `Line` parameter and a `Point` return value

Just describe what these functions do. Do not program them. For example, an answer to the first question is "sine" or "square root".

Exercise R4.2. True or false?

a. A function has exactly one return statement.

b. A function has at least one return statement.

c. A function has at most one return value.

d. A procedure (with return value void) never has a return statement.

e. When executing a return statement, the function exits immediately.

f. A function without parameters always has a side effect.

g. A procedure (with return value void) always has a side effect.

h. A function without side effects always returns the same value when called with the same parameter values.

Exercise R4.3. Write detailed function comments for the following functions. Be sure to describe all conditions under which the function cannot compute its result. Just write the comments, not the functions.

a. `double sqrt(double x)`

b. `string roman_numeral(int n)`

c. `bool is_leap_year(year y)`

d. `string weekday(int w)`

G   e. `Point midpoint(Point a, Point b)`

G   f. `double area(Circle c)`

G   g. `double slope(Line a)`

Exercise R4.4. Consider these functions:

```
double f(double x) { return g(x) + sqrt(h(x)); }
double g(double x) { return 4 * h(x); }
double h(double x) { return x * x + k(x) - 1; }
double k(double x) { return 2 * (x + 1); }
```

Without actually compiling and running a program, determine the results of the following function calls.

a. `double x1 = f(2);`

b. `double x2 = g(h(2));`

c. `double x3 = k(g(2) + h(2));`

d. `double x4 = f(0) + f(1) + f(2);`

e. `double x5 = f(-1) + g(-1) + h(-1) + k(-1);`

Exercise R4.5. What is a predicate function? Give a definition, an example of a predicate function, and an example of how to use it.

Exercise R4.6. What is the difference between a parameter value and a return value? What is the difference between a parameter value and a parameter variable? What is the difference between a parameter value and a value parameter?

Exercise R4.7. Ideally, a function should have no side effect. Can you write a program in which no function has a side effect? Would such a program be useful?

Exercise R4.8. For the following functions and procedures, circle the parameters that must be implemented as reference parameters.

   a. `y = sin(x);`

   b. `print_paycheck(harry);`

   c. `raise_salary(harry, 5.5);`

   d. `make_uppercase(message);`

   e. `key = uppercase(input);`

   f. `change_name(harry, "Horton");`

Exercise R4.9. For each of the variables in the following program, indicate the scope. Then determine what the program prints, without actually running the program.

```
int a = 0;
int b = 0;
int f(int c)
{
   int n = 0;
   a = c;
   if (n < c)
      n = a + b;
   return n;
}

int g(int c)
{
   int n = 0;
   int a = c;
   if (n < f(c))
      n = a + b;
   return n;
}

int main()
{
   int i = 1;
   int b = g(i);
   cout << a + b + i << "\n";
   return 0;
}
```

Exercise R4.10. We have seen three kinds of variables in C++: global variables, parameter variables, and local variables. Classify the variables of the preceding exercise according to these categories.

Exercise R4.11. Use the process of stepwise refinement to describe the process of making scrambled eggs. Discuss what you do if you do not find eggs in the refrigerator. Produce a call tree.

Exercise R4.12. How many parameters does the following function have? How many return values does it have? *Hint:* The C++ notions of "parameter" and "return value" are not the same as the intuitive notions of "input" and "output".

```cpp
void average(double& avg)
{
   cout << "Please enter two numbers: ";
   double x;
   double y;
   cin >> x >> y;
   avg = (x + y) / 2;
}
```

Exercise R4.13. What is the difference between a function and a procedure? A function and a program? The main procedure and a program?

Exercise R4.14. Perform a walkthrough of the int_name function with the following inputs:

a. 5

b. 12

c. 21

d. 321

e. 1024

f. 11954

g. 0

h. –2

Exercise R4.15. What preconditions do the following functions from the standard C++ library have?

a. sqrt

b. tan

c. log

d. exp

e. pow

f. fabs

Exercise R4.16. When a function is called with parameters that violate its precondition, it can terminate or fail safely. Give two examples of library functions (standard C++ or the library functions used in this book) that fail safely when called with invalid parameter values, and give two examples of library functions that terminate.

Exercise R4.17. Consider the following function:

```cpp
int f(int n)
{
   if (n <= 1) return 1;
   if (n % 2 == 0) // n is even
      return f(n / 2);
   else return f(3 * n + 1);
}
```

Perform walkthroughs of the computation f(1), f(2), f(3), f(4), f(5), f(6), f(7), f(8), f(9), and f(10). Can you conjecture what value this function computes for arbitrary n? Can you *prove* that the function always terminates? If so, please let the author know. At the time of this writing, this is an unsolved problem in mathematics, sometimes called the "$3n + 1$ problem" or the "Collatz problem".

Exercise R4.18. Consider the following procedure that is intended to swap the values of two integers:

```
void false_swap1(int& a, int& b)
{
   a = b;
   b = a;
}

int main()
{
   int x = 3;
   int y = 4;
   false_swap1(x, y);
   cout << x << " " << y << "\n";
   return 0;
}
```

Why doesn't the procedure swap the contents of x and y? How can you rewrite the procedure to work correctly?

Exercise R4.19. Consider the following procedure that is intended to swap the values of two integers:

```
void false_swap2(int a, int b)
{
   int temp = a;
   a = b;
   b = temp;
}

int main()
{
   int x = 3;
   int y = 4;
   false_swap2(x, y);
   cout << x << " " << y << "\n";
   return 0;
}
```

Why doesn't the procedure swap the contents of x and y? How can you rewrite the procedure to work correctly?

Exercise R4.20. Prove that the following procedure swaps two integers, without requiring a temporary variable, provided that a and b refer to different objects?

```
void tricky_swap(int& a, int& b)
{
   a = a - b;
   b = a + b;
   a = b - a;
}
```

What happens when the parameters refer to the same object?

Exercise R4.21. Define the terms *unit test* and *test harness*.

Exercise R4.22. If you want to test a program that is made up of four different functions, one of which is main, how many test harnesses do you need?

Exercise R4.23. What is an oracle?

Exercise R4.24. Define the terms *regression testing* and *test suite*.

Exercise R4.25. What is the debugging phenomenon known as "cycling"? What can you do to avoid it?

Exercise R4.26. Explain the differences between these debugger operations:

- Stepping into a function
- Stepping over a function

Exercise R4.27. Explain the differences between these debugger operations:

- Running until the current line
- Setting a breakpoint to the current line

Exercise R4.28. Explain in detail how to inspect the string stored in a string object in your debugger.

PROGRAMMING EXERCISES

Exercise P4.1. Enhance the program computing bank balances in Section 4.2 by prompting for the initial balance and the interest rate. Then print the balance after 10, 20, and 30 years.

Exercise P4.2. Write a procedure void sort2(int& a, int& b) that swaps the values of a and b if a is greater than b and otherwise leaves a and b unchanged. For example,

```
int u = 2;
int v = 3;
int w = 4;
int x = 1;
sort2(u, v); // u is still 2, v is still 3
sort2(w, x); // w is now 1, x is now 4
```

Exercise P4.3. Write a procedure sort3(int& a, int& b, int& c) that swaps its three inputs to arrange them in sorted order. For example,

```
int v = 3;
int w = 4;
int x = 1;
sort3(v, w, x); // v is now 1, w is now 3, x is now 4
```

Hint: Use sort2 of Exercise P4.2.

Exercise P4.4. Enhance the int_name function so that it works correctly for values ≤ 10,000,000.

Exercise P4.5. Enhance the int_name function so that it works correctly for negative values and zero. *Caution:* Make sure the improved function doesn't print 20 as "twenty zero".

Exercise P4.6. For some values (for example, 20), the int_name function returns a string with a leading space (" twenty"). Repair that blemish and ensure that spaces are inserted only when necessary. *Hint:* There are two ways of accomplishing this. Either ensure that leading spaces are never inserted, or remove leading spaces from the result before returning it.

Exercise P4.7. Write functions

```
double sphere_volume(double r);
double sphere_surface(double r);
double cylinder_volume(double r, double h);
double cylinder_surface(double r, double h);
double cone_volume(double r, double h);
double cone_surface(double r, double h);
```

that compute the volume and surface area of a sphere with radius r, a cylinder with a circular base with radius r and height h, and a cone with a circular base with radius r and height h. Then write a program that prompts the user for the values of r and h, calls the six functions, and prints the results.

Exercise P4.8. Write a function

```
double get_double(string prompt)
```

that displays the prompt string, followed by a space, reads a floating-point number in, and returns it. (In other words, write a console version of cwin.get_double.) Here is a typical usage:

```
salary = get_double("Please enter your salary:");
perc_raise =
   get_double("What percentage raise would you like?");
```

If there is an input error, abort the program by calling exit(1). (You will see in Chapter 5 how to improve this behavior.)

Exercise P4.9. *Leap years.* Write a predicate function

```
bool leap_year(int year)
```

that tests whether a year is a leap year: that is, a year with 366 days. Leap years are necessary to keep the calendar synchronized with the sun because the earth revolves around the sun once every 365.25 days. Actually, that figure is not entirely precise, and for all dates after 1582 the *Gregorian correction* applies. Usually years that are divisible by 4 are leap years, for example 1996. However, years that are divisible by 100 (for example, 1900) are not leap years, but years that are divisible by 400 are leap years (for example, 2000).

Exercise P4.10. *Julian dates.* Suppose you would like to know how many days ago Columbus was born. It is tedious to figure this out by hand, because months have different lengths and because you have to worry about leap years. Many people, such as astronomers, who deal with dates a lot have become tired of dealing with the craziness of the calendar and instead represent days in a completely different way: the so-called Julian day number. That value is defined as the number of days that have elapsed since Jan. 1, 4713 B.C. A convenient reference point is that October 9, 1995, is Julian day 2,450,000.

Here is an algorithm to compute the Julian day number: Set jd, jm, jy to the day, month, and year. If the year is negative, add 1 to jy. (There was no year 0. Year 1 B.C. was immediately followed by year A.D. 1) If the month is larger than February, add 1 to jm. Otherwise, add 13 to jm and subtract 1 from jy. Then compute

```
long jul = floor(365.25 * jy) + floor(30.6001 * jm) + jd
  + 1720995.0
```

We store the result in a variable of type long; simple integers may not have enough digits to hold the value. If the date was before October 15, 1582, return this value. Otherwise, perform the following correction:

```
int ja = 0.01 * jy;
jul = jul + 2 - ja + 0.25 * ja;
```

Now write a function

```
long julian(int year, int month, int day)
```

that converts a date into a Julian day number. Use that function in a program that prompts the user for a date in the past, then prints out how many days that is away from today's date.

Exercise P4.11. Write a procedure

```
void jul_to_date(long jul, int& year, int& month, int& day)
```

that performs the opposite conversion, from Julian day numbers to dates. Here is the algorithm. Starting with October 15, 1582 (Julian day number 2,299,161), apply the correction

```
long jalpha = ((jul - 1867216) - 0.25) / 36524.25;
jul = jul + 1 + jalpha - (int)(0.25 * jalpha);
```

Then compute

```
long jb = jul + 1524;
long jc = 6680.0 + (jb - 2439870 - 122.1)/365.25;
long jd = 365 * jc + (0.25 * jc);
int je = (jb - jd)/30.6001;
```

The day, month, and year are computed as

```
day = jb - jd - (long)(30.6001 * je);
month = je - 1;
year = (int)(jc - 4715);
```

If the month is greater than 12, subtract 12. If the month is greater than 2, subtract one from the year. If the year is not positive, subtract 1.

Use the function to write the following program. Ask the user for a date and a number n. Then print the date that is n days away from the input date. You can use that program to find out the exact day that was 100,000 days ago. The computation is simple. First convert the input date to the Julian day number, using the function of the preceding exercise, then subtract n, and then convert back using jul_to_date.

Exercise P4.12. In Exercise P3.6 you were asked to write a program to convert a number to its representation in Roman numerals. At the time, you did not know how to factor out common code, and as a consequence the resulting program was rather long. Rewrite that program by implementing and using the following function:

```
string roman_digit(int n, string one, string five,
    string ten)
```

That function translates one digit, using the strings specified for the one, five, and ten values. You would call the function as follows:

```
roman_ones = roman_digit(n % 10, "I", "V", "X");
n = n / 10;
roman_tens = roman_digit(n % 10, "X", "L", "C");
...
```

Exercise P4.13. Write a program that converts a Roman number such as MCMLXX-VIII to its decimal number representation. *Hint:* First write a function that yields the numeric value of each of the letters. Then convert a string as follows: Look at the first *two* characters. If the first has a larger value than the second, then simply convert the first, call the conversion function again for the substring starting with the second character, and add both values. If the first one has a smaller value than the second, compute the difference and add to it the conversion of the tail. This algorithm will convert "Pig Roman" numbers like "IC". Extra credit if you can modify it to process only genuine Roman numbers.

Exercise P4.14. Write a program that prints instructions to get coffee, asking the user for input whenever a decision needs to be made. Decompose each task into a procedure, for example:

```
void brew_coffee()
{
    cout << "Add water to the coffee maker.\n";
    cout << "Put a filter in the coffee maker.\n";
    grind_coffee();
    cout << "Put the coffee in the filter.\n";
    ...
}
```

Exercise P4.15. Consider the following buggy function:

```
Employee read_employee()
{
    cout << "Please enter the name: ";
    string name;
    getline(cin, name);
    cout << "Please enter the salary: ";
    double salary;
    cin >> salary;
    Employee r(name, salary);
    return r;
```

}

When you call this function once, it works fine. When you call it again in the same program, it won't return the second employee record correctly. Write a test harness that verifies the problem. Then step through the function. Inspect the contents of the string name and the Employee object r after the second call. What values do you get?

Exercise P4.16. *Postal bar codes.* For faster sorting of letters, the United States Postal Service encourages companies that send large volumes of mail to use a bar code denoting the zip code (see Figure 17).

The encoding scheme for a five-digit zip code is shown in Figure 18. There are full-height frame bars on each side. The five encoded digits are followed by a check digit, which is computed as follows: Add up all digits, and choose the check digit to make the sum a multiple of 10. For example, the zip code 95014 has a sum of 19, so the check digit is 1 to make the sum equal to 20.

Each digit of the zip code, and the check digit, is encoded according to the following table where 0 denotes a half bar and 1 a full bar.

	7	4	2	1	0
1	0	0	0	1	1
2	0	0	1	0	1
3	0	0	1	1	0
4	0	1	0	0	1
5	0	1	0	1	0
6	0	1	1	0	0
7	1	0	0	0	1
8	1	0	0	1	0
9	1	0	1	0	0
0	1	1	0	0	0

Note that they represent all combinations of two full and three half bars. The digit can be easily computed from the bar code using the column weights 7, 4, 2, 1, 0. For example, 01100 is $0 \times 7 + 1 \times 4 + 1 \times 2 + 0 \times 1 \times 0 \times 0 = 6$. The only exception is 0, which would yield 11 according to the weight formula.

Write a program that asks the user for a zip code and prints the bar code. Use : for half bars, | for full bars. For example, 95014 becomes

||:|:::|:|:||:::::::||:|::|:::|||

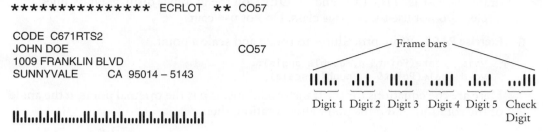

★ ★ ★ ★ ★ ★ ★ ★ ★ ★ ★ ★ ★ ★ ★ ECRLOT ★★ CO57

CODE C671RTS2
JOHN DOE   CO57
1009 FRANKLIN BLVD
SUNNYVALE   CA 95014 – 5143

IIılııılılıllIıııılIlılılılıııllılılılıllIlıltl

Figure 17 A Postal Bar Code

Digit 1 Digit 2 Digit 3 Digit 4 Digit 5 Check
                                                    Digit

Figure 18 Encoding for Five-Digit Bar Codes

Exercise P4.17. Write a program that reads in a bar code (with : denoting half bars and | denoting full bars) and prints out the zip code it represents. Print an error message if the bar code is not correct.

G **Exercise P4.18.** Write a program that displays the bar code, using actual bars, on your graphics screen. *Hint:* Write functions half_bar(Point start) and full_bar(Point start).

G **Exercise P4.19.** Write functions

```
double perimeter(Circle c);
double area(Circle c);
```

that compute the area and the perimeter of the circle c. Use these functions in a graphics program that prompts the user to specify a circle. Then display messages with the perimeter and area of the circle.

G **Exercise P4.20.** Write a function

```
double distance(Point p, Point q)
```

that computes the distance between two points. Write a test program that asks the user to select two points. Then display the distance.

G **Exercise P4.21.** Write a function

```
bool is_inside(Point p, Circle c)
```

that tests if a point is inside a circle. (You need to compute the distance between p and the center of the circle, and compare it to the radius.) Write a test program that asks the user to click on the center of the circle, then asks for the radius, then asks the user to click on any point on the screen. Display a message that indicates whether the user clicked inside the circle.

G **Exercise P4.22.** Write functions

```
display_H(Point p);
display_E(Point p);
display_L(Point p);
display_O(Point p);
```

that show the letters H, E, L, O on the graphics window, where the point p is the top left corner of the letter. Fit the letter in a 1 × 1 square. Then call the functions to draw the words "HELLO" and "HOLE" on the graphics display. Draw lines and circles. Do not use the Message class. Do not use cout.

G   **Exercise P4.23.** Write procedures to rotate and scale a point.

```
void rotate(Point& p, double angle);
void scale(Point& p, double scale);
```

Here are the equations for the transformations. If p is the original point, α the angle of the rotation, and q the point after rotation, then

$$q_x = p_x \cos\alpha + p_y \sin\alpha$$

$$q_y = -p_x \sin\alpha + p_y \cos\alpha$$

If p is the original point, s the scale factor, and q the point after scaling, then

$$q_x = sp_x$$

$$q_y = sp_y$$

However, note that your functions need to *replace* the point with its rotated or scaled image.

Now write the following graphics program. Start out with the point (5,5). *Rotate* it five times by 10 degrees, then scale it five times by 0.95. Then start with the point (–5,–5). Repeat the following five times.

```
rotate(b, 10 * PI / 180);
scale(b, 0.95);
```

That is, interleave the rotation and scaling five times.

Classes

CHAPTER GOALS

- To be able to implement your own classes
- To master the separation of interface and implementation
- To understand the concept of encapsulation
- To design and implement accessor and mutator member functions
- To understand object construction
- To learn how to distribute a program over multiple source files

At this point, you are familiar with using objects from existing classes, such as strings, streams, and the classes that were designed for this book. You have seen how to construct objects, and you have applied member functions with the dot notation.

In this chapter you will learn how to implement your own classes. You will see how to design classes that help you solve programming problems, and you will study the mechanics of defining classes, constructors, and member functions.

CHAPTER CONTENTS

5.1 Discovering Classes

A class represents a concept. Instead of groups of related variables, try designing a class for the underlying concept.

If you find yourself defining a number of related variables that all refer to the same concept, stop coding and think about that concept for a while. Then define a class that abstracts the concept and contains these variables as data fields.

Suppose you read in information about computers. Each record contains the model name, the price, and a score between 0 and 100. You are trying to find the "best bang for the buck": the product for which the value (score/price) is highest. The following program finds this information for you.

ch05/bestval.cpp

```
1   #include <iostream>
2   #include <string>
3
4   using namespace std;
5
6   int main()
7   {
8       string best_name = "";          ❶
9       double best_price = 1;
10      int best_score = 0;
```

```
11      bool more = true;
12      while (more)
13      {
14         string next_name;   ❷
15         double next_price;
16         int next_score;
17
18
19         cout << "Please enter the model name: ";
20         getline(cin, next_name);
21         cout << "Please enter the price: ";
22         cin >> next_price;
23         cout << "Please enter the score: ";
24         cin >> next_score;
25         string remainder; // Read remainder of line
26         getline(cin, remainder);
27
28         if (next_score / next_price > best_score / best_price)
29         {
30            best_name = next_name;
31            best_score = next_score;
32            best_price = next_price;
33         }
34
35         cout << "More data? (y/n) ";
36         string answer;
37         getline(cin, answer);
38         if (answer != "y") more = false;
39      }
40
41      cout << "The best value is " << best_name
42         << " Price: " << best_price
43         << " Score: " << best_score << "\n";
44
45      return 0;
46   }
```

Program Run

```
Please enter the model name: ACMA P600
Please enter the price: 995
Please enter the score: 75
More data? (y/n) y
Please enter the model name: Blackship NX-600
Please enter the price: 695
Please enter the score: 60
More data? (y/n) y
Please enter the model name: Kompac 690
Please enter the price: 598
Please enter the score: 60
More data? (y/n) n
The best value is Kompac 690 Price: 598 Score: 60
```

Pay special attention to the two sets of variables: best_name, best_price, best_score
1 and next_name, next_price, next_score **2**. The very fact that you have two sets
of these variables suggests that a common concept is lurking just under the surface.

Each of these two sets of variables describes a *product*. One of them describes the
best product, the other one the next product to be read in. In the following sections
we will develop a Product class to simplify this program. We will then define two
objects, best and next, of the Product class.

COMMON ERROR 5.1

Mixing >> and getline Input

It is tricky to mix >> and getline input. Consider how a product is being read in by the
bestval.cpp program:

```
cout << "Please enter the model name: ";
getline(cin, next_name);
cout << "Please enter the price: ";
cin >> next_price;
cout << "Please enter the score: ";
cin >> next_score;
```

The getline function reads an entire line of input, including the newline character at the end
of the line. It places all characters except for that newline character into the string next_name.
The >> operator reads all white space (that is, spaces, tabs, and newlines) until it reaches a
number. Then it reads only the characters in that number. It does not consume the character
following the number, typically a newline. This is a problem when a call to getline immediately follows a call to >>. Then the call to getline reads only the newline, considering it as
the end of an empty line.

Perhaps an example will make this clearer. Consider the first input lines of the product
descriptions. Calling getline consumes the colored characters.

$$cin = \boxed{A\ C\ M\ A\ \ \ P\ 6\ 0\ 0\ \backslash n}\ 9\ 9\ 5\ \backslash n\ 7\ 5\ \backslash n\ y\ \backslash n$$

After the call to getline, the first line has been read completely, including the newline at the
end. Next, the call to cin >> next_price reads the digits.

$$cin = \boxed{9\ 9\ 5}\ \backslash n\ 7\ 5\ \backslash n\ y\ \backslash n$$

After the call to cin >> next_price, the digits of the number have been read, but the newline
is still unread. This is not a problem for the next call to cin >> next_score. That call first
skips all leading white space, including the newline, then reads the next number.

$$cin = \backslash n\ \boxed{7\ 5}\ \backslash n\ y\ \backslash n$$

It again leaves the newline in the input stream, because the >> operators never read any more
characters than absolutely necessary. Now we have a problem. The next call to getline reads
a blank line.

$$cin = \boxed{\backslash n}\ y\ \backslash n$$

That call happens in the following context:

```
cout << "More data? (y/n) ";
string answer;
getline(cin, answer);
if (answer != "y") more = false;
```

It reads only the newline and sets answer to the empty string!

$$cin = \boxed{y \; \backslash n}$$

The empty string is not the string "y", so more is set to `false`, and the loop terminates.

This is a problem whenever an input with the >> operator is followed by a call to `getline`. The intention, of course, is to skip the rest of the current line and have `getline` read the next line. This purpose is achieved by the following statements, which must be inserted after the last call to the >> operator:

```
string remainder; // Read remainder of line
getline(cin, remainder);
// Now you are ready to call getline again
```

5.2 Interfaces

> Every class has a public interface: a collection of member functions through which the objects of the class can be manipulated.

To define a class, we first need to specify its public *interface*. The interface of the Product class consists of all functions that we want to apply to product objects. Looking at the program of the preceding section, we need to be able to perform the following:

- Make a new product object
- Read in a product object
- Compare two products and find out which one is better
- Print a product

The interface of a class is specified in the *class definition* (see Syntax 5.1 on page 234). Here is a partial definition of the Product class that describes the public interface:

```
class Product
{
public:
   Product();

   void read();

   bool is_better_than(Product b) const;
   void print() const;

private:
   implementation details—see Section 5.3
};
```

A constructor is used to initialize objects when they are created. A constructor with no parameters is called a default constructor.

The interface is made up of three parts. First we list the *constructors:* the functions that are used to initialize new objects. Constructors always have the same name as the class. The Product class has one constructor, with no parameters. Such a constructor is called a *default constructor.* It is used when you define an object without construction parameters, like this:

```
Product best; // Uses default constructor Product()
```

As a general rule, every class should have a default constructor. All classes used in this book do.

A mutator member function changes the state of the object on which it operates.

Then we list the *mutator functions*. A mutator is an operation that modifies the object. The Product class has a single mutator: read. After you call

```
p.read();
```

the contents of p have changed.

An accessor member function does not modify the object. Accessors must be tagged with const.

Finally, we list the *accessor functions*. Accessors just query the object for some information without changing it. The Product class has two accessors: is_better_than and print. Applying one of these functions to a product object does not modify the object. In C++, accessor operations are tagged as const. Note the position of the const keyword: after the closing parenthesis of the parameter list, but before the semicolon that terminates the function declaration. See Common Error 5.3 on page 240 for the importance of the const keyword.

Now we know *what* a Product object can do, but not *how* it does it. Of course, to use objects in our programs, we only need to use the interface. To enable any function to access the interface functions, they are placed in the public section of the class definition. As we will see in the next section, the variables used in the implementation will be placed in the private section. That makes them inaccessible to the users of the objects.

Figure 1 shows the interface of the Product class. The mutator functions are shown with arrows pointing inside the private data to indicate that they modify the data. The accessor functions are shown with arrows pointing the other way to indicate that they just read the data.

Now that you have this interface, put it to work to simplify the program of the preceding section.

Figure 1   The Interface of the Product Class

ch05/product1.cpp

```
 1  /*
 2      This program compiles but doesn't run.
 3      See product2.cpp for the complete program.
 4  */
 5
 6  #include <iostream>
 7  #include <string>
 8
 9  using namespace std;
10
11  class Product
12  {
13  public:
14      Product();
15
16      void read();
17
18      bool is_better_than(Product b) const;
19      void print() const;
20  private:
21  };
22
23  int main()
24  {
25      Product best;
26
27      bool more = true;
28      while (more)
29      {
30          Product next;
31          next.read();
32          if (next.is_better_than(best))
33              best = next;
34
35          cout << "More data? (y/n) ";
36          string answer;
37          getline(cin, answer);
38          if (answer != "y")
39              more = false;
40      }
41
42      cout << "The best value is ";
43      best.print();
44
45      return 0;
46  }
```

Wouldn't you agree that this program is much easier to read than the first version? Making Product into a class really pays off.

However, this program will not yet run. The interface definition of the class just *declares* the constructors and member functions. The actual code for these functions must be supplied separately. You will see how starting in Section 5.4.

SYNTAX 5.1 Class Definition

```
class ClassName
{
public:
   constructor declarations
   member function declarations
private:
   data fields
};
```

Example:

```
class Point
{
public:
   Point (double xval, double yval);
   void move(double dx, double dy);
   double get_x() const;
   double get_y() const;
private:
   double x;
   double y;
};
```

Purpose:

Define the interface and data fields of a class.

COMMON ERROR 5.2

Forgetting a Semicolon

Braces { } are common in C++ code, and usually you do not place a semicolon after the closing brace. However, class definitions always end in };. A common error is to forget that semicolon:

```
class Product
{
public:
   ...
private:
   ...
} // Forgot semicolon

int main()
{
   Product best; // Many compilers report the error in this line
   ...
}
```

This error can be extremely confusing to many compilers. There is syntax, now obsolete but supported for compatibility with old code, to define class types and variables of that type simultaneously. Because the compiler doesn't know that you don't use that obsolete construction, it tries to analyze the code wrongly and ultimately reports an error. Unfortunately, it may report the error *several lines away* from the line in which you forgot the semicolon.

If the compiler reports bizarre errors in lines that you are sure are correct, check that each of the preceding class definitions is terminated by a semicolon.

5.3 Encapsulation

Each object of a class stores certain values that are set in the constructor and that may change through the application of mutator functions. These values are collectively called the *state* of an object.

The state of a Product object consists of the name, price, and score of the product. These data items are defined as fields in the private section of the class definition.

```
class Product
{
public:
   Product();

   void read();

   bool is_better_than(Product b) const;
   void print() const;
private:
   string name;
   double price;
   int score;
};
```

Every product object has a name field, a price field, and a score field (see Figure 2). However, there is a catch. Because these fields are defined to be private, only the constructors and member functions of the class can access them.

> Every class has a private implementation: data fields that store the state of an object.

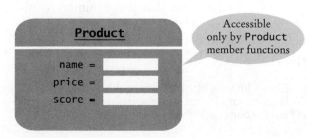

Figure 2   Encapsulation

You cannot access the data fields directly:

```
int main()
{
    ...
    cout << best.name; // Error—use print() instead
    ...
}
```

> Encapsulation is the act of hiding implementation details.

All data access must occur through the public interface. Thus, the data fields of an object are effectively hidden from the programmer. They are a part of the implementation details that are of no concern to the user of the class. The act of hiding implementation details is called *encapsulation*. While it is theoretically possible in C++ to leave data fields unencapsulated (by placing them into the public section), this is very uncommon in practice. We will always make all data fields private in this book.

The Product class is so simple that it is not obvious what benefit we gain from the encapsulation.

> Encapsulation protects the integrity of object data.

One benefit of the encapsulation mechanism is the guarantee that the object data cannot accidentally be put in an incorrect state. To understand that benefit better, consider the Time class:

```
class Time
{
public:
    Time();
    Time(int hrs, int min, int sec);

    void add_seconds(long s);

    int get_seconds() const;
    int get_minutes() const;
    int get_hours() const;
    long seconds_from() const;
private:
    ... // Hidden data representation
};
```

> By keeping the implementation private, we protect it from being accidentally corrupted.

Because the data fields are private, there are only three functions that can change these fields: the two constructors and the add_seconds mutator function. The four accessor functions cannot modify the fields, because the functions are declared as const.

Suppose that programmers could access data fields of the Time class directly. This would open the possibility of a type of bug, namely the creation of invalid times:

```
Time liftoff(19, 30, 0);

...
// Looks like the liftoff is getting delayed by another six hours
// Won't compile, but suppose it did
liftoff.hours = liftoff.hours + 6;
```

At first glance, there appears to be nothing wrong with this code. But if you look carefully, liftoff happens to be 19:30:00 before the hours are modified. Thus, it is 25:30:00 after the increment—an invalid time.

Fortunately, this error cannot happen with the Time class. The constructor that makes a time out of three integers checks that the construction parameters denote a valid time. If not, an error message is displayed and the program terminates. The Time() constructor sets a time object to the current time, which is always valid, and the add_seconds function knows about the length of a day and always produces a valid result. Since no other function can mess up the private data fields, we can *guarantee* that all times are always valid, thanks to the encapsulation mechanism.

> Encapsulation enables changes in the implementation without affecting users of a class.

There is a second benefit of encapsulation that is particularly important in larger programs. Typically, implementation details need to change over time. You want to be able to make your classes more efficient or more capable, without affecting the programmers that use your classes. As long as those programmers do not depend on the implementation details, you are free to change them at any time.

5.4 Member Functions

You must provide an implementation for every member function that is advertised in the class interface. Here is an example: the read function of the Product class.

```cpp
void Product::read()
{
    cout << "Please enter the model name: "
    getline(cin, name);
    cout << "Please enter the price: ";
    cin >> price;
    cout << "Please enter the score: ";
    cin >> score;
    string remainder; // Read the remainder of the line
    getline(cin, remainder);
}
```

The Product:: prefix makes it clear that we are defining the read function of the Product class. In C++ it is perfectly legal to have read functions in other classes as well, and it is important to specify exactly which read function we are defining. (See Syntax 5.2 on page 239.) You use the *ClassName*::read() syntax only when defining the function, not when calling it. When you call the read member function, the call has the form *object*.read().

> Use the const keyword when defining accessor member functions.

When defining an accessor member function, you must supply the keyword const following the closing parenthesis of the parameter list. For example, the call best.print() only inspects the object best without modifying it.

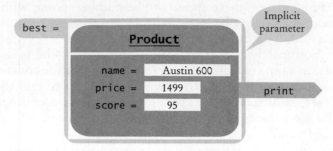

Figure 3   The Member Function Call `best.print()`

Hence `print` is an accessor function that should be tagged as `const`:

```
void Product::print() const
{
   cout << name
      << " Price: " << price
      << " Score: " << score << "\n";
}
```

Whenever you refer to a data field, such as `name` or `price`, in a member function, it denotes that data field *of the object for which the member function was called.* For example, when called with

```
best.print();
```

the `Product::print()` function prints `best.name`, `best.score`, and `best.price`. (See Figure 3.)

> The object on which a member function is applied is the implicit parameter. Every member function has an implicit parameter.

Note that the code for the member function makes no mention at all of the object to which a member function is applied. It is called the *implicit parameter* of the member function. You can visualize the code of the `print` function like this:

```
void Product::print() const
{
   cout << implicit_parameter.name
      << " Price: " << implicit_parameter.price
      << " Score: " << implicit_parameter.score << "\n";
}
```

> Explicit parameters of a member function are listed in the function definition.

In contrast, a parameter that is explicitly mentioned in the function definition, such as the `b` parameter of the `is_better_than` function, is called an *explicit parameter.* Every member function has exactly one implicit parameter and zero or more explicit parameters.

For example, the `is_better_than` function has one implicit parameter and one explicit parameter. In the call

```
if (next.is_better_than(best))
```

`next` is the implicit parameter and `best` is the explicit parameter (see Figure 4).

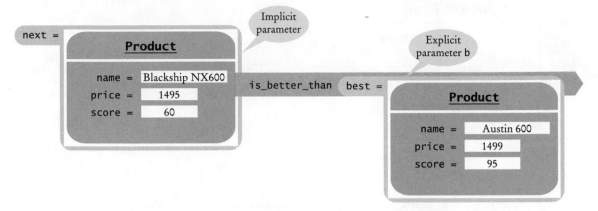

Figure 4 Implicit and Explicit Parameters of the Call next.is_better_than(best)

You may find it helpful to visualize the code of Product::is_better_than in this way:

```
bool Product::is_better_than(Product b) const
{
   if (implicit_parameter.price == 0) return true;
   if (b.price == 0) return false;
   return implicit_parameter.score / implicit_parameter.price
      > b.score / b.price;
}
```

SYNTAX 5.2 Member Function Definition

return_type ClassName::function_name(parameter₁, parameter₂, ...,
$\quad$ *parameterₙ)[const]ₒₚₜ*
{
$\quad$ *statements*
}

Example:

```
void Point::move(double dx, double dy)
{
   x = x + dx;
   y = y + dy;
}
double Point::get_x() const
{
   return x;
}
```

Purpose:

Supply the implementation of a member function.

COMMON ERROR 5.3

const Correctness

You should declare all accessor functions in C++ with the const keyword. (Recall that an accessor function is a member function that does not modify its implicit parameter.)

For example,

```
class Product
{
   ...
   void print() const;
   ...
};
```

If you fail to follow this rule, you build classes that other programmers cannot reuse. For example, suppose Product::print was not declared const, and another programmer used the Product class to build an Order class.

```
class Order
{
public:
   ...
   void print() const;
private:
   string customer;
   Product article;
   ...
};

void Order::print() const
{
   cout << customer << "\n";
   article.print(); // Error if Product::print not const
   ...
}
```

The compiler refuses to compile the expression article.print(). Why? Because article is an object of class Product, and Product::print is not tagged as const, the compiler suspects that the call article.print() may modify article. But article is a data field of Order, and Order::print promises not to modify any data fields of the order. The programmer of the Order class uses const correctly and must rely on all other programmers to do the same.

If you write a program with other team members who do use const correctly, it is very important that you do your part as well. You should therefore get into the habit of using the const keyword for all member functions that do not modify their implicit parameter.

5.5 Default Constructors

The purpose of a constructor is to initialize an object's data fields.

Every class should have one or more constructors. A constructor initializes the data fields of an object. By supplying constructors, you can ensure that all data fields are properly set before any member functions act on an object.

In this section, you will see how to define a default constructor—a constructor without parameters. The next section covers constructors with parameters.

A default constructor has no parameters.

As we already discussed, the name of a constructor is identical to the name of a class. Here is the definition of the default constructor for the `Product` class:

```
Product::Product()
{
   price = 1;
   score = 0;
}
```

Note the curious name of the constructor function: `Product::Product`. The `Product::` indicates that we are about to define a member function of the `Product` class. The second `Product` is the name of that member function.

Most default constructors set all data fields to a default value. The `Product` default constructor sets the score to 0 and the price to 1 (to avoid division by zero). The product name is automatically set to the empty string, as will be explained shortly. Not all default constructors act like that. For example, the `Time` default constructor sets the time object to the current time.

It is particularly important to initialize all numeric fields in a constructor because they are not automatically initialized.

In the code for the default constructor, you need to worry about initializing only *numeric* data fields. For example, in the `Product` class you must set `price` and `score` to a value, because numeric types are not classes and have no constructors. But the `name` field is automatically set to the empty string by the default constructor of the `string` class. In general, all data fields of class type are automatically constructed when an object is created, but the numeric fields must be set in the class constructors.

We now have all the pieces for the version of the product comparison program that uses the `Product` class. Here is the program:

ch05/product2.cpp

```
1   #include <iostream>
2   #include <string>
3
4   using namespace std;
5
6   class Product
7   {
8   public:
```

```
 9      /**
10          Constructs a product with score 0 and price 1.
11      */
12      Product();
13
14      /**
15          Reads in this product object.
16      */
17      void read();
18
19      /**
20          Compares two product objects.
21          @param b the object to compare with this object
22          @return true if this object is better than b
23      */
24      bool is_better_than(Product b) const;
25
26      /**
27          Prints this product object.
28      */
29      void print() const;
30   private:
31      string name;
32      double price;
33      int score;
34   };
35
36   Product::Product()
37   {
38      price = 1;
39      score = 0;
40   }
41
42   void Product::read()
43   {
44      cout << "Please enter the model name: ";
45      getline(cin, name);
46      cout << "Please enter the price: ";
47      cin >> price;
48      cout << "Please enter the score: ";
49      cin >> score;
50      string remainder; // Read remainder of line
51      getline(cin, remainder);
52   }
53
54   bool Product::is_better_than(Product b) const
55   {
56      if (price == 0) return true;
57      if (b.price == 0) return false;
58      return score / price > b.score / b.price;
59   }
60
61   void Product::print() const
62   {
```

```
63      cout << name
64          << " Price: " << price
65          << " Score: " << score;
66 }
67
68 int main()
69 {
70      Product best;
71
72      bool more = true;
73      while (more)
74      {
75          Product next;
76          next.read();
77          if (next.is_better_than(best))
78              best = next;
79
80          cout << "More data? (y/n) ";
81          string answer;
82          getline(cin, answer);
83          if (answer != "y")
84              more = false;
85      }
86
87      cout << "The best value is ";
88      best.print();
89
90      return 0;
91 }
```

RANDOM FACT 5.1

Programmer Productivity

If you talk to your friends in this programming class, you will find that some of them consistently complete their assignments much more quickly than others. Perhaps they have more experience. Even when comparing programmers with the same education and experience, however, wide variations in competence are routinely observed and measured. It is not uncommon to have the best programmer in a team be five to ten times as productive as the worst, using any of a number of reasonable measures of productivity [1].

That is a staggering range of performance among trained professionals. In a marathon race, the best runner will not run five to ten times faster than the slowest one. Software product managers are acutely aware of these disparities. The obvious solution is, of course, to hire only the best programmers, but even in recent periods of economic slowdown, the demand for good programmers has greatly outstripped the supply.

Fortunately for all of us, joining the ranks of the best is not necessarily a question of raw intellectual power. Good judgment, experience, broad knowledge, attention to detail, and superior planning are at least as important as mental brilliance. These skills can be acquired by individuals who are genuinely interested in improving themselves.

Even the most gifted programmer can deal with only a finite number of details in a given time period. Suppose a programmer can implement and debug one procedure every two hours, or one hundred procedures per month. (This is a generous estimate. Few programmers are this productive.) If a task requires 10,000 procedures (which is typical for a medium-sized program), then a single programmer would need 100 months to complete the job. Such a project is sometimes expressed as a "100-man-month" project. But as Brooks explains in his famous book [2], the concept of "man-month" is a myth. One cannot trade months for programmers. One hundred programmers cannot finish the task in one month. In fact, 10 programmers probably couldn't finish it in 10 months. First of all, the 10 programmers need to learn about the project before they can get productive. Whenever there is a problem with a particular procedure, both the author and its users need to meet and discuss it, taking time away from all of them. A bug in one procedure may have all of its users twiddling their thumbs until it is fixed.

It is difficult to estimate these inevitable delays. They are one reason why software is often released later than originally promised. What is a manager to do when the delays mount? As Brooks points out, adding more manpower will make a late project even later, because the productive people have to stop working and train the newcomers.

You will experience these problems when you work on your first team project with other students. Be prepared for a major drop in productivity, and be sure to set ample time aside for team communications.

There is, however, no alternative to teamwork. Most important and worthwhile projects transcend the ability of one single individual. Learning to function well in a team is as important for your education as it is to be a competent programmer.

5.6 Constructors with Parameters

It is common for a class to have multiple constructors. This allows you to define objects in different ways. Consider for example the Employee class that has two constructors:

```
class Employee
{
public:
   Employee();
   Employee(string employee_name, double initial_salary);

   void set_salary(double new_salary);

   string get_name() const;
   double get_salary() const;
private:
   string name;
   double salary;
};
```

Both constructors have the same name as the class, `Employee`. But the default constructor has no parameters, whereas the second constructor has a `string` and a `double` parameter. Whenever two functions have the same name but are distinguished by their parameter types, the function name is *overloaded*. (See Advanced Topic 5.2 on page 248 for more information on overloading in C++.)

> A function name is overloaded if there are different versions of the function, distinguished by their parameter types.

When you construct an object, the compiler chooses the constructor that matches the parameter values that you supply. For example,

```
Employee joe;
   // Uses default constructor
Employee lisa("Lisa Lee", 105000);
   // Uses Employee(string, double) constructor
```

Here is the implementation of the second constructor:

```
Employee::Employee(string employee_name, double initial_salary)
{
   name = employee_name;
   salary = initial_salary;
}
```

This is a straightforward situation; the constructor simply sets all data fields. Sometimes a constructor gets more complex because one of the data fields is itself an object of another class with its own constructor.

To see how to cope with this situation, suppose the `Employee` class stores the scheduled work hours of the employee:

```
class Employee
{
public:
   Employee(string employee_name, double initial_salary,
      int arrive_hour, int leave_hour);
   ...
private:
   string name;
   double salary;
   Time arrive;
   Time leave;
};
```

This constructor must set the `name`, `salary`, `arrive`, and `leave` fields. Since the last two fields are themselves objects of a class, they must be initialized with objects:

```
Employee::Employee(string employee_name, double initial_salary,
   int arrive_hour, int leave_hour)
{
   name = employee_name;
   salary = initial_salary;
   arrive = Time(arrive_hour, 0, 0);
   leave = Time(leave_hour, 0, 0);
}
```

The `Employee` class in the library of this book does not actually store the work hours. This is just an illustration to show how to construct a data field that is itself an object of a class.

SYNTAX 5.3 Constructor Definition

$ClassName::ClassName(parameter_1, parameter_2, ..., parameter_n)$
```
{
    statements
}
```

Example:
```
Point::Point(double xval, double yval)
{
    x = xval; y = yval;
}
```

Purpose:

Supply the implementation of a constructor.

COMMON ERROR 5.4

Forgetting to Initialize All Fields in a Constructor

Just as it is a common error to forget the initialization of a variable, it is easy to forget about data fields. Every constructor needs to ensure that all data fields are set to appropriate values.

Here is a variation on the Employee class. The constructor receives only the name of the employee. The class user is supposed to call set_salary explicitly to set the salary.

```
class Employee
{
public:
    Employee(string n);
    void set_salary(double s);
    double get_salary() const;
    ...
private:
    string name;
    double salary;
};

Employee::Employee(string n)
{
    name = n;
    // Oops—salary not initialized
}
```

If someone calls get_salary before set_salary has been called, a random salary will be returned. The remedy is simple: Just set salary to 0 in the constructor.

COMMON ERROR 5.5

Trying to Reset an Object by Calling a Constructor

The constructor is invoked only when an object is first created. You cannot call the constructor to reset an object:

```
Time homework_due(19, 0, 0);
...
homework_due.Time(); // Error
```

It is true that the default constructor sets a *new* time object to the current time, but you cannot invoke a constructor on an *existing* object.

The remedy is simple: Make a new time object and overwrite the current object stored in the variable.

```
homework_due = Time(); // OK
```

ADVANCED TOPIC 5.1

Calling Constructors from Constructors

Consider again the variation of the Employee class with work hour fields of type Time. There is an unfortunate inefficiency in the constructor:

```
Employee::Employee(string employee_name, double initial_salary,
    int arrive_hour, int leave_hour)
{
    name = employee_name;
    salary = initial_salary;
    arrive = Time(arrive_hour, 0, 0);
    leave = Time(leave_hour, 0, 0);
}
```

Before the constructor code starts executing, the default constructors are automatically invoked on all data fields that are objects. In particular, the arrive and leave fields are initialized with the current time through the default constructor of the Time class. Immediately afterwards, those values are overwritten with the objects Time(arrive_hour, 0, 0) and Time(leave_hour, 0, 0).

It would be more efficient to construct the arrive and leave fields with the correct values right away. That is achieved as follows with the form described in Syntax 5.4.

```
Employee::Employee(string employee_name, double initial_salary,
    int arrive_hour, int leave_hour)
    : arrive(arrive_hour, 0, 0),
    leave(leave_hour, 0, 0)
{
    name = employee_name;
    salary = initial_salary;
}
```

Many people find this syntax confusing, and you may prefer not to use it. The price you pay is inefficient initialization, first with the default constructor, and then with the actual initial value. Note, however, that this syntax is necessary to construct objects of classes that don't have a default constructor.

SYNTAX 5.4 Constructor with Field Initializer List

ClassName : : *ClassName* (*parameters*)
   : *field*₁ (*expressions*), ..., *field*ₙ (*expressions*)
{
   statements
}

Example:

```
Point::Point(double xval, double yval)
   : x(xval), y(yval)
{
}
```

Purpose:

Supply the implementation of a constructor, initializing data fields before the body of the constructor.

ADVANCED TOPIC 5.2

Overloading

When the same function name is used for more than one function, then the name is *overloaded*. In C++ you can overload function names provided the parameter types are different. For example, you can define two functions, both called print, one to print an employee record and one to print a time object:

```
void print(Employee e) ...
void print(Time t) ...
```

When the print function is called,

```
print(x);
```

the compiler looks at the type of x. If x is an Employee object, the first function is called. If x is a Time object, the second function is called. If x is neither, the compiler generates an error.

We have not used the overloading feature in this book. Instead, we gave each function a unique name, such as print_employee or print_time. However, we have no choice with constructors. C++ demands that the name of a constructor equal the name of the class. If a class has more than one constructor, then that name must be overloaded.

In addition to name overloading, C++ also supports *operator overloading*. You can define new meanings for the familiar C++ operators such as +, ==, and <<, provided at least one of the arguments is an object of some class. For example, we could overload the > operator to test whether one product is better than another. Then the test

```
if (next.is_better_than(best)) ...
```

could instead be written as

```
if (next > best) ...
```

To teach the compiler this new meaning of the > operator, we provide a member function called operator> as follows:

```
bool Product::operator>(Product b) const
{
    if (price == 0) return true;
    if (b.price == 0) return false;
    return score / price > b.score / b.price;
}
```

Operator overloading can make programs easier to read. See Chapter 14 for more information.

5.7 Accessing Data Fields

Private data fields can only be accessed by member functions of the same class.

Only member functions of a class are allowed to access the private data fields of objects of that class. All other functions—that is, member functions of other classes and functions that are not member functions of any class—must go through the public interface of the class.

For example, the raise_salary function of Chapter 4 cannot read and set the salary field directly:

```
void raise_salary(Employee& e, double percent)
{
    e.salary = e.salary * (1 + percent / 100); // Error
}
```

Instead, it must use the get_salary and set_salary functions:

```
void raise_salary(Employee& e, double percent)
{
    double new_salary = e.get_salary()
        * (1 + percent / 100);
    e.set_salary(new_salary);
}
```

These two member functions are extremely simple:

```
double Employee::get_salary() const
{
    return salary;
}

void Employee::set_salary(double new_salary)
{
    salary = new_salary;
}
```

In your own classes you should *not* automatically write accessor functions for *all* data fields. The less implementation detail you reveal, the more flexibility you have to improve the class. Consider, for example, the Product class. There was no need to supply functions such as get_score or set_price. Also, if you have a get_ function, don't feel obliged to implement a matching set_ function. For example, the Time class has a get_minutes function but not a set_minutes function.

Consider again the get_salary and set_salary functions of the Employee class. They simply get and set the value of the salary field. However, you should not assume that all functions with the prefixes get and set follow that pattern. For example, our Time class has three accessors get_hours, get_minutes, and get_seconds, but it does not use corresponding data fields hours, minutes, and seconds. Instead, there is a single data field

```
int time_in_secs;
```

The field stores the number of seconds from midnight (00:00:00). The constructor sets that value from the construction parameters:

```
Time::Time(int hour, int min, int sec)
{
    time_in_secs = 60 * 60 * hour + 60 * min + sec;
}
```

The accessors compute the hours, minutes, and seconds. For example,

```
int Time::get_minutes() const
{
    return (time_in_secs / 60) % 60;
}
```

This internal representation was chosen because it makes the add_seconds and seconds_from functions trivial to implement:

```
int Time::seconds_from(Time t) const
{
    return time_in_secs - t.time_in_secs;
}
```

Of course, the data representation is an internal implementation detail of the class that is invisible to the class user.

5.8 Comparing Member Functions with Nonmember Functions

Consider again the raise_salary function of Chapter 4.

```
void raise_salary(Employee& e, double percent)
{
    double new_salary = e.get_salary()
        * (1 + percent / 100);
    e.set_salary(new_salary);
}
```

This function is not a member function of the Employee class. It is not a member function of any class, in fact. Thus, the dot notation is not used when the function is called. There are two explicit arguments and no implicit argument.

```
raise_salary(harry, 7); // Raise Harry's salary by 7 percent
```

Let's turn raise_salary into a member function:

```
class Employee
{
public:
   void raise_salary(double percent);
   ...
};

void Employee::raise_salary(double percent)
{
   salary = salary * (1 + percent / 100);
}
```

Now the function must be called with the dot notation:

```
harry.raise_salary(7); // Raise Harry's salary by 7 percent
```

Which of these two solutions is better? It depends on the *ownership* of the class. If you are designing a class, you should make useful operations into member functions. However, if you are using a class designed by someone else, then you should not add your own member functions. The author of the class that you are using may improve the class and periodically give you a new version of the code. It would be a nuisance if you had to keep adding your own modifications back into the class definition every time that happened.

Inside main or another nonmember function, it is easy to differentiate between member function calls and other function calls. Member functions are invoked using the dot notation; nonmember functions don't have an *"object."* preceding them. Inside member functions, however, it isn't as simple. One member function can invoke another member function on its implicit parameter. Suppose we add a member function print to the Employee class:

```
class Employee
{
public:
   void print() const;
   ...
};

void Employee::print() const
{
   cout << "Name: " << get_name()
      << "Salary: " << get_salary()
      << "\n";
}
```

Now consider the call harry.print(), with implicit parameter harry. The call get_name() inside the Employee::print function really means harry.get_name().

Again, you may find it helpful to visualize the function like this:

```
void Employee::print() const
{
    cout << "Name: " << implicit_parameter.get_name()
        << "Salary: " << implicit_parameter.get_salary()
        << "\n";
}
```

In this simple situation we could equally well have accessed the name and salary data fields directly in the Employee::print function. In more complex situations it is very common for one member function to call another.

If you see a function call without the dot notation inside a member function, you first need to check whether that function is actually another member function of the same class. If so, it means "call this member function with the same implicit parameter".

If you compare the member and nonmember versions of raise_salary, you can see an important difference. The member function is allowed to modify the salary data field of the Employee object, even though it was not defined as a reference parameter.

Recall that by default, function parameters are value parameters, which the function cannot modify. You must supply an ampersand & to indicate that a parameter is a reference parameter, which can be modified by the function. For example, the first parameter of the nonmember version of raise_salary is a reference parameter (Employee&), because the raise_salary function changes the employee record.

The situation is exactly opposite for the implicit parameter of member functions. By default, the implicit parameter *can* be modified. Only if the member function is tagged as const must the default parameter be left unchanged.

The following table summarizes these differences.

	Explicit Parameter	**Implicit Parameter**
Value Parameter (no change)	No modifier void print(**Employee**)	Use const modifier void **Employee**::print() **const**
Reference Parameter (can be changed)	Use & modifier void raise_salary(**Employee&** e, double p)	No modifier void **Employee**::raise_salary(double p)

QUALITY TIP 5.1

File Layout

By now you have learned quite a few C++ features, all of which can occur in a C++ source file. Keep your source files neat and organize items in them in the following order:

- Included header files
- Constants
- Classes
- Global variables (if any)
- Functions

The member functions can come in any order. If you sort the nonmember functions so that every function is defined before it is used, then main comes last. If you prefer a different ordering, use function declarations (see Advanced Topic 4.1).

5.9 Separate Compilation

> The code of complex programs is distributed over multiple files.

When you write and compile small programs, you can place all your code into a single source file. When your programs get larger or you work in a team, that situation changes. You will want to split your code into separate source files. There are two reasons why this split becomes necessary. First, it takes time to compile a file, and it seems silly to wait for the compiler to keep translating code that doesn't change. If your code is distributed over several source files, then only those files that you changed need to be recompiled. The second reason becomes apparent when you work with other programmers in a team. It would be very difficult for multiple programmers to edit a single source file simultaneously. Therefore, the program code is broken up so that each programmer is solely responsible for a separate set of files.

If your program is composed of multiple files, some of these files will define data types or functions that are needed in other files. There must be a path of communication between the files. In C++, that communication happens through the inclusion of header files.

> Header files contain the definitions of classes and declarations of shared constants, functions, and variables.

A header file contains

- definitions of classes.
- declarations of constants.
- declarations of nonmember functions.
- declarations of global variables.

> Source files contain the function implementations.

The source file contains

- definitions of member functions.
- definitions of nonmember functions.
- definitions of global variables.

Let's consider a simple case first. We will create a set of two files, product.h and product.cpp, that contain the interface and the implementation of the Product class.

The header file contains the class definition. It also includes all headers that are necessary for defining the class. For example, the Product class is defined in terms of the string class. Therefore, you must include the <string> header as well. Any time you include a header from the standard library, you must also include the command

```
using namespace std;
```

ch05/prodtest/product.h

```
1   #ifndef PRODUCT_H
2   #define PRODUCT_H
3
4   #include <string>
5
6   using namespace std;
7
8   class Product
9   {
10  public:
11     /**
12         Constructs a product with score 0 and price 1.
13     */
14     Product();
15
16     /**
17         Reads in this product object.
18     */
19     void read();
20
21     /**
22         Compares two product objects.
23         @param b the object to compare with this object
24         @return true if this object is better than b
25     */
26     bool is_better_than(Product b) const;
27
28     /**
29         Prints this product object.
30     */
31     void print() const;
32  private:
33     string name;
34     double price;
35     int score;
36  };
37
38  #endif
```

Note the curious set of preprocessor directives that bracket the file.

```
#ifndef PRODUCT_H
#define PRODUCT_H
...
#endif
```

These directives are a guard against multiple inclusion. Suppose a file includes product.h and another header file that also includes product.h. Then the compiler sees the class definition twice, and it complains about two classes with the same name. (Sadly, it doesn't check whether the definitions are identical.)

The source file simply contains the definitions of the member functions (including constructors). Note that the source file product.cpp includes its own header file product.h. The compiler needs to know how the Product class is declared in order to compile the member functions.

ch05/prodtest/product.cpp

```cpp
1   #include <iostream>
2   #include "product.h"
3
4   using namespace std;
5
6   Product::Product()
7   {
8      price = 1;
9      score = 0;
10  }
11
12  void Product::read()
13  {
14     cout << "Please enter the model name: ";
15     getline(cin, name);
16     cout << "Please enter the price: ";
17     cin >> price;
18     cout << "Please enter the score: ";
19     cin >> score;
20     string remainder; // Read remainder of line
21     getline(cin, remainder);
22  }
23
24  bool Product::is_better_than(Product b) const
25  {
26     if (price == 0) return true;
27     if (b.price == 0) return false;
28     return score / price > b.score / b.price;
29  }
30
31  void Product::print() const
32  {
33     cout << name
34        << " Price: " << price
35        << " Score: " << score;
36  }
```

Note that the function comments are in the header file, since they are a part of the interface, not the implementation.

The product.cpp file does *not* contain a main function. There are many potential programs that might make use of the Product class. Each of these programs will need to supply its own main function, as well as other functions and classes.

Here is a simple test program that puts the Product class to use. Its source file includes the product.h header file.

ch05/prodtest/prodtest.cpp

```
1   #include <iostream>
2   #include "product.h"
3
4   int main()
5   {
6      Product best;
7
8      bool more = true;
9      while (more)
10     {
11        Product next;
12        next.read();
13        if (next.is_better_than(best))
14           best = next;
15
16        cout << "More data? (y/n) ";
17        string answer;
18        getline(cin, answer);
19        if (answer != "y")
20           more = false;
21     }
22
23     cout << "The best value is ";
24     best.print();
25
26     return 0;
27  }
```

To build the complete program, you need to compile both the prodtest.cpp and product.cpp source files. The details depend on your compiler. For example, with the Gnu compiler, you issue the commands

```
g++ -c product.cpp
g++ -c prodtest.cpp
g++ -o prodtest product.o prodtest.o
```

The first two commands translate the source files into object files that contain the machine instructions corresponding to the C++ code. The third command links together the object files, as well as all the required code from the standard library, to form an executable program.

You have just seen the simplest and most common case for designing header and source files. There are a few additional technical details that you need to know.

Place shared constants into the header file. For example,

product.h

```
1   const int MAX_SCORE = 100;
2   ...
```

To share a nonmember function, place the definition of the function into a source file and the function prototype (declaration) into the corresponding header file.

rand.h

```
1  void rand_seed();
2  int rand_int(int a, int b);
```

rand.cpp

```
1  #include "rand.h"
2
3  void rand_seed()
4  {
5     int seed = static_cast<int>(time(0));
6     srand(seed);
7  }
8
9  int rand_int(int a, int b)
10 {
11    return a + rand() % (b - a + 1);
12 }
```

Finally, it may occasionally be necessary to share a global variable among source files. For example, the graphics library of this book defines a global object cwin. It is declared in a header file as

```
extern GraphicWindow cwin;
```

The corresponding source file contains the definition

```
GraphicWindow cwin;
```

The extern keyword is required to distinguish the declaration from the definition.

RANDOM FACT 5.2

Programming—Art or Science?

There has been a long discussion whether the discipline of computing is a science or not. The field is called "computer science", but that doesn't mean much. Except possibly for librarians and sociologists, few people believe that library science and social science are scientific endeavors.

A scientific discipline aims to discover certain fundamental principles dictated by the laws of nature. It operates on the *scientific method:* by posing hypotheses and testing them with experiments that are repeatable by other workers in the field. For example, a physicist may have a theory on the makeup of nuclear particles and attempt to verify or falsify that theory by running experiments in a particle collider. If an experiment cannot be verified, such as the "cold fusion" research at the University of Utah, then the theory dies a quick death. (See http://physicsworld.com/cws/article/print/1258 for a history of that failed research.)

Some programmers indeed run experiments. They try out various methods of computing certain results, or of configuring computer systems, and measure the differences in performance. However, their aim is not to discover laws of nature.

Some computer scientists discover fundamental principles. One class of fundamental results, for instance, states that it is impossible to write certain kinds of computer programs, no matter how powerful the computing equipment is. For example, it is impossible to write a program that takes as its input any two C++ program files and as its output prints whether or not these two programs always compute the same results. Such a program would be very handy for grading student homework, but nobody, no matter how clever, will ever be able to write one that works for all input files. The majority of programmers write programs, however, instead of researching the limits of computation.

Some people view programming as an *art* or *craft*. A programmer who writes elegant code that is easy to understand and runs with optimum efficiency can indeed be considered a good craftsman. Calling it an art is perhaps far-fetched, because an art object requires an audience to appreciate it, whereas the program code is generally hidden from the program user.

Others call computing an *engineering discipline*. Just as mechanical engineering is based on the fundamental mathematical principles of statics, computing has certain mathematical foundations. There is more to mechanical engineering than mathematics, though, such as knowledge of materials and project planning. The same is true for computing.

In one somewhat worrisome aspect, computing does not have the same standing as other engineering disciplines. There is little agreement as to what constitutes professional conduct in the computer field. Unlike the scientist, whose main responsibility is the search for truth, the engineer must strive for the conflicting demands of quality, safety, and economy. Engineering disciplines have professional organizations that hold their members to standards of conduct. The computer field is so new that in many cases we simply don't know the correct method for achieving certain tasks. That makes it difficult to set professional standards.

What do you think? From your limited experience, do you consider the discipline of computing an art, a craft, a science, or an engineering activity?

CHAPTER SUMMARY

1. A class represents a concept. Instead of groups of related variables, try designing a class for the underlying concept.

2. Every class has a public interface: a collection of member functions through which the objects of the class can be manipulated.

3. A constructor is used to initialize objects when they are created. A constructor with no parameters is called a default constructor.

4. A mutator member function changes the state of the object on which it operates.

5. An accessor member function does not modify the object. Accessors must be tagged with const.

6. Every class has a private implementation: data fields that store the state of an object.

7. Encapsulation is the act of hiding implementation details.

8. Encapsulation protects the integrity of object data.

9. By keeping the implementation private, we protect it from being accidentally corrupted.

10. Encapsulation enables changes in the implementation without affecting users of a class.

11. Use the const keyword when defining accessor member functions.

12. The object on which a member function is applied is the implicit parameter. Every member function has an implicit parameter.

13. Explicit parameters of a member function are listed in the function definition.

14. The purpose of a constructor is to initialize an object's data fields.

15. A default constructor has no parameters.

16. It is particularly important to initialize all numeric fields in a constructor because they are not automatically initialized.

17. A function name is overloaded if there are different versions of the function, distinguished by their parameter types.

18. Private data fields can only be accessed by member functions of the same class.

19. The code of complex programs is distributed over multiple files.

20. Header files contain the definitions of classes and declarations of shared constants, functions, and variables.

21. Source files contain the function implementations.

FURTHER READING

1. W.H. Sackmann, W.J. Erikson, and E.E. Grant, "Exploratory Experimental Studies Comparing Online and Offline Programming Performance", *Communications of the ACM*, vol. 11, no. 1 (January 1968), pp. 3–11.

2. F. Brooks, *The Mythical Man-Month*, Addison-Wesley, 1975.

REVIEW EXERCISES

Exercise R5.1. List all classes that we have used so far in this book. Categorize them as
- Real-world entities
- Mathematical abstractions
- System services

Exercise R5.2. What is the *interface* of a class? What is the *implementation* of a class?

Exercise R5.3. What is a member function, and how does it differ from a nonmember function?

Exercise R5.4. What is a mutator function? What is an accessor function?

Exercise R5.5. What happens if you forget the const in an accessor function? What happens if you accidentally supply a const in a mutator function?

Exercise R5.6. What is an implicit parameter? How does it differ from an explicit parameter?

Exercise R5.7. How many implicit parameters can a member function have? How many implicit parameters can a nonmember function have? How many explicit parameters can a function have?

Exercise R5.8. What is a constructor?

Exercise R5.9. What is a default constructor? What is the consequence if a class does not have a default constructor?

Exercise R5.10. How many constructors can a class have? Can you have a class with no constructors? If a class has more than one constructor, which of them gets called?

Exercise R5.11. How can you define an object variable that is not initialized with a constructor?

Exercise R5.12. How are member functions declared? How are they defined?

Exercise R5.13. What is encapsulation? Why is it useful?

Exercise R5.14. Data fields are hidden in the private section of a class, but they aren't hidden very well at all. Anyone can read the private section. Explain to what extent the private keyword hides the private members of a class.

Exercise R5.15. You can read and write the salary field of the Employee class with the get_salary accessor function and the set_salary mutator function. Should every data field of a class have associated accessors and mutators? Explain why or why not.

Exercise R5.16. What changes to the Product class would be necessary if you wanted to make is_better_than into a nonmember function? (*Hint:* You would need to introduce additional accessor functions.) Write the class definition of the changed Product class, the definitions of the new member functions, and the definition of the changed is_better_than function.

Exercise R5.17. What changes to the Product class would be necessary if you wanted to make the read function into a nonmember function? (*Hint:* You would need to read in the name, price, and score and then construct a product with these properties.) Write the class definition of the changed Product class, the definition of the new constructor, and the definition of the changed read function.

Exercise R5.18. In a nonmember function, it is easy to differentiate between calls to member functions and calls to nonmember functions. How do you tell them apart? Why is it not as easy for functions that are called from a member function?

Exercise R5.19. How do you indicate whether the implicit parameter is passed by value or by reference? How do you indicate whether an explicit parameter is passed by value or by reference?

PROGRAMMING EXERCISES

Exercise P5.1. Implement all member functions of the following class:

```
class Person
{
public:
   Person();
   Person(string pname, int page);
   string get_name() const;
   int get_age() const;
private:
   string name;
   int age; // 0 if unknown
};
```

Exercise P5.2. Implement a class PEmployee that is just like the Employee class except that it stores an object of type Person as developed in Exercise P5.1.

```
class PEmployee
{
public:
   PEmployee();
   PEmployee(string employee_name, double initial_salary);
   void set_salary(double new_salary);
   double get_salary() const;
   string get_name() const;
private:
   Person person_data;
   double salary;
};
```

Exercise P5.3. Implement a class Address. An address has a house number, a street, an optional apartment number, a city, a state, and a postal code. Supply two constructors: one with an apartment number and one without. Supply a print function that prints the address with the street on one line and the city, state, and postal code on the next line. Supply a member function comes_before that tests whether one address comes before another when the addresses are compared by postal code.

Exercise P5.4. Implement a class Account. An account has a balance, functions to add and withdraw money, and a function to query the current balance. Charge a $5 penalty if an attempt is made to withdraw more money than available in the account.

Exercise P5.5. Enhance the Account class of Exercise P5.4 to compute interest on the current balance. Then use the Account class to implement the problem from the beginning of the book: An account has an initial balance of $10,000, and 6 percent annual interest is compounded monthly until the investment doubles.

Exercise P5.6. Implement a class Bank. This bank has two objects, checking and savings, of the type Account that was developed in Exercise P5.5. Implement four member functions:

```
void deposit(double amount, string account)
void withdraw(double amount, string account)
void transfer(double amount, string account)
void print_balances()
```

Here the account string is "S" or "C". For the deposit or withdrawal, it indicates which account is affected. For a transfer it indicates the account from which the money is taken; the money is automatically transferred to the other account.

Exercise P5.7. Implement a class SodaCan with functions get_surface_area() and get_volume(). In the constructor, supply the height and radius of the can.

Exercise P5.8. Implement a class Car with the following properties. A car has a certain fuel efficiency (measured in miles/gallon or liters/km—pick one) and a certain amount of fuel in the gas tank. The efficiency is specified in the constructor, and the initial fuel level is 0. Supply a function drive that simulates driving the car for a certain distance, reducing the fuel level in the gas tank, and functions get_gas, to return the current fuel level, and add_gas, to tank up. Sample usage:

```
Car my_beemer(29); // 29 miles per gallon
my_beemer.add_gas(20); // Tank 20 gallons
my_beemer.drive(100); // Drive 100 miles
cout << my_beemer.get_gas() << "\n"; // Print fuel remaining
```

Exercise P5.9. Implement a class Student. For the purpose of this exercise, a student has a name and a total quiz score. Supply an appropriate constructor and functions get_name(), add_quiz(int score), get_total_score(), and get_average_score(). To compute the latter, you also need to store the *number of quizzes* that the student took.

Exercise P5.10. Modify the Student class of Exercise P5.9 to compute grade point averages. Member functions are needed to add a grade, and get the current GPA. Specify grades as elements of a class Grade. Supply a constructor that constructs a grade from a string, such as "B+". You will also need a function that translates grades into their numeric values (for example, "B+" becomes 3.3).

Exercise P5.11. Define a class Country that stores the name of the country, its population, and its area. Using that class, write a program that reads in a set of countries and prints

- The country with the largest area
- The country with the largest population
- The country with the largest population density (people per square kilometer)

Exercise P5.12. Design a class `Message` that models an e-mail message. A message has a recipient, a sender, and a message text. Support the following member functions:

- A constructor that takes the sender and recipient and sets the time stamp to the current time
- A member function `append` that appends a line of text to the message body
- A member function `to_string` that makes the message into one long string like this: `"From: Harry Hacker\nTo: Rudolf Reindeer\n ..."`
- A member function `print` that prints the message text. *Hint:* Use `to_string`.

Write a program that uses this class to make a message and print it.

Exercise P5.13. Design a class `Mailbox` that stores e-mail messages, using the `Message` class of Exercise P5.12. You don't yet know how to store a collection of message objects. Instead, use the following brute force approach: The mailbox contains one very long string, which is the concatenation of all messages. You can tell where a new message starts by searching for a `From:` at the beginning of a line. This may sound like a dumb strategy, but surprisingly, many e-mail systems do just that.

Implement the following member functions:

```
void Mailbox::add_message(Message m);
Message Mailbox::get_message(int i) const;
void remove_message(int i);
```

What do you do if the message body happens to have a line starting with `"From: "`? Then the `to_string` function of the `Message` class should really insert a `>` in front of the `From:` so that it reads `>From:` . Again, this sounds dumb, but it is a strategy used by real e-mail systems. Extra credit if you implement this enhancement.

G   **Exercise P5.14.** Implement a class `Rectangle` that works just like the other graphics classes such as `Circle` or `Line`. A rectangle is constructed from two corner points. The sides of the rectangle are parallel to the coordinate axes:

You do not yet know how to define a `<<` operator to plot a rectangle. Instead, define a member function `plot`. Supply a function `move`. Pay attention to const. Then write a sample program that constructs and plots a few rectangles.

G   **Exercise P5.15.** Enhance the `Rectangle` class of Exercise P5.14 by adding member functions `perimeter` and `area` that compute the perimeter and area of the rectangle.

G   **Exercise P5.16.** Implement a class `Triangle` that works just like the other graphics classes such as `Circle` or `Line`. A triangle is constructed from three corner points. You do not yet know how to define a `<<` operator to plot a triangle. Instead, define a member function `plot`. Supply a function `move`. Pay attention to const. Then write a sample program that constructs and plots a few triangles.

G   **Exercise P5.17.** Enhance the `Triangle` class of Exercise P5.16 by adding member functions `perimeter` and `area` that compute the perimeter and area of the triangle.

G   **Exercise P5.18.** Design a class `House` that defines a house on a street. A house has a house number and an (x, y) location, where x and y are numbers between –10 and 10. The key member function is `plot`, which plots the house.

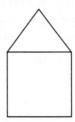

Next, design a class `Street` that contains a number of equally spaced houses. An object of type `Street` stores the first house, the last house (which can be anywhere on the screen), and the number of houses on the street. The `Street::plot` function needs to make the intermediate house objects on the fly, because you don't yet know how to store an arbitrary number of objects.

Use these classes in a graphics program in which the user clicks with the mouse on the locations of the first and last house, then enters the house numbers of the first and last house, and the number of houses on the street. Then the entire street is plotted.

G   **Exercise P5.19.** Design a class `Cannonball` to model a cannonball that is fired into the air. A ball has

- An x- and a y-position
- An x- and a y-velocity

Supply the following member functions:

- A constructor with an x-position (the y-position is initially 0)
- A member function `move(double sec)` that moves the ball to the next position (First compute the distance traveled in `sec` seconds, using the current velocities, then update the x- and y-positions; then update the y-velocity by taking into account the gravitational acceleration of –9.81 m/sec^2; the x-velocity is unchanged.)
- A member function `plot` that plots the current location of the cannonball
- A member function `shoot` whose parameters are the angle α and initial velocity v (Compute the x-velocity as $v \cos \alpha$ and the y-velocity as $v \sin \alpha$; then keep calling `move` with a time interval of 0.1 seconds until the x-position is 0; call `plot` after every move.)

Use this class in a program that prompts the user for the starting angle and the initial velocity. Then call `shoot`.

6

Vectors and Arrays

CHAPTER GOALS

- To become familiar with using vectors to collect objects
- To be able to access vector elements and resize vectors
- To learn how to use one- and two-dimensional arrays
- To learn about common array algorithms

In many programs, you need to collect multiple objects of the same type. In standard C++, the vector construct allows you to conveniently manage collections that automatically grow to any desired size. In this chapter, you will learn about vectors and common vector algorithms.

The standard vectors are built on top of the lower-level array construct. The last part of this chapter shows you how to work with arrays. Two-dimensional arrays are useful for representing tabular arrangements of data.

Chapter Contents

6.1 Using Vectors to Collect Data Items

In this section, we introduce the C++ vector construct. A vector allows you to conveniently store a sequence of data items.

Suppose you write a program that reads a list of salary figures and prints out the list, marking the highest value, like this:

```
32000
54000
67500
29000
35000
80000
115000 <= highest value
44500
100000
65000
```

Before you can determine which value to mark as the highest, the program must first read all data items. After all, the last value might be the highest one.

Could you simply store each value in a separate variable? If you know that there are ten inputs, then you can store the data in ten variables salary1, salary2, salary3, ..., salary10. However, such a sequence of variables is not very practical to use. You would have to write quite a bit of code ten times, once for each of the variables. In C++, a vector is a much better choice for storing the data.

A *vector* is a collection of data items of the same type. Every element of the collection can be accessed separately. Here we define a vector of ten employee salaries:

```
vector<double> salaries(10);
```

> Use a vector to collect multiple values of the same type.

This is the definition of a variable salaries whose type is vector<double>. That is, salaries stores a sequence of double values. The (10) indicates that the vector holds ten values. (See Figure 1.) In general, vector variables are defined as in Syntax 6.1 on page 268.

To get some data into salaries, you must specify which slot in the vector you want to use. That is done with the [] operator:

> Individual values in a vector are accessed by an integer *index* or *subscript*: v[i].

```
salaries[4] = 35000;
```

Now the slot with number 4 of salaries is filled with 35000. (See Figure 2). This "slot number" is called an *index* or *subscript*.

Because salaries is a vector of double values, a slot such as salaries[4] can be used just like any variable of type double:

```
cout << salaries[4] << "\n";
```

Before continuing, we must take care of an important detail of C++ vectors. If you look carefully at Figure 2, you will find that the *fifth* slot was filled with data when we changed salaries[4]. In C++, the slots of vectors are numbered *starting at 0*. That is, the legal slots for the salaries vector are

salaries[0], the first slot
salaries[1], the second slot
salaries[2], the third slot
salaries[3], the fourth slot
salaries[4], the fifth slot

...

salaries[9], the tenth slot

In "ancient" times there was a technical reason why this setup was a good idea. Because so many programmers got used to it, the vector construction imitates it. It is, however, a major source of grief for the newcomer.

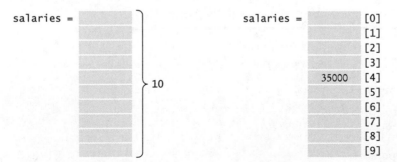

Figure 1
Vector of salaries

Figure 2
Vector Slot Filled with double Value

Valid values for the index range from 0 to one less than the size of the array.

You have to be careful about index values. Trying to access a slot that does not exist in the vector is a serious error. For example, if salaries holds ten values, you are not to allowed to access salaries[20]. Attempting to access a location that is not within the valid index range is called a *bounds error*. The compiler does not catch this type of error. Even the running program generates *no* error message. If you make a bounds error, you silently read or overwrite another memory location. As a consequence, your program may have random errors, and it can even crash.

The most common bounds error is the following:

A bounds error, which occurs if you supply an invalid index to a vector, can have serious consequences.

```
vector<double> salaries(10);
cout << salaries[10];
```

There is no salaries[10] in a vector with ten elements—the legal index values range from 0 to 9.

Another common error is to forget to size the vector.

```
vector<double> salaries; // No size given
salaries[0] = 35000;
```

The index can be any integer expression. It is very common to have a variable variable index such as salaries[i]. This allows you to access arbitrary locations in the vector (see Syntax 6.2 on page 269). For example, the following loop finds the highest salary:

```
double highest = salaries[0];
for (i = 1; i < 10; i++)
   if (salaries[i] > highest)
      highest = salaries[i];
```

By the way, the name *vector* originates from mathematics. You can have a vector in a plane with (x, y) coordinates; a vector in space with (x, y, z) coordinates; or a vector in a space with more than three dimensions, in which case the coordinates are no longer given separate letters x, y, z, but a single letter with subscripts (x_1, x_2, x_3, ..., x_{10}). Of course, in C++ the subscripts go from 0 to 9, not from 1 to 10, and the bracket operator x[i] is used since there is no easy way of writing a subscript x_i with a computer keyboard.

SYNTAX 6.1 Vector Variable Definition

```
vector<type_name> variable_name;
vector<type_name> variable_name(initial_size);
```

Example:

```
vector<int> scores;
vector<Employee> staff(20);
```

Purpose:

Define a new variable of vector type, and optionally supply an initial size.

CHAPTER 6 ■ Vectors and Arrays

> ## SYNTAX 6.2 Vector Subscript
>
> *vector_expression*[*integer_expression*]
>
> **Example:**
>
> salaries[i + 1]
>
> **Purpose:**
>
> Access an element in a vector.

6.2 Working with Vectors

In this section, you will learn how to visit all elements of a vector, and how to add elements to a vector.

When a vector is defined without a size parameter, it is empty and can hold *no* elements.

You can find out the size of a vector by calling the size function. For example, the loop of the preceding section,

```
for (i = 1; i < 10; i++)
   if (salaries[i] > highest)
      highest = salaries[i];
```

can be written as

```
for (i = 1; i < salaries.size(); i++)
   if (salaries[i] > highest)
      highest = salaries[i];
```

> Use the size function to obtain the current size of a vector.

Using size is actually a better idea than using the number 10. If the program changes, such as by allocating space for 20 employees in the salaries vector, the first loop is no longer correct, but the second loop automatically stays valid. This principle is another way to avoid magic numbers, as discussed in Quality Tip 2.3.

Note that i is a legal index for the vector v if $0 \le i$ and $i < $ v.size(). Therefore the for loop

```
for (i = 0; i < v.size(); i++)
   do something with v[i];
```

is extremely common for visiting all elements in a vector.

It is often difficult to know initially how many elements you need to store. For example, you may want to store all salaries that are entered in the salary chart program. You have no idea how many values the program user will enter. The function push_back allows you to start out with an empty vector and grow the vector whenever another employee is added:

```
vector<double> salaries;
...
```

```
double s;
cin >> s;
...
salaries.push_back(s);
```

The push_back command resizes the vector salary by adding one element to its end; then it sets that element to s. The strange name push_back indicates that s is *pushed* onto the *back* end of the vector.

> Use the push_back member function to add more elements to a vector. Use pop_back to reduce the size.

Although it is undeniably convenient to grow a vector on demand with push_back, it is also inefficient. More memory must be found to hold the longer vector, and all elements must be copied into the larger space. If you already know how many elements you need in a vector, you should specify that size when you define the vector, then fill it.

Another member function, pop_back, removes the last element of a vector, shrinking its size by one.

```
vector<double> salaries(10);
...
salaries.pop_back(); // Now salaries has size 9
```

Note that the pop_back function does not return the element that is being removed. If you want to know what that element is, you need to capture it first.

```
double last = salaries[salaries.size() - 1];
salaries.pop_back(); // Removes last from the vector
```

This is not very intuitive if you are familiar with the so-called *stack* data structure, whose pop operation returns the top value of the stack. Intuitive or not, the names push_back and pop_back are part of the standard for C++.

Now you have all the pieces to implement the program outlined at the beginning of the chapter. This program reads employee salaries and displays them, marking the highest salary.

ch06/salvect.cpp

```
1   #include <iostream>
2   #include <vector>
3
4   using namespace std;
5
6   int main()
7   {
8      vector<double> salaries;
9      cout << "Please enter salaries, 0 to quit:\n";
10     bool more = true;
11     while (more)
12     {
13        double s;
14        cin >> s;
15        if (s == 0)
16           more = false;
17        else
18           salaries.push_back(s);
```

```
19      }
20
21      double highest = salaries[0];
22      int i;
23      for (i = 1; i < salaries.size(); i++)
24         if (salaries[i] > highest)
25            highest = salaries[i];
26
27      for (i = 0; i < salaries.size(); i++)
28      {
29         cout << salaries[i];
30         if (salaries[i] == highest)
31            cout << " <== highest value";
32         cout << "\n";
33      }
34
35      return 0;
36   }
```

Program Run

```
Please enter salaries, 0 to quit:
32000
54000
67500
29000
35000
80000
115000
44500
100000
65000
0
32000
54000
67500
29000
35000
80000
115000 <== highest value
44500
100000
65000
```

For simplicity, this program stores the salary values in a vector<double>. However, it is just as easy to use vectors of objects. For example, you can create a vector of employees with a definition such as this one:

```
vector<Employee> staff(10);
```

You add elements by copying objects into the slots of the vector:

```
staff[0] = Employee("Hacker, Harry", 35000.0);
```

You can access any `Employee` object in the vector as `staff[i]`. Because the vector entry is an object, you can apply a member function to it:

```
if (staff[i].get_salary() > 50000.0) ...
```

COMMON ERROR 6.1

Bounds Errors

The most common vector error is accessing a nonexistent slot.

```
vector<double> data(10);
data[10] = 5.4;
    // Error—data has 10 elements with subscripts 0 to 9
```

If your program accesses a vector through an out-of-bounds subscript, there is no error message. Instead, the program will quietly (or not so quietly) corrupt some memory. Except for very short programs, in which the problem may go unnoticed, that corruption will make the program act flaky or cause a horrible death many instructions later. These are serious errors that can be difficult to detect.

PRODUCTIVITY HINT 6.1

Inspecting Vectors in the Debugger

Vectors are more difficult to inspect in the debugger than numbers or objects. Suppose you are running a program and want to inspect the contents of

```
vector<double> salaries;
```

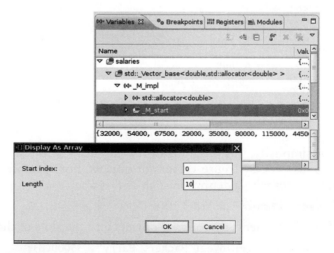

Figure 3 Display of Vector Elements

First, you tell the debugger to inspect the vector variable salaries. It shows you the inner details of an object. You need to find the data field that points to the vector elements (usually called start, _M_start, or _First or a similar name). That variable is a pointer—you will learn more about pointers in Chapter 7.

Try inspecting that variable. Depending on your debugger, you may need to click on it or select it and hit Enter. That shows you the *first* element in the vector. Then you must expand the range to show you as many elements as you would like to see. The commands to do so differ widely among debuggers. On one popular debugger, you must click on the field with the *right* mouse button and select "Range" from the menu. In another debugger, you need to type in an expression such as start[0]@10 to see ten elements. You will then get a display of all elements that you specified (see Figure 3).

Inspecting vectors is an important debugging skill. Read the debugger documentation, or ask someone who knows, such as your lab assistant or instructor, for details.

QUALITY TIP 6.1

Don't Combine Vector Access and Index Increment

It is possible to increment a variable that is used as an index, for example

```
x = v[i++];
```

That is a shortcut for

```
x = v[i];
i++;
```

Many years ago, when compilers were not very powerful, the v[i++] shortcut was useful, because it made the compiler generate faster code. Nowadays, the compiler generates the same efficient code for both versions. You should therefore use the second version, because it is clearer and less confusing.

ADVANCED TOPIC 6.1

Strings Are Vectors of Characters

A string variable is essentially a vector of characters. C++ has a basic data type char to denote individual characters. For example, the string greeting defined by

```
string greeting = "Hello";
```

can be considered a vector of five characters 'H', 'e', 'l', 'l', 'o'. Note that values of type char are enclosed in single quotes. 'H' denotes the individual character, "H" a string containing one character. An individual character can be stored in one byte. A string, even if it has length 1, needs to store both the contents and the length, which requires several bytes.

You can modify the characters in a string:

```
greeting[3] = 'p';
greeting[4] = '!';
```

Now the string is "Help!". Of course, the same effect can be achieved using string operations rather than direct character manipulation.

```
greeting = greeting.substr(0, 3) + "p!";
```

Manipulating the characters directly is more efficient than extracting substrings and concatenating strings. The [] operator is more convenient than the substr function if you want to visit a string one character at a time. For example, the following function makes a copy of a string and changes all characters to uppercase:

```
string uppercase(string s)
{
   string r = s;
   int i;
   for (i = 0; i < r.length(); i++)
      r[i] = toupper(r[i]);
   return r;
}
```

For example, uppercase("Hello") returns the string "HELLO". The toupper function is defined in the cctype header. It converts lowercase characters to uppercase.

RANDOM FACT 6.1

An Early Internet Worm

In November 1988, a college student at Cornell University launched a so-called virus program that infected about 6,000 computers connected to the Internet across the United States. Tens of thousands of computer users were unable to read their e-mail or otherwise use their computers. All major universities and many high-tech companies were affected. (The Internet was much smaller then than it is now.)

The particular kind of virus used in this attack is called a worm. The virus program crawled from one computer on the Internet to the next. The entire program is quite complex; its major parts are explained in [1]. However, one of the methods used in the attack is of interest here. The worm would attempt to connect to finger, a program in the UNIX operating system for finding information on a user who has an account on a particular computer on the network. Like many programs in UNIX, finger was written in the C language. C does not have array lists, only arrays, and when you construct an array in C, you have to make up your mind how many elements you need. To store the user name to be looked up (say, walters@cs.sjsu.edu), the finger program allocated an array of 512 characters, under the assumption that nobody would ever provide such a long input. Unfortunately, C does not check that an array index is less than the length of the array. If you write into an array, using an index that is too large, you simply overwrite memory locations that belong to some other objects. In some versions of the finger program, the programmer had been lazy and had not checked whether the array holding the input characters was large enough to hold the input. So the worm program purposefully filled the 512-character array with 536 bytes. The excess 24 bytes would overwrite a return address, which the attacker knew was stored just after the line buffer. When that function was finished, it didn't return to its caller but to code supplied by the worm (see Figure 4). That code ran under the same super-user privileges as finger, allowing the worm to gain entry into the remote system.

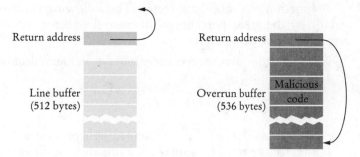

Figure 4 A "Buffer Overrun" Attack

Had the programmer who wrote finger been more conscientious, this particular attack would not be possible. In C++, as in C, all programmers must be very careful not to overrun array boundaries.

One may well speculate what would possess a skilled programmer to spend many weeks or months to plan the antisocial act of breaking into thousands of computers and disabling them. It appears that the break-in was fully intended by the author, but the disabling of the computers was a side effect of continuous reinfection and efforts by the worm to avoid being killed. It is not clear whether the author was aware that these moves would cripple the attacked machines.

In recent years, the novelty of vandalizing other people's computers has worn off, and there are fewer jerks with programming skills who write new viruses. Other attacks by individuals with more criminal energy, whose intent has been to steal information or money, have surfaced. See [2] for a very readable account of the discovery and apprehension of one such person.

6.3 Vector Parameters and Return Values

> Vectors can occur as the function parameters and return values.

This section contains several examples of functions that have vector parameters or return values. We start out with a function that computes the average of a vector of floating-point numbers:

```cpp
double average(vector<double> values)
{
   if (values.size() == 0) return 0;
   double sum = 0;
   for (int i = 0; i < values.size(); i++)
      sum = sum + values[i];
   return sum / values.size();
}
```

To visit each element of the vector values, the function needs to determine the size of values. It inspects all elements, with index starting at 0 and going up to, but not including, values.size(). See ch06/average.cpp for a complete sample program.

A function can modify a vector. The following function raises all values in the vector by the given percentage. Because the vector content is modified, you must use a reference parameter:

```
void raise_by_percent(vector<double>& values, double rate)
{
    for (int i = 0; i < values.size(); i++)
        values[i] = values[i] * (1 + rate / 100);
}
```

See ch06/raisesal.cpp for a complete sample program.

If a vector is passed by value, and a function modifies the vector, the modification affects the local copy of that value only, not the call parameter.

A function can return a vector. This is useful if a function computes a result that consists of a collection of values of the same type. Here is a function that collects all values that fall within a certain range:

```
vector<double> between(vector<double> values, double low, double high)
{
    vector<double> result;
    for (int i = 0; i < values.size(); i++)
        if (low <= values[i] && values[i] <= high)
            result.push_back(values[i]);
    return result;
}
```

See ch06/between.cpp for a complete sample program.

Now suppose you want to know *where* these values occur in the vector. Rather than returning the matching values, collect the positions of all matching values in a vector of integers. For example, if salaries[1], salaries[2], and salaries[4] are values matching your criterion, you would end up with a vector containing the integers 1, 2, and 4.

```
vector<int> between_locations(vector<double> values,
    double low, double high)
{
    vector<int> pos;
    for (int i = 0; i < values.size(); i++)
    {
        if (low <= values[i] && values[i] <= high)
            pos.push_back(i);
    }
    return pos;
}
```

Once you know where all matches occur, you can print just those:

```
vector<int> matches = between_locations(salaries, 45000.0, 65000.0);
for (int j = 0; j < matches.size(); j++)
    cout << salaries[matches[j]] << "\n";
```

Note the nested subscripts, salaries[matches[j]]. Here matches[j] is the subscript of the jth match. In our example, matches[0] is 1, matches[1] is 2, and matches[2] is 4. Thus, salaries[1], salaries[2], and salaries[4] are printed.

See ch06/matches.cpp for a complete sample program.

ADVANCED TOPIC 6.2

Passing Vectors by Constant Reference

Passing a vector into a function by value is unfortunately somewhat inefficient, because the function must make a copy of all elements. As explained in Advanced Topic 4.2, the cost of a copy can be avoided by using a constant reference.

```
double average(const vector<double>& values)
```

instead of

```
double average(vector<double> values)
```

This is a useful optimization that greatly increases performance.

6.4 Removing and Inserting Vector Elements

Suppose you want to *remove* an element from a vector. If the elements in the vector are not in any particular order, that task is easy to accomplish. Simply overwrite the element to be removed with the *last* element of the vector, then shrink the size of the vector. (See Figure 5.)

```
int last_pos = values.size() - 1;
values[pos] = values[last_pos];
values.pop_back();
```

See ch06/erase1.cpp for a complete sample program.

The situation is more complex if the order of the elements matters. Then you must move all elements following the element to be removed down (to a lower index) by one slot, and then shrink the size of the vector. (See Figure 6.)

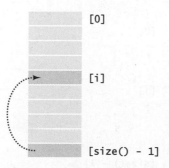

Figure 5   Removing an Element in an Unordered Vector

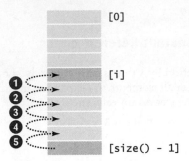

Figure 6
Removing an Element in an Ordered Vector

```
for (int i = pos; i < values.size() - 1; i++)
    values[i] = values[i + 1];
values.pop_back();
```

See ch06/erase2.cpp for a complete sample program.

Conversely, suppose you want to insert an element in the middle of a vector. Then you must add a new element at the end of the vector and move all elements above the insertion location up (to a higher index) by one slot. Note that the order of the movement is different: When you remove an element, you first move the next element down to a lower index, then the one after that, until you finally get to the end of the vector. When you insert an element, you start at the end of the vector, move that element up to a higher index, then move the one before that, and so on until you finally get to the insertion location (see Figure 7).

```
int last = values.size() - 1;
values.push_back(values[last]);
for (int i = last; i > pos; i--)
    values[i] = values[i - 1];
values[pos] = s;
```

See ch06/insert.cpp for a complete sample program.

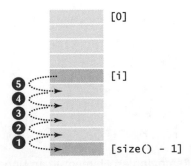

Figure 7   Inserting an Element in an Ordered Vector

QUALITY TIP 6.2

Make Parallel Vectors into Vectors of Objects

Sometimes, you find yourself using vectors of the same length, each of which stores a part of what conceptually should be an object. In that situation, it is a good idea to reorganize your program and use a single vector whose elements are objects.

For example, suppose you want to process a series of product data, and then display the product information, marking the best value (with the best score/price ratio):

```
ACMA P600 Price: 995 Score: 75
Alaris Nx686 Price: 798 Score: 57
Blackship NX-600 Price: 598 Score: 60 <= best value
Kompac 690 Price: 695 Score: 60
```

One solution is to keep three vectors, for the names, prices, and scores:

```
vector<string> names;
vector<double> prices;
vector<int> scores;
```

See ch06/bestval1.cpp for a complete program that uses this strategy.

Each of the vectors will have the same length, and the ith *slice* names[i], prices[i], scores[i], contains data that needs to be processed together. These vectors are called *parallel vectors* (see Figure 8).

Parallel vectors become a headache in larger programs. The programmer must ensure that the vectors always have the same length and that each slice is filled with values that actually belong together. Moreover, any function that operates on a slice must get all vectors as parameters, which is tedious to program.

The remedy is simple. Look at the slice and find the *concept* that it represents. Then make the concept into a class. In the example each slice contains a name, a price, and a score, describing a *product;* turn this into a class.

```
class Product
{
public:
   ...
private:
   string name;
   double price;
   int score;
};
```

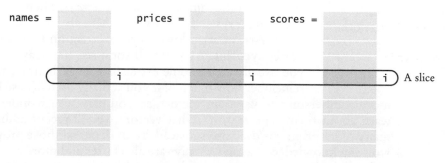

Figure 8 Parallel Vectors

> Avoid parallel vectors by changing them into vectors of objects.

This is, of course, precisely the Product class that we discovered in Chapter 5. You can now eliminate the parallel vectors and replace them with a single vector:

```
vector<Product> products;
```

Each slot in the resulting vector corresponds to a slice in the set of parallel vectors (see Figure 9).

See ch06/bestval2.cpp for the improved program.

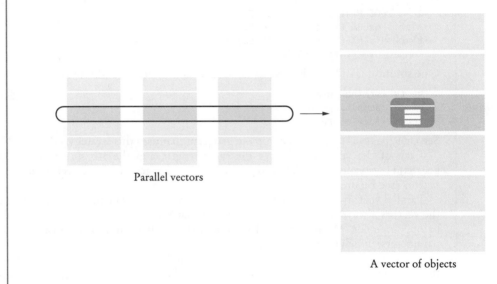

Parallel vectors

A vector of objects

Figure 9   Eliminating Parallel Vectors

6.5 Arrays

> Like vectors, arrays collect elements of the same type. Once the size of an array has been set, it cannot be changed.

In addition to vectors, C++ has a second mechanism for collecting elements of the same type, namely *arrays*. There are many similarities between arrays and vectors, but there are also some significant differences. Arrays are a lower-level abstraction than vectors, so they are less convenient. As you will soon see, an array cannot be resized—you usually create some extra space in each array, and then you must remember how much of it you actually used. These limits make arrays more cumbersome to use than vectors, so you may well wonder why you should learn about them. The reason is that vectors were a recent addition to C++, and many older programs use arrays instead. To understand those programs, you need a working knowledge of arrays. Arrays are also faster and more efficient than vectors. This can be important in some applications.

6.5.1 Defining and Using Arrays

Here is the definition of an array of ten floating-point numbers (see Syntax 6.3 on page 282):

```
double salaries[10];
```

This is very similar to a vector

```
vector<double> salaries(10);
```

Both the array and the vector have ten elements, `salaries[0]` ... `salaries[9]`.

Unlike a vector, an array can be filled with values when it is defined. For example,

```
double salaries[] = { 31000, 24000, 55000, 82000, 49000,
   42000, 35000, 66000, 91000, 60000 };
```

When you supply initialization values, you don't need to specify the array size. The compiler determines the size by counting the values.

Unlike a vector, an array can never change size. That is, the `salaries` array will always have exactly ten elements. You cannot use `push_back` to add more elements to it. Furthermore, the size of the array has to be known *when the program is compiled*. That is, you can't ask the user how many elements are needed and then allocate a sufficient number, as you could with a vector.

```
int n;
cin >> n;
double salaries[n]; // NO!
vector<double> salaries(n); // OK
```

When defining an array, you must come up with a good guess on the maximum number of elements that you need to store, and be prepared to ignore any more than the maximum. Of course, it may well happen that one wants to store more than ten salaries, so we use a larger size:

```
const int SALARIES_CAPACITY = 100;
double salaries[SALARIES_CAPACITY];
```

In a typical program run, less than the maximum size will be occupied by actual elements. The constant `SALARIES_CAPACITY` gives you only the *capacity* of the array; it doesn't tell you how much of the array is actually *used*. You must keep a *companion variable* that counts how many elements are actually used. Here we call the companion variable `salaries_size`. The following loop collects data and fills up the salaries array.

```
int salaries_size = 0;
while (more && salaries_size < SALARIES_CAPACITY)
{
   cout << "Enter salary or 0 to quit: ";
   double x;
   cin >> x;
   if (cin.fail())
      more = false;
   else
   {
```

```
        salaries[salaries_size] = x;
        salaries_size++;
    }
}
```

At the end of this loop, `salaries_size` contains the actual number of elements in the array. Note that you have to stop accepting inputs if the size of the array reaches the maximum size. The name `salaries_size` was chosen to remind you of the vector member function call `salaries.size()` which you would have used if `salaries` had been a vector. The difference between arrays and vectors is that you must create and manually update the `salaries_size` companion variable, whereas a vector automatically remembers how many elements it contains.

Here is a loop that computes the highest salary in the array. We can inspect only the elements with an index less than `salaries_size`, because the remaining elements have never been set and their contents are undefined.

```
double highest = 0;
if (salaries_size > 0)
{
    highest = salaries[0];
    int i;
    for (i = 1; i < salaries_size; i++)
        if (salaries[i] > highest)
            highest = salaries[i];
}
```

SYNTAX 6.3 Array Variable Definition

type_name variable_name[*size*];

Example:

```
int scores[20];
```

Purpose:

Define a new variable of an array type.

6.5.2 Array Parameters

When writing a function with an array parameter, you place an empty [] behind the parameter name:

```
double maximum(double a[], int a_size);
```

You also need to pass the size of the array to the function, because the function has no other way of querying the size of the array—there is no `size()` member function:

```
double maximum(double a[], int a_size)
{
```

```
    if (a_size == 0) return 0;
    double highest = a[0];
    int i;
    for (i = 1; i < a_size; i++)
        if (a[i] > highest)
            highest = a[i];
    return highest;
}
```

Array parameters are always passed by reference.

Unlike all other parameters, array parameters are *always passed by reference*. Functions can modify array parameters, and those modifications affect the array that was passed into the function. You never use an & when defining an array parameter. For example, the following function updates all elements in the array s:

```
void raise_by_percent(double s[], double s_size, double p)
{
    int i;
    for (i = 0; i < s_size; i++)
        s[i] = s[i] * (1 + p / 100);
}
```

It is considered good style to add the const keyword whenever a function does not actually modify an array:

```
double maximum(const double a[], int a_size)
```

If a function adds elements to an array, you need to pass three parameters to the function: the array, the maximum size, and the current size. The current size must be passed *as a reference parameter* so that the function can update it. Here is an example. The following function reads inputs into the array a (which has a capacity of a_capacity) and updates the variable a_size so that it contains the final size of the array when the end of input has been reached. Note that the function stops reading either at the end of input or when the array has been filled completely.

```
void read_data(double a[], int a_capacity, int& a_size)
{
    a_size = 0;
    while (a_size < a_capacity)
    {
        double x;
        cin >> x;
        if (cin.fail()) return;
        a[a_size] = x;
        a_size++;
    }
}
```

The return type of a function cannot be an array.

Although arrays can be function parameters, they cannot be function return types. If a function computes multiple values (such as the between function in Section 6.3), the caller of the function must provide an array parameter to hold the result.

```
void between(double values[], int values_size, double low, double high,
    double result[], double& result_size)
```

The following program reads salary values from standard input, then prints the maximum salary.

ch06/salarray.cpp

```
1   #include <iostream>
2
3   using namespace std;
4
5   /**
6       Reads data into an array, using 0 as a sentinel value.
7       @param a  the array to fill
8       @param a_capacity  the maximum size of a
9       @param a_size  filled with the size of a after reading the input
10  */
11  void read_data(double a[], int a_capacity, int& a_size)
12  {
13      a_size = 0;
14
15      bool more = true;
16      while (more)
17      {
18          double x;
19          cin >> x;
20          if (x == 0)
21              more = false;
22          else if (a_size == a_capacity)
23          {
24              cout << "Sorry--extra data ignored\n";
25              more = false;
26          }
27          else
28          {
29              a[a_size] = x;
30              a_size++;
31          }
32      }
33  }
34
35  /**
36      Computes the maximum value in an array.
37      @param a  the array
38      @param a_size  the number of values in a
39  */
40  double maximum(const double a[], int a_size)
41  {
42      if (a_size == 0)
43          return 0;
44      double highest = a[0];
45      for (int i = 1; i < a_size; i++)
46          if (a[i] > highest)
47              highest = a[i];
48      return highest;
49  }
50
```

```
51  int main()
52  {
53      const int SALARIES_CAPACITY = 100;
54      double salaries[SALARIES_CAPACITY];
55      int salaries_size = 0;
56      cout << "Please enter salaries, 0 to quit:\n";
57
58      read_data(salaries, SALARIES_CAPACITY, salaries_size);
59
60      double maxsal = maximum(salaries, salaries_size);
61      cout << "The maximum salary is " << maxsal << "\n";
62      return 0;
63  }
```

Program Run

```
Please enter salaries, 0 to quit:
32000
54000
67500
29000
0
The maximum salary is 67500
```

6.5.3 Character Arrays

Character arrays are arrays of values of the character type char.

Just as arrays predate vectors, there was a time when C++ had no string class. All string processing was carried out by manipulating arrays of the type char.

The char type denotes an individual character. Individual character constants are delimited by single quotes; for example,

```
char input = 'y';
```

Note that 'y' is a single character, which is quite different from "y", a string containing a single character. Each character is actually encoded as an integer value. For example, in the ASCII encoding scheme, which is used on the majority of computers today, the character 'y' is encoded as the number 121. (You should never use these actual numeric codes in your programs, of course.)

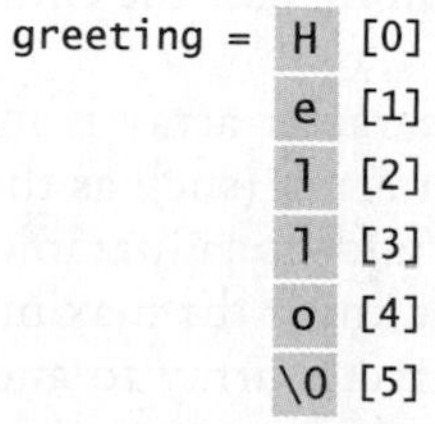

Figure 10 A Character Array

Here is a definition of a character array that holds the string "Hello":

```
char greeting[6] = "Hello";
```

The array contains six characters, namely 'H', 'e', 'l', 'l', 'o' and a *zero termi-nator* '\0'. (See Figure 10.) The terminator is a character that is encoded as the number zero—this is different from the character '0', the character denoting the zero digit. (Under the ASCII encoding scheme, the character denoting the zero digit is encoded as the number 48.)

If you initialize a character array variable with a character array constant (such as "Hello"), then you need not specify the size of the character array variable:

```
char greeting[] = "Hello";
    // Same as char greeting[6] = "Hello"
```

The compiler counts the characters of the initializer (including the zero terminator) and uses that count as the size for the array variable.

A character array constant (such as "Hello") always has a zero terminator. When you create your own character arrays, it is very important that you add the zero ter-minator—the string functions in the standard library depend on it:

```
char mystring[5];
for (i = 0; i < 4; i++)
    mystring[i] = greeting[i];
mystring[4] = '\0'; // Add zero terminator
```

It is an extremely common error to forget the space for this character. You can make this added space requirement more explicit if you always make character arrays MAXLENGTH + 1 characters long:

```
const int MYSTRING_MAXLENGTH = 4;
char mystring[MYSTRING_MAXLENGTH + 1];
```

Here is an implementation of the standard library function strlen that computes the length of a character array. The function keeps counting characters until it encounters a zero terminator.

```
int strlen(const char s[])
{
    int i = 0;
    while (s[i] != '\0')
        i++;
    return i;
}
```

As you can imagine, this function will misbehave if the zero terminator is not present. It will keep on looking past the end of the array until it happens to encoun-ter a zero byte.

Because the end of a character array is marked by a zero terminator, a function that reads from a character array (such as the strlen function above) does not need the size of the array as an additional parameter. However, any function that writes into a character array must know the maximum length. For example, here is a func-tion that appends one character array to another. The function reads from the sec-ond array and can determine its length by the zero terminator. However, the capacity of the first array, to which more characters are added, must be specified as an extra parameter. The s_maxlength value specifies the maximum length of the string stored in the array. It is expected that the array has one more byte to hold the zero terminator.

ch06/append.cpp

```cpp
1  #include <iostream>
2
3  using namespace std;
4
5  /**
6      Appends as much as possible from a string to another string.
7      @param s the string to which t is appended
8      @param s_maxlength the maximum length of s (not counting '\0')
9      @param t the string to append
10 */
11 void append(char s[], int s_maxlength, const char t[])
12 {
13     int i = strlen(s);
14     int j = 0;
15     // Append t to s
16     while (t[j] != '\0' && i < s_maxlength)
17     {
18         s[i] = t[j];
19         i++;
20         j++;
21     }
22     // Add zero terminator
23     s[i] = '\0';
24 }
25
26 int main()
27 {
28     const int GREETING_MAXLENGTH = 10;
29     char greeting[GREETING_MAXLENGTH + 1] = "Hello";
30     char t[] = ", World!";
31     append(greeting, GREETING_MAXLENGTH, t);
32     cout << greeting << "\n";
33     return 0;
34 }
```

Program Run

```
Hello, Wor
```

If you run this program, you will find that it doesn't print Hello, World! The output is truncated because the greeting character array can hold at most ten characters (plus the '\0' terminator). With the string class you never have this problem, because the class finds enough storage space to hold all characters that are added to a string.

Unfortunately, some of the standard library functions do not check whether they write past the end of a character array. For example, the standard function strcat works just like the append function given above, except that it does not check for space in the array to which the characters are appended. Thus, the following call will lead to disaster:

```
const int GREETING_MAXLENGTH = 10;
char greeting[GREETING_MAXLENGTH + 1] = "Hello";
char t[] = ", World!";
strcat(greeting, t); // NO!
```

Four more characters ('l', 'd', '!', and the zero terminator '\0') will be written past the end of the array greeting, overwriting whatever may be stored there. This is an exceedingly common and dangerous programming error.

The standard library has a second function, strncat, that is designed to avoid this problem. You specify the maximum number of characters to copy.

```
const int GREETING_MAXLENGTH = 10;
char greeting[GREETING_MAXLENGTH + 1] = "Hello";
char t[] = ", World!";
strncat(greeting, t, GREETING_MAXLENGTH - strlen(greeting));
```

Generally, it is best to avoid the use of character arrays—the string class is safer and far more convenient. For example, appending a string object to another is trivial:

```
string greeting = "Hello";
string t = ", World!";
greeting = greeting + t;
```

However, occasionally you need to convert a string into a character array because you need to call a function that was written before the string class was invented. In that case, use the c_str member function of the string class. For example, the cstdlib header declares a useful function

```
int atoi(const char s[])
```

that converts a character array containing digits into its integer value:

```
char year[] = "1999";
int y = atoi(year); // Now y is the integer 1999
```

This functionality is inexplicably missing from the string class, and the c_str member function offers an "escape hatch":

```
string year = "1999";
int y = atoi(year.c_str());
```

(In Chapter 9, you will see another method for converting strings to numbers.)

6.5.4 Two-Dimensional Arrays

Use a two-dimensional array to store tabular data.

It often happens that we want to store collections of numbers that have a two-dimensional layout. For example, consider a program that computes values of the pow function, as shown in the table on the next page. Such an arrangement, consisting of rows and columns of values, is called a *two-dimensional array*, or a *matrix*.

1	0	0	0	0	0
1	1	1	1	1	1
1	2	4	8	16	32
1	3	9	27	81	243
1	4	16	64	256	1024
1	5	25	125	625	3125
1	6	36	216	1296	7776
1	7	49	343	2401	16807
1	8	64	512	4096	32768
1	9	81	729	6561	59049
1	10	100	1000	10000	100000

C++ uses an array with two subscripts to store a two-dimensional array:

```
const int POWERS_ROWS = 11;
const int POWERS_COLS = 6;
double powers[POWERS_ROWS][POWERS_COLS];
```

Just as you specify the size of arrays when you define them, you must specify how many rows and columns you need. In this case, you ask for 11 rows and 6 columns.

> Individual elements in a two-dimensional array are accessed by double subscripts m[i][j].

To set a particular element in the two-dimensional array, you need to specify two subscripts in separate brackets to select the row and column, respectively (see Syntax 6.4 on page 291 and Figure 11):

```
powers[3][4] = pow(3, 4);
```

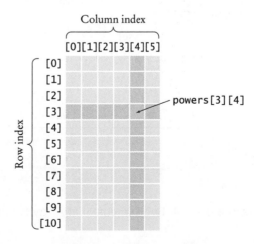

Figure 11
Accessing an Element in a
Two-Dimensional Array

Just as with one-dimensional arrays, you cannot change the size of a two-dimensional array once it has been defined.

To fill a two-dimensional array, you use two nested loops, like this:

```
for (int i = 0; i < POWERS_ROWS; i++)
   for (int j = 0; j < POWERS_COLS; j++)
      powers[i][j] = value for row i, column j;
```

Although these arrays appear to be two-dimensional, they are still stored as a sequence of elements in memory. Figure 12 shows how the powers array is stored, row by row. For example, to reach

```
powers[3][4]
```

the program must first skip past rows 0, 1, and 2 and then locate offset 4 in row 3. The offset from the start of the array is

```
3 * POWERS_COLS + 4
```

When passing a two-dimensional array to a function, you must specify the number of columns *as a constant* with the parameter type. The number of rows can be variable. For example,

```
void print_table(const double table[][POWERS_COLS], int table_rows)
{
   const int WIDTH = 10;
   cout << fixed << setprecision(0);
   for (int i = 0; i < table_rows; i++)
   {
      for (int j = 0; j < POWERS_COLS; j++)
         cout << setw(WIDTH) << table[i][j];
      cout << "\n";
   }
}
```

This function can print two-dimensional arrays with arbitrary numbers of rows, but the rows must have 6 columns. You have to write a different function if you want to print a two-dimensional array with 7 columns. The reason is that the compiler must be able to find the element

```
table[i][j]
```

by computing the offset

```
i * POWERS_COLS + j
```

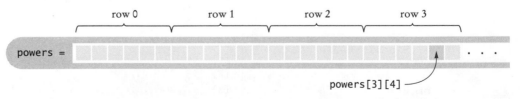

Figure 12   A Two-Dimensional Array Is Stored as a Sequence of Rows

The compiler knows to use POWERS_COLS as the number of columns in the computation of table[i][j] because it was specified in the definition of the table parameter as

```
double table[][POWERS_COLS]
```

If you like, you can specify the number of rows as well:

```
void print_table(double table[POWERS_ROWS][POWERS_COLS])
```

However, the compiler completely ignores the first index. When you access table[i][j], it does not check whether i is less than POWERS_ROWS. It does not check whether j is valid either. It merely computes the offset i * POWERS_COLS + j and locates that element.

Working with two-dimensional arrays is illustrated in ch06/matrix.cpp, a program that fills a two-dimensional array with data and then displays the contents.

SYNTAX 6.4 Two-Dimensional Array Definition

type_name variable_name[*size₁*][*size₂*];

Example:

```
double monthly_sales[NREGIONS][12];
```

Purpose:

Define a new variable that is a two-dimensional array.

QUALITY TIP 6.3

Name the Array Size and Capacity Consistently

It is a good idea to have a consistent naming scheme for array size and capacity. In this section, you always appended _size and _CAPACITY to the array name to denote the size and capacity for an array:

```
const int A_CAPACITY = 20;
int a[A_CAPACITY];
int a_size = 0;
...
int x;
cin >> x;
a[a_size] = x;
a_size++;
```

If you follow this naming convention or one similar to it, you always know how to inquire about the size and capacity of an array. Remember that you need to pass the size to all functions that read the array, and both the size and capacity to all functions that add values to the array.

COMMON ERROR 6.2

Omitting the Column Size of a Two-Dimensional Array Parameter

When passing a one-dimensional array to a function, you specify the size of the array as a separate parameter:

```
double maximum(const double a[], int a_size)
```

This function can compute the maximum of arrays of any size. However, for two-dimensional arrays you cannot simply pass the numbers of rows and columns as parameters:

```
void print(const double table[][], int table_rows,
    int table_cols) // NO!
```

You must know how many columns the two-dimensional array has, and specify the number of columns in the array parameter. This number must be a constant:

```
const int TABLE_COLS = 6;
void print(const double table[][TABLE_COLS],
    int table_rows) // OK
```

RANDOM FACT 6.2

International Alphabets

The English alphabet is pretty simple: upper- and lowercase *a* to *z*. Other European languages have accent marks and special characters. For example, German has three so-called *umlaut* characters, ä, ö, ü, and a *double-s* character ß. These are not optional frills; you couldn't write a page of German text without using these characters a few times. German computer keyboards have keys for these characters (see Figure 13).

This poses a problem for computer users and designers. The American standard character encoding (called ASCII, for American Standard Code for Information Interchange) specifies 128 codes: 52 upper- and lowercase characters, 10 digits, 32 typographical symbols, and 34 control characters (such as space, newline, and 32 others for controlling printers and other

Figure 13   The German Keyboard

Figure 14 The Thai Script

devices). The umlaut and double-s are not among them. Some German data processing systems replace seldom-used ASCII characters with German letters: [\]{|}~ are replaced with Ä Ö Ü ä ö ü ß. While most people can live without these characters, C++ programmers definitely cannot. Other encoding schemes take advantage of the fact that one byte can encode 256 different characters, of which only 128 are standardized by ASCII. Unfortunately, there are multiple incompatible standards for such encodings, resulting in a certain amount of aggravation among European computer users.

Many countries don't use the Roman script at all. Russian, Greek, Hebrew, Arabic, and Thai letters, to name just a few, have completely different shapes (see Figure 14). To complicate matters, Hebrew and Arabic are typed from right to left. Each of these alphabets has between 30 and 100 letters, and the countries using them have established encoding standards for them.

The situation is much more dramatic in languages that use the Chinese script: the Chinese dialects, Japanese, and Korean. The Chinese script is not alphabetic but *ideographic* (see Figure 15). A character represents an idea or thing. Most words are made up of one, two, or

CLASSIC SOUPS

			Sm.	Lg.
清燉雞湯 57.	House Chicken Soup (Chicken, Celery, Potato, Onion, Carrot)		1.50	2.75
雞飯湯 58.	Chicken Rice Soup		1.85	3.25
雞麵湯 59.	Chicken Noodle Soup		1.85	3.25
廣東雲吞 60.	Cantonese Wonton Soup		1.50	2.75
蕃茄蛋湯 61.	Tomato Clear Egg Drop Soup		1.65	2.95
雲吞湯 62.	Regular Wonton Soup		1.10	2.10
酸辣湯 63. 🦐	Hot & Sour Soup		1.10	2.10
蛋花湯 64.	Egg Drop Soup		1.10	2.10
雲蛋湯 65.	Egg Drop Wonton Mix		1.10	2.10
豆腐菜湯 66.	Tofu Vegetable Soup		NA	3.50
雞玉米湯 67.	Chicken Corn Cream Soup		NA	3.50
蟹肉玉米湯 68.	Crab Meat Corn Cream Soup		NA	3.50
海鮮湯 69.	Seafood Soup		NA	3.50

Figure 15 The Chinese Script

three of these ideographic characters. Over 50,000 ideographs are known, of which about 20,000 are in active use. Therefore, two bytes are needed to encode them. China, Taiwan, Japan, and Korea have incompatible encoding standards for them. (Japanese and Korean writing uses a mixture of native syllabic and Chinese ideographic characters.)

The inconsistencies among character encodings have been a major nuisance for international electronic communication and for software manufacturers vying for a global market. Starting in 1988, a consortium of hardware and software manufacturers developed a uniform 21-bit encoding scheme called *unicode* that is capable of encoding text in essentially all written languages of the world [3]. About 100,000 characters have been given codes, including more than 70,000 Chinese, Japanese, and Korean ideographs. There are even plans to add codes for extinct languages, such as Egyptian hieroglyphs.

CHAPTER SUMMARY

1. Use a vector to collect multiple values of the same type.

2. Individual values in a vector are accessed by an integer *index* or *subscript*: v[i].

3. Valid values for the index range from 0 to one less than the size of the array.

4. A bounds error, which occurs if you supply an invalid index to a vector, can have serious consequences.

5. Use the size function to obtain the current size of a vector.

6. Use the push_back member function to add more elements to a vector. Use pop_back to reduce the size.

7. Vectors can occur as the function parameters and return values.

8. Avoid parallel vectors by changing them into vectors of objects.

9. Like vectors, arrays collect elements of the same type. Once the size of an array has been set, it cannot be changed.

10. Array parameters are always passed by reference.

11. The return type of a function cannot be an array.

12. Character arrays are arrays of values of the character type char.

13. Use a two-dimensional array to store tabular data.

14. Individual elements in a two-dimensional array are accessed by double subscripts m[i][j].

FURTHER READING

1. Eugene H. Spafford, "The Internet Worm Program: An Analysis," Purdue Tehcnical Report CSD-TR-823, 1988, http://homes.cerias.purdue.edu/~spaf/tech-reps/823.pdf.

2. Cliff Stoll, *The Cuckoo's Egg*, Doubleday, 1989.

3. The Unicode Consortium, *The Unicode Standard*, Version 5.0, Addison-Wesley, 1996.

REVIEW EXERCISES

Exercise R6.1. Write code that fills a vector v with each sct of values below

  a. 1 2 3 4 5 6 7 8 9 10

  b. 0 2 4 6 8 10 12 14 16 18 20

  c. 1 4 9 16 25 36 49 64 81 100

  d. 0 0 0 0 0 0 0 0 0 0

  e. 1 4 9 16 9 7 4 9 11

Exercise R6.2. Write a loop that fills a vector v with ten random numbers between 1 and 100. Write code for two nested loops that fill v with ten *different* random numbers between 1 and 100.

Exercise R6.3. Write C++ code for a loop that simultaneously computes both the maximum and minimum of a vector.

Exercise R6.4. What is wrong with the following loop?

```
vector<int> v(10);
int i;
for (i = 1; i <= 10; i++) v[i] = i * i;
```

Explain two ways of fixing the error.

Exercise R6.5. What is an index of a vector or array? What are the legal index values? What is a bounds error?

Exercise R6.6. Write a program that contains a bounds error. Run the program. What happens on your computer?

Exercise R6.7. Write a program that fills a vector with the first ten square numbers 1, 4, 9, ..., 100. Compile it and launch the debugger. After the vector has been filled with three numbers, inspect it. Take a screen snapshot of the display that shows the ten slots of the vector.

Exercise R6.8. Write a loop that reads ten numbers and a second loop that displays them in the opposite order from which they were entered.

Exercise R6.9. Give an example of

    a. A useful function that has a vector of integers as a value parameter.

    b. A useful function that has a vector of integers as a reference parameter.

    c. A useful function that has a vector of integers as a return value.

Describe each function; do not implement them.

Exercise R6.10. A function that has a vector as a reference parameter can change the vector in two ways. It can change the contents of individual vector elements, or it can rearrange the elements. Describe two useful functions with vector<Product>& parameters that change a vector of products in each of the two ways just described.

Exercise R6.11. What are parallel vectors? Why are parallel vectors indications of poor programming? How can they be avoided?

Exercise R6.12. Design a class Staff that stores a collection of employees. What public member functions should you support? What advantages and disadvantages does a Staff class have over a vector<Employee>?

Exercise R6.13. Suppose v is a *sorted* vector of employees. Give pseudocode that describes how a new employee can be inserted in its proper position so that the resulting vector stays sorted.

Exercise R6.14. In many programming languages it is not possible to grow a vector. That is, there is no analog to push_back in those languages. Write code that reads a sequence of numbers into a vector without using push_back. First create a vector of a reasonable size (say 20). Also, use an integer variable length that tests how *full* the vector currently is. Whenever a new element is read in, increase length. When length reaches the *size* of the vector (20 at the outset), create a new vector of twice the size and copy all existing elements into the new vector. Write C++ code that performs this task.

Exercise R6.15. How do you perform the following tasks with vectors in C++?

    a. Test that two vectors contain the same elements in the same order.

    b. Copy one vector to another. (*Hint:* You may copy more than one element at a time.)

    c. Fill a vector with zeroes, overwriting all elements in it.

    d. Remove all elements from a vector. (*Hint:* You need not remove them one by one.)

Exercise R6.16. True or false?

    a. All elements of a vector are of the same type.

    b. Vector subscripts must be integers.

    c. Vectors cannot contain strings as elements.

    d. Vectors cannot use strings as subscripts.

    e. Parallel vectors must have equal length.

    f. Two-dimensional arrays always have the same numbers of rows and columns.

g. Two parallel arrays can be replaced by a two-dimensional array.

h. Elements of different columns in a two-dimensional array can have different types.

Exercise R6.17. True or false?

a. All vector parameters are reference parameters.

b. A function cannot return a two-dimensional array.

c. A function cannot change the dimensions of a two-dimensional array that is passed by value.

d. A function cannot change the length of a vector that is passed by reference.

e. A function can only reorder the elements of a vector, not change the elements.

PROGRAMMING EXERCISES

Exercise P6.1. Write a function

```
double scalar_product(vector<double> a, vector<double> b)
```

that computes the scalar product of two vectors. The scalar product is

$$a_0 b_0 + a_1 b_1 + \cdots + a_{n-1} b_{n-1}$$

Exercise P6.2. Write a function that computes the *alternating sum* of all elements in a vector. For example, if alternating_sum is called with a vector containing

$$1 \quad 4 \quad 9 \quad 16 \quad 9 \quad 7 \quad 4 \quad 9 \quad 11$$

then it computes

$$1 - 4 + 9 - 16 + 9 - 7 + 4 - 9 + 11 = -2$$

Exercise P6.3. Write a procedure reverse that reverses the sequence of elements in a vector. For example, if reverse is called with a vector containing

$$1 \quad 4 \quad 9 \quad 16 \quad 9 \quad 7 \quad 4 \quad 9 \quad 11$$

then the vector is changed to

$$11 \quad 9 \quad 4 \quad 7 \quad 9 \quad 16 \quad 9 \quad 4 \quad 1$$

Exercise P6.4. Write a function

```
vector<int> append(vector<int> a, vector<int> b)
```

that appends one vector after another. For example, if a is

$$1 \quad 4 \quad 9 \quad 16$$

and b is

$$9 \quad 7 \quad 4 \quad 9 \quad 11$$

then append returns the vector

$$1 \quad 4 \quad 9 \quad 16 \quad 9 \quad 7 \quad 4 \quad 9 \quad 11$$

Exercise P6.5. Write a function

```
vector<int> merge(vector<int> a, vector<int> b)
```

that merges two arrays, alternating elements from both arrays. If one array is shorter than the other, then alternate as long as you can and then append the remaining elements from the longer array. For example, if a is

1 4 9 16

and b is

9 7 4 9 11

then merge returns the array

1 9 4 7 9 4 16 9 11

Exercise P6.6. Write a function

```
vector<int> merge_sorted(vector<int> a, vector<int> b)
```

that merges two *sorted* vectors, producing a new sorted vector. Keep an index into each vector, indicating how much of it has been processed already. Each time, append the smallest unprocessed element from either vector, then advance the index. For example, if a is

1 4 9 16

and b is

4 7 9 9 11

then merge_sorted returns the vector

1 4 4 7 9 9 9 11 16

Exercise P6.7. Write a predicate function

```
bool equals(vector<int> a, vector<int> b)
```

that checks whether two vectors have the same elements in the same order.

Exercise P6.8. Write a predicate function

```
bool same_set(vector<int> a, vector<int> b)
```

that checks whether two vectors have the same elements in some order, ignoring multiplicities. For example, the two vectors

1 4 9 16 9 7 4 9 11

and

11 11 7 9 16 4 1

would be considered identical. You will probably need one or more helper functions.

Exercise P6.9. Write a predicate function

```
bool same_elements(vector<int> a, vector<int> b)
```

that checks whether two vectors have the same elements in some order, with the same multiplicities. For example,

1 4 9 16 9 7 4 9 11

and

11 1 4 9 16 9 7 4 9

would be considered identical, but

1 4 9 16 9 7 4 9 11

and

11 11 7 9 16 4 1

would not. You will probably need one or more helper functions.

Exercise P6.10. Write a function that removes duplicates from a vector. For example, if remove_duplicates is called with a vector containing

1 4 9 16 9 7 4 9 11

then the vector is changed to

1 4 9 16 7 11

Exercise P6.11. Write a program that asks the user to input a number n and prints all permutations of the sequence of numbers 1, 2, 3, ..., n. For example, if n is 3, the program should print

```
1   2   3
1   3   2
2   1   3
2   3   1
3   1   2
3   2   1
```

Hint: Write a function

```
permutation_helper(vector<int> prefix, vector<int> to_permute)
```

that computes all the permutations in the array to_permute and prints each permutation, prefixed by all numbers in the array prefix. For example, if prefix contains the number 2 and to_permute the numbers 1 and 3, then permutation_helper prints

```
2   1   3
2   3   1
```

The permutation_helper function does the following: If to_permute has no elements, print the elements in prefix. Otherwise, for each element e in to_permute, make an array to_permute2 that is equal to permute except for e and an array prefix2 consisting of prefix and e. Then call permutation_helper with prefix2 and to_permute2.

Exercise P6.12. Write a program that produces ten random permutations of the numbers 1 to 10. To generate a random permutation, you need to fill a vector with the numbers 1 to 10 so that no two entries of the vector have the same contents. You could do it by brute force, by calling rand_int until it produces a value that is not yet in the vector. Instead, you should implement a smart method. Make a second array and fill it with the numbers 1 to 10. Then pick one of those at random, remove it, and append it to the permutation vector. Repeat ten times.

Exercise P6.13. Write a program that prints out a bank statement. The program input is a sequence of transactions. Each transaction has the form

day amount description

For example,

```
15 -224 Check 2140
16 1200 ATM deposit
```

Your program should read in the descriptions and then print out a statement listing all deposits, withdrawals, and the daily balance for each day. You should then compute the interest earned by the account. Use both the *minimum daily balance* and the *average daily balance* methods for computing interest, and print out both values. Use an interest rate of 0.5 percent per month, and assume the month has 30 days. You may assume that the input data are sorted by the date. You may also assume that the first entry is of the form

```
1 1143.24 Initial balance
```

Exercise P6.14. Define a class

```
class Staff
{
public:
   ...
private:
   vector<Employee> members;
};
```

and implement the find and raise_salary procedures for the Staff data type.

Exercise P6.15. Design a class Student, or use one from a previous exercise. A student has a name and a birthday. Make a vector

```
vector<Student> friends;
```

Read a set of names and birthdays in from a file or type them in, thus populating the friends vector. Then print out all friends whose birthday falls in the current month.

Exercise P6.16. The following table can be found in the "West Suburban Boston, Area Code 617, 1990–1991" telephone book.

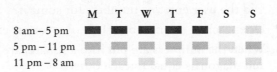

Dial direct		Weekday full rate		Evening 35% discount		Night & Weekend 60% discount	
Sample rates from city of **Waltham** to:	Mileage bands *Airline miles*	First minute	Each additional minute	First minute	Each additional minute	First minute	Each additional minute
Sudbury	0–10	.19	.09	.12	.05	.07	.03
Framingham	11–14	.26	.12	.16	.07	.10	.04
Lowell	15–19	.32	.14	.20	.09	.12	.05
Brockton	20–25	.38	.15	.24	.09	.15	.06
Worcester	26–33	.43	.17	.27	.11	.17	.06
Rockport	34–43	.48	.19	.31	.12	.19	.07
Fall River	44–55	.51	.20	.33	.13	.20	.08
Falmouth	56–70	.53	.21	.34	.13	.21	.08
Hyannis	71–85	.54	.22	.35	.14	.21	.08

Write a program that asks the user:
- The destination of the call
- The starting time
- The length of the call
- The weekday

The program should compute and display the charge. Note that the rate may vary. If the call starts at 4:50 P.M. and ends at 5:10 P.M., then half of it falls into the day rate and half of it into the evening rate.

Exercise P6.17. *Magic squares.* An $n \times n$ matrix that is filled with the numbers 1, 2, 3, . . ., n^2 is a magic square if the sum of the elements in each row, in each column, and in the two diagonals is the same value. For example,

16	3	2	13
5	10	11	8
9	6	7	12
4	15	14	1

Write a program that reads in n^2 values from the keyboard and tests whether they form a magic square when put into array form. You need to test three features:

1. Did the user enter n^2 numbers for some n?
2. Does each of the numbers 1, 2, ..., n^2 occur exactly once in the user input?
3. When the numbers are put into a square, are the sums of the rows, columns, and diagonals equal to each other?

Hint: First read the numbers into a vector. If the size of that vector is a square, test whether all numbers between 1 and n are present. Then fill the numbers into a matrix and compute the row, column, and diagonal sums.

Exercise P6.18. Implement the following algorithm to construct magic $n \times n$ squares; it works only if n is odd. Place a 1 in the middle of the bottom row. After k has been placed in the (i, j) square, place $k + 1$ into the square to the right and down, wrapping around the borders. However, if you reach a square that has already been filled, then you must move one square up instead. Here is the 5×5 square that you get if you follow this method:

11	18	25	2	9
10	12	19	21	3
4	6	13	20	22
23	5	7	14	16
17	24	1	8	15

Write a program whose input is the number n and whose output is the magic square of order n if n is odd.

G   **Exercise P6.19.** A *polygon* is a closed sequence of lines. To describe a polygon, store the sequence of its corner points. Because the number of points is variable, use a vector.

```
class Polygon
{
public:
    Polygon();
    void add_point(Point p);
    void plot() const;
private:
    vector<Point> corners;
};
```

Implement this class and supply a test harness that plots a polygon such as the following:

G Exercise P6.20. Enhance the `Polygon` class of Exercise P6.19 by adding member functions

```
double Polygon::perimeter() const
double Polygon::area() const
```

that compute the perimeter and the area of a polygon. To compute the perimeter, compute the distance between adjacent points, and total up the distances.

The area of a polygon with corners $(x_0, y_0), \ldots, (x_{n-1}, y_{n-1})$ is

$$\frac{1}{2}\left|x_0 y_1 + x_1 y_2 + \cdots + x_{n-1} y_0 - y_0 x_1 - y_1 x_2 - \cdots - y_{n-1} x_0\right|$$

As test cases, compute the perimeter and area of a rectangle and of a regular hexagon.

G Exercise P6.21. Enhance the `Polygon` class of Exercise P6.19 by adding member functions

```
void Polygon::move(double dx, double dy);
void Polygon::scale(double factor);
```

The first procedure moves all points of a polygon by the specified amounts in the x- and y-directions. The second procedure performs a scaling with the given scale factor and updates the coordinates of the points of the polygon accordingly. *Hint:* Use the move member function of the `Point` class. To scale a point, multiply both the x- and y-coordinate with the scale factor.

G Exercise P6.22. Write a procedure

```
void bar_chart(vector<double> data)
```

that displays a bar chart of the values in data. You may assume that all values in data are positive. *Hint:* You must figure out the maximum of the values in data. Set the coordinate system so that the x-range equals the number of bars and the y-range goes from 0 to the maximum.

G Exercise P6.23. Improve the `bar_chart` procedure of Exercise P6.22 to work correctly when data contains negative values.

G Exercise P6.24. Write a procedure

```
void pie_chart(vector<double> data)
```

that displays a pie chart of the values in data. You may assume that all values in data are positive.

G Exercise P6.25. Write a program that plays tic-tac-toe. The tic-tac-toe game is played on a 3 × 3 grid as in

The game is played by two players, who take turns. The first player marks moves with a circle, the second with a cross. The player who has formed a horizontal, vertical, or diagonal sequence of three marks wins. Your program should draw the game board, accept mouse clicks into empty squares, change the players after every successful move, and pronounce the winner.

Pointers

CHAPTER GOALS

- To learn how to declare, initialize, and use pointers
- To become familiar with dynamic memory allocation and deallocation
- To use pointers in common programming situations that involve optional and shared objects
- To avoid the common errors of dangling pointers and memory leaks
- To understand the relationship between arrays and pointers
- To be able to convert between string objects and character pointers
- To learn about function pointers and how they are used

An object variable *contains* an object, but a pointer specifies *where* an object is located. In C++, pointers are important for several reasons. Pointers can refer to objects that are allocated on demand. Pointers can be used for *shared access* to objects. Furthermore, as you will see in Chapter 8, pointers are necessary for implementing *polymorphism*, an important concept in object-oriented programming.

In C++, there is a deep relationship between pointers and arrays. You will see in this chapter how this relationship explains a number of special properties and limitations of arrays. Finally, you will see how to convert between string objects and char* pointers, which is necessary when interfacing with legacy code.

CHAPTER CONTENTS

7.1 Pointers and Memory Allocation

> Use dynamic memory allocation if you do not know in advance how many objects you need.

In many programming situations, you do not know beforehand how many objects you need. To solve this problem, you can use *dynamic allocation* and ask the C++ run-time system to create a new object whenever you need it. When you ask for a

```
new Employee
```

> The new operator allocates an object from the heap.

then a *memory allocator* finds a storage location for a new employee object. (See Syntax 7.1 on page 309.) The memory allocator keeps a large storage area, called the *heap*, for that purpose. The heap is a very flexible pool for memory. It can hold values of any type. You can equally ask for

```
new Time
new Product
```

The expression

```
new Employee
```

differs in an important way from a variable declaration

```
Employee harry;
```

The variable harry lives on the *stack*, a storage area that is associated with the function in which it is defined. When that function exits, the object is automatically reclaimed.

```
void f()
{
    Employee harry;  // Memory for employee allocated on the stack
    ...
} // Memory for employee automatically reclaimed
```

> Dynamically allocated objects live until they are explicitly reclaimed.

In contrast, the employee object that is allocated with

```
new Employee
```

stays alive until the programmer reclaims it. You will see in Section 7.2 how to explicitly deallocate the object.

This difference gives rise to another reason for using dynamic allocation: to produce objects that live longer than the function that created them.

> A pointer denotes the location of a value in memory.

When you allocate a new heap object, the memory allocator tells you where the object is located, by giving you the object's *memory address*. To manipulate memory addresses, you need to learn about a new C++ data type: the *pointer*. A pointer to an employee record,

```
Employee* boss;
```

contains the location or memory address for an employee object. A pointer to a time object,

```
Time* deadline;
```

stores the memory address for a time object. See Syntax 7.2 on page 309.

> The * operator locates the value to which a pointer points.

The types Employee* and Time* denote pointers to employee and time objects. The boss and deadline variables of type Employee* and Time* store the locations or memory addresses of employee and time objects. They cannot store actual employee objects or time objects, however (see Figure 1). As you look at that figure, also note that the pointer variables boss and deadline are allocated on the stack, whereas the objects to which they point are allocated on the heap.

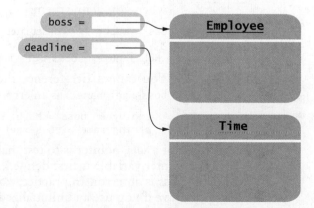

Figure 1
Pointers and the Objects to
Which They Point

When you create a new object on the heap, you usually want to initialize it. You can supply construction parameters, using the familiar syntax.

```
Employee* boss = new Employee("Lin, Lisa", 68000);
```

> Finding the value to which a pointer points is called dereferencing.

When you have a pointer to a value, you often want to access the value to which it points. That action—to go from the pointer to the value—is called *dereferencing*. In C++ the * operator is used to indicate the value associated with a pointer. For example, if boss is an Employee*, then *boss is an Employee value:

```
Employee* boss = ...;
raise_salary(*boss, 10);
```

Suppose you want to find out the name of the employee to which boss points:

```
Employee* boss =  ...;
string name = *boss.get_name(); // Error
```

Unfortunately, that is a syntax error. The dot operator has a higher precedence than the * operator. That is, the compiler thinks that you mean

```
string name = *(boss.get_name()); // Error
```

However, boss is a pointer, not an object. You can't apply the dot (.) operator to a pointer, and the compiler reports an error. Instead, you must make it clear that you first want to apply the * operator, then the dot:

```
string name = (*boss).get_name(); // OK
```

> Use the -> operator to access a data member or a member function through an object pointer.

Because this is such a common situation, the designers of C++ supply an operator to abbreviate the "dereference and access member" operation. That operator is written -> and usually pronounced as "arrow".

```
string name = boss->get_name(); // OK
```

Dereferencing of pointers and accessing members through pointers are summarized in Syntax 7.3 on page 309.

> The NULL pointer does not point to any object.

There is one special value, NULL, that can be used to indicate a pointer that doesn't point anywhere. Instead of leaving pointer variables uninitialized, you should always set pointer variables to NULL when you define them.

```
Employee* boss = NULL; // will set later
...
if (boss != NULL) name = boss->get_name(); // OK
```

> It is an error to dereference an uninitialized pointer or the NULL pointer.

You cannot dereference the NULL pointer. That is, calling *boss or boss->get_name() is an error as long as boss is NULL.

```
Employee* boss = NULL;
string name = boss->get_name(); // NO!! Program will crash
```

The purpose of a NULL pointer is to test that it doesn't point to any valid object.

When a pointer variable is first defined, it contains a random address. Using that random address is an error. In practice, your program will likely crash or mysteriously misbehave if you use an uninitialized pointer:

```
Employee* boss;
string name = boss->get_name(); // NO!! boss contains a random address
```

You must always initialize a pointer so that it points to an actual value before you can use it:

```
Employee* boss = new Employee("Lin, Lisa", 68000);
string name = boss->get_name(); // OK
```

SYNTAX 7.1 new Expression

new *type_name*
new *type_name*(*expression*$_1$, *expression*$_2$, ..., *expression*$_n$)

Example:

```
new Time
new Employee("Lin, Lisa", 68000)
```

Purpose:

Allocate and construct a value on the heap and return a pointer to the value.

SYNTAX 7.2 Pointer Variable Definition

type_name *variable_name*;
type_name *variable_name* = *expression*;

Example:

```
Employee* boss;
Product* p = new Product;
```

Purpose:

Define a new pointer variable, and optionally supply an initial value.

SYNTAX 7.3 Pointer Dereferencing

*pointer_expression
pointer_expression->class_member

Example:

```
*boss
boss->set_salary(70000)
```

Purpose:

Access the object to which a pointer points.

COMMON ERROR 7.1

Confusing Pointers with the Data to Which They Point

A pointer is a memory address—a number that tells where a value is located in memory. You can only carry out a small number of operations on a pointer:

- assign it to a pointer variable
- compare it with another pointer or the special value NULL
- dereference it to access the value to which it points

However, it is a common error to confuse the pointer with the value to which it points:

```
Employee* boss = ...;
raise_salary(boss, 10); // ERROR
```

Remember that the pointer boss only describes *where* the employee object is. To actually refer to the employee object, use *boss:

```
raise_salary(*boss, 10); // OK
```

COMMON ERROR 7.2

Declaring Two Pointers on the Same Line

It is legal in C++ to define multiple variables together, like this:

```
int i = 0, j = 1;
```

This style does *not* work with pointers:

```
Employee* p, q;
```

For historical reasons, the * associates only with the first variable. That is, p is a Employee* pointer, and q is an Employee object. The remedy is to define each pointer variable separately:

```
Employee* p;
Employee* q;
```

You will see some programmers group the * with the variable:

```
Employee *p, *q;
```

While it is a legal declaration, don't use that style. It makes it harder to tell that p and q are variables of type Employee*.

ADVANCED TOPIC 7.1

The this Pointer

Each member function has a special parameter variable, called this, which is a pointer to the implicit parameter. For example, consider the Product::is_better_than function of Chapter 5. If you call

```
next.is_better_than(best)
```

then the this pointer has type Product* and points to the next object.

You can use the `this` pointer inside the definition of a member function. For example,

```
bool Product::is_better_than(Product b)
{
    if (this->price == 0) return true;
    if (b.price == 0) return false;
    return this->score / this->price > b.score / b.price;
}
```

> In a member function, the `this` pointer points to the implicit parameter.

Here, the expression `this->price` refers to the `price` member of the object to which `this` points, that is, the `price` member of the implicit parameter, or `next.price`. The `this` pointer is not necessary, however, since by convention the expression `price` also refers to the field of the implicit parameter. Nevertheless, some programmers like to use the `this` pointer to make it explicit that `price` is a member and not a variable.

Note that `this` is a pointer whereas `b` is an object. Therefore, we access the `price` member of the implicit parameter as `this->price`, but for the explicit parameter we use `b.price`.

Very occasionally, a member function needs to pass the implicit parameter in its entirety to another function. Since `this` is a pointer to the implicit parameter, `*this` is the actual implicit parameter. For example, suppose someone defined a function

```
void debug_print(string message, Product p)
```

Then the code for the `is_better_than` function might start out with these statements:

```
debug_print("Implicit parameter:", *this);
debug_print("Explicit parameter:", b);
```

7.2 Deallocating Dynamic Memory

When your program no longer needs a value that you previously allocated with the `new` operator, you must reclaim it using the `delete` operator:

```
void g()
{
    Employee* boss;
    boss = new Employee(...); // Memory for employee allocated on the heap
    ...
    delete boss; // Memory for employee manually reclaimed
}
```

> You must reclaim dynamically allocated objects with the `delete` operator.

Actually, the foregoing example is a little more complex than that. There are two allocations: one on the stack and one on the heap. The variable `boss` is allocated on the stack. It is of type `Employee*`; that is, `boss` can hold the address of an employee object. Defining the pointer variable does not yet create an `Employee` object. The next line of code allocates an `Employee` object on the heap and stores its address in the pointer variable.

At the end of the block, the storage space for the pointer variable `boss` on the stack is automatically reclaimed. Reclaiming the pointer variable does not automatically reclaim the object to which it points. The memory address is merely forgotten.

(That can be a problem—see Common Error 7.4 on page 313). Therefore, you must manually delete the memory block holding the object.

Note that the pointer variable on the stack has a *name*, namely boss. But the employee object, allocated on the heap with new Employee, has no name! It can be reached only through the boss pointer. Values on the stack always have names; heap values do not.

After you delete the value attached to a pointer, you can no longer use that address! The storage space may already be reassigned to another value.

```
delete boss;
string name = boss->get_name(); // NO!! boss points to a deleted element
```

SYNTAX 7.4 delete Expression

delete *pointer_expression*;

Example:

delete boss;

Purpose:

Deallocate a value that is stored on the heap and allow the memory to be reallocated.

COMMON ERROR 7.3

Dangling Pointers

The most common pointer error is to use a pointer that has not been initialized, or that has already been deleted. Such a pointer is called a *dangling* pointer, because it does point somewhere, just not to a valid object. You can create real damage by writing to the location to which it points. Even reading from the location can crash your program.

> Using a dangling pointer (a pointer that has not been initialized or has been deleted) is a serious programming error.

An uninitialized pointer has a good chance of pointing to an address that your program doesn't own. On most operating systems, attempting to access such a location causes a processor error, and the operating system shuts down the program. You may have seen that happen to other programs—a dialog box with a bomb icon or a message such as "general protection fault" or "segmentation fault" comes up, and the program is terminated.

If a dangling pointer points to a valid address inside your program, then writing to it will damage some part of your program. You will change the value of one of your variables, or perhaps damage the control structures of the heap so that after several calls to new something crazy happens.

When your program crashes and you restart it, the problem may not reappear, or it may manifest itself in different ways because the random pointer is now initialized with a different random address. Programming with pointers requires iron discipline, because you can create true damage with dangling pointers.

Always initialize pointer variables. If you can't initialize them with the return value of new, then set them to NULL.

Never use a pointer that has been deleted. Some people immediately set every pointer to NULL after deleting it. That is certainly helpful:

```
delete first;
first = NULL;
```

However, it is not a complete solution.

```
second = first;
...
delete first;
first = NULL;
```

You must still remember that second is now dangling. As you can see, you must carefully keep track of all pointers and the corresponding heap objects to avoid dangling pointers.

COMMON ERROR 7.4

Memory Leaks

The second most common pointer error is to allocate memory on the heap and never deallocate it. A memory block that is never deallocated is called a *memory leak.*

If you allocate a few small blocks of memory and forget to deallocate them, this is not a huge problem. When the program exits, all allocated memory is returned to the operating system.

But if your program runs for a long time, or if it allocates lots of memory (perhaps in a loop), then it can run out of memory. Memory exhaustion will cause your program to crash. In extreme cases, the computer may freeze up if your program exhausted all available memory. Avoiding memory leaks is particularly important in programs that need to run for months or years, without restarting.

> Every call to new should have a matching call to delete.

Even if you write short-lived programs, you should make it a habit to avoid memory leaks. Make sure that every call to the new operator has a corresponding call to the delete operator.

ADVANCED TOPIC 7.2

The Address Operator

The new operator returns the memory address of a new value that is allocated on the heap. You can also obtain the address of an existing variable by applying the address (&) operator. For example,

```
Employee harry;
Employee* p = &harry;
```

See Figure 2.

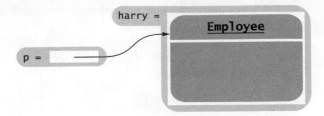

Figure 2
The Address Operator

However, you should never delete an address that you obtained in this way.

```
delete &harry; // ERROR!
```

Doing so would add a block of stack memory to memory that is managed by the heap. Later, that block of memory could be simultaneously allocated to a stack and a heap object. Mutating one of them would corrupt the other. This is a serious error that is very difficult to debug.

7.3   Common Uses for Pointers

In the preceding sections, you have seen how to define and use pointer variables. In this section, you will learn how pointers can be useful for solving common programming problems.

In our first example, we will model a Department class that describes a department in a company or university, such as the Shipping Department or the Computer Science Department. In our model, a department has

- a name of type string (such as "Shipping")
- an *optional* receptionist of type Employee

We will use a pointer to model the fact that the receptionist is optional:

```
class Department
{
   ...
private:
   string name;
   Employee* receptionist;
};
```

If a particular department has a receptionist, then the pointer will be set to the address of an employee object. Otherwise, the pointer will be the special value NULL. In the constructor, we set the value to NULL:

```
Department::Department(String n)
{
   name = n;
   receptionist = NULL;
}
```

The `set_receptionist` function sets the pointer to the address of an employee object:

```
void Department::set_receptionist(Employee* r)
{
   receptionist = r;
}
```

The `print` function prints either the name of the receptionist or the string `"None"`.

```
void Department::print() const
{
   cout << "Name: " << name
      << "\nReceptionist: ";
   if (receptionist == NULL)
      cout << "None";
   else
       cout << receptionist->get_name();
   cout << "\n";
}
```

Note the use of the -> operator when calling the `get_name` function. Since receptionist is a pointer, and not an object, it would be an error to use the dot operator.

> Pointers can be used to model optional values (by using a NULL pointer when the value is not present).

Here we take advantage of pointers to model a relationship in which one object may refer to 0 or 1 occurrences of another object. Without pointers, it would have been more difficult and less efficient to express the optional nature of the employee object. You might use a Boolean variable and an object, like this:

```
class Department // Modeled without pointers
{
   ...
private:
   string name;
   boolean has_receptionist;
   Employee receptionist;
};
```

Now those department objects that don't have a receptionist still use up storage space for an unused employee object. Clearly, pointers offer a better solution.

> Pointers can be used to provide shared access to a common value.

Another common use of pointers is *sharing*. Some departments may have a receptionist and a secretary; in others, one person does double duty. Rather than duplicating objects, we can use pointers to share the object (see Figure 3).

```
class Department
{
   ...
private:
   string name;
   Employee* receptionist;
   Employee* secretary;
};
```

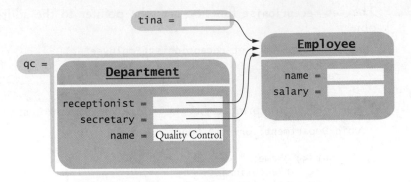

Figure 3   Three Pointers Share an Employee Object

Sharing is particularly important when changes to the object need to be observed by all users of the object. Consider, for example, the following code sequence:

```
Employee* tina = new Employee("Tester, Tina", 50000);
Department qc("Quality Control");
qc.set_receptionist(tina);
qc.set_secretary(tina);
tina->set_salary(55000);
```

Now there are three pointers to the employee object: `tina` and the `receptionist` and `secretary` pointers in the `qc` object. When raising the salary, the new salary is set in the shared object, and the changed salary is visible from all three pointers.

In contrast, we might have modeled the department with two employee objects, like this:

```
class Department // Modeled without pointers
{
    ...
private:
    string name;
    Employee receptionist;
    Employee secretary;
};
```

Now consider the equivalent code:

```
Employee tina("Tester, Tina", 50000);
Department qc("Quality Control");
qc.set_receptionist(tina);
qc.set_secretary(tina);
tina.set_salary(55000);
```

The department object contains two copies of the `tina` object. When raising the salary, the copies are not affected (see Figure 4).

This example shows that pointers are very useful to model a "$n : 1$" relationship, in which a number of different variables share the same object.

In Chapter 8, you will see another use of pointers, in which a pointer can refer to objects of varying types. That phenomenon, called *polymorphism*, is an important part of object-oriented programming.

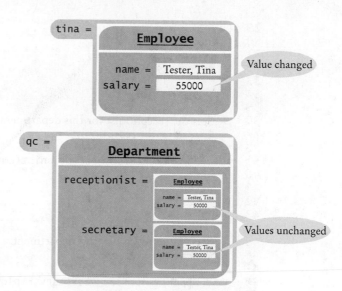

Figure 4
Separate Employee Objects

The following program gives a complete implementation of the Department class. Note how the pointers are used to express optional and shared objects.

ch07/department.cpp

```cpp
1  #include <string>
2  #include <iostream>
3
4  using namespace std;
5
6  #include "ccc_empl.h"
7
8  /**
9      A department in an organization.
10  */
11  class Department
12  {
13  public:
14     Department(string n);
15     void set_receptionist(Employee* e);
16     void set_secretary(Employee* e);
17     void print() const;
18  private:
19     string name;
20     Employee* receptionist;
21     Employee* secretary;
22  };
23
24  /**
25      Constructs a department with a given name.
26      @param n  the department name
27  */
28  Department::Department(string n)
```

```
29  {
30     name = n;
31     receptionist = NULL;
32     secretary = NULL;
33  }
34
35  /**
36     Sets the receptionist for this department.
37     @param e the receptionist
38  */
39  void Department::set_receptionist(Employee* e)
40  {
41     receptionist = e;
42  }
43
44  /**
45     Sets the secretary for this department.
46     @param e the secretary
47  */
48  void Department::set_secretary(Employee* e)
49  {
50     secretary = e;
51  }
52
53  /**
54     Prints a description of this department.
55  */
56  void Department::print() const
57  {
58     cout << "Name: " << name << "\n"
59        << "Receptionist: ";
60     if (receptionist == NULL)
61        cout << "None";
62     else
63        cout << receptionist->get_name() << " "
64           << receptionist->get_salary();
65     cout << "\nSecretary: ";
66     if (secretary == NULL)
67        cout << "None";
68     else if (secretary == receptionist)
69        cout << "Same";
70     else
71        cout << secretary->get_name() << " "
72           << secretary->get_salary();
73     cout << "\n";
74  }
75
76  int main()
77  {
78     Department shipping("Shipping");
79     Department qc("Quality Control");
80     Employee* harry = new Employee("Hacker, Harry", 45000);
81     shipping.set_secretary(harry);
82     Employee* tina = new Employee("Tester, Tina", 50000);
```

```
83    qc.set_receptionist(tina);
84    qc.set_secretary(tina);
85    tina->set_salary(55000);
86    shipping.print();
87    qc.print();
88    delete tina;
89    delete harry;
90    return 0;
91  }
```

Program Run

```
Name: Shipping
Receptionist: None
Secretary: Hacker, Harry 45000
Name: Quality Control
Receptionist: Tester, Tina 55000
Secretary: Same
```

ADVANCED TOPIC 7.3

References

In Section 4.8, you saw how to use *reference parameters* in functions that modify variables. For example, consider the function

```
void raise_salary(Employee& e, double by)
{
   double new_salary = e.get_salary() * (1 + by / 100);
   e.set_salary(new_salary);
}
```

This function modifies the first parameter but not the second. That is, if you call the function as

```
raise_salary(harry, percent);
```

then the value of harry may change, but the value of percent is unaffected.

A reference is a pointer in disguise. The function receives two parameters: the address of an Employee object and a copy of a double value. The function is logically equivalent to

```
void raise_salary(Employee* pe, double by)
{
   double new_salary = pe->get_salary() * (1 + by / 100);
   pe->set_salary(new_salary);
}
```

The function call is equivalent to the call

```
raise_salary(&harry, percent);
```

This is an example of sharing: the pointer variable in the function modifies the original object, and not a copy.

When you use references, the compiler automatically passes parameter addresses and dereferences the pointer parameters in the function body. For that reason, references are more convenient for the programmer than explicit pointers.

RANDOM FACT 7.1

Electronic Voting Machines

In the 2000 presidential elections in the United States, votes were tallied by a variety of machines. Some machines processed cardboard ballots into which voters punched holes to indicate their choices (see Figure 5). When voters were not careful, remains of paper—the now infamous "chads"—were partially stuck in the punch cards, causing votes to be miscounted. A manual recount was necessary, but it was not carried out everywhere due to time constraints and procedural wrangling. The election was very close, and there remain doubts in the minds of many people whether the election outcome would have been different if the voting machines had accurately counted the intent of the voters.

Subsequently, voting machine manufacturers have argued that electronic voting machines would avoid the problems caused by punch cards or optically scanned forms. In an electronic voting machine, voters indicate their preferences by pressing buttons or touching icons on a computer screen. Typically, each voter is presented with a summary screen for review before casting the ballot. The process is very similar to using an automatic bank teller machine (see Figure 6).

It seems plausible that these machines make it more likely that a vote is counted in the same way that the voter intends. However, there has been significant controversy surrounding some types of electronic voting machines. If a machine simply records the votes and prints out the totals after the election has been completed, then how do you know that the machine worked correctly? Inside the machine is a computer that executes a program, and, as you may know from your own experience, programs can have bugs.

In fact, some electronic voting machines do have bugs. There have been isolated cases where machines reported tallies that were impossible. When a machine reports far more or far fewer votes than voters, then it is clear that it malfunctioned. Unfortunately, it is then impossible to find out the actual votes. Over time, one would expect these bugs to be fixed in the software. More insidiously, if the results are plausible, nobody may ever investigate.

Figure 5   Punch Card Ballot

Figure 6   Touch Screen Voting Machine

Many computer scientists have spoken out on this issue and confirmed that it is impossible, with today's technology, to tell that software is error free and has not been tampered with. Many of them recommend that electronic voting machines should employ a *voter verifiable audit trail*. (A good source of information is http://verifiedvoting.org.) Typically, a voter-verifiable machine prints out a ballot. Each voter has a chance to review the printout, and then deposits it in an old-fashioned ballot box. If there is a problem with the electronic equipment, the printouts can be scanned or counted by hand.

As this book is written, this concept is strongly resisted both by manufacturers of electronic voting machines and by their customers, the cities and counties that run elections. Manufacturers are reluctant to increase the cost of the machines because they may not be able to pass the cost increase on to their customers, who tend to have tight budgets. Election officials fear problems with malfunctioning printers, and some of them have publicly stated that they actually prefer equipment that eliminates bothersome recounts.

What do you think? You probably use an automatic bank teller machine to get cash from your bank account. Do you review the paper record that the machine issues? Do you check your bank statement? Even if you don't, do you put your faith in other people who double-check their balances, so that the bank won't get away with widespread cheating?

At any rate, is the integrity of banking equipment more important or less important than that of voting machines? Won't every voting process have some room for error and fraud anyway? Is the added cost for equipment, paper, and staff time reasonable to combat a potentially slight risk of malfunction and fraud? Computer scientists cannot answer these questions—an informed society must make these tradeoffs. But, like all professionals, they have an obligation to speak out and give accurate testimony about the capabilities and limitations of computing equipment.

7.4 Arrays and Pointers

> The value of an array variable is a pointer to the starting element of the array.

There is an intimate connection between arrays and pointers in C++. Consider this declaration of an array:

```
int a[10];
```

The value of a is a pointer to the starting element (see Figure 7).

```
int* p = a; // Now p points to a[0]
```

You can dereference a by using the * operator: The statement

```
*a = 12;
```

has the same effect as the statement

```
a[0] = 12;
```

> Pointer arithmetic means adding an integer offset to an array pointer, yielding a pointer that skips past the given number of elements.

Moreover, pointers into arrays support *pointer arithmetic*. You can add an integer offset to the pointer to point at another array location. For example,

```
a + 3
```

is a pointer to the array element with index 3. Dereferencing that pointer yields the element a[3]. In fact, for any integer n, it is true that

```
a[n] == *(a + n)
```

> The array/pointer duality law states that a[n] is identical to *(a + n), where a is a pointer into an array and n is an integer offset.

This relationship is called the *array/pointer duality law*.

This law explains why all C++ arrays start with an index of zero. The pointer a (or a + 0) points to the starting element of the array. That element must therefore be a[0].

The connection between arrays and pointers becomes even more important when considering array parameters of functions. Consider the maximum function from Section 6.5.2.

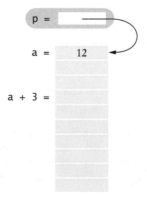

Figure 7 Pointers into an Array

```
double maximum(const double a[], int a_size)
{
   if (a_size == 0) return 0;
   double highest = a[0];
   for (int i = 0; i < a_size; i++)
      if (a[i] > highest)
         highest = a[i];
   return highest;
}
```

Call this function with a particular array:

```
double data[10];
... // Initialize data
double m = maximum(data, 10);
```

> When passing an array to a function, only the starting address is passed.

Note the value data that is passed to the maximum function. It is actually a pointer to the starting element of the array. In other words, the maximum function could have equally well been declared as

```
double maximum(const double* a, int a_size)
{
   ...
}
```

The const modifier indicates that the pointer a can only be used for reading, not for writing.

The parameter declaration of the first example

```
const double a[]
```

is merely another way of declaring a pointer parameter. The declaration gives the illusion that an entire array is passed to the function, but in fact the function receives only the starting address for the array.

It is essential that the function also knows where the array ends. The second parameter a_size indicates the size of the array that starts at a.

ADVANCED TOPIC 7.4

Using a Pointer to Step Through an Array

Now that you know that the first parameter of the maximum function is a pointer, you can implement the function in a slightly different way. Rather than incrementing an integer index, you can increment a pointer variable to visit all array elements in turn:

```
double maximum(const double* a, int a_size)
{
   if (a_size == 0) return 0;
   double highest = *a;
   const double* p = a + 1;
   int count = a_size - 1;
   while (count > 0)
   {
```

```
        if (*p > highest)
            highest = *p;
        p++;
        count--;
    }
    return highest;
}
```

Initially, the pointer p points to the element a[1]. The increment

```
p++;
```

moves it to point to the next element (see Figure 8).

It is a tiny bit more efficient to dereference and increment a pointer than to access an array element as a[i]. For this reason, some programmers routinely use pointers instead of indexes to access array elements. However, the efficiency gain is quite insignificant, and the resulting code is harder to understand, so it is not recommended. (See also Quality Tip 7.1 on page 324.)

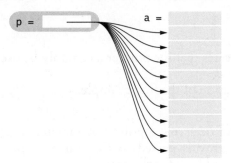

Figure 8   A Pointer Variable Traversing the Elements of an Array

QUALITY TIP 7.1

Program Clearly, Not Cleverly

Some programmers take great pride in minimizing the number of instructions, even if the resulting code is hard to understand. For example, here is a legal implementation of the maximum function:

```
double maximum(const double* a, int a_size)
{
    if (a_size == 0) return 0;
    double highest = *a;
    while (--a_size > 0)
        if (*++a > highest)
            highest = *a;
    return highest;
}
```

This implementation uses two tricks. First, the function parameters a and a_size are variables, and it is legal to modify them. Moreover, the expressions

    --a_size

and

    ++a

mean "decrement or increment the variable and return the new value". Therefore, *++a is the location to which a points after it has been incremented.

Please do not use this programming style. Your job as a programmer is not to dazzle other programmers with your cleverness, but to write code that is easy to understand and maintain.

COMMON ERROR 7.5

Confusing Array and Pointer Declarations

It can be confusing to tell whether a particular variable declaration yields a pointer variable or an array variable. There are four cases:

```
int* p; // p is a pointer
int a[10]; // a is an array
int a[] = { 2, 3, 5, 7, 11, 13 }; // a is an array
void f(int a[]); // a is a pointer
```

In the first case, you must initialize p to point somewhere before you use it.

COMMON ERROR 7.6

Returning a Pointer to a Local Array

Consider this function that tries to return a pointer to an array containing two elements, the minimum and the maximum value of an array.

```
double* minmax(const double a[], int a_size)
{
   assert(a_size > 0);
   double result[2];
   result[0] = a[0]; // result[0] is the minimum
   result[1] = a[0]; // result[1] is the maximum

   for (int i = 0; i < a_size; i++)
   {
      if (a[i] < result[0]) result[0] - a[i];
      if (a[i] > result[1]) result[1] = a[i];
   }
   return result; // ERROR!
}
```

The function returns a pointer to the starting element of the `result` array. However, that array is a local variable of the `minmax` function. The local variable is no longer valid when the function exits, and the values will soon be overwritten by other functions calls.

Unfortunately, it depends on various factors when the values are overwritten. Consider this test of the flawed `minmax` function:

```
double a[] = { 3, 5, 10, 2 };
double* mm = minmax(a, 4);
cout << mm[0] << " " << mm[1] << "\n";
```

One compiler yields the expected result:

```
2 10
```

However, another compiler yields:

```
1.78747e-307 10
```

It just happens that the other compiler chose a different implementation of the `iostream` library that involved more function calls, thereby clobbering the `result[0]` value sooner.

It is possible to work around this limitation, by returning a pointer to an array that is allocated on the heap. But the best solution is to avoid arrays and pointers altogether and to use vectors instead. As you have seen in Chapter 6, a function can easily and safely receive and return `vector<double>` objects:

```
vector<double> minmax(const vector<double>& a)
{
    assert (a.size() > 0);
    vector<double> result(2);
    result[0] = a[0]; // result[0] is the minimum
    result[1] = a[0]; // result[1] is the maximum

    for (int i = 0; i < a.size(); i++)
    {
        if (a[i] < result[0]) result[0] = a[i];
        if (a[i] > result[1]) result[1] = a[i];
    }
    return result; // OK!
}
```

ADVANCED TOPIC 7.5

Dynamically Allocated Arrays

You can allocate arrays of values from the heap. For example,

```
int staff_capacity = ...;
Employee* staff = new Employee[staff_capacity];
```

The `new` operator allocates an array of `staff_capacity` objects of type `Employee`, each of which is constructed with the default constructor. It returns a pointer to the starting element of the array. Because of array/pointer duality, you can access elements of the array with the `[]` operator: `staff[i]` is the `Employee` element with offset `i`.

To deallocate the array, you use the delete[] operator.

```
delete[] staff;
```

It is an error to deallocate an array with the delete operator (without the []). However, the compiler can't detect this error—it doesn't remember whether a pointer variable points to a single object or to an array of objects. Therefore, you must be careful and remember which pointer variables point to individual objects and which pointer variables point to arrays.

Heap arrays have one big advantage over array variables. If you declare an array variable, you must specify a fixed array size when you compile the program. But when you allocate an array on the heap, you can choose a different size for each program run.

If you later need more elements, you can allocate a bigger heap array, copy the elements from the smaller array into the bigger array, and delete the smaller array:

```
int bigger_capacity = 2 * staff_capacity;
Employee* bigger = new Employee[bigger_capacity];
for (int i = 0; i < staff_capacity; i++)
   bigger[i] = staff[i];
delete[] staff;
staff = bigger;
staff_capacity = bigger_capacity;
```

As you can see, heap arrays are more flexible than array variables. However, you should not actually use them in your programs. Use vector objects instead. A vector contains a pointer to a dynamic array, and it automatically manages it for you.

7.5 Pointers to Character Strings

C++ has two mechanisms for manipulating strings. The string class stores an arbitrary sequence of characters and supports many convenient operations such as concatenation and string comparison. However, C++ also inherits a more primitive level of string handling from the C language, in which strings are represented as arrays of char values.

While we don't recommend that you use character pointers or arrays in your programs, you occasionally need to interface with functions that receive or return char* values. Then you need to know how to convert between char* pointers and string objects.

> Low-level string manipulation functions use pointers of type char*.

In particular, literal strings such as "Harry" are actually stored inside char arrays, not string objects. When you use the literal string "Harry" in an expression, the compiler allocates an array of 6 characters (including a '\0' terminator—see Section 6.5.3). The value of the string expression is a char* pointer to the starting letter.

For example, the code

```
string name = "Harry";
```

is equivalent to

```
char* p = "Harry"; // p points to the letter 'H'
string name = p;
```

> You can construct string variables from char* pointers.

The string class has a constructor string(char*) that you can use to convert any character pointer or array to a safe and convenient string object. That constructor is called whenever you initialize a string variable with a char* object, as in the preceding example.

Here is another typical scenario. The tmpnam function of the standard library yields a unique string that you can use as the name of a temporary file. It returns a char* pointer:

```
char* p = tmpnam(NULL);
```

Simply turn the char* return value into a string object:

```
string name = p;
```

or

```
string name(p);
```

> You can use the c_str member function to obtain a char* pointer from a string object.

Conversely, some functions require a parameter of type char*. Then use the c_str member function of the string class to obtain a char* pointer that points to the first character in the string object.

For example, the tempnam function in the standard library, which also yields a name for a temporary file, lets the caller specify a directory. (Note that the tmpnam and tempnam function names are confusingly similar.) The tempnam function expects a char* parameter for the directory name. You can therefore call it as follows:

```
string dir = ...;
char* p = tempnam(dir.c_str(), NULL);
```

As you can see, you don't have to use character arrays to interface with functions that use char* pointers. Simply use string objects and convert between string and char* types when necessary.

COMMON ERROR 7.7

Failing to Allocate Memory

The most dangerous character pointer error is to copy a string into random memory.

```
char* p;
strcpy(p, "Harry");
```

This is not a syntax error. The strcpy function expects two character pointers. However, where is the string copied to? The target address p is an uninitialized pointer, pointing to a random location. The characters in the string "Harry" are now copied into that random location. There is a good chance that the operating system notices that the random memory location doesn't belong to the program. In that case, the operating system terminates the program with extreme prejudice. However, it is also possible that the random memory location happens to be accessible by the program. In that case some other, presumably useful, data will be overwritten.

There is an easy way to avoid this bug. Ask yourself, "Where does the storage for the target string come from?" Character arrays don't magically appear; you have to allocate them.

The target of the string copy must be a character array of sufficient size to accommodate the characters.

```
char buffer[100];
strcpy(buffer, "Harry"); // OK
```

COMMON ERROR 7.8

Confusing Character Pointers and Arrays

Consider the pointer declaration

```
char* p = "Harry";
```

Note that this declaration is entirely different from the array declaration

```
char s[] = "Harry";
```

The second declaration is just a shorthand for

```
char s[6] = { 'H', 'a', 'r', 'r', 'y', '\0' };
```

The variable p is a pointer that points to the starting character of the string. The characters of the string are stored elsewhere, not in p. In contrast, the variable s is an array of six characters. Perhaps confusingly, when used inside an expression, s denotes a pointer to the starting character in the array. But there is an important difference: p is a pointer *variable* that you can set to another character location. But the value s is *constant*—it always points to the same location. See Figure 9.

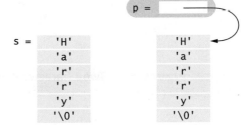

Figure 9
Character Pointers and Arrays

COMMON ERROR 7.9

Copying Character Pointers

There is an important difference between copying string objects and pointers of type char*. Consider this example:

```
string s = "Harry";
string t = s;
t[0] = 'L'; // now s is "Harry" and t is "Larry"
```

After copying s into t, the string object t contains a copy of the characters of s. Modifying t has no effect on s. However, copying character pointers has a completely different effect:

```
char* p = "Harry";
char* q = p;
q[0] = 'L'; // now both p and q point to "Larry"
```

After copying p into q, the pointer variable q contains the same memory address as p. The assignment to q[0] overwrites the starting letter in the string to which both p and q point (see Figure 10).

Note that you cannot assign one character array to another. The following assignment is illegal:

```
char a[] = "Harry";
char b[6];
b = a; // ERROR
```

The standard library provides the strcpy function to copy a character array to a new location:

```
strcpy(b, a);
```

The target pointer b must point to an array with sufficient space in it. It is a common beginner's error to try to copy a string into a character array with insufficient space. There is a safer function, strncpy, with a third parameter that specifies the maximum number of characters to copy:

```
strncpy(b, a, 5);
```

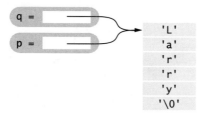

Figure 10   Two Character Pointers into the Same Character Array

7.6 Pointers to Functions

Sometimes, a function depends on another function. Here is a typical example: We want to print a table of values, like this:

```
  1 |     1
  2 |     4
  3 |     9
  4 |    16
...
 10 |   100
```

This particular table shows the values of the function $f(x) = x^2$. But you can use the exact same logic to print a table of the function $f(x) = x - 2$, or of any other function. We need a way of supplying the function f as a parameter to a function print_table.

In C++, this can be achieved by giving print_table a *function pointer*, that is, the location of the function code. Just as you get a pointer to an array by writing an array name without [], you get a function pointer by writing a function name without ().

> The name of a function without () denotes a function pointer.

For example,

```
sqrt
```

is a pointer to the sqrt function. To plot a table of square roots, simply pass the function pointer as a parameter:

```
print_table(sqrt);
```

To print a table of squares, you first need to make a square function, so that you have a function whose address you can pass to print_table:

```
double square(double x) { return x * x; }
...
print_table(square);
```

Now turn to the implementation of the print_table function. It has a parameter of type "function pointer", which we will explain later.

```
void print_table(DoubleFunPointer f)
{
    cout << setprecision(2);
    for (double x = 1; x <= 10; x++)
    {
        double y = f(x);
        cout << setw(10) << x << "|" << setw(10) << y << endl;
    }
}
```

You can use the variable f as if it were a regular function. The call f(x) tells the program to locate the code to which f points, and to call it with the parameter x. Some people prefer to write the call as

```
(*f)(x)
```

to make it clear that f is a pointer, not a function. Either notation is acceptable.

What remains is to define the function pointer type. Unfortunately, this is rather unsightly in C++. We want to declare f as a pointer, so that *f is a function. But we need to be precise about what function it is. It consumes a double value and returns a double value. The declaration looks like this:

```
double (*f)(double)
```

The parentheses are necessary. The definition

```
double *f(double)
```

denotes a function f (and not a function pointer) that consumes a double and returns a double* pointer.

You can define the `print_table` function as follows:

```
void print_table(double (*f)(double))
```

> Use typedef to make function pointer types easier to read.

Most people dislike this style because the variable `f` is buried inside a mess of type names and parentheses. The remedy is to use a *type definition*:

```
typedef double (*DoubleFunPointer)(double);
```

This declaration defines a type `DoubleFunPointer`, a thing whose * consumes a `double` and yields a `double`. In other words, a `DoubleFunPointer` is a pointer to a function that consumes and yields floating-point numbers. When you need a parameter that is a function pointer, simply use the type name:

```
void print_table(DoubleFunPointer f)
```

Function pointers are very useful whenever the behavior of a function depends on another function. They are also easy to use, provided you use the `typedef` mechanism to hide the messy pointer syntax.

SYNTAX 7.5 **typedef Statement**

typedef *declaration*;

Example:

typedef int (*IntFunPtr)(int);

Purpose:

Create an alias for a complicated type name.

RANDOM FACT 7.2

Embedded Systems

An *embedded system* is a computer system that controls a device. The device contains a processor and other hardware and is controlled by a computer program. Unlike a personal computer, which has been designed to be flexible and run many different computer programs, the hardware and software of an embedded system are tailored to a specific device. Computer controlled devices are becoming increasingly common, ranging from washing machines to medical equipment, cell phones, automobile engines, and spacecraft.

Several challenges are specific to programming embedded systems. Most importantly, a much higher standard of quality control applies. Vendors are often unconcerned about bugs in personal computer software, because they can always make you install a patch or upgrade to the next version. But in an embedded system, that is not an option. Few consumers would feel comfortable upgrading the software in their washing machines or automobile engines. If you ever handed in a programming assignment that you believed to be correct, only to have the instructor or grader find bugs in it, then you know how hard it is to write software that can reliably do its task for many years without a chance of changing it. Quality standards are especially important in devices whose failure would destroy property or human life. Many personal computer purchasers buy computers that are fast and have a lot of storage, because the investment is paid back over time when many programs are run on the same equipment. But the hardware for an embedded device is not shared.it is dedicated to one device. A separate processor, memory, and so on, are built for every copy of the device (see Figure 11). If it is possible to shave a few pennies off the manufacturing cost of every unit, the savings can add up quickly for devices that are produced in large volumes. Thus, the embedded-system programmer has a much larger economic incentive to conserve resources than the programmer of desktop software. Unfortunately, trying to conserve resources usually makes it harder to write programs that work correctly.

C and C++ are commonly used languages for developing embedded systems.

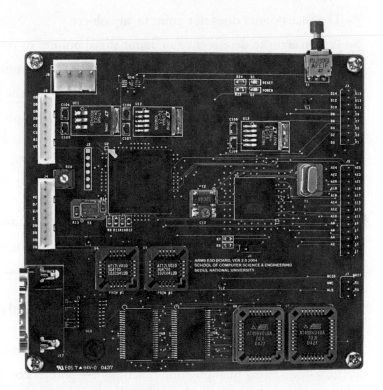

Figure 11   The Controller of an Embedded System

CHAPTER SUMMARY

1. Use dynamic memory allocation if you do not know in advance how many objects you need.

2. The new operator allocates an object from the heap.

3. Dynamically allocated objects live until they are explicitly reclaimed.

4. A pointer denotes the location of a value in memory.

5. The * operator locates the value to which a pointer points.

6. Finding the value to which a pointer points is called dereferencing.

7. Use the -> operator to access a data member or a member function through an object pointer.

8. The NULL pointer does not point to any object.

9. It is an error to dereference an uninitialized pointer or the NULL pointer.

10. In a member function, the this pointer points to the implicit parameter.

11. You must reclaim dynamically allocated objects with the delete operator.

12. Using a dangling pointer (a pointer that has not been initialized or has been deleted) is a serious programming error.

13. Every call to new should have a matching call to delete.

14. Pointers can be used to model optional values (by using a NULL pointer when the value is not present).

15. Pointers can be used to provide shared access to a common value.

16. The value of an array variable is a pointer to the starting element of the array.

17. Pointer arithmetic means adding an integer offset to an array pointer, yielding a pointer that skips past the given number of elements.

18. The array/pointer duality law states that a[n] is identical to *(a + n), where a is a pointer into an array and n is an integer offset.

19. When passing an array to a function, only the starting address is passed.

20. Low-level string manipulation functions use pointers of type char*.

21. You can construct string variables from char* pointers.

22. You can use the c_str member function to obtain a char* pointer from a string object.

23. The name of a function without () denotes a function pointer.

24. Use typedef to make function pointer types easier to read.

REVIEW EXERCISES

Exercise R7.1. Find the mistakes in the following code. Not all lines contain mistakes. Each line depends on the lines preceding it. Watch out for uninitialized pointers, NULL pointers, pointers to deleted objects, and confusing pointers with objects.

```
1   int* p = new int;
2   p = 5;
3   *p = *p + 5;
4   Employee e1 = new Employee("Hacker, Harry", 34000);
5   Employee e2;
6   e2->set_salary(38000);
7   delete e2;
8   Time* pnow = new Time();
9   Time* t1 = new Time(2, 0, 0);
10  cout << t1->seconds_from(pnow);
11  delete *t1;
12  cout << t1->get_seconds();
13  Employee* e3 = new Employee("Lin, Lisa", 68000);
14  cout << e3.get_salary();
15  Time* t2 = new Time(1, 25, 0);
16  cout << *t2.get_minutes();
17  delete t2;
```

Exercise R7.2. A pointer variable can contain a pointer to a valid object, a pointer to a deleted object, NULL, or a random value. Write code that creates and sets four pointer variables a, b, c, and d to show each of these possibilities.

Exercise R7.3. What happens when you dereference each of the four pointers that you created in Exercise R7.2? Write a test program if you are not sure.

Exercise R7.4. What happens if you forget to delete an object that you obtained from the heap? What happens if you delete it twice?

Exercise R7.5. What does the following code print?

```
Employee harry = Employee("Hacker, Harry", 35000);
Employee boss = harry;
Employee* pharry = new Employee("Hacker, Harry", 35000);
Employee* pboss = pharry;
boss.set_salary(45000);
(*pboss).set_salary(45000);
cout << harry.get_salary() << "\n";
cout << boss.get_salary() << "\n";
cout << pharry->get_salary() << "\n";
cout << pboss->get_salary() << "\n";
```

Exercise R7.6. Pointers are addresses and have a numerical value. You can print out the value of a pointer as cout << (unsigned long)(p). Write a program to compare p, p + 1, q, and q + 1, where p is an int* and q is a double*. Explain the results.

Exercise R7.7. In Chapter 2, you saw that you can use a cast (static_cast<int>) to convert a double value to an integer. Explain why casting a double* pointer to an int* pointer doesn't make sense. For example,

```
double values[] = { 2, 3, 5, 7, 11, 13 };
int* p = static_cast<int*>(values); // Why won't this work?
```

Exercise R7.8. Which of the following assignments are legal in C++?

```
void f(int p[])
{
    int* q;
    const int* r;
    int s[10];
    p = q;    ❶
    p = r;    ❷
    p = s;    ❸
    q = p;    ❹
    q = r;    ❺
    q = s;    ❻
    r = p;    ❼
    r = q;    ❽
    r = s;    ❾
    s = p;    ❿
    s = q;    ⓫
    s = r;    ⓬
}
```

Exercise R7.9. Given the definitions

```
double values[] = { 2, 3, 5, 7, 11, 13 };
double* p = values + 3;
```

explain the meanings of the following expressions:

a. values[1]

b. values + 1

c. *(values + 1)

d. p[1]

e. p + 1

f. p - values

Exercise R7.10. Explain the meanings of the following expressions:

a. "Harry" + 1

b. *("Harry" + 2)

c. "Harry"[3]

d. [4]"Harry"

Exercise R7.11. How can you implement a function minmax that computes both the minimum and the maximum of the values in an array of integers and stores the result in an int[2] array?

Exercise R7.12. What is the difference between the following two variable definitions?

a. `char a[] = "Hello";`

b. `char* b = "Hello";`

Exercise R7.13. What is the difference between the following three variable definitions?

a. `char* p = NULL;`

b. `char* q = "";`

c. `char r[] = { '\0' };`

Exercise R7.14. Consider this program segment:

```
char a[] = "Mary had a little lamb";
char* p = a;
int count = 0;
while (*p != '\0')
{
   count++;
   while (*p != ' ' && *p != '\0') p++;
   while (*p == ' ') p++;
}
```

What is the value of `count` at the end of the outer `while` loop?

Exercise R7.15. What are the limitations of the `strcat` and `strncat` functions when compared to the + operator for concatenating `string` objects?

Exercise R7.16. Using `typedef`, define a function pointer type for functions with a parameter `double` and no return value. Define a function `apply` that applies such a function to all elements of a `vector<double>`. For example, the call

```
void apply(data, print)
```

should print all `data` if the `print` function is defined as

```
void print(double x) { cout << x << endl; }
```

PROGRAMMING EXERCISES

Exercise P7.1. Implement a class `Person` with the following fields:

- the name
- a pointer to the person's best friend (a `Person*`)
- a popularity counter that indicates how many other people have this person as their best friend

Write a program that reads in a list of names, allocates a new `Person` for each of them, and stores them in a `vector<Person*>`. Then ask the name of the best friend for each of the `Person` objects. Locate the object matching the friend's name and call a set_best_friend member function to update the pointer and counter. Finally, print out all Person objects, listing the name, best friend, and popularity counter for each.

Exercise P7.2. Implement a class Person with two fields name and age, and a class Car with three fields:

- the model
- a pointer to the owner (a Person*)
- a pointer to the driver (also a Person*)

Write a program that prompts the user to specify people and cars. Store them in a vector<Person*> and a vector<Car*>. Traverse the vector of Person objects and increment their ages by one year. Finally, traverse the vector of cars and print out the car model, owner's name and age, and driver's name and age.

Exercise P7.3. Enhance the Employee class of Chapter 2 to include a pointer to a BankAccount. Read in employees and their salaries. Store them in a vector<Employee>. For each employee, allocate a new bank account on the heap, except that two consecutive employees with the same last name should share the same account. Then traverse the vector of employees and, for each employee, deposit 1/12th of their annual salary into their bank account. Afterwards, print all employee names and account balances.

Exercise P7.4. Enhance Exercise P7.3 to delete all bank account objects. Make sure that no object gets deleted twice.

Exercise P7.5. Write a function that computes the average value of an array of floating-point data:

```
double average(double* a, int a_size)
```

In the function, use a pointer variable, and not an integer index, to traverse the array elements.

Exercise P7.6. Write a function that returns a pointer to the maximum value of an array of floating-point data:

```
double* maximum(double a[], int a_size)
```

If a_size is 0, return NULL.

Exercise P7.7. Write a function that reverses the values of an array of floating-point data:

```
void reverse(double a[], int a_size)
```

In the function, use two pointer variables, and not integer indexes, to traverse the array elements.

Exercise P7.8. Implement the strncpy function of the standard library.

Exercise P7.9. Implement the standard library function

```
int strspn(const char s[], const char t[])
```

that returns the length of the initial portion of s consisting of characters in t (in any order).

Exercise P7.10. Write a function

```
void reverse(char s[])
```

that reverses a character string. For example, "Harry" becomes "yrraH".

Exercise P7.11. Using the strncpy and strncat functions, implement a function

```
void concat(const char a[], const char b[], char result[],
   int result_maxlength)
```

that concatenates the strings a and b to the buffer result. Be sure not to overrun the result. It can hold result_maxlength characters, not counting the '\0' terminator. (That is, the buffer has result_maxlength + 1 bytes available.) Be sure to provide a '\0' terminator.

Exercise P7.12. Add a member function

```
void Employee::format(char buffer[], int buffer_maxlength)
```

to the Employee class. The member function should fill the buffer with the name and salary of the employee. Be sure not to overrun the buffer. It can hold buffer_maxlength characters, not counting the '\0' terminator. (That is, the buffer has buffer_maxlength + 1 bytes available.) Be sure to provide a '\0' terminator.

Exercise P7.13. Write a program that reads lines of text and appends them to a char buffer[1000]. Stop after reading 1,000 characters. As you read in the text, replace all newline characters '\n' with '\0' terminators. Establish an array char* lines[100], so that the pointers in that array point to the beginnings of the lines in the text. Only consider 100 input lines if the input has more lines. Then display the lines in reverse order, starting with the last input line.

Exercise P7.14. The program in Exercise P7.13 is limited by the fact that it can only handle inputs of 1,000 characters or 100 lines. Remove this limitation as follows. Concatenate the input in one long string object. Use the c_str member function to obtain a char* into the string's character buffer. Establish the offsets of the beginnings of the lines as a vector<int>.

Exercise P7.15. Exercise P7.14 demonstrated how to use the string and vector classes to implement resizable arrays. In this exercise, you should implement that capability manually. Allocate a buffer of 1,000 characters from the heap (new char[1000]). Whenever the buffer fills up, allocate a buffer of twice the size, copy the buffer contents, and delete the old buffer. Do the same for the array of char* pointers—start with a new char*[100] and keep doubling the size.

Exercise P7.16. Modify the print_table function of Section 7.6 so that it prints the values of two functions. For example, the call print_table(square, sqrt) should yield a table like this:

```
1  |   1.00  |   1.00
2  |   4.00  |   1.41
```

Exercise P7.17. Implement a function

```
void fill_with_values(int a[], int size, IntFunPointer f)
```

that sets the ith element of the array to $f(i)$. Here IntFunPointer is a typedef for a pointer to a function that consumes an int and yields an int. Provide a main function in which you call the fill_with_values function so that an array of ten integers is filled with 1, 4, 9, 16, 25, ..., 100.

Chapter 8

Inheritance

CHAPTER GOALS

- To understand the concepts of inheritance and polymorphism
- To learn how inheritance is a tool for code reuse
- To learn how to call base-class constructors and member functions
- To understand the difference between static and dynamic binding
- To be able to implement dynamic binding with virtual functions

In this chapter you will learn two of the most important concepts in object-oriented programming: inheritance and polymorphism. Through inheritance, you will be able to define new classes that are extensions of existing classes.

Polymorphism allows you to take advantage of the commonality between related classes, while still giving each class the flexibility to implement specific behavior. Using polymorphism, it is possible to build very flexible and extensible systems.

CHAPTER CONTENTS

8.1 Derived Classes

> Inheritance is a mechanism for extending classes.

Inheritance is a mechanism for enhancing existing, working classes. If a new class needs to be implemented and a class representing a more general concept is already available, then the new class can *inherit* from the existing class. For example, suppose we need to define a class Manager. We already have a class Employee, and a manager is a special case of an employee. In this case, it makes sense to use the language construct of inheritance. Here is the syntax for the class definition:

```
class Manager : public Employee
{
public:
    new member functions
private:
    new data members
};
```

The : symbol denotes inheritance. The keyword public is required for a technical reason (see Common Error 8.1 on page 348).

> A derived class inherits from a base class and is a more specialized class.

The existing, more general class is called the *base class*. The more specialized class that inherits from the base class is called the *derived class*. In our example, Employee is the base class and Manager is the derived class.

> The derived class inherits all data fields and functions that it does not redefine.

In the Manager class definition you specify only new member functions and data members. All member functions and data members of the Employee class are automatically inherited by the Manager class. For example, the set_salary function automatically applies to managers:

```
Manager m;
m.set_salary(68000);
```

The general form of the definition of a derived class is shown in Syntax 8.1.

Figure 1 is a *class diagram* showing the relationship between these classes. In the preceding chapters, our diagrams focused on individual objects, which were drawn as rectangular forms that contained boxes for the class name and the data members. Since inheritance is a relationship between classes, not objects, we show two simple boxes joined by an arrow with a hollow head, which indicates inheritance.

To better understand the mechanics of programming with inheritance, consider a more interesting programming problem: modeling a set of clocks that display the times in different cities.

Start with a base class Clock that can tell the current local time. In the constructor, you can set the format to either "military format" (such as 21:05) or "am/pm" format (such as 9:05 pm). You then call the functions

```
int get_hours() const
int get_minutes() const
```

to get the hours and minutes. In military format, the hours range from 0 to 23. In "am/pm" format, the hours range from 1 to 12. You can use the function

```
bool is_military() const
```

to test whether the clock uses military time format. Finally, the function

```
string get_location() const
```

returns the fixed string "Local". We will later redefine it to return a string that indicates the location of the clock.

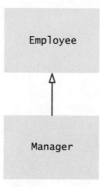

Figure 1   An Inheritance Diagram

The following program demonstrates the Clock class. The program constructs two Clock objects that display the time in both formats. If you run the program and wait a minute before answering y to the prompt, you can see that the clock advances.

ch08/clocks1/clock.h

```
 1  #ifndef CLOCK_H
 2  #define CLOCK_H
 3
 4  #include <string>
 5
 6  using namespace std;
 7
 8  class Clock
 9  {
10  public:
11     /**
12         Constructs a clock that can tell the local time.
13         @param use_military true if the clock uses military format
14     */
15     Clock(bool use_military);
16
17     /**
18         Gets the location of this clock.
19         @return the location
20     */
21     string get_location() const;
22
23     /**
24         Gets the hours of this clock.
25         @return the hours, in military or am/pm format
26     */
27     int get_hours() const;
28
29     /**
30         Gets the minutes of this clock.
31         @return the minutes
32     */
33     int get_minutes() const;
34
35     /**
36         Checks whether this clock uses military format.
37         @return true if military format
38     */
39     bool is_military() const;
40  private:
41     bool military;
42  };
43
44  #endif
```

ch08/clocks1/clock.cpp

```cpp
1   #include "ccc_time.h"
2   #include "clock.h"
3
4   Clock::Clock(bool use_military)
5   {
6       military = use_military;
7   }
8
9   string Clock::get_location() const
10  {
11      return "Local";
12  }
13
14  int Clock::get_hours() const
15  {
16      Time now;
17      int hours = now.get_hours();
18      if (military) return hours;
19      if (hours == 0)
20          return 12;
21      else if (hours > 12)
22          return hours - 12;
23      else
24          return hours;
25  }
26
27  int Clock::get_minutes() const
28  {
29      Time now;
30      return now.get_minutes();
31  }
32
33  bool Clock::is_military() const
34  {
35      return military;
36  }
```

ch08/clocks1/clocks1.cpp

```cpp
1   #include <iostream>
2   #include <iomanip>
3   #include <string>
4
5   using namespace std;
6
7   #include "clock.h"
8
9   int main()
10  {
11      Clock clock1(true);
12      Clock clock2(false);
13
```

```
14    bool more = true;
15    while (more)
16    {
17       cout << "Military time is "
18          << clock1.get_hours() << ":"
19          << setw(2) << setfill('0')
20          << clock1.get_minutes()
21          << setfill(' ') << "\n";
22       cout << "am/pm time is "
23          << clock2.get_hours() << ":"
24          << setw(2) << setfill('0')
25          << clock2.get_minutes()
26          << setfill(' ') << "\n";
27
28       cout << "Try again? (y/n) ";
29       string input;
30       getline(cin, input);
31       if (input != "y") more = false;
32    }
33    return 0;
34 }
```

Program Run

```
Military time is 21:05
am/pm time is 9:05
Try again? (y/n) y
Military time is 21:06
am/pm time is 9:06
Try again? (y/n) n
```

Now form a derived class `TravelClock` that can show the time in another location. Consider how travel clocks are different from basic `Clock` objects. Travel clocks store city names, and they show the time in those cities. The time is computed by taking the local time and adding the time difference between the local time and the time at the other location. For example, suppose the local time is Pacific Standard Time. Then you can make a clock for traveling to New York as follows:

```
TravelClock clock(true, "New York", 3);
cout << "The time in " << clock.get_location() << " is "
   << clock.get_hours() << ":" << clock.get_minutes();
```

The value 3 in the constructor denotes the fact that the time in New York is 3 hours ahead of Pacific Standard Time.

A `TravelClock` object differs from a `Clock` object in three ways:

- Its objects store the location name and time difference.
- The get_hours function of the `TravelClock` adds the time difference to the current time.
- The get_location function returns the actual location, not the string "Local".

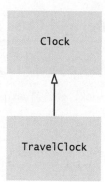

Figure 2
Inheritance Diagram for Clocks

When the TravelClock class inherits from the Clock class, it needs only to spell out these three differences:

```
class TravelClock : public Clock
{
public:
   TravelClock(bool mil, string loc, int diff);
   int get_hours() const;
   string get_location() const;
private:
   string location;
   int time_difference;
};
```

Figure 2 shows the inheritance diagram.

Figure 3 shows the layout of a TravelClock object. It inherits the military data field from the Clock base object, and it gains two additional data fields: location and time_difference.

It is important to note that the data members of the base class (such as the military field in our example) are present in each derived-class object, but they are not *accessible* by the member functions of the derived class. Since these fields are private data of the base class, only the base class has access to them. The derived class has no more access rights than any other class. In particular, none of the TravelClock member functions can access the military field.

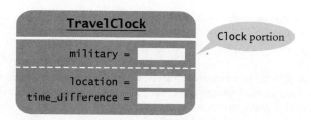

Figure 3   Data Layout of Derived Object

SYNTAX 8.1 Derived Class Definition

```
class DerivedClassName : public BaseClassName
{
    features
};
```

Example:

```
class Manager : public Employee
{
public:
    Manager(string name, double salary, string dept);
    string get_department() const;
private:
    string department;
};
```

Purpose:

Define a class that inherits features from a base class.

COMMON ERROR 8.1

Private Inheritance

It is a common error to forget the keyword `public` that must follow the colon after the derived-class name.

```
class Manager : Employee // Error
{
    ...
};
```

The class definition will compile. The `Manager` still inherits from `Employee`, but it inherits *privately*. That is, only the member functions of `Manager` get to call member functions of `Employee`. Whenever you invoke an `Employee` member function on a `Manager` object elsewhere, the compiler will flag this as an error:

```
int main()
{
    Manager m;
    ...
    m.set_salary(65000); // Error
}
```

This private inheritance is rarely useful. In fact, it violates the spirit of using inheritance in the first place—namely, to create objects that are usable just like the base-class objects. You should always use public inheritance and remember to supply the `public` keyword in the definition of the derived class.

8.2 Calling the Base-Class Constructor

The constructor of a derived class has two tasks:

- Initialize the base object
- Initialize all data members

The second task is fairly straightforward. In order to avoid negative values in the remainder computation of the get_hours function, add 24 to negative time differences until they become positive.

```
TravelClock::TravelClock(bool mil, string loc, int diff)
// Not complete
{
   location = loc;
   time_difference = diff;
   while (time_difference < 0)
      time_difference = time_difference + 24;
}
```

The first task is not as simple. You must construct the base object and tell it whether to use military time. However, the base class has no member function to set the clock format. The only way to set this value is through the Clock constructor. That is, you must somehow set the base object to

```
Clock(mil)
```

This is a common situation. Frequently, a derived-class constructor must invoke the base-class constructor before initializing the derived-class data. There is a special syntactical construct to denote the base construction:

```
TravelClock::TravelClock(bool mil, string loc, int diff)
   : Clock(mil)
{
   ...
}
```

The line

```
: Clock(mil)
```

means: Call the Clock constructor with parameter mil before executing the code inside the { }. The colon is supposed to remind you of inheritance.

> The constructor of a derived class can pass parameters to the base class constructors.

In general, the syntax for a derived-class constructor is shown in Syntax 8.2. (Actually, as explained in Advanced Topic 5.1, the same syntax can be used to invoke data field constructors as well, but then you place the name of the data field, not the name of the base class, after the colon. In this book, we choose not to use that syntax to initialize data fields.)

> If no parameters are passed explicitly, the default constructor of the base class is invoked.

If you omit the base-class constructor, then the base object is constructed with the default constructor of the base class. However, if the base class has no default constructor (such as the Clock class), then you have to explicitly call the base-class constructor in the derived-class constructor.

SYNTAX 8.2 Constructor with Base-Class Initializer

DerivedClassName::*DerivedClassName*(*expressions*)
  : *BaseClassName*(*expressions*)
{
   statements
}

Example:

```
Manager::Manager(string name, double salary, string dept)
   : Employee(name, salary)
{
   department = dept;
}
```

Purpose:

Supply the implementation of a constructor, initializing the base class before the body of the derived-class constructor.

8.3 Overriding Member Functions

> The derived class can override functions from the base class.

It is common for a derived class to redefine or *override* a member function of a base class. You want to override a base class member function whenever you are not satisfied with simply inheriting it.

Consider the get_hours function of the TravelClock class. It needs to override the base class get_hours function in order to take the time difference into account. Specifically, the derived class function needs to

- Get the hour value of the local time
- Adjust it by the time difference

Here is the pseudocode for the function.

```
int TravelClock::get_hours() const
{
   int h = local hour value;
   if (clock uses military time)
      return (h + time_difference) % 24;
```

```
    else
    {
        h = (h + time_difference) % 12;
        if (h == 0) return 12;
        else return h;
    }
}
```

First, we need to determine how to find out whether the clock uses military time. You can't just access the `military` field in the base class. While it is true that each object of type `TravelClock` inherits the `military` data field from the `Clock` base class, accessing this data field is not allowed. It is private to `Clock` and only accessible through the `Clock` member functions.

Fortunately, the `Clock` class has a member function, `is_military`, that reports the value of the `military` flag. You can call that member function. On which object? The clock that you are currently querying—that is, the implicit parameter of the `TravelClock::get_hours` function. As you saw in Chapter 5, if you invoke a member function on the implicit parameter, you don't specify the parameter but just write the member function name:

```
if (is_military()) ...
```

The compiler interprets

```
is_military()
```

as

implicit parameter`.is_military();`

Note that the `is_military` function is inherited from the base class, so you can call it through the *implicit parameter* object of the derived class.

But how do you get the local hour value? You can ask the `get_hours` function of the base class. Thus, you have to invoke `get_hours`:

```
int TravelClock::get_hours() const
{
    int h = get_hours(); // Not complete
    ...
}
```

But this won't quite work. Because the implicit parameter of `Travel-Clock::get_hours` is of type `TravelClock`, and there is a function named `get_hours` in the `TravelClock` class, that function will be called—but that is just the function you are currently writing! The function would call itself over and over, and the program would die in an infinite recursion.

Instead, you must be more specific which function named `get_hours` you want to call. You want `Clock::get_hours`:

```
int TravelClock::get_hours() const
{
    int h = Clock::get_hours();
    ...
}
```

> Use *BaseClass::function*
> notation to explicitly call a
> base-class function.

This version of the get_hours member function is correct. To get the hours of a travel clock, first get the hours of its underlying Clock, then add the time difference.

In general, suppose $B::f$ is a function in a base class. Then the derived class D can take three kinds of actions:

- The derived class can *extend* $B::f$ by supplying a new implementation $D::f$ that calls $B::f$. For example, the TravelClock::get_hours function is an extension of Clock::get_hours.

- The derived class can *replace* $B::f$ by supplying a new implementation $D::f$ that is unrelated to $B::f$. For example, the TravelClock::get_location function (which returns the location field) is a replacement for Clock::get_location (which only returns the string "Local").

- The derived class can *inherit* $B::f$, simply by not supplying an implementation for f. For example, the TravelClock class inherits Clock::get_minutes and Clock::is_military.

Here is the complete program that displays a plain Clock object and two Travel-Clock objects. As you can see, the TravelClock code is quite short. The files defining the Clock class, clock.h and clock.cpp, are the same as in Section 8.1, but clock.h is shown again here for comparison to the TravelClock code. This example shows how you can use inheritance to adapt existing code to a new purpose.

ch08/clocks2/clock.h

```
1   #ifndef CLOCK_H
2   #define CLOCK_H
3
4   #include <string>
5
6   using namespace std;
7
8   class Clock
9   {
10  public:
11     /**
12        Constructs a clock that can tell the local time.
13        @param use_military true if the clock uses military format
14     */
15     Clock(bool use_military);
16
17     /**
18        Gets the location of this clock.
19        @return the location
20     */
21     string get_location() const;
22
23     /**
24        Gets the hours of this clock.
25        @return the hours, in military or am/pm format
26     */
27     int get_hours() const;
```

```
28
29     /**
30         Gets the minutes of this clock.
31         @return  the minutes
32     */
33     int get_minutes() const;
34
35     /**
36         Checks whether this clock uses military format.
37         @return  true if military format
38     */
39     bool is_military() const;
40  private:
41     bool military;
42  };
43
44  #endif
```

ch08/clocks2/travelclock.h

```
1   #include <string>
2
3   using namespace std;
4
5   #include "clock.h"
6
7   class TravelClock : public Clock
8   {
9   public:
10     /**
11         Constructs a travel clock that can tell the time
12         at a specified location.
13         @param mil  true if the clock uses military format
14         @param loc  the location
15         @param diff  the time difference from the local time
16     */
17     TravelClock(bool mil, string loc, int diff);
18     string get_location() const;
19     int get_hours() const;
20  private:
21     string location;
22     int time_difference;
23  };
```

ch08/clocks2/travelclock.cpp

```
1   #include "travelclock.h"
2
3   TravelClock::TravelClock(bool mil, string loc, int diff)
4       : Clock(mil)
5   {
6       location = loc;
7       time_difference = diff;
```

```
 8      while (time_difference < 0)
 9         time_difference = time_difference + 24;
10  }
11
12  string TravelClock::get_location() const
13  {
14      return location;
15  }
16
17  int TravelClock::get_hours() const
18  {
19      int h = Clock::get_hours();
20      if (is_military())
21         return (h + time_difference) % 24;
22      else
23      {
24         h = (h + time_difference) % 12;
25         if (h == 0) return 12;
26         else return h;    }
27      }
28  }
```

ch08/clocks2/clocks2.cpp

```
 1  #include <iostream>
 2  #include <iomanip>
 3
 4  using namespace std;
 5
 6  #include "travelclock.h"
 7
 8  int main()
 9  {
10      Clock clock1(true);
11      TravelClock clock2(true, "Rome", 9);
12      TravelClock clock3(false, "Tokyo", -7);
13
14      cout << clock1.get_location() << " time is "
15         << clock1.get_hours() << ":"
16         << setw(2) << setfill('0')
17         << clock1.get_minutes()
18         << setfill(' ') << "\n";
19      cout << clock2.get_location() << " time is "
20         << clock2.get_hours() << ":"
21         << setw(2) << setfill('0')
22         << clock2.get_minutes()
23         << setfill(' ') << "\n";
24      cout << clock3.get_location() << " time is "
25         << clock3.get_hours() << ":"
26         << setw(2) << setfill('0')
27         << clock3.get_minutes()
28         << setfill(' ') << "\n";
29      return 0;
30  }
```

Program Run

```
Local time is 9:05
Rome time is 18:05
Tokyo time is 2:05
```

COMMON ERROR 8.2

Attempting to Access Private Base-Class Fields

A derived class inherits all fields from the base class. However, if the fields are private, the derived-class functions have no rights to access them. For example, suppose the salary of a manager is computed by adding a bonus to the annual salary:

```
double Manager::get_salary() const
{
   return salary + bonus;
      // Error—salary is private to Employee
}
```

The `Manager::get_salary` function has no more rights to access the private `Employee` fields than any other function. The remedy is to use the public interface of the base class:

```
double Manager::get_salary() const
{
   return Employee::get_salary() + bonus;
}
```

COMMON ERROR 8.3

Forgetting the Base-Class Name

A common error in extending the functionality of a base-class function is to forget the base-class name. For example, to compute the salary of a manager, get the salary of the underlying `Employee` object and add a bonus:

```
double Manager::get_salary() const
{
   double base_salary = get_salary();
      // Error—should be Employee::get_salary()
   return base_salary + bonus;
}
```

Here `get_salary()` refers to the `get_salary` function applied to the implicit parameter of the member function. The implicit parameter is of type `Manager`, and there is a `Manager::get_salary` function, so that function is called. Of course, that is a recursive call to the function that we are writing. Instead, you must be precise which `get_salary` function you want to call. In this case, you need to call `Employee::get_salary` explicitly.

Whenever you call a base-class function from a derived-class function with the same name, be sure to give the full name of the function, including the base-class name.

ADVANCED TOPIC 8.1

Protected Access

You ran into some degree of grief when trying to implement the get_hours member function of the TravelClock class. That member function needed access to the military data field of the base class. Your remedy was to have the base class provide the appropriate accessor function.

C++ offers another solution. The base class can declare the data field as protected:

```
class Clock
{
public:
   ...
protected:
   bool military

};
```

> Protected features can be accessed by the member functions of all derived classes.

Protected data and member functions can be accessed by the member functions of a class and all its derived classes. For example, TravelClock inherits from Clock, so its member functions can access the protected data fields of the Clock class.

Some programmers like the protected access feature because it seems to strike a balance between absolute protection (making all data members private) and no protection at all (making all data members public). However, experience has shown that protected data members are subject to the same kind of problems as public data members. The designer of the base class has no control over the authors of derived classes. Any of the derived-class member functions can corrupt the base-class data. Furthermore, classes with protected data members are hard to modify. Even if the author of the base class would like to change the data implementation, the protected data members cannot be changed, because someone might have written a derived class whose code depends on them.

It is best to leave all data private. If you want to grant access to the data only to derived-class member functions, consider making the *accessor* function protected.

8.4 Polymorphism

> Polymorphism (literally, "having multiple shapes") describes a set of objects of different classes with similar behavior.

In the preceding sections you saw one important use of inheritance: the reuse of existing code in a new problem. In this section you will see an even more powerful application of inheritance: to model variation in object behavior.

If you look into the main function of clocks2.cpp, you will find that there was quite a bit of repetitive code. It would be nicer if all three clocks were collected in a vector and one could use a loop to print the clock values:

```
vector<Clock> clocks;
clocks[0] = Clock(true);
clocks[1] = TravelClock(true, "Rome", 9);
clocks[2] = TravelClock(false, "Tokyo", -7);

for (int i = 0; i < clocks.size(); i++)
{
    cout << clocks[i].get_location() << " time is "
        << clocks[i].get_hours() << ":"
        << setw(2) << setfill('0')
        << clocks[i].get_minutes()
        << setfill(' ') << "\n";
}
```

Unfortunately, that does not work. The vector clocks holds objects of type Clock. The compiler realizes that a TravelClock is a special case of a Clock. Thus it permits the assignment from a travel clock to a clock:

```
clocks[1] = TravelClock(true, "Rome", 9);
```

However, a TravelClock object has three data fields, whereas a Clock object has just one field, the military flag. There is no room to store the derived-class data. That data simply gets *sliced away* when you assign a derived-class object to a base-class variable (see Figure 4).

If you run the resulting program, the output is:

```
Local time is 21:15
Local time is 21:15
Local time is 9:15
```

> When converting a derived class object to a base class, the derived class data is sliced away.

This problem is very typical of code that needs to manipulate objects from a mixture of data types. Derived-class objects are usually bigger than base-class objects, and objects of different derived classes have different sizes. A vector of objects cannot deal with this variation in sizes.

Instead, you need to store the actual objects elsewhere and collect their locations in a vector by storing pointers. (If you have skipped Chapter 7, you will now need to turn to Section 7.1 to learn about pointers. You can read that section independently of the remainder of Chapter 7.)

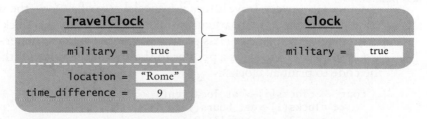

Figure 4   Slicing Away Derived-Class Data

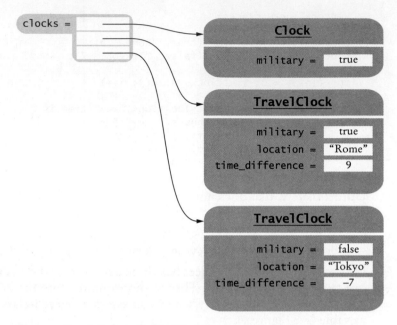

Figure 5   A Polymorphic Vector

Figure 5 shows the vector of pointers. The reason for using pointers is simple: Pointers to the various clock objects all have the same size—namely, the size of a memory address—even though the objects themselves may have different sizes.

Here is the code to set up the vector of pointers:

```
vector<Clock*> clocks;
// Populate clocks
clocks[0] = new Clock(true);
clocks[1] = new TravelClock(true, "Rome", 9);
clocks[2] = new TravelClock(false, "Tokyo", -7);
```

As the highlighted code shows, you simply declare the vector to hold pointers, and allocate all objects by calling new.

> A derived-class pointer can be converted to a base-class pointer.

Note that the last two assignments assign a derived-class pointer of type TravelClock* to a base-class pointer of type Clock*. This is perfectly legal. A pointer is the starting address of an object. Because every TravelClock is a special case of a Clock, the starting address of a TravelClock object is, in particular, the starting address of a Clock object. The reverse assignment—from a base-class pointer to a derived-class pointer—is an error.

Of course, clocks[i] is a pointer to the ith object, not the ith object itself. Thus, the code to print all clocks is

```
cout << clocks[i]->get_location() << " time is "
    << clocks[i]->get_hours() << ":"
    << setw(2) << setfill('0')
    << clocks[i]->get_minutes()
    << setfill(' ') << "\n";
```

Note the use of the -> operators because clocks[i] is a pointer.

Unfortunately, there remains a problem. The output is still

```
Local time is 21:15
Local time is 21:15
Local time is 9:15
```

As you can see, none of the travel clock code was executed. The compiler generated code only to call the Clock functions, not the functions that are appropriate for each object.

In the compiler's defense, it actually took the correct action. A member function call is compiled into a call to one particular function. It is the compiler's job to find the appropriate function that should be called. In this case, the pointer clocks[i] points to the implicit parameter; it is a pointer of type Clock*. Therefore, the compiler calls Clock member functions.

However, in this case you really do not want a simple function call. You want first to determine the actual type of the object to which clocks[i] points, which can be either a Clock or a TravelClock object, and then call the appropriate functions. This too can be arranged in C++. You must alert the compiler that the function call needs to be preceded by the appropriate function selection, which can be a different one for every iteration in the loop. You use the virtual keyword for this purpose:

```
class Clock
{
public:
   Clock(bool use_military);
   virtual string get_location() const;
   virtual int get_hours() const;
   int get_minutes() const;
   bool is_military() const;
private:
   ...
};
```

The virtual keyword must be used in the *base class*. All functions with the same name and parameter types in derived classes are then automatically virtual. However, it is considered good taste to supply the virtual keyword for the derived-class functions as well.

```
class TravelClock : public Clock
{
public:
   TravelClock(bool mil, string loc, int diff);
   virtual string get_location() const;
   virtual int get_hours() const;
private:
   ...
};
```

You do not supply the keyword virtual in the function definition:

```
string Clock::get_location() const // No virtual keyword
{
   return "Local";
}
```

When a virtual function is called, the version belonging to the actual type of the implicit parameter is invoked.

Whenever a virtual function is called, the compiler determines the type of the implicit parameter in the particular call at run time. The appropriate function for that object is then called. For example, when the get_location function is declared virtual, the call

```
clocks[i]->get_location();
```

always calls the function belonging to the actual type of the object to which clocks[i] points—either Clock::get_location or Travel-Clock::get_location.

When a virtual function is called, the exact function that is being executed is only determined at run time. Such a selection/call combination is called *dynamic binding*. In contrast, the traditional call, which always invokes the same function, is called *static binding*.

A dynamically bound function is selected at run time. A statically bound function is selected at compile time.

Only member functions can be virtual. A member function that is not tagged as virtual is statically bound. That is, the type of the implicit parameter, as it is known at compile time, is used to select one function, and that function is always called. Because static binding is less complex, it is the default in C++. You should use virtual functions only when you need the flexibility of dynamic binding at run time.

The clocks vector collects a mixture of both kinds of clock. Such a collection is called *polymorphic* (literally, "of multiple shapes"). Objects in a polymorphic collection have some commonality but are not necessarily of the same type. Inheritance is used to express this commonality, and virtual functions enable variations in behavior.

Virtual functions give programs a great deal of flexibility. The printing loop describes only the general mechanism: "Print the location, hours, and minutes of each clock". Each object knows on its own how to carry out the specific tasks: "Get your location" and "Get your hours".

Using virtual functions makes programs *easily extensible*. Suppose we want to have a new kind of clock for space travel. All we need to do is to define a new class SpaceTravelClock, with its own get_location and get_hours functions. Then we can populate the clocks vector with a mixture of plain clocks, travel clocks, and space travel clocks. The code that prints all clocks need not be changed at all! The calls to the virtual get_location and get_hours functions automatically select the correct member functions of the newly defined classes.

Here is the clock program again, using virtual functions. Not shown are clock.cpp (which is unchanged from the version shown on page 345) and travel-clock.cpp (unchanged from the version shown on page 353). When you run the program, you will find that the three Clock* pointers call the appropriate versions of the virtual functions.

ch08/clocks3/clock.h

```
1  #ifndef CLOCK_H
2  #define CLOCK_H
3
```

```
 4   #include <string>
 5
 6   using namespace std;
 7
 8   class Clock
 9   {
10   public:
11      /**
12          Constructs a clock that can tell the local time.
13          @param use_military true if the clock uses military format
14      */
15      Clock(bool use_military);
16
17      /**
18          Gets the location of this clock.
19          @return the location
20      */
21      virtual string get_location() const;
22
23      /**
24          Gets the hours of this clock.
25          @return the hours, in military or am/pm format
26      */
27      virtual int get_hours() const;
28
29      /**
30          Gets the minutes of this clock.
31          @return the minutes
32      */
33      int get_minutes() const;
34
35      /**
36          Checks whether this clock uses military format.
37          @return true if military format
38      */
39      bool is_military() const;
40   private:
41      bool military;
42   };
43
44   #endif
```

ch08/clocks3/travelclock.h

```
 1   #include <string>
 2
 3   using namespace std;
 4
 5   #include "clock.h"
 6
 7   class TravelClock : public Clock
 8   {
```

```
 9   public:
10      /**
11            Constructs a travel clock that can tell the time
12            at a specified location.
13            @param mil  true if the clock uses military format
14            @param loc  the location
15            @param diff  the time difference from the local time
16      */
17      TravelClock(bool mil, string loc, int diff);
18      virtual string get_location() const;
19      virtual int get_hours() const;
20   private:
21      string location;
22      int time_difference;
23   };
```

ch08/clocks3/clocks3.cpp

```
 1   #include <iostream>
 2   #include <iomanip>
 3   #include <vector>
 4
 5   using namespace std;
 6
 7   #include "travelclock.h"
 8
 9   int main()
10   {
11      vector<Clock*> clocks(3);
12      clocks[0] = new Clock(true);
13      clocks[1] = new TravelClock(true, "Rome", 9);
14      clocks[2] = new TravelClock(false, "Tokyo", -7);
15
16      for (int i = 0; i < clocks.size(); i++)
17      {
18         cout << clocks[i]->get_location() << " time is "
19            << clocks[i]->get_hours() << ":"
20            << setw(2) << setfill('0')
21            << clocks[i]->get_minutes()
22            << setfill(' ') << "\n";
23      }
24      return 0;
25   }
```

Program Run

```
Local time is 9:05
Rome time is 18:05
Tokyo time is 2:05
```

SYNTAX 8.3 Virtual Function Definition

```
class ClassName
{
    virtual return_type function_name(parameter₁, parameter₂, ..., parameterₙ);
    ...
};
```

Example:

```
class Employee
{
public:
    virtual double get_salary();
    ...
};
```

Purpose:

Define a dynamically-bound function that can be redefined in derived classes. When the function is called, the actual type of the implicit parameter determines which version of the function executes.

COMMON ERROR 8.4

Slicing an Object

In C++ it is legal to copy a derived-class object into a base-class variable. However, any derived-class information is lost in the process. For example, when a Manager object is assigned to a variable of type Employee, the result is only the employee portion of the manager data:

```
Manager m;
...
Employee e = m; // Holds only the Employee base data of m
```

Any information that is particular to managers is sliced off, because it would not fit into a variable of type Employee. This slicing may indeed be what you want. The code using the variable e may not care about the Manager part of the object and just needs to consider it as an employee. To avoid slicing, use pointers.

Note that the reverse assignment is not legal. That is, you cannot copy a base-class object into a derived-class variable.

```
Employee e;
...
Manager m = e; // Error
```

ADVANCED TOPIC 8.2

Virtual Self-Calls

Add the following print function to the Clock class:

```
void Clock::print() const
{
    cout << get_location() << " time is "
        << get_hours() << ":"
        << setw(2) << setfill('0')
        << get_minutes()
        << setfill(' ') << "\n";
}
```

Do *not* redefine the print function in the TravelClock class. Now consider the call

```
TravelClock rome_clock(true, "Rome", 9);
rome_clock.print();
```

Which get_location and get_hours function will the print function call? If you look inside the code of the Clock::print function, you can see that these functions are executed on the implicit object.

```
void Clock::print() const
{
    cout << implicit parameter.get_location() << " time is "
        << implicit parameter.get_hours() << ":"
        << setw(2) << setfill('0')
        << implicit parameter.get_minutes()
        << setfill(' ') << "\n";
}
```

The implicit parameter in our call is rome_clock, an object of type TravelClock. Because the get_location and get_hours functions are virtual, the TravelClock versions of the function are called automatically. This happens even though the print function is defined in the Clock class, which has no knowledge of the TravelClock class.

As you can see, virtual functions are a very powerful mechanism. The Clock class supplies a print function that specifies the common nature of printing, namely to print the location and time. How the location and time are determined is left to the derived classes.

RANDOM FACT 8.1

Operating Systems

Without an operating system, a computer would not be useful. Minimally, you need an operating system to locate files and to start programs. The programs that you run need services from the operating system to access devices and to interact with other programs. Operating systems on large computers need to provide more services than those on personal computers.
    Here are some typical services:

- *Program loading*. Every operating system provides some way of launching application programs. The user indicates what program should be run, usually by typing in the name of the program or by clicking on an icon. The operating system locates the program code, loads it in memory, and starts it.

- *Managing files.* A storage device such as a hard disk is, electronically, simply a device capable of storing a huge sequence of zeroes and ones. It is up to the operating system to bring some structure to the storage layout and organize it into files, folders, and so on. The operating system also needs to impose some amount of security and redundancy into the file system so that a power outage does not jeopardize the contents of an entire hard disk. Some operating systems do a better job in this regard than others.

- *Virtual memory.* Memory is expensive, and few computers have enough RAM to hold all programs and their data that a user would like to run simultaneously. Most operating systems extend the available memory by storing some data on the hard disk. The application programs do not realize what is happening. When a program accesses a data item that is currently not in memory, the processor senses this and notifies the operating system. The operating system swaps the needed data from the hard disk into RAM, simultaneously swapping out a memory block of equal size that has not been accessed for some time.

- *Handling multiple users.* The operating systems of large and powerful computers allow simultaneous access by multiple users. Each user is connected to the computer through a separate terminal. The operating system authenticates users by checking that they have a valid account and password. It gives each user a small *slice* of processor time, then serves the next user.

- *Multitasking.* Even if you are the sole user of a computer, you may want to run multiple applications—for example, to read your e-mail in one window and run the C++ compiler in another. The operating system is responsible for dividing processor time between the applications you are running, so that each can make progress.

Figure 6 A Graphical Software Environment for the Linux Operating System

- *Printing*. The operating system queues up the print requests that are sent by multiple applications. This is necessary to make sure that the printed pages do not contain a mixture of words sent simultaneously from separate programs.

- *Windows*. Many operating systems present their users with a desktop made up of multiple windows. The operating system manages the location and appearance of the window frames; the applications are responsible for the interior.

- *Fonts*. To render text on the screen and the printer, the shapes of characters must be defined. This is especially important for programs that can display multiple type styles and sizes. Modern operating systems contain a central font repository.

- *Communicating between programs*. The operating system can facilitate the transfer of information between programs. That transfer can happen through *cut and paste* or *interprocess communication*. Cut and paste is a user-initiated data transfer in which the user copies data from one application into a transfer buffer (often called a "clipboard") managed by the operating system and inserts the buffer's contents into another application. Interprocess communication is initiated by applications that transfer data without direct user involvement.

- *Networking*. The operating system provides protocols and services for enabling applications to reach information on other computers attached to the network.

Today, the most popular operating systems are Microsoft Windows, UNIX and its variants (such as Linux), and the Macintosh OS.

CHAPTER SUMMARY

1. Inheritance is a mechanism for extending classes.

2. A derived class inherits from a base class and is a more specialized class.

3. The derived class inherits all data fields and functions that it does not redefine.

4. The constructor of a derived class can pass parameters to the base class constructors.

5. If no parameters are passed explicitly, the default constructor of the base class is invoked.

6. The derived class can override functions from the base class.

7. Use *BaseClass::function* notation to explicitly call a base-class function.

8. Protected features can be accessed by the member functions of all derived classes.

9. Polymorphism (literally, "having multiple shapes") describes a set of objects of different classes with similar behavior.

10. When converting a derived class object to a base class, the derived class data is sliced away.

11. A derived-class pointer can be converted to a base-class pointer.

12. When a virtual function is called, the version belonging to the actual type of the implicit parameter is invoked.

13. A dynamically bound function is selected at run time. A statically bound function is selected at compile time.

REVIEW EXERCISES

Exercise R8.1. An object-oriented traffic simulation system has the following classes:

Vehicle	PickupTruck
Car	SportUtilityVehicle
Truck	Minivan
Sedan	Bicycle
Coupe	Motorcycle

Draw an inheritance diagram that shows the relationships between these classes.

Exercise R8.2. What inheritance relationships would you establish among the following classes?

```
Student
Professor
TeachingAssistant
Employee
Secretary
DepartmentChair
Janitor
SeminarSpeaker
Person
Course
Seminar
Lecture
ComputerLab
```

Exercise R8.3. Consider the following classes B and D:

```
class B
{
public:
   B();
   B(int n);
};

B::B()
{
   cout << "B::B()\n";
}

B::B(int n)
{
```

```
      cout << "B::B(" << n << ")\n";
}

class D : public B
{
public:
   D();
   D(int n);
private:
   B b;
};

D::D()
{
   cout << "D::D()\n";
}

D::D(int n) : B(n)
{
   b = B(-n);
   cout << "D::D("<< n <<")\n";
}
```

What does the following program print?

```
int main()
{
   D d(3);
   return 0;
}
```

Determine the answer by hand, not by compiling and running the program.

Exercise R8.4. What does the following program print?

```
class B
{
public:
   void print(int n) const;
};

void B::print(int n) const
{
   cout << n << "\n";
}

class D : public B
{
public:
   void print(int n) const;
};

void D::print(int n) const
{
   if (n <= 1) B::print(n);
   else if (n % 2 == 0) print(n / 2);
   else print(3 * n + 1);
```

```
   }

   int main()
   {
      D d;
      d.print(3);
      return 0;
   }
```

Determine the answer by hand, not by compiling and running the program.

Exercise R8.5. What is wrong with the following code?

```
class B
{
public:
   B();
   B(int n);
   void print() const;
private:
   int b;
};

B::B()
{
   b = 0;
}

B::B(int n)
{
   b = n;
}

void B::print() const
{
   cout << "B: " << b << "\n";
}

class D : public B
{
public:
   D();
   D(int n);
   void print() const;
};

D::D()
{
}

D::D(int n)
{
   b = n;
}
```

```
void D::print() const
{
    cout << "D: " << b << "\n";
}
```

How can you fix the errors?

Exercise R8.6. Suppose the class D inherits from B. Which of the following assignments are legal?

```
B  b;
D  d;
B* pb;
D* pd;
```

a. b = d;

b. d = b;

c. pd = pb;

d. pb = pd;

e. d = pd;

f. b = *pd;

g. *pd = *pb;

Exercise R8.7. Which of the following calls are statically bound, and which are dynamically bound? What does the program print?

```
class B
{
public:
    B();
    virtual void p() const;
    void q() const;
};

B::B() {}

void B::p() const
{
    cout << "B::p\n";
}

void B::q() const
{
    cout << "B::q\n";
}

class D : public B
{
public:
    D();
    virtual void p() const;
    void q() const;
};
```

```
D::D()
{
}

void D::p() const
{
    cout << "D::p\n";
}

void D::q() const
{
    cout << "D::q\n";
}

int main()
{
    B b;
    D d;
    B* pb = new B;
    B* pd = new D;
    D* pd2 = new D;

    b.p(); b.q();
    d.p(); d.q();
    pb->p(); pb->q();
    pd->p(); pd->q();
    pd2->p(); pd2->q();
    return 0;
}
```

Determine the answer by hand, not by compiling and running the program.

Exercise R8.8. True or false?

a. When a member function is invoked through a pointer, it is always statically bound.

b. When a member function is invoked through an object, it is always statically bound.

c. Only member functions can be dynamically bound.

d. Only nonmember functions can be statically bound.

e. When a function is virtual in the base class, it cannot be made nonvirtual in a derived class.

f. Calling a virtual function is slower than calling a nonvirtual function.

g. Constructors can be virtual.

h. It is good programming practice to make all member functions virtual.

PROGRAMMING EXERCISES

Exercise P8.1. Derive a class `Programmer` from `Employee`. Supply a constructor `Programmer(string name, double salary)` that calls the base-class constructor. Supply a function `get_name` that returns the name in the format `"Hacker, Harry (Programmer)"`.

Exercise P8.2. Implement a base class `Person`. Derive classes `Student` and `Instructor` from `Person`. A person has a name and a birthday. A student has a major, and an instructor has a salary. Write the class definitions, the constructors, and the member functions `print()` for all classes.

Exercise P8.3. Derive a class `Manager` from `Employee`. Add a data field, named `department`, of type `string`. Supply a function `print` that prints the manager's name, department, and salary. Derive a class `Executive` from `Manager`. Supply a function `print` that prints the string `Executive`, followed by the information stored in the `Manager` base object.

Exercise P8.4. Implement a base class `Account` and derived classes `Savings` and `Checking`. In the base class, supply member functions `deposit` and `withdraw`. Provide a function `daily_interest` that computes and adds the daily interest. For calculations, assume that every month has 30 days. Checking accounts yield interest of 3 percent monthly on balances over $1,000. Savings accounts yield interest of 6 percent on the entire balance. Write a driver program that makes a month's worth of deposits and withdrawals and calculates the interest every day.

Exercise P8.5. Measure the speed difference between a statically bound call and a dynamically bound call. Use the `Time` class to measure the time spent in one loop of virtual function calls and another loop of regular function calls.

Exercise P8.6. Write a base class `Worker` and derived classes `HourlyWorker` and `SalariedWorker`. Every worker has a name and a salary rate. Write a virtual function `compute_pay(int hours)` that computes the weekly pay for every worker. An hourly worker gets paid the hourly wage for the actual number of hours worked, if `hours` is at most 40. If the hourly worker worked more than 40 hours, the excess is paid at time and a half. The salaried worker gets paid the hourly wage for 40 hours, no matter what the actual number of hours is.

Exercise P8.7. Implement a base class `Appointment` and derived classes `Onetime`, `Daily`, `Weekly`, and `Monthly`. An appointment has a description (for example, "see the dentist") and a date and time. Write a virtual function `occurs_on(int year, int month, int day)` that checks whether the appointment occurs on that date. For example, for a monthly appointment, you must check whether the day of the month matches. Then fill a vector of `Appointment*` with a mixture of appointments. Have the user enter a date and print out all appointments that happen on that date.

Exercise P8.8. Improve the appointment book program of Exercise P8.7. Give the user the option to add new appointments. The user must specify the type of the appointment, the description, and the date and time.

Exercise P8.9. Improve the appointment book program of Exercises P8.7 and P8.8 by letting the user save the appointment data to a file and reload the data from a file. The saving part is straightforward: Make a virtual function save. Save out the type, description, date, and time. The loading part is not so easy. You must first determine the type of the appointment to be loaded, create an object of that type with its default constructor, and then call a virtual load function to load the remainder.

G **Exercise P8.10.** Implement a base class Vehicle and derived classes Car and Truck. A vehicle has a position on the screen. Write virtual functions draw that draw cars and trucks as follows:

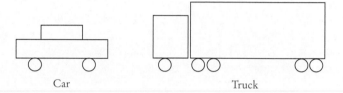

Car   Truck

Then populate a vector of Vehicle* pointers with a mixture of cars and trucks, and draw all of them.

G **Exercise P8.11.** Implement a base class Shape and derived classes Rectangle, Triangle, and Square. Derive Square from Rectangle. Supply virtual functions double area() and void plot(). Fill a vector of Shape* pointers with a mixture of the shapes, plot them all, and compute the total area.

G **Exercise P8.12.** Use Exercise P8.11 as the basis for a drawing program. Users can place various shapes onto the screen by first clicking on a shape icon and then clicking on the desired screen location:

Icons

Drawing area

Hint: Supply virtual functions make_shape(Point p) that return a new shape of default size anchored at the point p.

G **Exercise P8.13.** Extend the program of Exercise P8.12 by adding another shape type: CircleShape. (You cannot call it Circle, because there already is a Circle class in the graphics library.) Explain what changes you needed to make in the program to implement this extension. How do virtual functions help in making the program easily extensible?

G **Exercise P8.14.** Write a base class Chart that stores a vector of floating-point values. Implement derived classes, PieChart and BarChart, with a virtual plot function that can plot the data as a pie chart and as a bar chart.

Streams

CHAPTER GOALS

- To be able to read and write files
- To convert between strings and numbers using string streams
- To use stream manipulators to format output
- To learn how to process the command line
- To understand the concepts of sequential and random access
- To be able to build simple random-access database files
- To learn about encryption

All of the programs that you have written until now have read their input from the keyboard and displayed their output on the screen. However, many practical programs need to be able to use disk files for reading input and writing output. In this chapter, you will learn how to access files from C++ programs.

The C++ input/output library is organized in an object-oriented fashion, based on the concept of *streams*. An *input stream* is a source of data, and an *output stream* is a destination for data. Inheritance is used to provide classes for accessing files, strings, and other sources and destinations.

Chapter Contents

9.1 Reading and Writing Text Files

> To read or write disk files, you use objects of type fstream, ifstream, or ofstream.

To access a disk file, you need to open a file variable. File variables are variables of type ifstream (for input), ofstream (for output), or fstream (for both input and output). For example,

```
ifstream input_data;
```

You must include the header file fstream to use file variables.

To read anything from a file, you need to *open* it. When you open a file, you give the name of the disk file. Suppose you want to read data from a file named input.dat, located in the same directory as the program. Then you use the following command to open the file:

```
input_data.open("input.dat");
```

> When opening a file object, you supply the name of the disk file.

This procedure call associates the file variable input_data with the disk file named input.dat. Reading from the file is now completely straightforward: You simply use the same functions that you have always used.

```
int n;
double x;
input_data >> n >> x;
```

You read strings in the same way:

```
string s;
input_data >> s; // Read a word
getline(input_data, s); // Read a line
```

You read a single character with the get function:

```
char ch;
input_data.get(ch);
```

If you read a character and you regretted it, you can *unget* it, so that the next input operation can read it again. However, you can unget only one character at a time.

This is called *one-character lookahead:* At the next character in the input stream you can make a decision what you want to read in next, but not more than one character.

```
char ch;
input_data.get(ch);
if ('0' <= ch && ch <= '9') // It was a digit
{
    input_data.unget(); // Oops—didn't want to read it
    int n;
    input_data >> n; // Read integer starting with ch
}
```

Older implementations of the stream library do not have the unget member function. In that case you need to remember the last input character and call input_data.put_back(ch).

The fail function tells you whether input has failed. Just as for standard input, the file can be in a failed state because you reached the end of file or because of a formatting error. There can be yet another reason for a failed state: If you open a file and the name is invalid, or if there is no file of that name, then the file is also in a failed state. It is a good idea to test for failure whenever you open a file.

When you are done reading from a file, you should *close* it:

> When you are done using a file, you should close the file object.

```
input_data.close();
```

Writing to a file is just as simple. You open the file for writing:

```
ofstream output_data;
output_data.open("output.dat");
```

Now you send information to the output file in the usual way.

```
output_data << n << " " << x << "\n";
```

To write a single character, use

```
output_data.put(ch);
```

When you are finished with the output, remember to *close* the file.

```
output_data.close();
```

To open the same file for both reading and writing, you use an fstream variable:

```
fstream datafile;
datafile.open("employee.dat");
```

The file name that you give to the open command may be a string constant:

```
ifstream input_data;
input_data.open("input.dat");
```

If you want to pass a name that is stored in a string variable, use the c_str function to convert the string object to a character pointer.

```
string input_name;
cin >> input_name;
ifstream input_data;
input_data.open(input_name.c_str());
```

File names can contain directory path information, as in

```
~/homework/input.dat // UNIX
c:\homework\input.dat // Windows
```

When you specify the file name as a constant string, and the name contains back-slash characters (as in a Windows filename), you must supply each backslash *twice*:

```
input_data.open("c:\\homework\\input.dat");
```

Recall that a single backslash inside quoted strings is an *escape character* that is combined with another character to form a special meaning, such as \n for a newline character. The \\ combination denotes a single backslash. When the file name is entered into a string variable by the user, the user should not type the backslash twice.

Have a look at the maxtemp.cpp program in Section 4.6, which reads in temperature data and then displays the highest value. That program prompts the user to enter all data values. Of course, if the user makes a single mistake in a data value, then there is no going back. The user must then restart the program and reenter all data values. It makes more sense for the user to place the data values into a file using a text editor and then to specify the name of that file when the data values are to be used.

Here is the modified program that incorporates this improvement. The program queries the user for an input file name, opens a file variable, and passes that variable to the read_data function. Inside the function, we use the familiar >> operator to read the data values from the input file.

Note that the ifstream parameter of the read_data function is passed by *reference*. Reading from a file modifies the file variable. The file variable monitors how many characters have been read or written so far. Any read or write operation changes that data. For that reason, you must always pass file variables by reference.

ch09/maxval1.cpp

```
1  #include <string>
2  #include <iostream>
3  #include <fstream>
4
5  using namespace std;
6
7  /**
8      Reads numbers from a file and finds the maximum value.
9      @param in the input stream to read from
10     @return the maximum value or 0 if the file has no numbers
11  */
12  double read_data(ifstream& in)
13  {
14     double highest;
15     double next;
16     if (in >> next)
17        highest = next;
18     else
19        return 0;
20
```

```
21      while (in >> next)
22      {
23         if (next > highest)
24            highest = next;
25      }
26
27      return highest;
28   }
29
30   int main()
31   {
32      string filename;
33      cout << "Please enter the data file name: ";
34      cin >> filename;
35
36      ifstream infile;
37      infile.open(filename.c_str());
38
39      if (infile.fail())
40      {
41         cout << "Error opening " << filename << "\n";
42         return 1;
43      }
44
45      double max = read_data(infile);
46      cout << "The maximum value is " << max << "\n";
47
48      infile.close();
49      return 0;
50   }
```

Program Run

```
Please enter the data file name: data.txt
The maximum value is 34399
```

9.2 The Inheritance Hierarchy of Stream Classes

Stream classes inherit the operations <<, >>, getline, and fail from the istream and ostream classes.

The C++ input/output library consists of several classes that are related by inheritance. The most fundamental classes are the istream and ostream classes. An istream is a source of bytes. The get, getline, and >> operations are defined for istream objects. The ifstream class derives from the istream class. Therefore, it automatically inherits all istream operations. In Section 9.4, you will encounter another class, istringstream, that also derives from the istream class. It too inherits the istream operations. However, the open function is a member function of the ifstream class, not the istream class. You can only open file streams, not general input streams or string streams.

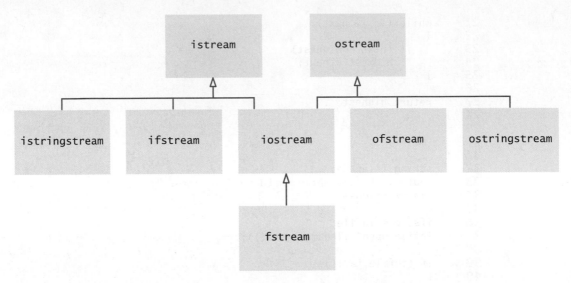

Figure 1   The Inheritance Hierarchy of Stream Classes

Similarly, an ostream is a destination for bytes. Several forms of the << operator are defined for ostream objects, to print out numbers, strings, and other types. The ofstream class derives from the ostream class and inherits the << operators.

An iostream combines the capabilities of an istream and ostream, by deriving from both classes (see Figure 1). The fstream class derives from iostream. (Note that, for technical reasons, fstream does *not* derive from ifstream or ofstream, even if it would make sense for it to do so.)

You should take advantage of the inheritance relationships between the stream classes whenever you write functions with stream parameters. Consider the read_data function in the preceding example program. It is declared as

```
double read_data(ifstream& in)
```

However, if you look inside the code of the function, you will see that the function never requires that the in parameter be a file stream. The function can equally well read data from any istream object. For that reason, you should declare such a function with a parameter of type istream, not ifstream:

```
double read_data(istream& in)
```

Now you can pass parameters of types other than ifstream, such as the cin object (which belongs to a derived class of istream but not to ifstream).

The following example program illustrates this concept. Note that the read_data function takes an istream parameter. In the main function, the program user can choose to supply the data in a file, or to type them in manually. The main function then calls the read_data function in one of two ways, either as

```
max = read_data(infile);
```

or

```
max = read_data(cin);
```

The `infile` and `cin` objects belong to different classes, but both classes inherit from `istream`.

As you already saw in the preceding section, the stream parameter must be passed by reference since the stream data structure is modified when you read from a stream. Now there is a second reason why you must use call by reference. If you used call by value,

```
double read_data(istream in) // Error! Missing &
```

then the parameter object would be *sliced* when copied into the parameter object `in` (see Common Error 8.4). Therefore, you must always use call by reference with stream parameters.

ch09/maxval2.cpp

```
1   #include <string>
2   #include <iostream>
3   #include <fstream>
4
5   using namespace std;
6
7   /**
8       Reads numbers from a file and finds the maximum value.
9       @param in the input stream to read from
10      @return the maximum value or 0 if the file has no numbers
11  */
12  double read_data(istream& in)
13  {
14      double highest;
15      double next;
16      if (in >> next)
17          highest = next;
18      else
19          return 0;
20
21      while (in >> next)
22      {
23          if (next > highest)
24              highest = next;
25      }
26
27      return highest;
28  }
29
30  int main()
31  {
32      double max;
33
34      string input;
35      cout << "Do you want to read from a file? (y/n) ";
36      cin >> input;
```

```
37
38      if (input == "y")
39      {
40         string filename;
41         cout << "Please enter the data file name: ";
42         cin >> filename;
43
44         ifstream infile;
45         infile.open(filename.c_str());
46
47         if (infile.fail())
48         {
49            cout << "Error opening " << filename << "\n";
50            return 1;
51         }
52
53         max = read_data(infile);
54         infile.close();
55      }
56      else
57         max = read_data(cin);
58
59      cout << "The maximum value is " << max << "\n";
60
61      return 0;
62   }
```

Program Run

```
Do you want to read from a file? (y/n) y
Please enter the data file name: data.txt
The maximum value is 34399
```

9.3 Stream Manipulators

You control stream formatting with stream manipulators.

To control how the output is formatted, you use stream *manipulators*. A manipulator is an object that is sent to a stream using the << operator, and that affects the behavior of the stream. The setprecision manipulator, which we already used, is a typical example. The statement

```
out << setprecision(2);
```

does not cause any immediate output, but it affects how the next floating-point number is written. In this section, you will learn about other manipulators in the standard C++ library. Table 1 summarizes the most commonly used stream manipulators.

Table 1 Stream Manipulators

Manipulator	Purpose	Example	Output
setw	Sets the field width of the next item only.	`out << setw(6) << 123;`	123
setfill	Sets the fill character for padding a field. (The default character is a space.)	`out << setfill('0') << setw(6)` `   << 123;`	000123
left	Selects left alignment.	`out << left << setw(6) << 123;`	123
right	Selects right alignment (default).	`out << right << setw(6) << 123;`	123
hex	Selects base 16 for integers.	`out << hex << 123;`	7b
dec	Selects base 10 for integers.	`out << dec << 123;`	123
fixed	Selects fixed format for floating-point numbers.	`double x = 123.4567;` `out << x << endl << fixed << x;`	123.457 123.456700

setprecision	Sets the number of significant digits for general format, the number of digits after the decimal point for fixed format.	`double x = 123.4567;`
		`out << setprecision(2) << x`
		`   << endl << fixed << x;`
			1.2e+02
			123.46

Occasionally, you need to pad numbers with leading zeroes, for example to print hours and minutes as 09:01. This is achieved with the `setfill` manipulator:

```
out << setfill('0') << setw(2) << hours
   << ":" << setw(2) << minutes << setfill(' ');
```

Now, a zero is used to pad the field. Afterwards, the space is restored as the fill character.

By default, the fill characters appear before the item:

```
out << setw(10) << 123 << endl << setw(10) << 4567;
```

produces

```
       123
      4567
```

The numbers line up to the right. That alignment works well for numbers, but not for strings. Usually, you want strings to line up on the left. You use the `left` and `right` manipulators to set the alignment. The following example uses left alignment for a string and then switches back to right alignment for a number:

```
out << left << setw(10) << str << right << setw(10) << num;
```

The hex and dec manipulators control the number base for integers, switching to hexadecimal (base 16) and decimal (base 10) numbers. (See Appendix F for a description of hexadecimal numbers.) For example,

```
out << hex << 10 << " " << dec << 10;
```

yields

```
a 10
```

The default format for floating-point numbers is called *general* format. That format displays as many digits as are specified by the *precision* (6 by default), switching to scientific notation for large and small numbers. For example,

```
out << 12.3456789 << " " << 123456789.0;
```

yields

```
12.3457 1.23457e+08
```

The *fixed* format prints all values with the same number of digits after the decimal point. In the fixed format, the numbers above are displayed as

```
12.345679 123456789.000000
```

Use the fixed manipulator to select that format, and the setprecision manipulator to change the precision.

For example,

```
out << fixed << setprecision(2) << 1.2 << " " << 1.235
```

yields

```
1.20 1.24
```

Note that the manipulators set the state of the stream object for all subsequent operations, with the exception of setw. After each output operation, the field width is reset to 0.

9.4 String Streams

Use string streams to read numbers that are contained in strings, or to convert between numbers and strings.

In the preceding section, you saw how the ifstream and ofstream classes can be used to read characters from a file and write characters to a file. In other words, you use a file stream if the source or the destination of the characters is a file. You can use other stream classes to read characters from a different source or to send them to a different destination.

The istringstream class reads characters from a string, and the ostringstream class writes characters to a string. That doesn't sound so exciting—we already know how to access and change the characters of a string. However, the string stream classes have the same *interface* as the other stream classes. In other words, using an istringstream you can read numbers that are stored in a string, simply by using the familiar >> operator. The string stream classes are defined in the sstream header.

Here is an example. The string `input` contains a date, and we want to separate it into month, day, and year. First, construct an `istringstream` object. The construction parameter is the string containing the characters that we want to read:

```
string input = "January 23, 1955";
istringstream instr(input);
```

Next, simply use the `>>` operator to read off the month name, the day, the comma separator, and the year:

```
string month;
int day;
string comma;
int year;
instr >> month >> day >> comma >> year;
```

Now `month` is `"January"`, `day` is 23, and `year` is 1955. Note that this input statement yields day and year as *integers*. Had we taken the string apart with `substr`, we would have obtained only strings, not numbers.

In fact, converting strings that contain digits to their integer values is such a common operation that it is useful to write a helper function for this purpose:

```
int string_to_int(string s)
{
   istringstream instr(s);
   int n;
   instr >> n;
   return n;
}
```

For example, `string_to_int("1999")` is the *integer* 1999.

By writing to a string stream, you can convert numbers to strings. First construct an `ostringstream` object:

```
ostringstream outstr;
```

Next, use the `<<` operator to add a number to the stream. The number is converted into a sequence of characters:

```
outstr << setprecision(5) << sqrt(2);
```

Now the stream contains the string `"1.41421"`. To obtain that string from the stream, call the `str` member function:

```
string output = outstr.str();
```

You can build up more complex strings in the same way. Here we build a data string of the month, day, and year:

```
string month = "January";
int day = 23;
int year = 1955;
ostringstream outstr;
outstr << month << " " << day << "," << year;
string output = outstr.str();
```

Now output is the string "January 23, 1955". Note that we converted the integers day and year into a string. Again, converting an integer into a string is such a common operation that is useful to have a helper function for it:

```
string int_to_string(int n)
{
   ostringstream outstr;
   outstr << n;
   return outstr.str();
}
```

For example, int_to_string(1955) is the string "1955".

A very common use of string streams is to accept input one line at a time and then to analyze it further. This avoids the complications that arise from mixing >> and getline that were discussed in Common Error 5.1. Simply call getline to read the input one line at a time, and then read items from the input lines by using string streams.

Here is an example. You prompt the user for a time, and want to accept inputs such as

```
21:30
9:30 pm
9 am
```

That is, the input line consists of a number, maybe followed by a colon and another number, maybe followed by am or pm. In the read_time procedure of the following program, you first read in the entire input line, then analyze what the user typed. The result is a pair of integers, hours and minutes, adjusted to military (24-hour) time if the user entered "pm".

In the time_to_string function, the integer values for hours and minutes are converted back to a string. Using the aforementioned int_to_string function, the integer values are converted to strings. A : separator is added between them. If the military parameter is false, an "am" or "pm" string is appended.

ch09/readtime.cpp

```
 1  #include <string>
 2  #include <iostream>
 3  #include <sstream>
 4
 5  using namespace std;
 6
 7  /**
 8     Converts an integer value to a string, e.g., 3 -> "3".
 9     @param s an integer value
10     @return the equivalent string
11  */
12  string int_to_string(int n)
13  {
14     ostringstream outstr;
15     outstr << n;
16     return outstr.str();
17  }
```

```
18
19   /**
20       Reads a time from standard input in the format hh:mm or
21       hh:mm am or hh:mm pm.
22       @param hours filled with the hours
23       @param minutes filled with the minutes
24   */
25   void read_time(int& hours, int& minutes)
26   {
27       string line;
28       getline(cin, line);
29       istringstream instr(line);
30
31       instr >> hours;
32
33       minutes = 0;
34
35       char ch;
36       instr.get(ch);
37
38       if (ch == ':')
39           instr >> minutes;
40       else
41           instr.unget();
42
43       string suffix;
44       instr >> suffix;
45
46       if (suffix == "pm")
47           hours = hours + 12;
48   }
49
50   /**
51       Computes a string representing a time.
52       @param hours the hours (0 ... 23)
53       @param minutes the minutes (0 ... 59)
54       @param military true for military format,
55       false for am/pm format
56   */
57   string time_to_string(int hours, int minutes, bool military)
58   {
59       string suffix;
60       if (!military)
61       {
62           if (hours < 12)
63               suffix = "am";
64           else
65           {
66               suffix = "pm";
67               hours = hours - 12;
68           }
69           if (hours == 0) hours = 12;
70       }
71       string result = int_to_string(hours) + ":";
```

```
72       if (minutes < 10) result = result + "0";
73       result = result + int_to_string(minutes);
74       if (!military)
75          result = result + " " + suffix;
76       return result;
77    }
78
79    int main()
80    {
81       cout << "Please enter the time: ";
82
83       int hours;
84       int minutes;
85
86       read_time(hours, minutes);
87
88       cout << "Military time: "
89          << time_to_string(hours, minutes, true) << "\n";
90       cout << "Using am/pm: "
91          << time_to_string(hours, minutes, false) << "\n";
92
93       return 0;
94    }
```

Program Run

```
Please enter the time: 1:05 pm
Military time: 13:05
Using am/pm: 1:05 pm
```

9.5 Command Line Arguments

Depending on the operating system and C++ development system used, there are different methods of starting a program—for example, by selecting "Run" in the compilation environment, by clicking on an icon, or by typing the name of the program at a prompt in a terminal or shell window. The latter method is called "invoking the program from the command line". When you use this method, you must of course type the name of the program, but you can also type in additional information that the program can use. These additional strings are called *command line arguments*. For example, if you start a program with the command line

```
prog -v input.dat
```

then the program receives two command line arguments: the strings "-v" and "input.dat". It is entirely up to the program what to do with these strings. It is customary to interpret strings starting with a - as options and other strings as file names.

Only text mode programs receive command line arguments; the graphics library that comes with this book does not collect them.

Programs that start from the command line can retrieve the name of the program and the command line arguments in the `main` function.

To receive command line arguments, you need to define the `main` function in a different way. You define two parameters: one integer and one with a type called `char*[]`, which denotes an array of pointers to C character arrays.

```
int main(int argc, char* argv[])
{
   ...
}
```

Here `argc` is the count of arguments, and `argv` contains the values of the arguments. Because they are character arrays, you should convert them to C++ strings. `string(argv[i])` is the `i`th command line argument, ready to use in C++.

In our example, `argc` is 3, and `argv` contains the three strings

```
string(argv[0]):   "prog"
string(argv[1]):   "-v"
string(argv[2]):   "input.dat"
```

Note that `string(argv[0])` is always the name of the program and that `argc` is always at least 1.

Let us write a program that *encrypts* a file—that is, scrambles it so that it is unreadable except to those who know the decryption method and the secret keyword. Ignoring 2000 years of progress in the field of encryption, we will use a method familiar to Julius Caesar. The person performing any encryption chooses an *encryption key*; here the key is a number between 1 and 25 that indicates the shift to be used in encrypting each letter. For example, if the key is 3, replace A with a D, B with an E, and so on (see Figure 2).

The program takes the following command line arguments:

- An optional -d flag to indicate decryption instead of encryption
- An optional encryption key, specified with a -k flag
- The input file name
- The output file name

If no key is specified, then 3 is used. For example,

```
caesar input.txt encrypt.txt
```

encrypts the file `input.txt` with a key of 3 and places the result into `encrypt.txt`.

```
caesar -d -k11 encrypt.txt output.txt
```

decrypts the file `encrypt.txt` with a key of 11 and places the result into `output.txt`.

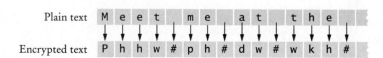

Figure 2 Caesar Cipher

Here is the program. When we find that the user has provided bad command line parameters (or none at all), the usage function prints a brief reminder of the correct usage. This behavior is common for command-line programs. Also note the use of the exit function for error handling. This function terminates the program and returns an error code to the operating system, just as if the main function had exited. When an error is detected, you can call exit to terminate the program immediately without having to first return to main.

ch09/caesar.cpp

```
1  #include <iostream>
2  #include <fstream>
3  #include <string>
4  #include <sstream>
5
6  using namespace std;
7
8  /**
9      Prints usage instructions.
10     @param program_name  the name of this program
11  */
12  void usage(string program_name)
13  {
14     cout << "Usage: " << program_name
15        << " [-d] [-kn] infile outfile\n";
16     exit(1);
17  }
18
19  /**
20     Prints file opening error message.
21     @param filename  the name of the file that could not be opened
22  */
23  void open_file_error(string filename)
24  {
25     cout << "Error opening file " << filename << "\n";
26     exit(1);
27  }
28
29  /**
30     Computes correct remainder for negative dividend.
31     @param a  an integer
32     @param n  an integer > 0
33     @return  the mathematically correct remainder r such that
34        a - r is divisible by n and 0 <= r and r < n
35  */
36  int remainder(int a, int n)
37  {
38     if (a >= 0)
39        return a % n;
40     else
41        return n - 1 - (-a - 1) % n;
42  }
43
```

```
44   /**
45       Encrypts a character using the Caesar cipher.
46       @param ch the character to encrypt
47       @param k the encryption key
48       @return the encrypted character
49   */
50   char encrypt(char ch, int k)
51   {
52       const int NLETTER = 'Z' - 'A' + 1;
53       if ('A' <= ch && ch <= 'Z')
54           return static_cast<char>(
55               'A' + remainder(ch - 'A' + k, NLETTER));
56       if ('a' <= ch && ch <= 'z')
57           return static_cast<char>(
58               'a' + remainder(ch - 'a' + k, NLETTER));
59       return ch;
60   }
61
62   /**
63       Encrypts a stream using the Caesar cipher.
64       @param in the stream to read from
65       @param out the stream to write to
66       @param k the encryption key
67   */
68   void encrypt_file(istream& in, ostream& out, int k)
69   {
70       char ch;
71       while (in.get(ch))
72           out.put(encrypt(ch, k));
73   }
74
75   /**
76       Converts a string to an integer, e.g., "3" -> 3.
77       @param s a string representing an integer
78       @return the equivalent integer
79   */
80   int string_to_int(string s)
81   {
82       istringstream instr(s);
83       int n;
84       instr >> n;
85       return n;
86   }
87
88   int main(int argc, char* argv[])
89   {
90       bool decrypt = false;
91       int key = 3;
92       int nfile = 0; // The number of files specified
93       ifstream infile;
94       ofstream outfile;
95
96       if (argc < 3 || argc > 5) usage(string(argv[0]));
97
```

```
 98      int i;
 99      for (i = 1; i < argc; i++)
100      {
101         string arg = string(argv[i]);
102         if (arg.length() >= 2 && arg[0] == '-')
103         // It is a command line option
104         {
105            char option = arg[1];
106            if (option == 'd')
107            decrypt = true;
108            else if (option == 'k')
109            key = string_to_int(arg.substr(2));
110         }
111         else
112         {
113            nfile++;
114            if (nfile == 1)
115            {
116               infile.open(arg.c_str());
117               if (infile.fail()) open_file_error(arg);
118            }
119            else if (nfile == 2)
120            {
121               outfile.open(arg.c_str());
122               if (outfile.fail()) open_file_error(arg);
123            }
124         }
125      }
126
127      if (nfile != 2) usage(string(argv[0]));
128
129      if (decrypt) key = -key;
130
131      encrypt_file(infile, outfile, key);
132      infile.close();
133      outfile.close();
134      return 0;
135   }
```

RANDOM FACT 9.1

Encryption Algorithms

The exercises at the end of this chapter give a few algorithms to encrypt text. Don't actually use any of those methods to send secret messages to your lover. Any skilled cryptographer can *break* these schemes in a very short time—that is, reconstruct the original text without knowing the secret keyword.

In 1978 Ron Rivest, Adi Shamir, and Leonard Adleman introduced an encryption method that is much more powerful. The method is called *RSA encryption*, after the last names of its inventors. The exact scheme is too complicated to present here, but it is not actually difficult to follow. You can find the details in [1].

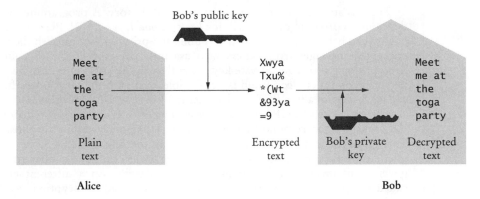

Bob's public key

Meet me at the toga party

Plain text

Xwya Txu% *(Wt &93ya =9

Encrypted text

Bob's private key

Meet me at the toga party

Decrypted text

Alice

Bob

Figure 3 Public-Key Encryption

RSA is a remarkable encryption method. There are two keys: a public key and a private key. (See Figure 3.) You can print the public key on your business card (or in your e-mail signature block) and give it to anyone. Then anyone can send you messages that only you can decrypt. Even though everyone else knows the public key, and even if they intercept all the messages coming to you, they cannot break the scheme and actually read the messages. In 1994, hundreds of researchers, collaborating over the Internet, cracked an RSA message encrypted with a 129-digit key. Messages encrypted with a key of 230 digits or more are expected to be secure.

The inventors of the algorithm obtained a *patent* for it. That means that anyone using it must seek a license from the inventors. They have given permission for most noncommercial usage, but if you implement RSA in a product that you sell, you must get their permission and probably pay them some amount of money.

A patent is a deal that society makes with an inventor. For a period of 17 years after the patent is awarded (or 20 years after the filing date), the inventor has an exclusive right for its commercialization, may collect royalties from others wishing to manufacture the invention, and may even stop competitors from marketing it altogether. In return, the inventor must publish the invention, so that others may learn from it, and must relinquish all claim to it after the protection period ends. The presumption is that in the absence of patent law, inventors would be reluctant to go through the trouble of inventing, or they would try to cloak their techniques to prevent others from copying their devices. The RSA patent expired on September 20, 2000.

What do you think? Are patents a fair deal? Unquestionably, some companies have chosen not to implement RSA, and instead chose a less capable method, because they could not or would not pay the royalties. Thus, it seems that the patent may have hindered, rather than advanced, commerce. Had there not been patent protection, would the inventors have published the method anyway, thereby giving the benefit to society without the cost of the 17-year monopoly? In this case, the answer is probably yes; the inventors were academic researchers, who live on salaries rather than sales receipts and are usually rewarded for their discoveries by a boost in their reputation and careers. Would their followers have been as active in discovering (and patenting) improvements? There is no way of knowing, of course. Is an algorithm even patentable, or is it a mathematical fact that belongs to nobody? The patent office did take the latter attitude for a long time. The RSA inventors and many others described their inventions in terms of imaginary electronic devices, rather than algorithms, to circumvent that restriction. Nowadays, the patent office will award software patents.

There is another fascinating aspect to the RSA story. A programmer, Phil Zimmermann, developed a program called PGP (for *Pretty Good Privacy*) [2]. PGP implements RSA. That is, you can have it generate a pair of public and private keys, publish the public key, receive encrypted messages from others who use their copy of PGP and your public key, and decrypt them with your private key. Even though the encryption can be performed on any personal computer, decryption is not feasible even with the most powerful computers. You can get a copy of a free PGP implementation from the GNU project [3].

The existence of PGP bothers the government to no end. They worry that criminals use the package to correspond by e-mail and that the police cannot tap those "conversations". Foreign governments can send communications that the National Security Agency (the premier electronic spy organization of the United States) cannot decipher. In the 1990s, the U.S. government unsuccessfully attempted to standardize on a different encryption scheme, called Skipjack, to which government organizations hold a decryption key that—of course—they promise not to use without a court order. There have been serious proposals to make it illegal to use any other encryption method in the United States. At one time, the government considered charging Zimmermann with breaching another law that forbids the unauthorized export of munitions as a crime and defines cryptographic technology as "munitions". They made the argument that, even though Zimmermann never exported the program, he should have known that it would immediately spread through the Internet when he released it in the United States.

What do you think? Will criminals and terrorists be harder to detect and convict once encryption of e-mail and phone conversations is widely available? Should the government therefore have a backdoor key to any legal encryption method? Or is this a gross violation of our civil liberties? Is it even possible to put the genie back into the bottle at this time?

9.6 Random Access

> You can access any position in a random access file by moving the *file pointer* prior to a read or write operation.

Consider a file that contains a set of employee data. You want to give some of the employees a raise. Of course, you can read all data into an array, update the information that has changed, and save the data out again. If the data set in the file is very large, you may end up doing a lot of reading and writing just to update a handful of records. It would be better if you could locate the changed information in the file and just replace it.

This is quite different from the file access that you programmed up to now. So far, you've read from a file an item at a time and written to a file an item at a time. That access pattern is called *sequential access*. Now we would like to access specific locations in a file and change only those locations. This access pattern is called *random access* (see Figure 4). There is nothing "random" about random access—the term simply means that you can read and modify any character stored at any location in the file.

Only disk files support random access; the cin and cout streams, which are attached to the keyboard and the terminal, do not. Each disk file has two special positions: the *get* position and the *put* position (see Figure 5). Normally, the put position is at the end of the file, and any output is appended to the end. However, if

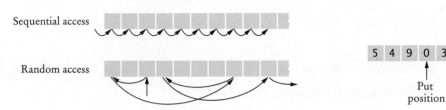

Figure 4   Sequential and Random Access   Figure 5   Get and Put Positions

you move the put position to the middle of the file and write to the file, the output overwrites what is already there. Normally, the get position starts at the beginning of the file and is moved toward the end as you read from the file. However, if you move the get position to another location, the next read command starts reading input at that location. Of course, you cannot move the get or put position beyond the last character currently in the file.

The following procedure calls move the get and put positions to character n counted from the beginning of the file fs.

```
fs.seekg(n, ios::beg);
fs.seekp(n, ios::beg);
```

To move to the position n characters away from the end of the file or the current position, use ios::end or ios::cur, respectively, instead of ios::beg. To determine the current position of the get and put positions (counted from the beginning of the file), use

```
n = fs.tellg();
n = fs.tellp();
```

Because files can be very large, the file positions are long integers. To find out the number of characters in a file, move the get position to the end and then find out the distance from the beginning of the file:

```
fs.seekg(0, ios::end);
long file_length = fs.tellg();
```

If you want to manipulate a data set in a file, you have to pay special attention to the formatting of the data. Suppose you just store the data as text:

If Harry's salary is increased by 5.5 percent, the new salary is $36,397.50. If one places the put position to the first character of the old value and simply writes out the new value, the result is

| H | a | c | k | e | r | , | | H | a | r | r | y | | 3 | 6 | 3 | 9 | 7 | . | 5 | r | a | c | k | e | r |

This does not work too well. The update overwrites some characters in the next record.

Variable-size records

Fixed-size records

Figure 6   Variable-Size and Fixed-Size Records

> Random access is most useful when all records in a file have the same size.

In order to be able to update a file, you must give each field a *fixed* size that is sufficiently large. As a result, every record in the file has the same size. This has another advantage: It is then easy to skip quickly to, say, the 50th record, without having to read in the first 49 records. Because records can be accessed at random when they all have the same size, a file with that structure is called a *random-access file*. (See Figure 6.)

To structure the data file in our example for random access, set the field lengths to the following dimensions:

Name: 30 characters

Salary: 10 characters

The file then looks as follows:

```
Hacker, Harry                           34500.00\n
Cracker, Carl V.                        61820.75\n
```

How large is each record? It would appear to be 30 + 10 = 40 bytes long. However, you must also count the newline character at the end of each line. Unfortunately, the Windows operating system stores a newline as two separate characters (called *carriage return* and *line feed*). Our programs never see that, because the input and output functions automatically convert between the '\n' character in strings and the carriage return/line feed combination in files. When counting file positions, though, you must take both characters into account, yielding a record length of 42 bytes. (See Advanced Topic 9.1 on page 398 for more information about this sordid topic.)

Now that you have determined the file layout, you can implement your random-access file functions. The following program asks the user to enter the position of the record that should be updated, and the price increase.

ch09/database.cpp

```
1   #include <iostream>
2   #include <iomanip>
3   #include <fstream>
4   #include <sstream>
5
```

```
6  using namespace std;
7
8  #include "ccc_empl.h"
9
10 const int NEWLINE_LENGTH = 2;
11 const int RECORD_SIZE = 30 + 10 + NEWLINE_LENGTH;
12
13 /**
14     Converts a string to a floating-point value, e.g.,
15     "3.14" -> 3.14.
16     @param s a string representing a floating-point value
17     @return the equivalent floating-point value
18 */
19 double string_to_double(string s)
20 {
21     istringstream instr(s);
22     double x;
23     instr >> x;
24     return x;
25 }
26
27 /**
28     Raises an employee salary.
29     @param e employee receiving raise
30     @param percent the percentage of the raise
31 */
32 void raise_salary(Employee& e, double percent)
33 {
34     double new_salary = e.get_salary() * (1 + percent / 100);
35     e.set_salary(new_salary);
36 }
37
38 /**
39     Reads an employee record from a file.
40     @param e filled with the employee
41     @param in the stream to read from
42 */
43 void read_employee(Employee& e, istream& in)
44 {
45     string line;
46     getline(in, line);
47     if (in.fail()) return;
48     string name = line.substr(0, 30);
49     double salary = string_to_double(line.substr(30, 10));
50     e = Employee(name, salary);
51 }
52
53 /**
54     Writes an employee record to a stream.
55     @param e the employee record to write
56     @param out the stream to write to
57 */
58 void write_employee(Employee e, ostream& out)
59 {
```

```
60    out << e.get_name()
61        << setw(10 + (30 - e.get_name().length()))
62        << fixed << setprecision(2)
63        << e.get_salary();
64 }
65
66 int main()
67 {
68    cout << "Please enter the data file name: ";
69    string filename;
70    cin >> filename;
71    fstream fs;
72    fs.open(filename.c_str());
73    fs.seekg(0, ios::end); // Go to end of file
74    int nrecord = fs.tellg() / RECORD_SIZE;
75
76    cout << "Please enter the record to update: (0 - "
77        << nrecord - 1 << ") ";
78    int pos;
79    cin >> pos;
80
81    const double SALARY_CHANGE = 5.0;
82
83    Employee e;
84    fs.seekg(pos * RECORD_SIZE, ios::beg);
85    read_employee(e, fs);
86    raise_salary(e, SALARY_CHANGE);
87    cout << "New salary: " + e.getSalary();
88    fs.seekp(pos * RECORD_SIZE, ios::beg);
89    write_employee(e, fs);
90
91    fs.close();
92    return 0;
93 }
```

Program Run

```
Please enter the data file name: employee.dat
Please enter the record to update: (0 - 9) 6
New salary: 130720
```

ADVANCED TOPIC 9.1

Binary Files

When a program saves numeric data to disk with the << operation, the data is saved in text format. For example, the floating-point number 314.7 is saved as 314.7 or perhaps 3.147E2. Actually, it is more efficient to save the number in the same format in which it is represented in the computer: as a sequence of bytes. That has the added advantage that the number automatically occupies a fixed size in the file, making random access easier.

When saving large data sets, it makes a lot of sense to use a binary format. For that reason, images and word processor documents are usually stored in binary files. We have not done that in this book. Writing binary output in a way that is portable across platforms requires a detailed understanding how binary numbers are stored on disk and in the processor memory.

A disadvantage of binary format is that it makes debugging *much* harder. When you look into a text file with a text editor, you can see exactly what is inside. To look inside a binary file, or to make a minor modification, you need special tools. We recommend using text files for saving data until an application is fully debugged. If the added efficiency of binary files is crucial, then rewrite just the input/output procedures to switch to binary format.

There is one common situation in which you will encounter the need for binary output. Suppose you write a C++ program that produces text output, and you want both the program and the output to be portable. That means, someone may compile the program under Unix or Windows, and someone may want to read the output in Windows even when the program was executed in Unix.

You will then want to generate the line endings in the Windows format as the "lowest common denominator". (Some Windows text editors deal poorly with "missing" carriage returns, but Unix text editors tend to be graceful about preserving additional carriage returns.)

In Windows, you produce such a line ending as out << "\n", but in Unix you have to use out << "\r\n". If you don't know on which platform your program will run, open the file stream in binary mode:

```
out.open(filename.c_str(), ios::out | ios::binary);
```

The ios::binary mode turns off the translation from '\n' to platform-dependent line endings. Then use

```
out << "\r\n";
```

to portably produce a Windows line ending.

RANDOM FACT 9.2

Databases and Privacy

Most companies use computers to keep huge data files of customer records and other business information. Special C++ database programs are used to search and update that information rapidly. This sounds like a straightforward extension of the techniques we learned in this chapter, but it does take special skills to handle truly massive amounts of data. You will likely take a course in database programming as part of your computer science education.

Databases not only lower the cost of doing business; they improve the quality of service that companies can offer. Nowadays it is almost unimaginable how time-consuming it used to be to withdraw money from a bank branch or to make travel reservations.

Today most databases are organized according to the *relational model*. Suppose a company stores your orders and payments. They will probably not repeat your name and address on every order; that would take unnecessary space. Instead, they will keep one file of all their customer names and identify each customer by a unique customer number. Only that customer number, not the entire customer information, is kept with an order record. (See Figure 7.)

To print an invoice, the database program must issue a *query* against both the customer and order files and pull the necessary information (name, address, articles ordered) from both.

Customers			Orders			
Cust. #:	Name		Order #:	Cust. #:	Item	
11439	Doe, John		59673	11439	DOS for Historians	
			59897	11439	C++ for Everyone	
			61013	11439	Big Java	

Figure 7   Relational Database Files

Frequently, queries involve more than two files. For example, the company may have a file of addresses of car owners and a file of people with good payment history and may want to find all of its customers who placed an order in the last month, drive an expensive car, and pay their bills, to send them another catalog. This kind of query is, of course, much faster if all customer files use the *same* key, which is why so many organizations in the United States try to collect the Social Security numbers of their customers.

The Social Security Act of 1935 provided that each contributor be assigned a Social Security number to track contributions into the Social Security Fund. These numbers have a distinctive format, such as 078-05-1120. (This particular number was printed on sample cards that were inserted in wallets. It actually was the Social Security number of the secretary of a vice president at the wallet manufacturer. When thousands of people used it as their own, the number was voided, and the secretary received a new number.) Figure 8 shows a Social Security card.

Figure 8   Social Security Card

Although they had not originally been intended for use as a universal identification number, Social Security numbers have become just that. The tax authorities and many other government agencies are required to collect the numbers, as are banks (for the reporting of interest income) and, of course, employers. Many other organizations find it convenient to use the number as well.

From a technical standpoint, Social Security numbers are a lousy method for indexing a database. There is a risk of having two records with the same number, because many illegal immigrants use fake numbers. Not everyone has a number—in particular, foreign customers. Because there is no checksum, a clerical error (such as transposing two digits) cannot be detected. (Credit card numbers have a checksum.) For the same reason, it is easy for anyone to make up a number.

Some people are very concerned about the fact that just about every organization wants to store their Social Security number. Unless there is a legal requirement, such as for banks, one can usually fight it or take one's business elsewhere. Even when an organization is required to collect the number, such as an employer, one can insist that the number be used only on tax and Social Security paperwork, not on the face of an ID card. Unfortunately, it usually takes near-superhuman effort to climb the organizational ladder to find someone with the authority to process paperwork with no Social Security number or to assign another identification number.

The discomfort that many people have about the computerization of their personal information is understandable. There is the possibility that companies and the government can merge multiple databases and derive information about us that we may wish they did not have or that simply may be untrue. An insurance company may deny coverage, or charge a higher premium, if it finds that you have too many relatives with a certain disease. You may be denied a job because of an inaccurate credit or medical report, and you may not even know the reason. These are very disturbing developments that have had a very negative impact for a small but growing number of people. See [4] for more information.

CHAPTER SUMMARY

1. To read or write disk files, you use objects of type `fstream`, `ifstream`, or `ofstream`.

2. When opening a file object, you supply the name of the disk file.

3. When you are done using a file, you should close the file object.

4. Stream classes inherit the operations `<<`, `>>`, `getline`, and `fail` from the `istream` and `ostream` classes.

5. You control stream formatting with stream manipulators.

6. Use string streams to read numbers that are contained in strings, or to convert between numbers and strings.

7. Programs that start from the command line can retrieve the name of the program and the command line arguments in the `main` function.

8. You can access any position in a random access file by moving the file pointer prior to a read or write operation.

9. Random access is most useful when all records in a file have the same size.

FURTHER READING

1. Bruce Schneier, *Applied Cryptography*, John Wiley & Sons, 1994.
2. Philip R. Zimmermann, *The Official PGP User's Guide*, MIT Press, 1995.
3. www.gnupg.org The GNU Project implementation of *Pretty Good Privacy*.
4. David F. Linowes, *Privacy in America*, University of Illinois Press, 1989.
5. Abraham Sinkov, *Elementary Cryptanalysis*, Mathematical Association of America, 1966.
6. Don Libes, *Obfuscated C and Other Mysteries*, John Wiley & Sons, 1993.

REVIEW EXERCISES

Exercise R9.1. Write C++ code to open a file with the name Hello.txt, store the message "Hello, World!" in the file, and close the file. Then open the same file again and read the message into a string variable. Close the file again.

Exercise R9.2. When do you open a file as an ifstream, as an ofstream, or as an fstream? Could you simply open all files as an fstream?

Exercise R9.3. What happens if you write to a file that you only opened for reading? Try it out if you don't know.

Exercise R9.4. What happens if you try to open a file for reading that doesn't exist? What happens if you try to open a file for writing that doesn't exist?

Exercise R9.5. What happens if you try to open a file for writing, but the file or device is write-protected (sometimes called read-only)? Try it out with a short test program.

Exercise R9.6. How do you open a file whose name contains a backslash, like temp\output.dat or c:\temp\output.dat?

Exercise R9.7. Why is the ifstream parameter of the read_data procedure in Section 9.2 a reference parameter and not a value parameter?

Exercise R9.8. How can you convert the string "3.14" into the floating-point number 3.14? How can you convert the floating-point number 3.14 into the string "3.14"?

Exercise R9.9. What is a command line? How can a program read its command line?

Exercise R9.10. If a program `woozle` is started with the command

```
woozle -DNAME=Piglet -I\eeyore -v heff.cpp a.cpp lump.cpp
```

what is the value of `argc`, and what are the values of `string(argv[0])`, `string(argv[1])`, and so on?

Exercise R9.11. How can you break the Caesar cipher? That is, how can you read a letter that was encrypted with the Caesar cipher, even though you don't know the key?

Exercise R9.12. What is the difference between sequential access and random access?

Exercise R9.13. What is the difference between a text file and a binary file?

Exercise R9.14. Some operating systems, in particular Windows, convert a `'\n'` character into a two-character sequence (carriage return/line feed) whenever writing a text file and convert the two-character sequence back into a newline when reading the text file back in. This is normally transparent to the C++ programmer. Why do we need to consider this issue in the database program of Section 9.6?

Exercise R9.15. What are the get and put positions in a file? How do you move them? How do you tell their current positions? Why are they `long` integers?

Exercise R9.16. How do you move the get position to the first byte of a file? To the last byte? To the exact middle of the file?

Exercise R9.17. What happens if you try to move the get or put position past the end of a file? What happens if you try to move the get or put position of `cin` or `cout`? Try it out and report your results.

PROGRAMMING EXERCISES

Exercise P9.1. Write a program that asks the user for a file name and displays the number of characters, words, and lines in that file. Then have the program ask for the name of the next file. When the user enters a file that doesn't exist (such as the empty string), the program should exit.

Exercise P9.2. *Random monoalphabet cipher.* The Caesar cipher, which shifts all letters by a fixed amount, is far too easy to crack. Here is a better idea. As the key, don't use numbers but words. Suppose the key word is FEATHER. Then first remove duplicate letters, yielding FEATHR, and append the other letters of the alphabet in reverse order:

F E A T H R Z Y X W V U S Q P O N M L K J I G D C B

Now encrypt the letters as follows:

A	B	C	D	E	F	G	H	I	J	K	L	M	N	O	P	Q	R	S	T	U	V	W	X	Y	Z
↓	↓	↓	↓	↓	↓	↓	↓	↓	↓	↓	↓	↓	↓	↓	↓	↓	↓	↓	↓	↓	↓	↓	↓	↓	↓
F	E	A	T	H	R	Z	Y	X	W	V	U	S	Q	P	O	N	M	L	K	J	I	G	D	C	B

Write a program that encrypts or decrypts a file using this cipher. For example,

```
crypt -d -kFEATHER encrypt.txt output.txt
```

decrypts a file using the keyword FEATHER. It is an error not to supply a keyword.

Exercise P9.3. *Letter frequencies.* If you encrypt a file using the cipher of Exercise P9.2, it will have all of its letters jumbled up, and will look as if there is no hope of decrypting it without knowing the keyword. Guessing the keyword seems hopeless too. There are just too many possible keywords. However, someone who is trained in decryption will be able to break this cipher in no time at all. The average letter frequencies of English letters are well known. The most common letter is E, which occurs about 13 percent of the time. Here are the average frequencies of the letters (see [5]).

A	8%	H	4%	O	7%	U	3%
B	<1%	I	7%	P	3%	V	<1%
C	3%	J	<1%	Q	<1%	W	2%
D	4%	K	<1%	R	8%	X	<1%
E	13%	L	4%	S	6%	Y	2%
F	3%	M	3%	T	9%	Z	<1%
G	2%	N	8%				

Write a program that reads an input file and displays the letter frequencies in that file. Such a tool will help a code breaker. If the most frequent letters in an encrypted file are H and K, then there is an excellent chance that they are the encryptions of E and T.

Exercise P9.4. *Vigenère cipher.* The trouble with a monoalphabetic cipher is that it can be easily broken by frequency analysis. The so-called Vigenère cipher overcomes this problem by encoding a letter into one of several cipher letters, depending on its position in the input document. Choose a keyword, for example TIGER. Then encode the first letter of the input text like this:

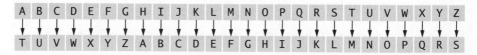

A	B	C	D	E	F	G	H	I	J	K	L	M	N	O	P	Q	R	S	T	U	V	W	X	Y	Z
↓	↓	↓	↓	↓	↓	↓	↓	↓	↓	↓	↓	↓	↓	↓	↓	↓	↓	↓	↓	↓	↓	↓	↓	↓	↓
T	U	V	W	X	Y	Z	A	B	C	D	E	F	G	H	I	J	K	L	M	N	O	P	Q	R	S

The encoded alphabet is just the regular alphabet shifted to start at T, the first letter of the keyword TIGER. The second letter is encrypted according to the following map.

The third, fourth, and fifth letters in the input text are encrypted using the alphabet sequences beginning with characters G, E, and R, and so on. Because the key is only five letters long, the sixth letter of the input text is encrypted in the same way as the first.

Write a program that encrypts or decrypts an input text according to this cipher.

Exercise P9.5. *Playfair cipher.* Another way of thwarting a simple letter frequency analysis of an encrypted text is to encrypt *pairs* of letters together. A simple scheme to do this is the Playfair cipher. You pick a keyword and remove duplicate letters from it. Then you fill the keyword, and the remaining letters of the alphabet, into a 5 × 5 square. (Since there are only 25 squares, I and J are considered the same letter.)

Here is such an arrangement with the keyword PLAYFAIR.

```
P L A Y F
I R B C D
E G H K M
N O Q S T
U V W X Z
```

To encrypt a letter pair, say AM, look at the rectangle with corners A and M:

```
P L A Y F
I R B C D
E G H K M
N O Q S T
U V W X Z
```

The encoding of this pair is formed by looking at the other two corners of the rectangle, in this case, FH. If both letters happen to be in the same row or column, such as GO, simply swap the two letters. Decryption is done in the same way.

Write a program that encrypts or decrypts an input text according to this cipher.

Exercise P9.6. *Junk mail.* Write a program that reads in two files: a *template* and a *database*. The template file contains text and tags. The tags have the form |1| |2| |3|... and need to be replaced with the first, second, third, ... field in the current database record.

A typical database looks like this:

```
Mr.|Harry|Hacker|1105 Torre Ave.|Cupertino|CA|95014
Dr.|John|Lee|702 Ninth Street Apt. 4|San Jose|CA|95109
Miss|Evelyn|Garcia|1101 S. University Place|Ann Arbor|MI|48105
```

And here is a typical form letter:

```
To:
|1| |2| |3|
|4|
|5|, |6| |7|

Dear |1| |3|:

You and the |3| family may be the lucky winners of $10,000,000 in the C++
compiler clearinghouse sweepstakes! ...
```

Exercise P9.7. The program in Section 9.6 only locates one record and updates the salary. Write a program that raises or lowers the salaries of all employees by a given percentage.

Exercise P9.8. The program in Section 9.6 asks the user to specify the record number. More likely than not, a user has no way of knowing the record number. Write a program that asks the user for the name of an employee, finds the record with that name, and displays the record. Then the program should give the following options to the user:

- Change the salary of this record
- View the next record
- Find another employee
- Quit

Exercise P9.9. To find a particular employee in a database file, the program needs to search one record at a time. If the records are *sorted*, there is a faster way. Count the number of records in the file, by dividing the length of the file by the length of each record. Set a variable first to 0, last to nrecords - 1. Compute mid = (first + last)/2. Read the record at mid. Maybe you are lucky, and you actually found the record you wanted. If so, print it and exit. Is its name before or after the name that you are searching? Adjust either last to mid - 1 or first to mid + 1 and repeat the search. This searching method is called a *binary search*, and it is much faster than a sequential search through all records. Implement this searching method.

Exercise P9.10. It is unpleasant to have to use the constant NEWLINE_LENGTH. One must remember to change the constant when porting the database program from UNIX to DOS. Implement the following strategy that avoids the problem. Write a function

```
int newline_length(fstream& fs)
```

Remember the current get position. Reset it to the beginning of the file. Keep calling tellg and reading characters. When the character is a '\n', check whether the get position jumps by 1 or 2. Return that value. If you don't find a newline in the entire file, then report 0. Before exiting, restore the get position to its original value.

Write this function and put it inside the database program.

Exercise P9.11. Write a program that keeps an employee database in a random-access file. Implement functions for adding and removing employees. You need not keep employees in sorted order. To remove an employee, just fill the entire record with spaces. When adding an employee, try to add it into one of those empty spots first before appending it to the end of the file.

Exercise P9.12. Write a program that manipulates three database files. The first file contains the names and telephone numbers of a group of people. The second file contains the names and Social Security numbers of a group of people. The third file contains the Social Security numbers and annual salaries of a group of people. The groups of people should overlap but need not be completely identical. Your program should ask the user for a telephone number and then print the name, Social Security number, and annual income, if it can determine that information.

Exercise P9.13. Write a program that prints out a student grade report. There is a file, `classes.txt`, that contains the names of all classes taught at a college, such as

classes.txt
```
1   CSC1
2   CSC2
3   CSC46
4   CSC151
5   MTH121
6   ...
```

For each class, there is a file with student numbers and grades:

csc2.txt
```
1   11234 A-
2   12547 B
3   16753 B+
4   21886 C
5   ...
```

Write a program that asks for a student ID and prints out a grade report for that student, by searching all class files. Here is a sample report

```
Student ID 16753
CSC2 B+
MTH121 C+
CHN1 A
PHY50 A-
```

Exercise P9.14. A bank keeps all bank accounts in a random access file in which each line has the format

account_number balance

Write a program that simulates an automatic teller machine. A user can deposit money to an account by specifying the account number and amount, withdraw money, query the account balance, or transfer money from one account to another.

Exercise P9.15. Write a program `copyfile` that copies one file to another. The file names are specified on the command line. For example,

```
copyfile report.txt report.sav
```

Exercise P9.16. Write a program that *concatenates* the contents of several files into one file. For example,

```
catfiles chapter1.txt chapter2.txt chapter3.txt book.txt
```

makes a long file book.txt that contains the contents of the files chapter1.txt, chapter2.txt, and chapter3.txt. The target file is always the last file specified on the command line.

Exercise P9.17. Write a program find that searches all files specified on the command line and prints out all lines containing a keyword. For example, if you call

```
find Tim report.txt address.txt homework.cpp
```

then the program might print

```
report.txt: discussed the results of my meeting with Tim T
address.txt: Torrey, Tim|11801 Trenton Court|Dallas|TX
address.txt: Walters, Winnie|59 Timothy Circle|Detroit|MI
homework.cpp: Time now;
```

The keyword is always the first command line argument.

Exercise P9.18. Write a program that checks the spelling of all words in a file. It should read each word of a file and check whether it is contained in a word list. A word list is available on most UNIX systems in the file /usr/dict/words. (If you don't have access to a UNIX system, your instructor should be able to get you a copy.) The program should print out all words that it cannot find in the word list.

Exercise P9.19. Write a program that opens a file for reading and writing, and replaces each line with its reverse. For example, if you run

```
reverse hello.cpp
```

then the contents of hello.cpp is changed to

```
>maertsoi< edulcni#
;dts ecapseman gnisu
()niam tni
{
;"n\!dlrow, olleH" << tuoc
;0 nruter
}
```

Of course, if you run reverse twice on the same file, then the original file is displayed.

Exercise P9.20. Exercise P9.19 shows a limitation of the hello.cpp program. If you reverse every line, it no longer is a legal C++ program. You may not think that this is much to worry about, but there are people who try hard to write programs that can be scrambled in various ways. For example, a winner of the 1989 Obfuscated C Contest wrote a program that can be reversed and still does something useful. The grand prize winner of the 1990 contest wrote a C program that can be sorted! The unsorted version solves a differential equation, whereas the version in which the lines are sorted in alphabetical order prints Fibonacci numbers. Look at [6] for a highly entertaining account of these contests.

Your task is to write a C++ program that turns into another legal C++ program when you reverse each line.

Chapter 10

Recursion

CHAPTER GOALS

- To learn about the method of recursion
- To understand the relationship between recursion and iteration
- To analyze problems that are much easier to solve by recursion than by iteration
- To learn to "think recursively"
- To be able to use recursive helper functions
- To understand when the use of recursion affects the efficiency of an algorithm

The method of recursion is a powerful technique to break up complex computational problems into simpler ones. The term "recursion" refers to the fact that the same computation recurs, or occurs repeatedly, as the problem is solved. Recursion is often the most natural way of thinking about a problem, and there are some computations that are very difficult to perform without recursion. This chapter shows you both simple and complex examples of recursion and teaches you how to "think recursively".

CHAPTER CONTENTS

10.1   Triangle Numbers

We begin this chapter with a very simple example that demonstrates the power of thinking recursively. In this example, we will look at triangle shapes such as this:

```
[]
[][]
[][][]
```

We will compute the area of a triangle of width n, assuming that each [] square has area 1. This value is sometimes called the *nth triangle number*. For example, as you can tell from looking at the above triangle, the third triangle number is 6.

You may know that there is a very simple formula to compute these numbers, but you should pretend for now that you don't know about it. The ultimate purpose of this section is not to compute triangle numbers, but to learn about the concept of recursion in a simple situation.

Here is the outline of the class that we will develop:

```
class Triangle
{
public:
   Triangle(int w);
   int get_area() const;
private:
   int width;
};

Triangle::Triangle(int w)
{
   width = w;
}
```

If the width of the triangle is 1, then the triangle consists of a single square, and its area is 1. Take care of this case first.

```
int Triangle::get_area()
{
   if (width == 1) return 1;
   ...
}
```

To deal with the general case, consider this picture.

```
[]
[][]
[][][]
[][][][]
```

Suppose you knew the area of the smaller, colored triangle. Then you could easily compute the area of the larger triangle as

```
smaller_area + width
```

How can you get the smaller area? Make a smaller triangle and ask it!

```
Triangle smaller_triangle(width - 1);
int smaller_area = smaller_triangle.get_area();
```

Now we can complete the get_area function:

```cpp
int Triangle::get_area() const
{
    if (width == 1) return 1;
    Triangle smaller_triangle(width - 1);
    int smaller_area = smaller_triangle.get_area();
    return smaller_area + width;
}
```

Here is an illustration of what happens when we compute the area of a triangle of width 4.

- The get_area function makes a smaller triangle of width 3.
  - It calls get_area on that triangle.
    - That function makes a smaller triangle of width 2.
      - It calls get_area on that triangle.
        - That function makes a smaller triangle of width 1.
        - It calls get_area on that triangle.
        - That function returns 1.
      - The function returns smaller_area + width = 1 + 2 = 3.
    - The function returns smaller_area + width = 3 + 3 = 6.
- The function returns smaller_area + width = 6 + 4 = 10.

> A recursive computation solves a problem by using the solution to the same problem with simpler inputs.

This solution has one remarkable aspect. To solve the area problem for a triangle of a given width, we use the fact that we can solve the same problem for a lesser width. This is called a *recursive* solution.

The call pattern of a recursive function looks complicated, and the key to the successful design of a recursive function is *not to think about it*. Instead, look at the get_area function one more time and notice how utterly reasonable it is. If the width is 1, then of course the area is 1. The next part is just as reasonable. Compute the area of the smaller triangle *and don't think about why that works*. Then the area of the larger triangle is clearly the sum of the smaller area and the width.

There are two key requirements to make sure that the recursion is successful:

- Every recursive call must simplify the computation in some way.
- There must be special cases to handle the simplest computations directly.

> For a recursion to terminate, there must be special cases for the simplest inputs.

The get_area function calls itself again with smaller and smaller width values. Eventually the width must reach 1, and there is a special case for computing the area of a triangle with width 1. Thus, the get_area function always succeeds.

Actually, you have to be careful. What happens when you call the area of a triangle with width −1? It computes the area of a triangle with width −2, which computes the area of a triangle with width −3, and so on. To avoid this, the get_area function should return 0 if the width is ≤ 0.

Recursion is not really necessary to compute the triangle numbers. The area of a triangle equals the sum

```
1 + 2 + 3 + ... + width
```

Of course, we can program a simple loop:

```
double area = 0;
for (int i = 1; i <= width; i++)
   area = area + i;
```

Many simple recursions can be computed as loops. However, loop equivalents for more complex recursions—such as the one in our next example—can be complex.

Actually, in this case, you don't even need a loop to compute the answer. The sum of the first n integers can be computed as

$$1 + 2 + \cdots + n = n \times (n + 1)/2$$

Thus, the area equals

```
width * (width + 1) / 2
```

Therefore, neither recursion nor a loop are required to solve this problem. The recursive solution is intended as a "warm-up" for the next section.

ch10/triangle.cpp

```
 1  #include <iostream>
 2
 3  using namespace std;
 4
 5  /**
 6     A class that describes triangle shapes like this:
 7     []
 8     [][]
 9     [][][]
10     . . .
11  */
12  class Triangle
13  {
```

```
14  public:
15      Triangle(int w);
16      int get_area() const;
17  private:
18      int width;
19  };
20
21  /**
22      Constructs a triangle with a given width.
23      @param w the width of the triangle base
24  */
25  Triangle::Triangle(int w)
26  {
27      width = w;
28  }
29
30  /**
31      Computes the area of the triangle shape.
32      @return the area
33  */
34  int Triangle::get_area() const
35  {
36      if (width <= 0) return 0;
37      if (width == 1) return 1;
38      Triangle smaller_triangle(width - 1);
39      int smaller_area = smaller_triangle.get_area();
40      return smaller_area + width;
41  }
42
43  int main()
44  {
45      Triangle t(4);
46      cout << "Area: " << t.get_area() << "\n";
47      return 0;
48  }
```

COMMON ERROR 10.1

Infinite Recursion

A common programming error is an infinite recursion: a function calling itself over and over with no end in sight. The computer needs some amount of memory for bookkeeping for each call. After some number of calls, all memory that is available for this purpose is exhausted. Your program shuts down and reports a "stack fault".

Infinite recursion happens either because the parameter values don't get simpler or because a terminating case is missing. For example, suppose the get_area function computes the area of a triangle with width 0. If it weren't for the special test, the function would have constructed triangles with width –1, –2, –3, and so on.

10.2 Permutations

In this section, we consider a more complex example of recursion that would be difficult to program with a simple loop. Our task is to generate all *permutations* of a string. A permutation is simply a rearrangement of the letters. For example, the string "eat" has six permutations (including the original string itself):

```
"eat"
"eta"
"aet"
"ate"
"tea"
"tae"
```

We will develop a function

```
vector<string> generate_permutations(string word)
```

that generates all permutations of a word.

Here is how you would use the function. The following code displays all permutations of the string "eat":

```
vector<string> v = generate_permutations("eat");
for (int i = 0; i < v.size(); i++)
    cout << v[i] << "\n";
```

Now you need a way to generate the permutations recursively. Consider the string "eat" and simplify the problem. First, generate all permutations that start with the letter 'e', then those that start with 'a', and finally those that start with 't'. How do you generate the permutations that start with 'e'? You need to know the permutations of the substring "at". But that's the same problem—to generate all permutations—with a simpler input, namely the shorter string "at". Using recursion generates the permutations of the substring "at". You will get the strings

```
"at"
"ta"
```

For each result of the simpler problem, add the letter 'e' in front. Now you have all permutations of "eat" that start with 'e', namely

```
"eat"
"eta"
```

Next, turn your attention to the permutations of "eat" that start with 'a'. You must create the permutations of the remaining letters, "et", namely:

```
"et"
"te"
```

Add the letter 'a' to the front of the strings and obtain

```
"aet"
"ate"
```

Generate the permutations that start with 't' in the same way.

That's the idea. To carry it out, you must implement a loop that iterates through the character positions of the word. Each loop iteration creates a shorter word that omits the current position:

```cpp
vector<string> generate_permutations(string word)
{
   vector<string> result;
   ...
   for (int i = 0; i < word.length(); i++)
   {
      string shorter_word = word.substr(0, i)
         + word.substr(i + 1);
         ...
   }
   return result;
}
```

The next step is to compute the permutations of the shorter word.

```cpp
vector<string> shorter_permutations
   = generate_permutations(shorter_word);
```

For each of the shorter permutations, add the omitted letter:

```cpp
for (int j = 0; j < shorter_permutations.size(); j++)
{
   string longer_word = word[i] + shorter_permutations[j];
   result.push_back(longer_word);
}
```

The permutation generation algorithm is recursive—it uses the fact that we can generate the permutations of shorter words. When does the recursion stop? You must build in a stopping point, a special case to handle words of length 1. A word of length 1 has a single permutation, namely itself. Here is the added code to handle a word of length 1.

```cpp
vector<string> generate_permutations(string word)
{
   vector<string> result;
   if (word.length() <= 1)
   {
      result.push_back(word);
      return result;
   }
   ...
}
```

The complete program is at the end of this section.

> For generating permutations, it is much easier to use recursion than iteration.

Could you generate the permutations without recursion? There is no obvious way of writing a loop that iterates through all permutations. Exercise P10.12 shows that there is an iterative solution, but it is far more difficult to understand than the recursive algorithm.

ch10/permute.cpp

```cpp
1   #include <iostream>
2   #include <string>
3   #include <vector>
4
5   using namespace std;
6
7   /**
8      Generates all permutations of the characters in a string.
9      @param word a string
10     @return a vector that is filled with all permutations
11     of the word
12  */
13  vector<string> generate_permutations(string word)
14  {
15     vector<string> result;
16     if (word.length() <= 1)
17     {
18        result.push_back(word);
19        return result;
20     }
21
22     for (int i = 0; i < word.length(); i++)
23     {
24        string shorter_word = word.substr(0, i)
25           + word.substr(i + 1);
26        vector<string> shorter_permutations
27           = generate_permutations(shorter_word);
28        for (int j = 0; j < shorter_permutations.size(); j++)
29        {
30           string longer_word = word[i] + shorter_permutations[j];
31           result.push_back(longer_word);
32        }
33     }
34     return result;
35  }
36
37  int main()
38  {
39     cout << "Enter a string: ";
40     string input;
41     getline(cin, input);
42     vector<string> v = generate_permutations(input);
43     for (int i = 0; i < v.size(); i++)
44        cout << v[i] << "\n";
45     return 0;
46  }
```

Program Run

```
Enter a string: arm
arm
amr
ram
```

```
rma
mar
mra
```

COMMON ERROR 10.2

Tracing Through Recursive Functions

Debugging a recursive function can be somewhat challenging. When you set a breakpoint in a recursive function, the program stops as soon as that program line is encountered in *any call to the recursive function*. Suppose you want to debug the recursive get_area function of the Triangle class. Run until the beginning of the get_area function (Figure 1). Inspect the width instance variable. It is 4.

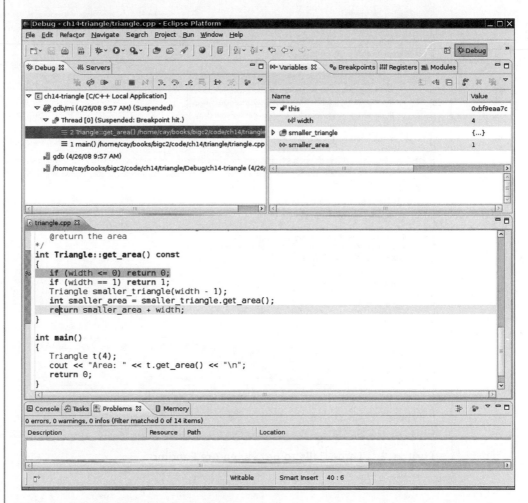

Figure 1   Debugging a Recursive Function

Remove the breakpoint and now run until the statement

```
return smaller_area + width;
```

When you inspect width again, its value is 2! That makes no sense. There was no instruction that changed the value of width! Is that a bug with the debugger?

No. The program stopped in the first *recursive* call to get_area that reached the return statement. If you are confused, look at the *call stack* (Figure 2). You will see that three calls to get_area are pending.

You can debug recursive functions with the debugger. You just need to be particularly careful, and watch the call stack to understand which nested call you currently are in.

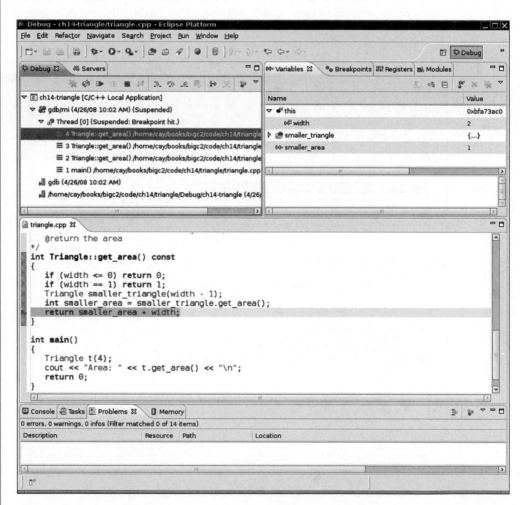

Figure 2   Three Calls to get_area Are Pending

10.3 Thinking Recursively

To solve a problem recursively requires a different mindset than to solve it by programming loops. In fact, it helps if you are, or pretend to be, a bit lazy and let others do most of the work for you. If you need to solve a complex problem, pretend that "someone else" will do most of the heavy lifting and solve the problem for all simpler inputs. Then you only need to figure out how you can turn the solutions with simpler inputs into a solution for the whole problem.

This section gives you a step-by-step guide to the method of recursion. To illustrate the steps, use the following problem to test whether a sentence is a *palindrome*—a string that is equal to itself when you reverse all characters. Typical examples of palindromes are

* rotor
* A man, a plan, a canal—Panama!
* Go hang a salami, I'm a lasagna hog

and, of course, the oldest palindrome of all:

* Madam, I'm Adam

Our goal is to implement the predicate function

```
bool is_palindrome(string s)
```

For simplicity, assume for now that the string has only lowercase letters and no punctuation marks or spaces. Exercise P10.13 asks you to generalize the function to arbitrary strings.

Step 1 Consider various ways for simplifying inputs.

In your mind, fix a particular input or set of inputs for the problem that you want to solve. Think how you can simplify the inputs in such a way that the same problem can be applied to the simpler input.

> The key step in finding a recursive solution is reducing the input to a simpler input for the same problem.

When you consider simpler inputs, you may want to remove just a little bit from the original input—maybe remove one or two characters from a string, or remove a small portion of a geometric shape. But sometimes it is more useful to cut the input in half and then see what it means to solve the problem for both halves.

In the palindrome test problem, the input is the string that we need to test. How can you simplify the input? Here are several possibilities:

* Remove the first character.
* Remove the last character.
* Remove both the first and the last character.
* Remove a character from the middle.
* Cut the string into two halves.

These simpler inputs are all potential inputs for the palindrome test.

Step 2 Combine solutions with simpler inputs to a solution of the original problem.

In your mind, consider the solutions of your problem for the simpler inputs that you have discovered in Step 1. Don't worry *how* those solutions are obtained. Simply have faith that the solutions are readily available. Just say to yourself: These are simpler inputs, so someone else will solve the problem for me.

Now think how you can turn the solution for the simpler inputs into a solution for the input that you are currently thinking about. Maybe you need to add a small quantity, related to the quantity that you lopped off to arrive at the simpler input. Maybe you cut the original input in two halves and have solutions for both halves. Then you may need to add both solutions to arrive at a solution for the whole.

Consider the methods for simplifying the inputs for the palindrome test. Cutting the string in half doesn't seem a good idea. If you cut

    "rotor"

in half, you get two strings:

    "rot"

and

    "or"

Neither of them is a palindrome. Cutting the input in half and testing whether the halves are palindromes seems a dead end.

The most promising simplification is to remove the first *and* last characters. Removing the r at the front and back of "rotor" yields

    "oto"

Suppose you can verify that the shorter string is a palindrome. Then *of course* the original string is a palindrome—we put the same letter in the front and the back. That's extremely promising. A word is a palindrome if

- The first and last letters match, and
- The word obtained by removing the first and last letters is a palindrome.

Again, don't worry how the test works for the shorter string. It just works.

Step 3 Find solutions to the simplest inputs.

A recursive computation keeps simplifying its inputs. Eventually it arrives at very simple inputs. To make sure that the recursion comes to a stop, you must deal with the simplest inputs separately. Come up with special solutions for them. That is usually very easy.

However, sometimes you get into philosophical questions dealing with *degenerate* inputs: empty strings, shapes with no area, and so on. Then you may want to investigate a slightly larger input that gets reduced to such a trivial input and see what value you should attach to the degenerate inputs so that the simpler value, when used according to the rules you discovered in Step 2, yields the correct answer.

Look at the simplest strings for the palindrome test:

- Strings with two characters
- Strings with a single character
- The empty string

You don't have to come up with a special solution for strings with two characters. Step 2 still applies to those strings—either or both of the characters are removed. But you do need to worry about strings of length 0 and 1. In those cases, Step 2 can't apply. There aren't two characters to remove.

A string with a single character, such as "I", is a palindrome.

The empty string is a palindrome—it's the same string when you read it backwards. If you find that too artificial, consider a string "oo". According to the rule discovered in Step 2, this string is a palindrome if the first and last character of that string match and the remainder—that is, the empty string—is also a palindrome. Therefore, it makes sense to consider the empty string a palindrome.

Thus, all strings of length 0 or 1 are palindromes.

Step 4 Implement the solution by combining the simple cases and the reduction step.

Now you are ready to implement the solution. Make separate cases for the simple inputs that you considered in Step 3. If the input isn't one of the simplest cases, then implement the logic you discovered in Step 2.

The following program shows the complete `is_palindrome` function.

ch10/palindrome.cpp

```
1   #include <iostream>
2   #include <string>
3   #include <vector>
4
5   using namespace std;
6
7   /**
8      Tests whether a string is a palindrome. A palindrome
9      is equal to its reverse, for example "rotor" or "racecar".
10     @param s a string
11     @return true if s is a palindrome
12  */
13  bool is_palindrome(string s)
14  {
15     // Separate case for shortest strings.
16     if (s.length() <= 1) return true;
17
18     // Get first and last character, converted to lowercase.
19     char first = s[0];
20     char last = s[s.length() - 1];
21
22     if (first == last)
23     {
```

```
24              string shorter = s.substr(1, s.length() - 2);
25              return is_palindrome(shorter);
26          }
27          else
28              return false;
29      }
30
31      int main()
32      {
33          cout << "Enter a string: ";
34          string input;
35          getline(cin, input);
36          cout << input << " is ";
37          if (!is_palindrome(input)) cout << "not ";
38          cout << "a palindrome\n";
39          return 0;
40      }
```

Program Run

```
Enter a string: aibohphobia
aibohphobia is a palindrome.
```

> When designing a recursive solution, do not worry about multiple nested calls. Simply focus on reducing a problem to a slightly simpler one.

You have now seen several recursive algorithms, all of which work on the same principle. When given a complex input, they first solve the problem with a simpler input. Then they turn the simpler result into the result for the more complex input. This process is quite intuitive as long as you think about the solution on that level only. However, behind the scenes, the function that computes the simpler input calls yet another function that works on even simpler input, which calls yet another, and so on, until one function's input is so simple that it can compute the results without further help. It is interesting to think about that process, but it can also be confusing. What's important is that you can focus on the one level that matters—putting a solution together from the slightly simpler problem, ignoring the fact that it also uses recursion to get its results.

10.4 Recursive Helper Functions

> Sometimes it is easier to find a recursive solution if you make a slight change to the original problem.

Sometimes it is easier to find a recursive solution if you change the original problem slightly. Then the original problem can be solved by calling a recursive helper function.

Here is a typical example. Consider the palindrome test of the preceding section. It is a bit inefficient to construct new string objects in every step. Now consider the following change in the problem. Rather than testing whether the entire sentence is a palindrome, check whether a substring is a palindrome:

```
/*
    Tests whether a substring of a string is a palindrome.
    @param s  the string to test
    @param start  the index of the first character of the substring
    @param end  the index of the last character of the substring
    @return  true if the substring is a palindrome
*/
bool substring_is_palindrome(string s, int start, int end)
```

This function turns out to be even easier to implement than the original test. In the recursive calls, simply adjust the start and end parameters to skip over matching letter pairs. There is no need to construct new string objects to represent the shorter strings.

```
bool substring_is_palindrome(string s, int start, int end)
{
    // Separate case for substrings of length 0 and 1
    if (start >= end) return true;

    if (s[start] == s[end])
        // Test substring that doesn't contain the first and last letters
        return substring_is_palindrome(s, start + 1, end - 1);
    else
        return false;
}
```

You should supply a function to solve the whole problem—the user of your function shouldn't have to know about the trick with the substring positions. Simply call the helper function with positions that test the entire string:

```
bool is_palindrome(string s)
{
    return substring is palindrome(s, 0, s.length() - 1);
}
```

Note that the is_palindrome function is *not* recursive. It just calls a recursive helper function.

Use the technique of recursive helper functions whenever it is easier to solve a recursive problem that is slightly different from the original problem.

10.5 Mutual Recursion

In a mutual recursion, a set of cooperating functions calls each other repeatedly.

In the preceding examples, a function called itself to solve a simpler problem. Sometimes, a set of cooperating functions calls each other in a recursive fashion. In this section, we will explore a typical situation of such a mutual recursion.

We will develop a program that can compute the values of arithmetic expressions such as

```
3 + 4 * 5
(3 + 4) * 5
1 - (2 - (3 - (4 - 5)))
```

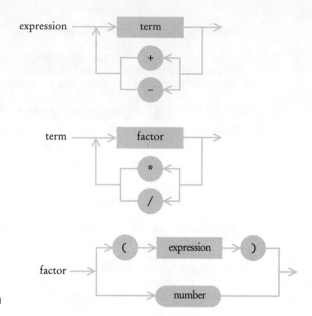

Figure 3
Syntax Diagrams for
Evaluating an Expression

Computing such an expression is complicated by the fact that * and / bind more strongly than + and -, and that parentheses can be used to group subexpressions.

Figure 3 shows a set of *syntax diagrams* that describes the syntax of these expressions. An expression is either a term, or a sum or difference of terms. A term is either a factor, or a product or quotient of factors. Finally, a factor is either a number or an expression enclosed in parentheses.

Figure 4 shows how the expressions 3 + 4 * 5 and (3 + 4) * 5 are derived from the syntax diagram.

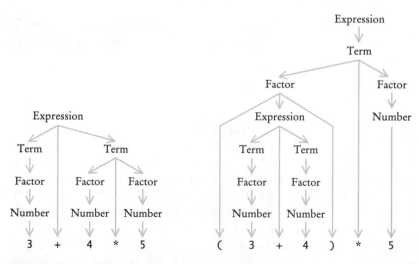

Figure 4   Syntax Trees for Two Expressions

Why do the syntax diagrams help us compute the value of the tree? If you look at the syntax trees, you will see that they accurately represent which operations should be carried out first. In the first tree, 4 and 5 should be multiplied, and then the result should be added to 3. In the second tree, 3 and 4 should be added, and the result should be multiplied by 5.

To compute the value of an expression, we implement three functions: `expression_value`, `term_value`, and `factor_value`. The `expression_value` function first calls `term_value` to get the value of the first term of the expression. Then it checks whether the next input character is one of + or -. If so, it calls `term_value` again and adds or subtracts it.

```cpp
int expression_value()
{
   int result = term_value();
   bool more = true;
   while (more)
   {
      char op = cin.peek();
      if (op == '+' || op == '-')
      {
         cin.get();
         int value = term_value();
         if (op == '+') result = result + value;
         else result = result - value;
      }
      else more = false;
   }
   return result;
}
```

The `term_value` function calls `factor_value` in the same way, multiplying or dividing the factor values.

Finally, the `factor_value` function checks whether the next input character is a '(' or a digit. In the latter case, the value is simply the value of the number. However, if the function sees a parenthesis, the `factor_value` function makes a recursive call to `expression_value`. Thus, the three functions are mutually recursive.

```cpp
int factor_value()
{
   int result = 0;
   char c = cin.peek();
   if (c == '(')
   {
      cin.get();
      result = expression_value();
      cin.get(); // read ")"
   }
   else // Assemble number value from digits
   {
      while (isdigit(c))
      {
         result = 10 * result + c - '0';
         cin.get();
         c = cin.peek();
```

```
            }
        }
        return result;
    }
```

As always with a recursive solution, you need to ensure that the recursion terminates. In this situation, that is easy to see. If `expression_value` calls itself, the second
call works on a shorter subexpression than the original expression. At each recursive call, at least some of the characters of the input are consumed, so eventually the
recursion must come to an end.

ch10/eval.cpp

```cpp
1   #include <iostream>
2   #include <cctype>
3
4   using namespace std;
5
6   int term_value();
7   int factor_value();
8
9   /**
10      Evaluates the next expression found in cin.
11      @return the value of the expression
12  */
13  int expression_value()
14  {
15      int result = term_value();
16      bool more = true;
17      while (more)
18      {
19          char op = cin.peek();
20          if (op == '+' || op == '-')
21          {
22              cin.get();
23              int value = term_value();
24              if (op == '+') result = result + value;
25              else result = result - value;
26          }
27          else more = false;
28      }
29      return result;
30  }
31
32  /**
33      Evaluates the next term found in cin.
34      @return the value of the term
35  */
36  int term_value()
37  {
38      int result = factor_value();
39      bool more = true;
```

```
40        while (more)
41        {
42           char op = cin.peek();
43           if (op == '*' || op == '/')
44           {
45              cin.get();
46              int value = factor_value();
47              if (op == '*') result = result * value;
48              else result = result / value;
49           }
50           else more = false;
51        }
52        return result;
53     }
54
55     /**
56        Evaluates the next factor found in cin.
57        @return the value of the factor
58     */
59     int factor_value()
60     {
61        int result = 0;
62        char c = cin.peek();
63        if (c == '(')
64        {
65           cin.get();
66           result = expression_value();
67           cin.get(); // Read ")"
68        }
69        else // Assemble number value from digits
70        {
71           while (isdigit(c))
72           {
73              result = 10 * result + c - '0';
74              cin.get();
75              c = cin.peek();
76           }
77        }
78        return result;
79     }
80
81     int main()
82     {
83        cout << "Enter an expression: ";
84        cout << expression_value() << "\n";
85        return 0;
86     }
```

Program Run

```
Enter an expression: 1+12*12*12
1729
```

10.6 The Efficiency of Recursion

As you have seen in this chapter, recursion can be a powerful tool to implement complex algorithms. On the other hand, recursion can lead to algorithms that perform poorly. In this section, we will analyze the question of when recursion is beneficial and when it is inefficient.

The Fibonacci sequence is a sequence of numbers defined by the equation

$$f_1 = 1$$
$$f_2 = 1$$
$$f_n = f_{n-1} + f_{n-2}$$

That is, each value of the sequence is the sum of the two preceding values. The first ten terms of the sequence are

```
1, 1, 2, 3, 5, 8, 13, 21, 34, 55
```

It is easy to extend this sequence indefinitely. Just keep appending the sum of the last two values of the sequence. For example, the next entry is 34 + 55 = 89.

We would like to write a function that computes f_n for any value of n. Suppose we translate the definition directly into a recursive function:

ch10/fibtest.cpp

```cpp
1   #include <iostream>
2
3   using namespace std;
4
5   /**
6       Computes a Fibonacci number.
7       @param n an integer
8       @return the nth Fibonacci number
9   */
10  int fib(int n)
11  {
12      if (n <= 2) return 1;
13      else return fib(n - 1) + fib(n - 2);
14  }
15
16  int main()
17  {
18      cout << "Enter n: ";
19      int n;
20      cin >> n;
21      int f = fib(n);
22      cout << "fib(" << n << ") = " << f << "\n";
23      return 0;
24  }
```

Program Run

```
Enter n: 6
fib(6) = 8
```

That is certainly simple, and the function will work correctly. But watch the output closely as you run the test program. For small input values, the program is quite fast. Even for moderately large values, though, the program pauses an amazingly long time between outputs. Try out some numbers between 30 and 50 to see this effect.

That makes no sense. Armed with pencil, paper, and a pocket calculator you could calculate these numbers pretty quickly, so it shouldn't take the computer long.

To determine the problem, insert trace messages into the function:

ch10/fibtrace.cpp

```
1   #include <iostream>
2
3   using namespace std;
4
5   /**
6      Computes a Fibonacci number.
7      @param n an integer
8      @return the nth Fibonacci number
9   */
10  int fib(int n)
11  {
12     cout << "Entering fib: n = " << n << "\n";
13     int f;
14     if (n <= 2) f = 1;
15     else f = fib(n - 1) + fib(n - 2);
16     cout << "Exiting fib: n - " << n
17        << " return value = " << f << "\n";
18     return f;
19  }
20
21  int main()
22  {
23     cout << "Enter n: ";
24     int n;
25     cin >> n;
26     int f = fib(n);
27     cout << "fib(" << n << ") = " << f << "\n";
28     return 0;
29  }
```

Program Run

```
Enter n: 6

Entering fib: n = 6
Entering fib: n = 5
Entering fib: n = 4
Entering fib: n = 3
Entering fib: n = 2
```

```
Exiting fib: n = 2 return value = 1
Entering fib: n = 1
Exiting fib: n = 1 return value = 1
Exiting fib: n = 3 return value = 2
Entering fib: n = 2
Exiting fib: n = 2 return value = 1
Exiting fib: n = 4 return value = 3
Entering fib: n = 3
Entering fib: n = 2
Exiting fib: n = 2 return value = 1
Entering fib: n = 1
Exiting fib: n = 1 return value = 1
Exiting fib: n = 3 return value = 2
Exiting fib: n = 5 return value = 5
Entering fib: n = 4
Entering fib: n = 3
Entering fib: n = 2
Exiting fib: n = 2 return value = 1
Entering fib: n = 1
Exiting fib: n = 1 return value = 1
Exiting fib: n = 3 return value = 2
Entering fib: n = 2
Exiting fib: n = 2 return value = 1
Exiting fib: n = 4 return value = 3
Exiting fib: n = 6 return value = 8

fib(6) = 8
```

Figure 5 shows the call tree.

Now it is becoming apparent why the function takes so long. It is computing the same values over and over. For example, the computation of fib(6) calls fib(4) twice and fib(3) three times. That is very different from the computation you would do with pencil and paper. There you would just write down the values as

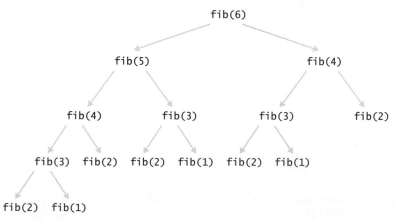

Figure 5   Call Pattern of the Recursive fib Function

they were computed and add up the last two to get the next one until you reached the desired entry; no sequence value would ever be computed twice.

If you imitate the pencil-and-paper process, then you get the following program.

ch10/fibloop.cpp

```cpp
1   #include <iostream>
2
3   using namespace std;
4
5   /**
6       Computes a Fibonacci number.
7       @param n  an integer
8       @return  the nth Fibonacci number
9   */
10  int fib(int n)
11  {
12      if (n <= 2) return 1;
13      int fold = 1;
14      int fold2 = 1;
15      int fnew;
16      for (int i = 3; i <= n; i++)
17      {
18          fnew = fold + fold2;
19          fold2 = fold;
20          fold = fnew;
21      }
22      return fnew;
23  }
24
25  int main()
26  {
27      cout << "Enter n: ";
28      int n;
29      cin >> n;
30      int f = fib(n);
31      cout << "fib(" << n << ") = " << f << "\n";
32      return 0;
33  }
```

This function runs *much* faster than the recursive version.

In this example of the fib function, the recursive solution was easy to program because it exactly followed the mathematical definition, but it ran far more slowly than the iterative solution, because it computed many intermediate results multiple times.

Can you always speed up a recursive solution by changing it into a loop? Frequently, the iterative and recursive solution have essentially the same performance. For example, here is an iterative solution for the palindrome test.

```
public bool is_palindrome(string s)
{
   int start = 0;
   int end = text.length() - 1;
```

```
    while (start < end)
    {
        if (s[start] != s[end]) return false;
        start++;
        end--;
    }
    return true;
}
```

This solution keeps two index variables: start and end. The first index starts at the beginning of the string and is advanced whenever a letter has been matched or a non-letter has been ignored. The second index starts at the end of the string and moves toward the beginning. When the two index variables meet, then the iteration stops.

Both the iteration and the recursion run at about the same speed. If a palindrome has n characters, the iteration executes the loop $n/2$ times. Similarly, the recursive solution calls itself $n/2$ times, because two characters are removed in each step.

In such a situation, the iterative solution tends to be a bit faster, because each recursive function call takes a certain amount of processor time. In principle, it is possible for a smart compiler to avoid recursive function calls if they follow simple patterns, but most compilers don't do that. From that point of view, an iterative solution is preferable.

> In many cases, a recursive solution is easier to understand and implement correctly than an iterative solution.

Often, recursive solutions are easier to understand and implement correctly than their iterative counterparts. There is a certain elegance and economy of thought to recursive solutions that makes them more appealing. As the computer scientist (and creator of the Ghost-Script interpreter for the PostScript graphics description language) L. Peter Deutsch put it: "To iterate is human, to recurse divine."

RANDOM FACT 10.1

The Limits of Computation

Have you ever wondered how your instructor or grader makes sure your programming homework is correct? In all likelihood, they look at your solution and perhaps run it with some test inputs. But usually they have a correct solution available. That suggests that there might be an easier way. Perhaps they could feed your program and their correct program into a program comparator, a computer program that analyzes both programs and determines whether they both compute the same results. Of course, your solution and the program that is known to be correct need not be identical—what matters is that they produce the same output when given the same input.

How could such a program comparator work? Well, the C++ compiler knows how to read a program and make sense of the classes, functions, and statements. So it seems plausible that someone could, with some effort, write a program that reads two C++ programs, analyzes what they do, and determines whether they solve the same task. Of course, such a program would be very attractive to instructors, because it could automate the grading process. Thus, even though no such program exists today, it might be tempting to try to develop one and sell it to universities around the world.

Figure 6   Alan Turing

However, before you start raising venture capital for such an effort, you should know that theoretical computer scientists have proven that it is impossible to develop such a program, *no matter how hard you try.*

There are quite a few of these unsolvable problems. The first one, called the *halting problem*, was discovered by the British researcher Alan Turing in 1936 (see Figure 6). Because his research occurred before the first actual computer was constructed, Turing had to devise a theoretical device, the *Turing machine*, to explain how computers could work. The Turing machine consists of a long magnetic tape, a read/write head, and a program that has numbered instructions of the form: "If the current symbol under the head is *x*, then replace it with *y*, move the head one unit left or right, and continue with instruction *n*" (see Figure 7).

Program

Instruction number	If tape symbol is	Replace with	Then move head	Then go to instruction
1	0	2	right	2
1	1	1	left	4
2	0	0	right	2
2	1	1	right	2
2	2	0	left	3
3	0	0	left	3
3	1	1	left	3
3	2	2	right	1
4	1	1	right	5
4	2	0	left	4

Control unit

Read/write head

Figure 7
A Turing Machine

Tape

Interestingly enough, with just these instructions, you can program just as much as with C++, even though it is incredibly tedious to do so. Theoretical computer scientists like Turing machines because they can be described using nothing more than the laws of mathematics.

Expressed in terms of C++, the halting problem states: "It is impossible to write a program with two inputs, namely the source code of an arbitrary C++ program P and a string I, that decides whether the program P, when executed with the input I, will halt without getting into an infinite loop". Of course, for some kinds of programs and inputs, it is possible to decide whether the programs halt with the given input. The halting problem asserts that it is impossible to come up with a single decision-making algorithm that works with all programs and inputs. Note that you can't simply run the program P on the input I to settle this question. If the program runs for 1,000 days, you don't know that the program is in an infinite loop. Maybe you just have to wait another day for it to stop.

Such a "halt checker", if it could be written, might also be useful for grading homework. An instructor could use it to screen student submissions to see if they get into an infinite loop with a particular input, and then not check them any further. However, as Turing demonstrated, such a program cannot be written. His argument is ingenious and quite simple.

Suppose a "halt checker" program existed. Let's call it H. From H, we will develop another program, the "killer" program K. K does the following computation. Its input is a string containing the source code for a program R. It then applies the halting checker on the input program R and the input string R. That is, it checks whether the program R halts if its input is its own source code. It sounds bizarre to feed a program to itself, but it isn't impossible. For example, the C++ compiler is written in C++, and you can use it to compile itself. Or, as a simpler example, you can use a word count program to count the words in its own source code.

When K gets the answer from H that R halts when applied to itself, it is programmed to enter an infinite loop. Otherwise K exits. In C++, the program might look like this:

```
int main
{
   string r = read program input;
   HaltChecker checker;
   if (checker.check(r, r))
      while (true) { } // infinite loop
   else
      return 0;
}
```

Now ask yourself: What does the halt checker answer when asked if K halts when given K as the input? Maybe it finds out that K gets into an infinite loop with such an input. But wait, that can't be right. That would mean that checker.check(r, r) returns false when r is the program code of K. As you can plainly see, in that case, the main function returns, so K didn't get into an infinite loop. That shows that K must halt when analyzing itself, so checker.check(r, r) should return true. But then the main function doesn't terminate—it goes into an infinite loop. That shows that it is logically impossible to implement a program that can check whether *every* program halts on a particular input.

It is sobering to know that there are *limits* to computing. There are problems that no computer program, no matter how ingenious, can answer.

Theoretical computer scientists are working on other research involving the nature of computation. One important question that remains unsettled to this day deals with problems that in practice are very time-consuming to solve. It may be that these problems are intrinsically hard, in which case it would be pointless to try to look for better algorithms.

Such theoretical research can have important practical applications. For example, right now, nobody knows whether the most common encryption schemes used today could be broken by discovering a new algorithm (see Random Fact 9.1 for more information on encryption algorithms). Knowing that no fast algorithms exist for breaking a particular code could make us feel more comfortable about the security of encryption.

CHAPTER SUMMARY

1. A recursive computation solves a problem by using the solution to the same problem with simpler inputs.

2. For a recursion to terminate, there must be special cases for the simplest inputs.

3. For generating permutations, it is much easier to use recursion than iteration.

4. The key step in finding a recursive solution is reducing the input to a simpler input for the same problem.

5. When designing a recursive solution, do not worry about multiple nested calls. Simply focus on reducing a problem to a slightly simpler one.

6. Sometimes it is easier to find a recursive solution if you make a slight change to the original problem.

7. In a mutual recursion, a set of cooperating functions calls each other repeatedly.

8. Occasionally, a recursive solution runs much slower than its iterative counterpart. However, in most cases, the recursive solution runs at about the same speed.

9. In many cases, a recursive solution is easier to understand and implement correctly than an iterative solution.

REVIEW EXERCISES

Exercise R10.1. Define the terms
- a. recursion
- b. iteration
- c. infinite recursion
- d. mutual recursion

Exercise R10.2. The factorial function counts the number of permutations of n objects. It is recursively defined by the equations

$$n! = (n-1)! \times n$$

and

$$0! = 1$$

Following this definition, determine the values for 1! and 2!. Explain why these are the correct counts for permutations of 1 and 2 objects.

Exercise R10.3. Outline, but do not implement, a recursive solution for finding the smallest value in an array.

Exercise R10.4. Outline, but do not implement, a recursive solution for sorting an array of numbers. *Hint:* First find the smallest value in the array.

Exercise R10.5. Outline, but do not implement, a recursive solution for generating all subsets of the set $\{1, 2, \ldots, n\}$.

Exercise R10.6. Exercise P10.12 shows an iterative way of generating all permutations of the sequence $(0, 1, \ldots, n-1)$. Explain why the algorithm produces the right result.

Exercise R10.7. Write a recursive definition of x^n, where $x \geq 0$, similar to the recursive definition of the Fibonacci numbers. *Hint:* How do you compute x^n from x^{n-1}? How does the recursion terminate?

Exercise R10.8. Write a recursive definition of $n! = 1 \times 2 \times \ldots \times n$, similar to the recursive definition of the Fibonacci numbers.

Exercise R10.9. Find out how often the recursive version of fib calls itself. Keep a global variable fib_count and increment it once in every call of fib. What is the relationship between fib(n) and fib_count?

Exercise R10.10. How many moves are required to move n disks in the "Towers of Hanoi" problem of Exercise P10.14? *Hint:* As described in the exercise,

moves(1) = 1
moves(n) = 2 · moves(n − 1) + 1

PROGRAMMING EXERCISES

Exercise P10.1. If a string has n letters, then the *number* of permutations is given by the factorial function:

$$n! = 1 \times 2 \times 3 \times \ldots \times n$$

For example, $3! = 1 \times 2 \times 3 = 6$ and there are six permutations of the three-character string "eat". Implement a recursive `factorial` function, using the definitions

$$n! = (n - 1)! \times n$$

and

$$0! = 1$$

Exercise P10.2. Write a recursive function `void reverse()` that reverses a sentence. For example:

```
Sentence greeting("Hello!");
greeting.reverse();
cout << greeting.get_text() << "\n";
```

prints the string "!olleH". Implement a recursive solution by removing the first character, reversing a sentence consisting of the remaining text, and combining the two.

Exercise P10.3. Redo Exercise P10.2 with a recursive helper function that reverses a substring of the message text.

Exercise P10.4. Implement the reverse function of Exercise P10.2 as an iteration.

Exercise P10.5. Use recursion to implement a function `bool find(string s, string t)` that tests whether a string t is contained in a string s:

```
bool b = s.find("Mississippi!", "sip"); // Returns true
```

Hint: If the text starts with the string you want to match, then you are done. If not, consider the sentence that you obtain by removing the first character.

Exercise P10.6. Use recursion to implement a function `int index_of(string s, string t)` that returns the starting position of the first substring of the string s that matches t. Return –1 if t is not a substring of s. For example,

```
int n = s.index_of("Mississippi!", "sip"); // Returns 6
```

Hint: This is a bit trickier than Exercise P10.5, because you need to keep track of how far the match is from the beginning of the sentence. Make that value a parameter of a helper function.

Exercise P10.7. Using recursion, find the largest element in a vector of integer values.

```
int maximum(vector<int> values)
```

Hint: Find the largest element in the subset containing all but the last element. Then compare that maximum to the value of the last element.

Exercise P10.8. Using recursion, compute the sum of all values in an array.

Exercise P10.9. Using recursion, compute the area of a polygon. Cut off a triangle and use the fact that a triangle with corners (x_1, y_1), (x_2, y_2), (x_3, y_3) has area $(x_1 y_2 + x_2 y_3 + x_3 y_1 - y_1 x_2 - y_2 x_3 - y_3 x_1)/2$.

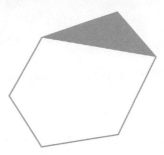

Exercise P10.10. Implement a function

```
vector<string> generate_substrings(string s)
```

that generates all substrings of a string. For example, the substrings of the string "rum" are the seven strings

```
"r", "ru", "rum", "u", "um", "m", ""
```

Hint: First enumerate all substrings that start with the first character. There are *n* of them if the string has length *n*. Then enumerate the substrings of the string that you obtain by removing the first character.

Exercise P10.11. Implement a function

```
vector<string> generate_subsets(string s)
```

that generates all subsets of characters of a string. For example, the subsets of characters of the string "rum" are the eight strings

```
"rum", "ru", "rm", "r", "um", "u", "m", ""
```

Note that the subsets don't have to be substrings—for example, "rm" isn't a substring of "rum".

Exercise P10.12. The following program generates all permutations of the numbers 0, 1, 2, ... , *n* – 1, without using recursion.

```
using namespace std;

void swap(int& x, int& y)
{
   int temp = x;
   x = y;
   y = temp;
}

void reverse(vector<int>& a, int i, int j)
{
   while (i < j)
   {
      swap(a[i], a[j]); i++; j--;
```

```
         }
      }

      bool next_permutation(vector<int>& a)
      {
         for (int i = a.size() - 1; i > 0; i--)
         {
            if (a[i - 1] < a[i])
            {
               int j = a.size() - 1;
               while (a[i - 1] > a[j]) j--;
               swap(a[i - 1], a[j]);
               reverse(a, i, a.size() - 1);
               return true;
            }
         }
         return false;
      }

      void print(const vector<int>& a)
      {
         for (int i = 0; i < a.size(); i++)
            cout << a[i] << " ";
         cout << "\n";
      }

      int main()
      {
         const int n = 4;
         vector<int> a(n);
         for (int i = 0; i < a.size(); i++) a[i] = i;
         print(a);
         while (next_permutation(a))
            print(a);
         return 0;
      }
```

The algorithm uses the fact that the set to be permuted consists of distinct numbers.
Thus, you cannot use the same algorithm to compute the permutations of the characters in a string. You can, however, use this technique to get all permutations of the
character positions and then compute a string whose ith character is s[a[i]]. Use
this approach to reimplement the generate_permutations function without recursion.

Exercise P10.13. Refine the is_palindrome function to work with arbitrary strings,
by ignoring non-letter characters and the distinction between upper- and lowercase
letters. For example, if the input string is

```
   "Madam, I'm Adam!"
```

then you'd first strip off the last character because it isn't a letter, and recursively
check whether the shorter string

```
   "Madam, I'm Adam"
```

is a palindrome.

Exercise P10.14. *Towers of Hanoi.* This is a well-known puzzle. A stack of disks of decreasing size is to be transported from the left-most peg to the right-most peg. The middle peg can be used as a temporary storage. (See Figure 8.) One disk can be moved at one time, from any peg to any other peg. You can place smaller disks only on top of larger ones, not the other way around.

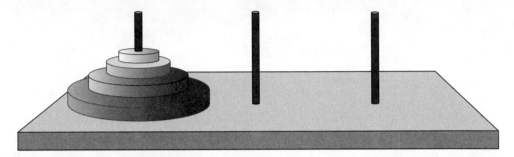

Figure 8   Towers of Hanoi

Write a program that prints the moves necessary to solve the puzzle for *n* disks. (Ask the user for *n* at the beginning of the program.) Print moves in the form

```
Move disk from peg 1 to peg 3
```

Hint: Write a helper function

```
void hanoi(int from, int to, int n)
```

that moves the top n disks from the peg from to the peg to. Then figure out how you can achieve that by first moving the pile of the top n - 1 disks to the third peg, moving the nth disk to the destination, and then moving the pile from the third peg to the destination peg, this time using the original peg as the temporary storage. Extra credit if you write the program to actually draw the moves using the graphics library or "ASCII art"!

Sorting and Searching

CHAPTER GOALS

- To compare the selection sort and merge sort algorithms

- To study the linear search and binary search algorithms

- To appreciate that algorithms for the same task can differ widely in performance

- To understand the big-Oh notation

- To learn how to estimate and compare the performance of algorithms

- To learn how to measure the running time of a program

One of the most common tasks in data processing is sorting. For example, a sequence of employees needs to be printed out in alphabetical order or sorted by salary. You will learn several sorting methods in this chapter and compare their performance.

Once a sequence of records is sorted, one can rapidly locate individual records. You will study the *binary search* algorithm that carries out this fast lookup.

CHAPTER CONTENTS

11.1 Selection Sort

> The selection sort algorithm sorts a sequence by repeatedly finding the smallest element of the unsorted tail region and moving it to the front.

A *sorting algorithm* rearranges the elements of a sequence so that they are stored in sorted order. In this section, we show you the first of several sorting algorithms, called *selection sort*. Consider the following vector a:

11 9 17 5 12

An obvious first step is to find the smallest element. In this case the smallest element is 5, stored in a[3]. You should move the 5 to the beginning of the vector. Of course, there is already an element stored in a[0], namely 11. Therefore you cannot simply move a[3] into a[0] without moving the 11 somewhere else. You don't yet know where the 11 should end up, but you know for certain that it should not be in a[0]. Simply get it out of the way by *swapping it* with a[3].

5 9 17 11 12

Now the first element is in the correct place. In the foregoing figure, color indicates the portion of the vector that is already sorted from the unsorted remainder.

Next take the minimum of the remaining entries a[1]...a[4]. That minimum value, 9, is already in the correct place. You don't need to do anything in this case, simply extend the sorted area by one to the right:

5 9 17 11 12

Repeat the process. The minimum value of the unsorted region is 11, which needs to be swapped with the first value of the unsorted region, 17.

Now the unsorted region is only two elements long; keep to the same successful strategy. The minimum element is 12. Swap it with the first value, 17.

That leaves you with an unprocessed region of length 1, but of course a region of length 1 is always sorted. You are done.

If speed was not an issue for us, we could stop the discussion of sorting right here. However, the selection sort algorithm shows disappointing performance when run on large data sets, and it is worthwhile to study better sorting algorithms.

Here is the implementation of the selection sort algorithm.

ch11/selsort/selsort.cpp

```cpp
1    #include <iostream>
2
3    #include "util.h"
4
5    /**
6       Gets the position of the smallest element in a vector range.
7       @param a the vector
8       @param from the beginning of the range
9       @param to the end of the range
10      @return the position of the smallest element in
11         the range a[from]...a[to]
12   */
13   int min_position(vector<int>& a, int from, int to)
14   {
15      int min_pos = from;
16      int i;
17      for (i = from + 1; i <= to; i++)
18         if (a[i] < a[min_pos]) min_pos = i;
19      return min_pos;
20   }
21
22   /**
23      Sorts a vector using the selection sort algorithm.
24      @param a the vector to sort
25   */
26   void selection_sort(vector<int>& a)
27   {
28      int next; // The next position to be set to the minimum
29
30      for (next = 0; next < a.size() - 1; next++)
31      {
```

```
32          // Find the position of the minimum
33          int min_pos = min_position(a, next, a.size() - 1);
34          if (min_pos != next)
35              swap(a[min_pos], a[next]);
36      }
37  }
38
39  int main()
40  {
41      rand_seed();
42      vector<int> v(20);
43      for (int i = 0; i < v.size(); i++)
44          v[i] = rand_int(1, 100);
45      print(v);
46      selection_sort(v);
47      print(v);
48      return 0;
49  }
```

ch11/selsort/util.h

```
1   #ifndef UTIL_H
2   #define UTIL_H
3
4   #include <vector>
5
6   using namespace std;
7
8   /**
9       Swaps two integers.
10      @param x  the first integer to swap
11      @param y  the second integer to swap
12   */
13  void swap(int& x, int& y);
14
15  /**
16      Prints all elements in a vector.
17      @param a  the vector to print
18   */
19  void print(vector<int> a);
20
21  /**
22      Sets the seed of the random number generator.
23   */
24  void rand_seed();
25
26  /**
27      Computes a random integer in a range.
28      @param a  the bottom of the range
29      @param b  the top of the range
30      @return a random integer x, a <= x and x <= b
31   */
32  int rand_int(int a, int b);
33
34  #endif
```

ch11/selsort/util.cpp

```cpp
 1  #include <iostream>
 2  #include <cstdlib>
 3  #include <ctime>
 4
 5  #include "util.h"
 6
 7  /**
 8      Swaps two integers.
 9      @param x the first integer to swap
10      @param y the second integer to swap
11  */
12  void swap(int& x, int& y)
13  {
14      int temp = x;
15      x = y;
16      y = temp;
17  }
18
19  /**
20      Prints all elements in a vector.
21      @param a the vector to print
22  */
23  void print(vector<int> a)
24  {
25      for (int i = 0; i < a.size(); i++)
26          cout << a[i] << " ";
27      cout << "\n";
28  }
29
30  /**
31      Sets the seed of the random number generator.
32  */
33  void rand_seed()
34  {
35      int seed = static_cast<int>(time(0));
36      srand(seed);
37  }
38
39  /**
40      Computes a random integer in a range.
41      @param a the bottom of the range
42      @param b the top of the range
43      @return a random integer x, a <= x and x <= b
44  */
45  int rand_int(int a, int b)
46  {
47      return a + rand() % (b - a + 1);
48  }
```

Program Run

```
60 47 70 39 6 12 96 93 83 53 36 29 50 97 94 95 38 17 8 26
 6 8 12 17 26 29 36 38 39 47 50 53 60 70 83 93 94 95 96 97
```

11.2 Profiling the Selection Sort Algorithm

To measure the performance of a program, one could simply run it and measure how long it takes by using a stopwatch. However, most of our programs run very quickly, and it is not easy to time them accurately in this way. Furthermore, when a program does take a noticeable time to run, a certain amount of that time may simply be used for loading the program from disk into memory (for which it should not be penalized) or for screen output (whose speed depends on the computer model, even for computers with identical CPUs). Instead we use the Time class. Recall that

```
Time now;
```

sets now to the current time.

Here is how to use the timer to measure the performance of the sorting algorithm. (See ch11/seltime.cpp.)

```cpp
int main()
{
   rand_seed();
   cout << "Enter vector size: ";
   int n;
   cin >> n;
   vector<int> v(n);
   for (int i = 0; i < v.size(); i++)
      v[i] = rand_int(1, 100);
   Time before;
   selection_sort(v);
   Time after;

   cout << "Elapsed time = " << after.seconds_from(before)
      << " seconds\n";
   return 0;
}
```

Table 1 Selection Sort	
n	**Seconds**
10,000	1
20,000	3
30,000	6
40,000	11
50,000	17
60,000	25

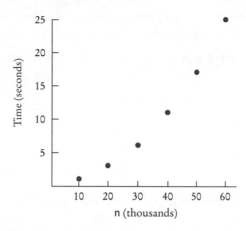

Figure 1   Time Taken by Selection Sort

By measuring the time just before the sorting and stopping it just afterwards, you don't count the time it takes to initialize the vector or the time during which the program waits for the user to type in n. Table 1 shows the results of some sample runs.

These measurements were obtained on a Pentium processor with a clock speed of 1.67 GHz running Linux. On another computer, the actual numbers will differ, but the relationship between the numbers will be the same. Figure 1 shows a plot of the measurements.

As you can see, doubling the size of the data set more than doubles the time needed to sort it.

11.3 Analyzing the Performance of the Selection Sort Algorithm

Let's count the number of operations that the program must carry out to sort a sequence using the selection sort algorithm. Actually, we don't know how many machine operations are generated for each C++ instruction or which of those instructions are more time-consuming than others, but we can make a simplification. Simply count how often an element is *visited*. Each visit requires about the same amount of work by other operations, such as incrementing subscripts and comparing values.

Let n be the size of the vector. First, you must find the smallest of n numbers. To achieve this, you must visit n elements. Then swap the elements, which takes two visits. (You may argue that there is a certain probability that you don't need to swap the values. That is true, and one can refine the computation to reflect that observation. As we will soon see, doing so would not affect the overall conclusion.) In the next step, you need to visit only $n - 1$ elements to find the minimum and then visit two of them to swap them. In the following step, $n - 2$ elements are visited to find the minimum. The last run visits two elements to find the minimum and requires two visits to swap the elements. Therefore, the total number of visits is

$$n + 2 + (n - 1) + 2 + \cdots + 2 + 2 = n + (n - 1) + \cdots + 2 + (n - 1) \cdot 2$$
$$= 2 + \cdots + (n - 1) + n + (n - 1) \cdot 2$$
$$= \frac{n(n + 1)}{2} - 1 + (n - 1) \cdot 2$$

because

$$1 + 2 + \cdots + (n - 1) + n = \frac{n(n + 1)}{2}$$

After multiplying out and collecting terms of n, you find that the number of visits is

$$\tfrac{1}{2}n^2 + \tfrac{5}{2}n - 3$$

This is a quadratic equation in n. That explains why the graph of Figure 1 looks approximately like a parabola.

Now simplify the analysis further. When you plug in a large value for n (for example, 1,000 or 2,000), then $\tfrac{1}{2}n^2$ is 500,000 or 2,000,000. The lower term, $\tfrac{5}{2}n - 3$, doesn't contribute much at all; it is just 2,497 or 4,997, a drop in the bucket compared to the hundreds of thousands or even millions of comparisons specified by the $\tfrac{1}{2}n^2$ term. Just ignore these lower-level terms. Next, ignore the constant factor $\tfrac{1}{2}$. You need not be interested in the actual count of visits for a single n. You need to compare the ratios of counts for different values of n^2. For example, you can say that sorting a sequence of 2,000 numbers requires four times as many visits as sorting a sequence of 1,000 numbers:

$$\frac{\left(\tfrac{1}{2} \cdot 2000^2\right)}{\left(\tfrac{1}{2} \cdot 1000^2\right)} = 4$$

The factor $\tfrac{1}{2}$ cancels out in comparisons of this kind. We will simply say, "The number of visits is of order n^2". That way, we can easily see that the number of comparisons increases fourfold when the size of the vector doubles: $(2n)^2 = 4n^2$.

To indicate that the number of visits is of order n^2, computer scientists often use *big-Oh notation:* The number of visits is $O(n^2)$. This is a convenient shorthand.

To turn an exact expression like

$$\tfrac{1}{2}n^2 + \tfrac{5}{2}n - 3$$

into big-Oh notation, simply locate the fastest-growing term, n^2, and ignore the constant coefficient $\tfrac{1}{2}$.

> Computer scientists use big-Oh notation to describe how fast a function grows.

In general, the expression $f(n) = O(g(n))$ means that f grows no faster than g, or, more formally, that for all n larger than some threshold, the ratio $f(n)/g(n)$ is less than a constant value C. The function g is usually chosen to be very simple, such as n^2 in our example.

You observed before that the actual number of machine operations, and the actual number of microseconds that the computer spends on them, is approximately proportional to the number of element visits. Maybe there are about 10 machine operations (increments, comparisons, memory loads, and stores) for every element visit. The number of machine operations is then approximately $10 \times \frac{1}{2}n^2$. Again, we aren't interested in the coefficient and can say that the number of machine operations, and hence the time spent on the sorting, is of the order of n^2 or $O(n^2)$.

> Selection sort is an $O(n^2)$ algorithm. Doubling the data set means a fourfold increase in processing time.

The sad fact remains that doubling the size of the vector causes a fourfold increase in the time required for sorting it. When the size of the sequence increases by a factor of 100, the sorting time increases by a factor of 10,000. To sort a sequence of a million entries, (for example, to create a telephone directory) takes 10,000 times as long as sorting 10,000 entries. If 10,000 entries can be sorted in about a second (as in our example), then sorting one million entries requires almost three hours. You will see in the next section how one can dramatically improve the performance of the sorting process by choosing a more sophisticated algorithm.

11.4 Merge Sort

In this section, you will learn about the merge sort algorithm, a much more efficient algorithm than selection sort. The basic idea behind merge sort is very simple. Suppose you have a vector of 10 integers. Engage in a bit of wishful thinking and hope that the first half of the vector is already perfectly sorted, and the second half is too, like this:

5 9 10 12 17   1 8 11 20 32

Now it is an easy matter to *merge* the two sorted sequences into a sorted sequence, simply by taking a new element from either the first or the second subvector and choosing the smaller of the elements each time:

5 9 10 12 17	1 8 11 20 32		1								
5 9 10 12 17	1 8 11 20 32		1	5							
5 9 10 12 17	1 8 11 20 32		1	5	8						
5 9 10 12 17	1 8 11 20 32		1	5	8	9					
5 9 10 12 17	1 8 11 20 32		1	5	8	9	10				
5 9 10 12 17	1 8 11 20 32		1	5	8	9	10	11			
5 9 10 12 17	1 8 11 20 32		1	5	8	9	10	11	12		
5 9 10 12 17	1 8 11 20 32		1	5	8	9	10	11	12	17	
5 9 10 12 17	1 8 11 20 32		1	5	8	9	10	11	12	17	20
5 9 10 12 17	1 8 11 20 32		1	5	8	9	10	11	12	17	20	32

In fact, you probably performed this merging before when you and a friend had to sort a pile of papers. You and the friend split up the pile in the middle, each of you sorted your half, and then you merged the results together.

This is all well and good, but it doesn't seem to solve the problem for the computer. It still has to sort the first and the second half of the sequence, because it can't very well ask a few buddies to pitch in. As it turns out, though, if the computer keeps dividing the vector into smaller and smaller subvectors, sorting each half and merging them back together, it carries out dramatically fewer steps than the selection sort requires.

Let us write a program that implements this idea. Because we will call the sort procedure multiple times to sort portions of the sequence, we will supply the range of elements that we would like to have sorted.

```cpp
void merge_sort(vector<int>& a, int from, int to)
{
    if (from == to) return;
    int mid = (from + to) / 2;

    // Sort the first and the second half
    merge_sort(a, from, mid);
    merge_sort(a, mid + 1, to);
    merge(a, from, mid, to);
}
```

The merge procedure is somewhat long but quite straightforward—see the following code listing for details.

ch11/mergesort/mergesort.cpp

```cpp
1   #include <iostream>
2
3   #include "util.h"
4
5   /**
6       Merges two adjacent ranges in a vector.
7       @param a  the vector with the elements to merge
8       @param from  the start of the first range
9       @param mid  the end of the first range
10      @param to  the end of the second range
11   */
12   void merge(vector<int>& a, int from, int mid, int to)
13   {
14       int n = to - from + 1; // Size of the range to be merged
15       // Merge both halves into a temporary vector b
16       vector<int> b(n);
17
18       int i1 = from;
19           // Next element to consider in the first half
20       int i2 = mid + 1;
21           // Next element to consider in the second half
22       int j = 0; // Next open position in b
23
```

```
24       // As long as neither i1 nor i2 is past the end, move the smaller
25       // element into b
26       while (i1 <= mid && i2 <= to)
27       {
28          if (a[i1] < a[i2])
29          {
30             b[j] = a[i1];
31             i1++;
32          }
33          else
34          {
35             b[j] = a[i2];
36             i2++;
37          }
38          j++;
39       }
40
41       // Note that only one of the two while loops below is executed
42
43       // Copy any remaining entries of the first half
44       while (i1 <= mid)
45       {
46          b[j] = a[i1];
47          i1++;
48          j++;
49       }
50       // Copy any remaining entries of the second half
51       while (i2 <= to)
52       {
53          b[j] = a[i2];
54          i2++;
55          j++;
56       }
57
58       // Copy back from the temporary vector
59       for (j = 0; j < n; j++)
60          a[from + j] = b[j];
61    }
62
63    /**
64       Sorts the elements in a range of a vector.
65       @param a the vector with the elements to sort
66       @param from start of the range to sort
67       @param to end of the range to sort
68    */
69    void merge_sort(vector<int>& a, int from, int to)
70    {
71       if (from == to) return;
72       int mid = (from + to) / 2;
73       // Sort the first and the second half
74       merge_sort(a, from, mid);
75       merge_sort(a, mid + 1, to);
76       merge(a, from, mid, to);
```

```
77  }
78
79  int main()
80  {
81      rand_seed();
82      vector<int> v(20);
83      for (int i = 0; i < v.size(); i++)
84          v[i] = rand_int(1, 100);
85      print(v);
86      merge_sort(v, 0, v.size() - 1);
87      print(v);
88      return 0;
89  }
```

11.5 Analyzing the Merge Sort Algorithm

The merge sort algorithm looks much more complicated than the selection sort algorithm, and it appears that it may well take much longer to carry out these repeated subdivisions. However, the timing results for merge sort look much better than those for selection sort (see ch11/mergetime.cpp and the table below). Sorting a sequence with 60,000 elements takes less than one second on our test machine, whereas the selection sort takes 25 seconds.

In order to get precise timing results, it is best to run the algorithm multiple times, and then divide the total time by the number of runs. Here are typical results:

n	Merge Sort (seconds)	Selection Sort (seconds)
10,000	0.012	1
20,000	0.025	3
30,000	0.038	6
40,000	0.052	11
50,000	0.066	17
60,000	0.081	25

Figure 2 shows a graph plotting the relationship. Note that the graph does not have a parabolic shape. Instead, it appears as if the running time grows approximately linearly with the size of the sequence.

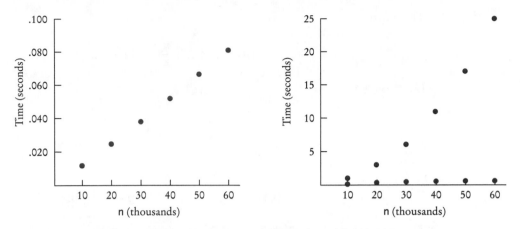

Figure 2 Merge Sort Timing (gray) versus Selection Sort (color)

To understand why the merge sort algorithm is such a tremendous improvement, let us estimate the number of sequence element visits. First, we tackle the merge process that happens after the first and second half have been sorted.

Each step in the merge process adds one more element to b. There are n elements in b. That element may come from the first or second half of a, and in most cases the elements from the two halves must be compared to see which one to take. Count that as 3 visits (one for b and one each for the two halves of a) per element, or 3n visits total. Then you must copy back from b to a, yielding another 2n visits, for a total of 5n.

If you let $T(n)$ denote the number of visits required to sort a range of n elements through the merge sort process, then you obtain

$$T(n) = T\left(\frac{n}{2}\right) + T\left(\frac{n}{2}\right) + 5n$$

because sorting each half takes $T(n/2)$ visits. (Actually, if n is not even, then you have one subsequence of size $(n-1)/2$ and one of size $(n+1)/2$. While it turns out that this detail does not affect the outcome of the computation, you can assume for now that n is a power of 2, say $n = 2^m$. This way, all subsequences can be evenly divided into two parts.)

Unfortunately, the formula

$$T(n) = 2T\left(\frac{n}{2}\right) + 5n$$

does not clearly tell you the relationship between n and $T(n)$. To understand the relationship, evaluate $T(n/2)$, using the same formula:

$$T\left(\frac{n}{2}\right) = 2T\left(\frac{n}{4}\right) + 5\frac{n}{2}$$

Therefore

$$T(n) = 2 \times 2T\left(\frac{n}{4}\right) + 5n + 5n$$

Do this again:

$$T\left(\frac{n}{4}\right) = 2T\left(\frac{n}{8}\right) + 5\frac{n}{4}$$

hence

$$T(n) = 2 \times 2 \times 2T\left(\frac{n}{8}\right) + 5n + 5n + 5n$$

This generalizes from 2, 4, 8, to arbitrary powers of 2:

$$T(n) = 2^k T\left(\frac{n}{2^k}\right) + 5nk$$

Recall that you assume that $n = 2^m$; hence, for $k = m$,

$$T(n) = 2^m T\left(\frac{n}{2^m}\right) + 5nm$$

$$= nT(1) + 5nm$$

$$= n + 5n\log_2(n)$$

Because $n = 2^m$, you have $m = \log_2(n)$.)

To establish the growth order, you drop the lower order term n and are left with $5n\log_2(n)$. Drop the constant factor 5. It is also customary to drop the base of the logarithm because all logarithms are related by a constant factor. For example,

$$\log_2(x) = \log_{10}(x)/\log_{10}(2) \approx \log_{10}(x) \times 3.32193$$

Hence we say that merge sort is an $O(n\log(n))$ algorithm.

Is the $O(n\log(n))$ merge sort algorithm better than an $O(n^2)$ selection sort algorithm? You bet it is. Recall that it took $100^2 = 10,000$ times as long to sort a million records as it took to sort 10,000 records with the $O(n^2)$ algorithm. With the $O(n\log(n))$ algorithm, the ratio is

> Merge sort is an $O(n\log(n))$ algorithm. The $n\log(n)$ function grows much more slowly than n^2.

$$\frac{1,000,000\log(1,000,000)}{10,000\log(10,000)} = 100\left(\frac{6}{4}\right) = 150$$

Suppose for the moment that merge sort takes the same time as selection sort to sort a sequence of 10,000 integers, that is, 1 second on the test machine. (Actually, as you have seen, it is much faster than that.) Then it would take about 150 seconds, or less than three minutes, to sort 1,000,000 integers. Contrast that with selection sort, which would take almost 3 hours for the same task. As you can see, even if it takes you several hours to learn about a better algorithm, that can be time well spent.

In this chapter you have barely begun to scratch the surface of this interesting topic. There are many sort algorithms, some with even better performance than the merge sort algorithm, and the analysis of these algorithms can be quite challenging. If you are a computer science major, you may revisit these important issues in a later computer science class.

ADVANCED TOPIC 11.1

The Quicksort Algorithm

Quicksort is a commonly used algorithm that has the advantage over merge sort that no temporary arrays are required to sort and merge the partial results.

The quicksort algorithm, like merge sort, is based on the strategy of divide and conquer. To sort a range a[from] . . . a[to] of the array a, first rearrange the elements in the range so that no element in the range a[from] . . . a[p] is larger than any element in the range a[p + 1] . . . a[to]. This step is called *partitioning* the range.

For example, suppose we start with a range

5 3 2 6 4 1 3 7

Here is a partitioning of the range. Note that the partitions aren't yet sorted.

3 3 2 1 4 | 6 5 7

You'll see later how to obtain such a partition. In the next step, sort each partition, by recursively applying the same algorithm on the two partitions. That sorts the entire range, because the largest element in the first partition is at most as large as the smallest element in the second partition.

1 2 3 3 4 | 5 6 7

Quicksort is implemented recursively as follows:

```
void sort(vector<int>& a, int from, int to)
{
   if (from >= to) return;
   int p = partition(a, from, to);
   sort(a, from, p);
   sort(a, p + 1, to);
}
```

Let us return to the problem of partitioning a range. Pick an element from the range and call it the *pivot*. There are several variations of the quicksort algorithm. In the simplest one, we'll pick the first element of the range, a[from], as the pivot.

Now form two regions a[from] . . . a[i], consisting of values at most as large as the pivot and a[j] . . . a[to], consisting of values at least as large as the pivot. The region a[i + 1] . . . a[j - 1] consists of values that haven't been analyzed yet. (See Figure 3.)

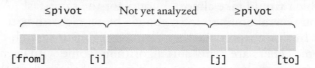

Figure 3   Partitioning a Range

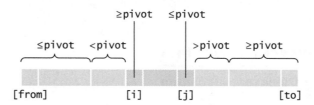

Figure 4   Extending the Partitions

At the beginning, both the left and right areas are empty; that is, i = from - 1 and j = to + 1.

Then keep incrementing i while a[i] < pivot and keep decrementing j while a[j] > pivot. Figure 4 shows i and j when that process stops.

Now swap the values in positions i and j, increasing both areas once more. Keep going while i < j. Here is the code for the partition method:

```
int partition(vector<int>& a, int from, int to)
{
   int pivot = a[from];
   int i = from - 1;
   int j = to + 1;
   while (i < j)
   {
      i++; while (a[i] < pivot) i++;
      j--; while (a[j] > pivot) j--;
      if (i < j) swap(a[i], a[j]);
   }
   return j;
}
```

On average, the quicksort algorithm is an $O(n \log(n))$ algorithm. Because it is simpler, it runs faster than merge sort in most cases. There is just one unfortunate aspect to the quicksort algorithm. Its *worst-case* runtime behavior is $O(n^2)$. Moreover, if the pivot element is chosen as the first element of the region, that worst-case behavior occurs when the input set is already sorted—a common situation in practice. By selecting the pivot element more cleverly, we can make it extremely unlikely for the worst-case behavior to occur. Such "tuned" quicksort algorithms are commonly used, because their performance is generally excellent. For example, the C library contains a function qsort that implements the quicksort algorithm.

RANDOM FACT 11.1

The First Programmer

Before pocket calculators and personal computers existed, navigators and engineers used mechanical adding machines, slide rules, and tables of logarithms and trigonometric functions to speed up computations. Unfortunately, the tables—for which values had to be computed by hand—were notoriously inaccurate. The mathematician Charles Babbage (1791–1871) had the insight that if a machine could be constructed that produced printed tables automatically, both calculation and typesetting errors could be avoided. Babbage set out to develop a machine for this purpose, which he called a *Difference Engine* because it used successive differences to compute polynomials. For example, consider the function $f(x) = x^3$. Write down the values for $f(1)$, $f(2)$, $f(3)$, and so on. Then take the *differences* between successive values:

```
1
     7
8
    19
27
    37
64
    61
125
    91
216
```

Repeat the process, taking the difference of successive values in the second column, and then repeat once again:

```
1
     7
8        12
    19        6
27       18
    37        6
64       24
    61        6
125      30
    91
216
```

Now the differences are all the same. You can retrieve the function values by a pattern of additions—you need to know the values at the fringe of the pattern and the constant difference. This method was very attractive, because mechanical addition machines had been known for some time. They consisted of cog wheels, with 10 cogs per wheel, to represent digits, and mechanisms to handle the carry from one digit to the next. Mechanical multiplication machines, on the other hand, were fragile and unreliable. Babbage built a successful prototype of the Difference Engine (see Figure 5) and, with his own money and government grants, proceeded to build the table-printing machine. However, because of funding problems and the difficulty of building the machine to the required precision, it was never completed.

While working on the Difference Engine, Babbage conceived of a much grander vision that he called the *Analytical Engine*. The Difference Engine was designed to carry out a limited set of computations—it was no smarter than a pocket calculator is today. But Babbage realized that such a machine could be made *programmable* by storing programs as well as data. The internal storage of the Analytical Engine was to consist of 1,000 registers of 50

Figure 5   Babbage's Difference Engine

decimal digits each. Programs and constants were to be stored on punched cards—a technique that was, at that time, commonly used on looms for weaving patterned fabrics.

Ada Augusta, Countess of Lovelace (1815–1852), the only child of Lord Byron, was a friend and sponsor of Charles Babbage. Ada Lovelace was one of the first people to realize the potential of such a machine, not just for computing mathematical tables but for processing data that were not numbers. She is considered by many the world's first programmer. The Ada programming language, a language developed for use in U.S. Department of Defense projects, was named in her honor.

11.6 Searching

Searching for an element in a sequence is an extremely common task. As with sorting, the right choice of algorithms can make a big difference.

Suppose you need to find the telephone number of your friend. If you have a telephone book, you can look up your friend's name quickly, because the telephone book is sorted alphabetically. However, now suppose you have a telephone number and you must know to whom it belongs (without actually calling the number). You could look through the telephone book, one number at a time, until you find the number. This would obviously be a tremendous amount of work.

This thought experiment shows the difference between a search through an unsorted data set and a search through a sorted data set.

> A linear search examines all values in a sequence until it finds a match or reaches the end.

If you want to find a number in a sequence of values that occur in arbitrary order, you must look through all elements until you have found a match or until you reach the end. This is called a *linear* or *sequential search.*

Here is a function that performs a linear search through a vector v of integers for a value, value (see ch11/lsearch.cpp). The function then returns the index of the match, or −1 if value does not occur in v.

```
int linear_search(vector<int> v, int value)
{
   for (int i = 0; i < v.size(); i++)
   {
      if (v[i] == value)
         return i;
   }
   return -1;
}
```

> A linear search locates a value in a sequence in $O(n)$ steps.

How long does a linear search take? If you assume that the element value is present in the vector v, then the average search visits $n/2$ elements. If it is not present, then all n elements must be inspected to verify the absence. Either way, a linear search is an $O(n)$ algorithm.

Now consider searching an item in a sequence that has been previously sorted. Of course, you could still do a linear search, but it turns out you can do much better than that.

Here is a typical example. The data set is:

```
[0] [1] [2] [3] [4] [5] [6] [7]
 14  43  76 100 115 290 400 511
```

and you want to see whether the value 123 is in the data set. The last point in the first half of the data set, v[3], is 100. It is smaller than the value you are looking for; hence, you should look in the second half of the data set for a match, that is, in the sequence

```
[0] [1] [2] [3] [4] [5] [6] [7]
 14  43  76 100 115 290 400 511
```

Now the last value of the first half of this sequence is 290; hence, the value must be located in the sequence

```
[0] [1] [2] [3] [4] [5] [6] [7]
 14  43  76 100 115 290 400 511
```

The last value of the first half of this very short sequence is 115, which is smaller than the value that you are searching, so you must look in the second half:

```
[0] [1] [2] [3] [4] [5] [6] [7]
 14  43  76 100 115 290 400 511
```

It is trivial to see that you don't have a match, because 123 ≠ 290. If you wanted to insert 123 into the sequence, you would need to insert it just before v[5].

A binary search locates a value in a sorted sequence by determining whether the value occurs in the first or second half, then repeating the search in one of the halves.

This search process is called a *binary search*, because the size of the search is cut in half in each step. That cutting in half works only because you know that the sequence of values is sorted.

The following function implements a binary search in a sorted sequence of integers (see ch11/bsearch.cpp). It returns the position of the match if the search succeeds, or −1 if the value is not found in v:

```
int binary_search(vector<int> v, int from, int to, int value)
{
    if (from > to)
        return -1;
    int mid = (from + to) / 2;
    if (v[mid] == value)
        return mid;
    else if (v[mid] < value)
        return binary_search(v, mid + 1, to, value);
    else
        return binary_search(v, from, mid - 1, value);
}
```

Now determine the number of element visits required to carry out a search. Use the same technique as in the analysis of merge sort. Because you look at the middle element, which counts as one comparison, and then search either the left or the right subsequence, you have

$$T(n) = T\left(\frac{n}{2}\right) + 1$$

Using the same equation,

$$T\left(\frac{n}{2}\right) = T\left(\frac{n}{4}\right) + 1$$

By plugging this result into the original equation, you get

$$T(n) = T\left(\frac{n}{4}\right) + 2$$

This generalizes to

$$T(n) = T\left(\frac{n}{2^k}\right) + k$$

As in the analysis of merge sort, you make the simplifying assumption that n is a power of 2, $n = 2^m$, where $m = \log_2(n)$. Then you obtain

$$T(n) = 1 + \log_2(n)$$

Therefore, binary search is an $O(\log(n))$ algorithm.

This result makes intuitive sense. Suppose that n is 100. Then after each search, the size of the search range is cut in half, to 50, 25, 12, 6, 3, and 1. After seven comparisons we are done. This agrees with our formula since $\log_2(100) \approx 6.64386$, and indeed the next larger power of 2 is $2^7 = 128$.

> A binary search locates a value in a sequence in $O(\log(n))$ steps.

Because a binary search is so much faster than a linear search, is it worthwhile to sort a sequence first and then use a binary search? It depends. If you only search the sequence once, then it is more efficient to pay for an $O(n)$ linear search than for an $O(n \log(n))$ sort and $O(\log(n))$ binary search. But if one makes a number of searches in the same sequence, then sorting it is definitely worthwhile.

11.7 Library Functions for Sorting and Binary Search

If you need to sort or search values in your own programs, there is no need to implement your own algorithms. You can simply use functions in the C++ library. This section gives you a brief overview of the library functions for sorting and binary search. For more information on using library algorithms, please turn to Chapter 20.

> The C++ library contains functions sort and binary_search.

You sort a vector v by calling

```
sort(v.begin(), v.end());
```

The expressions v.begin() and v.end() are *iterators* that denote the beginning and ending positions of the vector. (As you will see in the next chapter, an iterator denotes a position in a container.)

If the values are stored in an array a, then the call to the sort method looks slightly different. You supply a pointer to the beginning and the end of the array:

```
sort(a, a + size);
```

Here *size* is the size of the array. For example,

```
int a[5] = { 60, 47, 70, 39, 6 };
sort(a, a + 5); // Now a contains 6, 39, 47, 60, 70
```

If you have a sorted vector or array, you can use the binary_search function to test whether it contains a given value. For example, the call

```
binary_search(v.begin(), v.end(), value)
```

returns true if the vector v contains value. (Unlike our binary search function from the preceding section, the library function does not return the position where the value was found.)

To search an array, you call

```
binary_search(a, a + size, value)
```

To use the sort or binary_search functions, you must include the <algorithm> header.

ADVANCED TOPIC 11.2

Defining an Ordering for Sorting Objects

When you use the sort function, you must ensure that it is able to compare elements. Suppose that you want to sort a vector<Employee>. The compiler will complain that it does not know how to compare two employees.

There are several ways to overcome this problem. The simplest is to define the < operator for Employee objects:

```
bool operator<(const Employee& a, const Employee& b)
{
    return a.get_salary() < b.get_salary();
}
```

The curious name operator< indicates that this function defines a comparison operator. (See ch11/stlsort.cpp for an example program.) You will learn more about defining your own operators in Chapter 14.

This < operator compares employees by salary. If you call sort to sort a sequence of employees, they will be sorted by increasing salary.

Chapter 20 shows additional ways of specifying the comparison.

RANDOM FACT 11.2

Cataloging Your Necktie Collection

People and companies use computers to organize just about every aspect of their lives. On the whole, computers are tremendously good for collecting and analyzing data. In fact, the power offered by computers and their software makes them seductive solutions for just about any organizational problem. It is easy to lose sight of the fact that using a computer is not always the best solution to a problem.

In 1983, the author John Bear wrote about a person who had come up with a novel use for the personal computers that had recently become available. That person cataloged his necktie collection, putting descriptions of the ties into a database and generating reports that listed them by color, price, or style. We can hope he had another use to justify the purchase of a piece of equipment worth several thousand dollars, but that particular application was so dear to his heart that he wanted the world to know about it. Perhaps not surprisingly, few other computer users shared that excitement, and you don't find the shelves of your local software store lined with necktie-cataloging software.

The phenomenon of using technology for its own sake is quite widespread. In the "Internet bubble" of 2000, hundreds of companies were founded on the premise that the Internet made it technologically possible to order items such as groceries and pet food from a home computer, and therefore the traditional stores would be replaced by web stores. However, technological feasibility did not ensure economic success. Trucking groceries and pet food to households was expensive, and few customers were willing to pay a premium for the added convenience.

At the same time, many elementary schools spent tremendous resources to bring computers and the Internet into the classroom. Indeed, it is easy to understand why teachers, school administrators, parents, politicians and equipment vendors are in favor of computers in classrooms. Isn't computer literacy absolutely essential for youngsters in the new millennium? Isn't it particularly important to give low-income kids, whose parents may not be able to afford a home computer, the opportunity to master computer skills? However, schools have found that the total cost of running computers far exceeds the initial cost of the equipment. As schools purchased more equipment than could be maintained by occasional volunteers, they had to make hard choices—should they lay off librarians and art instructors to hire more computer technicians, or should they let the equipment become useless? Unfortunately, many schools were so caught up in the technology hype that they never asked themselves whether the educational benefits justified the expense. See [1] for more information.

As computer programmers, we like to computerize everything. As computer professionals, though, we owe it to our employers and clients to understand which problems they want to solve and to deploy computers and software only where they add more value than cost.

CHAPTER SUMMARY

1. The selection sort algorithm sorts a sequence by repeatedly finding the smallest element of the unsorted tail region and moving it to the front.

2. Computer scientists use big-Oh notation to describe how fast a function grows.

3. Selection sort is an $O(n^2)$ algorithm. Doubling the data set means a fourfold increase in processing time.

4. Merge sort is an $O(n \log(n))$ algorithm. The $n \log(n)$ function grows much more slowly than n^2.

5. A linear search examines all values in a sequence until it finds a match or reaches the end.

6. A linear search locates a value in a sequence in $O(n)$ steps.

7. A binary search locates a value in a sorted sequence by determining whether the value occurs in the first or second half, then repeating the search in one of the halves.

8. A binary search locates a value in a sequence in $O(\log(n))$ steps.

9. The C++ library contains functions sort and binary_search.

FURTHER READING

1. Oppenheimer, Todd. "The Computer Delusion," *The Atlantic Monthly* 280, no. 1 (July 1997): 45–62, available online at http://www.catholiceducation.org/articles/education/ed0026.html.

REVIEW EXERCISES

Exercise R11.1. *Checking against off-by-one errors.* When writing the selection sort algorithm of Section 11.1, a programmer must make the usual choices of < against <=, a.size() against a.size() - 1, and next against next + 1. This is fertile ground for off-by-one errors. Make code walkthroughs of the algorithm with vectors of length 0, 1, 2, and 3 and check carefully that all index values are correct.

Exercise R11.2. What is the difference between searching and sorting?

Exercise R11.3. For the following expressions, what is the order of the growth of each?

a. $n^2 + 2n + 1$

b. $n^{10} + 9n^9 + 20n^8 + 145n^7$

c. $(n + 1)^4$

d. $(n^2 + n)^2$

e. $n + 0.001n^3$

f. $n^3 - 1000n^2 + 10^9$

g. $n + \log(n)$

h. $n^2 + n \log(n)$

i. $2^n + n^2$

j. $\dfrac{(n^3 + 2n)}{(n^2 + 0.75)}$

Exercise R11.4. You determined that the actual number of visits in the selection sort algorithm is

$$T(n) = \tfrac{1}{2}n^2 + \tfrac{5}{2}n - 3$$

You then characterized this function as having $O(n^2)$ growth. Compute the actual ratios

$$T(2{,}000)/T(1{,}000)$$
$$T(5{,}000)/T(1{,}000)$$
$$T(10{,}000)/T(1{,}000)$$

and compare them with

$$f(2{,}000)/f(1{,}000)$$
$$f(5{,}000)/f(1{,}000)$$
$$f(10{,}000)/f(1{,}000)$$

where $f(n) = n^2$.

Exercise R11.5. Suppose algorithm A takes five seconds to handle a data set of 1,000 records. If the algorithm A is an $O(n)$ algorithm, how long will it take to handle a data set of 2,000 records? Of 10,000 records?

Exercise R11.6. Suppose an algorithm takes five seconds to handle a data set of 1,000 records. Fill in the following table, which shows the approximate growth of the execution times depending on the complexity of the algorithm.

	$O(n)$	$O(n^2)$	$O(n^3)$	$O(n \log(n))$	$O(2^n)$
1,000	5	5	5	5	5
2,000					
3,000		45			
10,000					

For example, since $3000^2/1000^2 = 9$, the $O(n^2)$ algorithm would take nine times as long, or 45 seconds, to handle a data set of 3,000 records.

Exercise R11.7. Sort the following growth rates from slowest growth to fastest growth.

$O(n)$ $O(n \log(n))$

$O(n^3)$ $O(2^n)$

$O(n^n)$ $O(\sqrt{n})$

$O(\log(n))$ $O(n\sqrt{n})$

$O(n^2 \log(n))$ $O(n^{\log(n)})$

Exercise R11.8. What is the order of complexity of the standard algorithm to find the minimum value of a sequence? Of finding both the minimum and the maximum?

Exercise R11.9. What is the order of complexity of the following function?

```cpp
int count(vector<int> a, int c)
{
   int count = 0;

   for (int i = 0; i < a.size(); i++)
   {
      if (a[i] == c) count++;
   }
   return count;
}
```

Exercise R11.10. Your task is to remove all duplicates from a vector. For example, if the vector has the values

$$4 \quad 7 \quad 11 \quad 4 \quad 9 \quad 5 \quad 11 \quad 7 \quad 3 \quad 5$$

then the vector should be changed to

$$4 \quad 7 \quad 11 \quad 9 \quad 5 \quad 3$$

Here is a simple algorithm. Look at a[i]. Count how many times it occurs in a. If the count is larger than 1, remove it. What is the order of complexity of this algorithm?

Exercise R11.11. Consider the following algorithm to remove all duplicates from a vector. Sort the vector. For each element, look at its two neighbors to decide whether it is present more than once. If so, remove it. Is this a faster algorithm than the one in Exercise R11.10?

Exercise R11.12. Develop a fast algorithm for removing duplicates from a vector if the resulting vector must have the same ordering as the original one.

Exercise R11.13. Consider the following sorting algorithm. To sort a vector a, make a second vector b of the same size. Then insert elements from a into b, keeping b in sorted order. For each element, call the binary search function of Exercise P11.6 to determine where it needs to be inserted. To insert an element into the middle of a vector, you need to move all elements above the insert location up.

Is this an efficient algorithm? Estimate the number of element visits in the sorting process. Assume that on average half of the elements of b need to be moved to insert a new element.

Exercise R11.14. Make a walkthrough of selection sort with the following data sets.
   a. 4   7   11   4   9   5   11 7   3   5
   b. –7 6   8   7   5   9   0   11 10 5   8

Exercise R11.15. Make a walkthrough of merge sort with the following data sets.
   a. 5   11 7   3   5   4   7   11 4   9
   b. 9   0   11 10 5   8   –7 6   8   7   5

Exercise R11.16. Make a walkthrough of the following:
   a. Linear search for 7 in   –7 1   3   3   4   7   11 13
   b. Binary search for 8 in   –7 2   2   3   4   7   8   11 13
   c. Binary search for 8 in   –7 1   2   3   5   7   10 13

PROGRAMMING EXERCISES

Exercise P11.1. Modify the selection sort algorithm to sort a vector of integers in descending order.

Exercise P11.2. Modify the selection sort algorithm to sort a vector of employees by salary.

Exercise P11.3. Write a program that generates the table of sample runs of the selection sort times automatically. The program should ask for the smallest and largest value of n and the number of measurements and then make all sample runs.

Exercise P11.4. Modify the merge sort algorithm to sort a vector of employees by salary.

Exercise P11.5. Write a telephone lookup program. Read a data set of 1,000 names and telephone numbers from a file that contains the numbers in random order. Handle lookups by name and also reverse lookups by phone number. Use a binary search for both lookups.

Exercise P11.6. Consider the binary search function in Section 11.7. If no match is found, the function returns –1. Modify the function so that it returns a `bool` value indicating whether a match was found. Add a reference parameter m, which is set to the location of the match if the search was successful. If a was not found, set m to the index of the next larger value instead, or to a.size() if a is larger than all the elements of the vector.

Exercise P11.7. Use the modification of the binary search function from Exercise P11.6 to sort a vector. Make a second vector of the same size as the vector to be sorted. For each element in the first vector, call binary search on the second vector to find out where the new element should be inserted. Then move all elements above the insertion point up by one slot and insert the new element. Thus, the second vector is always kept sorted. Implement this algorithm and measure its performance.

Exercise P11.8. Implement the `merge_sort` procedure without recursion, where the size of the vector is a power of 2. First merge adjacent regions of size 1, then adjacent regions of size 2, then adjacent regions of size 4, and so on.

Exercise P11.9. Implement the `merge_sort` procedure without recursion, where the size of the vector is an arbitrary number. *Hint:* Keep merging adjacent areas whose size is a power of 2, and pay special attention to the last area in the sequence.

Exercise P11.10. Write a program that sorts a vector of `Employee` objects by increasing salary and prints the results. Use the `sort` function from the C++ library.

Exercise P11.11. Write a program that sorts an array of `Time` objects and prints the results. Use the `sort` function from the C++ library.

Exercise P11.12. Write a program that keeps an appointment book. Make a class `Appointment` that stores a description of the appointment, the appointment day, the starting time, and the ending time. Your program should keep the appointments in a sorted vector. Users can add appointments and print out all appointments for a given day. When a new appointment is added, use binary search to find where it should be inserted in the vector. Do not add it if it conflicts with another appointment.

Exercise P11.13. Modify the binary search algorithm so that you can search the records stored in a *database file* without actually reading them into a vector. Use the employee database of Section 9.6, sort it by name, and make lookups for employees.

G   **Exercise P11.14.** Give a *graphical animation* of selection sort as follows: Fill a vector with a set of random numbers between 1 and 100. Set the window coordinate system to a.size() by 100. Draw each element as a stick, as in Figure 6. Whenever you change the vector, clear the screen and redraw.

Figure 6   Graphical Animation

G   **Exercise P11.15.** Write a graphical animation of merge sort.

G   **Exercise P11.16.** Write a graphical animation of binary search. Highlight the currently inspected element.

Chapter 12

Lists, Queues, and Stacks

- To become familiar with the list, queue, and stack data types
- To understand the implementation of linked lists
- To understand the efficiency of vector and list operations

In this chapter, we introduce a new data structure, the linked list. You will learn how to use lists and the related stack and queue types. You will study the implementation of linked lists and analyze when linked lists are more efficient than vectors.

CHAPTER CONTENTS

12.1 Linked Lists

A linked list is a data structure for collecting a sequence of objects, such that addition and removal of elements in the middle of the sequence is efficient.

To understand the need for such a data structure, imagine a program that maintains a vector of employee records, sorted by the last name of the employees. When a new employee is hired, an object needs to be inserted into the vector. Unless the company happens to hire employees in dictionary order, it is likely that a new employee object needs to be inserted into the middle of the vector. In that case, many other objects must be moved toward the end. Conversely, if an employee leaves the company, the hole in the sequence needs to be closed by moving all objects that came after it. Moving a large number of objects can involve a substantial amount of computer time. We would like to structure the data in a way that minimizes this cost.

> A linked list consists of a number of nodes, each of which has a pointer to the neighboring nodes.

Rather than storing the data in a single block of memory, a linked list uses a different strategy. Each value is stored in its own memory block, together with the locations of the neighboring blocks in the sequence (see Figure 1).

It is now an easy matter to add another value into the sequence, or to remove a value from the sequence, without moving the others (see Figures 2 and 3).

> Adding and removing elements in the middle of a linked list is efficient.

What's the catch? Linked lists allow speedy insertion and removal, but element access can be slow. For example, suppose you want to locate the fifth element. You must first traverse the first four. This is a problem if you need to access the elements in arbitrary order. The term *random access* is used in computer science to describe an access

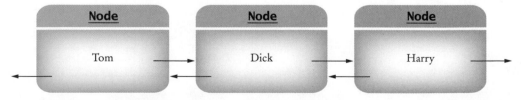

Figure 1 A Linked List

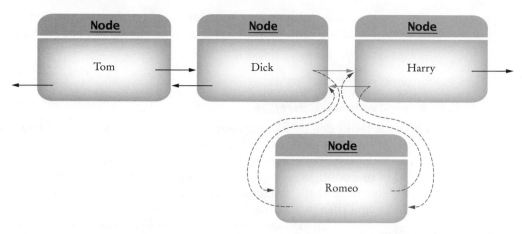

Figure 2 Adding a Node to a Linked List

pattern in which elements are accessed in arbitrary (not necessarily random) order. In contrast, sequential access visits the elements in sequence. For example, a binary search requires random access, whereas a linear search only requires sequential access.

> Visiting the elements of a linked list in sequential order is efficient, but random access is not.

Of course, if you mostly visit all elements in sequence (for example, to display or print the elements), the inefficiency of random access is not a problem. You use linked lists when you are concerned about the efficiency of inserting or removing elements and you rarely need element access in random order.

The standard C++ library has an implementation of the linked list container structure. In this section, you will learn how to use the standard linked list structure. Later you will look "under the hood" and find out how to implement linked lists. (The linked list of the standard C++ library has links going in both directions. Such a list is often called a *doubly-linked* list. A *singly-linked* list lacks the links to the predecessor elements.)

Just like vector, the standard list is a *template:* You can declare lists for different types. For example, to make a list of strings, define an object of type list<string>.

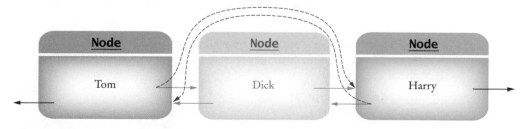

Figure 3 Removing a Node from a Linked List

Then you can use the push_back function to add strings to the end of the list. The following code segment defines a list of strings, names, and adds three strings to it:

```
list<string> names;

names.push_back("Tom");
names.push_back("Dick");
names.push_back("Harry");
```

This code looks exactly like the code that you would use to build a vector of strings. There is, however, one major difference. Suppose you want to access the last element in the list. You cannot directly refer to names[2]. Since the values are not stored in one contiguous block in memory, there is no immediate way to access the third element. Instead, you must visit each element in turn, starting at the beginning of the list and then proceeding to the next element.

> You can inspect and edit a linked list with an iterator. An iterator points to a node in a linked list.

To visit an element, you use a *list iterator*. An iterator marks a *position* in the list. To get an iterator that marks the beginning position in the list, you define an iterator variable, then call the begin function of the list class to get the beginning position:

```
list<string>::iterator pos;
pos = names.begin();
```

To move the iterator to the next position, use the ++ operator:

```
pos++;
```

You can also move the iterator backwards with the -- operator:

```
pos--;
```

You find the value that is stored in the position marked with the * operator:

```
string value = *pos;
```

You have to be careful to distinguish between the iterator pos, which represents a position in the list, and the value *pos, which represents the value that is stored in the list. For example, if you change *pos, then you update the contents in the list:

```
*pos = "Romeo";
    // The list value at the position is changed
```

If you change pos, then you merely change the current position.

```
pos = names.begin();
    // The position is again at the beginning of the list
```

To insert another string before the iterator position, use the insert function:

```
names.insert(pos, "Romeo");
```

The insert function inserts the new element *before* the iterator position, rather than after it. This convention makes it easy to insert a new element before the first value of the list:

```
pos = names.begin();
names.insert(pos, "Romeo");
```

That raises the question of how you insert a value after the end of the list. Each list has an *end position* that does not correspond to any value in the list but that points past the list's end. The end function returns that position:

```
pos = names.end(); // Points past the end of the list
names.insert(pos, "Juliet");
    // Insert past the end of the list
```

It is an error to compute

```
string value = *names.end(); // ERROR
```

The end position does not point to any value, so you cannot look up the value at that position. This error is equivalent to the error of accessing v[10] in a vector with 10 elements.

The end position has another useful purpose: it is the stopping point for traversing the list. The following code iterates over all elements of the list and prints them out:

```
pos = names.begin();
while (pos != names.end())
{
   cout << *pos << "\n";
   pos++;
}
```

The traversal can be described more concisely with a for loop:

```
for (pos = names.begin(); pos != names.end(); pos++)
   cout << *pos << "\n";
```

Of course, this looks very similar to the typical for loop for traversing a vector:

```
for (i = 0; i < v.size(); i++)
   cout << v[i] << "\n";
```

Finally, to remove an element from a list, you move an iterator to the position that you want to remove, then call the erase function. The erase function returns an iterator that points to the element after the one that has been erased.
The following code erases the second element of the list:

```
pos = names.begin();
pos++;
pos = names.erase(pos);
```

Now pos points to the element that was previously the third element and is now the second element.

Here is a short example program that adds elements to a list, inserts and erases list elements, and finally traverses the resulting list.

ch12/list1.cpp

```
1  #include <string>
2  #include <list>
3  #include <iostream>
4
5  using namespace std;
```

```
6
7   int main()
8   {
9      list<string> names;
10
11     names.push_back("Tom");
12     names.push_back("Dick");
13     names.push_back("Harry");
14     names.push_back("Juliet");
15
16     // Add a value in fourth place
17
18     list<string>::iterator pos;
19     pos = names.begin();
20     pos++;
21     pos++;
22     pos++;
23
24     names.insert(pos, "Romeo");
25
26     // Remove the value in second place
27
28     pos = names.begin();
29     pos++;
30
31     names.erase(pos);
32
33     // Print all values
34
35     for (pos = names.begin(); pos != names.end(); pos++)
36        cout << *pos << "\n";
37
38     return 0;
39  }
```

12.2 Implementing Linked Lists

The previous section showed you how to put linked lists to use. However, because the implementation of the list class is hidden from you, you had to take it on faith that the list values are really stored in separate memory blocks. We will now walk through an implementation of the list, node, and iterator classes.

For simplicity, we will implement linked lists of strings. To implement the linked list class in C++ that can hold values of arbitrary types, you need to know how to program with templates (Chapter 16). To implement iterators that behave exactly like the ones in the C++ library, you also need to know about operator overloading and nested classes (Chapters 17 and 18).

12.2.1 The Classes for Lists, Nodes, and Iterators

The list class of the standard library defines many useful member functions. For simplicity, we will only study the implementation of the most useful ones: push_back, insert, erase, and the iterator operations. We call our class List, with an uppercase L, to differentiate it from the standard list class template.

> When implementing a linked list, we need to define list, node, and iterator classes.

A linked list stores each value in a separate object, called a *node*. A node object holds a value, together with pointers to the previous and next nodes:

```
class Node
{
public:
   Node(string s);
private:
   string data;
   Node* previous;
   Node* next;
friend class List;
friend class Iterator;
};
```

A list node contains pointers to the next and previous nodes.

Note the friend declarations. They indicate that the List and Iterator member functions are allowed to inspect and modify the data members of the Node class, which we will write presently.

A class should not grant friendship to another class lightly, because it breaks the privacy protection. In this case, it makes sense, though, since the list and iterator functions do all the necessary work and the node class is just an artifact of the implementation that is invisible to the users of the list class. Note that no code other than the member functions of the list and iterator classes can access the node fields, so the data integrity is still guaranteed.

> A list object contains pointers to the first and last node.

A list object holds the locations of the first and last nodes in the list:

```
class List
{
public:
   List();
   void push_back(string data);
   void insert(Iterator pos, string s);
   Iterator erase(Iterator pos);
   Iterator begin();
   Iterator end();
private:
   Node* first;
   Node* last;
};
```

If the list is empty, then the first and last pointers are NULL. Note that a list object stores no data; it just knows where to find the node objects that store the list contents.

An iterator contains a pointer to the current node, and to the list that contains it.

Finally, an *iterator* denotes a position in the list. It holds a pointer to the node that denotes its current position, and a pointer to the list that created it. We use member functions get, next, and equals instead of operators *, ++, and ==. For example, we will call pos.next() instead of pos++.

```
class Iterator
{
public:
   Iterator();
   string get() const;
   void next();
   void previous();
   bool equals(Iterator b) const;
private:
   Node* position;
   List* container;
friend class List;
};
```

If the iterator points past the end of the list, then the position pointer is NULL. In that case, the previous member function uses the container pointer to move the iterator back from the past-the-end position to the last element of the list. (This is only one possible choice for implementing the past-the-end position. Another choice would be to store an actual dummy node at the end of the list. Some implementations of the standard list class do just that.)

12.2.2 Implementing Iterators

Iterators are created by the begin and end member functions of the List class. The begin function creates an iterator whose position pointer points to the first node in the list. The end function creates an iterator whose position pointer is NULL.

```
Iterator List::begin()
{
   Iterator iter;
   iter.position = first;
   iter.container = this;
   return iter;
}

Iterator List::end()
{
   Iterator iter;
   iter.position = NULL;
   iter.container = this;
   return iter;
}
```

The next function (which is the equivalent of the ++ operator) advances the iterator to the next position. This is a very typical operation in a linked list; let us study it in detail. The position pointer points to the current node in the list. That node has a

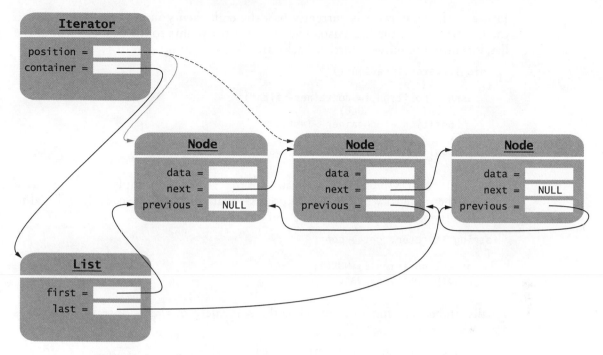

Figure 4 Advancing an Iterator

field next. Because position is a node pointer, the next field in the node to which position points is referred to as

```
position->next
```

That next field is itself a pointer, pointing to the next node in the linked list (see Figure 4). To make position point to that next node, write

```
position = position->next;
```

However, you can evaluate position->next only if position is not NULL, because it is an error to dereference a NULL pointer. That is, it is illegal to advance the iterator once it is in the past-the-end position.

Here is the complete code for the next function:

```
void Iterator::next()
{
   assert(position != NULL);
   position = position->next;
}
```

The previous function (which is the equivalent of the -- operator) is a bit more complex. In the ordinary case, you move the position backwards with the instruction

```
position = position->previous;
```

However, if the iterator is currently past the end, then you must make it point to the last element in the list. Also, when the iterator points to the first element in the list, it is illegal to move it further backward.

```
void Iterator::previous()
{
   assert(position != container->first);
   if (position == NULL)
      position = container->last;
   else
      position = position->previous;
}
```

The get function (which is the equivalent of the * operator) simply returns the data value of the node to which position points—that is, position->data. It is illegal to call get if the iterator points past the end of the list:

```
string Iterator::get() const
{
   assert(position != NULL);
   return position->data;
}
```

Finally, the equals function (which is the equivalent of the == operator) compares two position pointers:

```
bool Iterator::equals(Iterator b) const
{
   return position == b.position;
}
```

12.2.3 Implementing Insertion and Removal

In the last section you saw how to implement the iterators that traverse an existing list. Now you will see how to build up lists by adding and removing elements, one step at a time.

First, we will implement the push_back function. It appends an element to the end of the list (see Figure 5). Make a new node:

```
Node* new_node = new Node(s);
```

List nodes are allocated on the heap, using the new operator.

This new node must be integrated into the list after the node to which the last pointer points. That is, the next field of the last node (which is currently NULL) must be updated to new_node. Also, the previous field of the new node must point to what used to be the last node:

```
new_node->previous = last;  ❶
last->next = new_node;  ❷
```

Finally, you must update the last pointer to reflect that the new node is now the last node in the list:

```
last = new_node;  ❸
```

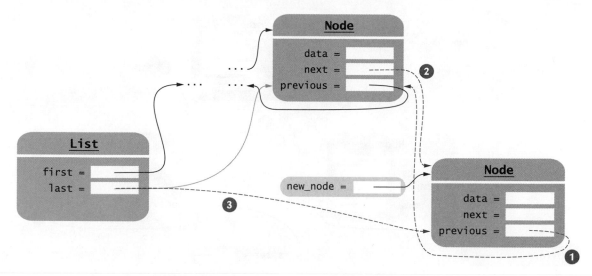

Figure 5   Appending a Node to the End of a Linked List

However, there is a special case when last is NULL, which can happen only when the list is empty. After the call to push_back, the list has a single node—namely, new_node. In that case, both first and last must be set to new_node:

```
void List::push_back(string data)
{
    Node* new_node = new Node(data);
    if (last == NULL) // List is empty
    {
        first = new_node;
        last = new_node;
    }
    else
    {
        new_node->previous = last;
        last->next = new_node;
        last = new_node;
    }
}
```

Inserting an element in the middle of a linked list is a little more difficult, because the node pointers in the *two* nodes surrounding the new node need to be updated. The function declaration is

```
void List::insert(Iterator iter, string s)
```

That is, a new node containing s is inserted before iter.position (see Figure 6).

Give names to the surrounding nodes. Let before be the node before the insertion location, and let after be the node after that. That is,

```
Node* after = iter.position;
Node* before = after->previous;
```

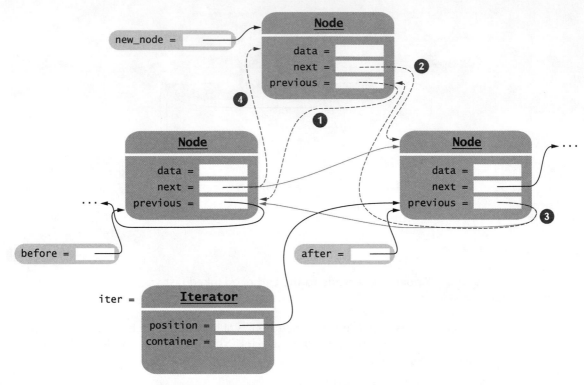

Figure 6   Inserting a Node into a Linked List

What happens if after is NULL? After all, it is illegal to apply -> to a NULL pointer. In this situation, you are inserting past the end of the list. Simply call push_back to handle that case separately. Otherwise, you need to insert new_node between before and after:

```
new_node->previous = before; ❶
new_node->next = after; ❷
```

You must also update the nodes from before and after to point to the new node:

```
after->previous = new_node; ❸
before->next = new_node;   // If before != NULL  ❹
```

However, you must be careful. You know that after is not NULL, but it is possible that before is NULL. In that case, you are inserting at the beginning of the list and need to adjust first:

```
if (before = NULL) // Insert at beginning
   first = new_node;
else
   before->next = new_node;
```

Here is the complete code for the insert function:

```
void List::insert(Iterator iter, string s)
{
   if (iter.position == NULL)
   {
      push_back(s);
      return;
   }

   Node* after = iter.position;
   Node* before = after->previous;
   Node* new_node = new Node(s);
   new_node->previous = before;
   new_node->next = after;
   after->previous = new_node;
   if (before == NULL) // Insert at beginning
      first = new_node;
   else
      before->next = new_node;
}
```

Finally, look at the implementation of the erase function:

```
Iterator List::erase(Iterator iter)
```

You want to remove the node to which iter.position points. It is illegal to erase the past-the-end position, so assert that iter.position points to an actual list element:

```
assert(iter.position != NULL);
```

As before, give names to the node to be removed, the node before it, and the node after it:

```
Node* remove = iter.position;
Node* before = remove->previous;
Node* after = remove->next;
```

You need to update the next and previous pointers of the before and after nodes to bypass the node that is to be removed (see Figure 7).

```
before->next = after;   // If before != NULL ❶
after->previous = before;  // If after != NULL ❷
```

However, as before, you need to cope with the possibility that before, after, or both are NULL. If before is NULL, you are erasing the first element in the list. It has no predecessor to update, but you must change the first pointer of the list. Conversely, if after is NULL, you are erasing the last element of the list and must update the last pointer of the list:

```
if (remove == first)
   first = after;
else
   before->next = after;
if (remove == last)
   last = before;
else
   after->previous = before;
```

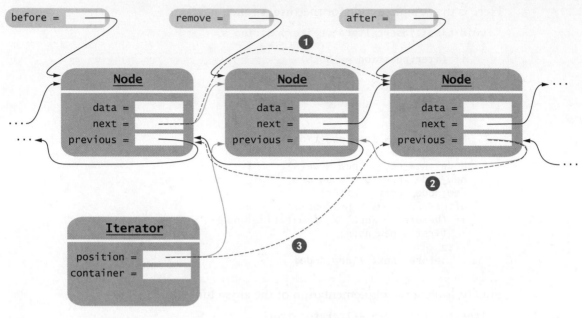

Figure 7   Removing a Node from a Linked List

You must adjust the iterator position so it no longer points to the removed element.

```
iter.position = after;  ❸
```

When a list node is erased, it is recycled to the heap with the delete operator.

Finally, you must remember to recycle the removed node:

```
delete remove;
```

Here is the complete erase function. Note that the function returns an iterator to the element following the erased one:

```
Iterator List::erase(Iterator iter)
{
   assert(iter.position != NULL);
   Node* remove = iter.position;
   Node* before = remove->previous;
   Node* after = remove->next;
   if (remove == first)
      first = after;
   else
      before->next = after;
   if (remove == last)
      last = before;
   else
      after->previous = before;
   delete remove;
   Iterator r;
   r.position = after;
   r.container = this;
   return r;
}
```

Implementing operations that modify a linked list is challenging—you need to make sure that you update all node pointers correctly.

Implementing these linked list operations is somewhat complex. It is also error-prone. If you make a mistake and misroute some of the pointers, you can get subtle errors. For example, if you make a mistake with a previous pointer, you may never notice it until you traverse the list backwards. If a node has been deleted, then that same storage area may later be reallocated for a different purpose, and if you have kept a pointer to it, following that invalid node pointer will lead to disaster. You must exercise special care when implementing any operations that manipulate the node pointers directly.

Here is a program that puts our linked list to use and demonstrates the insert and erase operations.

ch12/list2.cpp

```
1   #include <string>
2   #include <iostream>
3   #include <cassert>
4
5   using namespace std;
6
7   class List;
8   class Iterator;
9
10  class Node
11  {
12  public:
13     /*
14        Constructs a node with a given data value.
15        @param s the data to store in this node
16     */
17     Node(string s);
18  private:
19     string data;
20     Node* previous;
21     Node* next;
22  friend class List;
23  friend class Iterator;
24  };
25
26  class List
27  {
28  public:
29     /**
30        Constructs an empty list.
31     */
32     List();
33     /**
34        Appends an element to the list.
35        @param data the value to append
36     */
37     void push_back(string data);
```

```
38      /**
39          Inserts an element into the list.
40          @param iter the position before which to insert
41          @param s the value to append
42      */
43      void insert(Iterator iter, string s);
44      /**
45          Removes an element from the list.
46          @param iter the position to remove
47          @return an iterator pointing to the element after the
48          erased element
49      */
50      Iterator erase(Iterator iter);
51      /**
52          Gets the beginning position of the list.
53          @return an iterator pointing to the beginning of the list
54      */
55      Iterator begin();
56      /**
57          Gets the past-the-end position of the list.
58          @return an iterator pointing past the end of the list
59      */
60      Iterator end();
61  private:
62      Node* first;
63      Node* last;
64  friend class Iterator
65  };
66
67  class Iterator
68  {
69  public:
70      /**
71          Constructs an iterator that does not point into any list.
72      */
73      Iterator();
74      /**
75          Looks up the value at a position.
76          @return the value of the node to which the iterator points
77      */
78      string get() const;
79      /**
80          Advances the iterator to the next node.
81      */
82      void next();
83      /**
84          Moves the iterator to the previous node.
85      */
86      void previous();
87      /**
88          Compares two iterators.
89          @param b the iterator to compare with this iterator
90          @return true if this iterator and b are equal
91      */
92      bool equals(Iterator b) const;
```

```
 93  private:
 94     Node* position;
 95     List* container;
 96  friend class List;
 97  };
 98
 99  Node::Node(string s)
100  {
101     data = s;
102     previous = NULL;
103     next = NULL;
104  }
105
106  List::List()
107  {
108     first = NULL;
109     last = NULL;
110  }
111
112  void List::push_back(string data)
113  {
114     Node* new_node = new Node(data);
115     if (last == NULL) // List is empty
116     {
117        first = new_node;
118        last = new_node;
119     }
120     else
121     {
122        new_node->previous = last;
123        last->next = new_node;
124        last = new_node;
125     }
126  }
127
128  void List::insert(Iterator iter, string s)
129  {
130     if (iter.position == NULL)
131     {
132        push_back(s);
133        return;
134     }
135
136     Node* after = iter.position;
137     Node* before = after->previous;
138     Node* new_node = new Node(s);
139     new_node->previous = before;
140     new_node->next = after;
141     after->previous = new_node;
142     if (before == NULL) // Insert at beginning
143        first = new_node;
144     else
145        before->next = new_node;
146  }
```

```
147
148    Iterator List::erase(Iterator iter)
149    {
150       assert(iter.position != NULL);
151       Node* remove = iter.position;
152       Node* before = remove->previous;
153       Node* after = remove->next;
154       if (remove == first)
155          first = after;
156       else
157          before->next = after;
158       if (remove == last)
159          last = before;
160       else
161          after->previous = before;
162       delete remove;
163       Iterator r;
164       r.position = after;
165       r.container = this;
166       return r;
167    }
168
169    Iterator List::begin()
170    {
171       Iterator iter;
172       iter.position = first;
173       iter.container = this;
174       return iter;
175    }
176
177    Iterator List::end()
178    {
179       Iterator iter;
180       iter.position = NULL;
181       iter.container = this;
182       return iter;
183    }
184
185    Iterator::Iterator()
186    {
187       position = NULL;
188       container = NULL;
189    }
190
191    string Iterator::get() const
192    {
193       assert(position != NULL);
194       return position->data;
195    }
196
197    void Iterator::next()
198    {
199       assert(position != NULL);
200       position = position->next;
```

```
201    }
202
203    void Iterator::previous()
204    {
205       assert(position != container->first);
206       if (position == NULL)
207          position = container->last;
208       else
209          position = position->previous;
210    }
211
212    bool Iterator::equals(Iterator b) const
213    {
214       return position == b.position;
215    }
216
217    int main()
218    {
219       List staff;
220
221       staff.push_back("Tom");
222       staff.push_back("Dick");
223       staff.push_back("Harry");
224       staff.push_back("Juliet");
225
226       // Add a value in fourth place
227
228       Iterator pos;
229       pos = staff.begin();
230       pos.next();
231       pos.next();
232       pos.next();
233
234       staff.insert(pos, "Romeo");
235
236       // Remove the value in second place
237
238       pos = staff.begin();
239       pos.next();
240
241       staff.erase(pos);
242
243       // Print all values
244
245       for (pos = staff.begin(); !pos.equals(staff.end()); pos.next())
246          cout << pos.get() << "\n";
247
248       return 0;
249    }
```

12.3 The Efficiency of List and Vector Operations

In this section, we will formally analyze how efficient the fundamental operations on linked lists and vectors are. We will consider these operations:

- Getting the kth element
- Adding and removing an element at a given position (an iterator or index)
- Adding and removing an element at the end

To get the kth element of a linked list, you start at the beginning of the list and advance the iterator k times. Suppose it takes an amount of time T to advance the iterator once. This quantity is independent of the iterator position—advancing an iterator does some checking and then it follows the next pointer. Therefore, advancing the iterator to the kth element consumes kT time. Therefore, locating the kth element is an $O(k)$ operation.

To analyze the situation for vectors, we need to peek under the hood and see how the vector class is implemented.

A vector maintains a pointer to an array of elements termed the *buffer*. An integer field, called the *capacity*, is the maximum number of elements that can be stored in the current buffer. The buffer is usually larger than is necessary to hold the current elements in the collection. The *size* is the number of elements actually being held by the container. Because vectors use zero-based indexing, the size can also be interpreted as the first free location in the array. Figure 8 shows the internals of a vector.

To access the kth element, we simply use the expression buffer[k]. This is done in a constant amount of time that is independent of k. We say that accessing a vector element takes $O(1)$ time.

Next, consider the task of adding an element in the middle of a linked list. We assume that we already have an iterator to the insertion location. It might have taken some time to get there, but we are now concerned with the cost of insertion after the position has been established.

As shown in Figure 6, you add an element by modifying the previous and next pointers of the new node and the surrounding nodes. This operation takes a constant number of steps, independent of the position. The same holds for removing an element. We conclude that list insertion and removal are $O(1)$ operations.

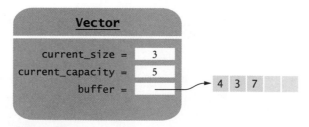

Figure 8   Internal Data Fields Maintained by Vector

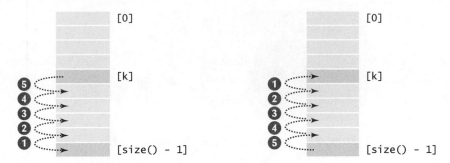

Figure 9 Inserting and Removing Vector Elements

For vectors, the situation is less rosy. To insert an element at position k, the elements with higher index values need to move (see Figure 9). How many elements are affected? For simplicity, we will assume that insertions happen at random locations. On average, each insertion moves $n / 2$ elements, where n is the size of the vector.

The same argument holds for removing an element. On average, $n / 2$ elements need to be move. Therefore, we say that vector insertion and removal are $O(n)$ operations.

There is one situation where adding an element to a vector isn't so costly: when the insertion happens at the end. The push_back member function carries out that operation.

If the size of the vector is less than the capacity, the new element is simply moved into place and the size is incremented, as shown in Figure 10. This is an $O(1)$ operation.

If, however, the size is equal to the capacity, it means that no more space is available. In order to make new space, a new and larger buffer is allocated. This new buffer is typically twice the size of the current buffer. (See Figure 11.) The existing elements are then copied into the new buffer, the old buffer is deleted, and insertion takes place as before. Reallocation is an $O(n)$ operation since all elements need to be copied to the new buffer.

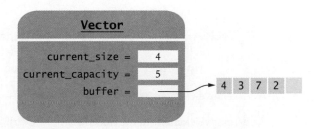

Figure 10 Vector After push_back

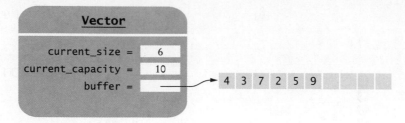

Figure 11   Vector After a Buffer Reallocation

If we carefully analyze the total cost of a sequence of push_back operations, it turns out that these reallocations are not as expensive as they first appear. The key observation is that reallocation does not happen very often. Suppose we start with a vector of capacity 10 and double the size with each reallocation. We must reallocate when the buffer reaches sizes 10, 20, 40, 80, 160, 320, 640, 1280, and so on.

Let us assume that one insertion without reallocation takes time T_1 and that reallocation of k elements takes time $k\,T_2$. What is the cost of 1280 push_back operations? Of course, we pay $1280 \cdot T_1$ for the insertions. The reallocation cost is

$$10T_2 + 20T_2 + 40T_2 + \cdots + 1280T_2 = (1 + 2 + 4 + \cdots + 128) \cdot 10 \cdot T_2$$
$$= 255 \cdot 10 \cdot T_2$$
$$< 256 \cdot 10 \cdot T_2$$
$$= 1280 \cdot 2 \cdot T_2$$

Therefore, the total cost is a bit less than

$$1280 \cdot (T_1 + 2T_2)$$

In general, the total cost of n push_back operations is less than $n \cdot (T_1 + 2T_2)$. Since the second factor is a constant, we conclude that n push_back operations take $O(n)$ time.

We know that it isn't quite true that an individual push_back operation takes $O(1)$ time. After all, occasionally a push_back is unlucky and must reallocate the buffer. But if the cost of that reallocation is distributed over the preceding push_back operations, then the surcharge for each of them is still a constant amount. We say that

Table 1 **Execution Times for Container Operations**		
Operation	**Vector**	**Linked List**
Add/remove element at end	$O(1)+$	$O(1)$
Add/remove element in the middle	$O(n)$	$O(1)$
Get kth element	$O(1)$	$O(k)$

push_back takes *amortized* $O(1)$ time, which is written as $O(1)+$. (Accountants say that a cost is amortized when it is distributed over multiple periods.)

Finally, we note that the push_back operation for a linked list takes $O(1)$ time, provided that the linked list implementation maintains a pointer to the last element of the list. Table 1 summarizes the execution times that we discussed in this section.

12.4 Queues and Stacks

In this section, you will consider two common data types that allow insertion and removal of items at the ends only, not in the middle.

> A queue is a container of items with "first in, first out" retrieval.

A *queue* lets you add items to one end of the queue (the *back*) and remove them from the other end of the queue (the *front*). To visualize a queue, simply think of people lining up (see Figure 12). People join the back of the queue and wait until they have reached the front of the queue. Queues store items in a *first in, first out* or *FIFO* fashion. Items are removed in the same order in which they have been added.

There are many uses of queues in computer science. For example, consider a printer that receives requests to print documents from multiple sources, either several computers or just several applications that print at the same time on one computer. If each of the applications sends printing data to the printer at the same time, then the printouts will be garbled. Instead, each application places all data that need to be sent to the printer into a file and inserts that file into the *print queue*. When

Figure 12 A Queue

the printer is done printing one file, it retrieves the next one from the queue. Therefore, print jobs are printed using the first in, first out rule, which is a fair arrangement for users of the shared printer.

The standard queue template implements a queue in C++. Following tradition, the addition and removal operations are called push and pop. The front member function yields the first element of the queue (that is, the next one to be removed). The back member function yields the element that was most recently added. You cannot access any other elements of the queue. Here is an example of using a queue:

```
queue<string> q;
q.push("Tom");
q.push("Dick");
q.push("Harry");
while (q.size() > 0)
{
    cout << q.front() << "\n";
    q.pop();
}
```

A stack is a container with "last in, first out" retrieval.

A *stack* lets you insert and remove elements at one end only, traditionally called the *top* of the stack. To visualize a stack, think of a stack of books (see Figure 13).

New items can be added to the top of the stack. Items are removed from the top of the stack as well. Therefore, they are removed in the order that is opposite from the order in which they have been added, also called *last in, first out* or *LIFO* order. For example, if you insert strings "Tom", "Dick", and "Harry" into a stack, and then remove them, then you will first see "Harry", then "Dick", and finally "Tom".

To obtain a stack in the standard C++ library, you use the stack template:

```
stack<string> s;
s.push("Tom");
s.push("Dick");
s.push("Harry");
while (s.size() > 0)
{
    cout << s.top() << "\n";
    s.pop();
}
```

Figure 13   A Stack of Books

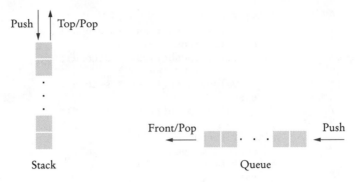

Figure 14 Stack and Queue Behavior

The pop member removes the top of the stack without returning a value. If you want to obtain the value before popping it, first call top, then pop.

Figure 14 contrasts the behaviors of the stack and queue data types. (ch12/fifolifo.cpp uses them in a sample program.)

A good example of the use of stack operations is a program that simulates the execution of a *Reverse Polish Notation* (RPN, or *postfix*) calculator. In RPN notation arguments are written before operators, so that an expression such as 3 + 4 * 7 would be written as 3 4 7 * +. This makes calculating the results easy. As each number is read it is pushed on a stack. As each operator is read two values are popped from the stack, the appropriate operation is performed, and the result is pushed back on the stack. The following program illustrates this technique. In addition to numbers and the four binary operators, it adds two one-character commands; the command p will print the current top of the stack, and the command q will halt the program.

ch12/calc.cpp

```cpp
1   #include <stack>
2   #include <iostream>
3   #include <cstdlib>
4
5   using namespace std;
6
7   int main()
8   {
9      stack<int> values;
10     string input;
11
12     while (cin >> input)
13     {
14        if (input == "+" || input == "-" || input == "*" || input == "/")
15        {
16           int second = values.top();
17           values.pop();
18           int first = values.top();
19           values.pop();
```

```
20              if (input == "+")
21                  values.push(first + second);
22              else if (input == "-")
23                  values.push(first - second);
24              else if (input == "*")
25                  values.push(first * second);
26              else
27                  values.push(first / second);
28          }
29          else if (input == "p")
30              cout << values.top() << "\n";
31          else if (input == "q")
32              return 0;
33          else // Convert input to integer
34              values.push(atoi(input.c_str()));
35      }
36  }
```

Program Run

```
1 2 4 * + p
9
3 - p
6
q
```

RANDOM FACT 12.1

Polish Notation

When you write arithmetic expressions you are used to operators with different levels of precedence that appear between the operands, except when parentheses are used to specify a different ordering. That is, an expression such as $3 + (4 - 2) \times 7$ is evaluated by first subtracting the 2 from the 4, then multiplying the result by 7, and finally adding the 3. Notice how the sequence of operations jumps around instead of being analyzed in a strict left to right or right to left order.

In the 1920s a Polish mathematician, Jan Łukasiewicz, noticed that if you wrote the operators first, before the operands, the need for both parentheses and precedence was eliminated and expressions could be read easily from left to right [1]. In Łukasiewicz's notation the expression would be written as $+ 3 \times - 4\ 2$. Table 2 shows some other examples.

Evaluating an expression in Łukasiewicz's form is a simple recursive algorithm. Examine the next term; if it is a constant, then that is your result; if it is a binary operator, then recursively examine the following two expressions, and produce their result. The scheme was termed Polish Notation in Łukasiewicz's honor (although one can argue it should be called Łukasiewicz Notation). Of course, an entrenched notation is not easily displaced, even when it has distinct disadvantages, and Łukasiewicz's discovery did not cause much of a stir for about 50 years.

In the 1950s, Australian computer scientist Charles Hamblin noted that an even better scheme would be to have the operators *follow* the operands [2]. This was termed *Reverse*

	Table 2	
Standard Notation	**Łukasiewicz Notation**	**RPN**
3 + 4	+ 3 4	3 4 +
3 + 4 × 5	+ 3 * 4 5	3 4 5 * +
3 × (4 + 5)	* 3 + 4 5	3 4 5 + *
(3 + 4) × 5	* + 3 4 5	3 4 + 5 *
3 + 4 + 5	+ + 3 4 5	3 4 + 5 +

Polish Notation, or RPN. The expression given would be written as 3 4 2 – 7× + in RPN. As you have seen, the evaluation of RPN is relatively simple if you have a stack. Each operand is pushed on the stack. Each operator pops the appropriate number of values from the stack, performs the operation, and pushes the result back onto the stack.

In 1972, Hewlett-Packard introduced the HP 35 calculator that used RPN. For example, to compute 3 + 4 * 5, you enter 3 4 5 * +. RPN calculators have no keys labeled with parentheses or an equals symbol. There is only a key labeled ENTER to push a number onto a stack. For that reason, Hewlett-Packard's marketing department used to refer to their product as "the calculators that have no equal". Indeed, the Hewlett-Packard calculators were a great advance over competing models that were unable to handle algebraic notation and left users with no other choice but to write intermediate results on paper.

Over time, developers of high quality calculators have adapted to the standard algebraic notation rather than forcing users to learn a new notation. However, those users who have made the effort of learning RPN tend to be fanatic proponents, and some Hewlett-Packard calculator models still support it.

CHAPTER SUMMARY

1. A linked list consists of a number of nodes, each of which has a pointer to the neighboring nodes.

2. Adding and removing elements in the middle of a linked list is efficient.

3. Visiting the elements of a linked list in sequential order is efficient, but random access is not.

4. You can inspect and edit a linked list with an iterator. An iterator points to a node in a linked list.

5. When implementing a linked list, we need to define list, node, and iterator classes.

6. A list object contains pointers to the first and last node.

7. An iterator contains a pointer to the current node, and to the list that contains it.

8. List nodes are allocated on the heap, using the `new` operator.

9. When a list node is erased, it is recycled to the heap with the `delete` operator.

10. Implementing operations that modify a linked list is challenging—you need to make sure that you update all node pointers correctly.

11. A queue is a container of items with "first in, first out" retrieval.

12. A stack is a container with "last in, first out" retrieval.

FURTHER READING

1. Jan Łukasiewicz, *Elementy Logiki Matematyczny*, Warsaw 1929; English translation: *Elements of Mathematical Logic*, Pergamon Press, London, 1963.

2. Charles L. Hamblin, "Translation to and from Polish notation", *Computing Journal*, 5:210–213, 1962.

REVIEW EXERCISES

Exercise R12.1. If a list has *n* elements, how many legal positions are there for inserting a new element? For erasing an element?

Exercise R12.2. What happens if you keep advancing an iterator past the end of the list? Before the beginning of the list? What happens if you look up the value at an iterator that is past the end? Erase the past-the-end position? All these are illegal operations, of course. What does the list implementation of your compiler do in these cases?

Exercise R12.3. Write a function that prints all values in a linked list, starting from the end of the list.

Exercise R12.4. The following code edits a linked list consisting of three nodes.

Draw a diagram showing how they are linked together after the following code is executed.

```
Node* p1 = first->next;
Node* p2 = first;
while (p2->next != NULL) p2 = p2->next;
first->next = p2;
p2->next = p1;
p1->next = NULL;
p2->previous = first;
p1->previous = p2;
last = p1;
```

Exercise R12.5. Explain what the following code prints.

```
list<string> names;
list<string>::iterator p = names.begin();
names.insert(p, "Tom");
p = names.begin();
names.insert(p, "Dick");
p++;
names.insert(p, "Harry");
for (p = names.begin(); p != names.end(); p++)
    cout << *p << "\n";
```

Exercise R12.6. The insert procedure of Section 12.2 inserts a new element before the iterator position. To understand the updating of the nodes, draw before/after node diagrams for the following four scenarios.

a. The list is completely empty.

b. The list is not empty, and the iterator is at the beginning of the list.

c. The list is not empty, and the iterator is at the end of the list.

d. The list is not empty, and the iterator is in the middle of the list.

Exercise R12.7. What advantages do lists have over vectors? What disadvantages do they have?

Exercise R12.8. Suppose you needed to organize a collection of telephone numbers for a company division. There are currently about 6,000 employees, and you know that the phone switch can handle at most 10,000 phone numbers. You expect several hundred lookups against the collection every day. Would you use a vector or a linked list to store the information?

Exercise R12.9. Suppose you needed to keep a collection of appointments. Would you use a linked list or a vector of Appointment objects?

Exercise R12.10. Suppose you write a program that models a card deck. Cards are taken from the top of the deck and given out to players. As cards are returned to the deck, they are placed on the bottom of the deck. Would you store the cards in a stack or a queue?

Exercise R12.11. Consider the efficiency of locating the kth element in a linked list of length n. If $k > n / 2$, it is more efficient to start at the end of the list and moving the iterator to the previous element. Why doesn't this increase in efficiency improve the big-Oh estimate of random access in a linked list?

Exercise R12.12. Explain why inserting an element into the middle of a list is faster than inserting an element into the middle of a vector.

Exercise R12.13. Explain why the push_back operation with a vector is usually constant time, but occasionally much slower.

Exercise R12.14. Suppose a vector implementation were to add 10 elements at each relocation instead of doubling the capacity. Show that the push_back operation no longer has amortized constant time.

Exercise R12.15. Write each of the following expressions in both Polish Notation and Reverse Polish Notation.

   a. $3 + 4$
   b. $1 \times 2 + 3$
   c. $1 \times (2 + 3)$
   d. $(2 - 4) \times (3 + 4)$
   e. $1 + 2 + 3 + 4$

Exercise R12.16. Suppose the strings "A" through "Z" are pushed onto a stack. Then they are popped off the stack and pushed onto a second stack. Finally, they are popped off the second stack and printed. In which order are the strings printed?

Exercise R12.17. What are the efficiencies of the push and pop operations of a stack when it is implemented using a linked list? Explain your answer.

Exercise R12.18. What are the efficiencies of the push and pop operations of a stack when it is implemented using a vector? Explain your answer.

Exercise R12.19. What are the efficiencies of the push and pop operations of a queue when it is implemented using a linked list? Explain your answer.

Exercise R12.20. What are the efficiencies of the push and pop operations of a queue when it is implemented using a vector? Explain your answer.

Exercise R12.21. Consider the following algorithm for traversing a maze such as this one:

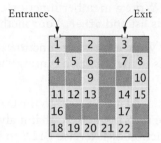

Make the cell at the entrance the current cell. Take the following actions, then repeat:
- If the current cell is adjacent to the exit, stop.
- Mark the current cell as visited.
- Add all unvisited neighbors to the north, east, south, and west to a queue.
- Remove the next element from the queue and make it the current cell.

In which order will the cells of the sample maze be visited?

Exercise R12.22. Repeat Exercise R12.21, using a stack instead of a queue.

PROGRAMMING EXERCISES

Exercise P12.1. Write a function

```
void downsize(list<string>& names)
```

that removes every second value from a linked list.

Exercise P12.2. Write a function `maximum` that computes the largest element in a `list<int>`.

Exercise P12.3. Write a function `sort` that sorts the elements of a linked list (without copying them into a vector).

Exercise P12.4. Write a function `merge` that merges two lists into one, alternating elements from each list until the end of one of the lists has been reached, then appending the remaining elements of the other list. For example, merging the lists containing A B C and D E F G H should yield the list A D B E C F G H.

Exercise P12.5. Provide a linked list of integers by modifying the `Node`, `List`, and `Iterator` classes of Section 12.2 to hold integers instead of strings.

Exercise P12.6. Write a member function `List::reverse()` that reverses the nodes in a list.

Exercise P12.7. Write a member function `List::push_front()` that adds a value to the beginning of a list.

Exercise P12.8. Write a member function `List::swap(List& other)` that swaps the elements of this list and `other`. Your method should work in $O(1)$ time.

Exercise P12.9. Write a member function `List::get_size()` that computes the number of elements in the list, by counting the elements until the end of the list is reached.

Exercise P12.10. Add a `size` field to the `List` class. Modify the `insert` and `erase` functions to update the `size` field so that it always contains the correct size. Change the `get_size()` function of Exercise P12.9 to take advantage of this data field.

Exercise P12.11. Turn the linked list implementation into a *circular list*: Have the previous pointer of the first node point to the last node, and the `next` pointer of the last node point to the first node. Then remove the `last` pointer in the `List` class since the value can now be obtained as `first->previous`. Reimplement the member functions so that they have the same effect as before.

Exercise P12.12. Turn the linked list implementation into a *singly-linked list*: Drop the `previous` pointer of the nodes and the `previous` member function of the iterator. Reimplement the other member functions so that they have the same effect as before. *Hint:* In order to remove an element in constant time, iterators should store the predecessor of the current node.

Exercise P12.13. Modify the linked list implementation to use a *dummy node* for the past-the-end position whose data field is unused. A past-the-end iterator should point to the dummy node. Remove the `container` pointer in the iterator class. Reimplement the member functions so that they have the same effect as before.

Exercise P12.14. Write a class `Polynomial` that stores a polynomial such as

$$p(x) = 5x^{10} + 9x^7 - x - 10$$

as a linked list of terms. A term contains the coefficient and the power of x. For example, you would store $p(x)$ as

$$(5,10),(9,7),(-1,1),(-10,0)$$

Supply member functions to add, multiply, and print polynomials. Supply a constructor that makes a polynomial from a single term. For example, the polynomial p can be constructed as

```
Polynomial p(Term(-10, 0));
p.add(Polynomial(Term(-1, 1)));
p.add(Polynomial(Term(9, 7)));
p.add(Polynomial(Term(5, 10)));
```

Then compute $p(x) \times p(x)$.

```
Polynomial q = p.multiply(p);
q.print();
```

Exercise P12.15. Implement a Stack class, using a linked list of strings. Supply operations size, push, pop, and top, just like in the standard stack template.

Exercise P12.16. Implement a Queue class, using a linked list of strings. Supply operations size, push, pop, front, and back, just like in the standard queue template.

Exercise P12.17. Using a queue of vectors, implement a non-recursive variant of the merge sort algorithm as follows. Start by inserting the entire vector to be sorted. We assume its size is a power of 2. Keep removing vectors from the queue, splitting them into two vectors of equal size, and adding the smaller vectors back into the queue. Once you encounter vectors of size 1, change to the following behavior: Remove pairs of vectors from the queue, merge them into a single vector and add the result back into the queue. Stop when the queue has size 1.

Exercise P12.18. Use a stack to enumerate all permutations of a string without using recursion. Suppose you want to find all permutations of the string meat. Push the string +meat on the stack. Now repeat the following operations until the stack is empty.

- Pop off the top of the stack.
- If that string ends in a + (such as tame+), remove the + and print the string
- Otherwise, remove each letter in turn from the right of the +, insert it just before the +, and push the resulting string on the stack. For example, after popping e+mta, you push em+ta, et+ma, and ea+mt.

Chapter 13

Sets, Maps, and Priority Queues

CHAPTER GOALS

- To become familiar with the set, map, and priority queue data types

- To understand the implementation of binary search trees and heaps

- To learn about the efficiency of operations on tree structures

In this chapter, we continue our presentation of common data structures. You will learn how to use the set, map, and priority queue types that are provided in the C++ library. You will see how these data structures are implemented as tree-like structures, and how they trade off sequential ordering for fast element lookup.

CHAPTER CONTENTS

13.1 Sets

Vectors and linked lists have one characteristic in common: These data structures keep the elements in the same order in which you inserted them. However, in many applications, you don't really care about the order of the elements in a collection. You can then make a very useful tradeoff: Instead of keeping elements in order, you can find them quickly.

> A set is an unordered collection of distinct elements.

In mathematics and computer science, an unordered collection of distinct items is called a *set*. As a typical example, consider a print server: a computer that has access to multiple printers. The server may keep a collection of objects representing available printers (see Figure 1). The order of the objects doesn't really matter.

The fundamental operations on a set are:

• Adding an element
• Removing an element
• Finding an element
• Traversing all elements

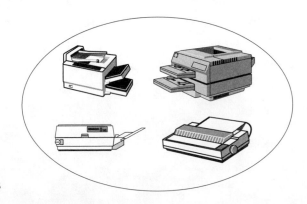

Figure 1
A Set of Printers

Sets don't have duplicates. Adding a duplicate of an element that is already present is ignored.

A set rejects duplicates. If an object is already in the set, an attempt to add it again is ignored. That's useful in many programming situations. For example, if we keep a set of available printers, each printer should occur at most once in the set. Thus, we will interpret the add and remove operations of sets just as we do in mathematics: Adding elements that are already in the set, as well as removing elements that are not in the set, are valid operations, but they do not change the set.

In C++, you use the set class to construct a set. As with vectors and lists, set requires a type parameter. For example, a set of strings is declared as follows:

```
set<string> names;
```

You use the insert and erase member functions to add and remove elements:

```
names.insert("Romeo");
names.insert("Juliet");
names.insert("Romeo"); // Has no effect: "Romeo" is already in the set
names.erase("Juliet");
names.erase("Juliet"); // Has no effect: "Juliet" is no longer in the set
```

To determine whether a value is in the set, use the count member function. It returns 1 if the value is in the set, 0 otherwise.

```
int c = names.count("Romeo"); // count returns 1
```

The standard C++ set class stores values in sorted order.

Finally, you can visit the elements of a set with an iterator. The iterator visits the elements in *sorted* order, not in the order in which you inserted them. For example, consider what happens when we continue our set example as follows.

```
names.insert("Tom");
names.insert("Dick");
names.insert("Harry");
set<string>::iterator pos;
for (pos = names.begin(); pos != names.end(); pos++)
   cout << *pos << " ";
```

The code prints the set elements in dictionary order:

```
Dick Harry Romeo Tom
```

A set cannot contain duplicates. A multiset (also called a bag) is an unordered container that can contain multiple copies of an element. An example is a grocery bag that contains some grocery items more than once (see Figure 2).

Figure 2
A Bag of Groceries

> A multiset (or bag) is similar to a set, but elements can occur multiple times.

In the C++ library, the `multiset` class implements this data type. You use a `multiset` in the same way as a set. When you insert an element multiple times, the element count reflects the number of insertions. Each call to erase decrements the element count until it reaches 0.

```
multiset<string> names;
names.insert("Romeo");
names.insert("Juliet");
names.insert("Romeo"); // Now names.count("Romeo") is 2
names.erase("Juliet"); // Now names.count("Juliet") is 0
names.erase("Juliet"); // Has no effect: "Juliet" is no longer in the bag
```

A good illustration of the use of sets is a program to check for misspelled words. Assume you have a file containing correctly spelled words (that is, a dictionary), and a second file you wish to check. The program simply reads the correctly spelled words into a set, then reads words from the second file and tests each in the set, printing the word if it is not found.

```
void spell_check(istream& dictionary, istream& text)
{
    set<string> words;
    string word;

    // First put all words from dictionary into set.
    while (dictionary >> word)
        words.insert(word);

    // Then read words from text
    while (text >> word)
        if (words.count(word) == 0)
            cout << "Misspelled word " << word << "\n";
}
```

ADVANCED TOPIC 13.1

Defining an Ordering for Container Elements

The set and multiset classes need to compare elements, and the map class needs to compare keys. By default, these classes use the < operator for comparisons.

Suppose that you want to build a set<Employee>. The compiler will complain that it does not know how to compare two employees.

To solve this problem you can overload the < operator for Employee objects:

```
bool operator<(Employee a, Employee b)
{
    return a.get_name() < b.get_name();
}
```

This < operator compares employees by name. You will learn more about overloading operators in Chapter 14. Chapter 20 shows additional ways of specifying the comparison.

13.2 Binary Search Trees

A set implementation is allowed to rearrange its elements in any way it chooses so that it can find elements quickly. Suppose a set implementation *sorts* its entries. Then it can use binary search to locate elements in $O(\log(n))$ steps, where n is the size of the set. There is just one wrinkle with this idea. We can't use an array to store the elements of a set, because insertion and removal in an array is slow; an $O(n)$ operation.

In this section we will introduce the simplest of many tree data structures that computer scientists have invented to overcome that problem.

> A binary tree consists of nodes, each of which has at most two child nodes.

A linked list is a one-dimensional data structure. Every node has a pointer to the next node. You can imagine that all nodes are arranged in a line. In contrast, a *binary tree* is made of nodes with *two* node pointers, called the *left* and *right children*. You should visualize it as a tree, except that it is traditional to draw the tree upside down, like a family tree or hierarchy chart (see Figure 3). In a binary tree, every node has at most two children; hence the name *binary*.

> All nodes in a binary search tree fulfill the property that the descendants to the left have smaller data values than the node data value, and the descendants to the right have larger data values.

Finally, a *binary search tree* is constructed to have the following important property:

- The data values of *all* descendants to the left of *any* node are less than the data value stored in that node, and *all* descendants to the right have greater data values.

The tree in Figure 3 has this property. To verify the binary search property, you must check each node. Consider the node "Juliet". All descendants to the left have data before "Juliet". All descendants on

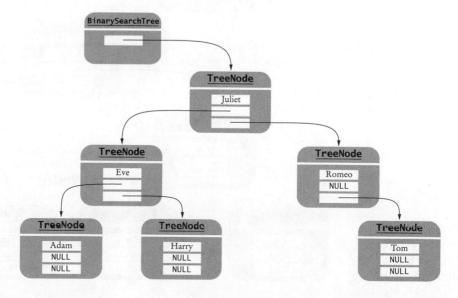

Figure 3
A Binary Search Tree

the right have data after "Juliet". Move on to "Eve". There is a child to the left, with data "Adam" before "Eve", and a single child to the right, with data "Harry" after "Eve". Check the remaining nodes in the same way.

Figure 4 shows a binary tree that is not a binary search tree. Look carefully—the root node passes the test, but its two children do not.

Let us implement these tree classes. Just as you needed classes for lists and their nodes, you need one class for the tree, containing a pointer to the *root node,* and a separate class for the nodes. Each node contains two pointers (to the left and right child nodes) and a data field. At the fringes of the tree, one or two of the child pointers are NULL.

```
class TreeNode
{
   ...
private:
   string data;
   TreeNode* left;
   TreeNode* right;
friend class BinarySearchTree;
};

class BinarySearchTree
{
   ...
private:
   TreeNode* root;
};
```

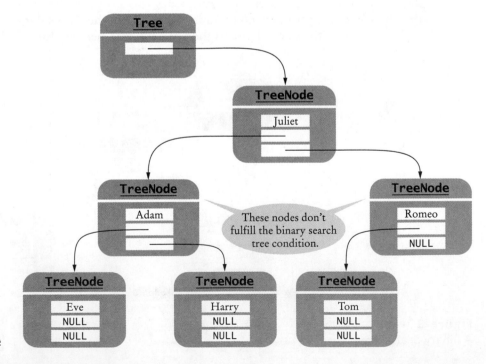

Figure 4
A Binary Tree
That Is Not a
Binary Search Tree

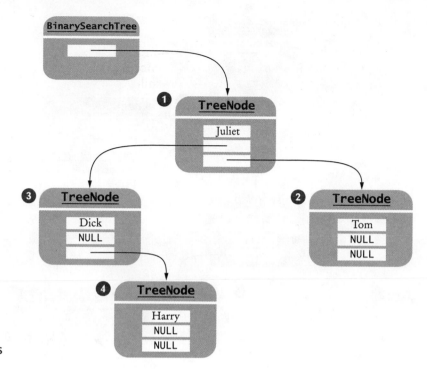

Figure 5
Binary Search Tree
After Four Insertions

To insert data into the tree, use the following algorithm:

• If you encounter a non-NULL node, look at its data value. If the data value of that node is larger than the one you want to insert, continue the process with the left child. If the existing data value is smaller, continue the process with the right child.

• If you encounter a NULL node, replace it with the new node.

For example, consider the tree in Figure 5. It is the result of the following statements:

```
BinarySearchTree tree;
tree.add("Juliet");   ❶
tree.add("Tom");      ❷
tree.add("Dick");     ❸
tree.add("Harry");    ❹
```

We want to insert a new element Romeo into it.

```
tree.add("Romeo");    ❺
```

Start with the root, Juliet. Romeo comes after Juliet, so you move to the right subtree. You encounter the node Tom. Romeo comes before Tom, so you move to the left subtree. But there is no left subtree. Hence, you insert a new Romeo node as the left child of Tom (see Figure 6).

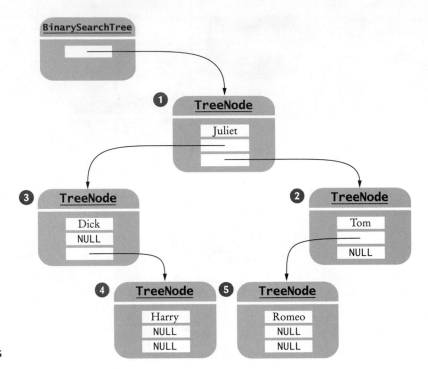

Figure 6
Binary Search Tree
After Five Insertions

You should convince yourself that the resulting tree is still a binary search tree. When Romeo is inserted, it must end up as a right descendant of Juliet—that is what the binary search tree condition means for the root node Juliet. The root node doesn't care where in the right subtree the new node ends up. Moving along to Tom, the right child of Juliet, all it cares about is that the new node Romeo ends up somewhere on its left. There is nothing to its left, so Romeo becomes the new left child, and the resulting tree is again a binary search tree.

Here is the code for the insert member function of the BinarySearchTree class:

```
void BinarySearchTree::insert(string data)
{
    TreeNode* new_node = new TreeNode;
    new_node->data = data;
    new_node->left = NULL;
    new_node->right = NULL;
    if (root == NULL) root = new_node;
    else root->insert_node(new_node);
}
```

> To insert a value in a binary search tree, recursively insert it into the left or right subtree.

If the tree is empty, simply set its root to the new node. Otherwise, you know that the new node must be inserted somewhere within the nodes, and you can ask the root node to perform the insertion. That node object calls the insert_node member function of the TreeNode class. That member function checks whether the new object is less than the object stored in the node. If so, the element is inserted in the left subtree. If it is larger than the object stored in the node, it is inserted in the right subtree:

```
void TreeNode::insert_node(TreeNode* new_node)
{
   if (new_node->data < data)
   {
      if (left == NULL) left = new_node;
      else left->insert_node(new_node);
   }
   else if (data < new_node->data)
   {
      if (right == NULL) right = new_node;
      else right->insert_node(new_node);
   }
}
```

Let us trace the calls to insert_node when inserting Romeo into the tree in Figure 5. The first call to insert_node is

```
root->insert_node(new_node)
```

Because root points to Juliet, you compare Juliet with Romeo and find that you must call

```
root->right->insert_node(new_node)
```

The node root->right contains Tom. Compare the data values again (Tom vs. Romeo) and find that you must now move to the left. Since root->right->left is NULL, set root->right->left to new_node, and the insertion is complete (see Figure 6).

We will now discuss the removal algorithm. Our task is to remove a node from the tree. Of course, we must first *find* the node to be removed. That is a simple matter, due to the characteristic property of a binary search tree. Compare the data value to be removed with the data value that is stored in the root node. If it is smaller, keep looking in the left subtree. Otherwise, keep looking in the right subtree.

Let us now assume that we have located the node that needs to be removed. First, let us consider an easy case, when that node has only one child (see Figure 7).

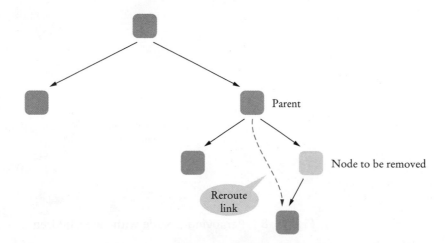

Figure 7
Removing a Node
with One Child

> When removing a node with only one child from a binary search tree, the child replaces the node to be removed.

> When removing a node with two children from a binary search tree, replace it with the smallest node of the right subtree.

To remove the node, simply modify the parent link that points to the node so that it points to the child instead.

If the node to be removed has no children at all, then the parent link is simply set to NULL.

The case in which the node to be removed has two children is more challenging. Rather than removing the node, it is easier to replace its data value with the next larger value in the tree. That replacement preserves the binary search tree property. (Alternatively, you could use the largest element of the left subtree—see Exercise P13.11).

To locate the next larger value, go to the right subtree and find its smallest data value. Keep following the left child links. Once you reach a node that has no left child, you have found the node containing the smallest data value of the subtree. Now remove that node—it is easily removed because it has at most one child. Then store its data value in the original node that was slated for removal. Figure 8 shows the details.

You will find the complete source code for the BinarySearchTree class at the end of the next section. Now that you have seen how to implement this complex data structure, you may well wonder whether it is any good. Like nodes in a list, tree nodes are allocated one at a time. No existing elements need to be moved when a new element is inserted in the tree; that is an advantage. How fast insertion is, how-

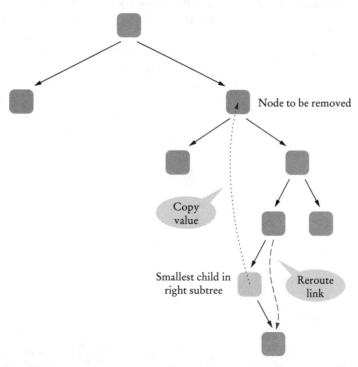

Figure 8   Removing a Node with Two Children

ever, depends on the shape of the tree. If the tree is *balanced*—that is, if each node has approximately as many descendants on the left as on the right—then insertion takes $O(\log(n))$ time, where n is the number of nodes in the tree. This is a consequence of the fact that about half of the nodes are eliminated in each step. On the other hand, if the tree happens to be *unbalanced*, then insertion can be slow—perhaps as slow as insertion into a linked list. (See Figure 9.)

> If a binary search tree is balanced, then inserting an element takes $O(\log(n))$ time.

If new elements are fairly random, the resulting tree is likely to be well balanced. However, if the incoming elements happen to be in sorted order already, then the resulting tree is completely unbalanced. Each new element is inserted at the end, and the entire tree must be traversed every time to find that end!

There are more sophisticated tree structures whose functions keep trees balanced at all times. In these tree structures, one can guarantee that finding, adding, and removing elements takes $O(\log(n))$ time. The standard C++ library uses *red-black trees*, a special form of balanced binary trees, to implement sets and maps.

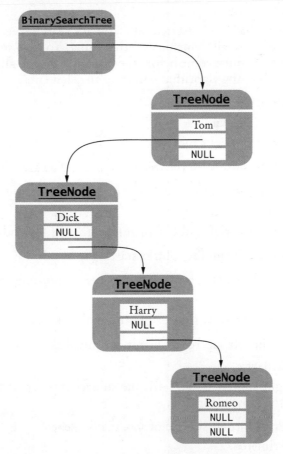

Figure 9   An Unbalanced Binary Search Tree

Table 1 summarizes the performance of the fundamental operations on vectors, lists, and balanced binary trees.

Table 1 Execution Times for Container Operations

Operation	Vector	Linked List	Balanced Binary Tree
Add/remove element at end	$O(1)$	$O(1)$	N/A
Add/remove element in the middle	$O(n)$	$O(1)$	$O(\log(n))$
Get kth element	$O(1)$	$O(k)$	N/A
Find value	$O(n)$	$O(n)$	$O(\log(n))$

13.3 Tree Traversal

Once data has been inserted into a binary search tree, it turns out to be surprisingly simple to print all elements in sorted order. You *know* that all data in the left subtree of any node must come before the node and before all data in the right subtree. That is, the following algorithm will print the elements in sorted order:

1. Print the left subtree.
2. Print the data.
3. Print the right subtree.

Let's try this out with the tree in Figure 6. The algorithm tells us to

1. Print the left subtree of Juliet; that is, Dick and descendants.
2. Print Juliet.
3. Print the right subtree of Juliet; that is, Tom and descendants.

How do you print the subtree starting at Dick?

1. Print the left subtree of Dick. There is nothing to print.
2. Print Dick.
3. Print the right subtree of Dick, that is, Harry.

That is, the left subtree of Juliet is printed as

Dick Harry

The right subtree of Juliet is the subtree starting at Tom. How is it printed? Again, using the same algorithm:

1. Print the left subtree of Tom, that is, Romeo.
2. Print Tom.
3. Print the right subtree of Tom. There is nothing to print.

Thus, the right subtree of Juliet is printed as

    Romeo Tom

Now put it all together: the left subtree, Juliet, and the right subtree:

    Dick Harry Juliet Romeo Tom

The tree is printed in sorted order.

Let us implement the print member function. You need a worker function print_nodes of the TreeNode class:

```cpp
void TreeNode::print_nodes() const
{
   if (left != NULL)
      left->print_nodes();
   cout << data << "\n";
   if (right != NULL)
      right->print_nodes();
}
```

To print the entire tree, start this recursive printing process at the root, with the following member function of the BinarySearchTree class.

```cpp
void BinarySearchTree::print() const
{
   if (root != NULL)
      root->print_nodes();
}
```

> Tree traversal schemes include preorder traversal, inorder traversal, and postorder traversal.

This visitation scheme is called *inorder traversal*. There are two other traversal schemes, called *preorder traversal* and *postorder traversal*.

In preorder traversal,

- Visit the root
- Visit the left subtree
- Visit the right subtree

In postorder traversal,

- Visit the left subtree
- Visit the right subtree
- Visit the root

These two traversals will not print the tree in sorted order. However, they are important in other applications of binary trees.

Tree traversals differ from an iterator in an important way. An iterator lets you visit a node at a time, and you can stop the iteration whenever you like. The traversals, on the other hand, visit all elements.

It turns out to be a bit complex to implement an iterator that visits the elements of a binary tree. Just like a list iterator, a tree iterator contains a pointer to a node. The iteration starts at the leftmost leaf. It then moves to the parent node, then to the right child, then to the next unvisited parent's leftmost child, and so on, until it reaches the rightmost leaf. Exercise P13.12 and Exercise P13.13 discuss two methods for implementing such a tree iterator.

ch13/bintree.cpp

```cpp
1   #include <iostream>
2   #include <string>
3
4   using namespace std;
5
6   class TreeNode
7   {
8   public:
9      void insert_node(TreeNode* new_node);
10     void print_nodes() const;
11     bool find(string value) const;
12  private:
13     string data;
14     TreeNode* left;
15     TreeNode* right;
16  friend class BinarySearchTree;
17  };
18
19  class BinarySearchTree
20  {
21  public:
22     BinarySearchTree();
23     void insert(string data);
24     void erase(string data);
25     int count(string data) const;
26     void print() const;
27  private:
28     TreeNode* root;
29  };
30
31  BinarySearchTree::BinarySearchTree()
32  {
33     root = NULL;
34  }
35
36  void BinarySearchTree::print() const
37  {
38     if (root != NULL)
39        root->print_nodes();
40  }
41
42  void BinarySearchTree::insert(string data)
43  {
44     TreeNode* new_node = new TreeNode;
45     new_node->data = data;
46     new_node->left = NULL;
47     new_node->right = NULL;
48     if (root == NULL) root = new_node;
49     else root->insert_node(new_node);
50  }
51
52  void TreeNode::insert_node(TreeNode* new_node)
53  {
```

```
54        if (new_node->data < data)
55        {
56           if (left == NULL) left = new_node;
57           else left->insert_node(new_node);
58        }
59        else if (data < new_node->data)
60        {
61           if (right == NULL) right = new_node;
62           else right->insert_node(new_node);
63        }
64    }
65
66    int BinarySearchTree::count(string data) const
67    {
68        if (root == NULL) return 0;
69        else if (root->find(data)) return 1;
70        else return 0;
71    }
72
73    void BinarySearchTree::erase(string data)
74    {
75        // Find node to be removed
76
77        TreeNode* to_be_removed = root;
78        TreeNode* parent = NULL;
79        bool found = false;
80        while (!found && to_be_removed != NULL)
81        {
82           if (to_be_removed->data < data)
83           {
84              parent = to_be_removed;
85              to_be_removed = to_be_removed->right;
86           }
87           else if (data < to_be_removed->data)
88           {
89              parent = to_be_removed;
90              to_be_removed = to_be_removed->left;
91           }
92           else found = true;
93        }
94
95        if (!found) return;
96
97        // to_be_removed contains data
98
99        // If one of the children is empty, use the other
100
101       if (to_be_removed->left == NULL || to_be_removed->right == NULL)
102       {
103          TreeNode* new_child;
104          if (to_be_removed->left == NULL)
105             new_child = to_be_removed->right;
106          else
107             new_child = to_be_removed->left;
```

```
108        if (parent == NULL) // Found in root
109           root = new_child;
110        else if (parent->left == to_be_removed)
111           parent->left = new_child;
112        else
113           parent->right = new_child;
114        return;
115     }
116
117     // Neither subtree is empty
118
119     // Find smallest element of the right subtree
120
121     TreeNode* smallest_parent = to_be_removed;
122     TreeNode* smallest = to_be_removed->right;
123     while (smallest->left != NULL)
124     {
125        smallest_parent = smallest;
126        smallest = smallest->left;
127     }
128
129     // smallest contains smallest child in right subtree
130
131     // Move contents, unlink child
132     to_be_removed->data = smallest->data;
133     if (smallest_parent == to_be_removed)
134        smallest_parent->right = smallest->right;
135     else
136        smallest_parent->left = smallest->right;
137  }
138
139  bool TreeNode::find(string value) const
140  {
141     if (value < data)
142     {
143        if (left == NULL) return false;
144        else return left->find(value);
145     }
146     else if (data < value)
147     {
148        if (right == NULL) return false;
149        else return right->find(value);
150     }
151     else
152        return true;
153  }
154
155  void TreeNode::print_nodes() const
156  {
157     if (left != NULL)
158        left->print_nodes();
159     cout << data << "\n";
160     if (right != NULL)
161        right->print_nodes();
```

```
162  }
163
164  int main()
165  {
166     BinarySearchTree t;
167     t.insert("D");
168     t.insert("B");
169     t.insert("A");
170     t.insert("C");
171     t.insert("F");
172     t.insert("E");
173     t.insert("I");
174     t.insert("G");
175     t.insert("H");
176     t.insert("J");
177     t.erase("A");  // Removing leaf
178     t.erase("B");  // Removing element with one child
179     t.erase("F");  // Removing element with two children
180     t.erase("D");  // Removing root
181     t.print();
182     cout << t.count("E") << "\n";
183     cout << t.count("F") << "\n";
184     return 0;
185  }
```

13.4 Maps

A map keeps associations between key and value objects.

A map is a data type that keeps associations between *keys* and *values*. Every key in the map has a unique value, but a value may be associated with several keys. Figure 10 gives a typical example: a map that associates names with colors. This map might describe the favorite colors of various people.

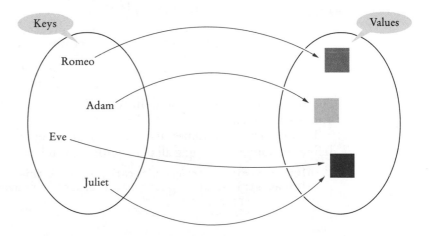

Figure 10
A Map

With the `map` class in the standard library, you use the `[]` operator to associate keys and values. Here is an example:

```
map<string, double> scores;
scores["Tom"] = 90;
scores["Dick"] = 86;
scores["Harry"] = 100;
```

You can read a score back with the same notation:

```
cout << "Tom's score: " << scores["Tom"];
```

To find out whether a key is present in the map, use the `find` member function. It yields an iterator that points to the entry with the given key, or past the end of the container if the key is not present.

The iterator of a `map<K, V>` with key type `K` and value type `V` yields elements of type `pair<K, V>`. The `pair` class is a simple class defined in the `<utility>` header that stores a pair of values. It has two public (!) data fields `first` and `second`.

Therefore, you have to go through this process to see if a key is present:

```
map<string, double>::iterator pos = scores.find("Harry"); // Call find
if (pos == scores.end()) // Check if there was a match
   cout << "No match for Harry";
else
   cout << "Harry's score: " << (*pos).second;
      // pos points to a pair<string, int>
```

As with pointers, you can write `pos->second` instead of `(*pos).second`.

The following loop shows how you iterate over the contents of a map:

```
map<string, double>::iterator pos;
for (pos = scores.begin(); pos != scores.end(); pos++)
{
   cout << "The score of " << pos->first << " is " <<
      pos->second << "\n";
}
```

> A multimap can have multiple values associated with the same key.

A multimap can have multiple values associated with the same key. Instead of using the `[]` operator, you insert and erase pairs. Here is an example:

```
multimap<string, string> friends;
friends.insert(make_pair("Tom", "Dick"));
   // Dick is a friend of Tom
friends.insert(make_pair("Tom", "Harry"));
   // Harry is also a friend of Tom
```

The `make_pair` function (also defined in the `<utility>` header) makes a `pair` object from its arguments.

To enumerate all values associated with a key, you obtain two iterators that define the range containing all pairs with a given key.

```
multimap<string, string>::iterator lower = friends.lower_bound("Tom");
multimap<string, string>::iterator upper = friends.upper_bound("Tom");
```

Then you visit all pairs in that range.

```
cout << "Tom's friends: ";
for (multimap<string, string>::iterator pos = lower; pos != upper; pos++)
   cout << pos->second << " ";
```

To erase a key/value association, locate it with an iterator, and then call the `erase` member function:

```
friends.erase(pos);
```

Maps and multimaps are implemented as binary trees whose nodes contain key/value pairs. The entries are ordered by increasing keys. You may need to define an `operator<` for the key type, as described in Advanced Topic 13.1.

A simple example to illustrate the use of maps and multimaps is a telephone database. The database associates names with telephone numbers. One member function inserts elements into the database. There are member functions to look up the number associated with a given name, and to carry out the inverse lookup of the names associated with a given number. Because two people can have the same number, we use a `multimap` for the inverse lookup. The member function `print_all` produces a listing of all entries. Because maps are stored in order based on their keys, this listing is naturally in alphabetical order according to name.

ch13/tele.cpp

```
1   #include <iostream>
2   #include <map>
3   #include <utility>
4   #include <string>
5   #include <vector>
6
7   using namespace std;
8
9   /**
10     TelephoneDirectory maintains a map of name/number pairs
11     and an inverse multimap of numbers and names.
12  */
13  class TelephoneDirectory
14  {
15  public:
16     /**
17        Adds a new name/number pair to database.
18        @param name the new name
19        @param number the new number
20     */
21     void add_entry(string name, int number);
22
23     /**
24        Finds the number associated with a name.
25        @param name the name being searched
26        @return the associated number, or zero
27        if not found in database
28     */
29     int find_entry(string name);
30
```

```
31     /**
32         Finds the names associated with a number.
33         @param number the number being searched
34         @return the associated names
35     */
36     vector<string> find_entries(int number);
37
38     /**
39         Prints all entries.
40     */
41     void print_all();
42  private:
43     map<string, int> database;
44     multimap<int, string> inverse_database;
45  };
46
47  void TelephoneDirectory::add_entry(string name, int number)
48  {
49     database[name] = number;
50     inverse_database.insert(make_pair(number, name));
51  }
52
53  int TelephoneDirectory::find_entry(string name)
54  {
55     map<string, int>::iterator p = database.find(name);
56     if (p == database.end())
57        return 0; // Not found
58     else
59        return p->second;
60  }
61
62  vector<string> TelephoneDirectory::find_entries(int number)
63  {
64     multimap<int, string>::iterator lower
65        = inverse_database.lower_bound(number);
66     multimap<int, string>::iterator upper
67        = inverse_database.upper_bound(number);
68     vector<string> result;
69
70     for (multimap<int, string>::iterator pos = lower;
71          pos != upper; pos++)
72        result.push_back(pos->second);
73     return result;
74  }
75
76  void TelephoneDirectory::print_all()
77  {
78     for (map<string, int>::iterator pos = database.begin();
79          pos != database.end(); pos++)
80     {
81        cout << pos->first << ": " << pos->second << "\n";
82     }
83  }
84
```

```
85  int main()
86  {
87      TelephoneDirectory data;
88      data.add_entry("Fred", 7235591);
89      data.add_entry("Mary", 3841212);
90      data.add_entry("Sarah", 3841212);
91      cout << "Number for Fred: " << data.find_entry("Fred") << "\n";
92      vector<string> names = data.find_entries(3841212);
93      cout << "Names for 3841212: ";
94      for (int i = 0; i < names.size(); i++)
95          cout << names[i] << " ";
96      cout << "\n";
97      cout << "All names and numbers:\n";
98      data.print_all();
99      return 0;
100 }
```

Program Run

```
Number for Fred: 7235591
Names for 3841212: Mary Sarah
All names and numbers:
Fred: 7235591
Mary: 3841212
Sarah: 3841212
```

ADVANCED TOPIC 13.2

Constant Iterators

If you carefully look at the source code of the preceding example, you will notice that the member functions for finding and printing dictionary entries were not marked as const. If you properly implement them as constant member functions, the compiler will complain that the iterators are not constant. That is a legitimate problem since you can modify a container through an iterator.

Each iterator type has a companion type for a constant iterator, similar to a constant pointer. Here is a const-correct implementation of the find_entry function:

```
int TelephoneDirectory::find_entry(string name) const
{
    map<string, int>::const_iterator p = database.find(name);
    if (p == database.end())
        return 0; // Not found
    else
        return p->second;
}
```

We will discuss iterators in more detail in Chapter 20.

13.5 Priority Queues

> A priority queue is a collection organized so as to permit fast access to and removal of the largest element.

The final container we will examine is the priority queue. A *priority queue* is a container optimized for one special task; quickly locating the element with highest priority. Prioritization is a weaker condition than ordering. In a priority queue the order of the remaining elements is irrelevant, it is only the highest priority element that is important.

Consider this example, where a priority queue contains strings denoting tasks:

```
priority_queue<string> tasks;
tasks.push("2 - Shampoo carpets");
tasks.push("9 - Fix overflowing sink");
tasks.push("5 - Order cleaning supplies");
```

The strings are formatted so that they start with a priority number. When it comes time to do work, we will want to retrieve and remove the task with the top priority:

```
string task = tasks.top(); // Returns "9 - Fix overflowing sink"
tasks.pop();
```

The term priority *queue* is actually a misnomer, because the priority queue does not have the "first in/first out" behavior as does a true queue. In fact the interface for the priority queue is more similar to a stack than to a queue. The basic three operations are push, pop and top. push places a new element into the collection. top returns the element with highest priority; pop removes this element.

One obvious implementation for a priority queue is a sorted set. Then it is an easy matter to locate and remove the largest element. However, another data structure, called a heap, is even more suitable for implementing priority queues. We will describe heaps in the next section.

Here is a simple program that demonstrates a priority queue. Instead of storing strings, we use a WorkOrder class. As described in Advanced Topic 13.1 on page 508, we supply an operator< function that compares work orders so that the priority queue can find the most important one.

ch13/pqueue.cpp

```
 1  #include <iostream>
 2  #include <queue>
 3
 4  using namespace std;
 5
 6  class WorkOrder
 7  {
 8  public:
 9     WorkOrder(int priority, string description);
10     int get_priority() const;
11     string get_description() const;
12  private:
13     int priority;
14     string description;
```

```
15  };
16
17  WorkOrder::WorkOrder(int pr, string descr)
18  {
19     priority = pr;
20     description = descr;
21  }
22
23  int WorkOrder::get_priority() const
24  {
25     return priority;
26  }
27
28  string WorkOrder::get_description() const
29  {
30     return description;
31  }
32
33  bool operator<(WorkOrder a, WorkOrder b)
34  {
35     return a.get_priority() < b.get_priority();
36  }
37
38  int main()
39  {
40     priority_queue<WorkOrder> tasks;
41     tasks.push(WorkOrder(2, "Shampoo carpets"));
42     tasks.push(WorkOrder(3, "Empty trash"));
43     tasks.push(WorkOrder(2, "Water plants"));
44     tasks.push(WorkOrder(1, "Remove pencil sharpener shavings"));
45     tasks.push(WorkOrder(4, "Replace light bulb"));
46     tasks.push(WorkOrder(9, "Fix overflowing sink"));
47     tasks.push(WorkOrder(1, "Clean coffee maker"));
48     tasks.push(WorkOrder(5, "Order cleaning supplies"));
49
50     while (tasks.size() > 0)
51     {
52        WorkOrder task = tasks.top();
53        tasks.pop();
54        cout << task.get_priority() << " - "
55           << task.get_description() << "\n";
56     }
57     return 0;
58  }
```

Program Run

```
9 - Fix overflowing sink
5 - Order cleaning supplies
4 - Replace light bulb
3 - Empty trash
2 - Water plants
2 - Shampoo carpets
1 - Remove pencil sharpener shavings
1 - Clean coffee maker
```

ADVANCED TOPIC 13.3

Discrete Event Simulations

A classic application of priority queues is in a type of simulation called a discrete event simulation. An event has a time at which it is scheduled to occur, and an action.

```
class Event
{
public:
   double get_time() const;
   virtual void act();
   ...
};
```

You form derived classes of the Event class for each event type. For example, an Arrival event can indicate the arrival of a customer, and a Departure event can indicate that the customer is departing. Each derived class overrides the act function. Typically, the act function of one event schedules additional events. For example, when one customer departs, another customer can be serviced. The act function of the Departure event generates a random time for the duration of the next customer's service and schedules that customer's departure.

The heart of the simulation is the event loop. This loop pulls the next event from the priority queue of waiting events. Two events are compared based on their time. The comparison is inverted, so that the element with highest priority is the one with the lowest scheduled time. Events can be inserted in any order, but are removed in sequence based on their time. As each event is removed, the "system clock" advances to the event's time, and the virtual act function of the event is executed:

```
while (event_queue.size() > 0)
{
   Event* next_event = event_queue.top();
   current_time = next_event->get_time();
   next_event->act(); // Typically adds new events
   delete next_event;
}
```

We face a technical issue when defining the event queue. The event queue holds Event* pointers that point to instances of derived classes. Since pointers already have a < operator defined, we cannot define an operator< that compares Event* pointers by their timestamp. Instead, we define a function for this purpose:

```
bool event_less(const Event* e1, const Event* e2)
{
   return e1->get_time() > e2->get_time();
      // The earliest event should have the largest priority
}
```

We then tell the priority queue to use this comparison function:

```
priority_queue<Event*, vector<Event*>,
   bool (*)(const Event*, const Event*)> event_queue(event_less);
```

Chapter 20 will demystify this declaration.

Exercise P13.15 asks you to simulate customers in a bank. Such simulations are important in practice because they give valuable information to business managers. For example, suppose you expect 60 customers per hour, each of whom needs to see a teller for an average of 5 minutes. Hiring 5 tellers should be enough to service all customers, but if you run the simulation, you may find that the average customer has to wait in line about 10 minutes. By running simulations, you can determine tradeoffs between unhappy customers and idle tellers.

13.6 Heaps

> A heap is an almost complete tree in which the values of all nodes are at least as large as those of their descendants.

A *heap* (or, for greater clarity, *max-heap*) is a binary tree with two special properties.

1. A heap is *almost complete*: all nodes are filled in, except the last level may have some nodes missing toward the right (see Figure 11).
2. The tree fulfills the *heap property:* all nodes store values that are at least as large as the values stored in their descendants (see Figure 12).

It is easy to see that the heap property ensures that the largest element is stored in the root.

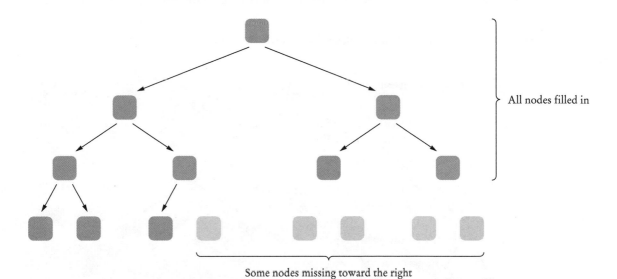

Figure 11   An Almost Complete Tree

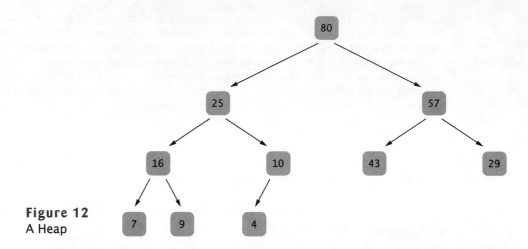

Figure 12
A Heap

A heap is superficially similar to a binary search tree, but there are two important differences.

1. The shape of a heap is very regular. Binary search trees can have arbitrary shapes.
2. In a heap, the left and right subtrees both store elements that are smaller than the root element. In contrast, in a binary search tree, smaller elements are stored in the left subtree and larger elements are stored in the right subtree.

Suppose we have a heap and want to insert a new element. Afterwards, the heap property should again be fulfilled. The following algorithm carries out the insertion (see Figure 13).

1. First, add a vacant slot to the end of the tree.

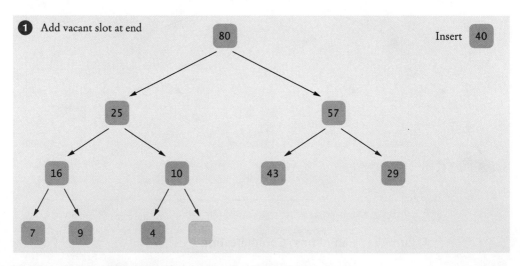

Figure 13 Inserting an Element into a Heap

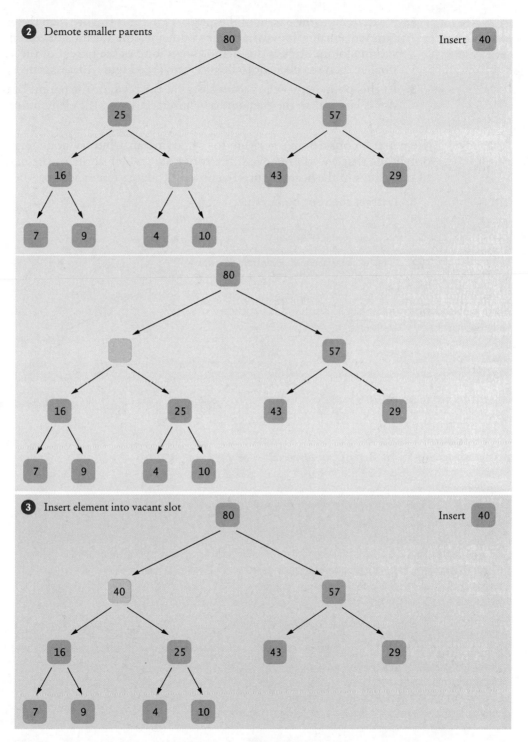

Figure 13 Inserting an Element into a Heap, continued

2. Next, demote the parent of the empty slot if it is smaller than the element to be inserted. That is, move the parent value into the vacant slot, and move the vacant slot up. Repeat this demotion as long as the parent of the vacant slot is smaller than the element to be inserted. (See Figure 13 continued.)

3. At this point, either the vacant slot is at the root, or the parent of the vacant slot is larger than the element to be inserted. Insert the element into the vacant slot.

We will not consider an algorithm for removing an arbitrary node from a heap. The only node that we will remove is the root node, which contains the maximum of all of the values in the heap. Figure 14 shows the algorithm in action.

1. Extract the root node value.

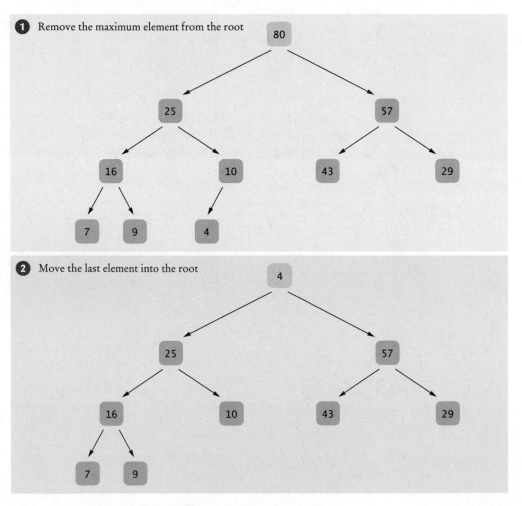

Figure 14 Removing the Maximum Value from a Heap

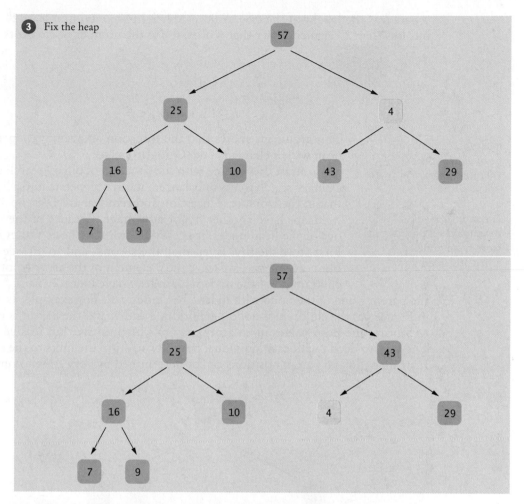

Figure 14 Removing the Maximum Value from a Heap, continued

2. Move the value of the last node of the heap into the root node, and remove the last node. Now the heap property may be violated for the root node, because one or both of its children may be larger.

3. Promote the larger child of the root node. (See Figure 14 continued.) Now the root node again fulfills the heap property. Repeat this process with the demoted child. That is, promote the larger of its children. Continue until the demoted child has no larger children. The heap property is now fulfilled again. This process is called "fixing the heap".

Inserting and removing heap elements is very efficient. The reason lies in the balanced shape of a heap. The insertion and removal operations visit at most h nodes, where h is the height of the tree. A heap of height h contains at least 2^{h-1} elements, but less than 2^h elements. In other words, if n is the number of elements, then

$$2^{h-1} \leq n < 2^h$$

or

$$h - 1 \leq \log_2(n) < h$$

Inserting or removing a heap element is an $O(\log(n))$ operation.

This argument shows that the insertion and removal operations in a heap with n elements take $O(\log(n))$ steps.

Contrast this finding with the situation of binary search trees. When a binary search tree is unbalanced, it can degenerate into a linked list, so that in the worst case insertion and removal are $O(n)$ operations.

The regular layout of a heap makes it possible to store heap nodes efficiently in an array.

Heaps have another major advantage. Because of the regular layout of the heap nodes, it is easy to store the node values in an array. First store the first layer, then the second, and so on (see Figure 15). For convenience, we leave the 0 element of the array empty. Then the child nodes of the node with index i have index $2 \cdot i$ and $2 \cdot i + 1$, and the parent node of the node with index i has index $i/2$. For example, as you can see in Figure 15, the children of node 4 are nodes 8 and 9, and the parent is node 2.

Storing the heap values in an array may not be intuitive, but it is very efficient. There is no need to allocate individual nodes or to store the links to the child nodes. Instead, child and parent positions can be determined by very simple computations.

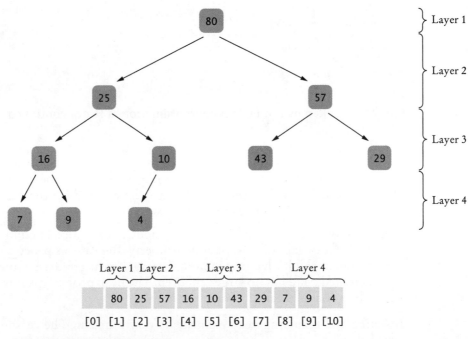

Figure 15 Storing a Heap in an Array

The program at the end of this section contains an implementation of a heap of integers. Using templates, it is easy to extend the class to a heap of any ordered type. (See Chapter 16 for information about templates.)

ch13/heap.cpp

```
1   #include <iostream>
2   #include <vector>
3
4   using namespace std;
5
6   /**
7       This class implements a heap.
8   */
9   class Heap
10  {
11  public:
12     /**
13         Constructs an empty heap.
14     */
15     Heap();
16
17     /**
18         Adds a new element to this heap.
19         @param new_element the element to add
20     */
21     void push(int new_element);
22
23     /**
24         Gets the maximum element stored in this heap.
25         @return the maximum element
26     */
27     int top() const;
28
29     /**
30         Removes the maximum element from this heap.
31     */
32     void pop();
33
34     /**
35         Returns the number of elements in this heap.
36     */
37     int size() const;
38  private:
39     /**
40         Turns the tree back into a heap, provided only the root
41         node violates the heap condition.
42     */
43     void fix_heap();
44
45     /**
46         Returns the index of the left child.
```

```
47            @param index  the index of a node in this heap
48            @return  the index of the left child of the given node
49        */
50        int get_left_child_index(int index);
51
52        /**
53            Returns the index of the right child.
54            @param index  the index of a node in this heap
55            @return  the index of the right child of the given node
56        */
57        int get_right_child_index(int index);
58
59        /**
60            Returns the index of the parent.
61            @param index  the index of a node in this heap
62            @return  the index of the parent of the given node
63        */
64        int get_parent_index(int index);
65
66        /**
67            Returns the value of the left child.
68            @param index  the index of a node in this heap
69            @return  the value of the left child of the given node
70        */
71        int get_left_child(int index);
72
73        /**
74            Returns the value of the right child.
75            @param index  the index of a node in this heap
76            @return  the value of the right child of the given node
77        */
78        int get_right_child(int index);
79
80        /**
81            Returns the value of the parent.
82            @param index  the index of a node in this heap
83            @return  the value of the parent of the given node
84        */
85        int get_parent(int index);
86
87        vector<int> elements;
88    };
89
90    Heap::Heap()
91    {
92        elements.push_back(0);
93    }
94
95    void Heap::push(int new_element)
96    {
97        // Add a new leaf
98        elements.push_back(0);
99        int index = elements.size() - 1;
100
```

```
101        // Demote parents that are smaller than the new element
102        while (index > 1
103            && get_parent(index) < new_element)
104        {
105            elements[index] = get_parent(index);
106            index = get_parent_index(index);
107        }
108
109        // Store the new element into the vacant slot
110        elements[index] = new_element;
111    }
112
113    int Heap::top() const
114    {
115        return elements[1];
116    }
117
118    void Heap::pop()
119    {
120        // Remove last element
121        int last_index = elements.size() - 1;
122        int last = elements[last_index];
123        elements.pop_back();
124
125        if (last_index > 1)
126        {
127            elements[1] = last;
128            fix_heap();
129        }
130    }
131
132    int Heap::size() const
133    [
134        return elements.size() - 1;
135    }
136
137    void Heap::fix_heap()
138    {
139        int root = elements[1];
140
141        int last_index = elements.size() - 1;
142        // Promote children of removed root while they are larger than last
143
144        int index = 1;
145        bool more = true;
146        while (more)
147        {
148            int child_index = get_left_child_index(index);
149            if (child_index <= last_index)
150            {
151                // Get larger child
152
153                // Get left child first
154                int child = get_left_child(index);
155
```

```
156              // Use right child instead if it is larger
157              if (get_right_child_index(index) <= last_index
158                 && get_right_child(index) > child)
159              {
160                 child_index = get_right_child_index(index);
161                 child = get_right_child(index);
162              }
163
164              // Check if smaller child is larger than root
165              if (child > root)
166              {
167                 // Promote child
168                 elements[index] = child;
169                 index = child_index;
170              }
171              else
172              {
173                 // Root is larger than both children
174                 more = false;
175              }
176           }
177           else
178           {
179              // No children
180              more = false;
181           }
182        }
183
184        // Store root element in vacant slot
185        elements[index] = root;
186  }
187
188  int Heap::get_left_child_index(int index)
189  {
190     return 2 * index;
191  }
192
193  int Heap::get_right_child_index(int index)
194  {
195     return 2 * index + 1;
196  }
197
198  int Heap::get_parent_index(int index)
199  {
200     return index / 2;
201  }
202
203  int Heap::get_left_child(int index)
204  {
205     return elements[2 * index];
206  }
207
```

```
208   int Heap::get_right_child(int index)
209   {
210       return elements[2 * index + 1];
211   }
212
213   int Heap::get_parent(int index)
214   {
215       return elements[index / 2];
216   }
217
218   int main()
219   {
220       Heap tasks;
221       tasks.push(2);
222       tasks.push(3);
223       tasks.push(2);
224       tasks.push(1);
225       tasks.push(4);
226       tasks.push(9);
227       tasks.push(1);
228       tasks.push(5);
229
230       while (tasks.size() > 0)
231       {
232           int task = tasks.top();
233           tasks.pop();
234           cout << task << "\n";
235       }
236       return 0;
237   }
```

Program Run

```
9
5
4
3
2
2
1
1
```

CHAPTER SUMMARY

1. A set is an unordered collection of distinct elements.

2. Sets don't have duplicates. Adding a duplicate of an element that is already present is ignored.

3. The standard C++ set class stores values in sorted order.

4. A multiset (or bag) is similar to a set, but elements can occur multiple times.

5. A binary tree consists of nodes, each of which has at most two child nodes.

6. All nodes in a binary search tree fulfill the property that the descendants to the left have smaller data values than the node data value, and the descendants to the right have larger data values.

7. To insert a value in a binary search tree, recursively insert it into the left or right subtree.

8. When removing a node with only one child from a binary search tree, the child replaces the node to be removed.

9. When removing a node with two children from a binary search tree, replace it with the smallest node of the right subtree.

10. If a binary search tree is balanced, then inserting an element takes $O(\log(n))$ time.

11. Tree traversal schemes include preorder traversal, inorder traversal, and post-order traversal.

12. A map keeps associations between key and value objects.

13. A multimap can have multiple values associated with the same key.

14. A priority queue is a collection organized so as to permit fast access to and removal of the largest element.

15. A heap is an almost complete tree in which the values of all nodes are at least as large as those of their descendants.

16. Inserting or removing a heap element is an $O(\log(n))$ operation.

17. The regular layout of a heap makes it possible to store heap nodes efficiently in an array.

REVIEW EXERCISES

Exercise R13.1. A school web site keeps a collection of web sites that are blocked at student computers. Should the program that checks for blocked sites use a vector, list, set, or map for storing the site addresses?

Exercise R13.2. A library wants to track which books are checked out to which patrons. Should they use a map or a multimap from books to patrons?

Exercise R13.3. A library wants to track which patrons have checked out which books. Should they use a map or a multimap from patrons to books?

Exercise R13.4. In an emergency, a case record is made for each incoming patient, describing the severity of the case. When doctors become available, they handle the most severe cases first. Should the case records be stored in a set, a map, or a priority queue?

Exercise R13.5. You keep a set of Point objects for a scientific experiment. (A Point has x and y coordinates.) Define a suitable operator< so that you can form a set<Point>.

Exercise R13.6. A set<T> can be implemented as a binary tree whose nodes store data of type T. How can you implement a multiset<T>?

Exercise R13.7. What is the difference between a binary tree and a binary search tree? Give examples of each.

Exercise R13.8. What is the difference between a balanced tree and an unbalanced tree? Give examples of each.

Exercise R13.9. The following elements are inserted into a binary search tree. Make a drawing that shows the resulting tree after each insertion.

```
Adam
Eve
Romeo
Juliet
Tom
Dick
Harry
```

Exercise R13.10. Insert the elements of Exercise R13.9 in opposite order. Then determine how the BinarySearchTree.print function prints out both the tree from Exercise R13.9 and this tree. Explain how the printouts are related.

Exercise R13.11. Consider the following tree. In which order are the nodes printed by the BinarySearchTree.print function?

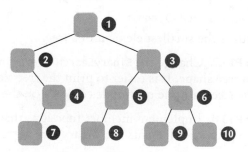

Exercise R13.12. How does a set achieve fast execution for insertions and removals?

Exercise R13.13. What properties of a binary tree make it a search tree? What properties make it a balanced tree?

Exercise R13.14. How is a map similar to a vector? How is it different?

Exercise R13.15. Why is a priority queue not, properly speaking, a queue?

Exercise R13.16. Prove that a heap of height h contains at least 2^{h-1} elements but less than 2^{h} elements.

Exercise R13.17. Suppose the heap nodes are stored in an array, starting with index 1. Prove that the child nodes of the heap node with index i have index $2 \cdot i$ and $2 \cdot i + 1$, and the parent heap node of the node with index i has index $i/2$.

PROGRAMMING EXERCISES

Exercise P13.1. Reimplement the Polynomial class of Exercise P12.14 by using a map<int, double> to store the coefficients.

Exercise P13.2. Write functions

```
set<int> set_union(set<int> a, set<int> b)
set<int> intersection(set<int> a, set<int> b)
```

that compute the set union and intersection of the sets a and b. (Don't name the first function union—that is a reserved word in C++.)

Exercise P13.3. Implement the *sieve of Eratosthenes*: a function for computing prime numbers, known to the ancient Greeks. Choose an integer n. This function will compute all prime numbers up to n. First insert all numbers from 1 to n into a set. Then erase all multiples of 2 (except 2); that is, 4, 6, 8, 10, 12, ... Erase all multiples of 3, that is, 6, 9, 12, 15, ... Go up to $\sqrt{n}$. The remaining numbers are all primes.

Exercise P13.4. Write a program that counts how often each word occurs in a text file. Use a multiset<string>.

Exercise P13.5. Repeat Exercise P13.4, but use a map<string, int>.

Exercise P13.6. Write a member function of the BinarySearchTree class

```
string smallest() const
```

that returns the smallest element of a tree.

Exercise P13.7. Change the BinarySearchTree.print member function to print the tree as a tree shape. It is easier to print the tree sideways. Extra credit if you instead print the tree with the root node centered on the top.

Exercise P13.8. Implement member functions that use preorder and postorder traversal to print the elements in a binary search tree.

Exercise P13.9. Implement a traversal function

```
void inorder(Action& a);
```

for inorder traversal of a binary search tree that carries out an action other than just printing the node data. The action should be supplied as a derived class of the class

```
class Action
{
public:
   virtual void act(string str) {}
};
```

Exercise P13.10. Use the `inorder` function of Exercise P13.9, and a suitable class derived from `Action`, to compute the sum of all lengths of the strings stored in a tree.

Exercise P13.11. In the `BinarySearchTree` class, modify the erase member function so that a node with two children is replaced by the largest child of the left subtree.

Exercise P13.12. Add a pointer to the parent node to the `TreeNode` class. Modify the insert and erase functions to properly set those parent nodes. Then define a `Tree-Iterator` class that contains a pointer to a `TreeNode`. The tree's begin member function returns an iterator that points to the leftmost leaf. The iterator's get member function simply returns the data value of the node to which it points. Its next member function needs to find the next element in inorder traversal. If the current node has a right child, then go to the leftmost leaf of the right child. Otherwise keep moving up to the parent until the previously traversed node is a left child.

Exercise P13.13. Implement a tree iterator as described in the preceding exercise without modifying the `TreeNode` class. *Hint:* The iterator needs to keep a stack of parent nodes.

Exercise P13.14. This problem illustrates the use of a discrete event simulation, as described in Advanced Topic 13.3 on page 528. Imagine you are planning on opening a small hot dog stand. You need to determine how many stools your stand should have. Too few stools and you will lose customers; too many and your stand will look empty most of the time.

There are two types of events in this simulation. An arrival event signals the arrival of a customer. If seated, the customer stays a randomly generated amount of time then leaves. A departure event frees the seat the customer was occupying. Simulate a hotdog stand with three seats. To initialize the simulation a random number of arrival events are scheduled for the period of one hour. The output shows what time each customer arrives and whether they stay or leave. The following is the beginning of a typical run:

```
time 0.13 Customer is seated
time 0.14 Customer is seated
time 0.24 Customer is seated
time 0.29 Customer finishes eating, leaves
time 0.31 Customer is seated
time 0.38 Customer finishes eating, leaves
time 0.41 Customer is seated
time 0.42 Customer is unable to find a seat, leaves
time 0.48 Customer is unable to find a seat, leaves
time 0.63 Customer is unable to find a seat, leaves
time 0.64 Customer is unable to find a seat, leaves
time 0.68 Customer finishes eating, leaves
time 0.71 Customer is seated
```

Exercise P13.15. Simulate the processing of customers at a bank with five tellers. Customers arrive on average once per minute, and they need an average of five minutes to complete a transaction. Customers enter a queue to wait for the next available teller.

Use two kinds of events. An arrival event adds the customer to the next free teller or the queue and schedules the next arrival event. When adding a customer to a free teller, also schedule a departure event. The departure event removes the customer from the teller and makes the teller service the next customer in the waiting queue, again scheduling a departure event.

For greater realism, use an exponential distribution for the time between arrivals and the transaction time. If m is the desired mean time and r a uniformly distributed random number between 0 and 1, then $-m \log(r)$ has an exponential distribution.

After each event, your program should print the bank layout, showing empty and occupied tellers and the waiting queue, like this:

```
c.cc.
```

if there is no queue, or

```
ccccc cccccccccccccccccc
```

if there is one. Simulate customer arrivals for 8 hours. At the end of the simulation, print the total number of customers served and the average time each customer spent in the bank. (Your Customer objects will need to track their arrival time.)

Exercise P13.16. In most banks, customers enter a single waiting queue, but most supermarkets have a separate queue for each cashier. Modify Exercise P13.15 so that each teller has a separate queue. An arriving customer picks the shortest queue. What is the effect on the average time spent in the bank?

Exercise P13.17. Modify the implementation of the Heap class so that the parent and child index positions are computed directly, without calling helper functions.

Exercise P13.18. Modify the implementation of the Heap class so that the 0 element of the array is not wasted.

Exercise P13.19. Modify the implementation of the Heap class so that it stores strings, not integers. Test your implementation with the tasks from the pqueue.cpp program.

14

Operator Overloading

- To learn about operator overloading
- To learn the various categories of operators, and their uses
- To learn how operator overloading is employed in the standard library
- To be able to implement overloaded operators in your own classes
- To learn how to avoid common errors in operator overloading

Operator overloading is both a powerful and error-prone aspect of programming in C++. Properly used, operators (such as + or <) can make a program intuitive and easy to understand. Improperly used, the same technique can confuse the reader and slow both understanding and execution. In this chapter you will learn how to define the meaning of operators when they are applied to objects. You will be introduced to the most common categories of operators. You will see how operators interact with conversions and the type system, and how operators are used in the standard library.

CHAPTER CONTENTS

14.1 Operator Overloading

The use of operators as a convenient shorthand notation predates computer science by several centuries. Because of this long acquaintance, most people find

```
a + b * c
```

much easier to grasp than

```
plus(a, times(b, c))
```

Minimalists insist that if you have a language that includes functions there is no need for operators because they serve much the same purpose. And there are languages (such as Lisp) that have only functions. But C++, like most computer languages, supports a rich set of operators for the simple reason that they make programs easier to read and understand.

You can define new meanings for C++ operators by defining functions whose name is operator followed by the operator symbol.

Where C++ is unusual is that it allows programmers to give new meanings to operators. Providing a new meaning to an operator is termed *operator overloading*. This ability is a powerful and sometimes subtle feature of the C++ language. An operator symbol may be easier to remember than a function name; for example, the use of the addition operator for string catenation is intuitive to many users, whereas they may not be able to remember whether the corresponding member function is named catenate, concatenate, append, combine, or something entirely different. (In the C++ string class it is append.) Defining an operator for a new data type may permit the reuse of an existing algorithm, such as one of the generic algorithms from the standard library that you will examine in Chapter 20. Finally, operators permit a more concise description of a task, without the clutter of parentheses associated with the function call syntax.

On the other hand, the fact that operators are concise can be a disadvantage. Because they provide so little context, the meaning attached to an operator may not be self evident. In this chapter we will present examples of both good and bad uses of operators.

The programmer is permitted to define new meanings for operators only if at least one argument has a class type. A programmer cannot, for example, change the meaning of the addition operator when it is used with integer arguments.

The language has a predefined set of operators, and the user is not allowed to create new ones. The set of valid operators that the user is allowed to overload is shown in Table 1.

In addition, the precedence and associativity among operators is fixed by the language and cannot be changed. A multiplication operator, for example, will always be performed prior to an addition operator in an expression in which they both occur, regardless of any new definitions for these two operators. Similarly, with the exception of the function call operator, the number of arguments required for each operator is fixed and cannot be altered. One cannot, for example, redefine the unary operator ! as a binary function. Operators and their precedence are listed in Appendix C.

Table 1 Overloadable Operators

+	-	*	/	%	^	&
|	~	!	=	<	>	+=
-=	*=	/=	%=	^=	&=	|=
<<	>>	>>=	<<=	==	!=	<=
>=	&&	||	++	--	->*	,
->	[]	()	new	new[]	delete	delete[]

14.1.1 Operator Functions

Operators in C++ can be overloaded in one of two ways. They can be defined as simple functions, separate from any class definition, or they can be defined as member functions within the body of a class definition. In the first form you overload an operator by defining a function whose name is operator followed by the operator symbol, as shown in Syntax 14.1. For example, suppose you want to define the *difference* between two Time objects as the number of seconds between them. The following operator- function lets you do that:

```
int operator-(const Time& a, const Time& b)
{
    return a.seconds_from(b);
}
```

Then you can simply use the - operator instead of calling seconds_from:

```
Time now;
Time morning(9, 0, 0);
int seconds_elapsed = now - morning;
```

Note that the operator- function is not a member function. It is a nonmember function with two parameters. The C++ language interprets the subtraction operator as a function call, as if the programmer had written

```
int seconds_elapsed = operator-(now, morning);
```

Can you use the + operator to *add* two times? Of course you can, simply by defining an operator+(const Time& a, const Time& b). But that doesn't mean you should. A Time object represents a *point in time*, not a duration. For example, 3 P.M. means "a particular time in the afternoon", which is quite different from "3 hours" or "15 hours". It does not make any sense to add two points in time. (For example, what should 3 P.M. + 1 P.M. be? 4 P.M.? How about 3 P.M. + 1 A.M.?)

SYNTAX 14.1 **Overloaded Operator Definition**

return_type operator*operator_symbol*(*parameters*)
{
   statements
}

Example:

```
int operator-(const Time& a, const Time& b)
{
    return a.seconds_from(b);
}
```

Purpose:

Supply the implementation of an overloaded operator.

However, it does make sense to add a number of seconds to a Time object, resulting in a new Time object. Here is an overloaded + operator for that task.

```
Time operator+(const Time& a, int sec)
{
   Time r = a;
   r.add_seconds(sec);
   return r;
}
```

For example:

```
Time now;
Time later = now + 60;   // 60 seconds later
```

Is this good programming practice? It depends. It is concise, and things should work well as long as everybody who will use the operator remembers that when an integer is added to a Time the units are seconds. But will they always remember? What if a programmer inadvertently thinks the integer refers to minutes? When using the function add_seconds the name makes this error unlikely. In the operator version, there is less context, and therefore less information to help the programmer remember. When using operators you need to carefully consider whether each use is appropriate and clear, and anticipate the possible sources of confusion.

14.1.2 Operator Member Functions

> Operators can be defined either as member or nonmember functions.

Instead of using a function, you could define the addition operator as a member function within the definition of the class Time. This would, however, require making a change to the original class definition.

```
class Time
{
   ...
   Time operator+(int sec) const;
};

Time Time::operator+(int sec) const
{
   Time r = *this;   // Copy the implicit parameter
   r.add_seconds(sec);
   return r;
}
```

Now when an addition operation is encountered involving a Time value and an integer, it is interpreted as a member function invocation of the left operand, passing as argument the value of the right operand. The statement

```
Time later = now + 60;   // 60 seconds later
```

becomes

```
Time later = now.operator+(60);
```

For this reason, even though you are implementing a binary operation, only one argument appears in the member function definition.

A few operators, such as the various forms of assignment, must be defined as member functions. For most operators, however, the programmer can choose to define it either as a nonmember or member function. Note that the syntax used to *invoke* the operator is the same whether it is defined as a nonmember function or a member function. There will be many examples of both throughout this chapter.

In deciding whether member or nonmember is preferable, there are two points to keep in mind.

- A nonmember function is normally not permitted access to the private portions of the class, whereas a member function is allowed such access. (The phrase "normally" is used because a friend function can override this restriction. You briefly encountered friend functions in Section 12.2.1, and will study the topic in more detail later in Chapter 18).

- Implicit conversions, say from integer or double to a user-defined type, will be performed for both right and left arguments if the operator is defined as a function, but only for the right argument if the operator is defined as a member function. You will see how conversions are defined in Section 14.8.

> Use a member function for an operator if you need access to private data.

> Use a nonmember function for an operator to allow type conversions for the left argument.

Thus, the member function form is preferable if the left argument is modified, as in assignment, or if the data fields to be manipulated are not easily accessible. Encapsulation is one of the primary concerns of a good object-oriented design, and should not be tossed away lightly. If an operator requires access to the internal state of a value, it should be made into a member function. On the other hand, the nonmember function version is preferable if the data fields being manipulated are easily accessible, if the left argument is not modified, or if conversions are permitted on both arguments. In many situations either form is acceptable.

SYNTAX 14.2 Overloaded Operator Member Function Definition

return_type ClassName::operator*operator_symbol*(*parameters*)
{
    statements
}

Example:

```
Time Time::operator+(int sec) const
{
    Time r = *this;
    r.add_seconds(sec);
    return r;
}
```

Purpose:

Supply the implementation of an overloaded operator member function.

14.2 Case Study: Fractional Numbers

Imagine you wish to implement a new data type that represents a fraction (a ratio of two integer values). Fractional numbers can be declared with both a numerator and denominator, or simply a numerator:

```
Fraction c; // Represents 0/1
Fraction b(7);  // Represents 7/1
Fraction a(3, 4);  // Represents 3/4
```

Constructors allow a Fraction to be formed with no arguments, one integer argument, or two integer arguments. In the first case the value is zero, in the second the denominator is assumed to be 1, and in the third case the Fraction is normalized to ensure that only the numerator can be negative and the value is in least common denominator form. (That is, a fraction such as 2/–4 would be converted into –1/2.) Part of the process of normalization is finding the greatest common divisor of two integer values. The algorithm to discover this value is discussed in Random Fact 14.1 on page 557.

You want fractions to act just like other numbers. That means you should be able to add and subtract fractional values, compare them to other fractions, perform input and output of fractions, and so on:

```
Fraction c(1, 2);
if (a < b)
   c = b - a;
else
   c = a - b;
cout << "Value is " << c << "\n";
```

Finally, you want to be able to mix fractions with integers:

```
c = a + 3;  // Should mean same as addition of 3/1
```

The Fraction data type is defined in the files fraction.h and fraction.cpp, and a test program is provided in fractiontest.cpp. We present the implementation here in its entirety, but will defer discussion of the implementation details to the following sections.

ch14/fraction.h

```
1  #ifndef FRACTION_H
2  #define FRACTION_H
3
4  #include <iostream>
5
6  using namespace std;
7
8  class Fraction
9  {
10 public:
11    /**
```

```
12              Constructs a fraction with numerator 0 and denominator 1.
13      */
14      Fraction();
15
16      /**
17              Constructs a fraction with numerator t and denominator 1.
18              @param t the numerator for the fraction
19      */
20      Fraction(int t);
21
22      /**
23              Constructs a fraction with given numerator and denominator.
24              @param t the initial numerator
25              @param b the initial denominator
26      */
27      Fraction(int t, int b);
28
29      /**
30              Returns the numerator.
31              @return the numerator value
32      */
33      int numerator() const;
34
35      /**
36              Returns the denominator.
37              @return the denominator value
38      */
39      int denominator() const;
40
41      /**
42              Updates a fraction by adding in another fraction value.
43              @param right the fraction to be added
44              @return the updated fraction value
45      */
46      Fraction& operator+=(const Fraction& right);
47
48      /**
49              Increments fraction by 1.
50      */
51      Fraction& operator++();   // Prefix form
52      Fraction operator++(int unused);   // Postfix form
53
54      /**
55              Compares one fraction value to another.
56              Result is negative if less than right, zero if equal, and
57              positive if greater than right.
58              @param right the fraction to be compared against
59      */
60      int compare(const Fraction& right) const;
61  private:
62      /**
63              Places the fraction in least common denominator form.
64      */
65      void normalize();
66
```

```
67      /**
68          Computes the greatest common denominator of two integer values.
69          @param n  the first integer
70          @param m  the second integer
71      */
72      int gcd(int n, int m);
73
74      int top;
75      int bottom;
76  };
77
78  Fraction operator+(const Fraction& left, const Fraction& right);
79  Fraction operator-(const Fraction& left, const Fraction& right);
80  Fraction operator*(const Fraction& left, const Fraction& right);
81  Fraction operator/(const Fraction& left, const Fraction& right);
82  Fraction operator-(const Fraction& value);
83
84  bool operator<(const Fraction& left, const Fraction& right);
85  bool operator<=(const Fraction& left, const Fraction& right);
86  bool operator==(const Fraction& left, const Fraction& right);
87  bool operator!=(const Fraction& left, const Fraction& right);
88  bool operator>=(const Fraction& left, const Fraction& right);
89  bool operator>(const Fraction& left, const Fraction& right);
90
91  ostream& operator<<(ostream& out, const Fraction& value);
92  istream& operator>>(istream& in, Fraction& r);
93
94  #endif
```

ch14/fraction.cpp

```
1   #include "fraction.h"
2   #include <cassert>
3   #include <stdexcept>
4
5   int Fraction::gcd(int n, int m)
6   {
7       // Euclid's Greatest Common Divisor algorithm
8       assert((n > 0) && (m > 0));
9       while (n != m)
10      {
11          if (n < m)
12              m = m - n;
13          else
14              n = n - m;
15      }
16      return n;
17  }
18
19  Fraction::Fraction(int t, int b) : top(t), bottom(b)
20  {
21      normalize();
22  }
23
```

```
24  Fraction::Fraction() : top(0), bottom(1) {}
25
26  Fraction::Fraction(int t) : top(t), bottom(1) {}
27
28  int Fraction::numerator() const
29  {
30     return top;
31  }
32
33  int Fraction::denominator() const
34  {
35     return bottom;
36  }
37
38  void Fraction::normalize()
39  {
40     // Normalize fraction by
41     // (a) moving sign to numerator
42     // (b) ensuring numerator and denominator have no common divisors
43     int sign = 1;
44     if (top < 0)
45     {
46        sign = -1;
47        top = -top;
48     }
49     if (bottom < 0)
50     {
51        sign = -sign;
52        bottom = -bottom;
53     }
54     assert(bottom != 0);
55     int d = 1;
56     if (top > 0) d = gcd(top, bottom);
57     top = sign * (top / d);
58     bottom = bottom / d;
59  }
60
61  Fraction operator+(const Fraction& left, const Fraction& right)
62  {
63     Fraction result(left.numerator() * right.denominator()
64        + right.numerator() * left.denominator(),
65        left.denominator() * right.denominator());
66     return result;
67  }
68
69  Fraction operator-(const Fraction& left, const Fraction& right)
70  {
71     Fraction result(left.numerator() * right.denominator()
72        - right.numerator() * left.denominator(),
73        left.denominator() * right.denominator());
74     return result;
75  }
76
```

```
77   Fraction operator*(const Fraction& left, const Fraction& right)
78   {
79       Fraction result(left.numerator() * right.numerator(),
80           left.denominator() * right.denominator());
81       return result;
82   }
83
84   Fraction operator/(const Fraction& left, const Fraction& right)
85   {
86       Fraction result(left.numerator() * right.denominator(),
87           left.denominator() * right.numerator());
88       return result;
89   }
90
91   Fraction operator-(const Fraction& value)
92   {
93       Fraction result(-value.numerator(), value.denominator());
94       return result;
95   }
96
97   int Fraction::compare(const Fraction& right) const
98   {
99       return numerator() * right.denominator()
100          - denominator() * right.numerator();
101      // Return the numerator of the difference
102  }
103
104  bool operator<(const Fraction& left, const Fraction& right)
105  {
106      return left.compare(right) < 0;
107  }
108
109  bool operator<=(const Fraction& left, const Fraction& right)
110  {
111      return left.compare(right) <= 0;
112  }
113
114  bool operator==(const Fraction& left, const Fraction& right)
115  {
116      return left.compare(right) == 0;
117  }
118
119  bool operator!=(const Fraction& left, const Fraction& right)
120  {
121      return left.compare(right) != 0;
122  }
123
124  bool operator>=(const Fraction& left, const Fraction& right)
125  {
126      return left.compare(right) >= 0;
127  }
128
129  bool operator>(const Fraction& left, const Fraction& right)
130  {
```

```
131         return left.compare(right) > 0;
132     }
133
134     ostream& operator<<(ostream& out, const Fraction& value)
135     {
136         out << value.numerator() << "/" << value.denominator();
137         return out;
138     }
139
140     istream& operator>>(istream& in, Fraction& r)
141     {
142         int t, b;
143         // Read the top
144         in >> t;
145         // If there is a slash, read the next number
146         char c;
147         in >> c;
148         if (c == '/')
149             in >> b;
150         else
151         {
152             in.unget();
153             b = 1;
154         }
155         r = Fraction(t, b);
156         return in;
157     }
158
159     Fraction& Fraction::operator++()
160     {
161         top += bottom;
162         return *this;
163     }
164
165     Fraction Fraction::operator++(int unused)
166     {
167         Fraction clone(top, bottom);
168         top += bottom;
169         return clone;
170     }
171
172     Fraction& Fraction::operator+=(const Fraction& right)
173     {
174         top = top * right.denominator() + bottom * right.numerator();
175         bottom *= right.denominator();
176         normalize();
177         return *this;
178     }
```

ch14/fractiontest.cpp

```
1   #include "fraction.h"
2
3   int main()
4   {
```

```
5      // Test constructors
6      Fraction a;   // Value is 0/1
7      Fraction b(4);   // Value is 4/1
8      Fraction c(6, 8);   // Value is 6/8, which is converted to 3/4
9      cout << "Constructed values " << a << " " << b << " " << c << "\n";
10     cout << "Value of c is " << c.numerator() << "/"
11         << c.denominator() << "\n";
12     // Test arithmetic instructions
13     Fraction d = b + c;
14     cout << "4 + 3/4 is " << d << "\n";
15     d = b - c;
16     cout << "4 - 3/4 is " << d << "\n";
17     Fraction e = (b + (-c));
18     cout << e << " done with negation\n";
19     if (d == e)
20        cout << "Subtraction test successful\n";
21     a = Fraction(6, 8);
22     b = Fraction(7, 8);
23     if (a < b)
24        cout << "Compare successful\n";
25     return 0;
26  }
```

Program Run

```
Constructed values 0/1 4/1 3/4
Value of c is 3/4
4 + 3/4 is 19/4
4 - 3/4 is 13/4
13/4 done with negation
Subtraction test successful
Compare successful
```

RANDOM FACT 14.1

The First Algorithm

The function normalize is used to reduce a fraction to a standard form, one in which the denominator is never negative and the numerator and denominator have no common factors. As part of the latter goal the function gcd is invoked. The letters in this function name stand for *greatest common divisor*.

The gcd algorithm was described by the Greek mathematician Euclid in the third century B.C. in his famous treatise on geometry, *The Elements*. Many authors consider the gcd to be one of the first formally developed algorithms [1]. In fact, until the rise of modern computers the word algorithm was used almost exclusively to refer to Euclid's gcd algorithm.

Although the logic behind the loop in the gcd algorithm may seem strange, it is not hard to explain. Imagine you want to find the greatest common divisor of two positive integer values n and m, and assume $n > m$. You know that such a number must exist, although you don't know what it is. Let us call the value d. Because d is a divisor, both n/d and m/d must be integers. This means that $n/d - m/d$ must also be an integer, and, by the rules of fractional subtraction, $(n - m)/d$ must be an integer. So any divisor of n and m must also be a divisor of $(n - m)$. So instead of finding the divisor of n and m, we could instead ask for the divisor of m and $(n - m)$. Since these two values are smaller than the original pair, we have reduced the problem to a simpler case. (You should contrast this with the type of analysis you performed when using recursion in Chapter 10.) The process continues until the two values are the same, in which case they both represent the desired divisor.

Although Euclid is credited with discovering the first algorithm, he did not invent the name "algorithm". Instead, the name derives from another mathematician and textbook author, Abu Ja'far Mohammed ibn Mûsâ al-Khowârizmî. In roughly 825 A.D. al-Khowârizmî wrote the book *Kitab al-jabr wa'l-muqabala* (Rules of restoration and reduction). Much of the mathematical knowledge of medieval Europe was discovered from Latin translations of this work. It may seem like a leap from al-Khowârizmî to "algorithm", but such is language. Interestingly, in addition to the word algorithm, the word algebra is derived from the title of this book.

EUCLID.

14.3 Overloading Simple Arithmetic Operators

The easiest overloaded operators to describe are the simple binary arithmetic operators; +, -, *, / and %. As you have already seen with the Time addition operator, each of these can be written either as a two-argument nonmember function, or as a one-argument member function.

For our Fraction data type, recall that the addition of a/b and c/d is defined to be $(a \cdot d + c \cdot b)/(b \cdot d)$. The following is used to implement the addition of two fractional values:

```
Fraction operator+(const Fraction& left, const Fraction& right)
{
```

```
    Fraction result(left.numerator() * right.denominator()
        + right.numerator() * left.denominator(),
        left.denominator() * right.denominator());
    return result;
}
```

The remaining operations are similarly defined. Note that when defining the arithmetic operators it is not necessary that the two arguments match in type. While they do for the fractional data type, they did not in the earlier example where seconds were added to a Time.

As mentioned earlier, a common example of overloading operators that is not related to arithmetic is the use of + to mean string catenation. The string data type in the standard library uses the + operator in this manner. However, as Productivity Hint 14.1 suggests, one should not go overboard with overloaded operators.

ADVANCED TOPIC 14.1

Returning Local Objects

Notice how the operator+ in Section 14.3 created a local variable named result, then immediately returned this object. Since the local variable is not used except as the value being returned, it is not actually necessary. Common practice among professional C++ programmers is not to create a variable in situations such as this, but rather to construct the result as an unnamed temporary:

```
Fraction operator+(const Fraction& left, const Fraction& right)
{
    return Fraction(left.numerator() + right.denominator()
        + right.numerator() * left.denominator(),
        left.denominator() * right.denominator());
}
```

PRODUCTIVITY HINT 14.1

Overload Operators Only to Make Programs Easier to Read

Some programmers are so enamored with operator overloading that they use it in ways that make programs hard to read. For example, some programmers might want to provide the ability to insert a value into a list by means of an operator, as in the following:

```
List staff;
staff += "Harry";
```

Maybe that's clever, but it can also be bewildering. It is best to overload operators to mimic existing use in mathematics or computer science. For example, it is reasonable to overload + and * for complex or matrix arithmetic, or to overload ++ and * to make iterators look like pointers.

14.3.1 Overloading Unary Arithmetic Operators

The operators +, -, * and & have both binary and unary forms. (Unary * is a pointer dereference, and unary & is the address operator.) To overload the unary form, simply reduce the number of arguments by one. For example, unary negation can be written as a function that takes one argument, instead of two:

```
Fraction operator-(const Fraction& value)
{
    Fraction result(-value.numerator(), value.denominator());
    return result;
}
```

A unary operator defined as a member function takes no arguments. You will see an example of this in Section 14.6.

14.4 Overloading Comparison Operators

Comparison operators are defined in a fashion analogous to the arithmetic operators, except that the results are typically Boolean. Two Time values are equal if the number of seconds between them is zero. Therefore, you can define:

```
bool operator==(const Time& a, const Time& b)
{
    return a.seconds_from(b) == 0;
}
```

Similarly, you can define the less than operator for Fraction values as follows:

```
bool operator<(const Fraction& left, const Fraction& right)
{
    return numerator() * right.denominator()
        < denominator() * right.numerator();
}
```

PRODUCTIVITY HINT 14.2

Define Comparisons in Terms of Each Other

The definitions of the six comparison operators are often very similar. Rather than writing six almost identical functions, a common technique is to write a single comparison method that returns an integer result. This result is negative if the first argument is less than the second, zero if they are equal, and positive if the first is greater than the second. Due to the way that fractions are normalized, the numerator of the difference of two fractions will satisfy the properties we seek.

```
int Fraction::compare(const Fraction& right) const
{
    return numerator() * right.denominator()
        - denominator * right.numerator();
    // Return the numerator of the difference
```

```
    }
```

Each of the six comparison operators can then be written as a simple test on the result yielded by the comparison function:

```
bool operator<(const Fraction& left, const Fraction& right)
{
    return left.compare(right) < 0;
}

bool operator==(const Fraction& left, const Fraction& right)
{
    return left.compare(right) == 0;
}

bool operator<=(const Fraction& left, const Fraction& right)
{
    return left.compare(right) <= 0;
}
```

ADVANCED TOPIC 14.2

Symmetry and Conversion

The comparison operators are normally defined as nonmember functions, not as member functions. To see why, imagine that you had instead defined the equality operator as a member function:

```
class Fraction
{
    ...
    bool operator==(const Fraction& right) const;
};

bool Fraction::operator==(const Fraction& right) const
{
    return numerator() * right.denominator()
        == right.numerator() * denominator();
}
```

Although we have written the equality operator only for fractions, a comparison between a Fraction and an integer will still work, since the integer will be implicitly converted into a fraction (see Section 14.8).

```
Fraction a(3,4);
if (a == 2) ... // Will work
```

However, for member functions automatic conversions are not applied to the left argument. Thus the following statement will not work

```
if (2 == a) ... // Error, no comparison between integer and Fraction
```

By defining the comparison operator as a nonmember function, both statements become legal.

14.5 Overloading Input and Output

The operators << and >> are overloaded in exactly the same fashion as the binary arithmetic operators. However, because their interpretation as shift operators is not common in other data types, these operators are often used to define operations completely unrelated to their original purpose as integer shift left and right. In fact, you are probably more familiar with these as the stream I/O operators, rather than as shift operators.

14.5.1 Stream Output

The use of operators in the stream input/output library makes it easy to extend input and output to new data types.

The output stream class, which you encountered in Chapter 9, provides the ability to write a single character to a file, string, or output device. All the remaining output routines are constructed using operator overloading and this basic ability. Among others, the stream library provides the following overloaded definitions:

```
ostream& operator<<(ostream& out, char value);
ostream& operator<<(ostream& out, int value);
ostream& operator<<(ostream& out, float value);
ostream& operator<<(ostream& out, double value);
ostream& operator<<(ostream& out, bool value);
ostream& operator<<(ostream& out, const char* value);
ostream& operator<<(ostream& out, string value);
```

Each of these operators takes an output stream as the left argument and another value as the right argument. When executed, each operator will, as a side effect, write the right argument to the stream, then return the stream value as the result. (Although we warned against functions having side effects in Section 4.6, output is one place where they are justified.) The fact that these functions return the stream argument is what allows a complex stream expression to be built out of parts. For example, consider the evaluation of the statement:

```
int i = 34;
cout << i << "\n";
```

The output statement is evaluated in stages left to right. First, the operator<<(ostream, int) is executed. This operator returns the output stream, so that next the operator<<(ostream, const char*) can be executed.

The ability to overload the << operator makes it simple to extend the output library to new data types. All that is needed to add the ability to write fractional values is to define yet another overloaded meaning for the output operator:

```
ostream& operator<<(ostream& out, const Fraction& value)
{
    out << value.numerator() << "/" << value.denominator();
    return out;
}
```

With this new ability the output of fractions can be intermixed with the output of other data types:

```
Fraction n(3, 4);
cout << "The value of n is " << n << "\n";
```

14.5.2 Stream Input

As you know, the >> operator is used for stream input. This operator can also be overwritten to work with new data types. For example, you can define an opera-tor>> to read a Time object from an input stream. For simplicity, assume that the Time value is entered as three separate integers, such as

9 15 00

Here is the definition of the >> operator for Time objects:

```
istream& operator>>(istream& in, Time& a)
{
   int hours;
   int minutes;
   int seconds;
   in >> hours >> minutes >> seconds;
   a = Time(hours, minutes, seconds);
   return in;
}
```

Note that the second argument must be a non-const reference parameter, since it is modified when it is filled with the input. The >> operator should return the input stream, just like the << operator. This allows a sequence of input operations to be chained together, as they were for output, and as is illustrated in the body of the Time::operator>> function itself.

ADVANCED TOPIC 14.3

Peeking at the Input

The stream I/O library allows the programmer to peek ahead one character in the input; if you decide you don't want the character you can put it back. For example, suppose you want to write an input function for Fraction values. You want to allow the input to be either a simple integer (such as 7) or a Fraction represented by an integer, a slash, and another integer (such as 3/4). If the next character after the numerator is not a slash, you want to push it back and return a Fraction with 1 as the denominator. You can write this function as follows:

```
istream& operator>>(istream& in, Fraction& r)
{
   int t, b;
   // Read the top
   in >> t;
```

```
            // If there is a slash, read the next number
            char c;
            in >> c;
            if (c == '/')
                in >> b;
            else
            {
                in.unget();
                b = 1;
            }
            r = Fraction(t, b);
            return in;
        }
```

14.6 Overloading Increment and Decrement Operators

As with their integer counterparts, the increment and decrement operators generally alter their argument value, in addition to producing a result. For this reason they are usually defined as member functions, not as ordinary functions. A second unusual characteristic of these operators is that there are two versions of each—a prefix version that produces a change before the result is determined:

```
++x
```

and a postfix form that yields the original value prior to the modification

```
x++
```

To distinguish these two cases, the C++ language introduces an extra argument to the postfix version of the operator. The value of this argument is not used. The following fragment illustrates the definition of these two operators for our Fraction data type:

```
class Fraction
{
    ...
    Fraction& operator++();   // Prefix form
    Fraction operator++(int unused); // Postfix form
    ...
};

Fraction& Fraction::operator++()
{
    top += bottom;
    return *this;
}
```

```
Fraction Fraction::operator++(int unused)
{
    Fraction clone(top, bottom);
    top += bottom;
    return clone;
}
```

Note that the prefix version is returning a reference, while the postfix version is returning a value. Reference results are more efficient, but care must be taken to avoid returning a reference to a local value. A good rule of thumb is if you return a value that exists outside the scope of the function (such as this) you should return a reference. If you return the value held by a local variable, return a value. The value will be duplicated before the local variable is destroyed. Finally, notice that the prefix increment operator does less work than the postfix version. This is typically true. Because it does less work, the prefix operation should be used whenever the programmer has a choice of the two forms (as, for example, in the increment portion of a for loop).

QUALITY TIP 14.1

Avoid Dependencies on Order of Evaluation

For numbers, both the prefix and postfix increment operators have the same effect: they increment x. However, they return different values: ++x evaluates to x *after* the increment, but x++ evaluates to x *before* the increment. You notice the difference only if you combine the increment expression with another expression. For example,

```
int i = 0;
int j = 0;
vector<double> s(10);
double a = s[i++];   // a is s[0], i is 1
double b = s[++j];   // b is s[1], j is 1
```

We do not recommend this style (see Quality Tip 6.1)—it is confusing and a common source of programming errors. Use ++ only to increment a variable and never use the return value; then it doesn't make any difference whether you use x++ or ++x.

More subtle errors occur because the order of binary operations is left unspecified in the C++ language definition. The following statement could produce either 10 or 11, depending on whether the increment is performed before or after the left argument of the addition is evaluated.

```
int i = 5;
int x = i + ++i;
```

Expressions with ambiguous meaning, such as this example, should be avoided. Unless the meaning is completely clear, increment a value in one statement, then use the resulting value in a separate statement.

COMMON ERROR 14.1

Inconsistent Operations

If you provide overloaded meanings for operators, make sure the meanings of different operators are consistent with each other. While nothing in the language definition requires it, most programmers would expect the following equivalences

```
i++              i = i + 1
++i              i = i + 1
i += c           i = i + c
i -= c           i = i - c
i - j            i + (-j)
- (-i)           i
```

There are many others. For example, a copy created by a constructor should match a copy created by an assignment. In general, try to make your classes as predictable as possible. This is sometimes termed the *principle of least astonishment*.

14.6.1 Iterators and Overloaded Operators

In Chapter 7 you learned how pointer values can be used to step through an array:

```
double sum(const double data[], int size)
{
   double* p = data;
   double* q = p + size;
   double sum = 0.0;
   while (p != q)
   {
      sum += *p;
      ++p;
   }
   return sum;
}
```

Let's list the pointer operations that were used in this function. First, there is the ability to set a pointer to the beginning of the collection, in this case, to the start of the array. Next, the ability to set another pointer to the end of the collection, which in this case was accomplished by adding an integer value to the pointer. The condition test in the while loop used the ability to compare one pointer to another. The next statement used the ability to access the value the pointer referenced, using the dereferencing operator *. The last statement in the loop incremented the pointer so that it would refer to the next element.

> Iterators use operators to create objects that simulate the behavior of pointers.

The fact that the operators such as addition, comparison, dereference, and increment can be overloaded with new meanings is used by the standard containers. In Section 12.2 you learned how iterators are used to loop over the elements in a container. All the standard containers provide functions to return an iterator representing the start of a collection, and a separate function to return an iterator representing the end of a collection. Contrast the sum function just defined with the same function as it would be written to analyze a collection stored in a list instead of an array:

```
double sum(const list<int>& data)
{
    list<int>::iterator p = data.begin();
    list<int>::iterator q = data.end();
    double sum = 0;
    while (p != q)
    {
        sum += *p;
        ++p;
    }
    return sum;
}
```

The only statements that have changed are those that define the initial values of p and q. The remaining operations (comparison, dereference, and increment) are all written in the same fashion as their pointer counterparts. Of course, they are implemented very differently. It is the technique of overloading that allows us to hide the different implementations behind a common symbol.

In Section 12.2 we implemented our own List and Iterator classes, using functions for the iterator operations. We could rewrite these functions as operators:

```
Iterator& Iterator::operator++(int)
{
    assert(position != NULL);
    position = position->next;
    return *this;
}

string Iterator::operator*() const
{
    assert(position != NULL);
    return position->data;
}

bool Iterator::operator==(const Iterator& b) const
{
    return position == b.position;
}

bool Iterator::operator!=(const Iterator& b) const
{
    return position != b.position;
}
```

Now you can write a loop just like the standard container loops:

```
Iterator start = names.begin();
Iterator stop = names.end();
while (start != stop)
{
    cout << *start << "\n";
    ++start;
}
```

14.7 Overloading the Assignment Operators

You might at first imagine that assignment would be one of the operators most commonly redefined. In fact, the assignment operator is very seldom given an explicit redefinition. This is because the assignment operator will be *automatically generated* should the programmer not override it. The default implementation will assign all data fields, a process termed a *member-wise assignment*. For most classes, such as our class Fraction, this is exactly the right action, and there is no need to do any more. Other functions that will be automatically provided include the default and copy constructors. You will see an example of this in Chapter 15.

In general the only reason to explicitly override the automatically generated assignment operator is when part of the assignment process involves dynamic memory management, as you will see in Chapter 15.

14.7.1 Overloading the Compound Assignment Operators

For primitive data values the operators +=, *=, and the like combine the operations of arithmetic and assignment. While the assignment operator will be automatically generated, these operators will not, even if the associated binary operator has been defined. If a binary operator, such as the addition operator +, is overloaded and if the assignment operator is appropriate (either the default implementation or an explicitly overloaded operator definition), the addition assignment operator += should be overloaded as well.

```
Fraction& Fraction::operator+=(const Fraction& right)
{
    top = top * right.denominator() + bottom * right.numerator();
    bottom *= right.denominator();
    normalize();
    return *this;
}
```

PRODUCTIVITY HINT 14.3

Define One Operator in Terms of Another

An easy way to ensure consistent behavior between an overloaded operator and the compound assignment operator is to define one in terms of the other. If the += operator and an appropriate constructor are defined, for example, the + operator can be easily implemented:

```
Fraction operator+(const Fraction& left, const Fraction& right)
{
    Fraction clone(left); // Copy the left argument
    clone += right;   // Add the right argument to it
    return clone;   // Return the updated value
}
```

Alternatively, the += operator can be defined using + and assignment:

```
Fraction& operator+=(Fraction& left, const Fraction& right)
{
    Fraction sum = left + right;
    left = sum;
    return left;
}
```

Notice in this case the left argument is declared as a reference parameter, as it is modified inside the function. This function also returns a reference, since the argument left is not a local variable, whereas the value clone in the previous function was local.

14.8 Overloading Conversion Operators

Operators can be used to control the conversion of values from one type to another.

C++ will perform a wide variety of *implicit* conversions; that is, conversions from one type to another in situations where no explicit request appears. You are familiar with this concept from the example of mixed-type arithmetic. In an expression such as

```
6 * 3.1415926
```

the left operand is an integer, while the right argument is a floating-point number. The integer value is implicitly converted to a floating-point equivalent, and the multiplication acts on these two values.

When dealing with new user-defined classes, there are two categories of type conversions to consider. The first is the conversion of a type to the new user-defined class, while the second is a conversion from the user-defined class to another type. The C++ language allows the programmer to define rules for both these situations.

Conversions of the first category, conversions *to* a user-defined type, are handled using constructors. For example, our Fraction class defines a constructor that takes a single integer argument. The C++ language rules allow this to be used to convert an integer value into a Fraction. For example, we have only defined the addition of two fractional values. Nevertheless, the C++ compiler will handle the addition of an integer to a Fraction:

```
Fraction a(3, 4);
a = a + 2;   // Addition of fraction and integer
```

The C++ compiler searches for a meaning to assign to the addition symbol. Since there is no explicit operator for adding a fraction to an integer, either the left or the right argument must be converted. There are two possibilities, converting the fraction to an integer and performing integer addition, or converting the integer to a fraction and performing fraction addition. Initially the compiler has no idea which, if either, is intended, and so will investigate both. We have not defined a rule that would convert a fraction into an integer, so that possibility is eliminated. That leaves only the addition of two fractions. To see whether this is possible the compiler searches for a conversion rule that could be used to change the right operand into a fractional value. It finds such a rule in the constructor. Using the constructor, the compiler creates an unnamed temporary value. That is, the statement is interpreted as if it had been written

```
a = a + Fraction(2);   // Convert right operand into fraction, then do addition
```

The second category of conversion involves changing a user-defined data type into another type. For example, suppose you want to provide the ability to convert a Fraction into a floating-point number. This is accomplished by writing a *conversion operator*. A conversion operator uses a type as the operator name, has no arguments, and does not specify a result type (since the result type is implicit in the name). Here is a conversion operator for converting a Fraction into a double:

```
Fraction::operator double() const
{
    // Convert numerator to double, then do division
    return static_cast<double>(top) / bottom;
}
```

The operator will be invoked for situations in which a conversion is required, for example in a mixed-type expression:

```
Fraction a(1, 2);
double d = 7.0;
double halfd = d * a;   // a is converted to double to do multiplication
cout << "one-half seven is " << halfd << "\n";
```

14.8.1 Stream Loops and Conversion Operators

An interesting and somewhat unorthodox use of conversion operators is found in the class istream. As you have seen in earlier chapters, a series of values can be read using a loop, as follows:

```
while (cin >> x)
    ...
```

The value returned by the >> operator is type istream. Since this is not a legal type for a while loop to test, the compiler searches for a conversion. A conversion operator provided by class istream will return a value that tests false on end of input or on error. The conversion is applied, and the loop executes as long as the stream is not exhausted.

QUALITY TIP 14.2

Conversion, Coercion, and Casts

The meanings of the terms coercion and conversion are easily confused, since both represent a change in type. A *conversion* denotes any change in type. If the type change is automatically carried out by the compiler, then we call the conversion a *coercion*. If the programmer explicitly requests the type change, then we call the conversion a *cast*. For example, in the expression

```
Fraction f = 10;
```

the compiler coerces the integer value 10 into the fraction f. In the expression

```
int n = static_cast<int>(x + 0.5);
```

the programmer casts the floating-point expression x + 0.5 into the integer n.

Conversions can either change the underlying representation (such as when an integer is converted into a floating-point number) or simply change the type without changing the representation, such as when a pointer to a derived class is changed into a pointer to the base class.

COMMON ERROR 14.2

Only One Level of Conversion

The C++ compiler does not perform more than one level of user-defined type conversion when trying to match an overloaded function. For example, suppose you define a Complex data type, and allow Complex values to be added to other Complex values. You also allow Complex values to be added to double values. This can most easily be performed by having a constructor for class Complex that takes an argument of type double. You cannot automatically expect that a value of type Complex can be combined with a Fraction.

```
Complex c(2, 3);
Fraction a(1, 3);
c = c + a;  // Compiler reports an error
```

For the latter statement to work, the compiler would have to detect the conversion from Fraction to double, then from double to Complex. To make this work you could either explicitly define an operator Complex in class Fraction, or add a constructor to class Complex that accepted a Fraction value.

COMMON ERROR 14.3

Ambiguous Conversions

If you look at the implementation of our Fraction class, you will note that we did not supply an operator double. If you supply too many type conversions, then the compiler cannot decide which conversion to choose, and it will report an error.

For example, consider the expression

```
Fraction(1, 2) * 2;
```

This can either mean

```
Fraction(1, 2).operator double() * 2
```

or

```
Fraction(1, 2) * Fraction(2)
```

Both choices are equally plausible to the compiler, and it reports an ambiguity. As a rule of thumb, you should supply conversions in only one direction: either from other types to your class, or from your class to other types.

For this reason, the string class has a constructor

```
string(const char*)
```

but no automatic conversion to a character pointer. You have to call the c_str member function if you want that conversion.

ADVANCED TOPIC 14.4

The explicit Keyword

Occasionally one would like a one-argument constructor to be used only for the creation of new values, and not used to provide a rule for the implicit conversion from one type to another. For this purpose C++ provides the explicit keyword. For example, in the class vector the constructor that takes an integer argument representing the vector size is declared as explicit:

```
class vector
{
    ...
    explicit vector(int v);
    ...
};
```

Without it, a failure to provide an index expression could lead to a very mysterious error

```
vector<int> v(10);
v = 5;  // Error—programmer intended to write v[0] = 5
```

The compiler will recognize that the assignment statement is operating on a value of type vector. It will then try to convert the right-hand side, the integer 5, into a value of this type. Without the explicit keyword, the compiler would interpret the constructor vector(int) as a method for converting integers into vectors. It would create a new vector of five elements, and replace the old vector v with this new collection, destroying the old value.

14.9 Overloading the Subscript Operator

We now continue the exposition of operator overloading with some operators that are not appropriate for the Fraction class case study. The first of these is the subscript operator. The *subscript operator* is often defined for classes that represent an indexable container, for example a vector or a map. In this case, the explicit argument represents the index and the result is the value stored at the given position. Like the assignment and the function call operator, this operator can only be defined as a member function.

A possible reason for overloading this operator would be to perform a range test on the index value, something that is not done by the C++ language for ordinary arrays. The following illustrates how this could be done. The class SafeArray is constructed either with a size, or with an existing array and size.

```
class SafeArray
{
public:
    SafeArray(int s);
    SafeArray(const int v[], int s);
    int& operator[](int i);
    int operator[](int i) const;
private:
    int size;
    int* values;
};

SafeArray::SafeArray(int s) : size(s), values(new int[size]) {}

SafeArray::SafeArray(const int v[], int s) : size(s)
{
    values = new int[size];
    for (int i = 0; i < size; i++)
        values[i] = v[i];
}

int& SafeArray::operator[](int index)
{
    assert((index >= 0) && (index < size));
    return values[i];
}

int SafeArray::operator[](int index) const;
{
    assert((index >= 0) && (index < size));
    return values[i];
}
```

The subscript operator checks the validity of the index value before returning the requested value. In the class SafeArray there are two definitions of the subscript operator. One returns a reference, so the value can be used for both the left and right sides of an assignment arrow:

```
SafeArray v(10);
v[2] = 7;
v[3] = v[2] + 12;
```

The second is declared as const, and is used when the variable is declared as constant. This version returns a value, and not a reference, and so can only be used to access a value, not to modify the array. (Returning a constant reference would have the same effect.)

```
int a[3];
a[2] = 17;
const SafeArray b(a, 3);
```

```
cout << "Value is " << b[2];   // OK
b[2] = 23;   // Error—result of subscript is not assignable
```

There is no operator[][] for double subscripts in the C++ language. As you have seen in Section 6.5.4, multiple subscripts can be treated as successive applications of single subscripts. When overloading, this means the first subscript must return a value (for example, MatrixRow) that is then a target for the second subscript operation. An alternative is to define the function call operator for multiple subscripts. We will illustrate both of these possibilities in Section 14.11.

14.10 Overloading the Function Call Operator

The function call operator permits the development of objects that are created using classes, but can be used as if they were functions. The advantage of this is that the class can, like all classes, encapsulate and carry its own data values.

The use of this operator is most easily illustrated with an example. Suppose you need a function that returns a random number between 1 and 100. This is easy to write:

```
int rand_100()
{
    return 1 + rand() % 100;
}
```

Now imagine that you need a similar function that returns a random value between a and b, where a and b are quantities that will not be known until run time. This is much harder to do with ordinary functions. The solution is to create a class, and initialize the values of a and b with the constructor:

```
class RandomInt
{
public:
    RandomInt(int ia, int ib);
    int operator()();
private:
    int a, b;
};

RandomInt::RandomInt(int ia, int ib) : a(ia), b(ib) {}

int RandomInt::operator()()
{
    return a + rand() % (b - a + 1);
}
```

You declare an instance of this class just like you would any other object. The difference is that once created, the object can be invoked just as you would a function:

```
RandomInt a(7, 15);   // Return random values from 7 to 15
cout << "one random value " << a() << "\n";
cout << "and another " << a() << "\n";
```

A function object defines the function call operator and so can be used in the fashion of a function, but it retains the properties of an object.

Because it can be used as if it were a function, such a value is termed a *function object*. As with assignment, this operator can only be defined as a member function. The function call operator is unique, in that it is the only operator in the C++ language for which the number of arguments is not fixed. Binary operators, such as operator <<, take only two arguments. Some operators, such as +, have both a one-argument and two-argument form. Like a function, the function call operator takes as many arguments as are specified in the function heading. This can be illustrated by the following generalization of the random number generator, which provides three different overloaded versions of the operator. When no arguments are specified it works as before. When one argument is given it is used as the new upper bound, and when two arguments are specified they are used as the lower and upper bounds:

```
class RandomInt
{
public:
    RandomInt(int ia, int ib);
    int operator()();
    int operator()(int nb);
    int operator()(int na, nb);
private:
    int a, b;
};

RandomInt::RandomInt(int ia, int ib) : a(ia), b(ib) {}

int RandomInt::operator()()
{
    return a + rand() % (b - a + 1);
}

int RandomInt::operator()(int nb)
{
    return a + rand() % (nb - a + 1);
}

int RandomInt::operator()(int na, int nb)
{
    return na + rand() % (nb - na + 1);
}
```

The function selected will be determined by the number of arguments provided:

```
RandomInt r(3, 7);
cout << "random value between 3 and 7 " << r() << "\n";
cout << "random value between 3 and 10 " << r(10) << "\n";
cout << "random value between 23 and 30 " << r(23, 30) << "\n";
```

Function objects are used extensively by various generic algorithms in the Standard Template Library (STL). We will return to function objects and the function call operator in more detail when we discuss the STL in Chapter 20.

ADVANCED TOPIC 14.5

Other Operators

There are a variety of operators that are not commonly used, and hence not commonly overloaded. The comma operator, for example, evaluates its operands left to right, then discards the left and returns the right. The operator has a precedence that is lower than assignment. Thus, the following expression will, perhaps surprisingly, assign the value of 7 to *x* and the value of 12 to *y*. (It is probable the programmer intended the comma to be a period.)

```
y = (x = 7,12);
```

The &, |, and ∧ operators provide bitwise and, or, and exclusive or operations when used with integers. (See Appendix G.) They can be overloaded to provide other meanings as ordinary binary operators. Note, however, that their precedence cannot be changed. Programmers often imagine that it would be useful to overload the ∧ operator so as to make it mean exponentiation. However, the statement

```
b = a ∧ 3 + 1   // DON'T—precedence is likely not what you think
```

does not, as one would like, compute $a^3 + 1$. Because + has a higher precedence than ∧, the expression is interpreted as a ∧ (3 + 1), thereby computing a^4.

As you learned in Section 3.5, the operators && and || provide the logical operations *and* and *or*. In their normal interpretation they use lazy evaluation; the right operand is not even evaluated if the result can be determined from the left alone. When overridden they become simple binary operators, and the lazy evaluation property is lost. When used as a unary operator, & produces the address of its argument (see Advanced Topic 7.2). This, too, can be overridden and provided with a new meaning.

The unary operators ~ and ! provide bitwise negation (when used with integers) and logical negation, respectively. Most users are more familiar with the latter, and thus it is a more common candidate for overloading.

The -> operator can be overloaded to create *smart pointers*, classes that perform similar to pointers. While this is frequent in professional C++ programs, the issues involved are complex and we will not explore them here. For more information on these technical issues, see [2].

The operators new and delete are used to control memory management, and will be discussed in the next chapter.

ADVANCED TOPIC 14.6

Inline Functions

When function bodies are very short, such as with the comparison operators in class Fraction, the execution time involved in the function call (pushing arguments on to the activation record stack, transfer of control, return from function, popping arguments off the stack) can often be greater than the execution time required by the body of the function itself. Moreover, many processors fetch and decode subsequent instructions as they execute an instruction. Branches and function calls slow down this mechanism.

When an inline function is invoked, the compiler expands the body of the function in place. This eliminates the execution cost of the function call, but results in multiple copies of the function body (one each time the function is called). For this reason, inline functions should only be used when the function body is very short.

To create an inline function the keyword `inline` is placed before the function body. The function definition is then placed in the interface file, not the implementation file:

```
inline bool operator<(const Fraction& left, const Fraction& right)
{
    return left.compare(right) < 0;
}
```

Member functions can also be inlined using a similar syntax:

```
inline Fraction& Fraction::operator++()
{
    top += bottom;
    return *this;
}
```

It is also possible to place the body of an inlined member function directly into a class declaration. In this case the `inline` keyword is not necessary:

```
class Fraction
{
    ...
    Fraction& Fraction::operator++()
    {
        top += bottom;
        return *this;
    }
    ...
};
```

However, this style can make reading the class definition difficult, since it combines interface and implementation features. In this book we will use only the first style.

A good rule of thumb is to use inlining when a function is three or fewer assignment statements, a single conditional (`if`) statement, and/or a return statement. Anything more complex should be written as a normal function.

Although we have not used inlining for functions in the `Fraction` case study (we have left that as an exercise), the `Matrix` case study in Section 14.11 contains several examples of function inlining.

14.11 Case Study: Matrices

To illustrate once more the technique of operator overloading we begin a case study that we will, in subsequent chapters, build on and expand with new features. Imagine you are developing a library of matrix algorithms. A matrix is a tabular arrangement of numbers, such as the following:

$$\begin{bmatrix} -0.15 & 0.28 & 1.4 \\ 0.26 & 0.24 & -3.36 \\ 0 & 0 & 1 \end{bmatrix}$$

Matrices are a very important tool in mathematics. Most science and engineering students take a course in linear algebra in which they learn about matrix arithmetic. Here is a brief refresher.

You add two matrices by adding the corresponding elements. For example,

$$\begin{bmatrix} 1 & 3 & 0 \\ 0 & 1 & 3 \\ 0 & 0 & 1 \end{bmatrix} + \begin{bmatrix} 1 & 0 & 0 \\ 4 & 1 & 0 \\ 0 & 4 & 1 \end{bmatrix} = \begin{bmatrix} 2 & 3 & 0 \\ 4 & 2 & 3 \\ 0 & 4 & 2 \end{bmatrix}$$

You can multiply a matrix with a number, simply by multiplying each element by the given number. This process is called scalar multiplication.

$$2 \cdot \begin{bmatrix} 1 & 3 & 0 \\ 0 & 1 & 3 \\ 0 & 0 & 1 \end{bmatrix} = \begin{bmatrix} 2 & 6 & 0 \\ 0 & 2 & 6 \\ 0 & 0 & 2 \end{bmatrix}$$

Finally, you can multiply two matrices. This operation is more complex. The (i, j) element of the product is formed by multiplying the ith row of the first matrix with the jth column of the second matrix. You multiply a row with a column by multiplying corresponding elements and adding up the products. Here is a product of a single row and a column.

$$\begin{bmatrix} 1 & 3 & 0 \end{bmatrix} \cdot \begin{bmatrix} 1 \\ 4 \\ 0 \end{bmatrix} = 1 \cdot 1 + 3 \cdot 4 + 0 \cdot 0 = 13$$

To form the matrix product, you carry out that operation for all rows of the first matrix and all columns of the second matrix.

$$\begin{bmatrix} 1 & 3 & 0 \\ 0 & 1 & 3 \\ 0 & 0 & 1 \end{bmatrix} \cdot \begin{bmatrix} 1 & 0 & 0 \\ 4 & 1 & 0 \\ 0 & 4 & 1 \end{bmatrix} = \begin{bmatrix} 13 & 3 & 0 \\ 4 & 13 & 3 \\ 0 & 4 & 1 \end{bmatrix}$$

If you never had a course in linear algebra, you will need to take it on faith that these operations are useful. At any rate, they are easy enough to program in C++.

In order to supply a matrix library, we need to choose a data type for matrices. The most obvious choice seems to be the two-dimensional arrays that were described in Section 6.5.4. However, you would encounter a number of problems. Array indexes are not checked. You need helper functions to copy two-dimensional arrays. Perhaps most importantly, you cannot use the standard mathematical symbols for matrix operations. Users of your library would have to use function calls such as

```
multiply(a, b, c)
```

instead of

```
c = a * b
```

Therefore, it is better to develop your own data type. Using overloaded operators, users of your library will be able to use the familiar mathematical notation.

The class Matrix maintains a collection of elements, in much the same fashion that the string class manages an array of character values. If ROWS and COLUMNS denote the dimensions of the matrix, then the matrix holds ROWS * COLUMNS elements. Because the number of rows and columns is variable, we cannot use a two-dimensional array to store the matrix elements. Instead, we use a one-dimensional array. Figure 1 shows the organization. The matrix element from row i and column j is found in the position

```
i * COLUMNS + j
```

The process of subscripting is fundamental to matrices. As was pointed out in Section 14.9, the C++ language does not directly support a two-dimensional subscript operator. There are two ways this is normally handled, and we will illustrate both. One way is to use the function call operator for subscripting.

```
class Matrix
{
   ...
   double& operator()(int i, int j);  // Return element [i][j]
};
```

The second solution is slightly more complicated. A subscript will return an intermediate value, an instance of class MatrixRow. This class will retain a pointer to the original matrix, and the row subscript. In a subscript expression, such as

```
Matrix m;
m[i][j] = 7.0;
```

The first subscript generates a MatrixRow, and it is this object that receives the second subscript, and ultimately produces the desired element.

As with the subscript operators described in Section 14.9, indexing a constant matrix will produce a value, while indexing a nonconstant matrix will produce a reference. In order to support this behavior, there is, in addition to MatrixRow, a second class ConstMatrixRow.

As described in Advanced Topic 14.6 on page 576, execution time can be improved by expanding small function bodies inline. Subscript operators, as well as other small functions, have all been given inline definitions. This means the function bodies are prefixed with the inline modifier and appear in the interface file, rather than in the implementation file.

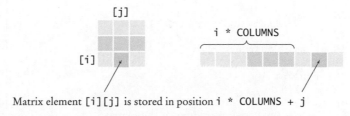

Matrix element [i][j] is stored in position i * COLUMNS + j

Figure 1   Storing Matrix Elements in an Array

In addition to the subscript operators, we supply operations such as += (an elementwise addition of one matrix to another), + (the element-wise addition of two matrices), and * (scalar or matrix product, depending on the parameters). A stream output operator produces a printed representation of the matrix.

In this chapter, we only implement 3 × 3 matrices. Variable dimensions will be introduced in Chapter 15. Subsequent chapters will make additional changes. The programming exercises suggest a number of additions to this class.

ch14/matrix1.h

```
1   #ifndef MATRIX1_H
2   #define MATRIX1_H
3
4   #include <iostream>
5   #include <cassert>
6
7   using namespace std;
8
9   /**
10      This class describes a row in a matrix.
11   */
12   class Matrix;   // Forward definition
13   class MatrixRow
14   {
15   public:
16      /**
17         Remembers a row for a given matrix.
18         @param m a pointer to the matrix
19         @param s the size of the row
20      */
21      MatrixRow(Matrix* m, int s);
22
23      /**
24         Accesses a row element.
25         @param j the column index
26         @return a reference to the element with the given index
27      */
28      double& operator[](int j);
29
30   private:
31      Matrix* mat;
32      int i;
33   };
34
35   /**
36      This class describes a row in a constant matrix.
37   */
38   class ConstMatrixRow
39   {
40   public:
41      /**
42         Constructs a row with a given start and size.
43         @param m a pointer to the matrix
```

```
44          @param s  the size of the row
45      */
46      ConstMatrixRow(const Matrix* m, int s);
47
48      /**
49          Accesses a row element.
50          @param j  the column index
51          @return a reference to the element with the given index
52      */
53      double operator[](int j) const;
54
55  private:
56      const Matrix* mat;
57      int i;
58  };
59
60  /**
61      This class describes a 3 × 3 matrix.
62  */
63  class Matrix
64  {
65  public:
66      /**
67          Constructs a matrix filled with zero elements.
68      */
69      Matrix();
70
71      /**
72          Accesses a matrix element.
73          @param i  the row index
74          @param j  the column index
75          @return a reference to the element with the given indexes
76      */
77      double& operator()(int i, int j);
78
79      /**
80          Accesses a matrix element.
81          @param i  the row index
82          @param j  the column index
83          @return the element with the given indexes
84      */
85      double operator()(int i, int j) const;
86
87      /**
88          Accesses a matrix row.
89          @param i  the row index
90          @return the row with the given index
91      */
92      MatrixRow operator[](int i);
93
94      /**
95          Accesses a matrix row.
96          @param i  the row index
```

```
 97            @return the row with the given index
 98        */
 99        ConstMatrixRow operator[](int i) const;
100
101        /**
102            Computes the matrix sum.
103            @param right another matrix
104            @return the updated matrix
105        */
106        Matrix& operator+=(const Matrix& right);
107
108        static const int ROWS = 3;
109        static const int COLUMNS = 3;
110
111    private:
112        double elements[ROWS * COLUMNS];
113    };
114
115    /**
116        Computes the matrix sum.
117        @param right another matrix
118        @return the sum of two matrices
119    */
120    Matrix operator+(const Matrix& left, const Matrix& right);
121
122    /**
123        Computes the matrix product.
124        @param right another matrix
125        @return the product of two matrices
126    */
127    Matrix operator*(const Matrix& left, const Matrix& right);
128
129    /**
130        Computes the scalar product of a scalar value and a matrix.
131        @param left a scalar value
132        @param right a matrix
133        @return the product of the given value and the given matrix
134    */
135    Matrix operator*(double left, const Matrix& right);
136
137    /**
138        Computes the scalar product of a matrix and a scalar value.
139        @param right a scalar value
140        @return the product of this matrix and the given value
141    */
142    Matrix operator*(const Matrix& left, double right);
143
144    /**
145        Prints a matrix to an output stream.
146        @param left an output stream
147        @param right a matrix
148        @return the given output stream
149    */
150    ostream& operator<<(ostream& left, const Matrix& right);
151
```

```
152    inline double& Matrix::operator()(int i, int j)
153    {
154       assert(0 <= i && i < ROWS && 0 <= j && j < COLUMNS);
155       return elements[i * COLUMNS + j];
156    }
157
158    inline double Matrix::operator()(int i, int j) const
159    {
160       assert(0 <= i && i < ROWS && 0 <= j && j < COLUMNS);
161       return elements[i * COLUMNS + j];
162    }
163
164    inline MatrixRow Matrix::operator[](int i)
165    {
166       return MatrixRow(this, i);
167    }
168
169    inline ConstMatrixRow Matrix::operator[](int i) const
170    {
171       return ConstMatrixRow(this, i);
172    }
173
174    inline MatrixRow::MatrixRow(Matrix* m, int s) : mat(m), i(s) {}
175
176    inline double& MatrixRow::operator[](int j)
177    {
178       return (*mat)(i, j);
179    }
180
181    inline ConstMatrixRow::ConstMatrixRow(const Matrix* m, int s)
182       : mat(m), i(s) {}
183
184    inline double ConstMatrixRow::operator[](int j) const
185    {
186       return (*mat)(i, j);
187    }
188
189    inline Matrix operator*(double left, const Matrix& right)
190    {
191       return right * left;
192    }
193
194    #endif
```

ch14/matrix1.cpp

```
1    #include <iomanip>
2    #include "matrix1.h"
3
4    Matrix::Matrix()
5    {
6       for (int i = 0; i < ROWS; i++)
7          for (int j = 0; j < COLUMNS; j++)
8             (*this)(i, j) = 0;
```

```
 9  }
10
11  Matrix& Matrix::operator+=(const Matrix& right)
12  {
13      for (int i = 0; i < ROWS; i++)
14        for (int j = 0; j < COLUMNS; j++)
15          (*this)(i, j) += right(i, j);
16      return *this;
17  }
18
19  Matrix operator+(const Matrix& left, const Matrix& right)
20  {
21      Matrix result = left;
22      result += right;
23      return result;
24  }
25
26  Matrix operator*(const Matrix& left, const Matrix& right)
27  {
28      Matrix result;
29      for (int i = 0; i < Matrix::ROWS; i++)
30        for (int j = 0; j < Matrix::COLUMNS; j++)
31          for (int k = 0; k < Matrix::COLUMNS; k++)
32            result(i, j) += left(i, k) * right(k, j);
33      return result;
34  }
35
36  Matrix operator*(const Matrix& left, double right)
37  {
38      Matrix result;
39      for (int i = 0; i < Matrix::ROWS; i++)
40        for (int j = 0; j < Matrix::COLUMNS; j++)
41          result(i, j) = left(i, j) * right;
42      return result;
43  }
44
45  ostream& operator<<(ostream& left, const Matrix& right)
46  {
47      const int WIDTH = 10;
48      for (int i = 0; i < Matrix::ROWS; i++)
49      {
50        for (int j = 0; j < Matrix::COLUMNS; j++)
51          left << setw(WIDTH) << right(i, j);
52        left << "\n";
53      }
54      return left;
55  }
```

The test program, matrixtest1.cpp, simply creates a matrix and exercises the arithmetic operations.

ch14/matrixtest1.cpp

```
1  #include "matrix1.h"
2
3  int main()
4  {
5     Matrix m;
6     m[0][0] = m[1][1] = m[2][2] = 1;
7     m(0, 1) = m(1, 2) = 2;
8     cout << 2 * m << "\n";
9     cout << m * m << "\n";
10    cout << 2 * m + m * m;
11    return 0;
12 }
```

CHAPTER SUMMARY

1. You can define new meanings for C++ operators by defining functions whose name is operator followed by the operator symbol.

2. Operators can be defined either as member or nonmember functions.

3. Use a member function for an operator if you need access to private data.

4. Use a nonmember function for an operator to allow type conversions for the left argument.

5. The use of operators in the stream input/output library makes it easy to extend input and output to new data types.

6. Iterators use operators to create objects that simulate the behavior of pointers.

7. Operators can be used to control the conversion of values from one type to another.

8. A function object defines the function call operator and so can be used in the fashion of a function, but it retains the properties of an object.

FURTHER READING

1. Donald Knuth, *The Art of Computer Programming: Vol 1: Fundamental Algorithms*, Addison-Wesley, 1973.

2. Bjarne Stroustrup, *The C++ Programming Language*, Special Ed., Addison-Wesley, 2000.

REVIEW EXERCISES

Exercise R14.1. To give an existing operator a new meaning, what property must the argument types possess?

Exercise R14.2. When would you choose an overloaded operator for a particular operation, and when would you choose a function?

Exercise R14.3. Overload the + operator to raise an employee salary. For example, harry + 5 gives Harry a 5 percent raise. Is this a good use for operator overloading?

Exercise R14.4. Could you overload the unary negation operator so that -T would decrement the Time value T by 60 seconds? Would this be a good idea or not?

Exercise R14.5. When should an operator function be a member function?

Exercise R14.6. Both of the following assignments are legal, but neither is likely to have the intended effect. Explain what values will be held by the two variables following the statements:

```
double pi = (3,14159);   // Comma, not period
double pi_two;
pi_two = 3,14159;
```

Exercise R14.7. To print an object, access to the private data fields is often necessary. Can the operator<< function be defined as a member function to grant this access? If so, give an example. If not, explain why not.

Exercise R14.8. Why are there two versions of the ++ and -- operator functions? Are there any other operators with two versions?

Exercise R14.9. Why should the prefix version of an increment operator be used instead of the postfix version whenever you have a choice between the two?

Exercise R14.10. What are the possible resulting values from the following three assignments?

```
i = 7;
j = ++i + i++;
k = j++ + ++j;
```

Exercise R14.11. What operators are necessary to use a value as an Iterator?

Exercise R14.12. What is the effect of declaring the assignment operator as private?

Exercise R14.13. Why do you seldom need to overload the assignment operator? In what situation is it necessary to define an assignment operator?

Exercise R14.14. What is the difference between a conversion and a coercion?

Exercise R14.15. How would you implement a conversion from float to Fraction? What problems do you run into?

Exercise R14.16. Imagine you have implemented a class Polynomial. How do you achieve the type conversion of a double to a Polynomial?

Exercise R14.17. What is the purpose of the `explicit` keyword? What potential error does the use of this keyword eliminate?

Exercise R14.18. Which operators does the `string` class overload?

Exercise R14.19. What unique characteristic makes the function call operator different from all other operators?

Exercise R14.20. What is a function object? How is a function object different from a function? What capabilities does a function object possess that an ordinary function does not?

PROGRAMMING EXERCISES

Exercise P14.1. Finish the implementation of the class `Fraction` by overloading the remaining arithmetic operations.

Exercise P14.2. Modify the class `Fraction` to permit fractions with a zero denominator. Change the stream output operator so that it will produce a special marker, *****, when such a value is printed. Add a conversion `operator bool` so as to test whether a `Fraction` is proper.

Exercise P14.3. Determine which functions in class `Fraction` are candidates for inlining. Rewrite the class to inline those you identify, and test the resulting application.

Exercise P14.4. Implement both the prefix and the postfix form of `Iterator::operator--` for the list class in Chapter 12.

Exercise P14.5. Define a class `Money`, which maintains two integer data fields, dollars and cents. Overload arithmetic operators, comparison operators, and input and output operators for your class. Should you overload the * and / operators? What argument types should they accept? Overload the % operator so that if n is a floating-point value, n % m yields n percent of the money amount m.

Exercise P14.6. Define a class `Complex` for complex numbers. Provide implementations for addition, subtraction, multiplication, and the stream input and output operators. Implement the compound assignment operators for each of the supported binary arithmetic operations.

Exercise P14.7. Define a class `BigInteger` that stores arbitrarily large integers by keeping their digits in a `vector<int>`. Supply a constructor `BigInteger(string)` that reads a sequence of digits from a string. Overload the +, -, and * operators to add, subtract, and multiply the digit sequences. Overload the << operator to send the big integer to a stream. For example,

```
BigInteger a("123456789");
BigInteger b("987654321");
cout << a * b;
```

prints 121932631112635269.

Exercise P14.8. Implement a class for polynomials. Store the coefficients in a vector of floating-point values. Then provide operators for addition, subtraction, multiplication, and output.

Exercise P14.9. Define a class Set that stores a finite set of integers. (In a set, the order of elements does not matter, and every element can occur at most once.) Supply add and remove member functions to add and remove set elements. Overload the | and & operators to compute the union and intersection of the set, and the << operator to send the set contents to a stream.

Exercise P14.10. Continue Exercise P14.9 and overload the ~ operator to compute the complement of a set. That is, ~a is the set of all integers that are not present in the set a. *Hint:* Add a bool field to the Set class to keep track of whether a set is finite or has a finite complement.

Exercise P14.11. Can you make the class vector<double> act like the mathematical concept of a vector? Implement the addition operator so as to compute the vector sum of two vectors. Why might it be more efficient to implement += as an operator that computes the vector sum in place in the left argument? Measure the difference in speed between v += w and v = v + w.

Exercise P14.12. Modify the class Matrix described in Section 14.11 to provide the following operations:

1. The negation of a matrix. This should yield the matrix in which every element is negated.
2. The compound assignment operator -=.
3. The subtraction operator -. Write this in two ways. First, just as the addition operator was written using +=, this can be written using -=. Second, write the operator using addition and unary negation.
4. The input of a matrix from an input stream.

Exercise P14.13. Extend the multiplication operator for class Matrix to allow matrices to be multiplied by vectors. As is conventional in mathematics, a matrix times a vector should multiply the matrix rows by the vector.

Exercise P14.14. Implement an associative array that uses strings for keys and stores values of type double. Overload the subscript operator (operator[]) to provide access as in the following example

```
AssociativeArray prices;
prices["Toaster Oven"] = 19.95;
prices["Car Vacuum"] = 24.95;
```

Memory Management

CHAPTER GOALS

- To learn about the different categories of memory
- To learn how to write and use constructors and destructors
- To be able to create classes that manage their own memory allocation and deallocation
- To understand how to avoid common memory management errors

In Chapter 7 you were introduced to the concepts of dynamic memory allocation using the new operator, and the need to release dynamic memory using the delete operator. These operations are part of the task termed memory management. In C++ memory management is explicitly under the direction of the programmer. If properly used, this can result in very efficient programs. But if improperly used (or, more often, ignored) memory management issues can make a program use more memory than is necessary, use more execution time than necessary, or cause mysterious errors that are nearly impossible to discover and correct. For this reason, writing effective C++ programs requires a clear understanding of how the memory management system operates.

CHAPTER CONTENTS

15.1 Categories of Memory

> Memory is divided into four areas: code, static data, the run-time stack, and the heap.

Memory in C++ programs is divided into four categories:

1. *Code.* This area contains machine instructions for all functions and member functions. As a program runs, instructions are read from memory and executed.
2. *Static Data.* This area contains all global variables, as well as any local variables or class data members that are declared using the static modifier.
3. *Run-time Stack.* This is the area used by most C++ variables. All local, non-static variables reside on the run-time stack.
4. *Free Store, or Heap.* This is the area for memory explicitly requested using the new operator.

15.1.1 Code Memory

The code memory contains the machine instructions that represent all functions and function members. Beginning programmers sometimes don't think of this as part of memory, because you generally cannot change these values once a function has been compiled. Nevertheless, they do occupy space in the computer memory.

It is possible to make a pointer reference a value in the code section of memory by using a function pointer. We discussed function pointers in Section 7.6.

15.1.2 Static Data Memory

This section of memory holds two categories of values, *global* and *static*. As you learned in Section 4.9, global variables are variables defined outside the scope of any functions or classes. Variables such as cin and cout are examples of global variables. For the memory management system, global variables have one important property. Within each name space, each name can be mapped one to one to an object. A local variable, in contrast, is created anew each time a function is executed. A recursive function, such as those you examined in Chapter 10, can cause the same name to be attached to several different currently active values. This will never happen with global variables. There is only one variable named cin. (In Chapter 18 we will return to the issue of name spaces and global names.) This means that each global variable can, prior to execution, be assigned a fixed-size block of memory.

Global variables can be initialized, either by an assignment or by using a constructor. The value is initialized only once, before execution of main begins. The following example function uses a global variable named counter to count the number of times that the function has been called, returning the updated count as the function result.

```
int counter = 0;

int counting_fun()
{
    // Count how many times the function is called
    counter++;
    return counter;
}
```

The second category of values in this portion of memory is static variables. Both local variables and data members can be declared to be static. An item with the static modifier, like a global variable, has only one value attached to the name. Again, like global variables, a static variable is assigned memory once, initialized before main begins execution, and will continue to exist until the end of execution. You could rewrite the counting function to use a static variable as follows:

```
int counting_fun()
{
    static int counter = 0;   // Will be initialized only once
    counter++;
    return counter;
}
```

15.1.3 The Run-time Stack

> Stack-based memory is tied to function entry and exit. Errors can occur if references continue to exist after a function exits.

Values in the run-time stack are tied to function entry and exit. Function invocations execute in an orderly fashion. If function f invokes function g, and function g in turn invokes function h, then function h must terminate before g will continue with execution, and g in turn must terminate before f will resume.

This last-in first-out behavior allows stack memory to be managed very efficiently. An internal pointer refers to the top of the run-time stack. When a function is invoked, the stack pointer is incremented, thereby allocating a block of memory. When a function returns, the stack pointer is decremented, allowing the memory to be reused by the next function call. The block of memory is termed the *activation record*. An activation record will maintain space for parameters, the return address (a pointer into code memory), space for saved internal registers and other machine-specific information, and space for local variables. If function f has called g, which in turn has called h, the most recent portion of the run-time stack will look like Figure 1.

The efficiencies of stack memory are not without cost. There are two major drawbacks to the use of the stack for storing local variables:

- The lifetime of stack-memory values is tied to function entry and exit. This means that stack-resident values cease to exist when a function returns. An attempt to use a stack-resident value after it has been deleted will cause an error.

- The size of stack-resident values must be known at compile time, which is when the structure of the activation record is laid out.

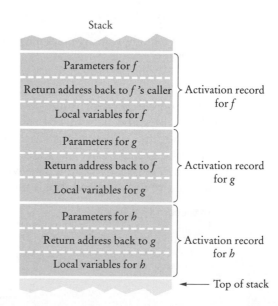

Figure 1
Activation Records on the Stack

You will examine the implications of these limitations later in this chapter when we discuss common memory errors.

15.1.4 Heap Memory

There are many situations where stack memory is inappropriate. It is often difficult or impossible to estimate beforehand how large an object should be—for example, how many elements an array needs to contain. It may also be difficult to determine how many items a program might require; for example, how many nodes will be contained in a linked list. Finally, it is also common that the lifetime of a value is not tied to procedure entry and exit. For example, when a value is placed into a linked list, the value will continue to exist even after the insertion function finishes execution. In such cases, local variables on the stack cannot be used, and dynamic allocation of storage is necessary. The *heap*—or *free store*—is the storage area for values explicitly requested using the new operator.

```
Employee* boss = new Employee("Lin, Lisa", 68000);
```

As you learned in Section 7.1, when you ask for a section of memory using this operator, a *memory allocator* finds a storage location for the new object in the heap. The memory allocator tells you where the object is located by returning the memory address for the value. This is termed *dynamic memory allocation*.

Dynamically allocated values are accessed through a pointer, which itself might reside either on the stack or on the heap. The statement above declares a pointer variable named boss that resides on the stack. The value of the pointer references a data area stored on the heap (see Figure 2).

Once you are finished with the dynamically allocated memory you must notify the memory allocator that it can be returned to the free store. This is done using the delete operator:

```
delete boss;
```

This statement deletes the heap memory that variable boss refers to.

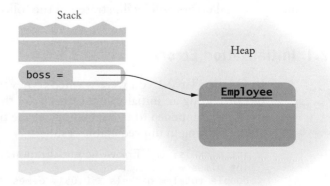

Figure 2   Values on the Stack and on the Heap

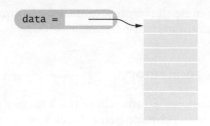

Figure 3   A Pointer to an Array

Allocation and deletion of arrays requires a slightly different syntax (see Figure 3):

```
double* data = new double[7]; // Allocate an array of 7 double cells
...
delete[] data; // Free the array
```

15.2 Common Memory Errors

> Pointers can refer to memory in all four areas.

Because the programmer is responsible for memory management in C++, and because pointers can refer to memory in any of the four areas, several errors are possible. These include the following:

- Using a value that has not been initialized.
- Using a pointer to reference a memory location that is no longer valid.
- Forgetting to delete a dynamically allocated section of memory.
- Deleting a memory value that was never allocated.
- Deleting a dynamically allocated section of memory more than once.

Each of these potential errors will be illustrated in the following sections.

15.2.1 Initialization Errors

> Initialization errors can occur for variables in any section of memory.

In Quality Tip 2.1 you were warned to never declare a variable without providing an initial value. Otherwise, the value of the variable is whatever happened to be in memory at the time the variable was created, resulting in unpredictable results:

```
int nickels;  // Error—no initialization
int dimes = 3;
double total = nickels * 0.05 + dimes * 0.10;
    // Error—unpredictable result
```

The use of constructors (which were introduced in Chapter 5, and which will be examined in more detail later in this chapter) alleviates this problem to some extent. A constructor ties together the operations of creation and initialization, ensuring that every value created is also initialized.

Pointers compound the problem of initialization. Now there are two data values to manage; the value of the pointer itself, and the data area it points to. Either data value can fail to be initialized. An initialization error occurs when the programmer forgets to allocate memory, but uses a pointer value anyway:

```
Employee* boss;
cout << "My boss earns " << boss->salary();
    // Error—almost certain crash, because pointer is undefined
```

Accessing this pointer will probably terminate the program. However, in particularly unfortunate circumstances, this value can refer to a valid section of memory, which may allow the program to proceed for a while longer, until the section of memory that the pointer references is used. However, the results are unpredictable, and almost always useless.

> Dynamically allocated memory introduces two potential pointer initialization errors: failure to initialize the pointer, and failure to initialize the space the pointer references.

Alternatively, a pointer for a dynamically allocated value can be properly initialized, but the space the pointer references still fails to be initialized.

```
int* coins = new int[3];
    // Array for counts of pennies, nickels, and dimes
    // Error—coins uninitialized
double total = coins[0] + coins[1] * 0.05 + coins[2] * 0.10;
```

Here the variable coins is properly set to point to an array of integer values. However, the array elements themselves are not initialized. By default, these dynamically allocated primitive values start out with random values.

15.2.2 Lifetime Errors

You must always remember that after a function returns from execution, the top of the stack pointer is decremented, and any local variables are no longer valid. Although the stack pointer is decremented, the memory occupied by the activation record will not be changed until overwritten by the next function call. This can be a source of subtle errors. A pointer to a local variable in a discarded activation record will no longer be valid, although it may appear to work for a short period of time — that is, until the next function call. Here is an example:

```
// Error—this function returns a reference to an invalid memory location
char* read_a_line()
{
   char buffer[200];   // Declare a buffer to hold the text
   cin >> buffer;      // Read a line of text
   return buffer;      // Return the text
}
...
char* p = read_a_line();
```

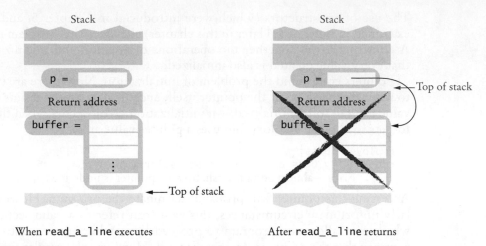

Figure 4   Creation of a Dangling Pointer

The read_a_line procedure returns a pointer to the array named buffer. However, memory for the buffer will be deleted once the function is finished executing. The pointer p will end up referencing values that may or may not be correct (see Figure 4), and will almost certainly be overwritten once the next function is called. As was noted in Common Error 7.3, a pointer that refers to a location that is no longer valid is termed a *dangling pointer*.

Returning a reference to a local variable is another common cause of lifetime errors:

```
Fraction& operator+(const Fraction& left, const Fraction& right)
{
   Fraction result(left.numerator() * right.denominator()
      + right.numerator() * left.denominator(),
      left.denominator() * right.denominator());
   return result; // Error—returns reference to a local variable
}
```

Some of the more sophisticated C++ compilers will warn about such errors, but you should not depend on this.

15.2.3 Array Bounds Errors

Global values and stack-resident arrays must have a size that is known at compile time. Often, programmers try to avoid this restriction by allocating an array with a size that is purposely too large. In the example in the previous section the programmer is reading lines of input from a file, and has allocated a character array to hold 200 elements. Why 200? When using arrays instead of vectors, one must make some fixed choice for the size. The programmer probably believed that no input line would have more than 200 characters. This is a dangerous assumption.

Problems can occur because array bounds are not checked in C++ at run time. Should a line longer than 200 characters be encountered, the buffer will simply be exceeded, and the values read will flow into whatever happens to follow the array in the activation record. This will have the effect of changing the values of other variables unpredictably, with generally undesirable results. This problem can be avoided by using a vector instead of an array whenever the size of the array cannot be determined at compile time.

QUALITY TIP 15.1

Avoid Buffer Overflow Errors

If you read the description of software patches or updates, you will often discover that a patch has been applied to overcome a "potential buffer overflow condition". What this means is that the original programmer has committed an error exactly like that described earlier, namely, allocating a fixed-size buffer, then reading a line of text of unknown size:

```
// Error—this function can potentially overwrite a fixed-size array
char buffer[200];   // Making array global avoids deletion error
char* read_a_line()
{
   cin >> buffer;
   return buffer;
}
```

The problem is only "potential", because it will only manifest itself when an input consisting of, in this case, more than 200 characters is encountered. When this occurs, whatever happens to follow the array in memory will be overwritten. Normally an error of this nature results in unpredictable garbage. However, malicious programmers, such as virus writers, have been known to use this behavior to their advantage. See Random Fact 6.1 for a case in which a programmer, by carefully analyzing how a compiler placed values into memory, discovered that the area following a global buffer was the return address for the activation record. By entering a carefully constructed, overly long line of text, it was possible to alter the return address. When the function finished, execution continued with the code supplied by the virus writer.

Avoid buffer overflow errors by never allocating a fixed-sized buffer. When doing string input and output, use the newer stream I/O classes and strings rather than the older character arrays. If you need a dynamically sized, indexed data structure, use a vector, not an array.

15.2.4 Object Slicing

In Section 8.4 you learned that a pointer declared as referencing an object of one class could, in fact, be referring to an object from a derived class. However, the behavior of pointers and nonpointers in this regard is subtly different, and it is important to understand what is going on.

Consider the following statements:

```
TravelClock* p = new TravelClock(true, "Rome", 9);  ❶
Clock* cp = p;  ❷
Clock c = *p;  ❸

cout << cp->get_location() << " time is " << cp->get_hours() << "\n";
cout << c.get_location() << " time is " << c.get_hours() << "\n";
```

If you run these statements, the output will be as follows:

```
Rome time is 6
Local time is 21
```

Both cases start from an object of type TravelClock. The first case assigned the address of this object to a variable declared as a pointer to an object of type Clock. This polymorphic assignment is permitted, because the class TravelClock is derived from Clock. In the second statement a simple assignment is used to copy the value from an instance of TravelClock to an instance of Clock. Given the similarities in the assignments, why are the results different?

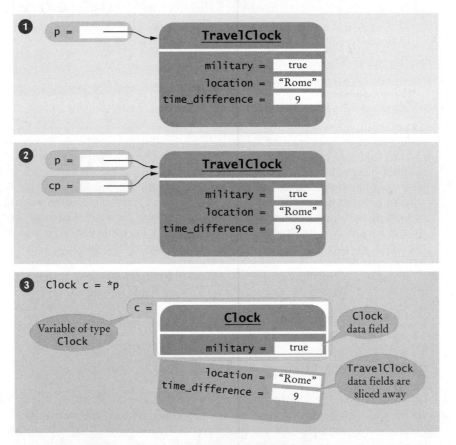

Figure 5   Data Fields Being Sliced by an Assignment

The answer is that the polymorphic behavior conflicts with the memory allocation model used by C++. Note that the objects of class TravelClock are larger than the objects of class Clock, since they include additional data members. This additional space was not taken into consideration when the activation record was constructed on the stack to hold the contents of the variable c. To maintain the efficiencies of the memory allocation, these additional fields are simply sliced away when the assignment takes place (see Figure 5). One way to remember this is to think that the object ceases to be an instance of the derived class and becomes an instance of the base class.

> Simple objects are not polymorphic in the way that pointers or references are. An assignment to such an object slices off data fields defined in the derived class.

When you understand the memory layout issues involved, it becomes clear why a member function call on an object is never polymorphic. For example, in the call

```
c.get_location()
```

there is no ambiguity about the type of c. It will always be a Clock. In contrast, the call

```
cp->get_location()
```

is polymorphic because cp might point to a Clock or an object of a derived class. Also note that the call

```
(*cp).get_location()
```

is polymorphic. Because the expression *cp is a reference to an object, not an actual object, it can refer to a derived class object.

Because of slicing, it is common in C++ to access objects in an inheritance hierarchy through pointers or references.

15.2.5 Memory Leaks

As was noted in Common Error 7.4, we say that a *memory leak* occurs when the programmer fails to return a dynamically allocated section of memory back to the memory manager using delete or delete[]. Often such a leak causes no harmful effect; however, in a long-running program, or if memory allocation occurs in a section of the program that is executed repeatedly, then a memory leak can cause a program to halt because the memory manager is unable to service a request for new memory. Memory leaks are often the result of successive assignments to the same pointer variables:

```
Clock* a_clock;
...
a_clock = new TravelClock(true, "Rome", 9);
...
a_clock = new TravelClock(true, "Tokyo", -7); // Leak, old memory is now lost
```

After the second assignment, both dynamically allocated objects remain on the heap, as shown in Figure 6. There are, however, no remaining pointers to the first object, so it cannot be recovered. The memory used by this object is lost.

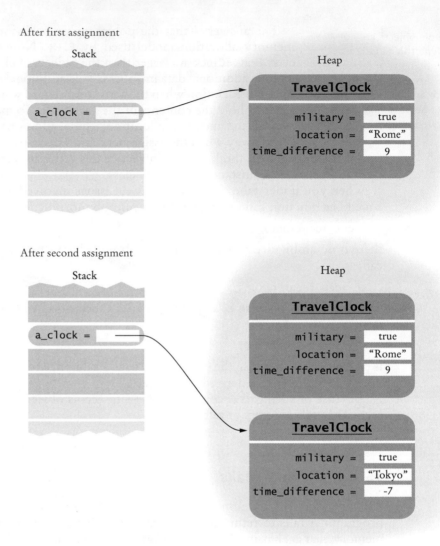

After first assignment

Figure 6 First Value Is Still on Heap, But Unreachable

15.2.6 Using Invalid Memory References

In an attempt to avoid memory leaks, programmers sometimes return a value to the memory manager before all references to the value have been deleted. As part of the process of managing and recycling heap-resident values, the heap manager often stores pertinent information in the values it manages. For example, the heap manager may keep a list of similarly sized blocks of memory, and store in each block a pointer to the next element. Reading such a value will produce garbage, and writing to such a value will confound the heap manager. Both errors are typically catastrophic.

Errors of this type are sometimes committed by a programmer forgetting that the update portion of a for loop is executed after the body of the loop, as in the following:

```
for (Node* p = ptr; p != NULL; p = p->next)
{
    delete p; // Error—p->next is referenced after p is deleted
}
```

The error occurs because the reference to p->next can be executed after the memory that p refers to has been recovered and, potentially, overwritten. The solution is to read this value first, before performing the deletion:

```
for (Node* p = ptr; p != NULL;)
{
    Node* q = p->next; // OK. Read p->next before deleting p
    delete p;
    p = q;
}
```

15.2.7 Deleting a Value More Than Once

If you call delete twice, chances are excellent that the heap is corrupted and that at some future point in time it will give out memory blocks twice or act unpredictably in some other way. These problems are extremely difficult to debug.

This error can sometimes be avoided by assigning a pointer a NULL value as soon as it is deleted. Using the delete statement with a NULL pointer has no effect. This practice can also help detect the previous error, using a dynamically allocated memory value after it has been deleted, because such uses will produce a NULL pointer error.

```
Clock* my_clock = new TravelClock(true, "Rome", 9);
...
delete my_clock;
my_clock = NULL; // Assign to NULL after deleting
...
cout << "Time is " << my_clock->get_hours << "\n";
// Error—using my_clock after it has been deleted
delete my_clock;   // However, delete on NULL pointer will have no effect
```

However, the assignment of a NULL value will not help if the same value is accessed by two different variables and both are deleted. This error is also common.

```
Clock* my_clock = new TravelClock(true, "Rome", 9);
Clock* your_clock = my_clock;
...
delete my_clock;
my_clock = NULL;
delete your_clock; // Same value being deleted twice
```

15.2.8 Deleting a Value That Was Never Allocated

Deleting a pointer that was never initialized and, therefore, contains a garbage value is a sure path to chaos. The heap manager may try to recover the memory returned by the pointer, which is likely not associated with the heap.

```
TravelClock* tc;
...
delete tc; // Error—attempting to delete garbage
```

On the other hand, the `delete` operator recognizes the value NULL, and will do nothing if a NULL pointer is deleted.

```
TravelClock* tc = NULL;
...
delete tc;   // This time OK, delete does nothing
```

This once again reinforces the rule that a variable should never be declared without being initialized.

15.3 Constructors

In Chapter 5 you were introduced to constructors. A *constructor* is a member function with the same name as the class in which it appears. In addition, a constructor does not specify a return type. The constructor is implicitly invoked as part of the process of object creation, and ties together the actions of memory allocation and initialization.

> Constructors tie together memory allocation and object initialization.

The purpose of a constructor is to ensure that every value created is also properly initialized. Along with destructors, which you will examine in Section 15.4, constructors encapsulate the management of the internal state of an object value behind the class definition, so that users of the class need not worry, or even be aware, of the implementation details. Often an important part of this task is the management of dynamically allocated memory.

A good illustration of this is the class `string`. You have been using string variables since the beginning of this book. What you may not have realized is that the contents of a string are not actually stored within the string value itself. Instead, a variable of type `string` holds a pointer to an array of character values. (That is, to a C style character array. See Section 7.5 for a discussion of C style strings.) The string value is typically stored on the stack, while the dynamically allocated character array is part of the heap, as shown in Figure 7.

Separating the string value from the character array allows the string to grow and shrink in response to string operations, such as catenation or substring, without running into the array fixed-size limitations. So effective is the job of hiding the management of this dynamic memory area within the `string` class, that many programmers using the `string` data type do not even know that it uses heap memory.

To see how this is done, imagine that the standard class `string` does not exist, and you want to write your own. Call the new class `String`. The following is the class

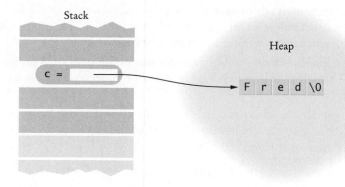

Figure 7 String Has Values on Both Stack and Heap

definition for this class. Some of the member functions have been labeled; the implementation of these will be discussed in following sections.

```
class String
{
public:
    String(); // Default constructor
    String(const char p[]); // Simple constructor
    String(const String& right); // Copy constructor
    ~String(); // Destructor
    String& operator=(const String& right); // Assignment operator
    String& operator+=(const String& right);
    int length() const;
    char& operator[](int index);
    char operator[](int index) const;
private:
    char* buffer;
    int len;
};
```

A constructor for class String will be called in the following situations.

- Execution enters a block in which a variable of class String is declared. Space for this variable will be created on the stack, and the constructor will be invoked before the block is executed.

- A global variable of class String is declared. Space for this variable is set aside in the static section of memory. The constructor is called before main starts.

- A static local variable of class String is declared. As with globals, static variables are assigned space in the static section of memory, and are initialized before main starts.

- An instance of class String is created on the heap by calling new String. The heap memory allocator creates a block of memory, then initializes the memory by invoking the constructor, before returning the address of the now initialized value.

- An unnamed temporary variable is created on the stack to hold the return value of a function, returning a value of type String. The constructor is called as part of the process of creating the temporary variable.
- A variable is being initialized that has a data field of type String. The constructor for the data field is invoked as part of the process of constructing the larger object.
- A variable is initialized that is from a class derived from String. The constructor for the base class is invoked as part of the construction and initialization of an instance of the derived class.

The various categories of constructors are examined in the following sections.

15.3.1 Constructors with Arguments

A constructor performs whatever tasks are necessary to initialize the newly created object. In our example we have purposely selected a class that must manage a dynamically allocated section of memory, namely the character array that will hold the underlying character values. Our constructor must see that this area is allocated and that it is properly initialized:

```
String::String(const char p[])
{
    // Determine number of characters in string
    len = 0;
    while (p[len] != '\0')
        len++;
    // Allocate buffer array, remember to make space for NULL character
    buffer = new char[len + 1];
    // Copy new characters
    for (int i = 0; i < len; i++)
        buffer[i] = p[i];
    buffer[len] = '\0';
}
```

We could have used the functions strlen and strcpy, described in Section 7.5, to manipulate the character array. However, for readers unfamiliar with these functions it is easier to understand the tasks being performed if they are spelled out in more detail.

The function length returns the length of the string, which is stored in a data field.

```
int String::length() const
{
    return len;
}
```

Access to each character in the string is provided by overloading the subscript operator. The second form will be used with constant values.

```
char& String::operator[](int index)
{
```

```
    assert((index >= 0) && (index < len));
    return buffer[index];
}

char String::operator[](int index) const
{
    assert((index >= 0) && (index < len));
    return buffer[index];
}
```

These two are combined in the implementation of the stream output operator:

```
ostream& operator<<(ostream& out, const String& right)
{
    int n = right.length();
    for (int i = 0; i < n; i++)
        out << right[i];
    return out;
}
```

COMMON ERROR 15.1

Forgetting the Dual Use of Single Argument Constructors

In Section 14.8 you learned that single argument constructors have a dual use. They are used to initialize a newly created value, but they are also used to convert a value from one type to another. Forgetting the second purpose can sometimes lead to strange errors, particularly given the complex C++ rules for conversion. For example, imagine that you had written a constructor for class String that takes an integer argument, producing the string representation of the integer:

```
class String
{
public:
    ...
    String(int n);
    ...
};

String::String(int a)
{
    char temp_buf[10];
    ostringstream outstr(temp_buf, 10);
    outstr << a;
    len = 0;
    while (temp_buf[len] != '\0')
        len++;
    buffer = new char[len + 1];
    for (int i = 0; i < len; i++)
        buffer[i] = temp_buf[i];
    buffer[len] = '\0';
}
```

Now imagine that you invoke a function that is looking for a String, passing it a character:

```
print_name('a');
```

You might imagine that the character value would be converted into a C string, which could then be used to initialize a temporary string. But there is no implicit conversion from character to string. There is, on the other hand, a conversion from character to integer, based on the ASCII value. (See Appendix D.) The ASCII value of character 'a' is 97. So this statement will use the constructor to convert the character to integer, and so will, perhaps surprisingly, pass to the function the string "97".

As you learned in Section 14.8, the use of constructors for the purpose of conversion can be avoided using the keyword explicit.

15.3.2 Default Constructors

As you learned in Chapter 5, a constructor with no arguments is known as a *default constructor*. If a local variable is declared with no arguments the default constructor will be invoked automatically:

```
String name; // Automatically initialized to empty string by default constructor
```

There are a number of other situations in which the default constructor will be invoked. For example, unless a field initializer is used, a data field will be initialized using a default constructor:

```
class Worker
{
public:
   ...
private:
   String name;
};
```

```
Worker fred;  // When created, fred.name will be empty string
```

When an array is created, the default constructor is called to initialize each array element.

```
String classmates[5]; // An array of five strings, all initialized to empty strings
```

While it is possible to write an array initializer for an array of primitive values (see Common Error 15.6 on page 627 for an example), there is no similar facility for arrays of objects. If a class has constructors, but no default constructor, then an attempt to allocate an array using the class will produce an error.

In our example class, the default constructor indicates a string with no characters. In this case it is not necessary to allocate memory for an array:

```
String::String()
{
   len = 0;
   buffer = NULL; // No need to allocate array to hold zero characters
}
```

SYNTAX 15.1 Default Constructor

ClassName::*ClassName*()
{
   statements
}

Example:

```
String::String()
{
    len = 0;
    buffer = NULL;
}
```

Purpose:

The default constructor will be invoked when a variable is declared with no arguments. In addition, it is used to initialize elements in an array, and to initialize data fields when no other initialization is provided.

COMMON ERROR 15.2

Default Constructor and Parentheses

Notice that the parentheses are omitted when invoking a default constructor.

```
String new_name;
```

This can be confusing, because a declaration that uses parentheses is syntactically correct, but has a different meaning. The following statement does not create, as you might expect, a new String initialized with the default constructor.

```
String new_name();
```

Instead, this statement is a function prototype. See Advanced Topic 4.1 for a discussion of prototypes. This statement is asserting that new_name is a function (defined elsewhere) that returns a value of type String.

The only place where parentheses are used to indicate a call on the default constructor is in the creation of an unnamed temporary. Such values are often used as arguments in a function call.

```
print_time(Time()); // Pass current time to print_time
```

15.3.3 Copy Constructors

> Copy constructors are used internally to create copies, or clones, of objects.

A constructor that takes as argument a reference to an object of the same class is termed a *copy constructor*. A copy constructor is used to create a copy, or clone, of a value:

```
String first("Fred");
String second(first);
    // second is initialized from first using copy constructor
String third = first; // Also uses copy constructor
```

The body of the copy constructor must do whatever is necessary to copy the value from the argument. In our example every String value manages its own dynamically allocated buffer. Therefore the copy constructor creates and initializes a new area:

```
String::String(const String& right)
{
   len = right.length();
   buffer = new char[len + 1];
   for (int i = 0; i < len; i++)
      buffer[i] = right[i];
   buffer[len] = '\0';
}
```

Copy constructors are invoked whenever a new object needs to be created as an exact copy of an existing object. This happens, for example, when an object is passed as an argument to a function that has declared a value parameter.

```
void print_line(String a)
{
   cout << a;
   a = "\n"; // Function modifies parameter variable
   cout << a;
}
```

```
String name("Fred");
print_line(name); // Argument is initialized by copy constructor
cout << name;
```

The fact that a copy has been created can be observed by noting that the value of name remains unchanged, even though the function modified the parameter variable. No copy constructor is used when you use a reference parameter.

```
void print_line2(String& a)
{
   cout << a;
   a = "\n";
   cout << a;
}
```

```
String name("Fred");
print_line2(name); // No copy is created because argument is by reference
cout << name; // Value is now changed
```

You can observe that no copy was created because the function changed the variable that was passed as a parameter.

SYNTAX 15.2 Copy Constructor

ClassName::*ClassName*(const *ClassName*& *parameter*)
{
    statements
}

Example:

```
String::String(const String& right)
{
   len = right.length();
   buffer = new char[len + 1];
   for (int i = 0; i < len; i++)
      buffer[i] = right[i];
   buffer[len] = '\0';
}
```

Purpose:

The copy constructor will be invoked when a variable is declared using another variable as an argument. In addition, copy constructors are used whenever an internal clone, or copy, of a value is needed. An example is creating a copy of an object to be passed to a value parameter.

QUALITY TIP 15.2

When to Use the System-Defined Copy Constructor

Unless the programmer provides one, the C++ compiler will automatically generate a copy constructor. This automatically generated function recursively invokes the copy constructor for each data field. This is termed a *memberwise copy*. In situations where a memberwise copy is appropriate (such as in the class Fraction), there is no need to write an explicit copy constructor or assignment operator. However, when classes use dynamically allocated memory (such as class String), this default behavior is usually not the desired action, and the functions should be defined.

15.3.4 Field Initializer Lists

As you learned in Advanced Topic 5.1, a data field can be assigned in a field initialization list. The unusual syntax for field initializers is found only in constructors (see Syntax 5.4).

```
class Employee
{
public:
   Employee(String employee_name, double initial_salary);
   ...
private:
   String name;
   double salary;
};

Employee::Employee(String employee_name, double initial_salary)
   : name(employee_name), salary(initial_salary)
{
}
```

Failing to use the field initializer list may result in a data field being modified twice; once by a default constructor, and the second time in the body of the constructor.

```
Employee::Employee(String employee_name, double initial_salary)
{
   // name is initialized first, using the default constructor for the String class
   name = employee_name; // Then it is reassigned here, using the assignment operator
   salary = initial_salary;
}
```

As noted in Section 8.2, a similar syntax is used for invoking the base-class constructor from the constructor in a derived class. The name of the base class replaces the name of the data field being initialized, as in the following example:

```
class TeachingAssistant : public Employee
{
public:
   TeachingAssistant(String student_name);
};

TeachingAssistant::TeachingAssistant(String student_name)
   // Teaching assistants all get same starting salary
   : Employee(student_name, 5000)
{
}
```

If you omit the invocation of the base-class constructor, the default constructor for the base class will be automatically invoked. In this case an error is reported if the base class has no default constructor.

Other data fields can be initialized using the same syntax. This form is required for data fields declared as constant, or for references (which, like constants, are assigned once and never modified). The notation is also necessary when assigning a size to a vector:

```
class PartDescription
{
public:
    PartDescription(String part_name, int inventory_number);
private:
    const String name;
    const int part_number:
    vector<PartDescription*> subcomponents;
};

PartDescription::PartDescription(String part_name, int inventory_number)
    : name(part_name), part_number(inventory_number), subcomponents(3)
{
}
```

ADVANCED TOPIC 15.1

Constructors Are Always Extensions

As you learned in Section 8.3, a derived class D can override a function in a base class B either as an extension or as a replacement. A member function $D::f$ is an extension if it invokes $B::f$ in the body of the function, otherwise the body of $D::f$ replaces that of $B::f$.

Although not the same mechanism, a constructor in a derived class does, in some fashion, override the constructor in the base class. However, a constructor is always an extension, never a replacement. The constructor for the derived class will always invoke the constructor for the base class, using the default constructor for the base class if no alternative is provided. It is not possible to avoid the execution of the constructor in the base class.

15.3.5 Assignment Operators

Although not technically a constructor, an assignment operator is similar to a constructor in the way it sets a variable to a new value. For this reason the tasks performed by an assignment operator are almost always very similar to those performed by the copy constructor. In the String class, the assignment operator must delete the old buffer, then create space for a new buffer and copy the character values.

```
String& String::operator=(const String& right)
{
    if (this != &right)
    {
        delete[] buffer; // Get rid of old buffer
        len = right.length();
        buffer = new char[len + 1];
        for (int i = 0; i < len; i++)
            buffer[i] = right[i];
        buffer[len] = '\0';
    }
    return *this;
}
```

Assignments should always check for the possibility of self assignment, assigning a variable to itself. As shown, this can be easily checked by comparing the value of this to the address of the argument. No action should be performed when a self assignment is detected. Assignments should also always return a reference to the current value, matching the action of the assignment operator for built-in types.

Other functions or operators may have similar actions. In the class String the += operator is overloaded to give it the meaning of catenation.

```
String& String::operator+=(const String& right)
{
    int n = length();
    int m = right.length();
    len = n + m;
    char* new_buffer = new char[len + 1];
    for (int i = 0; i < n; i++)
        new_buffer[i] = buffer[i];
    for (int j = 0; j < m; j++)
        new_buffer[n + j] = right[j];
    new_buffer[len] = '\0';
    delete[] buffer;
    buffer = new_buffer;
    return *this;
}
```

It is often convenient to make a single internal function to perform the common actions, and have both the copy constructor and the assignment operator call that function. You will see an example of this in Section 15.5.

QUALITY TIP 15.3

Observing Constructors

To observe when constructors and assignment statements (and destructors, which you will encounter shortly) are executed, simply place debugging messages into the body of the appropriate functions. For example, suppose this is done in our String example for each constructor and operator:

```
String::String(const char p[])
{
    cout << "Entering String::String(const char[])\n";
    ...
}
// And so on for all constructors and operators
```

Executing the following series of declarations and statements then allows us to observe the sequence of constructor invocations.

```
String one;
one = "Bert";
String two;
two = one;
one += " and Ernie";
```

The output would tell us which constructors or operators are being executed in these five statements:

```
Entering String()
Entering String(const char[])
Entering String::operator=(String)
Entering String()
Entering String::operator=(String)
Entering String(const char[])
Entering String::operator+=(String)
```

The execution performance can be improved by using initialization rather than assignment.

```
String one = "Bert";
String two = one;
two += " and Ernie";
```

Now there will be only three constructor calls and the append operator.

```
Entering String(const char[])
Entering String(const String&)
Entering String(const char[])
Entering operator+=(const String&)
```

If this small bit of code were to appear within a loop, the difference between seven operations and four could be very significant.

15.4 Destructors

Destructors are defined to take care of resource management when an object is deleted.

If the purpose of a constructor is to ensure that every allocated value is properly initialized, then the purpose of a destructor is to ensure that values are properly prepared for their deallocation. A *destructor* is a member function with the name ~*ClassName*, no arguments, and no return type. Like constructors, destructors are never directly invoked; instead they will be implicitly invoked when a value is destroyed. This can occur in the following situations:

- At the end of a block, destructors for any local variables will be invoked.
- At the end of a function, destructors for any arguments will be invoked.
- At the end of a statement, destructors for any named or unnamed temporary variables will be invoked.
- When a dynamically allocated value is deleted, the destructor is invoked before the memory is recovered.
- When main terminates, destructors for all static local and global values will be invoked.

- When an object variable is deleted, destructors for any data fields will be invoked.
- When an object variable from a derived class is deleted, destructors for the base class will be invoked.
- When an exception is thrown and execution leaves a block, destructors for any local variables will be invoked.

The purpose of a destructor is to perform any housekeeping tasks that may be necessary before a value is discarded. The most common housekeeping task is to avoid a memory leak by releasing any dynamically allocated memory, but other tasks that might appear in a destructor include closing files or releasing other system resources. If no destructor is provided, a default destructor will be automatically generated. The default destructor has an empty body; that is, it performs no actions. Destructors are much less common than constructors. While almost every class requires some initialization, a destructor is only necessary if an object requires some kind of resource management. There is no need for a destructor in class Fraction, for instance. When a Fraction is deleted (such as a local variable going out of scope), its memory is simply recovered and that is that.

The destructor for our String class is a good example. The destructor must ensure that when a value of type String is deleted, the dynamically allocated character array is returned to the heap memory manager.

```
String::~String()
{
    delete[] buffer;
}
```

Syntax 15.3 Destructor Definition

ClassName::~*ClassName*()
{
    statements
}

Example:

```
String::~String()
{
    delete[] buffer;
}
```

Purpose:

Perform any housekeeping tasks that should be performed before an object is deleted.

COMMON ERROR 15.3

Confusing Destruction and Deletion

Beginning programmers often confuse destruction and deletion. These concepts are closely related, but it is important that you separate them in your mind.

- Deletion means that a pointer is passed to the `delete` operator.
- Destruction means that a destructor (`~ClassName()`) is called when an object goes out of scope.

In other words, pointers are deleted and objects are destroyed.

Here are a couple of examples. Here, the `name` object goes out of scope:

```
{
   String name("Fred");
   ...
} // name.~String() automatically invoked here
```

The `name` object is destroyed. That is, the destructor is executed. As a consequence, the pointer `name.buffer` is deleted.

The next example is more complex. Consider this deletion of a pointer to a heap object.

```
String* p = new String("Alice");
...
delete p; // p->~String() automatically invoked here
```

The `delete` operator causes destruction of the object to which p points, which in turn causes the pointer p->buffer to be deleted. In other words, two blocks of memory are recycled to the heap: the `String` object and the internal buffer it contains. See Figure 8.

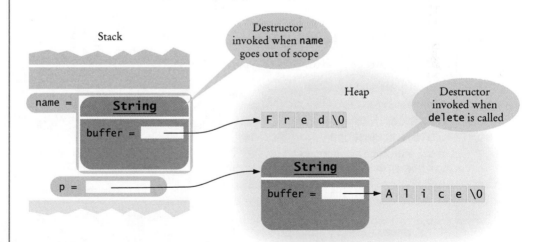

Figure 8   Destruction of Stack and Heap Objects

PRODUCTIVITY HINT 15.1

Tracing Execution

Earlier, you learned about the technique of placing output statements in a constructor as a means of seeing when and where constructors were being invoked. A useful programming tool can be built by extending this idea. Consider the following class definition:

ch15/trace.h

```
1   #ifndef TRACE_H
2   #define TRACE_H
3
4   #include <iostream>
1   #include <string>
2
3   using namespace std;
4
5   class Trace
6   {
7   public:
8      Trace(string n);
9      ~Trace();
10  private:
11     string name;
12  };
13
14  Trace::Trace(string n) : name(n)
15  {
16     cout << "Entering " << name << "\n";
17  }
18
19  Trace::~Trace()
20  {
21     cout << "Exiting " << name << "\n";
22  }
23
24  #endif
```

ch15/tracetest.cpp

```
1   #include <iostream>
2   #include "trace.h"
3
4   using namespace std;
5
6   int main()
7   {
8      int a = 5;
9      Trace one("TraceTest");
10     if (a < 10)
11     {
12        Trace two("if");
13        // ...
14     }
```

```
15    else
16    {
17        Trace three("else");
18        // ...
19    }
20    return 0;
21 }
```

The only purpose of the class is to display a message both when the constructor is invoked and when the destructor is executed. By creating local variables inside blocks, one can trace the flow of control inside a procedure. The output from variable **one** will be printed when execution of the function commences and when it terminates. The output from variable **two** will only appear if the condition tested by the if statement is true, while the output from variable **three** will be printed if the else branch is taken.

COMMON ERROR 15.4

Not Declaring Destructors Virtual

Whenever a class that is intended to serve as a base class for inheritance declares a destructor, the destructor should be declared as virtual. To illustrate, consider the following class declaration:

```
class Employee
{
public:
    ...
    virtual ~Employee();
private:
    char* name;
};

Employee::~Employee()
{
    delete[] name;
}

class TeachingAssistant : public Employee
{
    ...
private:
    string department;
};
```

At first glance, it doesn't look as if TeachingAssistant needs a destructor, but it has one, provided by the C++ compiler. That destructor invokes the string destructor on the department member.

Now imagine that you create and delete a polymorphic variable, as follows:

```
Employee* a = new TeachingAssistant();
delete a;
```

If the destructor in `Employee` is declared virtual, as shown, both the destructors in class `Employee` and class `TeachingAssistant` will be executed. If the `virtual` designation is omitted, only the function in class `Employee` will be performed. As a result, the memory of the `department` member will not be reclaimed.

QUALITY TIP 15.4

Include Virtual Destructors

Any class that includes at least one virtual member function should define a virtual destructor, even if it performs no explicit memory management. To illustrate, consider the following class declaration:

```
class Person
{
   ...
   // No destructor
private:
   int id;
};
```

No destructor has been provided, and of course, none is needed since the class does not manage heap memory or other resources. But now suppose that a derived class is formed.

```
class Employee : public Person
{
   ...
private:
   string name;
};
```

Now imagine that you create and delete a polymorphic variable, as follows:

```
Person* a = new Employee();
delete a;
```

The `Employee` class has a destructor, provided by the C++ compiler, that destroys the `name` member. But that destructor is not called when deleting the `Person*` pointer.

The remedy is to add a virtual do-nothing destructor to the `Person` class:

```
class Person
{
   ...
   virtual ~Person() {}
};
```

A good rule of thumb is to include a destructor (even if it does nothing) and declare it as `virtual` if there are any other virtual member functions in your class. Otherwise, destructors from any derived classes may not be executed.

QUALITY TIP 15.5

If Destructor, Then Copy Constructor and Assignment

The assignment operator, copy constructor, and destructor are collectively called the "big three". A simple rule of thumb is that if you define a destructor, then you should always provide a copy constructor and an assignment operator, and make sure all three perform in a similar fashion [1]. You must implement them for any class that manages heap memory. The equivalence of a copy constructor and the assignment operator should be clear; both are initializing a new value using an existing value. But the assignment operator is both deleting an old value, and creating a new one. You must make sure the first part of this task matches the actions of the destructor.

Imagine, for example, that our `String` class defined a destructor, but we had forgotten to define the copy constructor. In this case a default copy constructor would be automatically generated for us. This default would use memberwise initialization. An inadvertent copy could then produce a premature buffer deletion (see Figure 9):

```
String a = "Fred"; // Internal buffer is allocated here
{
    String b = a; // Error—memberwise copy produces shared buffer
} // Destructor b.~String() invoked, buffer is deleted
cout << a << "\n"; // Sure to cause error, because buffer is now deleted
```

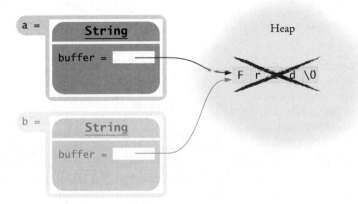

Figure 9   When b Is Deleted, Buffer for a Becomes Invalid

Here is a simple summary of the tasks for each of the big three.

Destructor
Free all dynamic memory that the object manages.

Copy Constructor
Initialize the object as a copy of the parameter object. For values with dynamic memory, this usually means allocating and initializing a duplicate copy of any dynamic memory values.

Assignment Operator

Check whether this == &right. *If so, do nothing.*

Free the dynamic memory of the object that is no longer needed. Copy the value of the argument. Again, this usually means allocating and initializing a duplicate copy of any dynamic memory values. Return *this.

Notice that the big three are actually constructed out of two lower level operations. If copy(right) is a member function that copies the argument, and free() a member function that frees dynamically allocated resources, the "big three" for class X can be described as follows:

```
X::X(const X& right)
{
    copy(right);
}

X& X::operator=(const X& right)
{
    if (this != &right)
    {
        free();
        copy(right);
    }
    return *this;
}

X::~X()
{
    free();
}
```

> Constructors, destructors, and the assignment operator must all be defined to work together to manage internally allocated dynamic memory.

Some authors refer to the "big four", including the default constructor in the group. What unites the big four is that they will all be automatically generated should the programmer not provide an alternative, and the automatically generated versions are generally incorrect if there are dynamically managed data fields. However, the default constructor is usually needed only if you are creating an array of values.

Finally, note that you only need to worry about the "big three" (or "big four") if your class manages heap memory. If you use the library classes, such as vector or list, there is nothing to worry about; these classes already implement the "big three" for you.

15.4.1 The Class auto_ptr

The relationship between a String object and the underlying buffer is a pattern that is repeated many times in programs. That is, there is an object that must dynamically allocate another memory value in order to perform its intended task. However, the lifetime of the dynamic value is tied to the lifetime of the original object; it exists as long as the original object exists, and should be eliminated when the original object ceases to exist.

To simplify the management of memory in this case, the standard library implements a useful type named auto_ptr. The definition of auto_ptr is found in file <memory>. When a variable declared as an auto_ptr is deleted, the dynamic memory associated with the variable is automatically recovered:

```
int f()
{
    auto_ptr<Employee> p = new Employee(...);
    ...
}   // Destructor of p will automatically delete Employee object
```

Local variables of type auto_ptr are useful in combination with exceptions, which we will examine in Chapter 17. When an exception terminates execution of a block, it still invokes the destructor of the auto_ptr, and the memory is properly recycled.

ADVANCED TOPIC 15.2

Overloading the Memory Management Operators

As we noted in Chapter 14, it is possible to overload the operators new and delete, thereby obtaining even more control over these tasks than is provided by the C++ run-time system. To illustrate the use of these operators, imagine that you wanted to change the allocation and recovery of nodes in the List class, so that deleted values would be stored in a global linked list. A request for a new Node would first check this list, removing the value if found, and otherwise asking the run-time system for a new value, as before:

```
class Node
{
public:
    Node(string s);
    void* operator new(size_t bytes);
    void operator delete(void* value);
private:
    string data;
    Node* previous;
    Node* next;
};

Node* free_store_list = NULL; // Global list, initially empty

void* Node::operator new(size_t types)
{
    if (free_store_list != NULL)
    {
        result = free_store_list;
        free_store_list = free_store_list->next;
    }
    else result = ::new Node;
    return result;
}

void Node::operator delete(void* value)
{
```

```
        Node* p = static_cast<Node*>(value);
        p->next = free_store_list;
        free_store_list = p;
    }
```

The arguments and return types to these operators must be as shown. The type `size_t` is a standard type used to represent the size of object values. The double colon preceding the `new` operator is a global qualifier, indicating that the global `new` operator should be used when the free store list contains no elements. The argument to `delete` is declared `void*`. This type will match any pointer type, in particular the pointer to `Node`. However, to be used as a pointer to `Node`, it must first be cast to the correct type. In a program with many allocations and removals the improvement in time for these simple functions over the standard memory allocation routines could be significant.

15.5 Reference Counting

> Reference counts can be used to manage memory when there is no clear owner for a dynamically allocated value.

A simple rule of thumb is that if an object allocates any dynamic memory it should be responsible for ensuring the memory is eventually freed when it is no longer useful. As is true in life, this simple rule of thumb becomes more complicated as soon as you introduce sharing. If two objects share a common data value, which one should be held responsible for ensuring the common data is freed?

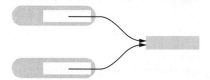

In some cases, one of the objects can be designated as the "owner" of the shared resource, but this is not always possible. In these cases, one common solution is to use a technique termed *reference counting*. The basic idea is to maintain a count, or reference, that indicates the number of references to the shared resource. When an object is first created, the reference count is one.

When the data value is shared with another object, the reference is incremented.

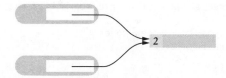

When an object is destroyed, or removes the reference to the value, the count is decremented.

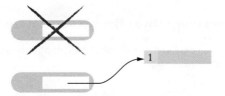

When the reference count is decremented to zero, it means that all objects using the shared value have been deleted and the shared data value itself can be deleted. To illustrate the idea of reference counts, imagine you wanted to change the semantics for the assignment of strings so that two strings would share a common internal data buffer. The following class declaration illustrates this technique. The main function prints each statement before it is executed.

ch15/sharedstring.cpp

```
1   #include <iostream>
2
3   using namespace std;
4
5   class SharedString
6   {
7   public:
8       SharedString();
9       SharedString(const char* right);
10      SharedString(const SharedString& right);
11      ~SharedString();
12      SharedString& operator=(const SharedString& right);
13  private:
14      class StringReference;
15      StringReference* p;
16      void reassign(StringReference*);
17  };
18
19  class SharedString::StringReference
20  {
21  public:
22      int count;
23      char* buffer;
24      StringReference(const char* right);
25      ~StringReference();
26  };
27
28  SharedString::SharedString() : p(NULL)
29  {
30      cout << "Entering SharedString() \n";
31  }
32
33  SharedString::SharedString(const char* right) : p(NULL)
34  {
```

```
35        cout << "Entering SharedString(const char*) ";
36        reassign(new StringReference(right));
37    }
38
39    SharedString::SharedString(const SharedString& right) : p(NULL)
40    {
41        cout << "Entering SharedString(const SharedString&) ";
42        reassign(right.p);
43    }
44
45    SharedString::~SharedString()
46    {
47        cout << "Entering ~SharedString() ";
48        reassign(NULL);
49    }
50
51    SharedString& SharedString::operator=(const SharedString& right)
52    {
53        cout << "Entering operator=(const SharedString&) ";
54        reassign(right.p);
55        return *this;
56    }
57
58    void SharedString::reassign(SharedString::StringReference* np)
59    {
60        if (np == NULL) // Print old values
61            cout << "value: " << p->buffer << " count: " << p->count << "\n";
62        if (np != NULL) // Increment count on the new value
63            np->count += 1;
64        if (p != NULL)   // Decrement reference count on old value
65        {
66            p->count -= 1;
67            if (p->count == 0)
68                delete p;
69        }
70        p = np;   // Change binding
71        if (p != NULL) // Print new values
72            cout << "value: " << p->buffer << " count: " << p->count << "\n";
73    }
74
75    SharedString::StringReference::StringReference(const char* right)
76    {
77        count = 0;
78        int n = 0;
79        while (right[n] != '\0')
80            n++;
81        buffer = new char[1 + n];
82        for (int i = 0; i < n; i++)
83            buffer[i] = right[i];
84        buffer[n] = '\0';
85    }
86
87    SharedString::StringReference::~StringReference()
88    {
89        delete[] buffer;
```

```
90  }
91
92  SharedString g; // Global value
93
94  int main()
95  {
96      cout << "Entering main\n";
97      cout << "SharedString a = \"Fred\";\n";
98  SharedString a = "Fred";
99      cout << "SharedString b = \"Alice\";\n";
100 SharedString b = "Alice";
101     cout << "SharedString c;\n";
102 SharedString c;
103     cout << "c = a;\n";
104 c = a;
105     cout << "a = b;\n";
106 a = b;
107     cout << "g = b;\n";
108 g = b;
109     cout << "Exiting main\n";
110     return 0;
111 }
```

Program Run

```
Entering SharedString()
Entering main
SharedString a = "Fred";
Entering SharedString(const char*) value: Fred count: 1
SharedString b = "Alice";
Entering SharedString(const char*) value: Alice count: 1
SharedString c;
Entering SharedString()
c = a;
Entering operator=(const SharedString&) value: Fred count: 2
a = b;
Entering operator=(const SharedString&) value: Alice count: 2
g = b;
Entering operator=(const SharedString&) value: Alice count: 3
Exiting main
Entering ~SharedString() value: Fred count: 1
Entering ~SharedString() value: Alice count: 3
Entering ~SharedString() value: Alice count: 2
Entering ~SharedString() value: Alice count: 1
```

The structure holding both the reference count and the buffer is defined by a nested class, StringReference, within the body of the SharedString class. References are managed by the function named reassign. This function is used by the constructors, the destructor, and by the assignment. It is not uncommon for these tasks to be very similar, and factoring their common aspects into a single internal function is good programming style. The function reassign takes as argument a pointer to a StringReference. This pointer could be NULL. If it is not NULL, the reference to the argument value is incremented. Then the reference to the current value is decremented. If the decremented reference becomes zero, the space for the internal character array is recovered.

The output illustrates how the various reference counts are incremented and decremented during the course of execution.

The default constructor is invoked even before the first statement is executed, in order to initialize the global variable named g. After the first statement, the value Fred has reference count 1. The second statement leaves the value Alice with a similar reference count of 1. The first assignment statement causes the value Fred to be shared, and hence the reference count is incremented to 2. The second assignment causes Alice to be incremented to 2. The reference on the original value in a is decremented to 1. The assignment to the global variable g means that there are now three variables that refer to the value Alice. After execution ends the three destructors are invoked to remove the three local variables. Finally, the destructor is invoked to remove the global variable g.

Reference counts may seem complex, but once mastered they can be implemented in a routine fashion. The following guidelines summarize the technique:

- Create separate classes for the clients (e.g., SharedString), reference (SharedString::StringReference), and the shared data (the character buffer inside of StringReference).

- Assignment among the clients of the shared data increments the reference count for the new value, and decrements the count for the old value. Note that assignment in C++ can occur in multiple ways, such as through the copy constructor as well as the assignment statement.

- When a client is destroyed, the reference to the shared resource is decremented. Destructors can be used to detect when the client is destroyed.

- When the reference count reaches zero, the shared resource is released.

COMMON ERROR 15.5

Self Assignment

We have been careful in our description of reference counting to insist that in an assignment the reference count for a new value is incremented first, and then the reference for the old value is decremented. A common error is to perform these tasks in the opposite order. This will often work until a self assignment is performed; that is, a statement such as the following:

```
SharedString a = "Fred";
a = a;
```

If the order of operations is reversed, the assignment will first decrement the reference count, which will then become zero, and the shared buffer will be deleted. Then the reference count will be incremented, but now it is too late, as the space for the shared buffer has already been deleted.

A simple solution to the problem of self assignment is to not do anything in this situation. A test for self assignment is to compare the argument to the value of this:

```
SharedString& SharedString::operator=(const SharedString& right)
{
   if (this != &right)
      reassign(right.p); // Only assign if not self assignment
   return *this;
}
```

COMMON ERROR 15.6

Reference Counting Fails in the Presence of Cycles

Reference counting is an excellent form of storage management for many applications. It does, however, have some drawbacks. Assignment, or copying a reference counted object, takes more time than simply copying a plain pointer. The updating of the reference count does extract a small performance cost. But this cost is typically negligible. Most importantly, reference counts do not work for complex data structures if they can ever produce a cycle. As Figure 10 illustrates, a cycle of shared values may never be deallocated, because each value references another, and so, even if there are no other references outside the cycle (and thus, the data could potentially be recovered), the reference counts will not reach zero.

Before using the technique of reference counting you should study your problem description carefully to ensure that cycles cannot arise.

Figure 10   A Reference Count Cycle

15.6 Case Study: Matrices, Continued

In this section we show how to extend the matrix case study we began in Section 14.11. Instead of 3×3 matrices, the class Matrix will now represent matrices with an arbitrary number of rows and columns. Because the size of the internal array cannot be determined at compile time, it is necessary to use dynamic memory allocation. The big three (copy constructor, assignment operator, and destructor) are written in the form described in Section 15.4. Access methods return the number of rows and columns in a matrix, which replace the static constants used in the earlier version. Smaller member functions have been inlined, as in Chapter 14. Other than these changes, the code is just as before. In the following listings the sections that are the same as before have been omitted.

ch15/matrix2.h

```
  1  #ifndef MATRIX2_H
  2  #define MATRIX2_H
  3
     ... Same as in matrix1.h
 59
 60  /**
 61      This class describes a matrix with arbitrary rows and columns.
 62  */
 63  class Matrix
 64  {
 65  public:
 66     /**
 67         Constructs a matrix filled with zero elements.
 68     */
 69     Matrix(int r, int c);
 70
 71     /**
 72         The big three: copy constructor, assignment operator, and destructor.
 73     */
 74     Matrix(const Matrix& other);
 75     Matrix& operator=(const Matrix& other);
 76     ~Matrix();
 77
 78     /**
 79         Gets the number of rows of this matrix.
 80         @return the number of rows
 81     */
 82     int get_rows() const;
 83
 84     /**
 85         Gets the number of columns of this matrix.
 86         @return the number of columns
 87     */
 88     int get_columns() const;
 89
     ...
126
127  private:
128     /**
129         Copies another matrix into this matrix.
130         @param other the other matrix
131     */
132     void copy(const Matrix& other);
133
134     /**
135         Frees the memory for this matrix.
136     */
137     void free();
138
```

```
139     int rows;
140     int columns;
141     double* elements;
142 };
143
    ...
180
181 inline Matrix::Matrix(const Matrix& other)
182 {
183     copy(other);
184 }
185
186 inline Matrix::~Matrix()
187 {
188     free();
189 }
190
191 inline int Matrix::get_rows() const
192 {
193     return rows;
194 }
195
196 inline int Matrix::get_columns() const
197 {
198     return columns;
199 }
200
201 inline void Matrix::free()
202 {
203     delete[] elements;
204 }
205
    ...
247
248 #endif
```

ch15/matrix2.cpp

```
1  #include <iomanip>
2  #include "matrix2.h"
3
4  Matrix::Matrix(int r, int c)
5      : rows(r), columns(c), elements(new double[rows * columns])
6  {
7      for (int i = 0; i < rows * columns; i++)
8          elements[i] = 0;
9  }
10
11 Matrix& Matrix::operator=(const Matrix& other)
12 {
13     if (this != &other)
14     {
```

```
15        free();
16        copy(other);
17     }
18     return *this;
19  }
20
21  void Matrix::copy(const Matrix& other)
22  {
23     rows = other.rows;
24     columns = other.columns;
25     elements = new double[rows * columns];
26     for (int i = 0; i < rows * columns; i++)
27        elements[i] = other.elements[i];
28  }
29
    ... Same as in matrix1.cpp
```

ch15/matrixtest2.cpp

```
1   #include "matrix2.h"
2
3   int main()
4   {
5      Matrix m(3, 3);
6      m[0][0] = m[1][1] = m[2][2] = 1;
7      m[0][1] = m[1][2] = 2;
8      Matrix a = 2 * m;
9      Matrix b(4, 4);
10     b = m * m;
11     cout << a << "\n";
12     cout << b << "\n";
13     cout << a + b;
14     return 0;
15  }
```

Program Run

```
    2        4        0
    0        2        4
    0        0        2

    1        4        4
    0        1        4
    0        0        1

    3        8        4
    0        3        8
    0        0        3
```

CHAPTER SUMMARY

1. Memory is divided into four areas: code, static data, the run-time stack, and the heap.

2. Stack-based memory is tied to function entry and exit. Errors can occur if references continue to exist after a function exits.

3. Pointers can refer to memory in all four areas.

4. Initialization errors can occur for variables in any section of memory.

5. Dynamically allocated memory introduces two potential pointer initialization errors: failure to initialize the pointer, and failure to initialize the space the pointer references.

6. Simple objects are not polymorphic in the way that pointers or references are. An assignment to such an object slices off data fields defined in the derived class.

7. Constructors tie together memory allocation and object initialization.

8. Copy constructors are used internally to create copies, or clones, of objects.

9. Destructors are defined to take care of resource management when an object is deleted.

10. Constructors, destructors, and the assignment operator must all be defined to work together to manage internally allocated dynamic memory.

11. Reference counts can be used to manage memory when there is no clear owner for a dynamically allocated value.

FURTHER READING

1. Marshall Cline and Greg A. Lomow, *C++ Frequently Asked Questions*, Addison-Wesley, 1995.

REVIEW EXERCISES

Exercise R15.1. When is memory for a local variable allocated? When is it recovered?

Exercise R15.2. Why might you want to allocate an array on the heap, rather than on the run-time stack?

Exercise R15.3. Describe the different named values in the following program, and explain in what category of memory each value resides.

```
int master_count = 0;

int counting_function(int increment)
{
   static int internal_count = 0;
   internal_count += increment;
   master_count += increment;
   return internal_count;
}

int main()
{
   for (int i = 0; i < 10; i++)
      if (master_count != counting_function(i))
         cout << "Why aren't these the same?";
   return 0;
}
```

Exercise R15.4. Show the state of the run-time stack and the location and value of each variable when execution reaches the output statement in the following program.

```
void print_result(int value)
{
   cout << "Final result is " << value << "\n";
}

void add_to(int start, int increment, int limit)
{
   if (start < limit)
      add_to(start + increment, increment, limit);
   else
      print_result(start + limit);
}

int main()
{
   add_to(5, 2, 10);
   return 0;
}
```

Exercise R15.5. What is the error in the following program fragment?

```
char* secret_message()
{
   char message_buffer[100];
   char* text = "Use the force, Luke!";
   int n = 0;
   while (text[n] != '\0')
      n++;
   for (int i = 0; i <= n; i++)
      message_buffer[i] = text[i];
   return message_buffer;
}
```

Exercise R15.6. Compile and execute the following program. Try inputting values of various lengths. Can you explain the results when the inputs are larger than four characters?

```
int main()
{
   char a[4], b[4], c[4];
   a[0] = b[0] = c[0] = '\0';
   cin >> b;
   cout << "a is " << a << "\n";
   cout << "b is " << b << "\n";
   cout << "c is " << c << "\n";
   return 0;
}
```

Exercise R15.7. Why is the initialization of pointers to dynamically allocated memory more complex than the initialization of simple variables?

Exercise R15.8. What error is being committed in the assignment operator for the following class?

```
class String
{
public:
   String(const char right[]);
   String& operator=(const String& right);
private:
   char* buffer;
};

String::String(const char right[])
{
   len = 0;
   while (right[len] != '\0')
      len++;
   buffer = new char[len + 1];
   for (int i = 0; i < len; i++)
      buffer[i] = right[i];
   buffer[len] = '\0';
}

String& String::operator=(const String& right)
{
   int n = right.length();
   for (int i = 0; i <= n; i++)
      buffer[i] = right.buffer[i];
   return *this;
}
```

Exercise R15.9. What is the error in the assignment operator for this class?

```
class String
{
public:
   String(const char right[]);
   String& operator=(const String& right);
```

```
private:
   char* buffer;
};

String::String(const char right[])
{
   len = 0;
   while (right[len] != '\0')
      len++;
   buffer = new char[len + 1];
   for (int i = 0; i < len; i++)
      buffer[i] = right[i];
   buffer[len] = '\0';
}

String& String::operator=(const String& right)
{
   if (this != &right)
   {
      delete[] buffer;
      len = right.length();
      char* buffer = new char[len + 1];
      for (int i = 0; i < len; i++)
         buffer[i] = right[i];
      buffer[len] = '\0';
   }
   return *this;
}
```

Exercise R15.10. What output will be printed by the following program?

```
class Base
{
public:
   virtual void display();
};

void Base::display()
{
   cout << "In base class \n";
}

class Derived : public Base
{
public:
   Derived(int v );
   virtual void display();
private:
   int value;
};

Derived::Derived(int v)
{
   value = v;
}
```

```
void Derived::display()
{
   cout << "In derived class, value is " << value << "\n";
}

int main()
{
   Base b;
   Derived d(4);
   b = d;
   b.display();
   Base* bp = new Derived(7);
   bp->display();
}
```

Exercise R15.11. What output will be printed by the following program?

```
class Base
{
public:
   Base();
   Base(int v);
   virtual void display();
private:
   int value;
};

Base::Base()
{
   value = 7;
}

Base::Base(int v)
{
   value = v;
}

void Base::display()
{
   cout << "In base class, value is " << value << "\n";
}

class Derived : public Base
{
public:
   Derived(int v);
   virtual void display();
private:
   int new_value;
};

Derived::Derived(int v)
{
   new_value = v;
}
```

```
void Derived::display()
{
   Base::display();
   cout << "In derived class, value is " << new_value << "\n";
}

int main()
{
   Derived d(5);
   d.display();
}
```

Exercise R15.12. Section 15.2.2 discusses the error that can arise when a function returns a reference to a local variable. To explore this further, imagine that the operator+ has been defined as shown in that section, and the statement a = (b + c) + d is being executed, where a, b, c, and d are variables of type Fraction. Remember that the operator has been redefined, so that this statement is internally the same as

```
Fraction temp& = operator+(b, c);
a = operator+(temp, d);
```

Draw a picture, similar to Figure 1, that shows the state of the stack prior to the statement, assuming that a, b, c, and d are all local variables. Then show the stack during the execution of the first operator, and again following the return of the second operator. Indicate the location of each variable on the stack. For reference variables, draw pointers to the location being referenced. Using these diagrams, explain why erroneous results are likely to be produced.

Exercise R15.13. Consider this code:

```
void f(int n)
{
   list<Employee*> e;
   for (int i = 1; i <= n; i++)
      e.push_back(new Employee());
}
```

At the end of the function, the list destructor will automatically delete the nodes of e. Why does the function still have a memory leak?

Exercise R15.14. The copy constructor for a class X has the form X(const X& b). Why is the parameter passed by reference? Explain why you can't define a constructor of the form X(X b)?

Exercise R15.15. What would be the implication of declaring a copy constructor private?

Exercise R15.16. What is the difference between destruction and deletion of an object?

Exercise R15.17. What problems could a programmer encounter if they defined a destructor for a class but no assignment operator? Illustrate your description with an example class.

Exercise R15.18. What problems could a programmer encounter if they defined a destructor for a class but no copy constructor? Illustrate your description with an example class.

Exercise R15.19. Which objects are destroyed when the following function exits? Which values are deleted?

```
void f(const Fraction& a)
{
   Fraction b = a;
   Fraction* c = new Fraction(3, 4);
   Fraction* d = &a;
   Fraction* e = new Fraction(7,8);
   Fraction* f = c;
   delete f;
}
```

Exercise R15.20. You can find the code for the vector template in the header file <vector>. Locate and copy the "big three" memory management functions in the class definition.

Exercise R15.21. Show the value of each reference count at the point the output statement is executed in the following program.

```
int main()
{
   SharedString one = "Fred";
   SharedString two = "Alice";
   SharedString three = one;
   SharedString four;
   four = three;
   three = two;
   cout << "What are the values here?\n";
}
```

Exercise R15.22. The nested class StringReference has a destructor, but no copy constructor or assignment operator. Explain why these are not needed.

PROGRAMMING EXERCISES

Exercise P15.1. Predict what the output will be in the following program, then test your prediction. Explain at what point in execution each message is generated.

```
void f(Trace t)
{
   cout << "Entering f \n";
}

int main()
{
   Trace tracer("main");
   f(tracer);
}
```

Exercise P15.2. Extend the class Trace with a copy constructor and an assignment operator, printing a short message in each. Use this class to demonstrate

a. the difference between initialization

```
Trace t("abc");
Trace u = t;
```

and assignment.

```
Trace t("abc");
Trace u("xyz");
u = t;
```

b. the fact that all constructed objects are automatically destroyed.

c. the fact that the copy constructor is invoked if an object is passed by value to a function.

d. the fact that the copy constructor is not invoked when a parameter is passed by reference.

e. the fact that the copy constructor is used to copy a return value to the caller.

Exercise P15.3. Continue the implementation of the String class. Add each of the following:

- A constructor String(int n, char c) that initializes the string with n copies of the character c.

- The + operator to perform concatenation of two String objects.

- A member function compare(String) that returns −1, 0, or 1 depending upon whether the string is lexicographically less than, equal to, or greater than the argument. Then, using this member function, provide definitions for the comparison operators <, <=, ==, !=, >, and >=.

- A function resize(int n, char c) that changes the size of the string to n, either truncating characters from the end, or inserting new copies of character c.

- The function call operator, so that s(int start, int length) returns a substring starting at the given position of the given size.

Exercise P15.4. Our String class always deletes the old character buffer and reallocates a new character buffer on assignment or in the copy constructor. This need not be done if the new value is smaller than the current value, and hence would fit in the existing buffer. Rewrite the String class so that each instance will maintain an integer data field indicating the size of the buffer, then only reallocate a new buffer when necessary. Abstract the common tasks from the assignment operator and the copy constructor, and place them into an internal method.

Exercise P15.5. Define a class Set that stores integers in a dynamically allocated array of integers.

```
class Set
{
public:
   void add(int n);
   bool contains(int n) const;
```

```
    int get_size() const;
    ...
private:
    int* elements;
    int size;
};
```

In a set, the order of elements does not matter, and every element can occur at most once.

Supply the add, contains, and get_size member functions and the "big three" memory management functions.

Exercise P15.6. Modify the class Matrix from Section 15.6 to provide the following operations:

1. The negation of a matrix. This should yield the matrix in which every element is negated.
2. The compound assignment operator -=.
3. The subtraction operator -. Write this in two ways. First, just as the addition operator was written using +=, this can be written using -=. Second, write the operator using addition and unary negation.
4. The addition and subtraction of a scalar value and a matrix. This should add or subtract the value from each element of the matrix.
5. The input of a matrix from an input stream.

Exercise P15.7. Implement operator[] in class SharedString. Can you write this operator so that changes to a character value alter only the target string and not any shared strings?

```
SharedString a = "Jim";
SharedString b = a;
b[0] = 'f';  // a should still have value Jim
```

Exercise P15.8. Lisp is a language that uses lists as a fundamental data type. Although the Lisp syntax is different, lists in Lisp are manipulated using three basic functions:

```
int car(const List& lst);
List cdr(const List& lst);
List cons(int n, const List& lst);
```

The function car returns the first element from a list. (Our lists will hold only integers. Lists in Lisp can, of course, hold any data type). The function cdr returns the argument list with the first element removed. The function cons returns a list in which the new element has been inserted at the front.

Unlike our lists in Chapter 12, lists in Lisp require only one data type, more or less analogous to our class Node. A NULL value is used to represent an empty list. Using reference counts, implement Lisp style lists. Function cons, for example, will add a new element to the existing list, increasing the reference for the original first element of the list.

Exercise P15.9. Write a class `OptionalEmployee` that stores an optional element of type `Employee*`. Here is a typical usage

```
class Department
{
private:
   ...
   OptionalEmployee secretary;
};
```

Supply a member function

```
bool exists() const
```

that tests whether the optional element exists, a member function

```
void set(Employee* t)
```

to set it, and

```
Employee* get() const
```

to get it. As an internal representation, use a field of type `Employee*`. Provide the necessary memory management functions to ensure that the data field is recovered when the enclosing object (for example, the instance of `Department`) is deleted.

Exercise P15.10. Add the "big three" memory management functions to the binary search tree in Chapter 13.

G   **Exercise P15.11.** Program a memory game. The game should display a playing surface of 12 square tiles, arranged 3 by 4, as follows

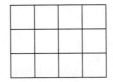

Each tile has a front side and a back side. The front side has various pictures of your own design, while the back side is blank. There are two instances of each image (that is, six images in the collection of twelve tiles). Initially all tiles display the blank back side.

You play the game by clicking on pairs of tiles. After you click the first tile, it is turned over (displaying the front side). After the second tile is clicked, if their pictures match they are both removed; otherwise they are both flipped back to the blank back side. The objective is to remove the tiles in the fewest possible steps.

Keep track of the number of steps and display the information at the end of the game. Store the tiles as pointers to instances of class `Tile`, and use appropriate memory management techniques to delete each tile as it is removed from the playing surface.

Chapter 16

Templates

CHAPTER GOALS

- To be able to use and define template classes and functions
- To learn how to use template parameters
- To distinguish between the polymorphic mechanisms of templates and inheritance
- To learn how to supply policies to templates

A function encapsulates a series of statements, allowing them to be executed with many different values. A template takes this idea to another level of abstraction. A template class or function can work with many different *types* of values. Templates permit the creation of general purpose, reusable tools and containers. Because the polymorphism of templates is handled at compile time rather than run time, templates are very efficient. In this chapter, you will explore the template mechanism in general. In Chapter 20, you will see how templates are used in the creation of the standard template library, the primary data structure library in C++.

CHAPTER CONTENTS

16.1 Template Functions

Suppose you want to write a printing function for an array of integers, so that a single call to the function will print all the values in the array with a comma between each element and square brackets around the whole. It's not hard to do; here is an example:

```cpp
void print(ostream& out, int data[], int count)
{
   out << "[";
   for (int i = 0; i < count; i++)
   {
      if (i > 0)
         out << ",";
      out << data[i];
   }
   out << "]";
}
```

The function works fine for this application. But in your next project, you need to do the same for an array of doubles. Can you reuse your previous work? One possibility is to simply copy the source code and edit it:

```cpp
void print(ostream& out, double data[], int count)
{
   out << "[";
   for (int i = 0; i < count; i++)
   {
```

```
        if (i > 0)
            out << ",";
        out << data[i];
    }
    out << "]";
}
```

This works, but is not entirely satisfactory, particularly if the function is more complex than our simple example. Cutting and pasting is notoriously error prone. What if you accidently delete a line? Would a casual examination of the code reveal this error? And there are other problems. For instance, which uses of the int keyword need to be replaced? Why was the second parameter in the function header changed and not the third? What if there were other int variables? Which ones would you need to change, and which ones would you keep as integer?

In your next program, you want a similar printing routine, but this time your array contains strings. Rather than copying and editing the source, you begin to think that there must be a better solution. Fortunately, there is.

Notice that the only difference between these functions is the parameter type. What you need is a way to abstract away the differences, and keep the parts that are the same. This is exactly what a template does.

> A template allows a function or class to work with a variety of types.

A *template* allows a function or a class definition to be parameterized by type. This is analogous to the way that function parameters allow the programmer to abstract an action to be performed and separate it from the values to be manipulated. The first version of the function print encapsulates a certain set of actions, that is, printing the elements in a certain way, and abstracts away through the parameters the elements held in the array. To generalize the operation, you need a similar way to parameterize the function; only this time the parameters will be *types* and not *values*.

> The template separates actions to be performed from the type of the values that the actions process.

To define a template, you first use the keyword template. This is followed by a list of *type parameters*. Together these are termed the template prefix, for example, template<typename T>. The type parameter list is surrounded by angle brackets, instead of the parentheses that surround a parameter list in a function. But like parameters, each type parameter is written as a keyword followed by a name.

```
template<typename T>
void print(ostream& out, T data[], int count)
{
    out << "[";
    for (int i = 0; i < count; i++)
    {
        if (i > 0)
            out << ",";
        out << data[i];
    }
    out << "]";
}
```

There is nothing special about the selection of the name T, it is just an arbitrary name, just like the selection of the name data for the function parameter. The keyword typename indicates that the value of T will be a type, and not a value. It could be a primitive type, such as `int`, or a class type, such as `string`. Earlier versions of C++ use the keyword `class` for this purpose, writing the template prefix as

```
template<class T>
```

The meaning is the same, and you will still often see this use. However, the keyword `class` could be easily misunderstood to imply that only class types could be used in this situation, and not primitive types. The keyword `typename` is for this reason more descriptive.

Within the body of the function the name `T` can be used wherever a type would be appropriate. For example, you can declare a variable as type `T` (or pointer to `T`, or vector of `T`'s) or you can make a parameter of type `T`, and so on.

> Template parameters are inferred from the values in a function invocation.

An interesting aspect of template functions is that the type attached to the template parameter is *inferred* from the parameter value:

```
int a[] = { 2, 4, 5 };
print(cout, a, 3);   // Will use int print
double b[] = { 3.14159, 2.7 };
print(cout, b, 2);   // Will use double print
string c[] = { "Fred", "Sally", "Alice" };
print(cout, c, 3);   // Will use string print
```

SYNTAX 16.1 **Template Function Definition**

```
template<typename type_variable₁, ..., typename type_variableₙ>
return_type function_name(parameters)
{
    statements
}
```

Example:

```
template<typename T>
void print(ostream& out, T data[], int count)
{
    out << "[";
    for (int i = 0; i < count; i++)
    {
        out << data[i];
        if (i + 1 < count)
            out << ",";
    }
    out << "]";
}
```

Purpose:

Define a function that can be reused with different types of parameters.

An error message will be generated if the compiler is unable to infer the template parameters from the parameter values.

COMMON ERROR 16.1

Invalid Type Parameters

The properties that a type parameter must satisfy are characterized only implicitly, by the way instances of the type are used in the body of the function itself. This can be illustrated by another simple template function, one that returns the maximum of two parameters:

```
template<typename T>
T max(const T& left, const T& right)
{
    if (left < right)
        return right;
    return left;
}
```

The function max (which is found in the standard library <algorithm>) can be used with any data type that implements the < operator. We know this not by looking at the function heading, but by examining the way that the variables left and right are used in the function body. For example, max can be used with integers or doubles:

```
int i = max(3, 4);
double d = max(3.14, 4.7);
```

Mixing types will not work, as the compiler is unable to decide which type the programmer wants to use:

```
double e = max(2, 3.13);   // Error—cannot infer type parameter
```

However, the programmer can explicitly provide the template parameter in order to avoid ambiguous situations:

```
double e = max<double>(2, 3.13);   // OK—integer will be converted into double
```

A common error is to use a value type that is not appropriate for the body of the function. For example, suppose you try to determine the "maximum" of two employees:

```
Employee mary("Mary Smith", 25000);
Employee fred("Fred Jones", 37500);
Employee big = max(mary, fred);  // Error—invalid types
```

An unfortunate fact is that many compilers will not report this error by pointing to the statement where the call is made, but will instead point to the line in the definition of the function where the error is discovered; namely, the point where the two employee values are compared. Because there is no operator< for Employee values, the compiler does not know how to interpret the programmer's intent.

You could get around this by providing an explicit meaning for the operation:

```
bool operator<(const Employee& a, const Employee& b)
{
    return a.salary() < b.salary();
}
```

Now it is perfectly acceptable to use the max function on two values of type Employee, and the function will return the employee with the largest salary.

```
Employee big = max(mary, fred);   // OK now, as < is well defined
```

Many template functions depend upon the type parameters having certain properties, such as recognizing operator< or operator==. Because these operations can themselves be given overloaded definitions, it is easy to use such functions with your own data types.

QUALITY TIP 16.1

Move from Concrete to Abstract

The development of most template functions follows the pattern given in our example. That is, the function is first created with fixed parameters (such as int), and later generalized by replacing the fixed types with a template type parameter. This is not necessarily a bad thing, as error messages from the template processing parts of C++ compilers are often misleading and obscure. The following is not an atypical error message. In this case, the error was caused by a single token mistake (a variable declared int that should have been string):

```
/usr/local/include/c++/3.2.2/bits/stl_algo.h: In function '_InputIter
   std::find_if(_InputIter, _InputIter, _Predicate,
   std::input_iterator_tag)
   [with _InputIter = std::_List_iterator<std::string, std::string&,
   std::string*>, _Predicate = std::binder2nd<std::greater<int> >]':
/usr/local/include/c++/3.2.2/bits/stl_algo.h:318:   instantiated from
   '_InputIter std::find_if(_InputIter, _InputIter, _Predicate) [with
   _InputIter = std::_List_iterator<std::string, std::string&,
   std::string*>, _Predicate = std::binder2nd<std::greater<int> >]'
test.cpp:11:   instantiated from here
/usr/local/include/c++/3.2.2/bits/stl_algo.h:188: no match for call to '(
   std::binder2nd<std::greater<int> >) (std::basic_string<char,
   std::char_traits<char>, std::allocator<char> >&)'
/usr/local/include/c++/3.2.2/bits/stl_function.h:395: candidates are:
   _Operation::result_type
   std::binder2nd<_Operation>::operator()
      (_Operation::first_argument_type&)
   const [with _Operation = std::greater<int>]
/usr/local/include/c++/3.2.2/bits/stl_function.h:401:
   _Operation::result_type
   std::binder2nd<_Operation>::operator()
      (_Operation::first_argument_type&)
   const [with _Operation = std::greater<int>]
```

Also, most programmers are more comfortable with a concrete type (for example, an array of integers) than with an abstract concept (an array of who-knows-what).

For both these reasons, debugging a nontemplate version of a function is often much easier than debugging a template function. Once the nontemplate version is working, then you can go back and generalize the concept by adding templates, knowing that the basic algorithms are correct.

16.2 Compile-Time Polymorphism

In Chapter 8 you learned how inheritance and overriding are used to address the problem of creating general purpose, reusable software components that can be specialized to fit new applications. Templates are another tool used to address the same issue. A template function or template class (which we will see shortly) can be instantiated in many different ways to fit the needs of individual applications. But while templates and inheritance share a common goal, there are significant differences in the two approaches.

Most importantly, the template mechanism does most of its work at compile time, while inheritance and overriding occur at run time. For this reason some authors use the term "compile-time polymorphism" to describe templates, and "run-time polymorphism" to describe inheritance/overriding [1].

Each different set of template parameters may cause the generation of an entirely different internal function definition. That is, the compiler will generate code for the function max<int> that is completely different from the code generated for max<double>. On the other hand, the compiler keeps track of which expansions have been produced. Two uses of the function max with integer parameters will share the same function; the compiler will not generate two copies of max<int>. (The word "may" in the first sentence reflects the fact that compilers are free to combine two expansions into one if they discover that they both use the same instructions, although few compilers are so intelligent.)

Most important, however, is that this expansion occurs at compile time. There are few run-time costs associated with the use of templates. This contrasts with inheritance and overriding, which is a powerful technique but which requires a run-time mechanism to select the correct member function to bind to each call.

In earlier chapters we have emphasized a distinction between function declarations and definitions, and between class declaration and definition. A declaration gives bare details, such as the function name and parameter types. A definition fills this out by providing a function body. Class declarations simply list the member function names and parameters, while later member function definitions provide function bodies. When files are compiled separately it is common to put declarations in header files (.h files), while the definitions appear in implementation files (.cpp files).

Templates create a third possibility. A function template is not, in fact, a function. It is instead a factory that can be used to produce functions. The functions produced by a function template are often termed template functions. (Similarly, the term *class template* is used to describe the generalization, while the term *template class* is used to describe the result of expanding the generalization.)

Shared template code should be placed into a header file.

Because function and class templates are expanded at compile time, they are commonly stored in header files and not in implementation files. That is, the entire template body of a function such as max will appear in a file ending with the suffix .h, and not in a file with extension .cpp. The header file will then be included in each file that uses the function.

ADVANCED TOPIC 16.1

Templates and Overloading

When two or more functions use the same name in a single scope, we say the function name is overloaded. In one sense templates always produce an overloaded name, because there can be an infinite set of replacements for the template parameters. However, template function names can also coexist with ordinary functions that use the same name. When the compiler must choose between the two, it will always select the nontemplate version over the template version. This policy allows the programmer to make special cases, or exceptions to template functions. This process is termed *specialization*.

> When a template and a nontemplate function with the same name can be used, the nontemplate function is selected.

For example, suppose you have added your new print template function to a project, but now need to print an array of Product values. The class Product does not have an output stream operator, but does have a member function named print. You can provide a function definition that will be used with only this parameter type as follows:

```
void print(ostream& out, Product data[], int count)
{
   out << "[";
   for (int i = 0; i < count; i++)
   {
      if (i > 0)
         out << ",";
      data[i].print(out);
   }
   out << "]";
}
```

When faced with the three-parameter form of print using an array of Product values, the compiler has two choices. It can expand the template version, substituting Product for the template parameter T, or it can use the specialized version. It will select the specialized version.

ADVANCED TOPIC 16.2

Forms of Polymorphism

The term *polymorphic* means, roughly, many forms (*poly* = many, *morph* = form). There are several different varieties of polymorphism. *Overloading*, where a single function name has many definitions that are distinguished at compile time based on their parameter types, is one form.

```
// Multiple meanings for same operation
ostream& operator<<(ostream& out, int value);
ostream& operator<<(ostream& out, double value);
ostream& operator<<(ostream& out, string value);
```

Overriding is another form of polymorphism. Overriding occurs when a function in a base class is declared virtual, and a function in a derived class has the same name and parameter signature. The determination of which function to execute is made at run time.

```
class Employee
{
   ...
   virtual double annual_income() const;
   ...
};

class Manager : public Employee
{
   ...
   virtual double annual_income() const;
   ...
};

Employee* e = new Manager("Sarah Smith", 67000, 2000);
// Although e is a pointer to Employee, it uses the Manager version of annual_income
cout << e->annual_income() << "\n";
```

Templates are a third form of polymorphism.

```
vector<int> dates;   // Vectors can hold integers
vector<double> data;   // or doubles, or any other type of value
```

Other types of languages, such as functional languages, have even more forms of polymorphism [2]. The common thread running through all these mechanisms is multiple meanings being attached to a single name.

16.3 Template Classes

Although template functions are useful and powerful, it is much more common to use templates in the creation of general purpose classes. Suppose, for example, you want to write a function that traverses a vector and simultaneously keeps track of the minimum and the maximum.

```
int min = v[0];
int max = v[0];
for (int i = 1; i < v.size(); i++)
{
   if (v[i] < min) min = v[i];
   if (v[i] > max) max = v[i];
}
```

To return both values, make a simple Pair class.

```
class Pair
{
```

```
public:
   Pair(int a, int b);
   int get_first() const;
   int get_second() const;
private:
   int first;
   int second;
};

inline Pair::Pair(int a, int b)
{
   first = a;
   second = b;
}

inline int Pair::get_first() const
{
   return first;
}

inline int Pair::get_second() const
{
   return second;
}
```

Now you can complete the function as follows:

```
Pair minmax(vector<int> v)
{
   ...
   return Pair(min, max);
}
```

The caller of the function retrieves both values like this:

```
Pair p = minmax(data);
cout << p.get_first() << " " << p.get_second() << "\n";
```

However, the Pair class is not very flexible. Suppose you want to gather a pair of double or string values. Then you need to define another class. Just as with the print function, you need a way to parameterize the class definition, allowing it to be used with many different types.

> When you declare a variable of a template class, you must specify the parameter types.

For this purpose, you can define a *class template*, which can produce pairs of particular types. Unlike template functions, the type parameters to a class template are not inferred. Instead, they must be explicitly named as part of the declaration. The template can be *instantiated* to classes Pair<int, int>, Pair<string, int>, and so on.

You can think of the Pair template as a factory for classes, and an instantiated class such as Pair<int, int> as a class produced by that factory. (The general class Pair is termed a class template, while an instantiated class such as Pair<int, int> is termed a template class.)

To define the template, denote the arbitrary types with type parameters F and S as shown in Syntax 16.2. Replace the types for the Pair's first and second data fields

> ## SYNTAX 16.2 Template Class Definition
>
> ```
> template<typename type_variable₁, ..., typename type_variableₙ>
> class ClassName
> {
>    features
> };
> ```
>
> **Example:**
>
> ```
> template<typename F, typename S>
> class Pair
> {
> public:
>    Pair(const F& a, const S& b);
>    F get_first() const;
>    S get_second() const;
> private:
>    F first;
>    S second;
> };
> ```
>
> **Purpose:**
>
> Define a class template with a type parameter.

with F and S. Finally, add a line `template<typename F, typename S>` before the class declaration:

```
template<typename F, typename S>
class Pair
{
public:
   Pair(const F& a, const S& b);
   F get_first() const;
   S get_second() const;
private:
   F first;
   S second;
};
```

Finally, you must turn *each* member function definition into a function template, as shown in Syntax 16.3:

```
template<typename F, typename S>
inline Pair<F, S>::Pair(const F& a, const S& b)
{
   first = a;
   second = b;
}
```

```
template<typename F, typename S>
inline F Pair<F, S>::get_first() const
{
    return first;
}

template<typename F, typename S>
inline S Pair<F, S>::get_second() const
{
    return second;
}
```

> Template classes allow the creation of containers that work with many different types of values.

Note that each function is turned into a separate template. Each function name is prefixed by the "Pair<F, S>::" qualifier. And, of course, the type variables F and S are used in place of the int type. The Pair template is a simplified version of a similar class named pair that appears in the standard library in the file <utility>.

The most common use of templates is in container classes. Of course, the standard vector and list constructs are templates.

SYNTAX 16.3 **Template Member Function Definition**

```
template<typename type_variable>
modifiers return_type ClassName<type_variable>::function_name(parameters) const_opt
{
    statements
}
```

Example:
```
template<typename T>
inline T Pair<T>::get_first() const
{
    return first;
}
```

Purpose:
Supply the implementation of a member function for a class template.

16.4 Turning a Class into a Template

In Chapter 12, you learned how to implement a linked list class. That class stored lists of strings. You now know how to store values of arbitrary types by turning the class into a template.

Because the List class uses the Node and the Iterator classes, you need to make templates for these classes as well. Start with the Node class. The original Node class stored a string value:

```
class Node
{
public:
   Node(string s);
private:
   string data;
   Node* previous;
   Node* next;
};
```

Replace each `string` with `T`. Prefix the class with `template<typename T>`. Change every `Node` to `Node<T>`, except for constructor names. The templatized version is

```
template<typename T>
class Node
{
public:
   Node(T s);
private:
   T data;
   Node<T>* previous;
   Node<T>* next;
};
```

You do the same with the `List` class:

```
template<typename T>
class List
{
public:
   List();
   void push_back(T s);
   void insert(Iterator<T> pos, T s);
   Iterator<T> erase(Iterator<T> pos);
   Iterator<I> begin();
   Iterator<T> end();
private:
   Node<T>* first;
   Node<T>* last;
};
```

Finally, turn *each* member function definition into a template, as shown in Syntax 16.3 on page 652:

```
template<typename T>
Iterator<T> List<T>::begin()
{
   Iterator<T> iter;
   iter.position = first;
   iter.last = last;
   return iter;
}
```

Remember that template class definitions commonly are stored in header files. In this case, because the only functions associated with lists are member functions, there is no `list.cpp` file. The completion of a template version of the class `List` is left as Exercise P16.5.

ADVANCED TOPIC 16.3

Nested Templates

Within the body of a template class, a member function or a nested class can have its own template definition, independent of the definition in the surrounding class. A simple example of the use of this feature in the standard library is the constructor that allows a container to be initialized from a collection defined by a pair of iterators. This occurs, for example, in class vector:

```
template<typename T>
class vector
{
public:
   template<typename ITR> vector(ITR start, ITR stop);
   ...
};

template<typename T> template<typename ITR>
vector<T>::vector(ITR start, ITR stop)
{
   // Vector initialization
   while (start != stop)
   {
      push_back(*start);
      ++start;
   }
}
```

This constructor allows the user to define a new vector, and initialize the vector with a collection defined by a pair of iterators. Because of the use of nested templates, this works even if the iterators are derived from an entirely different form of container, such as a list:

```
list<string> a;
a.push_back("one");
a.push_back("two");   // ... so on, to create the list
vector<string> b(a.begin(), a.end());
cout << b.front() << "\n";   // Will print first element of the vector
```

The invocations of a.begin and a.end will produce list iterators, which are quite different from vector iterators, but use the same iterator operations. The template parameter ITR will be bound to list<string>::iterator for the purposes of executing the constructor, which will copy the values from the list into the vector.

COMMON ERROR 16.2

Templates Don't Preserve Inheritance

Beginning students sometimes assume that because, for example, class Manager derives from Employee, that the class vector<Manager> must somehow be related to vector<Employee>. This is not true. There is no relationship between the two vector classes.

QUALITY TIP 16.2

Document Template Parameter Requirements

As Common Error 16.1 on page 645 shows, the requirements that template parameters must satisfy are implicitly defined by operations performed on values of the type by the member functions. If not properly handled, this can impose a heavy burden on a programmer who needs to use a template class created by another programmer, forcing them to read the entire class definition and all member function definitions to see what operations are invoked.

There is a subtlety in the requirement that template parameters provide the operations needed by class member functions—the code for member functions is only generated if the functions are used. For example, it is perfectly acceptable to instantiate a vector, for example, vector<Product>, with a class that does not have the equality operator (operator==), as long as functions that use this operator (such as find) are never invoked.

To avoid surprising the user with unanticipated requirements, you should always document the minimal set of operations necessary for any template parameters, placing the information in the comments that are part of the class definition:

```
/**
    A class to hold a collection of values.
    Type T must define a copy constructor.
    To use the find generic algorithm you must define the equality operator ==.
*/
template<typename T>
class vector
{
    ...
};


/**
    A collection of type value pairs.
    type K must have a copy constructor and the less than operator.
    type V must have a copy constructor and the equality operator.
*/
template<typename K, typename V>
class map
{
    ...
};
```

16.5 Nontype Template Parameters

> Template parameters can be type names or they can be constants.

The examples up to this point have all used types as template parameters, specified using the typename keyword. Although type names are the most common form of template parameter, there are other possibilities. Integer constants are a common example.

To illustrate, consider the matrix case study explored in several of the previous chapters. When the example was first described, the size was limited to 3 × 3 matrices so that space could be allocated with the object, instead of using dynamic heap memory. Later the 3 × 3 restriction was removed. To do this, the size of the matrix was specified by the constructor, but as a consequence, the space for the matrix values had to be dynamically managed. Template parameters provide a third alternative that is somewhere between these two. The size of the matrix could be specified by integer template parameters, as in the following:

```
template<typename T, int ROWS, int COLUMNS>
class Matrix
{
   ...
private:
   T data[ROWS][COLUMNS];
};
```

To create an instance of this matrix the programmer would specify both the element type and the size:

```
Matrix<double, 3, 4> a;   // A 3 × 4 matrix of double values
Matrix<string, 2, 2> b;
```

By using template parameters for the bounds, they become part of the type. This means that compatibility between variables of different sizes will be checked at compile time as part of the process of type checking, rather than needing to be checked at run time.

```
Matrix<int, 3, 4> a;
Matrix<double, 3, 4> b;
Matrix<int, 5, 7> c;
Matrix<int, 3, 4> d;

b = a;   // Error, element types don't match.
c = a;   // Error, sizes don't match, so types differ.
d = a;   // OK. Element types and sizes match.
```

Because the row and column sizes are known at compile time, the space for the elements can be allocated in an array, and does not need to be dynamically managed. But in this particular case the improvement in memory must be measured against a serious disadvantage—the requirements for operations such as matrix multiplication are now much more difficult to specify.

16.6 Setting Behavior Using Template Parameters

Template parameters can be used to set behavior, for example setting the comparison algorithm for sorted containers.

Template parameters can be used for a variety of purposes, not just as types for containers or bounds for arrays. An interesting use of template parameters is as a mechanism for specifying behavior, sometimes termed setting *policy*. We will illustrate this first with template functions, and then go on to consider template classes, where the technique is more commonly used.

Suppose you want to generalize the function max so that it will work with values that either do not support operator<, or that may have more than one way of ordering. Instances of class Employee, for example, might be compared either on name or on salary. To do this, the comparison is made into a template parameter, as follows:

```
template<typename T, typename CMP>
T max(const T& left, const T& right, CMP cmp)
{
    if (cmp(left, right))
        return right;
    return left;
}
```

The less than test has been replaced by a function call. This means the third parameter, cmp, must be able to be used in the fashion of a function call. As we saw in Chapter 14, this parameter could either actually be a function or, more likely, be a function object—a class that implements the function call operator, operator().

To use function objects as template parameters to compare values of type Employee either by salary or by name, develop the following two classes:

```
class CompareBySalary
{
public:
    bool operator()(const Employee& a, const Employee& b) const;
};

bool CompareBySalary::operator()(const Employee& a,
    const Employee& b) const
{
    return a.get_salary() < b.get_salary();
}

class CompareByName
{
public:
    bool operator()(const Employee& a, const Employee& b) const;
};

bool CompareByName::operator()(const Employee& a,
    const Employee& b) const
{
    return a.get_name() < b.get_name();
}
```

The types CompareBySalary and CompareByName represent two completely different orderings. Each is represented by a function object, a class that implements the function call operator. Using these, it is now possible to use the function max in either sense:

```
Employee alice("Alice Smith", 45000);
Employee fred("Fred Jones", 38500);

Employee one = max(alice, fred, CompareBySalary());
Employee two = max(alice, fred, CompareByName());
```

The same idea can be used in template class parameters. Consider the problem of maintaining a collection in sorted order. How do you specify the rules for comparing two elements? There are many ways to do this. Do not specify the sorting criteria in the container itself, because there may be many different types of elements and each may have its own rules for comparisons. As with the function max, the solution is to use template parameters to represent behavior. Imagine, for example, the following class definition for a sorted collection:

```
template<typename T, typename CMP>
class OrderedCollection
{
public:
   typedef Iterator<T> iterator;
   void add(T value);
   iterator begin();
   iterator end();
private:
   List<T> data;
   CMP comparator;
};
```

Within the class an instance of the comparison type is created as a private data field. An instance of this type is then used whenever a comparison is required. For example, when inserting a new element:

```
template<typename T, typename CMP>
void OrderedCollection<T, CMP>::insert(T value)
{
   iterator ptr = begin();
   while (ptr != end())
   {
      if (comparator(value, *ptr))
      {
         // Found place to insert
         data.insert(ptr, value);
         return;
      }
      ++ptr;
   }
   // Insert at end
   data.insert(ptr, value);
}
```

The creation of a sorted collection now requires two template parameters; the first identifying the element type, and the second giving the comparison algorithm. The two values with the same sorting algorithm match in type, while values with different sorting algorithms are separate types:

```
void f(OrderedCollection<Employee, CompareByName>& c)
{
   ...
}

OrderedCollection<Employee, CompareBySalary> a;
a.add(...);
OrderedCollection<Employee, CompareByName> b;
b.add(...);
```

```
f(a);   // Error—types don't match.
f(b);   // OK—type is OK.
```

In many situations a default policy can be identified—one that is only rarely replaced with an alternative. In this case, a default value can be associated with the template parameter. The default value is used when the programmer does not provide an explicit value. For sorting algorithms, a convenient default value would be the template class less<T>, provided in the standard library <functional>. This class has the following definition:

```
template<typename T>
class less
{
    bool operator()(const T& x, const T& y) const;
};

template<typename T>
bool less<T>::operator()(const T& x, const T& y) const
{
    return x < y;
}
```

That is, the less template class defines a function object that invokes the less than operator. This can be specified as the default template parameter to your sorted collection:

```
template<typename T, typename CMP = less<T> >
class OrderedCollection
{
    ...
};
```

Now if the user does not specify any other ordering, the default will be used, which will in turn use the "less than" operator.

```
OrderedCollection<int> data;   // Will use the less than operator
```

The standard container classes that depend upon ordering (map, multimap, and set) all set the ordering behavior in just this fashion. A template parameter that is used to set policy is called a *trait*. In addition to using traits to define comparison, the standard containers include traits that give the programmer control over the memory allocation for the container.

16.7 Case Study: Matrices, Continued

In previous chapters we developed the class Matrix for performing matrix manipulation. By making a template version of the class we allow the creation of matrices of strings or integers as well as matrices of doubles. In the code shown here we use template parameters only for the element type, and not for the row and column bounds as was discussed in Section 16.4. This makes it easier to overload the arithmetic operators.

To create the template version of the class, template prefixes were added to the class declarations and member function definitions. References to the class Matrix were then replaced by Matrix<T>. Member function definitions were moved into the header file.

Because zero may not be an appropriate value for all template parameter types (think of Matrix<string>), the loop that initializes elements in the constructor has been eliminated. Other than these, no further changes were necessary. The following listing shows typical changes.

ch16/matrix3.h

```
 1  #ifndef MATRIX3_H
 2  #define MATRIX3_H
    ... Same as in matrix2.h
 9
10  template <typename T> class Matrix;
11
12  /**
13      This class describes a row in a matrix.
14  */
15  template <typename T>
16  class MatrixRow
17  {
18  public:
19     /**
20         Remembers a row for a given matrix.
21         @param m  a pointer to the matrix
22         @param s  the size of the row
23     */
24     MatrixRow(Matrix<T>* m, int s);
25
26     /**
27         Accesses a row element.
28         @param j  the column index
29         @return  a reference to the element with the given index
30     */
31     T& operator[](int j);
32
33  private:
34     Matrix<T>* mat;
35     int i;
36  };
    ...
63
64  /**
65      This class describes a matrix with arbitrary rows and columns.
66  */
67  template <typename T>
68  class Matrix
69  {
```

```
 70  public:
 71     /**
 72         Constructs a matrix filled with zero elements.
 73     */
...
110
111     /**
112         Accesses a matrix row.
113         @param i  the row index
114         @return the row with the given index
115     */
116     MatrixRow<T> operator[](int i);
117

...
125     /**
126         Computes the matrix sum.
127         @param right another matrix
128         @return the updated matrix
129     */
130     Matrix<T>& operator+=(const Matrix<T>& right);
131
132  private:
...
143
144     int rows;
145     int columns;
146     T* elements;
147  };
148
149  /**
150     Computes the matrix sum.
151     @param right another matrix
152     @return the sum of two matrices
153  */
154  template <typename T>
155  Matrix<T> operator+(const Matrix<T>& left, const Matrix<T>& right);
156

...
271
272  template <typename T>
273  Matrix<T>::Matrix(int r, int c)
274     : rows(r), columns(c), elements(new T[rows * columns])
275  {
276  }
```
... Same as in `matrix2.cpp`
```
351
352  #endif
```

ch16/matrixtest3.cpp

```
1  #include <string>
2  #include "matrix3.h"
3
4  using namespace std;
5
```

```
 6  int main()
 7  {
 8     Matrix<double> m(3, 3);
 9     m[0][0] = m[1][1] = m[2][2] = 1;
10     m[0][1] = m[1][2] = 2;
11     m[0][2] = m[1][0] = m[2][0] = m[2][1] = 0;
12     cout << 2.0 * m + m * m << "\n";
13
14     Matrix<string> s(3, 2);
15     s[0][0] = "First"; s[0][1] = "Last";
16     s[1][0] = "Joan"; s[1][1] = "Jones";
17     s[2][0] = "Lisa"; s[2][1] = "Lin";
18     cout << s + s;
19
20     return 0;
21  }
```

Program Run

```
      3           8         4
      0           3         8
      0           0         3

  FirstFirst   LastLast
    JoanJoanJonesJones
    LisaLisa     LinLin
```

CHAPTER SUMMARY

1. A template allows a function or class to work with a variety of types.

2. The template separates actions to be performed from the type of the values that the actions process.

3. Template parameters are inferred from the values in a function invocation.

4. Shared template code should be placed into a header file.

5. When a template and a nontemplate function with the same name can be used, the nontemplate function is selected.

6. When you declare a variable of a template class, you must specify the parameter types.

7. Template classes allow the creation of containers that work with many different types of values.

8. Template parameters can be type names or they can be constants.

9. Template parameters can be used to set behavior, for example setting the comparison algorithm for sorted containers.

FURTHER READING

1. Bjarne Stroustrup, *The C++ Programming Language*, Special Ed., Addison-Wesley, 2000.
2. Adam Brooks Webber, *Modern Programming Languages: A Practical Introduction*, Franklin, Beedle & Associates, 2003.

REVIEW EXERCISES

Exercise R16.1. Why is the keyword `typename` preferable to the use of the keyword `class` in a template definition?

Exercise R16.2. Identify the errors in the following template function headers

    a. `template<typename T> f(int a)`

    b. `template<typename T, typename T> f(T* a)`

    c. `template<typename T1, typename T2> f(T1 a)`

Exercise R16.3. Why do you have to specify template parameters when you instantiate a class template, but not when you instantiate a function template?

Exercise R16.4. How is a template class different from a template function?

Exercise R16.5. How is a non-typename template parameter different from a type name parameter? When might you use such a value?

Exercise R16.6. Explain how template parameters can be used to set policy for a class.

Exercise R16.7. What happens when you change line 18 of `ch16/matrixtest3.cpp` to `cout << s * s; ?` Explain the error.

PROGRAMMING EXERCISES

Exercise P16.1. Rewrite the selection sort algorithm described in Section 11.1 as a template function, using the less than operator to compare two elements.

Exercise P16.2. Change your solution to Exercise P16.1 so that the comparison algorithm is also a template parameter. Use the standard class `less` as a default value.

Exercise P16.3. Rewrite the merge sort algorithm described in Section 11.4 as a template function. Use two template parameters, one to set the element type, and the second to define the ordering algorithm.

Exercise P16.4. Rewrite the binary search algorithm described in Section 11.7 as a template function.

Exercise P16.5. Finish the implementation of the template List<T> class described in Section 16.4.

Exercise P16.6. Finish the implementation of the class Matrix using integer template parameters from Section 16.5. Use the function call operator with two integer parameters to access each element in the matrix.

Exercise P16.7. Modify the class Pair in Section 16.3 so that the programmer can specify either one or two template parameters. *Hint:* Use a default value.

Exercise P16.8. Using the classes list<T> and Pair<T1, T2>, create a map abstraction. A map, you will recall, is a collection of key/value pairs. Keys are unique, and can be used to locate the associated values. Your map should implement the following interface:

```
insert(key, value)
bool contains_key(key)
value_of(key)
remove_key(key)
```

Exercise P16.9. Design a template class container that maintains a set. In a set, each element is unique, so adding an element to a set that already contains the value does nothing. Provide iterators as well as an addition and removal algorithm for your set.

Exercise P16.10. Create a template definition for a fixed-size array class. The declaration

```
Array<int, 10> data;
```

should create an array of 10 integer values. Override the subscript operator to provide access to the elements.

Exercise P16.11. Define an array class that allows the user to set a lower bound for index values that is different from zero. That is, a declaration such as

```
LBArray<int, 1955, 1975> data;
```

should create an array with 21 integer values, indexed using the integer values 1955 to 1975.

Exercise P16.12. The find algorithm in the standard library

```
find(begin, past_end, value)
```

yields an iterator pointing to the first occurrence of value in the given range, or past_end if the value is not present. Write a template function definition for find.

Chapter 17

Exception Handling

CHAPTER GOALS

- To understand how exceptional conditions can arise within a program

- To understand how dealing with exceptional conditions can make your programs more reliable and robust

- To learn how to use a variety of mechanisms to handle exceptional conditions

- To understand how to use try blocks and catch handlers in your own programs

Programs must always be prepared to handle exceptional conditions. The ability to gracefully deal with an exception is what separates robust and reliable programs from those that are fragile and difficult to use. In this chapter you will encounter the various mechanisms that are used to address exceptional conditions, and learn how to apply them in your own programs.

CHAPTER CONTENTS

17.1 Handling Exceptional Situations

Things sometimes go wrong. Programmers have always been forced to deal with error conditions and exceptional situations. The following are just a few types of errors commonly encountered:

- *User input errors.* A user enters invalid input, such as a file name that does not exist. An interactive program may be able to inform the user of the problem and await further input. The options for a noninteractive program may be much more limited.

- *Device errors.* A disk drive may be unavailable. A printer may be turned off. Such errors may cause a program to be aborted or suspended until the problem is fixed. Devices may fail in the middle of a task. For example, a printer may run out of paper in the middle of a long series of printing commands.

- *Physical limitations.* Disks can fill up. Available memory can become exhausted.

- *Component failures.* A function or class may perform incorrectly, or use other functions or classes incorrectly. For example, a function may use an illegal array index, or try to pop a value from an empty stack.

> Anomalous situations can be expected to occur, and programs should be written to be robust in the presence of errors.

From the very beginning, programmers and language designers have had to deal with problems such as these, and have developed a number of different approaches to address them. Some of these you have seen already, such as the predicate `fail` used by the stream I/O library to report an I/O error (Section 3.10), or the assert macro (Section 4.13). In this chapter you will examine a variety of other tools.

There are a variety of mechanisms that can be used to handle exceptional conditions. These include special return flags and assertions as well as the exception mechanism.

Some errors can be detected and resolved at the point they occur. An example might be an input format error. If a program is expecting a number and the user enters a name, the program can alert the user to the error and ask for a new value. Other errors are more difficult to deal with, because they are nonlocal. That is, the section of a program where an exceptional condition is discovered is not the section of a program where the resolution of the problem is best handled. To see why, we must first examine the nature of errors in a larger context.

The importance of exception handling has increased as the task of programming has evolved from a job pursued by a single programmer working in isolation to a communal activity requiring the combined effort of many—sometimes several hundred—programmers working together. One programmer, P1, will develop a function or a class that is being used by another programmer, P2.

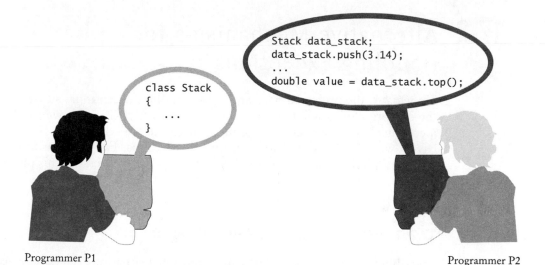

Programmer P1   Programmer P2

The management of exceptions becomes even more critical when software is developed by two or more programmers working on independent components.

Programmer P1 will have little control over how his or her software will be used by programmer P2. Thus a critical design goal for P1 should be to create robust components—software that will be tolerant of faults and be able to recover gracefully in the presence of errors.

Suppose programmer P1 develops a stack. Programmer P2 will be using the stack. Programmer P2 need not know how the stack is implemented (it could be implemented using a list, a vector, or a variety of other techniques). Instead, programmer P2 need only know how to use the set of operations provided:

```
Stack s;
s.push(3.14);
s.push(1.41);
s.push(2.76);
while (s.size() > 0)
{
```

```
        cout << s.top() << "\n";
        s.pop();
    }
```

Now imagine that something goes wrong. Perhaps P2 has misunderstood the interface, or perhaps the functions developed by P2 contain a logic error that causes them to use the component developed by P1 incorrectly. Suppose, for example, that P2 performs a pop on an empty stack. Programmer P1, who has little or no idea of the application at hand, will typically have no idea how to respond to the error. Programmer P2, on the other hand, has more information, and thus is in a better position to recover from the error. So the code developed by programmer P1 must somehow report back to the software written by P2 both the fact that an error has occurred, and the nature of the error.

17.2 Alternative Mechanisms for Handling Exceptions

Nowadays, the preferred mechanism for handling exceptional situations in C++ is the exception. You will examine exceptions in Section 17.3. However, the exception mechanism is a relatively recent addition to the C++ language. But programmers have always had to deal with exceptional situations. For this reason it is useful to start by examining a number of alternative ways of addressing this problem. Many of these alternatives are still used by functions in the C++ run-time library.

17.2.1 Assuming Errors Will Not Occur

Probably the worst way to deal with exceptional situations is to simply assume that they will not occur. Beginning programmers often make this mistake, by writing functions that will, for example, operate correctly on only a limited range of input values, and never bothering to check the legitimacy of their arguments. You saw this, for example, in the function future_value described in Chapter 4. What should this function do if either n or p is less than zero?

```
double future_value(double initial_balance, double p, int n)
{
    return initial_balance * pow(1 + p / 100, n);
}
```

Illegal inputs can lead to erroneous results that will likely lead to even more bizarre errors later in execution.

More often, mistakes arise not from a single function call, but as a consequence of the interaction between different member functions. For example, suppose programmer P1 has developed a stack container class. The programmer provides to programmer P2 a reasonable set of operations, such as the following:

```
class Stack
{
    Stack();
    void push(string value);
    double top();
    void pop();
    int size() const;
};
```

Programmer P1 may assume that a call on pop will never take place without a previous call on push to place a value on to the stack so the function doesn't test for this case. Programmer P1 has, after all, provided programmer P2 with the ability to check whether the stack is empty through the method size, so there is no excuse for such an error. Nevertheless, the error is almost certain to occur at some point. Whose fault is the error? Is it the fault of programmer P2, for not using the stack correctly, or is it the fault of programmer P1, for not anticipating the possibility of the error? Finger pointing aside, it is simply the case that the Stack data type would be more reliable and robust if programmer P1 had provided a better mechanism for dealing with errors.

While this description makes it sound as if no reasonable programmer would ever commit this type of mistake, it is a surprising fact that many parts of the C++ run-time library operate in just this fashion. The stack container in the Standard Template Library, for instance, simply assumes that a pop will not occur without a preceding push. The effect of this error is, according to the language definition, simply undefined. Many systems will fail with a confusing error message (such as "segmentation fault").

QUALITY TIP 17.1

Nobody Cares How Fast You Get the Wrong Answer

Efficiency is usually cited as the reason for creating components that neglect to check their data, such as the pop function in the STL class stack. The argument is that in those situations where reliability is a concern a good programmer will use the size function to check their data before calling pop, that one should not have to pay the execution time cost required by the check in situations where it is not needed, and that if checks are performed there will be a tendency to repeatedly check for the same error [1]. A similar argument is used to justify the fact that array index expressions in C++ programs are not checked.

As machines have become ever faster, however, the balance has shifted from efficiency to security as a primary concern. Programmers are notorious for not recognizing the possibility of error. In real terms the execution time cost of checks is small. And this small cost pales in comparison to the time spent hunting down mysterious errors that occur when "impossible" things happen. And even this pales in comparison to the millions of man years that have been spent combating computer viruses, many of which were made possible by the simple decision not to check array bounds in C and C++.

You should never assume that things will not go wrong—that your arguments will never be invalid, that two member functions will never be invoked in an incorrect sequence.

Program defensively. Assume that if something can go wrong, it will go wrong. Check for these conditions, then take appropriate actions when they occur.

17.2.2 Printing an Error Message

Printing a message to report an error may be reasonable in student programs or during the process of debugging.

```
double future_value(double initial_balance, double p, int n)
{
    if (p < 0 || n < 0)
    {
        cout << "Illegal values to future_value " << p << " " << n << "\n";
        return 0;
    }
    return initial_balance * pow(1 + p / 100, n);
}
```

It is also reasonable for an error message to ask a user to cure those error conditions that are within their power to remedy, such as closing a disk drive door or turning on a printer. However, in large systems there may not be enough information to produce a reasonable error message. Users of commercial software systems get extremely perturbed when a product emits an error message that is incomprehensible and does not indicate the appropriate remedy. Often a message such as "Error Code = −41" makes no more sense than "there was an error while your program was executing".

17.2.3 Special Return Values

One of the easiest ways to signal that an error has occurred in the processing of a function is to return a special value as the function result. Suppose the Stack class was implemented using an array of fixed size. This makes the code easy to write, but the stack will fill up when too many push operations are performed. To handle this, we define the push function so that it returns a special value (for example, a Boolean false) if it fails.

```
bool ok = my_stack.push(3.14);
if (!ok) cout << "Stack was full\n";
```

Of course, this leaves it to the programmer to check the resulting value. Using the stack without first checking the result value can be a source of confusing errors.

Note that this approach is not appropriate if the return type is not suitable for encoding an error flag; for example if the result is an Employee. It is also not applicable to functions that do not return a value, for example constructors.

Routines that yield numeric, string, or pointer results often return a special value, such as 0, -1, the empty string, or the NULL pointer when an error is encountered. For example, we may define Stack.top so that it returns zero if the stack is empty:

```
double s = my_stack.top();
if (s == 0) cout << "Stack was empty\n";
```

However, this introduces another problem. The number zero could be a legal value that was pushed onto the stack, or it could indicate an error.

The function `main` uses another example of special return values in C++. The `main` function returns a *status value*, which is zero if execution was successful, and a non-zero value if execution was not successful. Whether this value is communicated back to the user is dependent upon the platform. The function `exit` can be used to terminate execution and set the status value. A common way of responding to an error is printing a message and calling `exit`:

```
if (my_stack.size() == 0)
{
    cerr << "Stack Underflow Detected\n";
    exit(1); // Terminate with nonzero status flag
}
```

The stream I/O library uses a variation on the idea of a special return value. It does not return an error status directly, rather it provides a way to convert a value into an error status. Furthermore, unlike the earlier standard I/O library, it remembers error flags and will not try to perform an action in an exceptional situation, for example writing a value to a file that cannot be opened.

```
istream file_in("my_data.dat");
if (!file_in)
    Handle error case
```

Here it is not the case that `file_in` is itself a special flag, as it was in the earlier example. Rather, the `if` statement treats the `file_in` object as a `boolean`. This `boolean` value will tell if the file is currently in a valid state.

COMMON ERROR 17.1

Forgetting to Check Return Values

A surprisingly large number of programming errors are caused by the failure to check a return value. For example, it is common practice when writing functions that return a pointer to return a NULL pointer as an error indicator:

```
Employee* new_worker = read_employee();
```

If the programmer simply assumes the pointer is valid and goes on to use it without checking for NULL, subtle and difficult to debug errors will likely ensue.

17.2.4 External Flags

Sometimes programmers elect to return a status flag not as a function result, but through another variable. One way to do this is to use a reference parameter, which can be set to one value for correct outcomes and a different value on error.

```
Employee* read_employee_info(string name, bool& status)
{
    ...
}
bool read_ok = true;
Employee* new_employee = read_employee_info("Fred Smith", read_ok);
if (!read_ok) cout <<"Unable to read new employee information\n";
```

Another possibility is to return the error flag in a global variable. The latter approach is used by many of the standard mathematical routines. The global variable is named errno. The include file <cerrno> provides the declaration of the variable, as well as symbolic constants for a number of error conditions. Common conditions include EDOM (domain error) and ERANGE (range error). The value of errno is set by functions such as the square root routine:

```
#include <cerrno>
...
double x = ...;
errno = 0; // Clear the error flag
double d = sqrt(x);
if (errno == EDOM) // Test the global status flag
    Handle error case
```

The function atoi is another common function that uses errno. This function takes as argument a string of digits and returns the integer value the string represents. The flag errno is set to the symbolic constant ERANGE if the string does not represent a valid integer or if it is not in the range of values that can be represented by an int.

One disadvantage of this approach is that several functions that might set the global flag could appear in the same expression. Worse, it is possible that a function might *clear* the global flags:

```
// The function g clears the flag before attempting a calculation
double g(char* num_string)
{
    errno = 0; // Clear flags
    int n = atoi(num_string);
    if (errno == ERANGE)
        n = 0;
    return 3.14159 * sin(n * 3.14159);
}
```

```
// Is sqrt handled first or is g?
double d = sqrt(x) * g("34");
```

If the multiplication operator executes the square root function before invoking g, an error in calculating the square root could be masked by the function g clearing the error flag.

A more fundamental problem with this mechanism is that the variable errno is *global*. As was noted in Quality Tip 4.2, programmers have increasingly become aware that the use of global variables is inherently dangerous and error prone [2]. For example, it may be very difficult to trace how a global variable is being set or used. Because better mechanisms now exist, such as exceptions, they should be used.

17.2.5 Halting Execution with Assertions

One response to an exceptional condition is to simply halt execution. This can happen inadvertently, such as when pop on an empty stack causes a segmentation fault. Or it can happen by choice. The function exit(int) can be invoked to halt execution and set the return status value. The function exit, however, will not tell the programmer where the program was at the point of error. Furthermore, there is no guarantee that the user will check the return status. Since the program halted, the user might assume, incorrectly, that the program terminated normally.

A better alternative is the assert macro, which you encountered in Section 4.13. An assertion is simply a Boolean expression that can be evaluated at run time. Should the expression evaluate to false, a diagnostic error message is printed and the program is halted. The format for the diagnostic information is implementation-dependent, but it typically includes the text of the assertion that failed and the file name and line number at which the assertion appears:

```
#include <cassert>
...
double future_value(double initial_balance, double p, int n)
{
   assert(p >= 0);
   assert(n >= 0);
   return initial_balance * pow(1 + p / 100, n);
}
```

The assertion mechanism is hampered by the fact that assertion checking can be turned off at the discretion of the programmer simply by setting a compiler switch. Many programmers use assertions during program development and then, for the sake of efficiency, turn them off when a program goes into production. Unfortunately, errors occur in production programs as well as in programs under development, and such a short-sighted policy not only makes tracing errors more difficult, but also tends to make programs fail in even more mysterious ways.

More importantly, halting execution is often too radical a move to make in response to an error. Many errors can be handled if they are reported in a manner that the programmer can detect and analyze.

17.2.6 Error Handlers

Some libraries provide a mechanism for users to specify what should happen in case of an error. The library user installs an error handler function, and the library calls that function when an error occurs.

The standard C++ library allows you to install an error handler that is called when the new operator is unable to allocate more memory. You write a function with the action that should occur in that unfortunate event.

```
void out_of_memory_action()
{
   ...
}
```

Install the function by calling

```
set_new_handler(out_of_memory_action)
```

This seems like a flexible approach, but in practice it is very limited. There is very little you can do when the error occurs. Your function can't mint new transistors to make more memory. It is also difficult to save the state of the program because the error handler function will usually not have access to the program internals. For that reason, most error handlers simply print a message and exit the program.

In the past it was common to specify error handlers for tasks such as memory allocation. In recent years these have largely been replaced by the exception mechanism. In particular, if you don't install your own memory error handler, the C++ memory allocator will throw an exception when heap memory is exhausted.

17.3 Exceptions

> Use exceptions to transmit error conditions to special handlers.

Since the exception mechanism was added to the C++ language, it has tended to replace earlier techniques for dealing with exceptional conditions. This is due, in part, to the fact that exceptions interact well with other aspects of the language and avoid many of the problems of earlier mechanisms.

When a function detects an error, it can signal that condition to a handler by *throwing an exception* (see Syntax 17.1 on page 675). For example,

```
double future_value(double initial_balance, double p, int n)
{
    if (p < 0 || n < 0)
    {
        logic_error description("illegal future_value parameter");
        throw description;
    }
    return initial_balance * pow(1 + p / 100, n);
}
```

> When you detect an error condition, use the throw statement to signal the exception.

Here, `logic_error` is a standard exception class that is declared in the `<stdexcept>` header.

Many programmers don't bother to give the exception object a name and just throw an anonymous object, like this:

```
if (p < 0 || n < 0)
    throw logic_error("illegal future_value parameter");
```

The keyword `throw` indicates that the function exits immediately. However, the function does not return to its caller. Instead, it searches the caller, the caller's caller, and so forth, for a handler that specifies how to handle a logic error. When a handler is found, the associated `catch` clause is executed. The next section describes the syntax for writing `catch` clauses.

SYNTAX 17.1 Throwing an Exception

throw *expression*;

Example:

throw logic_error("illegal future_value parameter");

Purpose:

Abandon this function and throw a value to an exception handler.

17.3.1 Catching Exceptions

To handle an exception, supply a try block with a catch clause that matches the exception type.

You supply an exception handler with the try statement (see Syntax 17.2 on page 676):

```
try
{
    code
}
catch (logic_error& e)
{
    handler
}
```

If any of the functions in the try clause throws a logic_error, or calls another function that throws such an exception, then the code in the catch clause executes immediately.

For example, you can place a handler into the main function that tells the user that something has gone very wrong and offers a chance to try again with different inputs.

```
int main()
{
    bool more = true;
    while (more)
    {
        try
        {
            code
        }
        catch (logic_error& e)
        {
            cout << "A logic error has occurred: "
                << e.what() << "\n"
                << "Retry? (y/n)";
            string input;
            getline(cin, input);
            if (input == "n") more = false;
```

```
        }
      }
   }
```

This handler inspects the exception object that was thrown. Note that the catch clause looks somewhat like a function with a reference parameter variable e of type logic_error&. (You can give any name you like to the exception variable.) The catch clause then applies the what member function of the logic_error class to the exception object e. That function returns the string that was passed to the constructor of the error object in the throw statement.

SYNTAX 17.2 try Block

```
try
{
    statements
}
catch (type_name₁ variable_name₁)
{
    statements
}
catch (type_name₂ variable_name₂)
{
    statements
}
...
catch (type_nameₙ variable_nameₙ)
{
    statements
}
```

Example:

```
try
{
   List staff = read_list();
   process_list(staff);
}
catch (logic_error& e)
{
   cout << "Processing error " << e.what() << "\n";
}
```

Purpose:

Provide one or more handlers for types of exceptions that may be thrown when executing a block of statements.

17.3.2 Values Thrown and Caught

You can throw any type of value, primitive or object. For example, you can throw an integer value:

```
throw 3;
```

And later catch it with a clause that uses the same type:

```
try
{
    ...
}
catch (int a)
{
    ...
}
```

But while this is legal, it is usually not a good idea. What is the meaning of the value 3 as an error? Why not 4? There just isn't enough information in a primitive value to make sense of the error. Throwing enumerated constants or strings makes slightly more sense, but you must be careful. Implicit conversions, such as from int to double or from char* to string, are not performed when a value is thrown. The following will probably not operate as the programmer intended:

```
try
{
    ...
    throw "Stack Underflow";
    ...
}
catch (string err)
{
    cerr << err << "\n";
}
```

The reason is, as you learned in Chapter 7, the literal string is type char* (pointer to character). While this is often converted into a string, it is not the same type. Because thrown values are not converted, the catch clause will not be invoked.

> Throw and catch objects of classes that describe error conditions.

In order to avoid these problems, it is much more common for programs to throw and catch objects. Often programmers will create their own classes to represent errors.

For example:

```
class MyApplicationError
{
public:
    MyApplicationError(const string& r);
    string& what() const;
private:
    string reason;
};

MyApplicationError::MyApplicationError(const string& r) : reason(r) {}
```

```
    string& what() const
    {
        return reason;
    }
}
```

Errors are now indicated by throwing an instance of this class:

```
try
{
    ...
    throw MyApplicationError("illegal value");
    ...
}
catch (MyApplicationError& e)
{
    cerr << "Caught exception " << e.what() << "\n";
}
```

> The standard library provides a hierarchy of exception classes.

Note that an object is normally caught as a reference parameter. There are two reasons for this. First, it is more efficient, because it avoids the object being duplicated by means of a copy constructor. Second, it avoids the object-slicing problem that can occur if inheritance is used to define the class.

Why would inheritance be involved with exceptions? While the programmer is free to select any type of value to be used in a throw statement, it is often a good idea to reuse classes from the standard library. The standard library provides a hierarchy of standard exception classes, some of which are shown in Figure 1. The header for these classes is <stdexcept>. The classes can be used in two ways. One way is to simply create instances of these standard objects. This technique was illustrated in our initial example of the throw statement:

```
if (p < 0 || n < 0)
    throw logic_error("illegal future_value parameter");
```

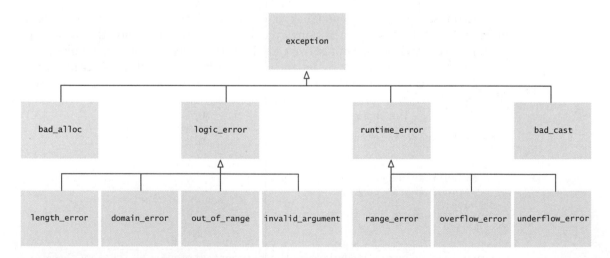

Figure 1   The Hierarchy of Standard Exception Types in C++

Another possibility is to use inheritance to define your own exception types as more specialized categories of the standard classes:

```
class FutureValueError : public logic_error
{
public:
    FutureValueError(string reason);
};

FutureValueError::FutureValueError(string reason)
    : logic_error(reason) {}
```

Use inheritance to organize exceptions into general and specialized classes.

With this declaration, the programmer declares that the Future-ValueError class is a subclass of logic_error. Notice that the Future-ValueError constructor passes the string parameter to the base class constructor. The future_value function can now throw a Future-ValueError object:

```
if (p < 0 || n < 0)
    throw FutureValueError("illegal parameter");
```

Because a FutureValueError is a logic_error, you can still catch it with a

```
catch (logic_error& e)
```

clause—that is the reason for using inheritance. Alternatively, you can supply a

```
catch (FutureValueError& e)
```

clause that only catches FutureValueError objects and not other logic errors. You can even do both:

```
try
{
    code
}
catch (FutureValueError& e)
{
    handler₁
}
catch (logic_error& e)
{
    handler₂
}
catch (bad_alloc& e)
{
    handler₃
}
```

In this situation, the first handler catches all future value errors, the second handler catches the logic errors that are not future value errors, and the third handler catches the bad_alloc exception that is thrown when the new operator runs out of memory. Within the catch clause the error string can be accessed using the member function what.

The order of catch clauses is important. When an exception occurs, the exception handling mechanism proceeds top to bottom to look for a matching handler and executes the first one found. You should match a derived class before matching its base class. If you reversed the handlers in the preceding code, then the `logic_error` handler would match a `FutureValueError`, and the handler for future value errors would never be executed.

A try block does not need to catch all exceptions. If an exception is thrown and not caught by any catch clause, the previous try block in the call sequence is examined. If that block does not have a catch clause of the appropriate type, the next most recent block is examined, and so on. Imagine that function `process_record` in the following invokes function `read`, which in turn invokes function `future_value`, which throws an exception.

```
double future_value(...)
{
    if (...) throw FutureValueError("illegal future_value parameter");
    ...
}

void read()
{
    try
    {
        ...
        double d = future_value(...);
        ...
    }
    catch (bad_alloc& e)
    {
        cout << "caught bad_alloc error " << e.what() << "\n";
    }
}

void process_record()
{
    try
    {
        read();
    }
    catch (logic_error& e)
    {
        cout << "caught logic_error " << e.what() << "\n";
    }
}
```

When the exception is thrown in the function `future_value` the exception handling system tries to find a matching catch clause. To do this it first examines the function `future_value` itself. But there is no catch clause in this function. So it next examines the caller, that is, the function `read`. But the argument type for the catch clause in function `read` does not match the type for the exception thrown. So the caller for `read`, namely function `process_record`, is examined. Here a catch clause of the correct type is found and executed. If the entire call stack is traversed and no catch clause with the appropriate type is found, the error handler function `terminate` is invoked. Normally this function halts execution. Programmers can specify their own actions by using the function `set_terminate` to set an error handler.

A catch clause consisting of three dots is used to catch any remaining exceptions. Since the exception itself is not named, it normally cannot be handled. A special form of the throw statement is therefore used to *rethrow* the exception, passing it on to another exception handler. Before the exception is rethrown, typically some error recovery tasks are performed, such as recovering dynamically allocated memory:

> *Rethrow any exception that you catch without fully handling it.*

```
try
{
    code
}
catch (FutureValueError& e)
{
    statements₁
}
catch (...) // Catch any remaining exceptions
{
    statements₂
    throw; // Rethrow the error
}
```

An example illustrating the use of this form of catch and rethrow will be presented in Section 17.3.3.

Quality Tip 17.2

Tie Exception Classes to the Standard Library

The C++ language permits a throw statement to represent an exception using any type of value. However, as a practical matter most programmers choose to throw objects. While it is sometimes sufficient to simply reuse one of the standard classes from Figure 1, more often than not programmers create their own exception classes. A user-defined class can more accurately represent the nature of the error in the application at hand and does not run the risk of being confused with errors arising from other sources.

However, it is useful to tie user-defined exception classes by inheritance to the standard class hierarchy. There are several advantages to doing this. First, the base class exception defines the big three memory management operations, freeing the programmer from this concern. The use of the standard class clearly indicates that the purpose is to describe an exception. Finally, the use of inheritance permits catch clauses to use polymorphism to catch an exception using a base class, such as logic_error, in place of the derived class.

As shown in Figure 1, the standard library distinguishes between "logic errors" and "run-time errors". When a logic error occurs, it never makes sense to retry the same operation, but a run-time error may have some chance of going away when the operation is attempted a second time. For example, logic dictates that getting data from an empty list is doomed to failure. But reading from a file on a networked file system may fail due to an intermittent network error, and then later work when the network is up again.

Some standard exceptions do not follow the logic error/run-time error dichotomy. For example, the exception bad_cast is thrown when a dynamic cast fails. The exception bad_alloc is thrown when memory becomes exhausted and a memory request cannot be satisfied. However, most user-defined exception classes fit into either the logic error or run-time error category, and hence are best handled by making them inherit from the appropriate standard class.

COMMON ERROR 17.2

Throwing Objects versus Throwing Pointers

A common source of error is to confuse throwing a pointer with throwing an object. There is a world of difference between

```
throw FutureValueError("illegal parameter");
```

and

```
throw new FutureValueError("illegal parameter");
```

A catch clause for the second must use a pointer value:

```
catch (FutureValueError* e) ...
```

The catch clause for the object will not catch a pointer value, nor will a catch clause for a pointer capture an object value. The two are separate types. Throwing an object is preferable to throwing a pointer, because it avoids a potential memory leak if you neglect to delete the exception object.

17.3.3 Stack Unwinding

One common use of exception handling is in functions that read input. Consider a function such as the Product::read function. It expects the name, price, and score of a product. What should happen if no price or score is given? This may be an indication of a corrupted file. In such a case, it makes sense to throw an exception.

```cpp
bool Product::read(fstream& fs)
{
    getline(fs, name);
    if (name == "") return false; // End of file
    fs >> price >> score;
    if (fs.fail())
        throw runtime_error("Error while reading product");
    string remainder;
    getline(fs, remainder);
    return true;
}
```

The read function shows the distinction between the *expected* end of file and an unexpected problem. All files must come to an end, and the function returns false if the end has been reached in the normal way. But if an error has occurred in the middle of a product record, then the function throws an exception. Therefore, the caller of the function only has to worry about the normal case and can leave the processing of the exceptional case to a specialized handler.

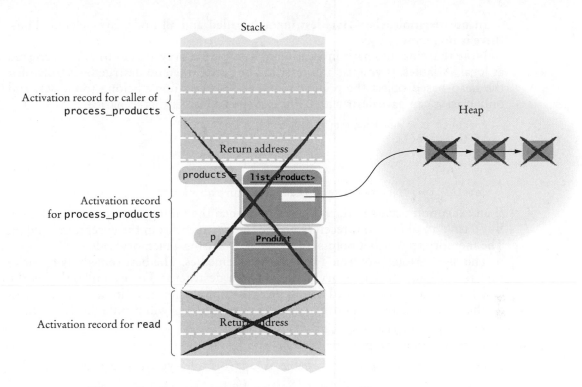

Figure 2   Run-Time Stack After Exception is Thrown

Consider this calling function:

```
void process_products(fstream& fs)
{
    list<Product> products;
    Product p;
    while (p.read(fs))
        products.push_back(p);
    do something with products
}
```

Now suppose that the read function throws an exception. Then the exception-handling mechanism abandons the process_products function and searches its callers for an appropriate handler.

But there is a problem. When the process_products function is abandoned, what happens to the memory in the products list? The list contains some number of nodes that were allocated on the heap and that need to be deleted (see Figure 2).

> When an object is removed from the stack through exception handling, its destructor is invoked.

The C++ exception-handling mechanism is prepared for this situation. An important aspect of exception-handling is the process of *unwinding the run-time stack*. When an exception is thrown, all function calls between the throw point and the try block are terminated. The exception handler invokes *all destructors of stack objects* before it abandons a function.

In our example, the ~list destructor is called and all nodes are deleted. Thus, there is no memory leak.

Note that this automatic invocation of destructors only applies to objects created as local variables. If you use a pointer in your code, then no destructor is called for the heap-based object the pointer refers to. Pointers don't belong to classes, and only classes can have destructors. For example, consider this scenario.

```
Product* p = new Product();
if (p->read())
{
   ...
}
delete p; // Never executes if read throws an exception
```

If an exception occurs in the read function, then the calling function is abandoned. But p isn't an object, so it receives no special treatment from the exception handler. The memory to which it points is not deleted, causing a memory leak.

This is a serious problem. There are two remedies. The best remedy is to make sure that all allocated memory is deleted in a destructor. For example, that is the case for the nodes of a linked list. Replacing a simple pointer with an auto_ptr will do the trick, because the destructor in the class auto_ptr will handle the deletion.

```
// Deletion now taken care of by auto_ptr destructor
auto_ptr<Product> p = new Product();
```

However, if a local pointer variable is unavoidable, you can use the following construct:

```
Product* p = NULL;
try
{
   p = new Product();
   if (p->read())
   {
      ...
   }
   delete p;
}
catch (...)
{
   delete p;
   throw;
}
```

As was noted in the previous section, the special clause catch (...) matches any exception. The handler contains the local cleanup, followed by the throw statement without an exception object. That special form of the throw statement *rethrows* the current exception. It is important to rethrow the exception so that a competent handler can process it. After all, the catch clause didn't properly handle the exception.

This local cleanup mechanism is clearly tedious, providing an excellent incentive to arrange your code in an object-oriented way. Place the pointer variables inside classes, and put the destructor in charge of cleanup.

17.3.4 Exceptions and Constructors / Destructors

Because a constructor does not return a value, the option of returning a status flag is not available. Throwing an exception is therefore a much cleaner way to indicate the failure of a constructor.

Objects are not considered to be "constructed" until the constructor completes execution. An exception thrown from within a constructor will not cause the destructor to be triggered. This leaves the programmer in charge of resource management inside the constructor. A subtle source of memory leaks arises from an exception being thrown after a dynamically allocated value is created:

```
class DataArray
{
public:
    DataArray(int s);
    ~DataArray();
    void init(int s);
private:
    int* data;
};

DataArray::DataArray(int s)
{
    data = new int[s];
    init(s); // What happens if init throws exception?
}

DataArray::~DataArray()
{
    delete[] data;
}
```

If the method init throws an exception, the dynamically allocated memory array will not be recovered, since the object is not yet considered to be constructed. To solve this problem, catch the error from within the constructor, delete the memory, then rethrow the exception:

```
DataArray::DataArray(int s)
{
    data = new int[s];
    try
    {
        init(s);
    }
    catch (...) // Catch any exception init throws
    {
        delete[] data;
        data = NULL;
        throw; // Rethrow exception
    }
}
```

Do not throw exceptions in a destructor.

Because destructors are invoked as part of the process of stack unwinding during the recovery from an exception, a destructor should never throw an exception. Doing so would yield two exceptions; the one currently being handled by the stack unwinding, and the one thrown by the destructor. Because it is unclear which exception should take priority, the program is immediately halted. This is almost never what the programmer intended.

COMMON ERROR 17.3

Exceptions During Construction of Global Variables

There is one caveat to the suggestion that exceptions be used to signal errors that occur during the execution of a constructor. Such use is not safe if the constructor in question is used to initialize a global variable. Because the initialization of global variables occurs before the function main is invoked, there can be no catch clause to capture any exceptions that may be generated. So any exceptions that are thrown will immediately terminate the program. This is yet another reason to avoid the use of global variables.

17.3.5 Exception Specifications

Exception specifications describe the exceptions that a function may throw.

If an exception is thrown and no catch clause exists to catch it then the program invokes an error handler to terminate the program. Furthermore, as you have seen in the preceding section, if an exception occurs, then some important code may not be executed. Therefore, it is somewhat dangerous to throw exceptions, or to call methods that can throw exceptions. In C++, a function can declare that it throws only exceptions of a certain type, or no exceptions at all. You can use that knowledge to make sure that it is safe to call certain functions, or to know which kinds of exceptions your program needs to catch.

A function signature can optionally be followed by the keyword throw and a parenthesized, comma-separated list of exception types (see Syntax 17.3 on page 687). For example:

```
void process_products(fstream& fs)
    throw (UnexpectedEndOfFile, bad_alloc)
```

To denote the fact that a function throws no exceptions, use an empty exception list.

```
void print_products(const list<Product>& products)
    throw ()
```

A function without a throw specification is allowed to throw any exception.

Exception specifications are checked at run time. An unexpected exception terminates the program.

You must be careful when using exception specifications. The compiler does not enforce them. If a function calls another function, and the called function throws an exception that is not caught, then an exception that is not on the specification list can end up propagating through the function. If a function with an exception specification throws an unexpected exception object whose type is not in the list, the exception handling mechanism invokes an error handler to terminate the program.

Exception specifications are not tied to function signatures during inheritance. A function in a derived class that overrides a function in a base class can throw an exception that is not specified in the base class definition. An examination of the base class will therefore not reveal this possibility.

SYNTAX 17.3 Exception Specification

return_type function_name(parameters)
    throw (*type_name$_1$, type_name$_2$, ..., type_name$_n$*)

Example:

```
void process_products(fstream& fs)
    throw (UnexpectedEndOfFile, bad_alloc)
```

Purpose:

List the types of all exceptions that a function can throw.

QUALITY TIP 17.3

Use Exceptions for Exceptional Cases

Consider the read function of the Product class. It returns false at the end of the stream. Why doesn't it throw an exception?

The designer of this function realized that every stream must come to an end. In other words, the end of input is a normal condition, not an exceptional one. Whenever you attempt to read a data record, you must be prepared to deal with the possibility that you reached the end. However, if the end of input occurs inside a data record that should be complete, then you can throw an exception to indicate that the input came to an *unexpected* end. This must have been caused by some exceptional event, perhaps a corrupted file.

In particular, you should *never* use an exception as a "break statement on steroids". Don't throw an exception to exit a deeply nested loop or a set of recursive method calls; this is considered an abuse of the exception mechanism. A good tutorial on the use of exceptions is [3].

QUALITY TIP 17.4

Throwing an Exception Is Not a Sign of Shame

Some programmers prefer to patch a problem locally rather than throw an exception, because they consider it irresponsible not to handle all problems. For example, some programmers may implement the `Iterator::get` method to return an empty string when the iterator is in an invalid position. However, that view is short-sighted. By supplying a false return value, a program may muddle through for a while, but it will likely produce unexpected and useless results. Furthermore, suppressing the error report deprives an exception handler of effectively dealing with the problem.

It is entirely honorable to throw exceptions to indicate failures that a function cannot competently handle. Of course, it is a good idea to document these exceptions.

RANDOM FACT 17.1

The Ariane Rocket Incident

The European Space Agency, Europe's counterpart to NASA, developed a rocket model called Ariane that it had successfully used several times to launch satellites and scientific experiments into space. However, when a new version, the Ariane 5, was launched on June 4, 1996, from ESA's launch site in Kourou, French Guiana, the rocket veered off course approximately 40 seconds after liftoff. Flying at an angle of more than 20 degrees, rather than straight up, exerted such an aerodynamic force that the boosters separated, which triggered the automatic self-destruction mechanism. The rocket blew itself up.

The ultimate cause of this accident was an unhandled exception! The rocket contained two identical devices (called inertial reference systems) that processed flight data from measuring devices and turned the data into information about the rocket position. The onboard computer used the position information for controlling the boosters. The same inertial reference systems and computer software had worked fine on the Ariane 4 predecessor.

However, due to design changes of the rocket, one of the sensors measured a larger acceleration force than had been encountered in the Ariane 4. That value, computed as a floating-point value, was stored in a 16-bit integer. Unlike C++, the Ada language, used for the device software, generates an exception if a floating-point number is too large to be converted to an integer. Unfortunately, the programmers of the device decided that this situation would never happen and didn't provide an exception handler.

When the overflow did happen, the exception was triggered and, because there was no handler, the device shut itself off. The onboard computer sensed the failure and switched over to the backup device. However, that device had shut itself off for exactly the same reason, something that the designers of the rocket had not expected. They figured that the devices might fail for mechanical reasons, and the chances of two devices having the same mechanical failure was considered remote. At that point, the rocket was without reliable position information and went off course (see Figure 3).

Would it have been better if the software hadn't been so thorough? If it had ignored the overflow, the device wouldn't have been shut off. It would have just computed bad data. But then the device would have reported wrong position data, which could have been equally fatal. Instead, a correct implementation should have caught overflow exceptions and come

Figure 3 The Explosion of the Ariane Rocket

up with some strategy to recompute the flight data. Clearly, ignoring an exception was not a reasonable option in this context.

17.4 Case Study: Matrices, Continued

In Chapters 14 through 16 we developed classes to be used in matrix algorithms. To modify these classes to use exceptions we first define a pair of exception classes. The class MatrixMismatchException inherits from the standard class invalid_argument, while the class MatrixIndexException inherits from out_of_range. By using the standard library classes that inherit from class exception, both of these exception classes can be caught by a single catch clause, as shown in the test program. In order to provide a more meaningful error message we include the out of range index value as an argument to the constructor for the class MatrixIndexException. Because the base exception class requires a string, the index value is formatted using a private internal method before the constructor for the base class is called:

ch17/matrix4.h

```
1   #ifndef MATRIX4_H
2   #define MATRIX4_H
3
4   #include <iostream>
5   #include <stdexcept>
6
7   using namespace std;
8
9   /**
10      Matrix exception class for indexing error.
11  */
12  class MatrixIndexException : public out_of_range
13  {
14  public:
15     MatrixIndexException(int i);
16  private:
17     string format_message(int i);
18  };
19
```

```
20  /**
21      Matrix exception class for mismatched argument error.
22  */
23  class MatrixMismatchException : public invalid_argument
24  {
25  public:
26      MatrixMismatchException();
27  };
28
29  /**
30      This class describes a row in a matrix.
31  */
32  class Matrix;
33  class MatrixRow
34  {
    ... Same as in matrix2.h
48      double& operator[](int j) throw (MatrixIndexException);
    ...
53  };
    ...
80  /**
81      This class describes a matrix with arbitrary rows and columns.
82  */
83  class Matrix
84  {
85  public:
    ...
116     double& operator()(int i, int j) throw (MatrixIndexException);
    ...
131     MatrixRow operator[](int i) throw (MatrixIndexException);
    ...
145     Matrix& operator+=(const Matrix& right)
146         throw (MatrixMismatchException);
147
148 private:
    ...
163 };
    ...
170 Matrix operator+(const Matrix& left, const Matrix& right)
171     throw (MatrixMismatchException);
    ...
178 Matrix operator*(const Matrix& left, const Matrix& right)
179     throw (MatrixMismatchException);
    ...
203
204 inline MatrixIndexException::MatrixIndexException(int idx)
205     : out_of_range(format_message(idx)) {}
206
207 inline MatrixMismatchException::MatrixMismatchException()
208     : invalid_argument("Matrix arguments have incompatible sizes")  {}
209
    ...
235 inline MatrixRow Matrix::operator[](int i) throw (MatrixIndexException)
236 {
```

```
237      return MatrixRow(this, i);
238  }
239

     ...
247
248  inline double& MatrixRow::operator[](int j)
         throw (MatrixIndexException)
249  {
250      return (*mat)(i,j);
251  }
     ...
267  #endif
```

Methods that used assert in the previous version have been rewritten in matrix4.cpp to throw exceptions on error. Notice that the matrix addition function is declared as potentially throwing an exception even though none appears in the body, because the exception from the operator += can propagate through the function. The same is true for the subscript operators in MatrixRow and ConstMatrixRow.

ch17/matrix4.cpp

```
1   #include <iomanip>
2   #include <sstream>
3
4   #include "matrix4.h"
5
6   string MatrixIndexException::format_message(int n)
7   {
8       ostringstream outstr;
9       outstr << "Matrix index " << n << " out of range";
10      return outstr.str();
11  }
12

    ... Same as in matrix2.cpp
38
39  double& Matrix::operator()(int i, int j) throw (MatrixIndexException)
40  {
41      if (i < 0 || i >= rows)
42          throw MatrixIndexException(i);
43      if (j < 0 || j >= columns)
44          throw MatrixIndexException(j);
45      return elements[i * get_columns() + j];
46  }
    ...
56
57  Matrix& Matrix::operator+=(const Matrix& right)
58      throw (MatrixMismatchException)
59  {
60      if (rows != right.rows || columns != right.columns)
61          throw MatrixMismatchException();
62      for (int i = 0; i < rows; i++)
63          for (int j = 0; j < columns; j++)
64              (*this)(i, j) += right(i, j);
```

```
65        return *this;
66   }
67
68   Matrix operator+(const Matrix& left, const Matrix& right)
69        throw (MatrixMismatchException)
70   {
71       Matrix result = left;
72       result += right;
73       return result;
74   }
75
76   Matrix operator*(const Matrix& left, const Matrix& right)
77        throw (MatrixMismatchException)
78   {
79       if (left.get_columns() != right.get_rows())
80           throw MatrixMismatchException();
81       Matrix result(left.get_rows(), right.get_columns());
82       for (int i = 0; i < left.get_rows(); i++)
83           for (int j = 0; j < right.get_columns(); j++)
84               for (int k = 0; k < left.get_columns(); k++)
85                   result(i, j) += left(i, k) * right(k, j);
86       return result;
87   }
     ...
```

ch17/matrixtest4.cpp

```
1    #include "matrix4.h"
2
3    int main()
4    {
5        try
6        {
7            Matrix m(4, 3);
8            m[0][0] = m[1][1] = m[2][2] = 1;
9            m[0][1] = m[1][2] = m[2][3] = 2;
10           cout << m * m;
11       }
12       catch (exception& e)
13       {
14           cout << "Caught exception: " << e.what() << "\n";
15       }
16       return 0;
17   }
```

Program Run

```
Caught exception: Matrix index 3 out of range
```

CHAPTER SUMMARY

1. Anomalous situations can be expected to occur, and programs should be written to be robust in the presence of errors.

2. There are a variety of mechanisms that can be used to handle exceptional conditions. These include special return flags and assertions as well as the exception mechanism.

3. The management of exceptions becomes even more critical when software is developed by two or more programmers working on independent components.

4. Use exceptions to transmit error conditions to special handlers.

5. When you detect an error condition, use the throw statement to signal the exception.

6. To handle an exception, supply a try block with a catch clause that matches the exception type.

7. Throw and catch objects of classes that describe error conditions.

8. The standard library provides a hierarchy of exception classes.

9. Use inheritance to organize exceptions into general and specialized classes.

10. Rethrow any exception that you catch without fully handling it.

11. When an object is removed from the stack through exception handling, its destructor is invoked.

12. Do not throw exceptions in a destructor.

13. Exception specifications describe the exceptions that a function may throw.

14. Exception specifications are checked at run time. An unexpected exception terminates the program.

FURTHER READING

1. Bjarne Stroustrup, *The C++ Programming Language*, Special Ed., Addison-Wesley, 2000.

2. William A. Wulf and Mary Shaw, "Global Variable Considered Harmful", *Sigplan Notices*, 8(2): 28–43, 1973.

3. Herb Sutter, *Exceptional C++*, Addison-Wesley, 2000.

REVIEW EXERCISES

Exercise R17.1. Give three examples not mentioned in the chapter of exceptional conditions that a program could encounter.

Exercise R17.2. Explain why the handling of exceptional conditions is often nonlocal.

Exercise R17.3. What is the argument usually cited for not bothering to check for exceptional conditions? What is the counter-argument?

Exercise R17.4. What are the dangers inherent in returning an error status value as a function return value?

Exercise R17.5. Give two reasons why returning an error status value through a global variable is not a good idea.

Exercise R17.6. What dangers are there in simply halting execution by calling `exit` when an error is encountered?

Exercise R17.7. What is the advantage of using `assert` rather than testing a condition and calling `exit`? What are two drawbacks to the use of `assert`?

Exercise R17.8. What are the advantages of using exceptions in place of other means of error processing described in this chapter?

Exercise R17.9. Write the statements to throw

    a. a `runtime_error` with an explanation "Network failure"

    b. a string `"Network failure"`

    c. the unlucky number 13

Exercise R17.10. Write the statements to catch the exceptions of Exercise R17.9.

Exercise R17.11. If no exceptions are thrown within a try block, where does execution continue after the statements complete execution?

Exercise R17.12. What happens if an exception is thrown and no matching catch clause can be found?

Exercise R17.13. What happens if a value being thrown matches several catch clauses?

Exercise R17.14. What happens when a `throw` statement occurs inside a catch handler?

Exercise R17.15. Write the statements to catch

    a. any `logic_error`

    b. any `ListError` or `runtime_error`

    c. any exception

Exercise R17.16. What is the advantage to creating your own exception class? What is the benefit of using inheritance from the standard exception class hierarchy?

Exercise R17.17. When do you use the `throw;` statement without argument?

Exercise R17.18. Consider the following code:

```
void f()
{
   List a;
   List* b = new List();
   throw runtime_error("");
}
```

Which objects are destroyed? Are there any memory leaks?

Exercise R17.19. What is the difference between

```
void f();
```

and

```
void f() throw ();
```

Exercise R17.20. How do you denote a function that throws only `bad_alloc` exceptions? A function that throws no exceptions at all? A function that can throw exceptions of any type?

Exercise R17.21. What happens in your programming environment if you throw an exception that is never caught? What happens if you throw an exception that violates an exception specification?

PROGRAMMING EXERCISES

Exercise P17.1. One argument used to justify the fact that the `stack` data structure in the standard library does not throw exceptions is that it is easy to add these facilities. Create a class `SafeStack` that implements a stack of strings. Use an instance of `stack<string>` to hold the underlying values, and implement the same interface as that data type. However, your class should throw an exception if an attempt is made to remove a value from an empty stack.

Exercise P17.2. Use the class you developed in Exercise P17.1 to measure the execution cost of throwing an exception. Create an empty stack and, within a loop, repeatedly execute the following `try` block:

```
try
{  // DON'T—this is not a good idea, just being used for timing
   stack.pop();
}
catch (StackError& s)
{
   ...
}
```

Compare the execution time to the simpler statement that avoids the exception altogether

```
if (!stack.empty())
   stack.pop();
```

Exercise P17.3. Demonstrate that a try block need not catch every type of error that could be generated within the block. What happens to exceptions that are not caught?

Exercise P17.4. Enhance the List class of Chapter 12 to throw an exception whenever an error condition occurs. Use exception specifications for all functions.

Exercise P17.5. Modify the class Fraction of Chapter 14 to throw an exception if a zero denominator is specified. What would be an appropriate category for this exception?

Exercise P17.6. Using the class Trace developed in Chapter 15, verify that destructors will be properly invoked when an exception is thrown from a function many levels deep in a function call.

Exercise P17.7. Write a program that can be used to demonstrate that the order in which catch clauses are listed is important.

Exercise P17.8. Change the Product class of Chapter 5 so that the read member function reads a product record from a file and throws an exception when there is an unexpected problem. Change the main function of the product2.cpp program to prompt the user for a file name, read the file, and print the best product. However, if an error occurs during reading the file, offer the user the choice of entering another file name. Test your program with a file that you purposely corrupted.

Exercise P17.9. Change the database.cpp program of Chapter 9 so that the read_employee function throws an exception when there is an unexpected problem. If an error occurs during reading the file, offer the user the choice of entering another file name. Test your program with a file that you purposely corrupted.

Exercise P17.10. In Exercises P8.7–8.9, you implemented an appointment calendar. Revisit that design and change it so that the program throws an exception when input is entered in an incorrect format.

Exercise P17.11. In Exercises P8.7–8.9, you implemented an appointment calendar. Revisit that design and change it so that the program throws an exception when there is

- an error reading the appointment data (for example, because the input file is missing or corrupted).
- an error saving the appointment data (for example, because the disk is full).

Chapter 18

Name Scope Management

- To understand how the management of names is tied to the management of values

- To understand the concepts of scope and visibility, and the various scopes found in C++ programs

- To learn how to use protected visibility

- To understand the use of friends, nested classes, and private inheritance

- To learn how to use name spaces

The complexity of large programs comes not from their algorithmic details (such as finding a better way to sort numbers), but from the management of communication. For example, how can one programmer avoid using the same names as another programmer working in a different section of the program? How much (or how little) information does one programmer need to understand to use the software created by another programmer? Such complexity is controlled through the management of names, thereby reducing the amount of information that must be shared. The C++ language provides a number of mechanisms for name management; each of these will be examined in this chapter.

CHAPTER CONTENTS

18.1 Encapsulation

> Encapsulation helps reduce the number of visible names, thereby helping to manage complexity.

Encapsulation is one of the primary tools programmers use to control complexity. As you learned in Section 5.3, part of what *encapsulate* means is to hide or restrict access to a data field or to a member function. When a data field is declared as private, it is said to be encapsulated within the class definition. The term conjures up an image of a capsule, or container—a view of an object as a unit, rather than a collection of parts.

```
class Product
{
public:
   Product();

   void read();

   bool is_better_than(Product b) const;

   void print() const;
private:
   string name;
   double price;
   int score;
};
```

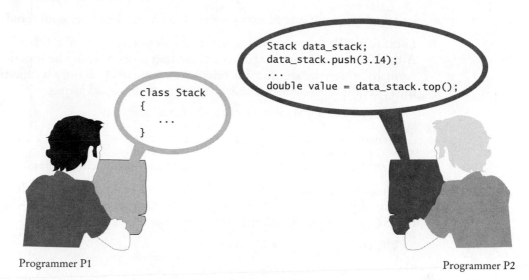

Figure 1 Programming Viewed as a Collaborative Task

What encapsulation does is restrict access to *names*. When you create a Product, the values associated with the private data fields name, price, and score are part of the object; it is only the names that are hidden within the class definition. But restricting the use of names is effectively the same as restricting access to values—if you cannot name a value, you cannot use it.

As you saw in the last chapter, many issues in the control of complexity are put into sharp focus when you imagine a program as being the end result of many programmers working together (see Figure 1).

Suppose programmer P2 uses a code library that was authored by programmer P1. Encapsulation limits the information that the second programmer, programmer P2, must know and understand in order to use the library. Any data fields encapsulated in the class definitions written by P1 are inaccessible to the code developed by P2, and this inaccessibility means that they need not even be known to programmer P2.

Encapsulation also addresses the problem of name collision. *Name collision* occurs when two programmers use the same name for different purposes in their independently-developed sections of code. By encapsulating the names, the two uses can coexist without conflict.

18.2 Name Scopes

Scope is the section of a program in which a name is visible.

A concept closely related to encapsulation is the notion of *scopes*. As you learned in Section 4.9, a scope is the part of a program in which a name is visible and has a given meaning. A variable defined in a function header, for example, is meaningful only within that function. Such a variable is said to have *local scope*.

Local scope is just one of many scopes you have already encountered:

- *Local scope.* Parameter variable names are defined as part of a function heading. Although the associated argument *value* may exist outside the function, the *name* by which the argument is referenced is meaningful only within the body of the function. Therefore it is said that the name has local scope.

```
double future_value(double p) // p has local scope
{
    double b = 1000 * pow(1 + p / 100, 10);   // b has block scope
    return b;
} // Neither p nor b has any meaning outside the function definition
```

- *Block scope.* As you learned in Section 3.7, a variable declared inside a for loop is meaningful only within the bounds of the loop. It is created when the loop begins, persists for the execution of the loop, and is then destroyed.

```
for (int i = 1; i <= 10; i++)
{
    cout << "Hello number " << i << "\n";
} // i no longer defined here
```

More generally, a variable with block scope can be declared within any block statement. The name is meaningful from the point of declaration to the closing brace of the block. The name is attached to the variable only for the body of the block, and the variable itself exists only for the duration of the statement.

```
{
    int t = x; // t is created here
    x = y;
    y = t;
} // t no longer defined here
```

Because a function body is a special case of a block statement, local scope is actually a special case of block scope.

- *Class scope.* A data field or member function of a class is said to have class scope.

```
class Product
{
public:
    ...
private:
    string name; // name, price, and score have class scope
    double price;
    int score;
};
```

- *Global scope.* Variables declared outside of function and class definitions are said to have global scope. Global scope extends from the point of definition until the end of the file in which the variable appears. Such variables can be used anyplace, in any function or member function definition. For this reason, knowing how a global variable is assigned or used may be difficult, making programs hard to understand. Problems with the use of global variables were one reason for the introduction of name spaces, which will be discussed in Section 18.7.

There are other names that have global scope. When a class is defined at the top level (that is, outside of any other function or class definition), the class name is given global scope.

- *File Scope.* As you read in Section 5.9, large projects are often divided into several files. In part this is so that individual programmers can work on their own files, and still contribute to a large multiprogrammer project. Global variables declared as static have file scope, which means they are meaningful only within the file in which they are declared. Those not declared as static may be shared among many files. To do so, the global variable must be declared extern in each file in which it is used but not defined. The name is then meaningful from the point of declaration until the end of the file. The use of file scope has now largely been replaced by the introduction of name spaces.

Notice that scopes overlap with each other. The body of a member function, for example, has access to variables from the scope of its class as well as local variables.

The two most important scopes that you have not yet seen are *protected* scope and *namespace* scope. These will be examined later in this chapter.

We have been careful to point out that the meaning attached to a name extends from the point of definition until the end of the scope. The following bit of code is perverse, but entirely legal:

```
int count = 0; // Create a global variable
...
int count_items()
{
    int orig_count = count; // orig_count initialized to value in global variable
    int count = 0; // A different variable named count is being created
    for (...)
        count++; // Increment the local variable
    return count + orig_count;
    // Returning value of local variable count + global count contained in orig_count
}
// Local count and orig_count are no longer available, global variable count accessible
```

18.2.1 Shadows and Qualification

The example above illustrates an important principle. A name can hide, or block, a name from a surrounding scope. Such a name is said to *shadow* the previous definition. After exit from the scope, the blocked name resumes its previous meaning. The following is even more perverse than the previous example but is again perfectly legal.

```
// DON'T WRITE CODE SUCH AS THE FOLLOWING!
double balance; // balance has global scope
class BankAccount
{
public:
    BankAccount(double balance); // Parameter variable balance has local scope
private:
    double balance; // Data field balance has class scope
```

```
};

BankAccount::BankAccount(double balance)
{
    this->balance = balance; // Assign data field balance using parameter value
    ::balance = balance; // Assign global variable using parameter value
}
```

> A variable that hides another variable of the same name in a different scope is said to shadow the hidden name.

Within the class definition the data field named balance shadows the global variable with the same name. Within the definition of the constructor the parameter variable named balance shadows both the data field and the global variable.

Access to names that have been shadowed can sometimes be circumvented using qualified names. For instance, while within the body of the constructor the name balance refers to the parameter variable, the data field can be referred to as this->balance. (See Advanced Topic 7.1 for a discussion of the this pointer.) Similarly, the pair of colons are referred to as the *global qualifier*, and are used to indicate that a name should be taken from the global scope, not the local scope. The return statement in the function count_items could have been written as follows:

```
return count + ::count; // Return sum of local and global values
```

Qualification eliminates the need for the local variable orig_count entirely. Qualification is used whenever a name could potentially have many meanings. This occurs in the definition of a member function, as well as when a member function in a derived class needs to invoke the function of the same name in the parent class:

```
int TravelClock::get_hours() const
{
    int h = Clock::get_hours(); // Qualify which get_hours is intended
    ...
}
```

ADVANCED TOPIC 18.1

Overriding, Shadowing, and Scopes

The concept of a shadow becomes slightly more subtle when applied to member functions and inheritance. As you learned in Chapter 8, when a derived class declares a virtual member function with the same arguments as a member function in the base class, the derived function *overrides* the base class function. However, if the argument list is changed then overriding does not occur, and instead the function name shadows the function in the base class. But this shadowing does not imply an overloading.

When the C++ compiler is searching for a member function to match a particular invocation, it first locates a scope in which the function is defined. Having found a scope, the compiler then tries to match the argument list to the available functions in that scope. Because the sequence of steps is to first locate a scope, then select a function, a function that changes an argument list can hide a function in the base class, even one with a different argument type signature, because they occur in different scopes. This is true whether or not the base class function is declared virtual.

In the following example, the base class `Employee` declares a function named `set_salary`. The derived class `Manager` defines a function using the same name but a different signature. If both of these were declared in the same scope, they would exist as two independent functions, and both would be available. But because they are found in separate scopes, the function in the derived class hides the function in the base class.

```
class Employee
{
    ...
    virtual void set_salary(int new_salary);
};

class Manager : public Employee
{
    ...
    virtual void set_salary(int new_salary, int yearly_bonus);
};

Manager m;
m.set_salary(45000); // Error—function requires two arguments
```

To avoid this problem you can overload the function in the derived class, so that *both* declarations appear in the same scope:

```
class Manager : public Employee
{
    ...
    virtual void set_salary(int new_salary);
    void set_salary(int new_salary, int yearly_bonus);
};
```

Although the derived class needs to define the function inherited from the base class, it does not need to reimplement the function. It can simply use a qualified name to invoke the base class function:

```
void Manager::set_salary(int new_salary)
{
    Employee::set_salary(new_salary)   // Invoke the base class function
}
```

QUALITY TIP 18.1

Don't Pollute the Global Scope

Names with global scope are known throughout a program. In large, multiprogrammer projects, this means they are potentially accessible to every programmer. Names in each scope must be unique, which means that two programmers cannot independently use the same name. For this reason it is important to minimize the number of names in the global scope.

In Quality Tip 4.2 you have already been warned against the use of global variables. Not only do they populate the global scope, but the assignment and use of global variables is difficult to track.

Global constants do not change, and so tracking modifications to such values is not a problem. But they, too, populate the global scope. One programmer may think that the name WM_SIZE is perfectly understandable. But is it a size used somehow for window messages, or for a widget map? Placing the definition for a constant inside a class definition makes the name have class scope, rather than global scope. If the definition is public, it is still available to other programmers by means of a qualified name. Even better, the qualification now provides a context to understand the meaning.

```
class WindowMessage
{
public:
   static const int WM_SIZE = 400;
      // Can be referenced as WindowMessage::WM_SIZE
   ...
};
```

Class names are another item in the global scope. Auxiliary classes, such as Node, may be found in several different types of container. Using a nested class (see Section 18.5) moves the class name from the global scope to a class scope. This avoids conflicts with other similarly named classes.

```
class List
{
   ...
   class Node; // Name Node now has class scope
   ...
};

class List::Node // Name must be fully qualified
{
   ...
};
```

Finally, name spaces (Section 18.7) can be used to move functions from a global scope to a more restricted namespace scope, where they will not interfere with other programmers' names.

COMMON ERROR 18.1

Confusing Scope and Lifetime

Don't confuse the two concepts of *scope* and *lifetime*. Scope is a static characteristic; it indicates in what sections of a program a name is visible. Lifetime is a dynamic characteristic; it refers to how long during execution a variable will exist.

An example students often find confusing is the use of a static local variable. A static local, such as the variable counter in the following example, has local scope. The name is meaningful only within the body of the function. However, the variable has global lifetime, meaning it is stored in the section of memory reserved for global variables, and exists as long as the program is executing.

```
int counting_fun()
{
```

```
        static int counter = 0; // Local scope, global lifetime
        counter = counter + 1;
        return counter;
    }
```

ADVANCED TOPIC 18.2

Forward References

In any scope, names are meaningful from the point at which they are defined until the end of their scope. Occasionally it is necessary to introduce a name before a full definition would be appropriate. This is termed a *forward reference*.

You have seen already some examples of forward references. A function prototype, discussed in Advanced Topic 4.1, is one form of forward reference. The prototype provides the function header, and is sufficient to *declare* the function. Later, the function *definition* provides the body of the function. However, the function can be called knowing only the declaration at any time after the declaration. This allows functions to be mutually recursive, as you saw in Section 10.5.

```
int term_value(); // Forward reference
int factor_value(); // Forward reference

int expression_value()
{
    int result = term_value();
    ...
}

int term value()
{
    int result = factor_value();
    ...
}

int factor_value()
{
    ...
    if (c == '(')
    {
        result = expression_value(); // Recursive call
    }
    ...
}
```

Class names can also be declared using a forward reference. Again, the forward reference allows two classes to be mutually recursive:

```
class Person; // Forward reference

class BankAccount
{
    ...
```

```
private:
    Person* owner; // Permitted, because name Person has been declared
};

class Person
{
    ...
private:
    BankAccount retirement_account;
};
```

Nested classes, which you will examine in Section 18.5, are also often first declared with a forward reference and defined later.

18.3 Protected Scope

The relationship between a derived class and a base class can be subtle. In Chapter 8 you examined a class TravelClock that inherited from class Clock. An instance of the derived class inherits the data fields from the Clock base class, although it is not allowed access to these fields (see Figure 2).

Up to this point it has appeared as if the designer of a class had two choices. He or she could declare data fields and member functions as public, in which case they were open to the world, or he or she could declare these features as private, in which case they were accessible only within the class itself. But often the designer of a class would like something between these two extremes.

Imagine, for example, a class Chart that stores an array of numbers. Derived classes PieChart, BarChart, and so on will each display the data in a different fashion.

```
class Chart
{
public:
    virtual void draw() const;
    ...
protected:
    vector<double> data;
};

class PieChart : public Chart
{
public:
    virtual void draw() const;
    ...
};
```

Data fields and member functions declared as protected are accessible to derived classes.

If the data in the base class is declared private, the derived class cannot access it. If it is declared public, anybody can access it, which is probably not a good idea. What is needed is an indication that derived classes, and only derived classes, are allowed access. That purpose is achieved with the keyword protected. Features declared with

Figure 2   A Derived Class Maintains Data from the Base Class

protected scope are accessible from within a base class or within any derived class, but are not accessible outside of class definitions.

With the introduction of protected, there are now three different faces, or interfaces, that a class projects. There is the public face, the interface to the rest of the world. There is the private face, the interface to the member functions within the class itself. And finally there is the protected face, the interface to derived classes. Users of a class and developers of derived classes can both be considered to be clients. But the two groups have very different needs and requirements. Users of a class need to know how to use the services the class provides. Developers of derived classes want to know how to specialize a class to make it fit a new purpose. The protected keyword allows the class designer to control what information is available to each group.

SYNTAX 18.1 Protected Members

```
class ClassName
{
   ...
protected:
   member functions and data fields
};
```

Example:

```
class Chart
{
   ...
protected:
   vector<double> data;
   double value_at(int index) const;
};
```

Purpose:

Declare member functions and data fields that are visible to derived classes.

QUALITY TIP 18.2

Use Accessor Functions for Protected Access to Data

Although both data fields and member functions can be declared protected, many style guides suggest that protected data fields are usually a bad idea. The argument against protected data fields is similar to the argument against global variables and against declaring public data fields. By making a data field protected, the class designer is giving control to the authors of the derived classes. There is nothing to prevent a derived class member function from corrupting the base-class data. A better alternative is to leave the data fields private, and provide derived classes with a protected accessor function:

```
class Chart
{
public:
    virtual void draw() const;
    ...
protected:
    double value_at(int index) const; // ... only allows access, not modification
    ...
private:
    vector<double> data; // Now data is safely private
};
```

Because a class has no control over who will derive from it, protected operations should be written with the same care as public operations.

18.4 Friends

The modifiers private, protected, and public give the programmer control over access to names, which implicitly gives the programmer control over access to their associated data values. However, the three possibilities of public, protected, and private cannot cover all situations. Oftentimes a programmer would like to make a data field or member function accessible to another function or another class that is not a derived class, and to do so without making the name accessible in a public fashion. The solution in this case is to declare a *friend*.

> A friend is a class or function that is allowed access to all features in another class.

> Friends must be explicitly declared as part of a class definition.

A friend can be either another class or a function. The friend must be explicitly named within a class definition. By naming the friend, the class is granting access to all the private features of the class. Declaring a class as friend means that all member functions in the friend class are friends. Needless to say, this is a dangerous mechanism because it exposes the encapsulated state of a class to outside modification. Friendship is not something that should be given away freely. But because friends are named, and because friends are allowed direct access to internal data fields, friendship is a more precise and efficient mechanism than, for example, the creation of accessor functions.

You have seen an example of friends in Section 12.2.1. In the implementation of linked lists there were three classes, `List`, `Node`, and `Iterator`. The data fields in class `Node` were encapsulated behind a private declaration. Normally, this would make the data inaccessible outside the class declaration. But by declaring the classes `List` and `Iterator` as friends, these classes, and *only these classes*, were allowed to view and modify the data fields.

```
class Node
{
public:
   Node(string s);
private:
   string data;
   Node* previous;
   Node* next;
   friend class List;
   friend class Iterator;
};
```

SYNTAX 18.2 Friends

```
class ClassName
{
   ...
friend class ClassName;
friend return_type function_name(parameter list);
};
```

Example:

```
class Node
{
public:
   Node(string s);
private:
   string data;
   Node* previous;
   Node* next;
friend class List;
friend class Iterator;
};

class Employee
{
   ...
friend ostream& operator<<(ostream& out, const Employee& e);
};
```

Purpose:

Allow other classes and functions to access the private features of a class.

A common example of a function being declared as a friend is an output stream operator. Often the output operator requires access to the inner state of an object.

```
class Employee
{
public:
   Employee(string employee_name, double initial_salary);
   ...
private:
   string name;
   double salary;
friend ostream& operator<<(ostream& out, const Employee& e);
};

ostream& operator<<(ostream& out, const Employee& e)
{
   out << "Employee: " << e.name;
   return out;
}
```

Note that even though the description of a friend function appears in a class definition, the friend is not a member function. Also, the placement of the friend designation is unimportant. A friend will have access to all data fields, including private ones, regardless whether the friend declaration appears in the public, private, or protected portions of a class definition.

QUALITY TIP 18.3

Friendship Is Granted, Not Taken

The designer of a class explicitly names the classes and functions that are to be considered friends. It is not possible to attach a new class or function as a friend to an existing class without changing the original class. Friendship is also not symmetric; if class Iterator is a friend of class List, it does not imply that class List is a friend of class Iterator. Friendship is not transitive. If List is a friend to Node, and Node a friend to Iterator, it does not automatically make List a friend to Iterator. Finally, friendship is not inherited. If a base class is friend to another class, it does not mean that derived classes are friends.

Friendship opens a crack in the encapsulation provided by the class mechanism, allowing modification to a class state from outside the class boundary. For this reason, the use of friends and friendship should be carefully considered when classes are designed. Oftentimes a careful design, or the use of nested classes discussed in the next section, can avoid the necessity of declaring friends.

On the positive side, friends are conveniently listed in the class definition. If the implementation of a class changes, both member functions and friends may need to be modified. Derived classes may also need to be changed, but they are not so easy to find, as the base class contains no reference to derived classes.

18.5 Nested Classes

In Chapter 12 you examined the development of three classes, List, Node, and Iterator. There is a difference between these classes and those in the standard C++ library version of linked lists. In Chapter 12, we defined an iterator as

```
Iterator pos = staff.begin();
```

However, with the standard library classes, you use a different syntax:

```
list<string>::iterator pos = staff.begin();
```

> A nested class is defined inside another class to limit the nested class's names to the outer class's scope.

In the standard library, the iterator class is *nested* inside the list class (see Syntax 18.3 on page 713). The use of a nested class (sometimes called a *member class* [1]) allows other collection classes, such as vectors, maps, and sets, to define their own iterators. All of these iterators have different internal implementations. They just share the same name, iterator, because they represent the same concept. To avoid name conflicts, each of the container classes uses nesting to make sure it owns the name for its iterator. Nested names are expressed with a qualified name, as follows:

```
vector<double>::iterator p = a.begin();
list<string>::iterator q = b.begin();
```

Let's do the same for the List and Iterator classes from Chapter 12, namely nest the Iterator class inside the List class and then use it as

```
List::Iterator pos = staff.begin();
```

To nest a class inside another involves two steps. First, declare the nested class with a forward reference inside the outer class:

```
class List
{
    ...
    class Iterator; // Forward reference
    ...
};
```

Then define the class and its member functions, always referring to the class by its full name (such as List::Iterator).

```
class List::Iterator
{
public:
    Iterator();
    string get() const;
    ...
private:
    ...
};

List::Iterator::Iterator()
{
    ...
```

```
    }

    string List::Iterator::get() const
    {
       ...
    }
```

Note that the name of the class is List::Iterator, but the name of the constructor is still just Iterator.

Except for the nesting of the names, nested classes act exactly the same as regular classes. A nested class has no right to access private members of the outer class (unless it has been declared as a friend), and the outer class has no right to access private members of the inner class.

It is legal to include the *entire* definition of the nested class *inside* the definition of the outer class:

```
    class List
    {
       ...
       class Iterator
       {
       public:
          Iterator();
          string get() const;
          ...
       };
       ...
    };
```

This looks quite confusing, and it makes it appear as if the List object contains an Iterator object inside it. That is not the case. The List class merely owns the Iterator class, or, in other words, the name Iterator is in the scope of the List class. The List member functions can simply refer to it as Iterator, all other functions must refer to it as List::Iterator.

In general, you use nested classes for just one reason: to place the name of a class inside the scope of another class. Nested classes need not be in the public portion of a class definition. Declaring a nested class as private encapsulates the entire class definition. It means that instances of the nested class can only be manipulated by functions that are permitted to access private members of the outer class. You saw an example of this in Chapter 15.

```
    class SharedString
    {
       ...
    private:
       class StringReference;
       ...
    };

    class SharedString::StringReference
    {
    public:
       int count;
       char* buffer;
```

```
        StringReference(const char* right);
        ~StringReference();
};
```

The class `StringReference` is private to `SharedString`. There is no danger in making the data members public since the class itself a private nested class.

QUALITY TIP 18.4

Manage Encapsulation

The C++ programmer has a variety of tools that are used to manage encapsulation. These include class definitions; access modifiers, such as `private` and `public`; nested classes; and name spaces. Often several mechanisms could potentially be used to address the same problem. For example, the class `Node` could be declared as `friend` to class `List`, as in Chapter 12. An alternative is to declare the class `Node` as nested within class `List` (see Exercise P18.1). How should you select among various design alternatives?

There are several considerations, all of which can be summarized as ways to manage encapsulation. Loosening access control can compromise the encapsulation of a class. If a class names a single function as a friend, this is normally not a problem. The friend function is listed in the class definition, and becomes part of the interface. If the class implementation is changed, the friend must track the change just as all other functions declared in the class definition.

Declaring another class a friend is more dangerous. By doing this, the designer of the class agrees that all operations in the friend class, whether they exist now or will be added later, will have access to all private features. This should only be carried out to join closely related classes, such as `Node` and `List`. Friendship should seldom cross programmer boundaries; that is, a class being developed by one programmer should almost never declare as friend a class being developed by another programmer.

The designer of a class usually knows what friends are going to do, but cannot predict what a derived class might do. Hence access to protected features should be guarded even more closely than friendship. This is not to say that protected operations are a bad idea. Protected member functions (and, rarely, data fields) divide an interface into three parts. There are those features known to all users, the public part. There are those features known to developers of derived classes, the protected part. And finally there is the private part, accessible only to the class itself. As always, planning and careful thought are the key to creating a good design.

18.6 Private Inheritance

Normally inheritance is used to create a more specialized version of an existing abstraction. This idea is captured in a rule of thumb, called the "is-a" test (see Section 22.5). The *is-a* test says to form the English sentence "a B is an A". If the sentence sounds right to your ear, then inheritance is very likely an acceptable mechanism for forming a new class for B out of an existing class for A. So, for example, saying that "a manager is an employee" makes sense, as does "a travel clock is a clock". Saying "a company is an employee" does not make sense, although a company may have employees. So, a class that represents a company would likely not be constructed using inheritance from class `Employee`.

Another variation on the *is-a* test is the *substitution principle*. The substitution principle says that if you are expecting an instance of class A, your code should continue to work if you are given an instance of class B instead. If you were expecting a `Clock`, would your code continue to work if you were given a `TravelClock` instead? Because a `TravelClock` has all the functionality of the class `Clock`, you would hope that the answer is yes.

A practical consequence of this view of inheritance is that the interface of the base class becomes the basis for the interface of the derived class. One way to think of this is that names for member functions in the base class flow through to the derived class, to emerge as member functions in the derived class. This is true even if the member functions are not redefined in the derived class.

Occasionally it seems desirable to use inheritance to form a new class using an existing class—even when the *is-a* and substitution tests fail. Generally this occurs when the functionality of the base class is useful, but the new class and the base class do not fit the *is-a* relationship.

To illustrate, assume you need a class to represent the concept of a set. A set is a collection of unordered elements, with no element repeated. Imagine you have already written the class `List`, and you want to reuse the `List` class in order to simplify the creation of the class `Set`. The substitution principle fails for this example; you would not imagine that code designed to deal with a `List` would continue to work if presented with a Set. Similarly there are member functions in the interface for List that do not seem appropriate to a Set. Nevertheless, the functionality of class List seems useful in the construction of a set.

A solution is to declare that the class Set inherits privately from the class List. In a *private inheritance*, the functionality of the base class is still available to the new derived class. But the interface for the base class does not flow through to the derived class, and it does not automatically become the interface for the new class.

```
class Set : private List
{
public:
    void add(string s);
    Iterator erase(Iterator pos);
    Iterator begin();
    Iterator end();
};

void Set::add(string s)
{
    Iterator iter = begin();
    Iterator stop = end();
    while (iter != stop)
    {
        if (s.equals(iter.get()))
            return; // Already in set, don't add
    }
    push_back(s); // Can use inherited push_back function
}

Iterator Set::erase(Iterator pos)
{
    List::erase(pos);
}

Iterator Set::begin()
{
    return List::begin();
}

Iterator Set::end()
{
    return List::end();
}
```

Private inheritance uses a base class for the functionality it provides. But the interface of the base class does not become the interface for the new class.

Notice how it is legal to call push_back from within a function in class Set. However, because inheritance is private, this function does not become part of the interface for class Set:

```
Set a_set;
a_set.add("Sally"); // legal
a_set.push_back("Fred"); // Error
    // push_back not part of interface for Set
```

While private inheritance is legal, it is rare that it is actually useful. In this example the same effect could have been achieved by having class Set maintain its own private internal data field of type List. The amount of work involved in the implementation would be about the same, and would be much easier to understand.

It is also possible to declare a class to use protected inheritance, although this is even less common than private inheritance. You will encounter private inheritance again in the next chapter, when you examine the relationship between this mechanism and polymorphism.

SYNTAX 18.4 Private Inheritance

```
class DerivedClassName : private BaseClassName
{
    features
};
```

Example:

```
class Set : private List
{
public:
    void add(string s);
    Iterator erase(Iterator pos);
    Iterator begin();
    Iterator end();
};
```

Purpose:

To allow the derived class access to the functionality of the base class, without declaring the derived class as a specialized form of the base class.

18.7 Name Spaces

In larger programming projects, you should place the names of classes, global functions, and global variables in a name space with a unique name.

Name spaces are another mechanism used to avoid naming conflicts. For example, in a large software project, it is quite possible that several programmers come up with names for functions or classes that conflict with another. Suppose a programmer comes up with a class called map—perhaps to denote a map in a computer game—unaware that there is already a map class in the standard library. By using name spaces, it becomes possible to use both classes in the same program. The standard library classes are in the std name space. You can unambiguously reference the standard map class using the qualified name std::map. If the other map class is in a different name space, say acme, then you can specify it as acme::map.

To add classes, functions, or variables to a name space, surround their declarations with a namespace block (see Syntax 18.5 on page 718):

```
namespace acme
{
   class map
   {
      ...
   };

   void draw(map m);
}
```

Unlike classes, name spaces are *open*. You can add as many items to a name space as you like, simply by starting another namespace block.

```
namespace acme
{
   class maze
   {
      ...
   };
}
```

This is how, for example, the container classes are added to the standard name space:

```
namespace std
{
   class string
   {
      ...
   };
}
```

Of course, it is tedious to prefix all standard classes with the std:: qualifier if there are no name conflicts. Therefore, your programs start out with the directive

```
using namespace std;
```

The purpose of that directive is to specify that all names should be looked up in the std name space. For example, when the compiler sees cout, it will find the declaration of std::cout in the iostream header, and know that you really want to use that variable. If you want to use just one or two names you can instruct the compiler to include only those, instead of the entire name space:

```
using std::cout; // Include only the name cout from the std name space
```

In one important aspect, the std name space is atypical. Because you use name spaces to avoid name clashes, you normally want to use name space names that are truly unambiguous and therefore long, such as ACME_Software_San_Jose_CA_US. At first glance, this looks very tedious—programmers would not be happy to type

```
ACME_Software_San_Jose_CA_US::map
```

To solve this problem, you can define a short alias for a long name space (see Syntax 18.6 on page 719). For example

```
namespace acme = ACME_Software_San_Jose_CA_US;
```

> Use name space aliases to conveniently refer to long name space names.

Then you can use the alias, such as acme::map, in your program and the compiler automatically translates the alias to the complete name of the name space. Different aliases can be used for the same name space in different source files, avoiding a conflict of alias names.

In professional programs, it is an excellent idea to use name spaces, particularly if you build libraries for other programmers. Follow these rules:

- Come up with long and unique names for your name spaces.
- Use the alias feature to establish short aliases.
- Don't use the using directive for name spaces other than std.

It is best to avoid using and namespace alias declarations in a header (.h) file. Otherwise, every programmer who includes the header file is forced to live with those declarations. A better approach is to use only fully qualified names in the header file, such as

```
void print(std::ostream& out)
```

In the case study described in Section 18.8, we illustrate this technique, placing fully qualified names into the header file and employing a using statement only in the implementation file.

SYNTAX 18.5 Name Space Definition

```
namespace name_space_name
{
    feature₁
    feature₂
    ...
    featureₙ
}
```

Example:

```
namespace ACME_Software_San_Jose_CA_US
{
    class map
    {
        ...
    };
}
```

Purpose:

Include a class, function, or variable in a name space.

SYNTAX 18.6 Name Space Alias

namespace *alias_name* = *name_space_name*;

Example:

namespace acme = ACME_Software_San_Jose_CA_US;

Purpose:

Introduce a short alias for the long name of a name space.

QUALITY TIP 18.5

Use Unambiguous Names for Name Spaces

Some programmers use their initials or the initials of a product or company as names for name spaces. Searching on the Web, one can find C++ libraries with name spaces such as MRI and IPL. This is not a good practice—it is just a matter of time before Irene P. Lee uses her initials for her name space, and then needs to use the Image Processing Library that does the same.

Use a long name, such as

Image_Proc_Lib_ACME_Software_San_Jose_CA_US

for the library name space. Programmers using the library can easily use a convenient alias of their own choosing.

ADVANCED TOPIC 18.3

Local Name Space Declaration

A using statement is subject to the same scope rules as declaration statements. This can sometimes be useful. For example, suppose ACME software distributes their own form of stack. You want to use this stack within the body of a function, but outside the function declaration, you want to use the standard library container. To do this, nest the using statement for ACME inside the function definition:

```
using namespace std; // Allows stack to mean the standard library

void f(double data)
{
   using acme::stack; // ACME version now shadows std::stack
   ...
}
```

18.8 Case Study: Matrices, Continued

In this section we continue the matrix case study started in previous chapters. In order to improve encapsulation, the classes MatrixRow and ConstMatrixRow (now renamed simply Row and ConstRow) have been changed to nested classes and moved inside the class definition for Matrix. They are declared as private, as there is never any need for instances of these classes to be created outside the matrix class itself. In the class definition in the interface file, and everywhere in the implementation file, references to MatrixRow are replaced by Matrix::Row (the class Row that appears inside class Matrix).

Similarly, the two classes that describe exceptional conditions, MatrixIndex-Exception and MatrixMismatchException, have been renamed IndexException and MismatchException and are now nested inside the class. This means that the catch clause in the test program must use a qualified name Matrix::IndexException to describe the exception value being caught.

We have also added a second name space. The class Matrix is defined in its own name space, BigCPlusPlus_Matrix. Notice how both the interface and implementation classes place definitions in this name space. As suggested in Section 18.6, the interface file does not import the entire standard name space, but uses qualified names for those features it requires (the exception classes std::out_of_range and std::invalid_argument, and the stream class std::ostream). The implementation file (matrix5.cpp) on the other hand, imports the entire std name space, and so can refer to these values by the simpler names out_of_range, invalid_argument, and ostream.

The application file matrixtest5.cpp could have included both complete name spaces, using the following statements:

```
using namespace std;
using namespace BigCPlusPlus_Matrix;
```

We have instead simply included the one feature from the standard name space that is required (std::cout), defined an alias for the matrix name space, and used qualified names.

ch18/matrix5.h

```
 1   #ifndef MATRIX5_H
 2   #define MATRIX5_H
 3
 4   #include <iostream>
 5   #include <stdexcept>
 6
 7   namespace BigCPlusPlus_Matrix
 8   {
 9
10   /**
11       This class describes a matrix with arbitrary rows and columns.
12   */
13   class Matrix
14   {
```

```
15    private:
16       /**
17           Forward reference for classes Row and ConstRow.
18       */
19       class Row;
20       class ConstRow;
21
22    public:
      ... Same as in matrix4.h
62
63       /**
64           Accesses a matrix row.
65           @param i  the row index
66           @return  the row with the given index
67       */
68       Row operator[](int i);
69
70       /**
71           Accesses a matrix row.
72           @param i  the row index
73           @return  the row with the given index
74       */
75       ConstRow operator[](int i) const;
   ...
83
84       /**
85           Forward reference for classes MismatchException and IndexException.
86       */
87       class MismatchException;
88       class IndexException;
89
90    private:
      ...
106   };
107
108   /**
109       This class describes a row in a matrix.
110   */
111   class Matrix::Row
112   {
      ...
156   };
157
158   /**
159       Matrix exception class: Indexing error
160   */
161   class Matrix::IndexException : public std::out_of_range
162   {
163   public:
164      IndexException(int i);
165   private:
166      std::string format_message(int i);
167   };
168
```

```
169   /**
170       Matrix exception class: Mismatched Argument error
171   */
172   class Matrix::MismatchException : public std::invalid_argument
173   {
174   public:
175       MismatchException();
176   };
177
      ...
213   std::ostream& operator<<(std::ostream& left, const Matrix& right);
214
215   inline Matrix::IndexException::IndexException(int idx)
216       : out_of_range(format_message(idx)) {}
217
218   inline Matrix::MismatchException::MismatchException()
219       : invalid_argument("Matrix arguments have incompatible sizes")   {}
      ...
256   inline Matrix::Row::Row(Matrix* m, int s) : mat(m), i(s) { }
257
258   inline double& Matrix::Row::operator[](int j)
259   {
260       return (*mat)(i,j);
261   }
262
      ...
276   }
277   #endif
```

ch18/matrix5.cpp

```
 1    #include <iomanip>
 2    #include <sstream>
 3    #include "matrix5.h"
 4
 5    using namespace std;
 6
 7    namespace BigCPlusPlus_Matrix
 8    {
 9
10    string Matrix::IndexException::format_message(int n)
11    {
12        ostringstream outstr;
13        outstr << "Matrix index " << n << " out of range";
14        return outstr.str();
15    }
16
      ... Same as in matrix4.cpp
44
45    double& Matrix::operator()(int i, int j)
46    {
47        if (i < 0 || i >= rows)
48            throw Matrix::IndexException(i);
```

```
49        if (j < 0 || j >= columns)
50            throw Matrix::IndexException(j);
51        return elements[i * get_columns() + j];
52    }
53
      ...
110
111   }
```

ch18/matrixtest5.cpp

```cpp
1   #include "matrix5.h"
2
3   using std::cout;
4   namespace mat = BigCPlusPlus_Matrix;
5
6   int main()
7   {
8       mat::Matrix m(3, 3);
9       m[0][0] = m[1][1] = m[2][2] = 1;
10      m[0][1] = m[1][2] = 2;
11      cout << 2 * m + m * m;
12      try
13      {
14          m[4][2] = 7; // Purposeful subscript error
15      }
16      catch (mat::Matrix::IndexException& e)
17      {
18          cout << "Caught exception: " << e.what() << "\n";
19      }
20      return 0;
21  }
```

Program Run

```
        3        8        4
        0        3        8
        0        0        3
Caught exception: Matrix index 4 out of range
```

CHAPTER SUMMARY

1. Encapsulation helps reduce the number of visible names, thereby helping to manage complexity.

2. Scope is the section of a program in which a name is visible.

3. A variable that hides another variable of the same name in a different scope is said to shadow the hidden name.

4. Data fields and member functions declared as protected are accessible to derived classes.

5. A friend is a class or function that is allowed access to all features in another class.

6. Friends must be explicitly declared as part of a class definition.

7. A nested class is defined inside another class to limit the nested class's names to the outer class's scope.

8. Private inheritance uses a base class for the functionality it provides. But the interface of the base class does not become the interface for the new class.

9. In larger programming projects, you should place the names of classes, global functions, and global variables in a name space with a unique name.

10. Use name space aliases to conveniently refer to long name space names.

FURTHER READING

1. Bjarne Stroustrup, *The C++ Programming Language*, Special Ed., Addison-Wesley, 2000.

REVIEW EXERCISES

Exercise R18.1. What does encapsulation mean? How does encapsulation help control the complexity of multiprogrammer applications?

Exercise R18.2. Identify the scope of each variable in the following:

```cpp
vector<int> v;

namespace Acme_Search
{
    const int maxdata = 100;

    int binary_search(int from, int to, int a)
    {
        if (from > to)
            return -1;
        int mid = (from + to) / 2;
        if (v[mid] == a)
            return mid;
        else if (v[mid] < a)
            return binary_search(mid + 1, to, a);
        else
            return binary_search(from, mid - 1, a);
    }
}
```

Exercise R18.3. What does it mean for one variable to shadow another?

Exercise R18.4. How is protected visibility different from private or public visibility?

Exercise R18.5. What does friendship mean? What are the positive benefits and negative consequences of friendship?

Exercise R18.6. In what ways is a nested class similar to a friend class? In what ways is it different?

Exercise R18.7. How is private inheritance different from public inheritance?

Exercise R18.8. In what situation is private inheritance preferable to public inheritance?

Exercise R18.9. Explain in which sense classes are closed while name spaces are open.

Exercise R18.10. When would you define a class as a nested class, and when would you define it in a name space?

Exercise R18.11. Suppose Harry J. Hacker develops a code library that he wants others to use. Why would it not be a good idea to place it into a name space hjh? What name space name might be appropriate?

Exercise R18.12. Why is it acceptable to use short aliases for name spaces, even though short names for name spaces are not appropriate?

PROGRAMMING EXERCISES

Exercise P18.1. In Section 18.5 you saw how to make the class Iterator a nested class within List, rather than a friend. Do the same with class Node. What accessibility should the nested class Node possess?

Exercise P18.2. Finish the implementation of classes Chart and BarChart from Section 18.3. Class BarChart should display a simple textual representation of the data, similar to the following:

```
3 ***
5 *****
2 **
7 *******
```

Exercise P18.3. Modify the application you created for Exercise P18.2 and add a nested Iterator class and public member functions begin and end to the Chart class. These functions should yield iterator objects, allow a user to write an iterator loop to access the elements of the chart.

Exercise P18.4. Define output operators for Clock and TravelClock. Modify the classes Clock and TravelClock to declare the output operators as friends.

Exercise P18.5. Implement a 2 × 2 Matrix class that holds four floating-point numbers, and a Vector class that holds two floating-point numbers. Supply constructors and print operators, but do not expose the values of either class. Overload the multiplication operator so that a Matrix can be multiplied by a Vector object. To do this you will need to make Vector a friend of Matrix.

Exercise P18.6. Redo the implementation of class Fraction from Section 14.2, but remove the member functions numerator and denominator. What operators must now be declared as friends?

Exercise P18.7. Implement two classes, Stack and Queue, using private inheritance from class List. Note that you can access both the front and the back of a list by manipulating the iterators returned from begin and end.

Exercise P18.8. Define two functions

```
void cout(string& s)
void cin(string& s)
```

The first one removes all consonants from the string s. The second removes all vowels from the string s. Place both functions into a name space whose name is your name and student ID number. Then write a program that prompts the user to enter a string and prints the result of applying both functions.

Exercise P18.9. Define two functions

```
bool endl(string s)
void setw(string& s, char c)
```

The first function returns true if s ends in a lowercase letter. The second function changes all white space in s to the character c. Place both functions into a name space whose name is your name and student ID number. Then write a program that prompts the user to enter a string and prints the result of applying both functions.

G **Exercise P18.10.** Modify the application you created for Exercise P18.2 using the graphical library from Chapter 2. Create derived classes PieChart and BarChart that display the chart information in graphical format.

Chapter 19

Class Hierarchies

CHAPTER GOALS

- To be able to group classes into a class hierarchy
- To work with abstract classes
- To understand the concept of run-time type identification
- To learn how to use multiple inheritance
- To study the design of software frameworks

Hierarchies of classes are common in large programs. In this chapter, you will study advanced features of C++ that facilitate working with class hierarchies, such as abstract classes, run-time type identification, and multiple inheritance. We conclude this chapter with a discussion of software frameworks.

CHAPTER CONTENTS

19.1 Class Inheritance Hierarchies

In the real world, you often categorize concepts using a hierarchy. Businesses use corporate hierarchies, which describe the supervisor/worker relationship (who reports to whom). Family relationships are described using family trees, which describe child, parent, and marriage relationships. As these examples illustrate, hierarchies are usually represented as trees, with the most general concepts at the root of the hierarchy, and more specialized ones forming the branches. Figure 1 shows a typical example. Note that the shape is inverted, with the root at the top.

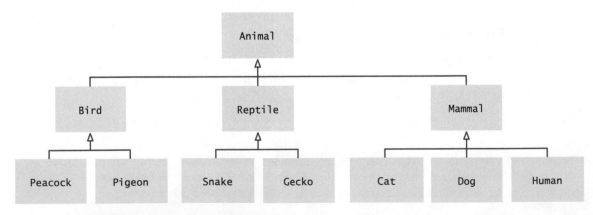

Figure 1   A Typical Hierarchy

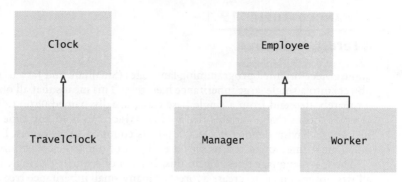

Figure 2   Simple Class Hierarchies

> Classes can be organized into inheritance hierarchies based on the base class/derived class inheritance relationship.

The class inheritance relationship fits this hierarchical pattern. Base classes appear at the top of the diagram, and derived classes fall below. Levels in the tree are linked by the *is-a* relationship—each derived class is a more specialized form of the base class. Some class hierarchies are very short, as shown in Figure 2.

But other class hierarchies can be quite complex. For example, suppose you are representing regular shapes for a drawing program; you might end up with a hierarchy as shown in Figure 3.

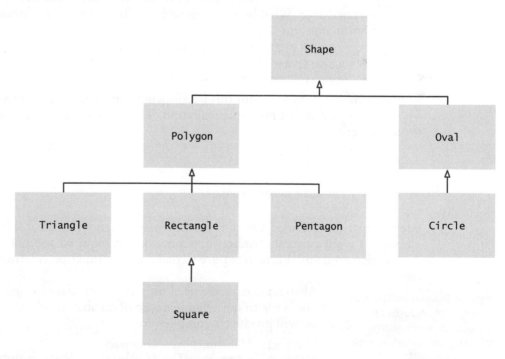

Figure 3   A More Complex Class Hierarchy

A Forest, Not a Tree

Some object-oriented programming languages (Smalltalk and Java to name just two) place all objects into a single large inheritance hierarchy. This means that all objects in these languages ultimately descend from a single base class, usually named `Object`. This has certain advantages. It means that a variable declared as `Object` can hold any type of value. It also means that any behavior defined in class `Object` is common to all values. But it also makes classes much more interconnected, as they are all part of one large collection.

The C++ language does not do this. Instead of requiring a single large inheritance tree, it allows programmers to create a forest of many small inheritance trees.

19.2 Abstract Classes

> An abstract class contains at least one virtual function that is declared but not defined.

In designing a class hierarchy, it may sometimes be the case that a certain behavior should be attached to a base class, but no implementation of that behavior makes sense. An example might be computing the area of a shape. For each concrete derived class it is possible to describe how to determine an area, so each class might define an appropriate member function. But in order to be used with the polymorphic variable of class `Shape`, the base class must also define the member function named `area`. What behavior should this function have? Without a concrete representation, no value makes sense.

```
Shape* s = new Triangle(4, 5, 6); // First s is a triangle
s = new Square(3, 4); // Now it is a square
cout << "Area is " << s.area() << "\n";
```

The C++ language provides for this by allowing a member function to be described by a prototype that has no implementation. This is indicated by an equal sign and the value zero:

```
class Shape
{
    ...
    virtual double area() const = 0;
};
```

Such a function is termed a *pure virtual member function*. While it is legal to define a body for a pure virtual member function, it is not required and not usually done. A class that contains at least one pure virtual member function is termed an *abstract class*.

> It is not legal to create an instance of an abstract class, although you may use a pointer or reference to an abstract class.

Abstract classes are used only as a base class for inheritance. It is not possible to create an instance of an abstract class. Attempting to do so will produce a compiler error:

```
Shape s1; // Error, Shape is abstract
Shape* s2 = new Shape(); // Also error, Shape is abstract
Shape* s3 = new Square(3, 4); // But this is OK
```

> ## SYNTAX 19.1 Pure Virtual Member Function
>
> ```
> class ClassName
> {
>    ...
>    virtual return_type function_name(parameters) = 0;
>    ...
> };
> ```
>
> **Example:**
>
> ```
> class Shape
> {
>    ...
>    virtual double area() const = 0;
> };
> ```
>
> **Purpose:**
>
> Declare a member function with no definition. A class that contains at least one pure virtual function is termed abstract. Derived classes must override the function and provide their own definition or they themselves will be considered abstract.

A class that consists *entirely* of pure virtual member functions is sometimes termed an *interface*. An interface describes desired behaviors as a set of functions but does not define how the behaviors should be implemented.

19.3 Obtaining Run-Time Type Information

> The dynamic type of a polymorphic variable can be tested using a dynamic cast.

When you have a pointer or reference that can refer to an object of multiple classes in a hierarchy, you occasionally need to obtain the actual type of an object. There are two common ways that this is done. A *dynamic cast* verifies that the pointer or reference can be safely converted to a pointer or reference of a derived class. The typeid operator yields the exact type of an object. We describe both features in the following sections.

19.3.1 Dynamic Casts

The dynamic_cast operator requires a type as a template parameter, followed by a parameter that must be a pointer or reference (see Syntax 19.2 on page 732).

```
// Implicitly converts from Manager to Employee
Employee* e = new Manager("Sarah Smith", 67000, 2000);
// Explicitly converts from Employee to Manager
Manager* m = dynamic_cast<Manager*>(e);
```

The dynamic cast succeeds if the template type matches the actual type of the pointer or reference. In that case, the dynamic_cast operator returns the pointer or reference, converted to the template type. If the type is not correct, a NULL pointer is returned. Comparing the result to NULL is therefore equivalent to testing the type of the parameter.

```
for (int i = 0; i < department.size(); i++)
{
    Manager* m = dynamic_cast<Manager*>(department[i]);
    if (m != NULL)
    {
        cout << "Employee " << department[i]->get_name()
            << " is a manager.\n";
        m->set_bonus(2000); // Can now invoke manager member functions
    }
    else
        cout << "Employee " << department[i]->get_name()
            << " is not a manager.\n";
}
```

The assignment of a Manager value to an Employee variable is sometimes termed an *upcast*, because you are moving "up" the class hierarchy. Similarly, the use of the dynamic cast, which does just the reverse, is termed a *downcast*, because you are moving down the class hierarchy as it is written on the page.

If the dynamic_cast operation is used with a reference, instead of a pointer, a failure results in a bad_cast exception being thrown, rather than a NULL pointer, because there is no equivalent to a NULL pointer when using references.

To use a dynamic cast, objects must belong to a class with at least one virtual function.

A static_cast is similar, but performs no run-time check on the result. If the programmer has made a mistake and the change in type is not valid, no indication will be given. This makes static casts much more dangerous than dynamic casts. A static cast should only be used for primitive types (for example, converting an integer into a double) or non-polymorphic types.

```
int max = 42;
double dmax = static_cast<double>(max); // One way to convert to double
```

SYNTAX 19.2 Dynamic Cast

dynamic_cast<*type_name*>(*expression*)

Example:

Manager* m = dynamic_cast<Manager*>(department[i]);

Purpose:

Safely test the type of a polymorphic variable, converting to derived class type if appropriate, returning a NULL pointer if not.

19.3.2 The typeid Operator

The typeid operator yields a type_info object that describes a type.

A dynamic cast tests whether a pointer or reference can be safely converted to a given type, but it does not give the actual type of the object that is being referenced. To obtain that specific type, you can use the typeid operator. This operator takes as parameter either an expression or a class name. It returns an object of type type_info, which is defined in the header file <typeinfo>. (Note that the type name contains an underscore, the header file name does not.) Among other things, the type_info object contains the name of a class as a string.

For example, executing the following:

```
for (int i = 0; i < department.size(); i++)
   cout << typeid(*department[i]).name() << "\n";
```

will produce

```
Manager
Employee
Employee
```

An alternative way to test the type of an object is to compare the typeinfo value to that of a known class type:

```
for (int i = 0; i < department.size(); i++)
{
   if (typeid(*department[i]) == typeid(Manager))
      cout << "Employee " << department[i]->get_name()
         << " is a manager. \n";
   else
      cout << "Employee " << department[i]->get_name()
         << " is not a manager. \n";
}
```

However, both dynamic casts and the typeid operator should be avoided whenever possible in favor of virtual member functions (see Common Error 19.1 on page 734).

SYNTAX 19.3 typeid

typeid(*expression*)
typeid(*type_name*)

Example:

```
#include <typeinfo>
if (typeid(*department[i]) == typeid(Manager)) ...
```

Purpose:

Obtain dynamic type information from a polymorphic expression.

COMMON ERROR 19.1

Taking Type of Pointer, Not Object

Note carefully that the expressions in the previous example dereferenced the pointer values before using them as a parameter to typeid. This resulted in accessing the type of value the pointer referred to, not the type of the pointer itself:

```
Employee* e = new Manager("Sarah Smith", 67000, 2000);
typeid(*e); // Returns description of type of object pointed to by e, Manager
typeid(e); // Returns description of type of pointer, Employee*
```

A common error is to compare a pointer type to a class type. This will never succeed:

```
// Error—cannot be true, because e is a pointer
if (typeid(e) == typeid(Manager))
```

COMMON ERROR 19.2

Using Type Tests Instead of Polymorphism

Beginning programmers often perform explicit type tests as part of a complex conditional statement, as in the following:

```
void give_raise(Employee* e, double percent)
{
    if (typeid(*e) == typeid(Employee))
    {
        ... // Do actions specific to Employee
    }
    else if (typeid(*e) == typeid(Manager))
    {
        ... // Do actions specific to Manager
    }
}
```

Such code is a sign of poor design. What happens if the type of e is neither an Employee nor a Manager? What happens if later a new derived type, say HourlyEmployee, is added to the system? When this occurs you will have to go back and locate all the places where the conditional statements are used and add new code to handle the new class.

A far better alternative is to use polymorphism. Create a virtual member function in the base class, and override it in each of the derived classes.

```
class Employee
{
    virtual void give_raise(double percent);
};

class Manager : public Employee
{
    virtual void give_raise(double percent);
};
```

Now instead of testing the type of the value, you can simply invoke the virtual member function. Even better, when a new derived class is created, the new class simply overrides the member function, and no change is necessary in the calling function.

ADVANCED TOPIC 19.2

Virtual Function Tables

You may wonder how the compiler can generate code at compile time that will, when executed at run time, select the correct virtual function to execute. In order to accomplish this the compiler creates a special table for each class, called the virtual function table, or *vtable*. The vtable maintains pointers to each virtual member function implemented by the class. Each object is then augmented with an additional hidden data field, termed the *vtable pointer*, that points to the virtual function table appropriate to the class of the value currently being held by the variable. Instances of the same class point to the same vtable, while instances of a derived class will have a different vtable (Figure 4).

To see how the virtual function table is used, imagine that a variable declared as a pointer to Employee actually holds a value that is type Manager:

```
Employee* emp = new Manager("Sarah Smith", 67000, 2000);
```

The value of the pointer will point to a section in memory where the data for the object is stored. Along with the data fields for the object (name, salary, and so on) will be the vtable

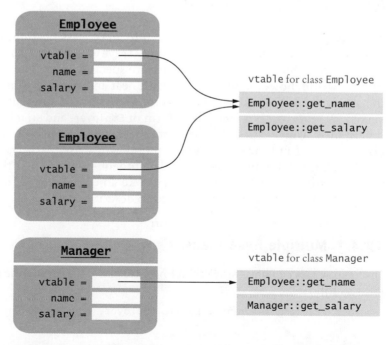

Figure 4 Instances of the Same Class Share a Virtual Function Table

pointer. This value will point to the virtual function table for Manager, the type used in the new statement that created the data (see Figure 5). If a member function is inherited from the base class, as is get_name in Figure 4, then the vtable in the derived class points to the same function as the vtable in the base class. If a member function is overridden, as is get_salary, then the entry in the vtable points to the derived class function. Code generated for a call on a virtual function, such as get_salary, examines the virtual function table and transfers control to the correct function. Just as the same function can execute differently based on differences in data values, the same code generated by the compiler will at different times transfer to different functions, depending on the contents of the vtable pointer.

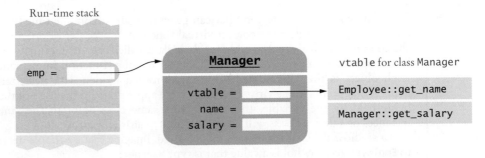

Figure 5   The vtable Is Used to Locate a Member Function at Run Time

19.4 Multiple Inheritance

You have seen inheritance described as a form of classification. A derived class is a more specialized type of the base class. A TravelClock, for example, is a specialized form of Clock. Similarly, a Manager is a more specialized form of Employee. Objects in the real world, however, seldom fit such a neat and simple pattern. Consider modeling a university. You will want a class for Employee, to represent workers at the university. A Professor is a specialized form of Employee, and so might be derived using inheritance. Universities also have students, which might be represented by the class Student. But how should you represent the class TeachingAssistant? A teaching assistant is both an employee and a student—instances of the class will exhibit characteristics of both (earning a salary like an employee, taking classes like a student). Multiple inheritance can be used to describe such classes.

19.4.1 Multiple Base Classes

In C++, a class can have more than one base class. We can define a teaching assistant class as follows:

```
class TeachingAssistant : public Employee, public Student
{
    ...
};
```

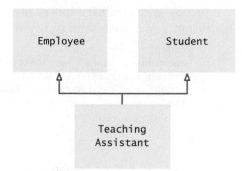

Figure 6
TeachingAssistant Inherits from
Both Employee and Student

A class that inherits from two or more base classes is said to use multiple inheritance.

A TeachingAssistant is a blending of the behavior of the classes Employee and Student. A class, such as TeachingAssistant, that inherits from two or more base classes is said to exhibit *multiple inheritance* (see Figure 6).

When multiple inheritance is used, the class inheritance diagram is no longer a tree. But neither is it an arbitrary graph; there are some restrictions. No class can be its own direct or indirect parent, for example. This prevents the inheritance diagram from ever having cycles. A directed graph with no cycles is termed a *directed acyclic graph*, or DAG. Class diagrams for classes with multiple inheritance are one example of a DAG.

Instances of derived classes maintain the data fields associated with base classes. An instance of Manager, for example, maintains the data fields associated with class Employee. In the same fashion, an instance of class TeachingAssistant will maintain the data fields associated with both base classes Employee and Student, as shown in Figure 7.

The idea of polymorphic assignment works for each of the base classes. That is, a pointer to a value of type TeachingAssistant can be assigned either to a variable declared as a pointer to a Student, or as a pointer to an Employee.

```
TeachingAssistant* fred = new TeachingAssistant();
Employee* new_hire = fred; // Legal, because a TeachingAssistant is-a Employee
Student* advisee = fred; // Legal, because a TeachingAssistant is-a Student
```

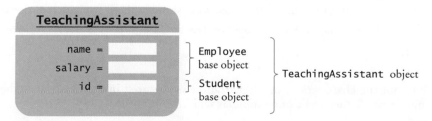

Figure 7 A TeachingAssistant Object Holds Data Fields from Both Base Classes

Just as with ordinary inheritance, a dynamic cast can be used to determine if an instance of Student is in reality an instance of TeachingAssistant:

```
Student* mary = ...;
TeachingAssistant* lab_instructor = dynamic_cast<TeachingAssistant*>(mary);
if (lab_instructor != NULL)
    cout << "Yes, mary is a TeachingAssistant. \n";
else
    cout << "No, mary is not a TeachingAssistant. \n";
```

SYNTAX 19.4 Multiple Inheritance

class *DerivedClassName* : public *BaseClass*$_1$, ..., public *BaseClass*$_n$
{
    features
};

Example:

class TeachingAssistant : public Student, public Employee
{
    ...
};

Purpose:

Define a class that inherits features from two or more base classes.

COMMON ERROR 19.3

Failing to Preserve the Is-a Relationship

The use of multiple inheritance does not mean you should abandon the *is-a* relationship that is the defining characteristic of single inheritance hierarchies. The new abstraction must be a specialization of *each* of the base classes. (A TeachingAssistant is-a Student, and a TeachingAssistant is-an Employee.)

A common error is to use multiple inheritance as a tool for composition rather than for specialization. Just because a car has an engine and also has a transmission as well as a body, it does not mean that a class that models a car should inherit from each of these:

```
class Car : public Engine, public Transmission, public Body // Error
{
    ...
};
```

Without the characteristic of specialization as captured in the *is-a* relationship, the use of inheritance (either single or multiple) is seldom appropriate.

19.4.2 Name Ambiguities

A common difficulty arising from the use of multiple inheritance is that similar names can be used for different operations in the base classes. For example, it is likely that employees have identification numbers, and so class Employee might have a member function get_id. But students also have identification numbers, and so class Student might easily have a similar function. There is no reason to expect that the two identification numbers would be the same, (unless the university has made the mistake of using Social Security numbers for student identification numbers, see Random Fact 9.2). If you invoke the function get_id with an instance of class TeachingAssistant, which one should be executed?

```
TeachingAssistant* fred = new TeachingAssistant();
cout << "Your number is " << fred->get_id() << "\n";
   // Error, ambiguous member function name
```

The C++ compiler cannot determine which function is intended—the get_id function in class Employee or the get_id function in class Student. There are two ways to get around this problem. One solution is to use a fully qualified function name:

```
TeachingAssistant* fred = new TeachingAssistant();
cout << "Your teaching assistant is " << fred->Employee::get_id() << "\n";
```

A better solution is to redefine the ambiguous function in the new class, and hide the use of the qualified name within the body of the function.

```
class TeachingAssistant : public Student, public Employee
{
public:
   string get_id() const;
   string student_id() const;
};

// get_id will return Employee identification number
string TeachingAssistant::get_id()
{
   return Employee::get_id();
}

string TeachingAssistant::student_id()
   // Make student value available by a different name
{
   return Student::get_id();
}
```

19.4.3 Replicated Base Classes

It is not legal to specify the same base class more than once in a class heading:

```
class MultiplePartTime : public Employee, public Employee // Error
{
   ...
};
```

However, nothing prevents the same class from appearing indirectly more than once as a consequence of inheritance. To illustrate, imagine that you had a class Person used to maintain information such as a name:

```
class Person
{
public:
    Person(string n);
    string get_name() const;
private:
    string name;
};
```

It would make perfectly good sense to have both Student and Employee derive from the base class Person, as both students and employees have names:

```
class Student : public Person
{
    ...
};
class Employee : public Person
{
    ...
};
```

The problem now arises when you create the class TeachingAssistant that inherits from both Employee and Student. In addition to the function name ambiguity problem you have already considered, there is a problem associated with the data field in class Person. Remember that an instance of a derived class contains the memory associated with the parent class. An instance of Employee contains the data for class Person.

An instance of Student also contains the data for class Person.

Should an instance of class TeachingAssistant contain one copy of the data fields from class Person, or two?

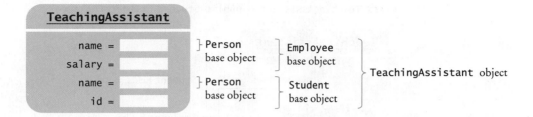

There is no single right answer to this question. One can imagine situations where separate data fields might be appropriate, as well as situations where a single data field seems called for. In this case, for example, the latter seems most likely (unless you want to allow teaching assistants to have one name when they are sitting in class, and another name when they are in front of the class).

The C++ language allows the programmer to control which of these two possibilities occurs. The default behavior is to generate separate copies of the data members of all base classes, as previously described. To avoid the duplication of base class data members, the programmer must specify the inheritance as virtual, as in the following.

```
class Student : virtual public Person
{
    ...
};

class Employee : virtual public Person
{
    ...
};

class TeachingAssistant : public Student, public Employee
{
    ...
};
```

Figure 8 shows the effect on the data layout. The virtual derived class gains a pointer that points to the Person part of the class. When forming another derived class that inherits twice from Person, that class has two copies of that pointer, one

class Student : virtual public Person   class Employee : virtual public Person

Student
id =
name =

Fields defined in
} Student
} Person fields

Employee
salary =
name =

Fields defined in
} Employee
] Person fields

Figure 8   Virtual Inheritance Alters Placement of Base Class Data

```
class TeachingAssistant : public Student, public Employee
```

Figure 9   Virtual Inheritance Combines Data from Common Base Classes

from each of its parents, but only one copy of the Person data. The pointers are adjusted so that they both point to the shared data members (see Figure 9)

Notice that the virtual keyword must be used in the intermediate classes Student and Employee, and not in the class TeachingAssistant where the conflict actually occurs.

QUALITY TIP 19.1

Avoid Multiple Inheritance

Multiple inheritance is much more complex than single inheritance. We have only hinted at the numerous possibilities for confusion that arise from the use of multiple inheritance (both from the programmers' and the compiler writers' points of view). True uses for this feature are exceedingly rare. Some authors, and some programming languages, go so far as to say that multiple inheritance should never be used [1].

Often multiple inheritance can be eliminated by using other mechanisms. The class TeachingAssistant might, for example, simply maintain a data field of type Student, or one of type Employee. This prevents the polymorphic assignment of a TeachingAssistant value to a variable of type Employee, but often this is not important. Alternatively, a Teaching-Assistant might have a *nested class* that is derived from class Employee. The nested class can maintain an instance of the outer class, and can be used polymorphically with Employee.

```
class TeachingAssistant : public Student
{
   ...
private:
   class EmployeePart;
   EmployeePart* employee_ptr;
};

class TeachingAssistant::EmployeePart : public Employee
{
```

```
public:
    EmployeePart(TeachingAssistant&);
    ...
private:
    TeachingAssistant* ta_part; // Allows access back to outer class
};

TeachingAssistant::TeachingAssistant()
{
    employee_ptr = new EmployeePart(this); // Pass pointer to implicit parameter
}

TeachingAssistant::EmployeePart::EmployeePart(TeachingAssistant* taval)
    : ta_part(taval) {}
```

Ruling out multiple inheritance altogether goes too far. There are legitimate uses for the technique. Inheriting from several interfaces (classes that consist entirely of pure virtual functions) can never cause the ambiguity problems described here. Classes that cannot share any common data areas are also safe. Nevertheless, the careful programmer will always consider the alternatives before using this technique.

19.5 Software Frameworks

A software framework is a collection of classes that capture the common features of a task.

A hallmark of modern programming is an emphasis on software reuse. The idea of *software reuse* is to develop general purpose software components that can be carried from one project to the next without needing to be rewritten. This makes software development more like other engineering fields, such as mechanical engineering, where reusable components such as girders or bolts are put together in a variety of ways, or electrical engineering where the reusable components are capacitors and resistors.

But there is a fundamental conflict inherent in the notion of a reusable software component. To be reusable the component must be general purpose—it must not require details that are specific to any one application. But the component must also be useful, it must address and solve the problem at hand, which often requires very individual detail in each new application. How can this tension between general purpose use and specific application be resolved?

Programmers specialize the behavior by overriding member functions.

One solution in object-oriented languages makes use of polymorphism. A very general base class can be developed and distributed across many projects. This base class can be quite complex, but must not contain any information specific to any given application. The developers for each new application then use inheritance to create specialized versions of the general purpose classes. It is in these specialized classes that the details specific to each application are contained.

An easy example to envision, and the example that drove the development of object-oriented programming as a useful programming technique, is the creation of a graphical user interface. As you will see in Chapter 25, programming a GUI is a nontrivial task. First there is the sheer number of different components, such as buttons, scroll bars, text areas, windows, and dialog boxes. Furthermore, each of these can have complex behavior. A window can be moved, resized, iconified, or have menus. Windows can overlap, and must be repainted when an overlapping window is removed.

Rewriting all this behavior for each new application would be almost impossibly difficult. Fortunately, it does not have to be done. Instead, developers use a software framework. A framework is nothing more than a collection of reusable classes and functions (often termed a *toolkit*) that developers employ as a starting point in the creation of new applications. In Chapter 25 you will learn about the wxWidgets toolkit.

Consider the basic task of putting a window up on a screen. The concept of the window is generic, and a lot of code can be written to handle general purpose tasks, such as moving the window, handling menu bars, and so on. But a fundamental problem remains: the general purpose class does not know how to render (or paint) the contents of the window, or how to respond to events such as mouse clicks. To overcome this, the base class simply leaves these tasks as member functions and provides either a pure virtual member function or a simple default behavior (such as doing nothing):

```
class wxWindow
{
public:
    ...
    // Pure virtual member function
    virtual void OnPaint(wxPaintEvent& event) = 0;
    virtual void OnMouseEvent(wxMouseEvent& event);
    ...
};

void wxWindow::OnMouseEvent(wxMouseEvent& event)
{
    // Default behavior, do nothing
}
```

Each new application uses inheritance to construct a special purpose class that derives from wxWindow. The new class can then fill in the application-specific details, such as what a mouse event means in the context of this given application.

```
class ClockWindow : public wxWindow
    // ClockWindow will be developed in Chapter 25
{
public:
    ...
    virtual void OnPaint(wxPaintEvent& event);
    virtual void OnMouseEvent(wxMouseEvent& event);
    ...
};

void ClockWindow::OnMouseEvent(wxMouseEvent& event)
{
```

```
    ... // Implement mouse events for this specific application
}
```

By using inheritance, the vast majority of the code needed to handle the manipulation of windows is reused across many applications. By overriding key member functions, this general behavior is then specialized in each new application. Polymorphism is important, because the framework itself thinks of the application as an instance of wxWindow, while the programmer views the application as an instance of the new application class (such as ClockWindow). This combination of inheritance, overriding, and polymorphism is repeated many times on many different levels in the development of a GUI. You will see more of this in Chapter 25.

QUALITY TIP 19.2

Design Your Own Software Frameworks

A framework is a skeleton application, a structure onto which specialized details can be added while avoiding the repetition of common features. Any time you anticipate creating several programs that are variations on a common theme you should think about the possibility of creating your own software framework. To create a framework, ask yourself

- What features are common to most or all example problems?
- What features must be specialized in each new application?

For example, in a game framework common features might be the use of a board, a mechanism to keep and display a score, and the fact that play flips from one player to another (or perhaps from one player to the computer). Variations include the actual display of the board, and the actions to be performed on each turn.

   You then determine how those aspects in the second category can be described as a series of one or more member function invocations. For example, you might create a member function to paint the display of the board, another to update the score for each player, and yet a third to perform the actions of one turn.

   You then develop the framework by concentrating on the common features, ignoring the aspects that are particular to each different application. If you are successful, it makes the creation of new applications that fit the pattern of your framework much easier, as each new application need not rewrite all the common code.

RANDOM FACT 19.1

Functional Programming

The C++ language encourages a style of programming termed object-oriented, which is in turn often considered to be a special category of a more general style of programming termed *imperative programming*. Imperative programming is based on the idea of a command, or instruction, telling the computer to do something. An assignment statement is the best example of an imperative. Each command makes a small change in memory, and computation consists of ensuring that a long sequence of commands are executed one after the other in the proper sequence.

There are, however, other styles of programming. The most widely used alternative is *functional programming*. Functional programming is based not on commands, but on expressions. A functional program is nothing more than the evaluation of a single large expression. In order to manage complexity, functions are used to break expressions into smaller and easier to understand units. Functional programs do not have variables and assignment statements, in the sense of identifiers that change over time. Instead, functional programs have identifiers (parameters or local variables) that can be set once and thereafter do not change. When a task needs to be performed repeatedly, functional programs use recursion in place of loops. The following function is a typical example. The function is written in the language ML, and computes the number of ways that m items can be selected from a group of n:

```
fun comb(n, m) =
    if m = 0 orelse m = n then 1
    else comb(n-1, m) + comb(n-1, m-1)
```

Other than the use of orelse instead of || as the or symbol the meaning is not difficult to understand. To compute the number of combinations of m things from a group of n, if m is 0 or m is the entire collection then the answer is 1. Otherwise two recursive calls are performed, and their sum is the result.

Notice there are no assignment statements. Recursion is used for repetition, instead of loops. Functions in ML and other functional languages possess a property termed *referential transparency*. What this means is that the same parameters given to a function will always produce the same result. Because of this property, ML interpreters are free to cache the results of a recursive function call, and if the same parameters later arise they can return the cached value. Another interesting characteristic of ML is that it does not use declaration statements. Instead, the types of identifiers are inferred from their use. Here, n and m are being compared to integers, and hence they must themselves be integers.

Most functional programming languages use lists as their basic data structures. Programs that manipulate lists tend to be highly recursive. The following program to generate the reverse of a list illustrates these characteristics, as well as the syntax used by ML:

```
fun reverse(L) =
    if L = nil then nil
    else reverse(tl(L)) @ [hd(L)];
```

The value nil represents the empty list. The function hd returns the head of a list, that is, the first element. The function tl returns the tail, that is, the list that remains once the head is removed. The square brackets are making a list out of a single item, while the @ symbol appends two lists. So this function can be read as follows: to produce the reverse of a list, if the list is empty then return the empty list. Otherwise, remove the first element, reverse the rest of the list, and append the head of the list to the end. Notice that once again there are neither assignment statements nor variables, and the outcome is simply the result of evaluating an expression.

Type inference on this function illustrates an unusual property. The use of the built-in functions hd and tl, and the comparison to nil all tell the compiler that L is a list. But a list of what? Because nothing is done with the head of the list except to make a new list, there is no way to tell. But rather than report an error, the ML compiler is satisfied to record the type of the variable L as "list of alpha", where alpha is an unknown type. This is similar in many ways to the C++ template parameter. A function, such as reverse, that will work with incompletely specified types is termed polymorphic. The function reverse does not care what type of elements the list is maintaining, and will work just the same with a list of integers or a list of strings, or even a list of lists.

Finally, functional programming languages incorporate an idea termed a *higher order function*. A higher order function uses a function as parameter in the course of evaluating another function. A simple example is the function map, which is written as follows:

```
function map(F, L) =
    if L = nil then nil
    else [F(hd(L))] @ map(F, tl(L))
```

The function map takes two values as parameter, the first is a function and the second a list. If it is given an empty list it returns the empty list. Otherwise, it applies the function to the first element of the list, and appends the result to the list generated by the recursive call on the remainder. To illustrate, consider the following function that adds 3 to its parameter:

```
fun addThree(X) = X + 3
```

A call on map(addThree, [2 4 7]) would produce the list [5 7 10]. Note how the function addThree is being used as a value that is passed as a parameter to map. This is similar (although there are some technical differences) to the use of function objects and the overloading of the function call operator in C++.

Further information on ML can be found in [2]. Another functional language that is widely used is Haskell [3].

CHAPTER SUMMARY

1. Classes can be organized into inheritance hierarchies based on the base class/ derived class inheritance relationship.

2. An abstract class contains at least one virtual function that is declared but not defined.

3. It is not legal to create an instance of an abstract class, although you may use a pointer or reference to an abstract class.

4. The dynamic type of a polymorphic variable can be tested using a dynamic cast.

5. The typeid operator yields a type_info object that describes a type.

6. A class that inherits from two or more base classes is said to use multiple inheritance.

7. A software framework is a collection of classes that capture the common features of a task.

8. Programmers specialize the behavior by overriding member functions.

FURTHER READING

1. Tom Cargill, *C++ Programming Style*, Addison-Wesley, 1992.
2. Jeffrey D. Ullman, *Elements of ML Programming*, Prentice-Hall, 1994.
3. Simon Thompson, *Haskell: The Craft of Functional Programming*, Addison-Wesley, 1996.

REVIEW EXERCISES

Exercise R19.1. Explain the relationship between levels in an inheritance tree.

Exercise R19.2. What does it mean to say that the C++ language allows the programmer to create an inheritance forest, and not a tree?

Exercise R19.3. What is a pure virtual member function? What is an abstract class?

Exercise R19.4. What is a dynamic cast? What is the purpose of this operation?

Exercise R19.5. What are the problems that arise with statements that branch on different types? Why is it better to use polymorphism in this situation?

Exercise R19.6. When an overridden virtual member function is executed, the `vtable` helps determine which function to execute. Explain how this mechanism works.

Exercise R19.7. What does it mean to say that a class uses multiple inheritance?

Exercise R19.8. Why are the function name and data ambiguity problems inherent in multiple inheritance not an issue with single inheritance?

Exercise R19.9. What is virtual inheritance? What problem does this feature address?

Exercise R19.10. Investigate the use of multiple inheritance in the `iostream` hierarchy. Why does `iostream` inherit from both `istream` and `ostream`? Why doesn't `fstream` inherit from `ifstream` and `ofstream`?

Exercise R19.11. Exercise P6.25 asked you to implement a tic-tac-toe game. Suppose you now want to make a software framework for several different board games. What functions would you keep in class `Game`? How would those functions be specialized in an application-specific class, such as `TicTacToeGame`?

Exercise R19.12. What is a software framework? How does the use of a software framework simplify the creation of new applications?

PROGRAMMING EXERCISES

Exercise P19.1. Design a class hierarchy that links the classes Bicycle, Boat, Bus, Airplane, Horse, and Automobile.

Exercise P19.2. Finish the implementation of the Shape hierarchy started in Figure 3, adding member functions to compute the area of each. Write a function that takes a vector of shapes and computes the total area of the collection.

Exercise P19.3. Does it make sense for class Square to be a subclass of class Rectangle, or for class Rectangle to be a subclass of class Square? Write both versions, keeping track of appropriate data values. The first is termed using inheritance for specialization, and the other is sometimes termed using inheritance for extension. Which organization makes more sense? Why?

Exercise P19.4. Rewrite the clocks3 program from Chapter 8 to use dynamic casts instead of virtual function calls. (This is not a good idea; the purpose of this exercise is only to become familiar with dynamic casts.)

Exercise P19.5. Rewrite the clocks3 program from Chapter 8 to use the typeid operator and static casts instead of virtual function calls. (This is not a good idea; the purpose of this exercise is only to become familiar with run-time type identification.)

Exercise P19.6. Finish the implementation of the class TeachingAssistant. Show that the same TeachingAssistant value can appear both in a vector of Students and in a vector of Employees.

Exercise P19.7. Change the class TeachingAssistant to use nested classes. Add a member function as_employee to the class TeachingAssistant that will return an object of type Employee, and the member function as_student that will, from this value, return the Student object. Again show how to use the same value on a list of Students and a list of Employees. Is this technique easier or more difficult to use than the multiple inheritance technique?

Exercise P19.8. Design a framework for solitaire card games. What features are common to many different solitaire games? What features are unique to each game?

Exercise P19.9. Design a framework for discrete event simulations, as described in Chapter 13. Make Event into an abstract class. The main function should be a part of your framework and not supplied by the framework user.

G **Exercise P19.10.** Create an abstract class Chart that maintains a collection of integer data values stored in a vector. Include a member function draw(Point& p) as a pure virtual member function to display the data at the given point. Create derived classes PieChart and BarChart that each display the data in the indicated format.

G   **Exercise P19.11.** Create a class StringRectangle that inherits from both string and Rectangle. When displayed, the output should be the text of the string contained within a rectangle, like this:

G   **Exercise P19.12.** Create the class ShadedRectangle that draws a Rectangle with lines across it, like this:

Then create the class ShadedStringRectangle that inherits from both ShadedRectangle and StringRectangle from Exercise P19.11. A ShadedStringRectangle should draw the text of a string inside a shaded rectangle.

G   **Exercise P19.13.** Design a framework for animation. The framework should clear the graphics window between each frame, and pause for a short time after each new frame is displayed. Derived classes are responsible for drawing the images. A simple way to pause is to have a loop that executes many times, but does nothing. Use your framework to create an animation of a car driving around the edges of the window.

The Standard Template Library

The **Standard Template** Library, or STL, is a library of collection classes and associated functions. These collections are of the sort commonly found in almost all nontrivial applications. Using these standard container data structures simplifies the creation of new applications and promotes the portability of the resulting code.

Each of the standard containers can produce iterators that provide access to the elements in a collection. A large library of standard algorithms can be used to manipulate containers through the use of iterators. You will learn about the variety of iterators, and the generic algorithms and functions that make use of iterators.

CHAPTER CONTENTS

20.1 The STL

> The Standard Template Library, or STL, is a library of container classes.

Almost all nontrivial computer programs maintain a collection of elements of one type or another. Because such collections are so common, the study of data structures used to store collections is a fundamental part of any computer science curriculum. Over the years, computer programmers have identified a small set of collection data structures that occur repeatedly across many different problem domains and applications. These basic data structures, or container classes, are therefore ideal candidates to be developed as reusable abstractions. A reusable library of data structures allows programs to be developed more easily, since the container classes do not have to be rewritten in each new application. They promote reliability, because library classes are extensively used and debugged, and portability, because a standard library is the same on every platform. For this reason most programming languages now come with libraries of common data structures.

The Standard Template Library, or STL, is the C++ library of data structures and their associated algorithms. As one would expect in an object-oriented language, containers are represented by classes. However, one of the most interesting features of the STL is the use of "generic algorithms". Rather than placing a large amount of functionality in each container, the STL provides container classes that have relatively small interfaces. These small interfaces make it easier to understand and use the classes.

> Each class in the STL supports a relatively small set of operations.

> This basic functionality can be extended though the use of generic algorithms.

This minimal functionality is greatly extended by a library of functions. A simple example is the function count, which counts the number of specific elements in a collection. The number of 7s that occur in a list of integers could be calculated as follows:

```
int seven_count = count(numbers.begin(), numbers.end(), 7);
```

Through the use of templates, these generic algorithms can be used with many different types of containers. That is why they are termed "generic".

Alex Stepanov, the principal designer of the STL, has said that the reason the container data structures and algorithms in the STL can work together seamlessly is that they do not know anything about each other. The containers do not know what algorithms they will be used with. This reduces the size of the interface for each container, because the algorithms are not part of the container operations. The containers provide iterators, and that is all.

The algorithms, on the other hand, never actually manipulate the containers directly. Instead, algorithms operate only through the use of a middleman, the iterator. By working in this indirect fashion, an algorithm need not know what sort of container the data is derived from, only the operations for the iterators it requires.

> Through the use of iterators, generic algorithms can be made to work with a variety of containers.

The use of iterators as mediators makes the coupling between containers and algorithms extremely loose, and is what allows containers and algorithms to be mixed in an almost infinite variety of ways.

Like the container classes, iterators and algorithms in the STL are generalized by the use of template parameters. This allows these features to operate with a wide variety of types. Just as important, the compile-time polymorphism of templates means that the majority of work needed to specialize a generic algorithm to a specific application is performed at compile time. This results in fast execution times for the algorithms in the STL library.

20.2 Iterators

> Iterators are high-level abstractions that serve the same role as pointers, but can be applied to a variety of data structures.

Fundamental to the use of the container classes in the STL and their associated algorithms is the concept of an iterator. As you learned in Chapter 12, an iterator is simply an object used to cycle through the elements stored in a container. By means of operator overloading, iterators can use the same syntax as pointers. In fact, for some containers, iterators *are* simply pointers.

Like a pointer, an iterator can be used in variety of different ways. An iterator can be used to denote a specific location, in the same way that a pointer is used to reference a specific memory address. Just as the * operator is used to indicate the value associated with a pointer (see Section 7.1) the same operator is used to access the value associated with an iterator. The following will, for example, print the first element in a vector of integers:

```
vector<int>::iterator p = a_vector.begin();
cout << *p << "\n";
```

On the other hand, a *pair* of iterators can be used to describe a range of values. This is analogous to the way in which two pointers can be used to describe a contiguous region of memory, such as the values in an array. Imagine you have declared an array of integers. If a is a pointer to an array, then a + n is the address of the nth element in the array. A pair of pointers describes a range in the array:

```
int a[10];
int* p = a + 2;
int* q = a + 5;
```

When two pointers describe a range, it is conventional that the ending pointer is not considered to be part of the range. For example, one would normally interpret the values p and q in Figure 1 as describing the range consisting of the three elements a[2], a[3], and a[4]. Notice that q points to the element after a[4], which is *not* considered to be part of the range. In fact, to describe the entire collection, the ending pointer will be the value just beyond the last element in the array. Because subscript bounds are not checked in C++, this can be written as a + 10. This memory address is not part of the array a, it is simply a place holder, a marker for the end of the array.

Iterators work in the same fashion. The only difference is that the values referenced by iterators need not be in adjacent memory locations. But in the same fashion as pointers, iterators are used to describe a starting location and a *past-the-end* location. For container classes, the member function begin returns a starting iterator, and the member function end returns a past-the-end location, a special marker to indicate the end of the collection. For a linked list, we could imagine these two locations as shown in Figure 2.

As the past-the-end pointer for the array shows, a pointer can fail to reference a legal value in the collection. Just as it is improper to try to dereference and obtain a value from a past-the-end pointer, it is improper to dereference a past-the-end iterator of a container. However, just as pointer bounds are not checked, iterators are not obligated to check for illegal use, and so it is up to you, the programmer, to ensure that no illegal dereference operations are performed.

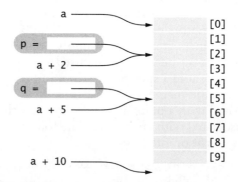

Figure 1   Pointers Referencing an Array

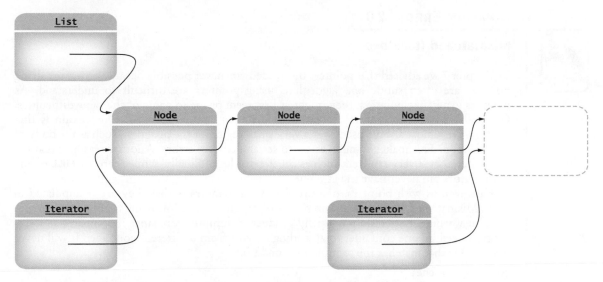

Figure 2 Iterators for a Linked List

When two iterators refer to a range of values, a loop is sometimes used to access each value in the range. The increment operator (operator++) is used to move from one element to the next, and the equality operators (operator== and operator!=) are used to terminate the loop.

```
for (p = start; p != past_end; ++p)
{
    Process *p;
}
```

In Chapter 7, we recommended the use of index values instead of pointers to create loops for arrays, because many programmers find them easier to understand and less error prone. However, in this chapter, you will see how the use of array pointers can unify algorithms, so that they work using the same syntax for arrays and for STL containers. Through the application of operator overloading, exactly the same operators are used to describe an iterator loop for each of the STL containers.

Ranges can be used to describe the entire contents of a container, by constructing an iterator to the initial element and the special ending iterator. But just as pointers p and q in the earlier example described a portion of the larger container, ranges can also be used to describe subsequences within a container. The first iterator describes the first value in the subsequence, while the second iterator serves as the past-the-end value for the subsequence.

Recall from Chapter 14 that there are two forms of the ++ operator. Both forms increment their argument, but the prefix form (++p) yields the value after the increment, whereas the postfix form (p++) yields the value before the increment. Since iterators can be more heavyweight than numbers or pointers, it is a good idea to avoid the postfix form unless you really want to capture the old value. For that reason, we will use ++p whenever we advance an iterator.

COMMON ERROR 20.1

Mismatched Iterators

In Chapter 7 we advised that pointers be avoided whenever possible because errors involving pointers are often subtle and algorithms using pointers are difficult to understand. As iterators generalize pointers, they might at first seem prone to some of the same difficulties. Generally, however, iterators are easier to use than simple pointers. One reason is that iterators are almost always used over a very small region of the program, such as the body of a single loop. This makes it much easier to see and correct errors. Another reason is that the use of iterators is very stylized, such as the iterator loop. Finally, while there are NULL pointers, iterators can never have a NULL value.

However, as with pointers, one problem with iterators is that they are manipulated in pairs. Mismatching a pair is a certain source of problems. The following bit of code compiles without warning, but could potentially produce an infinite loop, since it compares an iterator produced by one container to an ending iterator from a different container. It will never find a value that matches the termination condition.

```
list<int> one;
list<int> two;
...
list<int>::iterator p = one.begin();
while (p != two.end())
{
    ...
    ++p;
}
```

Care must be taken to ensure that elements of an iterator pair always come from the same container.

COMMON ERROR 20.2

Assuming the Ending Iterator Is Included in a Range

In mathematics there is a concept called a half-open interval, often represented as [a,b). The description [1,5), for example, represents the range of numbers starting from *and including* 1, up to but *not including* 5. (If we are discussing integers, it would be the values 1, 2, 3, and 4.) When iterators are used to represent a range of elements they can be imagined as a type of half-open interval. The first iterator denotes an element that is included in the collection, and the collection extends to but does not include the element denoted by the second iterator.

This is easy to remember when the iterators are produced using the member functions begin and end, but students are sometimes confused when iterators are used to represent a range that is a part of a collection. For example, suppose you have a list of words, and you want to print all the words between "ant" and "bee". Using the find algorithm you encountered in earlier chapters, this could be written as follows:

```
list<string> words;
// words is initialized with a list of words
list<string>::iterator pos = find(words.begin(), words.end(), "ant");
if (pos != words.end())
{
   list<string>::iterator end = find(pos, words.end(), "bee");
   while (pos != end)
   {
      cout << "word is " << *pos << "\n";
      ++pos;
   }
}
```

The word "bee", if it occurs at all in the list, will not be printed by the loop. The iterator that describes the location of bee is a marker for the end of the range, and is not part of the range.

20.2.1 Varieties of Iterators

Up to this point we have used only four operators with our iterators. The * operator is used to access the value associated with an iterator, the ++ operator is used to advance an iterator to the next element, and the equality operators (operator== and operator!=) are used to compare two iterators for equality or inequality. But certain containers provide iterators that support a wider range of operations. In Section 12.1 we noted that list iterators support both operator++ and operator--, allowing iterators to move both forward and backward through the container. And just as regular pointers can be subscripted (see Chapter 7), vector iterators recognize the subscript operator:

```
vector<int> a(10);
vector<int>::iterator p = a.begin();
++p;
++p;
cout << p[3] << "\n";   // Prints out a[5]!
```

Recall that for a pointer p, the expression p[n] is the same as *(p + n). The addition in the latter is not normal arithmetic addition, but instead indicates a reference to the nth element after p. Ordinary pointers can also be subtracted; the expression q - p returning the number of elements between p and q.

Finally, recall that for a pointer, the expression p->m is the same as (*p).m, where m is a data member or member function. The same relationship holds for iterators. This is useful if you have an iterator that points to an object. For example,

```
vector<string>::iterator p = names.begin();
int n = p->length(); // The length of the string *p
```

Not all operations are recognized by all iterators. List iterators, for example, do not support the subscript operator and will generate a compiler error if you attempt to use one. This is because lists do not support constant time access to arbitrary elements. The iterators in the STL can be divided into five different categories according to the operators they support. These five categories are described in Table 1.

<table>
<tr><th colspan="2">Table 1   Categories of Iterators</th></tr>
<tr><th>Iterators</th><th>Operators</th></tr>
<tr><td>Input Iterator</td><td>Supports operators ==, !=, ++, *, and -> only for returning a value</td></tr>
<tr><td>Output Iterator</td><td>Supports operators ==, !=, ++, *, and -> only for assignment</td></tr>
<tr><td>Forward Iterator</td><td>Supports operators ==, !=, ++, *, and -></td></tr>
<tr><td>Bidirectional Iterator</td><td>Supports operators ==, !=, ++, --, *, and -></td></tr>
<tr><td>Random Access Iterator</td><td>Supports operators ==, !=, ++, --, [], *, -> as well as iterator + n and iterator - iterator. As with pointers, iterator + n references the next n^{th} value following the iterator, and iterator - iterator the number of elements between two iterators</td></tr>
</table>

Member functions in the classes `vector` and `deque` return random access iterators. Lists, sets, and maps return bidirectional iterators. We have not yet seen examples of the other categories, however, later in this chapter we will see how some of these are produced.

A container declared as constant, such as a const vector, will return a type of iterator termed a `const_iterator`. A `const_iterator` can be used to access a value, but not to make changes to the underlying container.

20.3 The Fundamental Containers

The three fundamental sequential data structures are the vector, list, and deque.

Containers in the STL can be divided into three categories. The first category represents fundamental containers, sometimes termed *sequential* containers. The three fundamental containers are the vector, list, and deque. The second category consists of classes called *adapters*, which are layered on top of the fundamental containers. The three collection types in this category are the stack, the queue, and the priority queue. Finally, there are the *associative containers*. In an associative container, elements are ordered in a way that allows for fast retrieval. The two collection types in this category are the set and the map. Except for the deque (which will be described in Section 20.3.3), you have encountered these containers in Chapters 12 and 13.

An interesting feature of the STL is the degree to which the operations provided by these three containers overlap. This is shown in Table 2. Many operations are supported by all three containers, and most of the remainder are supported by two of the three. This means that programs written with one container in mind can often

Table 2 Operations Provided by the Fundamental Containers

Operation	Vector	List	Deque
container()	$O(1)$	$O(1)$	$O(1)$
container(*size*)	$O(1)$	$O(n)$	$O(1)$
container(*size*, *value*)	$O(n)$	$O(n)$	$O(n)$
container(*iterator*, *iterator*)	$O(n)$	$O(n)$	$O(n)$
at(int)	$O(1)$		$O(1)$
back()	$O(1)$	$O(1)$	$O(1)$
begin()	$O(1)$	$O(1)$	$O(1)$
capacity()	$O(1)$		
clear()	$O(1)$	$O(1)$	$O(1)$
empty()	$O(1)$	$O(1)$	$O(1)$
end()	$O(1)$	$O(1)$	$O(1)$
erase(*iterator*)	$O(n)$	$O(1)$	$O(n)$
erase(*iterator*, *iterator*)	$O(n)$	$O(1)$	$O(n)$
front()	$O(1)$	$O(1)$	$O(1)$
insert(*iterator*, *value*)	$O(n)$	$O(1)$	$O(n)$
pop_back()	$O(1)$	$O(1)$	$O(1)$
pop_front()		$O(1)$	$O(1)$
push_back(*value*)	$O(1)+$	$O(1)$	$O(1)+$
push_front(*value*)		$O(1)$	$O(1)+$
rbegin()	$O(1)$	$O(1)$	$O(1)$
rend()	$O(1)$	$O(1)$	$O(1)$
resize(*size*, *value*)	$O(n)$		$O(n)$
size()	$O(1)$	$O(1)$	$O(1)$
operator[](int)	$O(1)$		$O(1)$
operator=(*container*)	$O(n)$	$O(n)$	$O(n)$

use any of the three. For example, invoking begin with any container will yield an iterator. This iterator can be used to cycle over the elements in the container, and the loop will be the same regardless of the container type. The element that an iterator references can be erased from a collection using the same operation, and so on.

The following loop removes all even numbers from a vector of integers. If the container had been a list or deque, rather than a vector, the only difference would be the declaration type of the iterator. Without reading this declaration, it is impossible to infer from the operations involved what type of container is being used.

```
vector<int>::iterator current = a_container.begin();
while (current != a_container.end())
{
    // Number is even if remainder is zero after division by two
    if (0 == *current % 2)
        current = a_container.erase(current);
    else
        ++current;
}
```

All the containers support a variety of constructors. The default constructor creates an empty collection. An integer argument creates a container with the indicated number of elements, initialized to the default value for the element type. A second form of this constructor allows the user to explicitly set an initial value for the elements. Finally, a collection can be initialized using another collection specified by a pair of iterators.

The function at, supported by both vectors and deques, checks the index for validity, unlike operator[], which performs no checking. The functions front and back return references to the first and last elements in the collection. The function empty returns true if the container has no elements. An element referenced by an iterator can be erased, as can a range of elements specified by a pair of iterators. The value returned by erase is the iterator that references the next element in sequence (that is, the element after the erased value). Elements can be inserted at a location specified by an iterator, however the efficiency of this operation varies by data structure. The functions push_front and push_back insert values at the front and back of a collection, while the operations pop_front and pop_back remove them. (Vectors don't support push_front and pop_front because adding and removing values at the beginning of an array is inefficient.) The functions rbegin and rend return iterators that traverse the collection in reverse order.

In addition to the operations provided by member functions in each of the three classes, the utility of these data structures is greatly extended by the use of generic algorithms. A few of these, such as the generic algorithm find, you have seen. You will examine more of these in Section 20.8.

The similarity of operations among these three containers does not mean that the container types are identical. Often there is a difference in the big-Oh execution time between containers for the same operation. Recall the discussion of execution times from Section 11.5. Some operations are constant time, meaning they take the same amount of time in a container holding ten elements as they would in a container holding ten thousand. Constant time operations are often described as $O(1)$. Other operations are linear time, meaning the time they take is proportional to the size of the container. This is written as $O(n)$. A linear time operation would take approximately a thousand times longer on a container with ten thousand elements as it would on a container with ten elements. Between these two are various other timings. In the sections on sets and maps (Sections 20.5.1 and 20.5.2) you will encounter logarithmic time, which is in practice almost as fast as constant time. And finally there is amortized constant time, which in Table 2 is written $O(1)+$. Amortized constant time means that the operation is fast (that is, constant time) most of the time. However, this property is not guaranteed, and once in a while the operation may require more than constant time (usually, $O(n)$ time). It must be the case, however, that in any sufficiently long sequence of operations, the *average* amount of time required for the operation remains constant. Insertion at the end of a vector is a good example of an operation that requires amortized constant time, as you saw in Section 12.3 on the implementation of the vector.

Selecting an appropriate container for any problem requires knowing what operations the problem demands, the approximate size of the collection being held by the container, and how often (at least in relative terms) each operation will be performed. A task that requires indexed access could use either a vector or a deque. However, if elements are frequently inserted at the front of the container, the $O(1)$ performance of the deque for push_front is preferable to the $O(n)$ cost of placing an element at the front of a vector using insert. On the other hand, if indexing is not used, but elements are frequently being placed into the middle of the collection using insert, then the $O(1)$ performance of the list for this operation is better than the $O(n)$ time required by vectors or deques.

QUALITY TIP 20.1

Experimentally Evaluate Execution Times

Selecting a container for any task should depend first upon the operations required and second upon an evaluation of big-Oh execution times. That is, if the key part of an application is a loop that will be repeated performing an insertion in the middle of a collection, then the $O(1)$ versus $O(n)$ difference between insertions for lists and insertions for vectors or deques dominates any other consideration.

However, having performed this analysis, it is often the case that two or more containers appear to be acceptable candidates for use. If the difference between using a vector or using a deque is simply one or two declaration statements, collecting actual execution times is an appealing alternative. Using a small sample of test data, try executing the program using first one container, then another. Gather the resulting execution times, and select the container with the fastest time.

20.3.1 Vners

As you know, a vector is an indexed container. The fundamental operation is subscripting, using `operator[]`. However, elements can also be added to the end of the vector using the member function `push_back`. The interface for the vector was described in Table 2.

The implementation of the vector maintains both the size and the capacity as integer data fields. The buffer is a simple array, accessed using a pointer. (See Section 7.4 for a discussion of array and pointer equivalences). Iterators can be represented by pointers into the buffer.

> The vector and deque are indexed data structures; they support efficient access to each element based on an integer key.

```
template <typename T>
class vector
{
public:
   typedef T* iterator;
   vector();
   ...
private:
   T* buffer;
   int current_size;
   int current_capacity;
};
```

The implementation of the remaining operations is explored in programming exercises at the end of the chapter.

20.3.2 Lists

> A list supports efficient insertion into or removal from the middle of a collection. Lists can also be merged with other lists.

As you have seen in Chapter 12, lists are implemented as linked lists. This allows rapid insertions into either the front or the back of the list. By means of iterators, elements can be inserted into the middle of lists.

Of the three fundamental data structures, the list is the only one that supports constant time insertions into the middle of a collection. (The constant time efficiency assumes that the insertion point is known. If it is not known, finding a location in a linked list may require $O(n)$ steps. This is still more efficient on average than adding an element to the middle of a vector, which is always an $O(n)$ operation even if the insertion point is known.)

Lists also support a number of operations, defined in Table 3, that are not recognized by the other two containers. Some of these operations are similar to functions provided by the generic algorithms we will examine later in this chapter. For example, while sorting is a member function for a list, the same task is performed using a generic algorithm for a vector. Where this is true, it is because the list-specific member functions use a technique that is more efficient than the container-independent generic algorithm.

Table 3   List Operations Not Found in Other Container Classes

Operation	Description
merge(*list*)	Merge the current list, which is assumed to be sorted, with the argument list, which is also assumed to be sorted
remove(*value*)	Remove all instances of the given value
remove(*pred*)	Remove values for which predicate returns true
reverse()	Reverse order of elements
sort()	Place the values into sorted order
sort(*cmp*)	Place values into order using the given comparison
splice(*iterator*, *list*)	Splice the values of the argument list into the list at the given location
unique()	Remove duplicate copies of values from a sorted list
unique(*pred*)	Compare adjacent values in a sorted list using predicate; when true remove second value

20.3.3 Deque

A deque provides random access and insertions at the front and back in constant time.

The name *deque* (pronounced "deck") is short for *double-ended queue*. Like a vector, a deque is indexed. Like a list, it provides constant time insertions at either the front or the back of the collection. However, insertions into the middle are not as fast as insertions into the front or back.

A deque is not as commonly used as a vector or list, but there are situations where it is preferable:

- If you need random access into the middle of the container and also frequently add and remove elements at both ends, use a deque. If you only add and remove elements at one end, use a vector.

- If you have a long queue (with insertion and removal only at the ends), a deque is more efficient than a linked list since a deque does not maintain a link field for each element.

On the plus side, because it does not maintain a link field for each element, the deque uses less memory than a list containing the same number of elements.

The implementation of the deque is not specified by the language standard, however one approach is to use a variation on the vector. (A more complicated, but also more efficient, alternative for implementing the deque is described in [1].) As in the vector, elements are stored in an underlying array. The capacity is the size of this

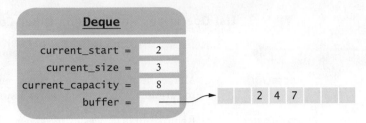

Figure 3   Internal Data Fields Maintained by Deque

array. Another integer data field holds the current size of the collection. A third data field represents the current start of the collection in the array. Unlike the vector, this starting location need not be the beginning of the array. Elements continue from the starting location one after another, as in Figure 3.

From Figure 3 it is easy to see why, as with the vector, the push_back operation is generally fast, but not always so. If no buffer reallocation is necessary, adding an element is simply a matter of incrementing an index and copying the element. It is only when the entire buffer is full that the operation requires a significant amount of time. Furthermore, push_front is also generally fast, which was not true for the vector. All that is needed is to move the starting location back one position, and place the new element at the front of the container (see Figure 4).

However, a complication is that elements can "wrap around" the end of the underlying array. The starting location could be near the end of the buffer. If the number of remaining positions is smaller than the size, the elements continue at the start of the array, as in Figure 5.

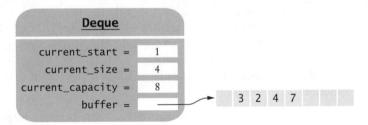

Figure 4   Deque after push_front

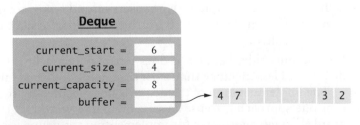

Figure 5   Deque Data Wrapping Around Internal Buffer

The need to handle the possibility of wrapping around makes the implementation of the deque slightly more complicated than the vector. This is explored in programming assignments at the end of the chapter.

ADVANCED TOPIC 20.1

Memory Allocation Traits

If you examine the template definition for the fundamental containers in the standard library, you will see that they contain an additional template argument that we have not discussed.

```
template <typename T, typename A = allocator<T> >
class list
{
    ...
};
```

The argument A is termed the memory allocator trait. (Recall from Section 16.6 that a trait is a template argument used to set policy.) The allocator is used to allocate and reclaim the memory used by the data structure, such as the nodes of a linked list and the memory blocks of a vector. In most applications, the default memory allocator will work fine and there should be little reason to replace it with an alternative. Further information on allocators can be found in [1].

20.4 Container Adapters

As you learned in Chapters 12 and 13, stacks and queues are data structures that support a FIFO (first in, first out) or LIFO (last in, first out) data access. Priority queues yield data with the highest priority. Data is placed into the container by the operation push, returned by either top (stack and priority queue) or front (queue), and removed by the pop operation.

> Stacks, queues, and priority queues are adapters built on top of the fundamental collections.

An interesting feature of stacks, queues, and priority queues in the STL is that they are not, in fact, containers in their own right, but adapters built on top of one of the fundamental containers. An adapter is a wrapper, a class that uses another container to maintain elements, but that changes the interface for the underlying class. Operations for the adapter are ultimately performed by passing a request to the class it is holding. To illustrate this, the following is a slightly simplified implementation of the class stack:

```
template <typename T, typename C = deque<T> >
class stack
{
public:
    int size() const;
    void push(const T& x);
```

```
      T& top();
      void pop();
protected:
      C values;
};

template <typename T, typename C>
int stack<T, C>::size() const
{
    return values.size();
}

template <typename T, typename C>
void stack<T, C>::push(const T& x)
{
    values.push_back(x);
}

template <typename T, typename C>
T& stack<T, C>::top()
{
    return values.back();
}

template <typename T, typename C>
void stack<T, C>::pop()
{
    values.pop_back();
}
```

The data field named `values` is the container that is holding the elements. Each stack operation is implemented by making a further call to a member function for this container. Notice that this class description has two template arguments, while the declarations in Chapter 16 used only one. This is because the second argument, the type of the actual underlying container, has a default value that depends upon the first argument. The declaration

```
stack<int> data;
```

is the same as

```
stack<int, deque<int> > data;
```

If for some reason you do not want to use the deque as the underlying container, then you can simply provide a different template argument for the second value:

```
stack<int, vector<int> > data;   // Will use a vector instead of a deque
```

Stacks work with either vectors or deques, and queues work with either lists or deques. The deque is the default for both. Notice how all operations are implemented using operations for the underlying container. The implementation of queue is a programming exercise at the end of the chapter.

Priority queues use a vector or deque to build a heap, as described in Chapter 13. The default is a vector.

20.5 Associative Containers

An associative container maintains elements in an order that is optimized for fast insertion, removal, and finding of elements.

An associative container does not keep its elements in the order in which they were inserted, but it is optimized for fast insertion, removal, and finding of elements. The STL has four associative containers: set, multiset, map, and multimap.

20.5.1 Sets and Multisets

A set is an associative container that does not allow the same element to appear more than once. If an existing element is added to a set, the second addition is ignored. A variation included in the STL, called a multiset, eliminates this restriction, instead providing a count of how many additions have occurred. Sets support the operations shown in Table 4.

To understand better the need for the set data structure, compare the use of a set to the use of a list. To determine whether or not a list contains a specific element requires in the worst case examining every value in the collection, a potentially

Table 4 Operations Provided by the Set Container

Operation	Description
set()	Construct an empty set
set(*iterator*, *iterator*)	Construct a set from the given range of values
begin()	Return iterator for set
count(*value*)	Return number of instances of value
empty()	Return true if set is empty
end()	Return ending iterator for set
erase(*iterator*)	Erase position from set
erase(*value*)	Erase value from set
find(*value*)	Return iterator for value
insert(*value*)	Insert value into set
rbegin()	Return iterator for values in reverse order
rend()	Return ending iterator for values in reverse order
size()	Return number of elements in set

costly $O(n)$ time operation. The same task can be performed with a set in $O(\log(n))$ time.

But the fast execution time of set operations is not attained without difficulty. The set is able to achieve fast execution by maintaining elements in sequence, that is, in sorted order. As you saw in Chapter 13, maintaining a collection in sorted order permits the use of efficient data structures, such as binary search trees. Because of the need to establish an ordering, sets can only be used with values that can be compared with each other. The need to order elements was not a requirement for any of the fundamental containers.

The template arguments for class set are as follows:

```
template <typename T, typename CMP = less<T> >
class set
{
    ...
};
```

The first template argument is, as always, the element type. The second argument is the strategy that will be used to compare two elements. The default value for this argument is the type of the standard less function object, which uses the < operator. (Function objects were introduced in Section 14.10.) If the element ordering is given by the < operator, you need only specify the element type of a set, not the comparator:

```
set<int> a;
set<string> b;
```

There are three ways to form sets of a new object type. Suppose we want to maintain elements of type Employee in a set. One approach is to override operator< and thereby allow the normal declaration:

```
bool operator<(const Employee& a, const Employee& b)
{
    return a.salary() < b.salary();
}

set<Employee> workers; // Will be sorted by salary
```

Another approach is to use a pointer to a comparison function.

```
bool salary_less(const Employee& a, const Employee& b)
{
    return a.salary() < b.salary();
}

set<Employee, bool (*)(const Employee&, const Employee&)>
    workers(salary_less); // Will be sorted by calling the salary_less function
```

The second template parameter is the type of the comparison function.

A third approach is to provide an explicit function object that defines the ordering. Notice that the function object is a class that implements the function call operator, and not operator<.

```
class SortByName
{
public:
    bool operator()(const Employee& a, const Employee& b) const;
};

bool SortByName::operator()(const Employee& a, const Employee& b) const
{
    return a.get_name() < b.get_name();
}
```

The class that defines the sorting algorithm can then be used as the second template argument in the set definition:

```
set<Employee, SortByName> workers; // Now sorted by name
```

20.5.2 Maps and Multimaps

Maps and multimaps associate keys with values. Keys can belong to any ordered data type.

A map is an indexed data structure, similar to a vector or a deque. However, maps differ from vectors or deques in two important respects. First, in a map, unlike a vector or deque, the indices (called the keys) need not be integers, but can be any ordered data type. For example, maps can be indexed by strings, or by real numbers. Any data type for which a comparison operator can be defined can be used as a key.

As with a vector or deque, elements can be accessed for both insertion and retrieval through the use of the subscript operator, although there are other techniques. Like a set, a map is an ordered data structure. This means that elements are maintained in sequence, the order being determined by the keys. Because a map maintains elements in order, it can very rapidly find the element specified by a given key.

There are two varieties of maps provided by the standard library. The map data structure demands unique keys. That is, there is a one-to-one association between keys and their corresponding values. A multimap, on the other hand, permits multiple entries to be indexed by the same key. The operations of the map data structure are listed in Table 5.

The map data type has three template arguments. The first two are the key and value types. The third is the comparison for keys. This third argument defaults to the simple less than comparison for keys.

```
template <typename K, typename V, typename CMP = less<K> >
class map
{
    ...
};
```

Should the user wish to use a comparison algorithm that is different from the less than operator, he or she can explicitly provide it as the third argument, just as with the set.

The implementation of the map is simplified by the fact that a map can be considered to be a set that maintains a collection of pairs. Each key/value pair is stored in

Table 5   Operations Provided by the Map Container

Operation	Description
map()	Construct an empty map
map(*iterator*, *iterator*)	Construct a map from the given range of values
begin()	Return iterator for map
count(*key*)	Return number of entries with key (always 0 or 1 for map)
empty()	Return true if collection is empty
end()	Return ending iterator for map
erase(*iterator*)	Erase value at indicated location
erase(*iterator*, *iterator*)	Erase range of values
find(*key*)	Return iterator to value with given key
insert(*element*)	Insert element, which must be a key/value pair
lower_bound(*key*)	Return iterator for first entry with given key (multimap only)
rbegin()	Return iterator for map in reverse order
rend()	Return ending iterator for map in reverse order
size()	Return number of elements in container
upper_bound(*key*)	Return iterator for past-the-end entry with given key (multimap only)
operator[*key*]	Return value associated with given key

an element of type pair. When an entry is inserted into the map, it must first be written as a pair. Iterators for maps produce a sequence of pairs. The key and value can each be accessed as part of the pair:

```
map<string, int> database;
...
map<string, int>::iterator current = database.begin();
while (current != database.end())
{
   pair<string, int> element = *current;
   cout << "key is " << element.first << ", value is " <<
      element.second << "\n";
   ++current;
}
```

20.6 Case Study: Dijkstra's Shortest Algorithm

We will use a typical application to illustrate the use of several different forms of container in one program. Imagine a bus company that runs buses in triangular routes to various cities. The routes are labeled with their associated costs in Figure 6. The problem is to determine the minimum cost to travel from one city, for example Pierre, to each of the other cities.

To begin with, we need a way to represent a destination and the cost associated with traveling there. We could use a pair for this purpose, but because we also need to override the comparison operator it is just as easy to define a new class:

```
class DistanceToCity
{
public:
    DistanceToCity(string n, int d);
    string name;
    int distance;
    bool operator<(const DistanceToCity& right) const;
};

DistanceToCity::DistanceToCity(string n, int d)
{
    name = n;
    distance = d;
}

bool DistanceToCity::operator<(const DistanceToCity& right) const
{
    return right.distance < distance;
}
```

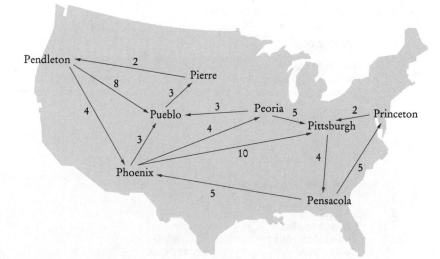

Figure 6   A Typical Directed Graph

A single instance of this class represents a destination and the cost (represented as distance) to travel to the destination. Our graph can then be represented as a type of map. The key will be a city name, and an element will be an instance of Distance-ToCity. Because some cities are origins for several different possible destinations (from Pendleton you can travel to either Phoenix or Pueblo, for example), we must use a multimap.

```
multimap<string, DistanceToCity> CityMap;
```

The class DistanceFinder will hide the details of the actual map by providing two member functions. The first adds a single link to the graph. The second takes a source node, and fills in a map of destinations and their minimal costs.

The algorithm used to find the shortest distance is known as Dijkstra's shortest path algorithm. The algorithm, named for its inventor Edsger Dijkstra, is relatively simple. A priority queue is used to represent the list of possible destinations and the cost associated with traveling to them. This priority queue is sorted on smallest distance. Initially, the source is placed in the queue with distance zero. A loop then pulls elements from the queue. If the item pulled from the queue represents a city that has not yet been visited (a fact that is determined by seeing if there is an entry in the shortest distance map with the given key) then the value and cost is placed into the map because it represents the least distance to the new city. Knowing the distance to the city, and by consulting the graph to discover the distance to get from that city to the next, new entries are then placed into the queue. Some of these may represent cities that have already been visited. If so, when they are removed from the priority queue the shortest distance map will already have an entry for the given key, and they will be ignored.

In the middle of the inner loop, as new entries are being placed into the queue, the distance from the current city to the next is found in the multimap named cities. The function lower_bound returns the first entry, while the function upper_bound returns the iterator just past the last entry. The characteristic iterator loop is used to examine each element in between.

ch20/dijkstra.cpp

```cpp
1  #include <map>
2  #include <queue>
3  #include <iostream>
4
5  using namespace std;
6
7  /**
8      A utility class representing distance to a given city.
9  */
10 class DistanceToCity
11 {
12 public:
13    DistanceToCity();
14    DistanceToCity(string n, int d);
15    bool operator<(const DistanceToCity& right) const;
16    string get_name() const;
```

```
17       int get_distance() const;
18   private:
19       string name;
20       int distance;
21   };
22
23   DistanceToCity::DistanceToCity()
24   {
25       name = "";
26       distance = 0;
27   }
28
29   DistanceToCity::DistanceToCity(string n, int d)
30   {
31       name = n;
32       distance = d;
33   }
34
35   bool DistanceToCity::operator<(const DistanceToCity& right) const
36   {
37       return right.distance < distance;
38   }
39
40   inline string DistanceToCity::get_name() const { return name; }
41
42   inline int DistanceToCity::get_distance() const { return distance; }
43
44   /**
45      A framework for finding shortest paths
46      using Dijkstra's shortest path algorithm.
47   */
48   class DistanceFinder
49   {
50   public:
51      /**
52         Sets the distance between two cities.
53         @param from originating city
54         @param to destination city
55         @param distance distance between cities
56      */
57      void set_distance(string from, string to, int distance);
58
59      /**
60         Produces map of shortest distances.
61         @param start originating city
62         @param shortest map of shortest distances from start
63      */
64      void find_distance(string start, map<string, int>& shortest);
65
66   private:
67      typedef multimap<string, DistanceToCity> CityMap;
68      typedef CityMap::iterator Citr;
69      CityMap cities;
70   };
```

```
71
72    void DistanceFinder::set_distance(string from, string to, int distance)
73    {
74        cities.insert(CityMap::value_type(from, DistanceToCity(to,
75          distance)));
76    }
77
78    void DistanceFinder::find_distance(string start,
79        map<string, int>& shortest)
80    {
81        priority_queue<DistanceToCity> que;
82        que.push(DistanceToCity(start, 0));
83
84        while (!que.empty())
85        {
86            DistanceToCity new_city = que.top();
87            que.pop();
88            if (shortest.count(new_city.get_name()) == 0)
89            {
90                int d = new_city.get_distance();
91                shortest[new_city.get_name()] = d;
92                Citr p = cities.lower_bound(new_city.get_name());
93                Citr stop = cities.upper_bound(new_city.get_name());
94                while (p != stop)
95                {
96                    DistanceToCity next_destination = (*p).second;
97                    int total_distance = d + next_destination.get_distance();
98                    que.push(DistanceToCity(next_destination.get_name(),
99                        total_distance));
100                   ++p;
101                }
102           }
103       }
104   }
105
106   int main()
107   {
108       DistanceFinder d;
109       d.set_distance("Pendleton", "Phoenix", 4);
110       d.set_distance("Pendleton", "Pueblo", 8);
111       d.set_distance("Pensacola", "Phoenix", 5);
112       d.set_distance("Peoria", "Pittsburgh", 5);
113       d.set_distance("Peoria", "Pueblo", 3);
114       d.set_distance("Phoenix", "Peoria", 4);
115       d.set_distance("Phoenix", "Pittsburgh", 10);
116       d.set_distance("Phoenix", "Pueblo", 3);
117       d.set_distance("Pierre", "Pendleton", 2);
118       d.set_distance("Pittsburgh", "Pensacola", 4);
119       d.set_distance("Princeton", "Pittsburgh", 2);
120       d.set_distance("Pueblo", "Pierre", 3);
121
122       map<string, int> shortest;
123       d.find_distance("Pierre", shortest);
124       map<string, int>::iterator current = shortest.begin();
```

```
125     map<string, int>::iterator stop = shortest.end();
126     while (current != stop)
127     {
128        pair<string, int> p = *current;
129        cout << "distance to " << p.first << " is " << p.second << "\n";
130        ++current;
131     }
132     return 0;
133 }
```

We will trace the first few steps of the algorithm in order to illustrate its behavior. Initially the starting city, Pierre, is placed into the priority queue with distance zero. Because this is the only element in the priority queue, it is removed. From Pierre the next city is Pendleton, which is placed into the queue with cost 2. Removing Pendleton, the next two possible cities are Pueblo (cost 10) and Phoenix (cost 6). Because the latter has a smaller cost than the former, it will be the element examined next. From Phoenix one can reach Pueblo (cost 9), Peoria (cost 10), and Pittsburgh (cost 16). At this point the priority queue has four items, Pueblo with cost 10 reachable from Pendleton, Pueblo with cost 9 reachable from Phoenix, Peoria (cost 10), and Pittsburgh (cost 16). The smallest entry will be Pueblo with cost 9. Notice that later when Pueblo with cost 10 is removed from the queue it will be noted that the city has already been reached, and no further processing of the city will be performed. Execution continues in this fashion until all reachable cities have been examined.

20.7 Functions, Generators, and Predicates

Many of the generic algorithms provided in the standard library require functions or function objects as arguments. A simple example is the algorithm for_each, which has the following definition:

```
template<typename Iterator, typename Action>
void for_each(Iterator current, Iterator stop, Action action)
{
   while (current != stop)
   {
      action(*current);
      ++current;
   }
}
```

Many generic algorithms take functions or function objects as arguments.

There are two template arguments. The first is used to match the pair of iterators that describe the sequence of values in the collection. Because these are tied to template arguments, the same algorithm can be used with iterators from any type of container. The second template argument matches the action, which must be a function or function object.

The following, for example, declares a list of integers, then invokes the function print_element on each value in the list:

```
void print_element(int value)
{
    cout << value << "\n";
}

list<int> a_list;
...
for_each(a_list.begin(), a_list.end(), print_element);
```

Each value from the list is passed, in turn, as an argument to the print_element function.

20.7.1 Predicates

A predicate is a function that returns a Boolean value.

A *predicate* is simply a function that returns a true/false value. This can be a bool type (the preferred technique) or, because C++ interprets integer values as Boolean, an int. In the latter case an integer zero is interpreted as false, and anything nonzero as true. (Characters and pointers can also be interpreted as Boolean values.)

The following are some example predicates. The first takes an integer value and returns true if it has a zero remainder when divided by two—that is, if the number is even. The second takes an integer that represents a year, returns true if the year is a leap year, and returns false otherwise:

```
bool is_even(int val)
{
    return 0 == val % 2;
}

bool is_leap_year(int year)
{
    if (0 == year % 400) return true; // Every 400 years is a leap year
    if (0 == year % 100) return false; // Otherwise centuries are not
    if (0 == year % 4) return true; // Every fourth year is
    return false; // Otherwise not
}
```

An example of a generic algorithm that uses a predicate is find_if. This algorithm returns the first value that satisfies the predicate, returning the second argument (which is generally the end-of-range value) if no such element is found. Using this algorithm, the following locates the first leap year in a list of years:

```
list<int>::iterator first_leap = find_if(a_list.begin(), a_list.end(),
    is_leap_year);
if (first_leap != a_list.end()) ... // Found it
```

Predicates are also often created using function objects, which we will describe shortly.

20.7.2 Generators

A generator is a function with no arguments that returns a different value each time it is called.

A *generator* is a function that takes no arguments and that returns a value, possibly a different value, each time it is invoked. The most common generator is the random number generator rand, which you learned about in Section 3.11. Each time rand is executed, it returns a new random integer value.

An example of a generic algorithm that uses a generator is the function generate. This function replaces each element in a sequence with a new value returned by the generator. The following, for example, creates a vector with ten random integers.

```
vector<int> a(10);
generate(a.begin(), a.end(), rand);
```

Suppose that instead of random integers you needed to create random integers between 1 and 100. Using the same logic as the rand_int function (Section 3.11) you could write this as follows:

```
int rand_one_hundred()
{
    return 1 + rand() % 100;
}
```

You could then use this new generator to create a vector of values between 1 and 100:

```
vector<int> b(50);
generate(b.begin(), b.end(), rand_one_hundred);
```

Generators, like predicates, are also often written as function objects.

20.7.3 Function Objects

A function object is an object of a class that implements the function call operator, and hence can be used in the same manner as a function.

A *function object* is an instance of a class that defines the function call operator. Because the class defines this operator, its objects can be invoked using the same syntax as an ordinary function. There are a number of reasons why you might want to define a function object, rather than simply writing an ordinary function. Being an object, a function object can be stored in a variable, passed as an argument, or returned as a result from a function. Function objects can be expanded inline, for more efficient execution. Most importantly, function objects can carry state. This means they can be initialized and can remember values from creation until they are used, or from one invocation to the next.

A simple example will illustrate the difference between a function and a function object. The function rand returns random integers. The function rand_one_hundred uses rand and returns random values between 1 and 100. Suppose you wanted to generalize this so that you could generate random values between *a* and *b*, where *a* and *b* are values set at run time. You know how to create a single random number in this form, using the function `rand_int`. But now you need a generator, that is, a function that takes no arguments and will return a different random value each time it is invoked. But how to set the values of *a* and *b*? The solution is to create a class, and set the values of *a* and *b* in the constructor:

```
class RandomInt
{
public:
   RandomInt(int ia, int ib);
   int operator()();
private:
   int a, b;
};

RandomInt::RandomInt(int ia, int ib)
{
   a = ia;
   b = ib;
}

inline int RandomInt::operator()()
{
   return a + rand() % (b - a + 1);
}
```

If you create an instance of this class, then each time you invoke the function call operator you will get a different random number:

```
RandomInt r10(1, 10);
cout << "one random number " << r10() << "\n";
cout << "and another " << r10() << "\n";
```

You could use this class to, for example, create a vector of random values between 1 and 10. One way would be to pass an instance of the class to the generator:

```
vector<int> a(10);
generate(a.begin(), a.end(), r10);
```

More commonly, the instance is created as an unnamed temporary, a value that will exist only for the duration of the function call, and will then be destroyed:

```
vector<int> b(10);
generate(b.begin(), b.end(), RandomInt(1, 10));
```

Predicates are also often written as function objects. Suppose you want to generalize the function even to a divisible-by-*n* predicate, where *n* is a value that is not known until run time. The following shows how this can be done:

```
class DivisibleBy
{
public:
   DivisibleBy(int in);
   bool operator()(int x);
private:
   int n;
};
```

```
DivisibleBy::DivisibleBy(int in) : n(in) {}

inline bool DivisibleBy::operator()(int x)
{
    return 0 == x % n;
}
```

With this class, the value of the divisor can be set by the constructor when an instance of the class is created. Afterward, the object can be used in the fashion of a function, and will return true if the argument is a multiple of the value. For example, imagine you had a list of integers, and you needed to find the first value after the initial element that is divisible by the initial element. You could do this as follows:

```
list<int> a_list;
...
list<int>::iterator current = a_list.begin();
DivisibleBy pred(*current); // Create the predicate
++current; // Advance to next element
list<int>::iterator ele = find_if(current, a_list.end(), pred);
if (ele != a_list.end()) // Found it
```

Another reason to use a function object in place of a function is when each invocation must remember some state set by earlier invocations. Suppose, for example, that you need a generator that will produce the sequence 1, 2, 3, and so on, returning a different integer value on each call. This sequence generator could be written as:

```
class SequenceGenerator
{
public:
    SequenceGenerator(int sv); // Can set starting value
    int operator()();
private:
    int current;
};

SequenceGenerator::SequenceGenerator(int sv)
{
    current = sv;
}

inline int SequenceGenerator::operator()()
{
    int r = current;
    current++;
    return r;
}
```

Using this class, a twenty-element vector could be initialized to the values 1 to 20:

```
vector<int> a(20); // Declare a new vector
generator(a.begin(), a.end(), SequenceGenerator(1)); // Initialize it
```

There are a number of function objects that are already defined in the standard library. These will be described in the next section, when we explore some of the generic algorithms that make them useful.

20.7.4 Standard Function Objects and Binders

The STL provides predefined function objects for arithmetic and relational operators, and a mechanism for combining function objects.

The standard library provides a number of predefined function objects in the header file `<functional>`. These can often be combined with generic algorithms to extend their utility without having to write new code.

Earlier in this chapter you encountered the binary predicate `less<T>`, which was a predicate version of the operator `<`. The class `less` is a template class, from which a function object can be produced. There are predicate versions of all the standard relational operators. These are named `equal_to`, `not_equal_to`, `greater`, `less`, `greater_equal`, and `less_equal`. One place these can be used is as the comparison arguments in the standard containers. For instance, to create a set that stores values in decreasing order rather than increasing order, you can write the following declaration:

```
set<int, greater<int> > new_set;
```

Another group of function objects encapsulate the standard arithmetic operations. These include `plus`, `minus`, `multiplies`, `divides`, `modulus`, and `negate`. These can be used with generic algorithms. For example, the default version of the `accumulate` function calculates the sum of the values in a range. But the binary function used in this algorithm need not be summation. An alternative can be explicitly passed as argument.

The `accumulate` function has four arguments: two iterators denoting a range, the default value that is returned when the range is empty, and a function that defaults to `plus<T>`. The following returns the product of a vector of integers instead of their sum.

```
int prod = accumulate(a.begin(), a.end(), 1, multiplies<int>());
```

While the use of these function objects can simplify certain tasks, it is often the case that a needed predicate or function is a minor variation of an existing function. For example, suppose you are searching for the first negative number in a collection of values. The predicate you need can be expressed as "less than zero". But this is a minor variation on "less than", with the second argument bound to zero.

This idea is termed a *binder*. In other languages the same concept is often termed a *curry*, after a logician, Haskell Curry, who investigated the use of this technique in the 1950s. There are two binders in C++. The first, `bind1st`, takes a two-argument function and binds the first argument, yielding a one-argument function. The function `bind2nd` does the same, but binds the second argument. Using these, our search for the first element less than zero could be written as follows:

```
list<int>::iterator first_negative =
    find_if(a.begin(), a.end(), bind2nd(less<int>(), 0));
```

Another category of binder is a *negator*. An example is the negator not1. This function takes a unary (one argument) Boolean predicate, and inverts the sense of the result. Finding the first value larger than or equal to zero could be written as:

```
list<int>::iterator first_positive =
    find_if(a.begin(), a.end(), not1(bind2nd(less<int>(), 0)));
```

20.8 Generic Algorithms

Generic algorithms can be used to initialize a container, transform a collection, search for a value within a container, remove elements from a container, or other tasks.

In Chapter 1 you learned that an *algorithm* is a solution technique that is unambiguous, executable, and terminating. Later, you learned that algorithms could be represented by functions, and that these functions could be generalized by parameters, so that they could work with a wide variety of values. In Chapter 16 you learned about function templates. A function template not only allows a function to work with a wide variety of values, but also allows the function to work with a variety of different *types*. A *generic algorithm* takes this concept one step further. A generic algorithm is an algorithm that has been generalized so that it can operate not only with a wide variety of values and a variety of types, but also with multiple types of containers.

Two features, *templates* and *iterators*, are key to the development of generic algorithms. Templates allow algorithms to work with multiple types. Template parameter values are matched at compile time, and do not impose any additional run-time overhead. Iterators are used to tie the algorithms to containers, and allow the same algorithm to work with many different containers.

In the generic algorithms these two features come together. In the container classes, the template arguments were generally used to represent the type of element the container was holding. For generic algorithms, the template arguments typically represent the type of iterator the algorithm will use. You saw this in the definition of the for_each algorithm:

```
template<typename Iterator, typename Action>
void for_each(Iterator current, Iterator stop, Action action)
{
    while (current != stop)
    {
        action(*current);
        ++current;
    }
}
```

Notice that neither template argument indicates the type of element being held in the container. This information, as well as knowledge of the kind of container the loop is cycling over, is only implicitly defined by the type of the iterator. As we noted at the beginning of the chapter, this makes an extremely loose connection between the generic algorithm and the container classes.

There are several dozen generic algorithms in the standard library. We will present only the most common and useful. A more complete description can be found in reference manuals for the standard library, such as [1]. In order to simplify the presentation of these algorithms, we will divide them into several categories. First you will examine algorithms that are mainly used to initialize a sequence. The algorithm generate is an example of this category. The next category is algorithms used to make transformations. A third category is those used for searching. The generic algorithms find and find_if that you have seen already are examples of this variety. Next are algorithms used to remove values from a collection. All the generic algorithms described are defined in the header file <algorithm>.

20.8.1 Initialization Algorithms

A container can be initialized by filling, copying, or generating. To *fill* means to initialize with a single fixed value. To *copy* means to duplicate values from one container in order to fill a second. Finally, to *generate* means, as we have seen, to execute a function repeatedly and use the resulting values to initialize a container.

There are two algorithms that can be used to fill a container. The first, fill, takes as arguments an iterator range and a value, and assigns each element in the range the given value. The following illustrates this function being used to initialize a ten-element vector with the value 1.

```
vector<int> a(10);
fill(a.begin(), a.end(), 1);
```

The second algorithm, fill_n, takes an iterator, an integer count, and a value. It initializes the number of positions specified by the count with the given value. The following will fill the first five positions in the previous vector with the value 2.

```
fill_n(a.begin(), 5, 2);
```

It is important to note that both of these algorithms reassign an existing element in a container. As shown they cannot be used to, for example, create new values in an empty list. When using fill_n you must be careful that the container can hold the given number of elements.

The generic algorithm copy is used to copy one collection into another. It takes three arguments, the first two specifying the range of the input container, and the third indicating the starting location for the destination container. It is assumed, but not checked, that the destination is large enough to accommodate the input.

```
vector<int> b(20);
copy(a.begin(), a.end(), b.begin()); // Will initialize first 10 positions of b
```

You have already seen how the generic algorithm generate can be used to initialize a container using a generator. The following assigns a twenty-element vector with random values between 50 and 75.

```
vector<int> c(20);
generate(c.begin(), c.end(), RandomInt(50, 75));
```

The function generate_n can be used to generate a fixed number of values. Surprisingly, there is no copy_n algorithm.

```
generate_n(c.begin(), 10, RandomInt(10, 20)); // Overwrite first 10 positions
```

In Section 20.9, you will see how the utility of the initialization algorithms can be greatly extended through the use of inserters.

20.8.2 Transformations

The category of algorithms in the standard library used to transform a sequence into a new sequence has two subcategories. Some, like reverse, change a sequence in place, overwriting the original values. Others, such as transform, are normally used to produce a new sequence.

Sorting is a common task for computer programs. The list container provides for sorting as a member function. Sets and maps are ordered already and cannot be sorted. But it is frequently necessary to sort collections stored in a vector, deque, or ordinary array. For this purpose you can use the sort generic algorithm:

```
vector<int> a(10);
generate(a.begin(), a.end(), rand); // Create list of random numbers
sort(a.begin(), a.end()); // Then sort them
```

An advantage of sorted containers is that they can be rapidly searched. We will return to this when we discuss the searching algorithms in the standard library. The sort algorithm cannot be used with lists, because it requires the use of random-access iterators, which are not provided by lists. But this is not a significant limitation because, as we have noted already, the class list provides a member function for sorting, which uses a different algorithm.

The algorithm reverse reverses the elements in a sequence, so that the last element becomes the new first, and the first element the new last, and so on. Note that lists provide this same action as a member function.

```
vector<int> a(10);
generate(a.begin(), a.end(), SequenceGenerator(1)); // Initially 1, 2, ... 10
reverse(a.begin(), a.end()); // Now 10, 9, 8, ... 2, 1
```

The algorithm random_shuffle randomly rearranges the elements in a collection. This could be useful, for example, in sorting a deck of playing cards. The arguments must be random access iterators, which means that the function is only useful with vectors, deques, or ordinary arrays. It cannot be used with lists, sets, or maps. In the playing card example, the deck might be represented by a vector of elements of type Card instead of type int.

```
vector<int> a(10);
generate(a.begin(), a.end(), SequenceGenerator(1)); // Initially 1, 2, ... 10
random_shuffle(a.begin(), a.end());
```

It is impossible to predict what the resulting sequence will be. One potential sequence is 4, 7, 2, 3, 5, 8, 9, 1, 10, 6.

There are a number of transformations that are less commonly encountered in practice. For example, the algorithm rotate provides a rotation around a point that is specified by an iterator. A *rotation* of a sequence divides the sequence into two sections, then swaps the order of the sections, maintaining the relative ordering of the elements within the sections. Suppose, for example, we have a vector containing the values 1 to 10, and we rotate around the element 7.

```
vector<int> a(10);
generate(a.begin(), a.end(), SequenceGenerator(1));
vector<int>::iterator rotate_point = find(a.begin(), a.end(), 7);
rotate(a.begin(), rotate_point, a.end());
```

The result places the values 7 to 10, the values from the rotation point to the end, at the beginning of the sequence. The values 1 to 6, the elements before the rotation point, are moved to the end. Note that the two subsequences need not be the same length, and that the rotation point argument appears between the starting and ending iterators in the argument list.

7 8 9 10 1 2 3 4 5 6

A *partition* is formed by moving all the elements that satisfy a predicate to one end of a sequence, and all the elements that fail to satisfy the predicate to the other end. For example, suppose you start with a vector of values 1 to 10, and partition using the predicate is_even:

```
vector<int> a(10);
generate(a.begin(), a.end(), SequenceGenerator(1));
partition(a.begin(), a.end(), is_even);
```

10 6 8 4 2 3 1 7 5 9

The result is that all the even values will be moved to the front, and all the non-even values moved to the end. The relative order of the elements within a partition in the resulting container may not be the same as the values in the original sequence. A second version of partition, named stable_partition, is not as fast but guarantees the ordering of the resulting values. The stable partition of the example would be 2 4 6 8 10 1 3 5 7 9. Partitioning is one step in a famous and very fast sorting algorithm termed Quicksort that you saw in Advanced Topic 11.1. You can learn more about Quicksort in any data structures textbook [2].

The transform algorithm is an example of a generic algorithm that can be used to generate a new sequence. There are two versions of this algorithm. The first takes an input sequence (specified by a starting and ending iterator), an output destination (specified by a single iterator), and a unary function. It applies the function to each element in the input to form the output. For example, by writing the following you could use this algorithm to form the squares of the first ten integers:

```
int square(int n)
{
    return n * n;
}
```

```
vector<int> a(10);
generate(a.begin(), a.end(), SequenceGenerator(1));
vector<int> b(10);
transform(a.begin(), a.end(), b.begin(), square);
```

The second form takes two sequences, and applies a binary function in a pair-wise fashion to corresponding elements. The function assumes, but does not check, that the second sequence has at least as many elements as the first. The result is placed into a third sequence, which also must have sufficient space for the result:

```
int add(int a, int b)
{
    return a + b;
}


vector<int> c(10);
transform(a.begin(), a.end(), b.begin(), c.begin(), add);
```

When we discussed the list container earlier in this chapter we noted that two lists of sorted values can be merged to form a new sorted collection. The merge algorithm generalizes this to other containers. It is assumed the inputs are sorted. It is also assumed that the target has enough space to store the values.

```
vector<int> a(10);
vector<int> b(20);
generate_n(a.begin(), 10, SequenceGenerator(1));
generate_n(b.begin(), 20, SequenceGenerator(1));
vector<int> c(30);
merge(a.begin(), a.end(), b.begin(), b.end(), c.begin());
```

One of the more unusual transformation algorithms is next_permutation. A permutation is a reordering of values in a sequence. There are, for example, six permutations of the values 1 2 3. These are 1 2 3, 1 3 2, 2 1 3, 2 3 1, 3 1 2, and 3 2 1. In general an n element sequence will have $n!$ permutations. Note that in the first permutation the values appear in increasing order, while in the last they appear in decreasing order. This idea can be generalized and used to order the series of permutations. The algorithm next_permutation transforms a sequence into the next permutation in this series. The function returns a Boolean value indicating whether there was or was not a next permutation. This allows the function to be executed in a loop, as follows:

```
vector<int> a(4);
generate(a.begin(), a.end(), SequenceGenerator(1)); // Initialize 1, 2, 3, 4
while (next_permutation(a.begin(), a.end()))
{
    cout << "Output permutation ";
    for (vector<int>::iterator p = a.begin(); p!= a.end(); ++p)
    {
        cout << *p << " ";
    }
    cout << "\n";
}
```

You can compare this loop to the recursive algorithm for permutations described in Section 10.1. A permutation of a word is termed an *anagram*. Permutations of the word *able*, for example, include *beal*, *bela*, and *bale* (as well as *aleb*, *aelb*, *aebl*, and a variety of other nonsense words). The entire series of permutations can be generated using the following:

```
char word[] = "able";
char* p = word; // Beginning iterator
char* q = word + strlen(word); // Ending iterator
sort(p, q); // Initially sort letters into increasing order
while (next_permutation(p, q))
    cout << word << "\n";
```

20.8.3 Searching Algorithms

The next category of algorithms includes those that are used to locate elements within a sequence. Rather than returning actual values from a container, the searching algorithms return an iterator that describes a position. Among other benefits, this allows these algorithms to produce a sensible result when given an empty sequence. (They will return the past-the-end iterator in this case). The first two algorithms we describe are max_element and min_element. These two algorithms generalize the standard library routines max and min, allowing them to operate with an entire collection.

```
vector<int> d(10);
generate(d.begin(), d.end(), rand); // Generate ten random numbers
vector<int>::iterator mx =
    max_element(d.begin(), d.end()); // Find largest value
vector<int>::iterator mn =
    min_element(d.begin(), d.end()); // Find smallest value
if (mx != d.end()) // Will fail for empty vector
    cout << "Largest is " << *mx << " and smallest is " << *mn << "\n";
```

Another common searching algorithm is find. This function returns an iterator that identifies the first element that matches a given element. For example, the following call returns an iterator to the first element in the list that equals 7. If there is no matching element, the past-the-end iterator is returned.

```
list<int> values;
...
list<int>::iterator p = find(values.begin(), values.end(), 7);
```

A variation on the find algorithm is find_if. This generic algorithm takes a predicate and returns the first value that satisfies the predicate. The following would return the first leap year in a list of years:

```
list<int> years;
...
list<int>::iterator first_leap =
    find_if(years.begin(), years.end(),is_leap_year);
```

A sequential search such as those used by find and find_if is inefficient for large collections. But as you learned in Chapter 11, searching can be very fast in a sorted collection. Imagine trying to discover whether or not a certain value occurs in a collection of 10,000 elements. A sequential search would require an examination of all

10,000 values. If, however, the container were sorted, a binary search would give you the same information after examining only 14 elements.

There are a number of generic algorithms that operate on sorted sequences. The function binary_search returns a Boolean value indicating whether or not the value is found in the container. The function lower_bound performs a similar task, but returns an iterator indicating where a value can be inserted so as to maintain ordering. That is, the iterator refers either to the first element larger than or equal to the search key, or to the ending iterator if no element is larger than the search key. The function upper_bound does the same, but locates the first element strictly larger than the search key. If a collection already contains multiple copies of the search key, the subrange indicated by these two values describes the section of the container in which the values are found.

```
vector<int> a(20);
generate(a.begin(), a.end(), RandomInt(1, 10));
sort(a.begin(), a.end());
if (binary_search(a.begin(), a.end(), 7))
{
    vector<int>::iterator p = lower_bound(a.begin(), a.end(), 7);
    vector<int>::iterator q = upper_bound(a.begin(), a.end(), 7);
    while (p != q)
    {
        cout << "found " << *p << "\n";
        ++p;
    }
}
```

A number of other generic algorithms treat a sorted collection as if it were a set, and produce values such as the set union, intersection, or difference. These are explored in exercises at the end of the chapter.

There are yet more algorithms that search for values of a specialized nature. We will mention some of these, but not describe them in detail. The function adjacent_find returns the position of the first element that is equal to the next immediately following element. For example, if a sequence contained the values 1 4 2 5 6 6 7 5, it would return an iterator corresponding to the first 6 value. The algorithm search is used to locate the beginning of a subsequence within a larger sequence. The function equal works with two sequences of similar size, and returns true if the associated elements are each equal, while the algorithm mismatch takes a similar pair of sequences and returns a pair of iterators that together indicate the first positions where the sequences have differing elements.

20.8.4 Removal and Replacement Algorithms

Removal algorithms can be categorized in two different ways. First, they can be categorized as to whether they operate with a fixed value or use a predicate. This is analogous to the difference between find (which searches for a specific value) and find_if (which searches for an element that satisfies a predicate). Next, there are those algorithms that work in place, changing a container directly, in contrast to those that copy their result to a new container.

These possibilities can be illustrated by the various forms of remove. The function remove_copy takes a specific value as argument, and copies to another container the sequence of the original container with all instances of the value removed. For example, suppose a is an eight-element vector with the values shown below, and b is a vector with all zero values:

a = | 1 | 2 | 3 | 2 | 4 | 2 | 5 | 6 |

b = | 0 | 0 | 0 | 0 | 0 | 0 | 0 | 0 |

An invocation of remove_copy(a.begin(), a.end(), b.begin(), 2) would copy all values *except* the 2s, resulting in the following:

a = | 1 | 2 | 3 | 2 | 4 | 2 | 5 | 6 |

b = | 1 | 3 | 4 | 5 | 6 | 0 | 0 | 0 |

Notice that the resulting sequence is smaller than the original. The function returns the iterator to b that indicates the end of the result sequence.

An invocation of remove_copy_if(a.begin(), a.end(), b.begin(), DivisibleBy(2)) would copy all values *except* those divisible by 2, resulting in the following:

a = | 1 | 2 | 3 | 2 | 4 | 2 | 5 | 6 |

b = | 1 | 3 | 5 | 0 | 0 | 0 | 0 | 0 |

You may have noticed that these examples did not change the size of the result container, b, even though only the initial portion was being used. In general, generic algorithms do not alter the size of the containers they operate on. This can be somewhat confusing when using those algorithms that operate in place, such as remove. Consider the call remove(a.begin(), a.end(), 2) using the same input as before. The purpose of this call is to remove all instances of the value 2. After this call, the sequence will be as shown below, and the value returned will be an iterator pointing to the indicated element:

a = | 1 | 3 | 4 | 5 | 6 | 2 | 5 | 6 |

Notice that the initial portion, the values before the iterator, are the desired result. The values from the iterator to the end are just the original elements in the container. To eliminate the unwanted values it is necessary to use the erase function provided by the container:

```
vector<int>::iterator p = remove(a.begin(), a.end(), 2);
a.erase(p, a.end());   // Remove the remaining values
```

The function remove_if is similar, but uses a predicate:

```
vector<int>::iterator = remove_if(a.begin(), a.end(), DivisibleBy(2));
a.erase(p, a.end()); // Collection is now 1, 3, 5
```

The following illustrates a use of remove_if in an implementation of the Sieve of Eratosthenes algorithm, which was described in Exercise P13.3. The container being manipulated is initially a collection of values from 2 to the upper bound. On each recursive call, we extract the first value from the container. A call to remove_if then eliminates all the multiples of this value. Recall that calling remove_if does not shrink the size of the container. This is accomplished by the subsequent call to erase. We then recursively call the function again, and upon its return restore the extracted value to the front.

```
void sieve(deque<int>& numbers)
{
    if (numbers.empty())
        return;
    int n = numbers.front();
    numbers.pop_front();
    deque<int>::iterator p =
        remove_if(numbers.begin(), numbers.end(), DivisibleBy(n));
    numbers.erase(p, numbers.end());
    sieve(numbers);
    numbers.push_front(n);
}

deque<int> a(100);
generate_n(a.begin(), 100, SequenceGenerator(2));
sieve(a);
```

The algorithm unique is similar to the member function of the same name in the list container. The algorithm searches for adjacent elements that are the same. When found, the second (and any successive) values are removed. The sequence 1 3 3 3 2 2 5 4 4 would, after processing by unique, become 1 3 2 5 4. Note that the values need not be sorted. As with remove, no values from the container are actually deleted, instead the iterator that refers to the end of the new sequence is returned. Any remaining values must then be removed using the erase function provided by the container.

```
list<int>::iterator p = unique(a.begin(), a.end());
a.erase(p, a.end()); // Remove the remaining values
```

The member function unique in the list container does not require the erase operation. A variation on unique, named unique_copy, makes a copy of the transformed collection, instead of making the modification in place. An example of the use of unique_copy will be shown in the case study examined in Section 20.10.

The algorithms replace and replace_if are used to replace occurrences of certain elements with a new value. For both functions, the new value is fixed when the function is invoked, and will replace all instances of the specified value, no matter how many replacements are performed. In replace the test is against a constant value, for example replacing all 3s with 4s. In replace_if the test is provided by a predicate, for example replacing all even numbers with zero:

```
vector<int> a(10);
generate(a.begin(), a.end(), RandomInt(1, 5));
replace(a.begin(), a.end(), 3, 4);
replace_if(a.begin(), a.end(), is_even, 0);
```

COMMON ERROR 20.3

Forgetting to Erase Removed Elements

Because the generic algorithms manipulate containers indirectly through iterators, they never change the size of a container they are iterating over. A common error is to assume that operations such as unique or remove will actually alter the size of the underlying container, forgetting to supply the additional erase step. For example, suppose that vector x is initialized with the values 1 2 2 3 3 3 4 4 4 4. Performing the operation

```
unique(x.begin(), x.end());
```

will leave x holding the values 1 2 3 4 3 3 4 4 4 4. The unwanted ending parts of this collection are eliminated by using a subsequent erase operation:

```
vector<int>::iterator p = unique(x.begin(), x.end());
x.erase(p, x.end()); // Now x will hold 1 2 3 4
```

20.8.5 Other Algorithms

Two counting algorithms are count and count_if. These are used to count the number of values in a collection, or to count the number of values that satisfy a predicate:

```
int three_count = count(a.begin(), a.end(), 3);
int even_count = count_if(a.begin(), a.end(), is_even);
cout << "number of 3's " << three_count <<
    ", number even " << even_count << "\n";
```

A few numeric algorithms are described in the header file <numeric>, rather than <algorithm>. An example is the function accumulate which forms the sum of a range.

```
list<double> data;
double sum  = accumulate(data.begin(), data.end(), 0);
// Now sum contains the sum of the elements in the list
```

The same function works if you have a container of strings:

```
vector<string> words;
string longword = accumulate(words.begin(), words.end(), "");
```

The last argument is the starting value of the summation. This value is returned when the range is empty.

You can optionally supply a function other than summation (which is the default)—see Section 20.7.4 for an example.

Other more specialized numeric algorithms include those that find inner products and partial sums of sequences.

20.9 Iterator Adapters

Adapters allow you to reuse algorithms for new situations. For example, through the use of an adapter, you can use an algorithm that is designed to fill a container to send data to an output stream. The following sections discuss the algorithm adapters provided by the STL.

20.9.1 Inserters

Algorithms such as `fill`, `copy`, or `generate` are normally used to overwrite the contents of an existing location. For example, the following creates a ten-element vector, then reassigns the first five locations using the function `fill_n`:

```
vector<int> a(10);
fill(a.begin(), a.end(), 1); // Fill all ten locations with 1
fill_n(a.begin(), 5, 0); // Reassign first five locations with 0
```

Even lists can be overwritten in this fashion, but only if they already have elements to be given new values by the operation. It would be useful, however, if the functionality provided by `fill`, `copy`, or `generate` could be used to create or insert new elements into the container.

> Many algorithms assign values to a container using an iterator. An inserter can be used to replace this assignment action with an insertion into a container.

In the STL this is accomplished by defining an adapter called an *inserter*. An adapter, as you saw in Section 20.4 when you encountered the stack and queue adapters, is a class that wraps around an existing class and changes the interface. A typical inserter is `back_inserter`. The `back_inserter` function takes a container (typically a vector or list) as argument. It creates a class that satisfies the iterator interface. But unlike the iterator, when a value is assigned to the inserter, instead of changing an existing location, the value is inserted into the container using the function `push_back`. An example will illustrate this. Create an initially empty list, then copy the values from the vector into the list using the following commands:

```
list<int> b;
copy(a.begin(), a.end(), back_inserter(b));
```

The copy algorithm that we normally use to copy elements from one container into another is now being used to *insert* values into an empty container using the push_back operation. The `front_inserter` does the same, but uses the operation `push_front` instead of `push_back`. (Because vectors do not support the `push_front` operation, they cannot be used to form a `front_inserter`.) Using this adapter, the following example takes an initially empty list and initializes it using twenty random values between 2 and 10.

```
list<int> c;
generate_n(front_inserter(c), 20, RandomInt(2, 10));
```

20.9.2 Stream Iterators

A stream iterator changes iterator operations into those that manipulate an I/O stream.

A stream iterator is another form of adapter that is used to convert iterator operations into I/O stream operations. An example is ostream_iterator. This class implements the operations of an iterator. However, each time the iterator is assigned, the value is not stored, it is output into the stream. This allows operations such as copy to be used to print an entire collection, as in the following:

```
copy(c.begin(), c.end(), ostream_iterator<int>(cout));
```

When executed, each value from the list c will be copied to the standard output. An optional second argument to the constructor is a string that will be used as a separator between the values:

```
copy(c.begin(), c.end(), ostream_iterator<int>(cout, "\n"));
```

Input stream iterators are similar. An input stream iterator implements the iterator interface. However, each time a value is requested from the iterator, a new element is instead read from the input stream. The sequence ends when the input stream is exhausted. The default value from the class is used to represent the end-of-sequence iterator. The following, for example, reads integer values from the standard input and copies them into a list:

```
list<int> d;
copy(istream_iterator<int>(cin), istream_iterator<int>(),
    back_inserter(d));
```

Simple file transformation programs can be created by combining input and output stream iterators and the various algorithms provided by the standard library. The following short program reads a file of integers from the standard input, removes all the even numbers, and copies those that are not even to the standard output, separating each value with a newline:

```
int main()
{
    vector<int> x;
    copy(istream_iterator<int>(cin), istream_iterator(), back_inserter(x));
    vector<int>::iterator p = remove_if(x.begin(), x.end(), is_even);
    x.erase(p, x.end());
    copy(x.begin(), x.end(), ostream_iterator<int>(cout, "\n"));
    return 0;
}
```

20.10 Case Study: File Merge Sort

Imagine that you want to make a list of all the words used in a document, such as this book. You have the input as a text file, but most words are used more than once. You want to eliminate duplicates, and list each word only once. But there is another problem; the source file is so large (or your computer memory so small)

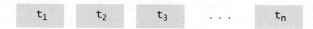

Figure 7   Temporary Files after Phase 1

that you cannot store all the words in a single container in memory. The solution is to use a variation on a technique termed a *file merge sort*.

The general approach works in two phases. In the first phase the input is divided into smaller units that can be held in memory. In this example we will read the input in blocks of 1,000 words. After the given number of words are read, the input is sorted, and repeated words removed. The remaining values are then written to a temporary file. This process is repeated until all the input has been read. (See Figure 7.) At that point the input has been divided into some number of temporary files, each of which holds a sorted sequence of words. These are stored in a queue.

Now phase two begins. The first two temporary files are opened, and their names removed from the queue. The contents of these files are merged to form a new sorted file of words. (See Figure 8.) Merging two files can be performed holding only a few elements from each collection in memory. This means the merge can be accomplished even if the collection is too large to represent in memory. But there is a problem with this. The merge can now contain repeated words. To remove these, a second pass over the input using the algorithm unique is required. This removes the repeated words. (Exercise P20.23 suggests an alternative solution to this problem.) Once the files are merged, the new temporary is added to the end of the queue, and the process repeated.

This continues until there is only a single file remaining. Because at each step two files are merged into one, this must eventually occur. At this point the final file represents the desired result, and it can be copied to the standard output.

A variety of generic algorithms are used in this application. In the first phase a generator is used to initialize a vector of words. This generator reads words from the standard input. Because there is no standard library function to do this, a function object named WordGen is written for this purpose. WordGen returns an empty string when the end of input is detected. After initialization with the list of words, the vector is sorted (using the generic algorithm sort) and duplicate words removed (using the algorithm unique). The resulting values are then copied into a temporary file. A utility function temp_name creates file names using an output stream. The copy generic algorithm is then employed to copy the vector to the temporary file. To use

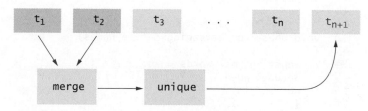

Figure 8   Temporary Files Being Merged in Phase 2

copy an output iterator is necessary. The output iterator changes the assignment operations in the copy algorithm into file output commands. This entire process repeats until the input is exhausted.

ch20/filesort.cpp

```
1   #include <algorithm>
2   #include <fstream>
3   #include <iostream>
4   #include <iterator>
5   #include <queue>
6   #include <sstream>
7   #include <vector>
8
9   using namespace std;
10
11  /**
12      Creates a temporary file name.
13  */
14  string temp_name()
15  {
16      static int file_count = 0;
17      ostringstream name;
18      name << "temp" << file_count;
19      file_count++;
20      return name.str();
21  }
22
23  /**
24      A generator for strings from standard input.
25  */
26  class WordGen
27  {
28  public:
29      string operator()();
30  };
31
32  string WordGen::operator()()
33  {
34      string in;
35      if (cin >> in)
36      {
37          return in;
38      }
39      return "";
40  }
41
42  void phase1(queue<string>& file_names)
43  {
44      const int max_words = 10;
45      WordGen wgen;
46      while (cin)
47      {
```

```
48        // Read max_words into vector, sort them, write to temp file
49        vector<string> a;
50        generate_n(back_inserter(a), max_words, wgen);
51        sort(a.begin(), a.end());
52
53        vector<string>::iterator p = unique(a.begin(), a.end());
54        a.erase(p, a.end());
55
56        string tname = temp_name();
57        file_names.push(tname);
58        ofstream out_file(tname.c_str());
59        copy(a.begin(), a.end(),
60           ostream_iterator<string>(out_file, "\n"));
61        out_file.close();
62     }
63 }
64
65 void phase2(queue<string>& file_names)
66 {
67     while (file_names.size() > 1)
68     {
69        // Merge two temp files into one
70        string t1 = file_names.front();
71        file_names.pop();
72        string t2 = file_names.front();
73        file_names.pop();
74
75        ifstream f1(t1.c_str());
76        ifstream f2(t2.c_str());
77        string tname = temp_name();
78        ofstream out_file(tname.c_str());
79
80        merge(istream_iterator<string>(f1),
81           istream_iterator<string>(),
82           istream_iterator<string>(f2),
83           istream_iterator<string>(),
84           ostream_iterator<string>(out_file, "\n"));
85
86        f1.close();
87        f2.close();
88        out_file.close();
89
90        // Now remove duplicates from resulting file
91        ifstream in_file(tname.c_str());
92        string tname2 = temp_name();
93        ofstream out_file2(tname2.c_str());
94
95        unique_copy(istream_iterator<string>(in_file),
96           istream_iterator<string>(),
97           ostream_iterator<string>(out_file2, "\n"));
98
99        in_file.close();
100        out_file2.close();
101        file_names.push(tname2);
```

```
102        }
103  }
104
105  int main()
106  {
107      queue<string> file_names;
108
109      phase1(file_names);
110      phase2(file_names);
111
112      string tname = file_names.front();
113      ifstream in_file(tname.c_str());
114      copy(istream_iterator<string>(in_file),
115          istream_iterator<string>(),
116          ostream_iterator<string>(cout, "\n"));
117
118      return 0;
119  }
```

In phase two the file names are removed from the file_names queue and the associated files are opened. The contents of the files are then merged, using the algorithm merge. Note that both of the input iterators for this algorithm are file-input iterators, while the output is a file-output iterator. The resulting file may now contain repeated elements. To eliminate these the file is opened once more, this time for reading. The generic algorithm unique_copy performs the task of eliminating repeated elements as the values are copied to the output. The resulting file is sorted and contains no duplicates. The name of this file is placed back in the queue, and the process is repeated until only one file remains.

When phase two finishes the last file contains the desired results. A final call on the generic algorithm copy is used to copy the values from this file to the standard output.

CHAPTER SUMMARY

1. The Standard Template Library, or STL, is a library of container classes.

2. Each class in the STL supports a relatively small set of operations.

3. This basic functionality can be extended though the use of generic algorithms.

4. Through the use of iterators, generic algorithms can be made to work with a variety of containers.

5. Iterators are high-level abstractions that serve the same role as pointers, but can be applied to a variety of data structures.

6. Pairs of iterators can be used to refer to a complete collection of values, or a subportion of a collection.

7. The three fundamental sequential data structures are the vector, list, and deque.

8. The vector and deque are indexed data structures; they support efficient access to each element based on an integer key.

9. A list supports efficient insertion into or removal from the middle of a collection. Lists can also be merged with other lists.

10. A deque provides random access and insertions at the front and back in constant time.

11. Stacks, queues, and priority queues are adapters built on top of the fundamental collections.

12. An associative container maintains elements in an order that is optimized for fast insertion, removal, and finding of elements.

13. Sets and multisets keep elements in sorted order.

14. Maps and multimaps associate keys with values. Keys can belong to any ordered data type.

15. Many generic algorithms take functions or function objects as arguments.

16. A predicate is a function that returns a Boolean value.

17. A generator is a function with no arguments that returns a different value each time it is called.

18. A function object is an object of a class that implements the function call operator, and hence can be used in the same manner as a function.

19. The STL provides predefined function objects for arithmetic and relational operators, and a mechanism for combining function objects.

20. Generic algorithms can be used to initialize a container, transform a collection, search for a value within a container, remove elements from a container, or other tasks.

21. Many algorithms assign values to a container using an iterator. An inserter can be used to replace this assignment action with an insertion into a container.

22. A stream iterator changes iterator operations into those that manipulate an I/O stream.

FURTHER READING

1. Nicolai M. Josuttis, *The C++ Standard Library: A Tutorial and Reference*, Addison-Wesley, 1999.

2. Timothy Budd, *Data Structures in C++ Using the Standard Template Library*, Addison-Wesley, 1997.

REVIEW EXERCISES

Exercise R20.1. In what way is an iterator similar to a pointer? In what way is it different?

Exercise R20.2. What is a past-the-end value? How is it different from a regular pointer or iterator?

Exercise R20.3. Explain how pairs of iterators are used to describe a sequence of values or a subsequence of values in a container.

Exercise R20.4. What are the different varieties of iterators? What operations are recognized by each? What type of iterator is used by a list? By a vector? By a deque?

Exercise R20.5. What is a container class?

Exercise R20.6. What does it mean to say an operation is $O(1)$? $O(n)$? $O(1)+$?

Exercise R20.7. Explain why inserting an element into the middle of a list is faster than inserting an element into the middle of a vector.

Exercise R20.8. Explain why the push_back operation with a vector is usually constant time, but occasionally much slower.

Exercise R20.9. What does the term *deque* stand for?

Exercise R20.10. What is a container adapter? How does this term apply to the stack and queue containers?

Exercise R20.11. How does a set achieve fast execution for insertions and removals?

Exercise R20.12. How is a map similar to a vector? How is it different?

Exercise R20.13. Why is a priority queue not, properly speaking, a queue?

Exercise R20.14. What is a generator? Give an example of the use of a generator in a generic algorithm.

Exercise R20.15. What is a predicate? Give an example of the use of a predicate in a generic algorithm.

Exercise R20.16. What is a function object? What can a function object do that an ordinary function cannot?

Exercise R20.17. What are the three forms of initialization provided by the generic algorithms in the standard library? Give an example of each.

Exercise R20.18. List four example transformations provided by the standard library.

Exercise R20.19. How is the search performed by find different from that performed by lower_bound? What are the requirements for the use of the first? For the use of the second?

Exercise R20.20. What is an inserter? How does an inserter change the execution of a generic algorithm such as copy?

Exercise R20.21. What is a stream iterator? How does a stream iterator change the execution of a generic algorithm such as copy?

Exercise R20.22. What is a binder? Show how to use a binder to find values in a list that are less than 10.

PROGRAMMING EXERCISES

Exercise P20.1. Section 20.3.1 described in general terms the implementation of the vector data type. Complete the implementation of the vector by providing definitions for the following operations:

- A default constructor, which should create a buffer with capacity 5 and size 0.
- A constructor that takes an integer argument, and creates a buffer with the given size and capacity.
- A member function set_capacity(int), which changes the capacity to the indicated limit, copying elements from the current buffer. If the new capacity is larger than the current size, the size remains unchanged; otherwise the size is made the same as the new capacity.
- The operation at, which returns the element at the given location in the buffer.
- The operation push_back, which adds the element to the end of the buffer, increasing the size, and invoking set_capacity to increase the capacity of the buffer if necessary.

Exercise P20.2. Section 12.3 described why the vector function push_back is said to have amortized constant time cost. Print the average number of assignments to the buffer for 50 consecutive push_back operations and an initial buffer size of 0. Repeat for 12 push_back operations and an initial buffer size of 10.

Exercise P20.3. Using the implementation of the class List you developed in Chapter 12, add the following operations:

- remove(*value*) — remove all instances of the given value
- reverse() — reverse the order of elements in the list
- unique() — remove all but the first instance of any adjacent similar values

Exercise P20.4. Add the following operations to the implementation of the List data type in Chapter 12.

- merge(*list*) — assuming both current and argument lists are sorted, merge two lists into one
- splice(*iterator*, *list*) — splice the argument list at the indicated location, removing all values from the argument list

Exercise P20.5. Building on the description of the deque presented in Section 20.3.3, implement the deque and provide a default constructor, subscript operator, and the functions push_front, pop_front, push_back, and pop_back.

Exercise P20.6. Show how a queue adapter can be written on top of the deque or list containers.

Exercise P20.7. Show how a map can be implemented using a set that maintains a collection of pairs by implementing the specialized map using strings for keys, integers for values, and the operations at(*key*), at_put(*key*, *value*).

Exercise P20.8. Many of the generic algorithms have almost trivial implementations, no more complicated than the definition of for_each given in Section 20.7. Using for_each as a model, provide implementations for the following algorithms:

  a. copy
  b. fill
  c. generate
  d. replace
  e. count
  f. find
  g. remove_copy

Exercise P20.9. Like fill, the implementation of fill_n is a loop, but instead of an iterator loop it uses a simple integer loop. Provide implementations for the following algorithms:

  a. fill_n
  b. generate_n

Exercise P20.10. The predicate versions of the algorithms have a similar structure to those you wrote in Exercise P20.8, but invoke a predicate function to test each element. Show implementations for each of the following:

  a. find_if
  b. count_if
  c. replace_if
  d. remove_copy_if

Exercise P20.11. Show how to implement find using find_if. Can you do this without writing any additional functions other than those provided by the standard library?

Exercise P20.12. The standard library does not include the function copy_if, that copies only those elements that satisfy a predicate. Provide an implementation of this algorithm, and test your implementation with both vectors and lists.

Exercise P20.13. Show how copy_if can be implemented using a combination of remove_copy_if and a negator.

Exercise P20.14. Write an implementation for reverse. You can assume the iterator arguments are bidirectional iterators; that is, they recognize both the increment operator ++ and the decrement operator --. Make certain your algorithm works for both even and odd length collections. Test your algorithm with both lists and vectors.

Exercise P20.15. Write an implementation for unique_copy. Test your implementation using both vectors and lists.

Exercise P20.16. Using the fact that iterators for vectors and deques support subscripting and subtraction (that is, *iterator - iterator* returns the number of positions between the two iterators), rewrite the binary_search function described in Section 11.7 to provide an implementation of the generic algorithms lower_bound, upper_bound, and binary_search.

Exercise P20.17. Because the sort algorithm requires random-access iterators it cannot be used with lists. This is normally not a problem, because list includes this task as a member function. Assume, however, that lists did not have this member function, and you needed to have the ability to sort a list. Show how a list can be sorted:

1. Using only generic algorithms, inserters, binders, and a temporary vector.
2. Using only generic algorithms, inserters, binders, and a temporary set.

Exercise P20.18. Write a program that produces anagrams of sentences; that is, permutations of the words in a sentence, rather than permutations of the letters in the words.

Exercise P20.19. When generated using next_permutation, the last permutation is always one in which values are listed in decreasing order. Using this observation, show how to implement what must surely be one of the *slowest* sorting algorithms ever devised.

Exercise P20.20. Write a program that that removes duplicate adjacent words from from a text file. How would this program have fixed the previous sentence?

Exercise P20.21. The following is a simplified implementation of the algorithm merge. This algorithm takes two sorted sequences, and produces a new sorted sequence containing the combined elements of each. Notice how it uses only the less than operator, and assumes that if two values are not less than each other, then they are equal.

```
template<typename T1, typename T2, typename T3>
merge(T1 first, T1 endfirst, T2 second, T2 endsecond, T3 destination)
{
    while ((first != endfirst) && (second != endsecond))
    {
        if (*first < *second)
        {
            *destination = *first;
            ++destination;
            ++first;
```

```
        }
        else if (*second < *first)
        {
            *destination = *second;
            ++destination;
            ++second;
        }
        else
        { // They are equal
            *destination = *first;
            ++destination;
            ++first;
        }
    }
    // Copy remaining values
    while (first != endfirst)
    {
        *destination = *first;
        ++destination;
        ++first;
    }
    while (second != endsecond)
    {
        *destination = *second;
        ++destination;
        ++second;
    }
}
```

Variations on this algorithm can be used to implement a set. The standard library includes four algorithms that implement the classic set operations. A set is represented with an ordered sequence in which *no element is repeated*. A set_union produces in the output a new set containing the combined elements from the two collections (with duplicates, of course, removed). A set_intersection produces only those values found in both sets. A set_difference produces those values that are members of the first set but not the second. Finally, the subset test includes returns true if every member of the first set is also found in the second. Each of these can be written as a relatively simple variation on the merge algorithm. Show the implementations of each. Test your algorithms using both vectors and lists.

Exercise P20.22. Two problems in the case study described in Section 20.10 are that (a) words are defined by white space, so that punctuation is included as part of a word (e.g., "lists." and "lists" are treated as two different words), and (b) words are case sensitive (e.g., "Lists" and "lists" are treated as two different words). Show how both of these problems can be solved by expanding the definition of the operator() in the generator WordGen.

Exercise P20.23. There are several alternative techniques that could have been used in the implementation of the case study described in Section 20.10. Investigate and implement each of the following, and test the resulting program.

1. In phase1 we could have used a list to hold the collection of words, rather than a vector. What statements would have been altered by this change?

2. In phase1 we could have used a set, rather than a vector of words. How would this have simplified the function? What tasks could then be avoided?

3. In phase2 we could have used a set_union, rather than a merge. How would this have simplified the function? What tasks could then be avoided?

4. Suppose we had used a deque, rather than a queue, for the file names. What features of the program would have been changed? What if we had used a list?

Exercise P20.24. The application examined in Section 20.10 was described as a variation on a file merge sort. A true file merge sort produces a sorted representation of the input, using each line as a separate value, and without bothering to remove duplicates. Rewrite the program to produce this effect.

Exercise P20.25. A *concordance* is an index of a text file that indicates on which line (or lines) each word appears. Write a program that produces a concordance using the same ideas as in the application described in Section 20.10. You will find it useful to read the input line by line, keeping track of the line numbers. A string input stream can then be used to break the line into words, remembering the line number with each word. In the second phase, instead of removing duplicated words, merge the line numbers for duplicated words.

Chapter 21

Features of the C++0x Standard

CHAPTER GOALS

- To introduce features that will be part of the next revision of the C++ language definition, currently scheduled for 2010

- To learn how automatic type inference, range-based for statements, and lambda expressions will simplify common programming situations

- To understand how new constructor features will aid in the development of classes with multiple constructors

- To learn about new data structures, such as the unordered_map

If you have ever attended a play written by William Shakespeare you know that the English language has evolved over time, as many of the words and phrases common in Shakespeare's day are now unfamiliar. Computer languages experience a similar process of evolution, but at a much faster rate. In this chapter, we will describe some of the more notable changes that will be forthcoming in the new C++ standard.

CHAPTER CONTENTS

21.1 C++0x Design Objectives

C++0x will extend the C++ language with new features, but will not eliminate any portion of the existing language.

The C++ language has undergone many transformations since it was first defined in 1984. For example, the original language did not have streams (Chapter 9). The template feature (Chapter 16) appeared around 1993, but the standard template library (Chapter 20) did not become part of the language until 1998. The defining document for the language was updated again in 2003. Now the language is once more undergoing a major transformation.

The term C++0x is the informal name used to describe the new standard, as the planned release date was to be 2008 or 2009. However, delays in the process now seem to indicate that the new standard will not be ready before 2010, and it will probably be a few years before all the new features become available in most implementations.

In developing the new standard, the committee applied some general guidelines:

- Maintain stability and compatibility with earlier definitions of the language, and with the older C language, whenever possible.

- Introduce new features through the standard library, rather than by adding new syntax to the base language.

- Where changes to the language are necessary, use them to facilitate systems and library design, rather than introducing new features that are useful only for specific applications.

- Increase type safety by providing alternatives to current unsafe practices.
- Improve performance of programs that use multiple threads of execution.
- Provide libraries for common programming tasks.
- Support the "zero overhead" principle, which states that the cost (for example in run-time execution) of a feature should be borne only if the feature is used.
- Make the C++ language easy to teach, learn, and understand, without removing any features or utilities needed by expert programmers.

The following sections will describe only a few of the proposed changes. Further details on other features can be found in [1] or [2].

21.2 Automatic Type Inference

The feature of the new standard likely to be used most is known as automatic *type inference*, or *type determination*. If you examine any of the code samples from Chapter 20, you will notice that type names can become exceedingly long and complicated, particularly when using qualified names for iterators combined with template classes. For example:

```
vector<int>::iterator current = a_container.begin();
map<string, int>::iterator current = database.begin();
multimap<string, DistanceToCity>::iterator p =
    cities.lower_bound(new_city.get_name());
```

> The auto keyword allows a declaration statement to infer the type from an initializing expression.

The type names needed for these declarations can be difficult for the programmer to determine, and they are unnecessary. When a variable is being both declared and initialized, the compiler can easily determine the type by examining the expression being used on the right-hand side of the initialization. In the new language standard, the keyword auto can be used in place of a type name when a variable is being both declared and initialized; the type will be inferred automatically from the initializing expression:

```
auto current = a_container.begin();
auto current = database.begin()
auto p = cities.lower_bound(new_city.get_name());
```

The resulting statements are shorter, and typically easier to understand, particularly when the variables are used only to create an iterator loop. Instead of writing:

```
for (vector<int>::const_iterator itr = my_vec.begin();
    itr != my_vec.end(); ++itr)
{
    ...
}
```

the programmer can use the shorter:

```
for (auto itr = my_vec.begin(); itr != my_vec.end(); ++itr)
{
    ...
}
```

> The decltype keyword allows a declaration statement to infer the type of a new variable from the type of an existing variable.

A related new feature is a pseudo-function named `decltype`. This function takes as argument a variable and returns the type associated with the variable. It is used in creating a variable with the same type as another:

```
map<string::int>::iterator start_point;
decltype(start_point) end_point;
    // Ensure end_point has same type as start_point
```

SYNTAX 21.1 Auto Initialization

auto *variable_name* = *initial_value*;

Example:

```
auto current = a_container.begin();
```

Purpose:

Define a new variable with a particular initial value, avoiding having to explicitly declare the type for the new variable. The type of the variable will be automatically inferred from the type of the initial value.

SYNTAX 21.2 Type Duplication

decltype(*variable_name*) *variable_name*;
decltype(*variable_name*) *variable_name* = *initial_value*;

Example:

```
decltype(start_point) end_point;
```

Purpose:

To copy the type of an existing variable to create a second variable of the same type.

21.3 Range-based for Loop

As you learned in Chapter 20, iterators are the preferred means of looping over the values stored in a container. The statement used to create an iterator loop has a typical format:

```
for (vector<int>::const_iterator itr = my_vec.begin();
   itr != my_vec.end(); ++itr)
{
```

```
    ... // Do something with the value *itr
}
```

A loop in this form requires the programmer to create a new variable to hold the iterator, and then to dereference the iterator using the * operator to obtain the current value. A new version of the for statement allows the programmer to specify the value of the container directly, and avoid the declaration of the iterator variable altogether:

```
for (int x : my_vec)
{
    ... // Do something with the value x
}
```

A range-based for loop is used to sequentially examine the values from an iterable expression, such as a collection.

The first part of the new for statement declares a variable that will be used to loop over the values in the collection. The second part of the statement, after the colon, must represent a value that can be iterated over, for example an instance of a container class. Behind the scenes, the compiler will produce an iterator variable and do the same actions as before, but the new version is much easier to read and understand.

If the loop variable is declared as a reference, then the underlying container values can be modified as well as accessed. The following, for example, will modify an array data by doubling each element.

```
int data[] = {3, 4, 6};

for (int& x : data)
{
    x = x * 2; // Double each value
}
```

SYNTAX 21.3 Range-based for Loop

```
for (type_name variable_name : iterable_expression)
{
    statements
}
```

Example:

```
for (int x : my_vec)
{
    sum = sum + x;
}
```

Purpose:

Create a new variable that will cycle through all the values of an iterable expression. Each result produced by the iteration will be assigned to the variable in turn, and the associated statement will be executed.

21.4 New Constructor Features

There are several new ways to use class constructors. The first allows constructors in a class definition to invoke other constructors for the same class. This is termed a *forwarding constructor*. The syntax is a simple extension of the syntax described in Section 5.6. That example presented a class with both a default constructor and a constructor that required explicit arguments:

```
class Employee
{
public:
    Employee();
    Employee(string employee_name, double initial_salary);
    ...
};
```

The implementation of the second constructor sets the appropriate fields:

```
Employee::Employee(string employee_name, double initial_salary)
{
    name = employee_name;
    salary = initial_salary;
}
```

> Forwarding constructors allow one constructor to invoke a second constructor, thereby simplifying the coding of classes that have multiple constructors.

With the new syntax, the default constructor can simply invoke the more general constructor using default values:

```
Employee::Employee() : Employee("no name", 1.00) { }
```

The advantage of doing so is that the statements used to initialize the newly-created object are written only once. The default constructor then calls on the code of the second constructor to perform its task. Among other advantages, if it is later necessary to modify the statements used in doing initialization, there is only one function body to change. Compare the syntax for forwarding constructors to the syntax shown for base-class constructors in Section 8.2. The only difference is that the "base class" can now be the current class, rather than a parent class.

The initializer list is a feature that can be used in several new ways in the new standard. In some situations it will be able to replace the parentheses in a constructor:

```
Employee alice{"Alice Smith", 25.5}; // Create and initialize new employee record
```

Initializer lists can also be used to create an array of object values. For example, the following creates an array of Employee records, invoking the constructor for each with the given values.

```
Employee staff[4] = {{"Fred", 12.5}, {"Sally", 32.5}, {"Sam", 19.2},
    {"Alice", 9.5}};
```

In other places, the initializer list can be used to create a new unnamed value. For example, suppose we define a function that will look up the employee record for a given name. If no employee of the given name is found, one possibility would be to create and return a default Employee object:

Syntax 21.4 **Constructor Chaining**

ClassName::*ClassName*(*expressions*) : *ClassName*(*expressions*)
{
    statements
}

Example:

```
Employee::Employee() : Employee("no name", 1.00) { }
```

Purpose:

A constructor for a class can invoke other constructors for the same class by supplying appropriate arguments. This can simplify the definition of multiple constructors for the same class.

```
Employee find_employee(string name)
{
    if (...)
    { // Look up and return the employee
    }
    return {"no name", 1.00};
}
```

Notice there is no type name or explicit constructor syntax appearing with the return statement. Because the compiler knows that the return type must be an Employee, it looks for a constructor of that type that matches the values found in the initializer list.

Another, and probably more common, use of initializer lists occurs when a class can take an arbitrary number of arguments, such as a container. It has always been possible to initialize a simple array by listing the elements in the array:

```
double data[] = {2.5, 2.7, 9.1, 7.6};
```

The statement creates a new array named data, and initializes it with the four values shown. A similar syntax can now be used to initialize standard collection objects, such as a vector:

```
vector<double> data({2.5, 2.7. 9.1, 7.6});
```

The statement creates a new vector, then inserts the four values shown. In this example, the values between the braces create a value of a new data type (termed std::initializer_list), and that value is then passed to the constructor. The constructor uses the value to initialize the vector.

You can use the new initializer list data type with your own classes. It could be used, for example, to add a new constructor to the class Matrix (Section 14.11) that initializes the values in the 3 × 3 matrix:

```
class Matrix
{
```

```
public:
   Matrix();
   Matrix(std::initializer_list<double> data);
   ...
};

Matrix::Matrix(std::initializer_list<double> data)
{
   int i = 0;
   int j = 0;
   for (double d : data)
   {
      (*this)(i, j++) = d;
      if (j >= 3)
      {
         i++;
         j = 0;
      }
   }
}
```

Note the use of the new range-based for statement to cycle over the values in the initializer list. Using this form, a new matrix can be both declared and initialized in a single statement:

```
Matrix upper_left({1.0, 2.5, 3.7, 0.0, 5.2, 3.4, 0.0, 0.0, 1.7});
```

Because std::initializer_list is an actual type, it can be used in more places than class constructors. Ordinary functions can, for example, take an initializer list as an argument. The following simple function computes the sum of the elements in the initializer list argument.

```
double sum_list(std::initializer_list<double> data)
{
   double sum = 0.0;
   for (double d : data)
      sum = sum + d;
   return sum;
}
```

The function would be invoked by passing the entire list as an argument, as follows:

```
cout << "The sum is " << sum_list({2.4, 7.6, 9.3, 1.7});
```

SYNTAX 21.5 Array Initializer List Construction

type_name variable_name[*size*] = { *expressions* };

Example:

```
Point box[4] = {{4, 5}, {6, 5}, {4, 2}, {6, 2}};
```

Purpose:

Provide constructor arguments to be used to initialize elements of an array of object types.

21.5 Regular Expressions

Regular expressions are used in a number of programming languages and tools. They are a concise yet powerful way to describe patterns.

Productivity Hints 4.2 and 4.3 introduced you to the idea of regular expressions. Regular expressions are extremely valuable in searching strings for substrings that match various patterns. Two proposed new standard types, regex and match, and a pair of functions regex_search and regex_match, can be used to perform regular expression matching. The following illustrates their use:

```
regex pattern("i[sp]+i"); // Pattern is any number of s's or p's between i's
match result;
if (regex_match("Mississippi", result, pattern))
{
    for (int i = 0; i < result.size(); i++)
        cout << "found " << result[i] << "\n";
}
```

A match is a type that records information about the matching values, such as their starting location and size. It can be indexed just like an array. The outcome of this expression would be

```
found issi
found issi
found ippi
```

Regular expressions can be used for all sorts of searching operations. The following table lists some common patterns accepted by the regular expression library. For more information on regular expressions, consult one of the many tutorials on the Internet (such as [4]).

Text	Matches Literal
^	Start of string
$	End of string
(...)*	Zero or more occurrences
(...)+	One or more occurrences
(...)?	Optional (zero or one)
[chars]	One character from range
[^chars]	One character not from range
Pat | pat	Alternative (one or the other)
(...)	Group
.	Any character except newline

21.6 Lambda Functions

A lambda function is an unnamed function used as an expression, typically one passed as argument to another function.

In Section 20.7.3 you learned about *function objects*. A function object is an instance of a class that defines the function call operator. Because the class defines this operator, instances of the class can be invoked using the same syntax as an ordinary function.

The most common use for function call operators is to create arguments for use with generic functions. For instance, Section 20.7.3 contained the following class definition:

```
class DivisibleBy
{
public:
   DivisibleBy(int n);
   bool operator()(int x);
private:
   int n;
};


DivisibleBy::DivisibleBy(int in) : n(in) {}

inline bool DivisibleBy::operator()(int x)
{
   return 0 == x % n;
}
```

The value of the divisor n can be used by the constructor when an instance of this class is created. This instance can then be used as a function, one that will return true when the argument is divisible by the given amount. For example, invoking the function find_if we can discover the first element (if any), that is divisible by 17:

```
list<int> a_list;
...
auto itr = find_if(a_list.begin(), a_list.end(), DivisibleBy(17));
if (itr != a_list.end()) ... // Found it
```

The need to construct the class DivisibleBy solely for the purpose of creating one simple function seems heavy-handed. A new alternative allows the programmer a simpler way of creating functions as expressions. These are termed *lambda functions*. The syntax for lambda functions is an empty pair of square brackets, followed by an argument list and the function body. The function has no name, and so is typically used only as an argument. The equivalent of our divisor-finding example would look something like the following:

```
auto itr =
   find_if(a_list.begin(), a_list.end(), [](int x) { return 0 == x % 17; });
if (itr != a_list.end()) ... // Found it
```

Through the use of the lambda function, there is no need to construct an explicit class just for the purpose of creating a single instance.

Another example of a lambda function being used for a common operation is the comparison function in a sort. The use of comparison functions was described in

Section 16.6. For instance, suppose you want to sort a vector of `Employee` records based on their salaries. You can do this as follows:

```
vector<Employee> data;
...
    // Sort using the given comparison
data.sort([](Employee& x, Employee& y)
    { return x.get_salary < y.get_salary; });
```

A lambda is allowed to access variables from the surrounding scope, but the names of such variables must be explicitly listed inside the square brackets that begin the lambda function. Variable names that begin with an ampersand are treated as references. This means that the variable in the lambda function is the same as the variable in the surrounding scope, so changes to one will alter both. For example, the following could be used to determine the sum of the salaries of the individuals in the previously defined vector of `Employee` records:

```
double salary_sum = 0;
for_each(data.begin(), data.end(),
    [&salary_sum](Employee& x) { salary_sum = salary_sum + x.salary; });
```

The change to the variable `salary_sum` inside the lambda function changes the variable of the same name, resulting in the sum of the salary fields being placed into the variable.

SYNTAX 21.6 Lambda Function

[] (*parameter*$_1$, *parameter*$_2$, ... , *parameter*$_n$) { *statements* }

Example:

```
[](int x) { return 0 == x % 17; }
```

Purpose:

Define a nameless function that can be used as an expression, most commonly as an argument to another function.

21.7 Controlling Default Implementations

In Quality Tip 15.2 we warned that the C++ compiler will automatically create a copy constructor if the programmer fails to provide one. Default constructors, assignment operators, and destructors will similarly be created automatically if an explicit version is not provided. In the new language standard, the programmer can indicate that they are aware of this possibility and approve of it using the `default` keyword. To do this, the body of the new class is created using an assignment operator and the keyword:

```
template class Box<typename T>
{
```

```
public:
    Box(T init) { value = init; }
    Box(const Box<T>& right) = default;
    void operator=(const Box<T>& right) = default;
private:
    T value;
};
```

In the example shown, the programmer has provided one implementation of the constructor, and marked that the copy constructor and the assignment operator should be given their default meanings. Since this would have happened in any case, this use of the keyword is really just documenting the class, to make it easier to read and understand.

An alternative is to explicitly disable certain features of a class. The keyword delete indicates that the associated function cannot be invoked, not even using a default implementation. For example, the following class definition creates a type of object that cannot be copied using either an assignment statement or a copy constructor:

```
template class Box<typename T>
{
public:
    Box(T init) { value = init; }
    Box(const Box<T>& right) = delete;
    void operator=(const Box<T>& right) = delete;
private:
    T value;
};
```

Any attempt to copy an instance of this class will be flagged by the compiler as an error.

SYNTAX 21.7 Default/Deleted Implementations

return_type ClassName::function_name(parameter$_1$, parameter$_2$, ..., parameter$_n$) = default;
return_type ClassName::function_name(parameter$_1$, parameter$_2$, ..., parameter$_n$) = delete;

Example:

```
void operator=(const Box<T>& right) = default;
void operator=(const Box<T>& right) = delete;
```

Purpose:

To indicate that the default implementation of a copy constructor, default constructor, assignment operator, or destructor should be instantiated (if the default keyword is used), or to indicate that the default implementations should not be created (if the delete keyword is used).

21.8 Hash Tables

Section 13.4 introduced the standard library data type termed the map. A map is an indexed data structure, associating every value with a key used to access the value. Strings are typically used as keys, as in this telephone database example:

```
map<string, string> telephone_numbers;
telephone_numbers["Fred Smith"] = "7347829";
cout << "Number for Fred Smith is " << telephone_numbers["Fred Smith"];
```

> Use an unordered_map, which is implemented as a hash table, if the keys in a map cannot be compared in magnitude. Otherwise use a simple map.

Up to now the map implementation used a data structure that required keys be comparable to each other using the relational operator <. The new library will include a new implementation of the map interface, termed an unordered_map, that will permit keys that are not ordered. The unordered_map is based on a data structure termed a hash table. Details concerning hash tables can be found in any data structures textbook.

21.9 Concepts

> A concept identifies the operations that must be provided by a template argument.

Quality Tip 16.1 warned that the error messages from the use of templates can be extremely confusing. This is due to the fact that errors are only discovered after a template class has been instantiated with given type arguments, and even then the error messages refer back to the template definition, and not to the point at which the specific instantiation was declared. To address this problem the new language definition includes a feature termed a *concept*. A concept is similar to a class definition, but it is used to characterize the requirements that a template argument must satisfy.

To illustrate the use of concepts, suppose you have written a simple function to sum the values of an array:

```
double sum(double array[], int n)
{
    double result = 0;
    for (int i = 0; i < n; i++)
        result = result + array[i];
    return result;
}
```

You decide you want to generalize the function, and so your first idea is to simply replace the arguments that were declared as double with a template value:

```
template<typename T>
T sum(T array[], int n)
{
    T result = 0;
    for (int i = 0; i < n; i++)
        result = result + array[i];
    return result;
}
```

Using a concept allows the compiler to send a clearer error message when invalid template arguments are used.

The problem is that if you try to instantiate this function with a type that does not understand the addition operator, the compiler will produce an error message, but that message will refer to the template class and not to the declaration. Using concepts, we can ensure that any arguments used to expand the template must know how to invoke the addition operator.

First, we need to describe the functions we need, like this:

```
auto concept Addable<typename T>
{
    T operator+(T x, T y);
};
```

SYNTAX 21.8 Concept Definition

```
auto concept ConceptName
{
    function declarations
    operator declarations
};
```

Example:

```
auto concept Addable<typename T>
{
    T operator+(T x, T y);
};
```

Purpose:

To define what operations a template argument must implement.

SYNTAX 21.9 Template Function Concept Binding

```
template <typename type_variable₁, ..., typename type_variableₙ>
requires concept₁, ..., conceptₙ
return_type function_name(parameters)
{
    statements
}
```

Example:

```
template<typename T> requires Addable<T>
T sum(T array[], int n) { ... }
```

Purpose:

To indicate that template parameters to a template function definition must satisfy certain properties.

> ### SYNTAX 21.10 Template Class Concept Binding
>
> ```
> template <typename type_variable₁, ..., typename type_variableₙ>
>    requires concept₁, ... , conceptₙ
> class ClassName
> {
>    features
> };
> ```
>
> **Example:**
>
> ```
> template<typename T> requires Addable<T>
> class Accumulator
> {
> public:
>    Accumulator() { result = 0; }
>    void add(T value) { result = result + value; }
>    T get_result() { return result; }
> private
>    T result;
> };
> ```
>
> **Purpose:**
>
> To indicate that template parameters to a template class definition must satisfy certain
> properties.

Notice that the concept is similar to a class definition. The concept itself may take
template arguments. Any functions that we require our argument to understand
must be expressed as a concept.

Next, the declaration of our original class is modified to indicate that any value
used in the template parameter must satisfy the Addable property:

```
template<typename T> requires Addable<T>
T sum(T array[], int n)
{
   T result = 0;
   for (int i = 0; i < n; i++)
      result = result + array[i];
   return result;
}
```

The satisfaction of the Addable concept can be checked at the point the template
class is used, instead of during the process of expanding the template class.

```
Employee[3] employees;
...
Employee sum = sum(employees, 3)
error: Template argument Employee does not satisfy the Addable concept
```

Once the programmer knows where the problem originates (that is, with the class
Employee and not with the sum function) this problem can then be easily solved by
providing an implementation for the required operation. The standard library will

include concepts that define the requirements for a variety of containers, iterators, and algorithms. For example, the concept `EqualityComparable` ensures that class `A` understands the equality testing operator, while the concept `Addable` ensures that class `A` understands the addition operator.

21.10 Other Minor Changes

The `>>` operator is used for right shifts and stream output. In the past, the inadvertent use of this syntax as part of a complicated template definition would result in confusing error messages:

```
vector<pair<int, real>> data; // Error
vector<pair<int, real> > data; // Ok
```

The new language standard allows the `>>` symbol to be used in this situation and the complier will detect the use and do the correct thing.

The type `long long int` (representing an integer that is at least 64 bits) has for many years been supported by most C compilers. It will now be part of the C++ language definition as well.

RANDOM FACT 21.1

Programming Languages

Many hundreds of programming languages exist today, which is actually quite surprising. The idea behind a high-level programming language is to provide a medium for programming that is independent from the instruction set of a particular processor, so that one can move programs from one computer to another without rewriting them. Moving a program from one programming language to another is a difficult process, however, and it is rarely done. Thus, it seems that there would be little use for so many programming languages.

Unlike human languages, programming languages are created with specific purposes. Some programming languages make it particularly easy to express tasks from a particular problem domain. Some languages specialize in database processing; others in "artificial intelligence" programs that try to infer new facts from a given base of knowledge; others in multimedia programming. The Pascal language was purposefully kept simple because it was designed as a teaching language. The C language was developed to be translated efficiently into fast machine code, with a minimum of housekeeping overhead. The C++ language builds on C by adding features for object-oriented programming. The Java language was designed for securely deploying programs across the Internet. The Ada language (named for Ada Augusta, the Countess of Lovelace, a friend and student of Charles Babbage who was discussed in Random Fact 11.1), was designed for use in embedded systems software.

The initial version of the C language was designed around 1972. Unlike Ada, C is a simple language that lets you program "close to the machine". It is also quite unsafe. Because different compiler writers added different features, the language actually sprouted various dialects. Some programming instructions were understood by one compiler but rejected by another. Such divergence is an immense pain to a programmer who wants to move code from one computer to another, and an effort got underway to iron out the differences and come up with a standard version of C. The design process ended in 1989 with the completion of the ANSI (American National Standards Institute) Standard. In the meantime, Bjarne Stroustrup of AT&T added features of the language Simula (an object-oriented language designed for carrying out simulations) to C. The resulting language was called C++. From 1985 until today, C++ has grown by the addition of many features, and a standardization process was completed in 1998. The new standard, when it is finally approved, will eventually supersede and replace the 1998 standard.

C++ has been enormously popular because programmers can take their existing C code and move it to C++ with only minimal changes. In order to keep compatibility with existing code, every innovation in C++ had to work around the existing language constructs, yielding a language that is powerful but still true to its roots.

Keep in mind that a programming language is only part of the technology for writing programs. To be successful, a programming language needs feature-rich libraries, powerful tools, and a community of knowledgeable and enthusiastic users. Several very well-designed programming languages have withered on the vine, whereas other programming languages whose design was merely "good enough" have thrived in the marketplace.

CHAPTER SUMMARY

1. C++0x will extend the C++ language with new features, but will not eliminate any portion of the existing language.

2. The auto keyword allows a declaration statement to infer the type from an initializing expression.

3. The decltype keyword allows a declaration statement to infer the type of a new variable from the type of an existing variable.

4. A range-based for loop is used to sequentially examine the values from an iterable expression, such as a collection.

5. Forwarding constructors allow one constructor to invoke a second constructor, thereby simplifying the coding of classes that have multiple constructors.

6. Regular expressions are used in a number of programming languages and tools. They are a concise yet powerful way to describe patterns.

7. A lambda function is an unnamed function used as an expression, typically one passed as argument to another function.

8. Use an unordered_map, which is implemented as a hash table, if the keys in a map cannot be compared in magnitude. Otherwise use a simple map.

9. A concept identifies the operations that must be provided by a template argument.

10. Using a concept allows the compiler to send a clearer error message when invalid template arguments are used.

FURTHER READING

1. www.research.att.com/~bs/rules.pdf An article about the design goals of the C++0x standard.

2. www.open-std.org/jtc1/sc22/wg21/ The web site of the C++0x standards committee.

3. www.generic-programming.org/languages/conceptcpp/tutorial/

4. www.zvon.org/other/PerlTutorial/Output A dynamic tutorial for regular expressions.

REVIEW EXERCISES

Exercise R21.1. What is the purpose of the auto keyword when used in a declaration? How does it simplify the creation of declaration statements?

Exercise R21.2. What type of values can be used in a range-based for loop?

Exercise R21.3. In Section 7.6 you learned how to use the typedef keyword to avoid long type names in declarations. Typedefs are often used to address the problem of overly long type names discussed in Section 21.2, as in the following example:

```
// Define a name to represent an iterator over city map
typedef multimap<string, DistanceToCity>::iterator cityIterator;
...
// Now use previously defined type name to create an iterator
cityIterator p = cities.lower_bound(new_city.get_name());
```

Compare and contrast the use of the auto feature to the use of typedef. Which form do you think is easier to read and understand?

Exercise R21.4. Compare the syntax for constructor chaining to the syntax used for base class initialization described in Syntax 8.2. How are they similar? How are they different?

Exercise R21.5. Describe a regular expression for the letter c followed by a vowel followed by the letter t. What three letter words would this pattern match?

Exercise R21.6. What is a lambda function? How are they commonly used?

Exercise R21.7. Hash tables are used to implement a new data structure that has an interface similar to that of the existing map container class. What feature of the new container is different from that of the map?

PROGRAMMING EXERCISES

Exercise P21.1. In Exercise P5.2 you implemented a class PEmployee that defined two constructors, a default constructor and a constructor with explicit arguments. Rewrite the class definition so that the default constructor uses constructor chaining to invoke the second constructor.

Exercise P21.2. Rewrite the function sum described in Section 14.6.1 to use template arguments and declare the iterator variables using the auto keyword.

Exercise P21.3. In Section 14.2 you investigated the implementation of a class for fractional numbers. Rewrite the constructors for that class to use constructor chaining, so that the constructors with zero or one argument simply call the constructor with two arguments.

Exercise P21.4. In Section 6.2 you examined a simple program to manipulate vectors. Rewrite the program salvect.cpp to use range-based for loops (rather than subscripts) to examine vector elements.

Exercise P21.5. Rewrite the two-argument form of the RandomInt function in Section 14.10 as a lambda function.

Exercise P21.6. Rewrite the function max, described in Common Error 16.1, to use concepts and in so doing, avoid the potential error described in that section.

Object-Oriented Design

CHAPTER GOALS

- To learn about the software life cycle
- To learn how to discover classes and member functions
- To understand the concepts of cohesion and coupling
- To learn the CRC card method
- To gain an understanding of UML class diagrams
- To learn how to use object-oriented design to build complex programs
- To study examples of the object-oriented design process

To implement a software system successfully, be it as simple as your next homework project or as complex as the next air traffic monitoring system, some amount of planning, design, and testing is required. In fact, for larger projects, the amount of time spent on planning is much higher than the amount of time spent on programming and testing.

If you find that most of your homework time is spent in front of the computer, keying in code and fixing bugs, you are probably spending more time on your homework than you should. You could cut down your total time by spending more on the planning and design phase. This chapter tells you how to approach these tasks in a systematic manner.

CHAPTER CONTENTS

22.1 The Software Life Cycle

> The life cycle of software encompasses all activities from initial analysis until obsolescence.

In this section we will discuss the *software life cycle*: the activities that take place between the time a software program is first conceived and the time it is finally retired.

Many software engineers break the development process down into the following five phases:

- analysis
- design
- implementation
- testing
- deployment

In the *analysis* phase, you decide *what* the project is supposed to accomplish; you do not think about *how* the program will accomplish its tasks. The output of the analysis phase is a *requirements document*, which describes in complete detail what the program will be able to do once it is completed. Part of this requirements document can be a user manual that tells how the user will operate the program to derive the promised benefits. Another part sets performance criteria—how many inputs the program must be able to handle in what time, or what its maximum memory and disk storage requirements are.

In the *design* phase, you develop a plan for how you will implement the system. You discover the structures that underlie the problem to be solved. When you use object-oriented design, you decide what classes you need and what their most important member functions are. The output of this phase is a description of the classes and member functions, with diagrams that show the relationships among the classes.

In the *implementation* phase, you write and compile program code to implement the classes and member functions that were discovered in the design phase. The output of this phase is the completed program.

In the *testing* phase, you run tests to verify that the program works correctly. The output of this phase is a report describing the tests that you carried out and their results.

In the *deployment* phase, the users of the program install it and use it for its intended purpose.

A formal process for software development describes phases of the development process and gives guidelines for how to carry out the phases.

When managing a large software project, it is not obvious how to organize these phases. A manager needs to know when to stop analyzing and start designing, when to stop coding and start testing, and so on. *Formal processes* have been established to help in the management of software projects. A formal process identifies the activities and deliverables of different phases and gives guidelines how to carry out the phases and when to move from one phase to the next.

When formal development processes were first established in the early 1970s, software engineers had a very simple visual model of these phases. They postulated that one phase would run to completion, its output would spill over to the next phase, and the next phase would begin. This model is called the *waterfall model* of software development (Figure 1).

The waterfall model of software development describes a sequential process of analysis, design, implementation, testing, and deployment.

In an ideal world the waterfall model has a lot of appeal: You figure out what to do; then you figure out how to do it; then you do it; then you verify that you did it right; then you hand the product to the customer. When rigidly applied, though, the waterfall model simply did not work. It was very difficult to come up with a perfect requirements specification. It was quite common to discover in the design phase that the requirements were not consistent or that a small change in the requirements would lead to a system that was

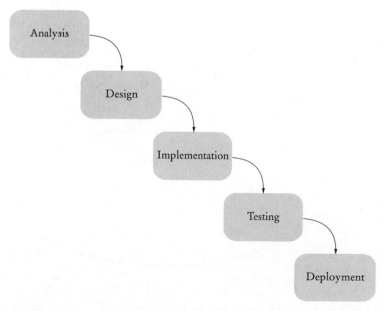

Figure 1 The Waterfall Model

both easier to design and more useful for the customer, but the analysis phase was over, so the designers had no choice—they had to take the existing requirements, errors and all. This problem would repeat itself during implementation. The designers may have thought they knew how to solve the problem as efficiently as possible, but when the design was actually implemented, it turned out that the resulting program was not as fast as the designers had thought. The next transition is one with which you are surely familiar. When the program was handed to the quality assurance department for testing, many bugs were found that would best be fixed by reimplementing, or maybe even redesigning, the program, but the waterfall model did not allow for this. Finally, when the customers received the finished product, they were often not at all happy with it. Even though the customers typically were very involved in the analysis phase, often they themselves were not sure exactly what they needed. After all, it can be very difficult to describe how you want to use a product that you have never seen before. But when the customers started using the program, they began to realize what they would have liked. Of course, then it was too late, and they had to live with what they got.

> The spiral model of software development describes an iterative process in which design and implementation are repeated.

Having some level of iteration is clearly necessary. There simply must be a mechanism to deal with errors from the preceding phase. The spiral model, proposed by Barry Boehm in 1988, breaks down the development process into multiple phases (Figure 2). Early phases focus on the construction of *prototypes*. A prototype is a small system that shows some aspects of the final system. Because prototypes model only a part of a system and do not need to withstand customer abuse, they can be implemented quickly. It is common to build a *user*

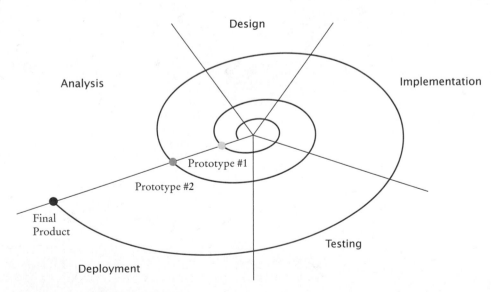

Figure 2   The Spiral Model

interface prototype that shows the user interface in action. This gives customers an early chance to become more familiar with the system and to suggest improvements before the analysis is complete. Other prototypes can be built to validate interfaces with external systems, to test performance, and so on. Lessons learned from the development of one prototype can be applied to the next iteration of the spiral.

By building in repeated trials and feedback, a development process that follows the spiral model has a greater chance of delivering a satisfactory system. However, there is also a danger. If engineers believe that they don't have to do a good job because they can always do another iteration, then there will be many iterations, and the process will take a very long time to complete.

Figure 3 (from [1]) shows activity levels in the "Rational Unified Process", a commonly used development process methodology for large projects. You can see that this is a complex process involving multiple iterations.

In your first programming course, you will not develop systems that are so complex that you need a full-fledged methodology to solve your homework problems. This introduction to the development process should, however, show you that successful software development involves more than just coding. In the remainder of this chapter, we will have a closer look at the design phase of the software development process.

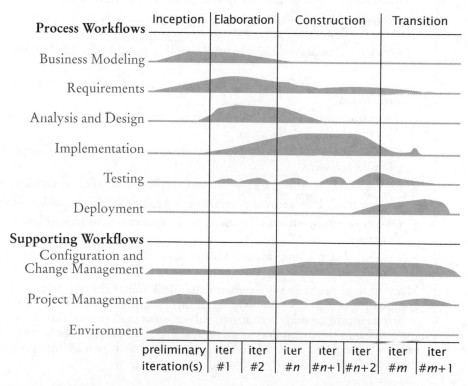

Figure 3 Activity Levels in the Rational Unified Process Methodology

RANDOM FACT 22.1

Extreme Programming

Even complex development processes with many iterations have not always met with success. In fact, there have been many reports of spectacular failures. Unsuccessful project teams followed the guidelines of their chosen methodology. They produced reams of analysis and design documentation. Unfortunately, it is very difficult for development managers to distinguish between good and bad designs. When a naive design turns out to be unimplementable, much time is wasted, often greatly surprising the managers who put their faith in the formal process.

> Extreme programming strives for simplicity by removing formal structure and focusing on best practices.

In 1999, Kent Beck published an influential book [2] on *extreme programming*, a development methodology that strives for simplicity by cutting out most of the formal trappings of a traditional development methodology and instead focusing on a set of *practices*:

- *Pair programming:* Put programmers together in pairs, and require each pair to write code on a single computer. (You may want to try this out—many programmers have found that it is surprisingly effective to have one pair of hands and two pairs of eyes on the computer.)

- *Realistic planning:* Customers are to make business decisions, programmers are to make technical decisions. Update the plan when it conflicts with reality.

- *Small releases:* Release a useful system quickly, then release updates on a very short cycle.

- *Metaphor:* All programmers should have a simple shared story that explains the system under development.

- *Simplicity:* Design everything to be as simple as possible instead of preparing for future complexity.

- *Testing:* Both programmers and customers are to write test cases. The system is continuously tested.

- *Refactoring:* Programmers are to restructure the system continuously to improve the code and eliminate duplication.

- *Collective ownership:* All programmers are to have permission to change all code as it becomes necessary.

- *Continuous integration:* Whenever a task is completed, build the entire system and test it.

- *40-hour week:* Don't cover up unrealistic schedules with bursts of heroic effort.

- *On-site customer:* An actual customer of the system is to be accessible to team members at all times.

- *Coding standards:* Programmers are to follow standards that emphasize self-documenting code.

Many of these practices are common sense. Beck claims that the value of the extreme programming approach lies in the synergy of these practices—the sum is bigger than the parts.

Extreme programming is controversial—it is not at all proven that this set of practices by itself will consistently produce good results. For many projects, the best management policy may be to combine good practices with a development process that does not overwhelm developers with unnecessary activities.

22.2 CRC Cards

In object-oriented design, you discover classes, determine responsibilities of classes, and describe relationships between classes.

In the design phase of software development, your task is to discover structures that make it possible to implement a set of tasks on a computer. When you use the object-oriented design process, you carry out the following tasks:

1. Discover classes.
2. Determine the responsibilities of each class.
3. Describe the relationships between the classes.

A class represents some useful concept. You have seen classes for concrete entities such as products, circles, and clocks. Other classes represent abstract concepts such as streams and strings. A simple rule for finding classes is to look for nouns in the task description. For example, suppose your job is to print an invoice such as the one in Figure 4. Obvious classes that come to mind are Invoice, LineItem, and Customer. It is a good idea to keep a list of candidate classes on a whiteboard or a sheet of paper. As you brainstorm, simply put all ideas for classes on the list. You can always cross out the ones that weren't useful.

INVOICE

Sam's Small Appliances
100 Main Street
Anytown, CA 98765

Item	Qty	Price	Total
Toaster	3	$29.95	$89.85
Hair Dryer	1	$24.95	$24.95
Car Vacuum	2	$19.99	$39.98

AMOUNT DUE: $154.78

Figure 4 An Invoice

Once a set of classes has been identified, you need to define the behavior for each class. That is, you need to determine what member functions each object needs to carry out to solve the programming problem. A simple rule for finding these functions is to look for verbs in the task description, and then match the verbs to the appropriate objects. For example, in the invoice program, some class needs to compute the amount due. Now you need to figure out which class is responsible for this function. Do customers compute what they owe? Do invoices total up the amount due? Do the items total themselves up? The best choice is to make "compute amount due" the responsibility of the Invoice class.

> A CRC card describes a class, its responsibilities, and its collaborating classes.

An excellent way to carry out this task is the so-called CRC card method. "CRC" stands for "classes", "responsibilities", "collaborators". In its simplest form, the method works as follows. Use an index card for each class (see Figure 5). As you think about verbs in the task description that indicate member functions, you pick the card of the class that you think should be responsible, and write that responsibility on the card. For each responsibility, you record which other classes are needed to fulfill it. Those classes are the collaborators.

For example, suppose you decide that an invoice should compute the amount due. Then you write "compute amount due" on the left-hand side of an index card with the title Invoice.

If a class can carry out that responsibility all by itself, you do nothing further. But if the class needs the help of other classes, you write the names of those collaborators on the right-hand side of the card.

To compute the total, the invoice needs to ask each line item about its total price. Therefore, the LineItem class is a collaborator.

This is a good time to look up the index card for the LineItem class. Does it have a "get total price" member function? If not, add one.

How do you know that you are on the right track? For each responsibility, ask yourself how it can actually be done, using just the responsibilities written on the

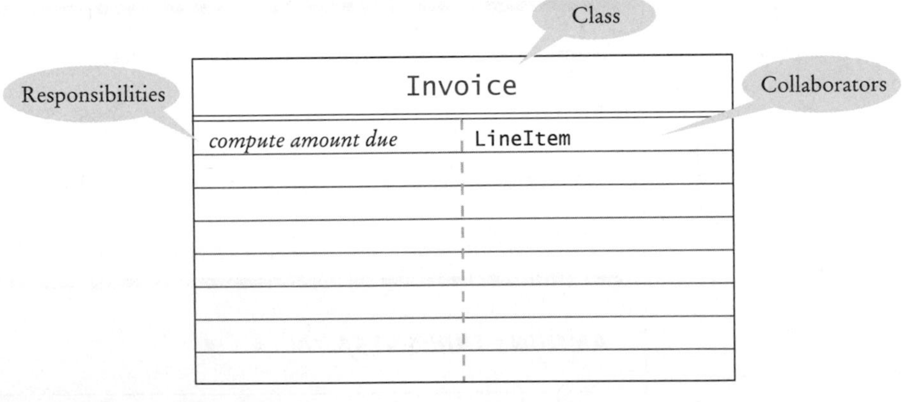

Figure 5   A CRC Card

various cards. Many people find it helpful to group the cards on a table so that the collaborators are close to each other, and to simulate tasks by moving a token (such as a coin) from one card to the next to indicate which object is currently active. Keep in mind that the responsibilities that you list on the CRC card are on a high level. Sometimes a single responsibility may need two or more member functions for carrying it out. Some researchers say that a CRC card should have no more than three distinct responsibilities.

The CRC card method is informal on purpose, so that you can be creative and discover classes and their properties. Don't be afraid to cross out, move, split, or merge responsibilities. Rip up cards if they become too messy. This is an informal process.

You are done when you have walked through all major tasks and satisfied yourself that they can all be solved with the classes and responsibilities that you discovered.

22.3 Cohesion

You have used a good number of classes in the preceding chapters and probably designed a few classes yourself as part of your programming assignments. Designing a class can be a challenge—it is not always easy to tell how to start or whether the result is of good quality.

Students who have prior experience with programming in a non-object-oriented style are used to programming *functions*. A function carries out an action. In object-oriented programming, however, each function belongs to a class. Classes are collections of objects, and objects are not actions—they are entities. So you have to start the programming activity by identifying objects and the classes to which they belong.

Remember the rule of thumb from Section 22.2: Class names should be nouns, and member function names should be verbs.

> A class should represent a single concept from the problem domain, such as business, science, or mathematics.

What makes a good class? Most importantly, a class should *represent a single concept*. Some of the classes that you have seen represent concepts from mathematics or physics:

- Point
- Circle
- Time

Other classes are abstractions of real-life entities.

- Product
- Employee

For these classes, the properties of a typical object are easy to understand. A Circle object has a center and radius. Given an Employee object, you can raise the salary. Generally, concepts from the part of the universe that our program concerns, such as science, business, or a game, make good classes. The name for such a class should be a noun that describes the concept.

What might not be a good class? If you can't tell from the class name what an object of the class is supposed to do, then you are probably not on the right track. For example, your homework assignment might ask you to write a program that prints paychecks. Suppose you start by trying to design a class PaycheckProgram. What would an object of this class do? An object of this class would have to do everything that the homework needs to do. That doesn't simplify anything. A better class would be Paycheck. Then your program can manipulate one or more Paycheck objects.

Another common mistake, particularly by students who are used to writing programs that consist of functions, is to turn an action into a class. For example, if your homework assignment is to compute a paycheck, you may consider writing a class ComputePaycheck. But can you visualize a "ComputePaycheck" object? The fact that "ComputePaycheck" isn't a noun tips you off that you are on the wrong track. On the other hand, a Paycheck class makes intuitive sense. The word "paycheck" is a noun. You can visualize a paycheck object. You can then think about useful member functions of the Paycheck class, such as compute_net_pay, that help you solve the assignment.

> The public interface of a class is cohesive if all of its features are related to the concept that the class represents.

Let's return to the observation that a class should represent a single concept. The member functions and constants that the public interface exposes should be *cohesive*. That is, all interface features should be closely related to the single concept that the class represents.

If you find that the public interface of a class refers to multiple concepts, then that is a good sign that it may be time to use separate classes instead. Consider, for example, the public interface of a CashRegister class:

```
class CashRegister
{
public:
   void add_nickels(int count);
   void add_dimes(int count);
   void add_quarters(int count);
   double get_total() const;
   ...
};
```

There are really two concepts here: a cash register that holds coins and computes their total, and the individual coins, each with their own names and values. It would make more sense to have a separate Coin class. Each coin should be responsible for knowing its name and value.

```
class Coin
{
public:
   Coin(double v, string n);
   double get_value() const;
private:
   ...
};
```

Then the CashRegister class can be simplified:

```
class CashRegister
{
public:
    void add(Coin c);
    double get_total() const;
    ...
};
```

This is clearly a better solution, because it separates the concepts of the cash register and the coins. Each of the resulting classes is more cohesive than the original CashRegister class was.

22.4 Coupling

> The "uses" or dependency relationship denotes that a class uses objects of another class.

Many classes need other classes to do their job. For example, the restructured CashRegister class of the preceding section *depends on* the Coin class. In general, a class depends on another if one of its member functions uses an object of the other class in some way.

In particular, the "collaborators" column of the CRC cards tell you which classes depend on another.

We will follow the notation of the Unified Modeling Language (UML) when drawing *class diagrams* that show the relationships between classes. In a UML class diagram, you denote dependency by a dashed line with an open arrow tip that points to the dependent class. Figure 6 shows a class diagram that indicates that the CashRegister class depends on the Coin class.

Note that the Coin class does *not* depend on the CashRegister class. Coins have no idea that they are being collected in cash registers, and they can carry out their work without ever calling any member function in the CashRegister class.

If many classes of a program depend on each other, then we say that the *coupling* between classes is high. Conversely, if there are few dependencies between classes, then we say that the coupling is low (Figure 7).

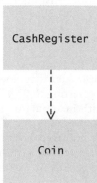

Figure 6
Dependency Relationship Between the CashRegister and Coin Classes

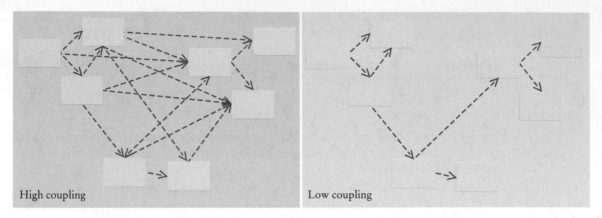

High coupling   Low coupling

Figure 7 High and Low Coupling Between Classes

It is a good practice to minimize the coupling (i.e., dependency) between classes.

Why does coupling matter? If the Coin class changes in the next release of the program, all the classes that depend on it may be affected. If the change is drastic, the coupled classes must all be updated. Furthermore, if you would like to use the class in another program, you have to take with it all the classes on which it depends. Thus, in general, you want to remove unnecessary coupling between classes.

QUALITY TIP 22.1

Consistency

In the preceding sections, you learned two criteria that are used to analyze the quality of the public interface of a class. You should maximize cohesion and remove unnecessary coupling. There is another criterion that you should pay attention to—consistency. When you have a set of member functions, follow a consistent scheme for their names and parameters. This is simply a sign of good craftsmanship.

Sadly, you can find any number of inconsistencies in the standard library. Here is an example. To set the precision of an output stream, you use the setprecision manipulator:

```
cout << setprecision(2);
```

To set the field width, you call

```
cout << setw(8);
```

Why not setwidth? And why does the setting for precision persist until you change it, while the width keeps reverting to 0? Why the inconsistency? It would have been an easy matter to supply a setwidth manipulator that exactly mirrors setprecision. There is probably no good reason why the designers of the C++ library made these decisions. They just happened, and then nobody bothered to clean them up.

Inconsistencies such as these are not a fatal flaw, but they are an annoyance, particularly because they can be so easily avoided. When designing your own classes, you should make an effort to periodically inspect them for consistency.

22.5 Relationships Between Classes

When designing a program, it is useful to document the relationships between classes. This helps you in a number of ways. For example, if you find classes with common behavior, you can save effort by placing the common behavior into a base class. If you know that some classes are *not* related to each other, you can assign different programmers to implement each of them, without worrying that one of them has to wait for the other.

You have seen the inheritance relationship between classes in Chapter 8. Inheritance is a very important relationship between classes, but, as it turns out, it is not the only useful relationship, and it can be overused.

> Inheritance (the "is-a" relationship) is a relationship between a more specialized class and a more general class.

Inheritance is a relationship between a more general class (the base class) and a more specialized class (the derived class). This relationship is often described as the *is-a* relationship. Every car *is a* vehicle. Every savings account *is a* bank account.

> Aggregation (the "has-a" relationship) denotes the fact that objects of a class contain objects of another class.

Another important relationship between classes is *aggregation*. When the objects of one class contain objects of another, then we say that the first class aggregates the other. For example, if a class Car stores objects of class Tire, then we say that there is an aggregation relationship between the classes Car and Tire. This relationship is also described as the *has-a* relationship. Every car *has* tires.

In the UML notation, aggregation is denoted by a solid line with a diamond next to the aggregating class. Figure 8 shows a class diagram with an inheritance and an aggregation relationship.

> Inheritance is sometimes inappropriately used when aggregation would be more appropriate.

It is tempting to use inheritance even if it is not appropriate to do so. For example, consider a Tire class that describes a car tire. Should the class Tire inherit from the class Circle? It sounds convenient. There are probably quite a few useful member functions in the Circle class—for example, the Tire class may inherit member functions that compute the radius, perimeter, and center point. All that should come

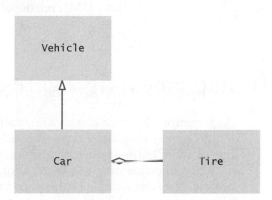

Figure 8 UML Notation for Inheritance and Aggregation

Table 1 UML Relationship Symbols			
Relation- ship	Symbol	Line Style	Arrow Style
Inheritance	———————▷	Solid	Closed triangle
Aggregation	◇———————	Solid	Diamond (at aggregating end)
Dependency	- - - - - - - ▹	Dotted	Open arrow

in handy when drawing tire shapes. Yet, though it may be convenient for the programmer, this arrangement makes no sense conceptually. Tires are not circles. Tires are car parts, whereas circles are geometric objects.

It would be more appropriate to use aggregation: A tire *has a* circle as its boundary.

> "Is-a", "has-a", and "uses" are the three key dependencies between classes.

The third key relationship between classes is the *uses* or *dependency* relationship, which you saw in the preceding section. Recall that a class depends on another if one of its member functions uses an object of the other class in some way. Aggregation is a stronger form of dependency. If a class aggregates another, it certainly uses the other class.

However, the converse is not true. If a class depends on another, it comes in contact with objects of the other class in some way, not necessarily through aggregation. Even though a physical cash register contains coins, the same need not be true for a CashRegister object. It is entirely possible that the add member function simply adds the coin value to the total without storing any actual coin objects.

> You need to be able to distinguish the UML notations for inheritance, aggregation, and dependency.

As you saw in the preceding section, the UML notation for dependency is a dashed line with an open arrow that points to the dependent class.

The arrows in the UML notation can get confusing. Table 1 shows the three UML relationship symbols that we discussed in this section.

22.6 Implementing Aggregations

Aggregations between classes are usually implemented as data fields. For example, if the Company class aggregates the Employee class, a company object needs to store one or more Employee objects or pointers.

When implementing the aggregation, you need to make two important choices. Should you store a single Employee or a vector of Employee objects? Should you store objects or pointers? To answer these questions, ask yourself two questions.

First, what is the *multiplicity* of the aggregation? The three most common choices are

- 1 : many (for example, every company has many employees)
- 1 : 1 (for example, every bank account has one owner)
- 1 : 0 or 1 (for example, every department has 0 or 1 receptionist)

For a "1 : many" relationship, you need to use a vector (or some other data structure—see Chapter 12).

Next, you need to ask whether you store objects or pointers. You must use pointers in three circumstances:

- For a "1 : 0 or 1" relationship (see Chapter 7)
- For object sharing (see Chapter 7)
- For polymorphism, to refer to an object that may belong to a base class or a derived class (see Chapter 8)

Consider a few examples. Consider a `BankAccount` class that needs to store a `Person` object, the owner of the account. (In real life, there are accounts with multiple owners, but for simplicity, we will assume that each account has only one owner.) Should you store a `Person` object, or a pointer of type `Person*`? Since multiple bank accounts can share the same owner, it makes sense to use a pointer:

```
class BankAccount
{
   ...
private:
   Person* owner;
};
```

On the other hand, consider a `Car` class that is associated with the `Tire` class. A car has multiple tires, so you would use a vector to store them. Should you store objects or pointers? A particular tire can only be a part of a single car, so you can store objects.

```
class Car
{
   ...
private:
   vector<Tire> tires;
};
```

22.7 Case Study: Printing an Invoice

In this chapter, we discuss a five-part development process that is particularly well suited for beginning programmers:

1. Gather requirements.
2. Use CRC cards to find classes, responsibilities, and collaborators.

3. Use UML class diagrams to record class relationships.
4. Document classes and member functions.
5. Implement your program.

There isn't a lot of notation to learn. The class diagrams are simple to draw. The deliverables of the design phase are immediately useful for the implementation phase. Of course, as your projects get more complex, you will want to learn more about formal design methods. There are many techniques to describe object scenarios, call sequencing, the large-scale structure of programs, and so on, that are very beneficial even for relatively simple projects. *The Unified Modeling Language User Guide* [1] gives a good overview of these techniques.

In this section, we will walk through the object-oriented design technique with a very simple example. In this case, the methodology may feel overblown, but it is a good introduction to the mechanics of each step. You will then be better prepared for the more complex example that follows.

22.7.1 Requirements

The task of this program is to print an invoice. An invoice describes the charges for a set of products in certain quantities. (Complexities such as dates, taxes, and invoice and customer numbers are omitted.) The program simply prints the billing address, all line items, and the amount due. Each line item contains the description and unit price of a product, the quantity ordered, and the total price.

```
                       I N V O I C E

    Sam's Small Appliances
    100 Main Street
    Anytown, CA 98765

    Description              Price  Qty  Total
    Toaster                  29.95   3   89.85
    Hair dryer               24.95   1   24.95
    Car vacuum               19.99   2   39.98

    AMOUNT DUE: $154.78
```

Also, in the interest of simplicity, no user interface is required. Simply use a test harness that adds items to the invoice and then prints it.

22.7.2 CRC Cards

First, you need to discover classes. Classes correspond to nouns in the requirements description. In this problem, it is pretty obvious what the nouns are:

```
    Invoice
    Address
    LineItem
    Product
```

```
Description
Price
Quantity
Total
Amount Due
```

(Of course, Toaster doesn't count—it is the description of a LineItem object and therefore a data value, not the name of a class.)

Description and price are fields of the Product class. What about the quantity? The quantity is not an attribute of a Product. Just as in the printed invoice, let's have a class LineItem that records the product and the quantity (such as "3 toasters").

The total and amount due are computed—not stored anywhere. Thus, they don't lead to classes.

After this process of elimination, four candidates for classes are left:

```
Invoice
Address
LineItem
Product
```

Each of them represents a useful concept, so make them all into classes.

The purpose of the program is to print an invoice. Record that responsibility in a CRC card:

Invoice
print the invoice

How does an invoice print itself? It must print the billing address, print all items, and then add the amount due. How can the invoice print an address? It seems best to leave this responsibility to the Address class. This leads to a second CRC card:

Address
print the address

Similarly, printing of an item is the responsibility of the LineItem class.

The print member function of the Invoice class calls the print member functions of the Address and LineItem classes. Whenever a member function uses another class, you list that other class as a collaborator. In other words, Address and LineItem are collaborators of Invoice:

Invoice	
print the invoice	Address
	LineItem

When formatting the invoice, the invoice also needs to compute the total amount due. To obtain that amount, it must ask each line item about the total price of the item.

How does a line item obtain that total? It must ask the product for the unit price, and then multiply it by the quantity. That is, the Product class must reveal the unit price, and it is a collaborator of the LineItem class.

Product	
get description	
get unit price	

LineItem	
print the item	Product
get total price	

Finally, the invoice must be populated with products and quantities, so that it makes sense to print the result. This too is a responsibility of the Invoice class. Simply list the responsibilities in the left column and the collaborators in the right column, and don't worry about how they line up.

Invoice	
print the invoice	Address
add a product and quantity	LineItem
	Product

You now have a set of CRC cards that completes the CRC card process.

There are a few points to keep in mind when using CRC cards. It is not easy to reason about objects and scenarios at a high level. It can be extremely difficult to distinguish between operations that are easy to implement and those that sound easy but actually pose significant implementation challenges. The only solution to this problem is lots of practice.

Also, don't be deceived by the seemingly logical progression of thoughts in this section. Generally, when using CRC cards, there are quite a few false starts and detours. Describing them in a book would be pretty boring, so the process descriptions that you get in books tend to give you a false impression. One purpose of CRC cards is to fail *early*, to fail *often*, and to fail *inexpensively*. It is a lot cheaper to tear up a bunch of cards than to reorganize a large amount of source code.

22.7.3 Class Diagrams

The dependency relationships come from the collaboration column in the CRC cards. Each class depends on the classes with which it collaborates. In our example, the Invoice class collaborates with the Address, LineItem, and Product classes. The LineItem class collaborates with the Product class.

Now ask yourself which of these dependencies are actually aggregations. How does an invoice know about the address, line item, and product objects with which it collaborates? An invoice object must hold the address and the items when it prints the invoice. But an invoice object need not hold a product object when adding a product. The product is turned into a line item, and then it is the line item's responsibility to hold it.

Therefore, the Invoice class aggregates the Address class and the LineItem class, but not the Product class. An invoice doesn't store products directly—they are stored in the LineItem objects. The LineItem class aggregates the Product class.

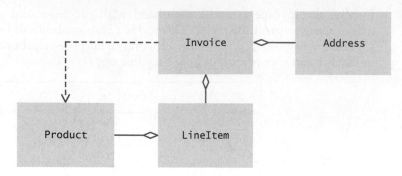

Figure 9   The Relationships Between the Invoice Classes

There is no inheritance in this example. Figure 9 shows the class relationships between the invoice classes.

22.7.4 Class and Function Comments

> Use documentation comments (with the bodies of the functions left blank) to record the behavior of classes and member functions.

The final step of the design phase is to write the documentation of the discovered classes and member functions. You could write this documentation in a word processor or a Wiki, but there is an easier alternative: Simply write C++ code with documentation comments (but without implementing any functions).

You can then run a comment extraction program to obtain a prettily formatted version of your documentation in HTML format (see Figure 10). One such program is doxygen [3].

As you produce the documentation, you will need to fill in some details. The CRC cards only contain the member functions in a high-level description. You need to come up with reasonable parameters and return types.

Here is the documentation for the invoice classes.

```cpp
/**
    Describes an invoice for a set of purchased products.
*/
class Invoice
{
public:
    /**
        Adds a charge for a product to this invoice.
        @param p the product that the customer ordered
        @param quantity the quantity of the product
    */
    void add(Product p, int quantity);

    /**
        Prints the invoice.
    */
    void print() const;
```

```
};

/**
    Describes a quantity of an article to purchase and its price.
*/
class LineItem
{
public:
    /**
        Computes the total cost of this line item.
        @return the total price
    */
    double get_total_price() const;

    /**
        Prints this line item.
    */
    void print() const;
};

/**
    Describes a product with a description and a price.
*/
class Product
{
public:
    /**
        Gets the product description.
        @return the description
    */
    string get_description() const;

    /**
        Gets the product price.
        @return the unit price
    */
    double get_price() const;
};

/**
    Describes a mailing address.
*/
class Address
{
public:
    /**
        Prints the address.
    */
    void print() const;
};
```

This approach for documenting your classes has a number of advantages. You can share the documentation with others if you work in a team. You use a format that is immediately useful—C++ files that you can carry into the implementation phase.

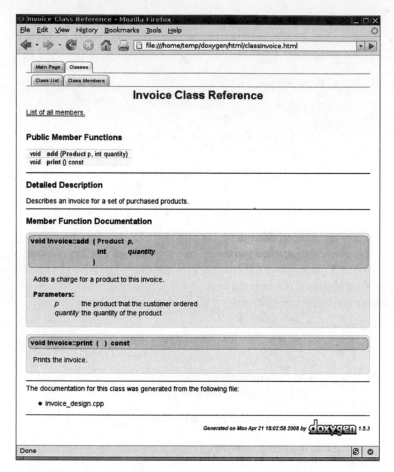

Figure 10 The Class Documentation in the HTML Format

And, most importantly, you supply the comments for the key member functions—a task that less prepared programmers leave for later, and then often neglect for lack of time.

22.7.5 Implementation

Finally, you are ready to implement the classes.

You already have the member function signatures and comments from the previous step. Now look at the aggregation relationships in the class diagram to add data fields. Start with the `Invoice` class which aggregates `Address` and `LineItem`. Every invoice has one billing address, but it can have many items. To store multiple `LineItem` objects, you use a vector. Now you have the data fields of the `Invoice` class:

```
class Invoice
{
```

```
    ...
private:
   Address billing_address;
   vector<LineItem> items;
};
```

As you can see from the class diagram, the LineItem class aggregates Product. Also, you need to store the product quantity, which leads to the following data fields:

```
class LineItem
{
   ...
private:
   Product prod;
   int quantity;
};
```

The member functions themselves are now very easy. Here is a typical example. You already know what the get_total_price member function of the LineItem class needs to do—get the unit price of the product and multiply it with the quantity.

```
double LineItem::get_total_price()
{
   return prod.get_price() * quantity;
}
```

The other member functions are equally straightforward and won't be discussed in detail.

Finally, you need to supply constructors, another routine task.

Here is the entire program. It is a good practice to go through it in detail and match up the classes and member functions against the CRC cards and class diagram.

ch22/invoice.cpp

```
 1  #include <iostream>
 2  #include <iomanip>
 3  #include <string>
 4  #include <vector>
 5
 6  using namespace std;
 7
 8  /**
 9     Describes a product with a description and a price.
10  */
11  class Product
12  {
13  public:
14     Product();
15     Product(string d, double p);
16
17     /**
18        Gets the product description.
19        @return the description
20     */
21     string get_description() const;
22
```

```
23     /**
24         Gets the product price.
25         @return the unit price
26     */
27     double get_price() const;
28 private:
29     string description;
30     double price;
31 };
32
33 Product::Product()
34 {
35     price = 0;
36 }
37
38 Product::Product(string d, double p)
39 {
40     description = d;
41     price = p;
42 }
43
44 string Product::get_description() const
45 {
46     return description;
47 }
48
49 double Product::get_price() const
50 {
51     return price;
52 }
53
54 /**
55     Describes a quantity of an article to purchase and its price.
56 */
57 class LineItem
58 {
59 public:
60     LineItem();
61     LineItem(Product p, int q);
62
63      /**
64         Computes the total cost of this line item.
65         @return the total price
66     */
67     double get_total_price() const;
68
69     /**
70         Prints this line item.
71     */
72     void print() const;
73 private:
74     Product prod;
75     int quantity;
76 };
```

```
77
78   LineItem::LineItem()
79   {
80      quantity = 0;
81   }
82
83   LineItem::LineItem(Product p, int q)
84   {
85      prod = p;
86      quantity = q;
87   }
88
89   double LineItem::get_total_price() const
90   {
91      return prod.get_price() * quantity;
92   }
93
94   void LineItem::print() const
95   {
96      cout << left << setw(28)
97         << prod.get_description()
98         << right << fixed << setprecision(2)
99         << setw(7) << prod.get_price()
100        << setw(5) << quantity
101        << setw(7) << get_total_price() << "\n";
102  }
103
104  /**
105     Describes a mailing address.
106  */
107  class Address
108  {
109  public:
110     Address();
111     Address(string n, string s, string c, string st, string z);
112
113     /**
114        Prints the address.
115     */
116     void print() const;
117  private:
118     string name;
119     string street;
120     string city;
121     string state;
122     string zip;
123  };
124
125  Address::Address() {}
126
127  Address::Address(string n, string s, string c, string st, string z)
128  {
129     name = n;
130     street = s;
```

```
131        city = c;
132        state = st;
133        zip = z;
134    }
135
136    void Address::print() const
137    {
138        cout << name << "\n" << street << "\n"
139            << city << ", " << state << " " << zip << "\n";
140    }
141
142    /**
143        Describes an invoice for a set of purchased products.
144    */
145    class Invoice
146    {
147    public:
148        Invoice(Address a);
149
150        /**
151            Adds a charge for a product to this invoice.
152            @param p the product that the customer ordered
153            @param quantity the quantity of the product
154        */
155        void add(Product p, int quantity);
156
157        /**
158            Prints the invoice.
159        */
160        void print() const;
161    private:
162        Address billing_address;
163        vector<LineItem> items;
164    };
165
166    Invoice::Invoice(Address a)
167    {
168        billing_address = a;
169    }
170
171    void Invoice::add(Product p, int q)
172    {
173        LineItem it(p, q);
174        items.push_back(it);
175    }
176
177    void Invoice::print() const
178    {
179        cout << "                    I N V O I C E\n\n";
180        billing_address.print();
181        cout <<
182            "\n\nDescription                 Price  Qty  Total\n";
183        for (int i = 0; i < items.size(); i++)
184            items[i].print();
```

```
185
186        double amount_due = 0;
187        for (int i = 0; i < items.size(); i++)
188            amount_due = amount_due + items[i].get_total_price();
189
190        cout << "\nAMOUNT DUE: $" << amount_due;
191    }
192
193    int main()
194    {
195        Address sams_address("Sam's Small Appliances",
196            "100 Main Street", "Anytown", "CA", "98765");
197
198        Invoice sams_invoice(sams_address);
199        sams_invoice.add(Product("Toaster", 29.95), 3);
200        sams_invoice.add(Product("Hair dryer", 24.95), 1);
201        sams_invoice.add(Product("Car vacuum", 19.99), 2);
202
203        sams_invoice.print();
204        return 0;
205    }
```

22.8 Case Study: An Educational Game

This example uses the optional graphics library that is described in Chapter 2.

22.8.1 Requirements

Your task is to write a game program that teaches your baby sister how to read the clock (see Figure 11). The game should do the following: randomly generate a time, draw a clock face with that time, and ask the player to type in the time. The player

Figure 11
The Screen Display of
the Clock Program

gets two tries before the game displays the correct time. Whenever the player gets the right answer, the score increases by one point. There are four levels of difficulty. Level 1 teaches full hours, level 2 teaches 15-minute intervals, level 3 teaches 5-minute intervals, and level 4 displays all times. When the player has reached a score of five points on one level, the game advances to the next level.

At the beginning, the game asks for the player's name and the desired starting level. After every round, the player is asked whether he or she wants to play more. The game ends when the player decides to quit.

22.8.2 CRC Cards

What classes can you find? You need to look at nouns in the problem description; here are several:

```
Player
Clock
Time
Level
Game
Round
```

Not all nouns that you find make useful objects. For example, the Level is just an integer between 1 and 4; it doesn't really do anything. At this time, the best course of action is to leave it in the list of possible classes and to abandon it later if it turns out not to have any useful actions.

Start with a simple class: the Clock class. The clock object has one important responsibility: to draw the clock face.

Clock		
draw		

When a clock draws itself, it must draw the hour and minute hands to show the current times. To get the hours and minutes of the current time, it must collaborate with the Time class.

How does the clock know what time it is? You need to tell it:

Clock	
draw	Time
set time	

Next, take up the Time class. You need to get the hours and minutes of a given time, and be able to tell when two times are the same.

Time	
get hours and minutes	
check if equal to another	
	Time *object*

Now look at the player. A player has a name, a level, and a score. Every time the player gets a correct answer, the score must be incremented.

Player	
increment score	

After every five score increments, the level is incremented as well. Let the *increment score* function take care of that. Of course, then you must find out what the current level is.

Player
increment score
get level

Now you are in a fairly typical situation. You have a mess of classes, each of which seems to do interesting things, but you don't know how they will all work together.

A good plan is to introduce a class that represents the entire program—in our case, the game:

Game
play

Unlike the previously discovered functions, it is not at all obvious how the play function works. You must use the process of stepwise refinement, which we discussed in Chapter 4. What does it mean to play the game? The game starts by asking the player's name and level. Then the player plays a round, the game asks whether the player wants to play again, and so on.

Play the Game:

```
read player information
do
{
    play a round
    ask whether player wants to play again
}
while (player wants to play again);
```

A couple of new actions are required: to get player information and to play a round. Add *read player information* to the Game class:

Game
play
read player information

Now, how about *play a round*? Should the Game class or the Player class implement this function? What is involved in playing a round? You must make a time, depending on the selected level. You must draw the clock, ask for input, check whether the input is correct, play again if it is not, and increment the player's score if it is.

The responsibility can be assigned either way. In this discussion, let the Game class take care of playing the round. It informs the player about the game progress, which makes the Player class a collaborator. Note that the game must draw a clock face when playing a round, so Clock is a collaborator. Furthermore, the game generates Time objects, which makes Time another collaborator.

Game	
play	Player
read player information	Clock
play round	Time

So far there is no need for the classes Round and Level that were tentatively noted in the class discovery step, so do not implement them.

22.8.3 Class Diagrams

From the collaborator columns of the CRC cards, you can determine that the Game class uses the Player, Clock, and Time classes, and the Clock class uses the Time class.

Next, ask yourself whether any of these dependencies are actually aggregations. Does a Game object contain a Player object? Or do the Game member functions only

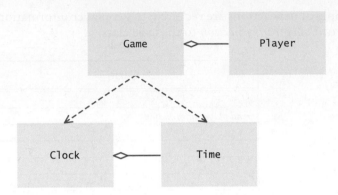

Figure 12   The Relationships Between the Clock Game Classes

use local or parameter variables of type Player? Since the same player object must be manipulated during several rounds, one can't just construct local player objects in each round. That is, there must be a Player object that persists during the lifetime of the game. Conceivably, that Player object might be passed as a parameter to the *play round* function, but that seems far-fetched. It makes much more sense for the Game object to have a data field of type Player, to initialize that object in the "read player information" function, and to have the *play round* function modify its state. Thus, you may conclude that the Player class is associated with the Game class.

On the other hand, there is no pressing need for the Clock and Time classes to be aggregated with the Game class. The *play round* function can construct local Clock and Time objects.

Since the Clock CRC card shows a *set time* function, you can conclude that the Time class is aggregated with the Clock class.

Figure 12 shows the class diagram for the clock game classes.

22.8.4 Class and Function Comments

Translating the responsibilities from the CRC cards to member functions is straightforward. Following are the commented Clock, Player, and Game classes.

```
/**
    A clock that can draw its face.
*/
class Clock
{
public:
    /**
        Sets the current time.
        @param t the time to set
    */
    void set_time(Time t);
```

```
    /**
        Draws the clock face, with tick marks and hands.
    */
    void draw() const;
};

/**
    The player of the clock game.
*/
class Player
{
public:
    /**
        Increments the score. Moves to next level if current
        level complete.
    */
    void increment_score();

    /**
        Gets the current level.
        @return the level
    */
    int get_level() const;
};

/**
    The clock game.
*/
class Game
{
public:
    /**
        Plays the game while the player wants to continue.
    */
    void play();

    /**
        Reads player name and level.
    */
    void read_player_information();

    /**
        Plays a round, with up to two guesses.
    */
    void play_round();
};
```

Now turn to the Time class. You will need the following functionality:

- Get the hours and minutes of a Time object.
- Check whether two Time objects are identical.

This class seems to be similar to the Time class that is a part of the library of this book (see Chapter 2). Rather than reinventing the wheel, determine whether you can use this class. That class stores seconds in addition to hours and minutes. Of course, you can set the seconds to zero. To see whether two times are identical, check whether there are zero seconds from the first to the second time; that is, test whether `time1.seconds_from(time2)` is 0. It is, so you can use the library class and don't need to write a new one.

Now you have a set of classes, with reasonably complete interfaces. Is the design complete? In practice, that is not always an easy question to answer. It is quite common to find during the implementation phase that a particular task cannot be carried out with the interface functions. Then one needs to go back and revise the classes and interfaces.

22.8.5 Implementation

Start with the `Clock` class. The clock must remember the time that is set with `set_time` so that it can draw the clock face. It must also remember where to draw the clock. Store the current time, the center point, and the radius of the clock face.

```
class Clock
{
    ...
private:
    Time current_time;
    Point center;
    double radius;
};
```

Here is the `set_time` function:

```
void Clock::set_time(Time t)
{
    current_time = t;
}
```

The draw function is more complex. Use the process of stepwise refinement to simplify it.

Draw the Clock:

> *draw a circle*
> *draw the hour "ticks"*
> *draw the minute "ticks"*
> *draw the hour hand*
> *draw the minute hand*

You need a function to draw a tick and a function to draw a hand. Each of these functions takes two parameters: the angle of the line segment to draw and its length. For convenience, the angle is measured clockwise, in multiples of six degrees (the angle between two adjacent minute ticks), starting from the 12 o'clock position.

```
void Clock::draw_tick(double angle, double length) const
{
```

```
    double alpha = PI / 2 - 6 * angle * PI / 180;
    Point from(
        center.get_x() + cos(alpha) * radius * (1 - length),
        center.get_y() + sin(alpha) * radius * (1 - length));
    Point to(center.get_x() + cos(alpha) * radius,
        center.get_y() + sin(alpha) * radius);
    cwin << Line(from, to);
}

void Clock::draw_hand(double angle, double length) const
{
    double alpha = PI / 2 - 6 * angle * PI / 180;
    Point from = center;
    Point to(center.get_x() + cos(alpha) * radius * length,
        center.get_y() + sin(alpha) * radius * length);
    cwin << Line(from, to);
}
```

Then the function to draw the clock face is relatively simple:

```
void Clock::draw() const
{
    cwin << Circle(center, radius);
    const double HOUR_TICK_LENGTH = 0.2;
    const double MINUTE_TICK_LENGTH = 0.1;
    const double HOUR_HAND_LENGTH = 0.6;
    const double MINUTE_HAND_LENGTH = 0.75;
    for (int i = 0; i < 12; i++)
    {
        draw_tick(i * 5, HOUR_TICK_LENGTH);
        for (int j = 1; j <= 4; j++)
            draw_tick(i * 5 + j, MINUTE_TICK_LENGTH);
    }

    draw_hand(current_time.get_minutes(), MINUTE_HAND_LENGTH);
    draw_hand((current_time.get_hours() +
        current_time.get_minutes() / 60.0) * 5,
        HOUR_HAND_LENGTH);
}
```

The draw function illustrates an important point. Object-oriented design does not replace the process of stepwise refinement. It is quite common to have member functions that are complex and need to be refined further. Because the helper functions draw_tick and draw_hand are only meant to be called by draw, they should be placed in the private section of the class.

The Clock constructor constructs a clock from a given center and radius:

```
Clock::Clock(Point c, double r)
{
    center = c;
    radius = r;
}
```

Now we turn to the Player class. A player needs to store the current level and score:

```
class Player
{
```

```
    ...
private:
    int level;
    int score;
};
```

The constructor and the get_level function are straightforward—see the code at the end of this section.

The increment_score function is more interesting. Of course, it increments the score. When the score becomes a multiple of five, and the level is less than four, the level is also incremented:

```
void Player::increment_score()
{
    score++;
    if (score % 5 == 0 and level < 4)
        level++;
}
```

The last class to consider is the Game class. What data fields does the game need? It needs a player. How about the clock and the time? Each round generates a new random time, and the time is not needed in the other functions. Therefore, do not make the clock and time data fields of the Game class. They will just be local variables of the play_round function.

You already saw the pseudocode for the play procedure. Here is the full C++ code:

```
void Game::play()
{
    rand_seed();
    read_player_information();
    string response;
    do
    {
        play_round();
        response = cwin.get_string(
            "Do you want to play again? (y/n)");
    }
    while (response == "y");
}
```

Here is the read_player_information function:

```
void Game::read_player_information()
{
    string name = cwin.get_string("What is your name?");
    int initial_level;
    do
    {
        initial_level = cwin.get_int(
            "At what level do you want to start? (1-4)");
    }
    while (initial_level < 1 || initial_level > 4);
    player = Player(name, initial_level);
}
```

Not unexpectedly, the play_round function is the hardest. Here is a refinement:

Play a Round:

make a random time
show the time
get a guess
`if` *(guess is not correct)*
  get a guess
`if` *(guess is correct)*
`{`

  congratulate player
  increment score

`}`
`else`
  give correct answer

The *random time* depends on the level. If the level is 1, then the time must be a full hour—that is, a multiple of 60. If the level is 2, then the number of minutes is a multiple of 15. If the level is 3, then the number of minutes is a multiple of 5. Otherwise, it can be any number.

```
Time Game::random_time()
{
   int level = player.get_level();

   int minutes;
   if (level == 1) minutes = 0;
   else if (level == 2) minutes = 15 * rand_int(0, 3);
   else if (level == 3) minutes = 5 * rand_int(0, 11);
   else minutes = rand_int(0, 59);
   int hours = rand_int(1, 12);
   return Time(hours, minutes, 0);
}
```

Since *get a guess* occurs twice, make that into a separate function:

```
Time Game::get_guess()
{
   int hours;
   do
   {
      hours = cwin.get_int("Please enter hours: (1-12)");
   }
   while (hours < 1 || hours > 12);
   int minutes;
   do
   {
      minutes = cwin.get_int("Please enter minutes: (0-59)");
   }
   while (minutes < 0 || minutes > 59);

   return Time(hours, minutes, 0);
}
```

You are now ready to implement the play_round function.

```
void Game::play_round()
{
   cwin.clear();
   Time t = random_time();
   const double CLOCK_RADIUS = 5;
   Clock clock(Point(0, 0), CLOCK_RADIUS);
   clock.set_time(t);
   clock.draw();

   Time guess = get_guess();
   if (t.seconds_from(guess) != 0)
      guess = get_guess();

   string text;
   if (t.seconds_from(guess) == 0)
   {
      text = "Congratulations, " + player.get_name()
         + "! That is correct.";
      player.increment_score();
   }
   else
      text = "Sorry, " + player.get_name()
         + "! That is not correct.";

   cwin <<
      Message(Point(-CLOCK_RADIUS, CLOCK_RADIUS + 1), text);
}
```

There is, however, a slight problem. We want to be friendly and congratulate the player by name:

```
Congratulations, Susan! That is correct.
```

However, if you look at the Player class, you won't find a get_name function. This was an oversight; it is easy to remedy:

```
class Player
{
public:
   ...
   /**
      Gets the player's name.
      @return the name
   */
   string get_name() const;
   ...
};

string Player::get_name() const
{
   return name;
}
```

When designing a collection of collaborating classes, as you are doing to implement this game, it is quite common to discover imperfections in some of the classes. This is not a problem. Revisiting a class to add more member functions is perfectly acceptable.

The main program is now quite short. You need to make a Game object and call play:

```cpp
int ccc_win_main()
{
    Game clock_game;
    clock_game.play();

    return 0;
}
```

This is actually quite anticlimactic after the complicated development of the classes and member functions. As a consistency check, here is a call tree that shows how the program unfolds. (We do not list constructors or very simple accessor functions such as get_minutes.)

```
main
    ├── Game::play
    ├── Game::get_player_information
    └── Game::play_round
            ├── Game::random_time
            ├── Clock::set_time
            ├── Clock::draw
            ├── Game::get_guess
            └── Player::increment_score
```

This example shows the power of the methods of finding objects and stepwise refinement. It also shows that designing and implementing even a moderately complex program is a lot of work.

Here is the entire program—the longest program we have developed in this book:

ch22/clock.cpp

```cpp
1   #include <cstdlib>
2   #include <cmath>
3   #include <ctime>
4
5   using namespace std;
6
7   #include "ccc_win.h"
8   #include "ccc_time.h"
9
10  const double PI = 3.141592653589793;
11
12  /**
13      A clock that can draw its face.
14  */
15  class Clock
16  {
17  public:
```

```
18       /**
19           Constructs a clock with a given center and radius.
20           @param c the center of the clock
21           @param r the radius of the clock
22       */
23       Clock(Point c, double r);
24
25       /**
26           Sets the current time.
27           @param t the time to set
28       */
29       void set_time(Time t);
30
31       /**
32           Draws the clock face, with tick marks and hands.
33       */
34       void draw() const;
35   private:
36       /**
37           Draw a tick mark (hour or minute mark).
38           @param angle the angle in minutes (0 ... 59, 0 = top)
39           @param length the length of the tick mark
40       */
41       void draw_tick(double angle, double length) const;
42
43       /**
44           Draw a hand, starting from the center.
45           @param angle the angle in minutes (0 ... 59, 0 = top)
46           @param length the length of the hand
47       */
48       void draw_hand(double angle, double length) const;
49
50       Time current_time;
51       Point center;
52       double radius;
53   };
54
55   /**
56       The player of the clock game.
57   */
58   class Player
59   {
60   public:
61       /**
62           Constructs a player with no name, level 1, and score 0.
63       */
64       Player();
65
66       /**
67           Constructs a player with given name and level.
68           @param player_name the player name
69           @param initial_level the player's level (1 ... 4)
70       */
71       Player(string player_name, int initial_level);
```

```
72
73      /**
74          Increments the score. Moves to next level if current
75          level complete.
76      */
77      void increment_score();
78
79      /**
80          Gets the current level.
81          @return the level
82      */
83      int get_level() const;
84
85      /**
86          Gets the player's name.
87          @return the name
88      */
89      string get_name() const;
90   private:
91      string name;
92      int score;
93      int level;
94   };
95
96   /**
97       The clock game.
98   */
99   class Game
100  {
101  public:
102      /**
103          Constructs the game with a default player.
104      */
105      Game();
106
107      /**
108          Plays the game while the player wants to continue.
109      */
110      void play();
111
112      /**
113          Reads player name and level.
114      */
115      void read_player_information();
116
117      /**
118          Plays a round, with up to two guesses.
119      */
120      void play_round();
121  private:
122      /**
123          Makes a random time, depending on the level.
124          @return the random time
125      */
126      Time random_time();
```

```
127
128      /**
129          Gets a time input from the user.
130          @return the time guessed by the user
131      */
132      Time get_guess();
133
134      Player player;
135  };
136
137  /**
138      Sets the seed of the random number generator.
139  */
140  void rand_seed()
141  {
142      int seed = static_cast<int>(time(0));
143      srand(seed);
144  }
145
146  /**
147      Returns a random integer in a range.
148      @param a the bottom of the range
149      @param b the top of the range
150      @return a random number x, a <= x and x <= b
151  */
152  int rand_int(int a, int b)
153  {
154      return a + rand() % (b - a + 1);
155  }
156
157  Clock::Clock(Point c, double r)
158  {
159      center = c;
160      radius = r;
161  }
162
163  void Clock::set_time(Time t)
164  {
165      current_time = t;
166  }
167
168  void Clock::draw_tick(double angle, double length) const
169  {
170      double alpha = PI / 2 - 6 * angle * PI / 180;
171      Point from(
172          center.get_x() + cos(alpha) * radius * (1 - length),
173          center.get_y() + sin(alpha) * radius * (1 - length));
174      Point to(center.get_x() + cos(alpha) * radius,
175          center.get_y() + sin(alpha) * radius);
176      cwin << Line(from, to);
177  }
178
179  void Clock::draw_hand(double angle, double length) const
180  {
181      double alpha = PI / 2 - 6 * angle * PI / 180;
```

```
182        Point from = center;
183        Point to(center.get_x() + cos(alpha) * radius * length,
184           center.get_y() + sin(alpha) * radius * length);
185        cwin << Line(from, to);
186     }
187
188     void Clock::draw() const
189     {
190        cwin << Circle(center, radius);
191        const double HOUR_TICK_LENGTH = 0.2;
192        const double MINUTE_TICK_LENGTH = 0.1;
193        const double HOUR_HAND_LENGTH = 0.6;
194        const double MINUTE_HAND_LENGTH = 0.75;
195        for (int i = 0; i < 12; i++)
196        {
197           draw_tick(i * 5, HOUR_TICK_LENGTH);
198           int j;
199           for (j = 1; j <= 4; j++)
200              draw_tick(i * 5 + j, MINUTE_TICK_LENGTH);
201        }
202        draw_hand(current_time.get_minutes(), MINUTE_HAND_LENGTH);
203        draw_hand((current_time.get_hours() +
204           current_time.get_minutes() / 60.0) * 5, HOUR_HAND_LENGTH);
205     }
206
207     Player::Player()
208     {
209        level = 1;
210        score = 0;
211     }
212
213     Player::Player(string player_name, int initial_level)
214     {
215        name = player_name;
216        level = initial_level;
217        score = 0;
218     }
219
220     int Player::get_level() const
221     {
222        return level;
223     }
224
225     string Player::get_name() const
226     {
227        return name;
228     }
229
230     void Player::increment_score()
231     {
232        score++;
233        if (score % 5 == 0 && level < 4)
234           level++;
235     }
```

```
236
237  Game::Game()
238  {
239  }
240
241  void Game::play()
242  {
243     rand_seed();
244     read_player_information();
245     string response;
246     do
247     {
248        play_round();
249        response = cwin.get_string(
250           "Do you want to play again? (y/n)");
251     }
252     while (response == "y");
253  }
254
255  void Game::read_player_information()
256  {
257     string name = cwin.get_string("What is your name?");
258     int initial_level;
259     do
260     {
261        initial_level = cwin.get_int(
262           "At what level do you want to start? (1-4)");
263     }
264     while (initial_level < 1 || initial_level > 4);
265     player = Player(name, initial_level);
266  }
267
268  Time Game::random_time()
269  {
270     int level = player.get_level();
271     int minutes;
272     if (level == 1) minutes = 0;
273     else if (level == 2) minutes = 15 * rand_int(0, 3);
274     else if (level == 3) minutes = 5 * rand_int(0, 11);
275     else minutes = rand_int(0, 59);
276     int hours = rand_int(1, 12);
277     return Time(hours, minutes, 0);
278  }
279
280  Time Game::get_guess()
281  {
282     int hours;
283     do
284     {
285        hours = cwin.get_int("Please enter hours: (1-12)");
286     }
287     while (hours < 1 || hours > 12);
288     int minutes;
```

```
289    do
290    {
291       minutes = cwin.get_int("Please enter minutes: (0-59)");
292    }
293    while (minutes < 0 || minutes > 59);
294
295    return Time(hours, minutes, 0);
296 }
297
298 void Game::play_round()
299 {
300    cwin.clear();
301    Time t = random_time();
302    const double CLOCK_RADIUS = 5;
303    Clock clock(Point(0, 0), CLOCK_RADIUS);
304    clock.set_time(t);
305    clock.draw();
306
307    Time guess = get_guess();
308    if (t.seconds_from(guess) != 0)
309       guess = get_guess();
310
311    string text;
312    if (t.seconds_from(guess) == 0)
313    {
314       text = "Congratulations, " + player.get_name()
315          + "! That is correct.";
316       player.increment_score();
317    }
318    else
319       text = "Sorry, " + player.get_name()
320          + "! That is not correct.";
321    cwin << Message(Point(-CLOCK_RADIUS, CLOCK_RADIUS + 1), text);
322 }
323
324 int ccc_win_main()
325 {
326    Game clock_game;
327    clock_game.play();
328
329    return 0;
330 }
```

CHAPTER SUMMARY

1. The life cycle of software encompasses all activities from initial analysis until obsolescence.

2. A formal process for software development describes phases of the development process and gives guidelines for how to carry out the phases.

3. The waterfall model of software development describes a sequential process of analysis, design, implementation, testing, and deployment.

4. The spiral model of software development describes an iterative process in which design and implementation are repeated.

5. Extreme programming strives for simplicity by removing formal structure and focusing on best practices.

6. In object-oriented design, you discover classes, determine responsibilities of classes, and describe relationships between classes.

7. A CRC card describes a class, its responsibilities, and its collaborating classes.

8. A class should represent a single concept from the problem domain, such as business, science, or mathematics.

9. The public interface of a class is cohesive if all of its features are related to the concept that the class represents.

10. The "uses" or dependency relationship denotes that a class uses objects of another class.

11. It is a good practice to minimize the coupling (i.e., dependency) between classes.

12. Inheritance (the "is-a" relationship) is a relationship between a more specialized class and a more general class.

13. Aggregation (the "has-a" relationship) denotes the fact that objects of a class contain objects of another class.

14. Inheritance is sometimes inappropriately used when aggregation would be more appropriate.

15. "Is-a", "has-a", and "uses" are the three key dependencies between classes.

16. You need to be able to distinguish the UML notations for inheritance, aggregation, and dependency.

17. Use documentation comments (with the bodies of the functions left blank) to record the behavior of classes and member functions.

FURTHER READING

1. Grady Booch, James Rumbaugh, and Ivar Jacobson, *The Unified Modeling Language User Guide*, 2nd ed. Addison-Wesley, 2005.

2. Kent Beck, *Extreme Programming Explained*, Addison-Wesley, 1999.

3. www.stack.nl/~dimitri/doxygen/ Web site for comment extraction program.

REVIEW EXERCISES

Exercise R22.1. What is the software life cycle?

Exercise R22.2. Explain the process of object-oriented design.

Exercise R22.3. Give a rule of thumb for how to find classes when designing a program.

Exercise R22.4. Give a rule of thumb for how to find member functions when designing a program.

Exercise R22.5. After discovering a function, why is it important to identify the object that is *responsible* for carrying out the action?

Exercise R22.6. Consider the following problem description:

> Users place coins in a vending machine and select a product by pushing a button. If the inserted coins are sufficient to cover the purchase price of the product, the product is dispensed and change is given. Otherwise, the inserted coins are returned to the user.

What classes should you use to implement it?

Exercise R22.7. Consider the following problem description:

> Employees receive their biweekly paycheck. They are paid their hourly wage for each hour worked; however, if they worked more than 40 hours per week, they are paid overtime at 150 percent of their regular wage.

What classes should you use to implement it?

Exercise R22.8. Consider the following problem description:

> Customers order products from a store. Invoices are generated to list the items and quantities ordered, payments received, and amounts still due. Products are shipped to the shipping address of the customer, and invoices are sent to the billing address.

What classes should you use to implement the problem?

Exercise R22.9. Suppose a vending machine contains products, and users insert coins into the vending machine to purchase products. Draw a class diagram showing the dependencies between the classes VendingMachine, Coin, and Product.

Exercise R22.10. What relationship is appropriate between the following classes: aggregation, inheritance, or neither?

   a. University–Student
   b. Student–TeachingAssistant
   c. Student–Freshman
   d. Student–Professor
   e. Car–Door
   f. Truck–Vehicle

g. `Traffic–TrafficSign`

h. `TrafficSign–Color`

Exercise R22.11. Suppose every Volkswagen is a car. Should a class `Volkswagen` inherit from the class `Car`? Volkswagen is a car manufacturer. Does that mean that the class `Volkswagen` should inherit from the class `CarManufacturer`?

Exercise R22.12. Some books on object-oriented programming recommend deriving the class `Circle` from the class `Point`. Then the `Circle` class inherits the `set_location` function from the `Point` base class. Explain why the `set_location` function need not be redefined in the derived class. Why is it nevertheless not a good idea to have `Circle` inherit from `Point`? Conversely, would deriving `Point` from `Circle` fulfill the "is-a" rule? Would it be a good idea?

PROGRAMMING EXERCISES

Exercise P22.1. Write a program that implements a different game, to teach arithmetic to your baby brother. The program tests addition and subtraction. In level 1 it tests only addition of numbers less than 10 whose sum is less than 10. In level 2 it tests addition of arbitrary one-digit numbers. In level 3 it tests subtraction of one-digit numbers with a nonnegative difference. Generate random problems and get the player input. The player gets up to two tries per problem. As in the clock game, advance from one level to the next when the player has achieved a score of five points.

Exercise P22.2. In the clock game program, we assigned the `play_round` function to the `Game` class. That choice was somewhat arbitrary. Modify the clock program so that the `Player` class is responsible for `play_round`.

Exercise P22.3. Design a simple e-mail messaging system. A message has a recipient, a sender, and a message text. A mailbox can store messages. Supply a number of mailboxes for different users and a user interface for users to log in, send messages to other users, read their own messages, and log out. Follow the design process described in this chapter.

Exercise P22.4. Write a program that allows an instructor to keep a grade book. Each student has scores for exams, homework assignments, and quizzes. Grading scales convert the total scores in each category into letter grades (e.g., 100–94 = A, 93–91 = A–, 90–88 = B+, etc.) To determine the final grade, the category grades are converted to numeric values (A = 4.0, A– = 3.7, B+ = 3.3, etc.). Those scores are weighted according to a set of weights (e.g., exams 40%, homework 35%, quizzes 25%), and the resulting numeric value is again converted into a letter grade. Design a user interface that firms up the requirements, use CRC cards to discover classes and methods, provide class diagrams, and implement your program.

Exercise P22.5. Write a program that simulates a vending machine. Products can be purchased by inserting the correct number of coins into the machine. A user selects a product from a list of available products, adds coins, and either gets the product or gets the coins returned if insufficient money was supplied or if the product is sold out. Products can be restocked and money removed by an operator. Follow the design process that was described in this chapter.

Exercise P22.6. Write a program to design an appointment calendar. An appointment includes the appointment day, starting time, ending time, and a description; for example,

```
2010/10/1 17:30 18:30 Dentist
2010/10/2 08:30 10:00 CS1 class
```

Supply a user interface to add appointments, remove canceled appointments, and print out a list of appointments for a particular day. Follow the design process that was described in this chapter.

Exercise P22.7. *Airline seating*. Write a program that assigns seats on an airplane. Assume the airplane has 20 seats in first class (5 rows of 4 seats each, separated by an aisle) and 180 seats in economy class (30 rows of 6 seats each, separated by an aisle). Your program should take three commands: add passengers, show seating, and quit. When passengers are added, ask for the class (first or economy), the number of passengers traveling together (1 or 2 in first class; 1 to 3 in economy), and the seating preference (aisle or window in first class; aisle, center, or window in economy). Then try to find a match and assign the seats. If no match exists, print a message. Your user interface can be text-based or graphical. Follow the design process that was described in this chapter.

Exercise P22.8. Write a tic-tac-toe game that lets a human player play against the computer. Your program will play many turns against a human opponent, and it will learn. When it is the computer's turn, the computer randomly selects an empty field, except that it won't ever choose a losing combination. For that purpose, your program must keep an array of losing combinations. Whenever the human wins, the immediately preceding combination is stored as losing. For example, suppose that x = computer and o = human. Suppose the current combination is

Now it is the human's turn, who will of course choose

The computer should then remember the preceding combination

```
 O | X | X
---+---+---
   | O |
---+---+---
   |   |
```

as a losing combination. As a result, the computer will never again choose that combination from

```
 O | X |
---+---+---
   | O |
---+---+---
   |   |
```

or

```
 O |   | X
---+---+---
   | O |
---+---+---
   |   |
```

Discover classes and supply a class diagram before you begin to program.

G   **Exercise P22.9.** Write a bumper car game with the following rules. Bumper cars are located in grid points (x, y), where x and y are integers between -10 and 10. A bumper car starts moving in a random direction, either left, right, up, or down. If it reaches the boundary of its track (that is, x or y is 10 or -10), then it reverses direction. If it is about to bump into another bumper car, it reverses direction. Model a track with two bumper cars. Make each of them move 100 times, alternating between the two cars. Display the movement on the graphics screen. Use at least two classes in your program. There should be no global variables.

G   **Exercise P22.10.** Write a program that can be used to design a suburban scene, with houses, streets, and cars. Users can add houses and cars of various sizes to a street. Design a user interface that firms up the requirements, use CRC cards to discover classes and methods, provide class diagrams, and implement your program.

The Unified Modeling Language

In Chapter 22 you were introduced to a small portion of a powerful design methodology called the Unified Modeling Language, or UML. In this chapter we will continue to explore this technique, learning about more advanced diagrams in the UML, such as state diagrams, and more advanced analysis techniques, such as use cases. By the end of the chapter you will see how these techniques are combined in the development of a small, but realistic, case study of a voice mail system.

CHAPTER CONTENTS

23.1 The Unified Modeling Language

> The UML notation is the unification of several notations for object-oriented design diagrams.

Graphical notations are very useful for conveying design information. It is easier to extract relationship information by looking at a diagram than by reading documentation. In the first several chapters you were introduced to flowcharts. While useful for describing the behavior in very small examples, flowcharts do not scale well to large problems. When object-oriented design was first developed, a number of researchers proposed their own design notations. Unfortunately, these diagramming conventions differed greatly in their visual appearance. That problem was resolved when three well-known researchers, Booch, Rumbaugh, and Jacobson, got together to unify their disparate notations. The result was the Unified Modeling Language or UML [1].

In Chapter 22, you encountered class diagrams, one of the diagram types standardized in the UML. In the remainder of this section, you will learn about some of the advanced features of class diagrams. In subsequent sections, we introduce several additional diagram types.

23.1.1 Attributes and Member Functions in UML Class Diagrams

Sometimes it is useful to indicate class attributes and member functions in a class diagram. An *attribute* is an externally observable property that objects of a class have. For example, name and price would be attributes of the Product class. Usually, attributes correspond to data fields. But they don't have to—a class may have a different way of organizing its data. Consider the Time class from the library for this

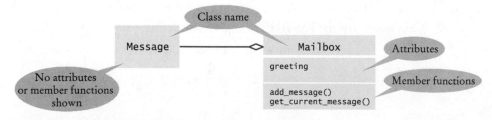

Figure 1   Attributes and Member Functions in a Class Diagram

book. Conceptually, it has attributes seconds, minutes, and hours, but it doesn't actually store the minutes and hours in separate data members. Instead, it stores the number of seconds since midnight and computes the minutes and hours from it.

You can indicate attributes and member functions in a class diagram by dividing a class rectangle into three compartments, with the class name in the top, attributes in the middle, and member functions in the bottom (see Figure 1). You need not list *all* attributes and member functions in a particular diagram. Just list the ones that are helpful for understanding the point you are making with a particular diagram.

Also, don't list as an attribute what you also draw as an aggregation. If you denote by aggregation the fact that a Mailbox has Message objects, don't add an attribute messages.

To distinguish the attributes from the member functions, it is common to add parentheses after function names, as we did in Figure 1.

Sometimes it is useful to indicate the types of attributes and member functions. Unlike in C++, where the type precedes a variable, the official UML format is *attribute : type_name*, for example, greeting : string. After all, UML is a language-neutral notation that describes designs, not implementations in a particular language. While most UML tools use this formal notation, programmers who draw diagrams by hand will often use the familiar C++ notation string greeting.

Similarly, in the formal notation for specifying parameter and return types of a member function, you put the parameter type after each parameter, and the return type after the name of the function. For example,

```
add_message(msg : Message) : void
```

Keep in mind that you should only include the type information when it is helpful. Too much irrelevant information makes a UML diagram hard to read.

23.1.2 Multiplicities

It is very useful to indicate multiplicities of relationships between classes. You simply write the multiplicities at the ends of the edge that indicates the relationship. For example, Figure 2 denotes that a mailbox can hold any number of messages, and a message is in exactly one mailbox.

The most common choices for multiplicity are:

- any number (zero or more): *
- one or more: 1..*
- zero or one: 0..1
- exactly one: 1

Figure 2   Multiplicities of an Aggregation Relationship

23.1.3 Aggregation, Composition, and Association

Classes are joined by various kinds of connections (see Figure 3). Some designers differentiate between aggregation and composition. *Composition* is a stronger form of aggregation where the contained objects do not have an existence independent of their containers. The UML notation for composition is a line with a solid diamond at the end corresponding to the class doing the aggregation (see Figure 4).

Consider our voice mail system. As you will see later in this chapter, a mailbox contains two *message queues*, one for new messages and one for saved messages. These queues are permanently contained in the mailboxes—a message queue never exists outside a mailbox. On the other hand, messages get moved from one queue to another. Thus, message queues are contained in mailboxes, and messages are merely aggregated in message queues. We will not make a distinction between aggregation and composition in this book, but you may encounter it elsewhere.

Some designers do not like the aggregation and composition/containment relationships because they consider them too implementation-specific. UML defines a more general *association* between classes. An association is drawn as a solid line without a diamond. You can write *roles* at the ends of the lines (see Figure 5).

Here we model the fact that students register for courses and courses have students as participants. Early in a design, this general relationship makes a lot of sense. As you move closer to implementation, you will want to resolve whether a Course object manages a collection of students, a Student object manages a collection of courses, or both courses and students manage collections of each other.

The relationship between courses and students is bidirectional—Course objects will need to know about the students in the course, and Student objects need to know about the courses for which they are registered. Quite often, an association is directed, that is, it can only be navigated in one way. For example, a message queue needs to be able to locate the messages inside, but a message need not know in which queue it is. A directed association is drawn with an open arrow tip (see Figure 6). It is easy to confuse that connector with inheritance—you have to pay close attention to the shapes of the arrow tips when drawing UML diagrams.

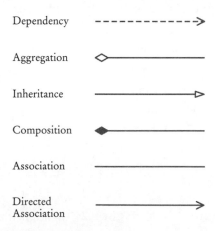

Figure 3   UML Connectors

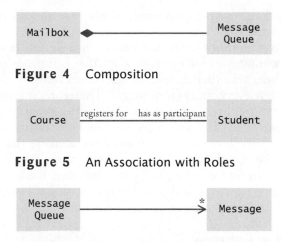

Figure 4　Composition

Figure 5　An Association with Roles

Figure 6　A Directed Association

Frankly, the differences between association, aggregation, and composition are subtle and can be confusing, even to experienced designers. If you find the distinctions helpful, by all means use them. But don't lose sleep pondering the differences between these concepts.

23.2 Use Cases

> Use cases assist problem analysis by providing concrete scenarios from which general action can be abstracted.

Use cases are an *analysis technique* used to describe in a formal way how a computer system should work. Each use case focuses on a specific scenario, a description of a hypothetical use of the intended application. Each scenario describes the steps that are necessary to bring it to successful completion. Each step in a use case represents an interaction with people or entities outside the computer system (the *actors*) and the system itself. For example, in our voice mail system the use case "Leave a message" describes the steps that a caller must take to dial an extension and leave a message. The use case "Retrieve messages" describes the steps needed to listen to the messages in the mailbox. In the first case, the actor is the caller leaving a message. In the second case, the actor is the mailbox owner.

An essential aspect of a use case is that it must describe a scenario that completes to a point that is of some *value* to one of the actors. In the case of "Leave a message", the value to the caller is the fact that the message is deposited in the appropriate mailbox. In contrast, merely dialing a telephone number and listening to a menu would not be considered a valid use case because it does not by itself have value to anyone.

Of course, most scenarios that potentially deliver a valuable outcome can also fail for one reason or another. Perhaps the message queue is full, or a mailbox owner entered the wrong password. A use case should include *variations* that describe these situations.

It is common for one use case to *include* another. For example, consider a caller who wants to leave a message. The caller first needs to reach the recipient's extension. But there are other reasons to reach the extension, for example, to talk to someone, or to retrieve your own messages. Therefore, it makes sense to factor out the common action of reaching an extension into a separate use case. The use cases "Leave a message" and "Retrieve messages" include the use case "Reach an extension".

Minimally, a use case should have a name that describes it concisely, a main sequence of actions, and, if appropriate, variants to the main sequence. Some analysts prefer a more formal write-up that numbers the use cases, calls out the actors, refers to related use cases, and so on. In this book we'll keep use cases as simple as possible.

Here are two sample use cases for the voice mail system.

Reach an Extension

1. The caller dials the main number of the voice mail system.
2. The voice mail system speaks a prompt.

   `Enter mailbox number followed by #.`
3. The caller types in the extension number of the message recipient.
4. The voice mail system speaks.

   `You have reached mailbox xxxx. Please leave a message now.`

Variation #1

1.1. In Step 3, the user enters an invalid extension number.
1.2. The voice mail system speaks.

   `You have typed an invalid mailbox number.`
1.3. Continue with Step 2.

Leave a Message

1. The caller carries out **Reach an Extension**.
2. The caller speaks the message.
3. The caller hangs up.
4. The voice mail system places the recorded message in the recipient's mailbox.

Variation #1

1.1. After Step 1, the caller hangs up instead of speaking a message.
1.2. The voice mail system discards the empty message.

The "meat" of a use case lies in its textual description. As an adjunct to that description, the UML defines a notation for use case diagrams (see Figure 7).

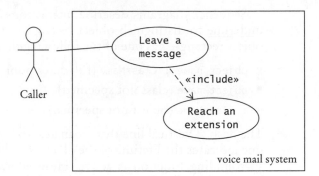

Figure 7
A UML Use Case Diagram

The diagrams denote the following:

- Actors (drawn as stick figures) for the human users of a system
- Use cases (drawn as ovals)
- Relationships between use cases, in particular, the "includes" relationship
- System boundaries (drawn as rectangles)

Figure 7 only has one actor, the person leaving a message, and one system—the voice mail system. There are two use cases, one included in the other.

Keep in mind that use case diagrams can never replace the textual description of a use case. If you have many use cases, the use case diagrams can give you a "bird's eye" overview.

23.3 Sequence Diagrams

> Sequence diagrams record the dynamic interaction between objects.

Class diagrams are static—they display the relationships among the classes that exist throughout the lifetime of the system. In contrast, a sequence diagram shows the dynamics of a particular scenario. You use sequence diagrams to describe communication relationships among objects. Figure 8 shows the key elements of a sequence diagram—a function call from one object to another.

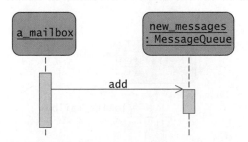

Figure 8 A Sequence Diagram

Sequence diagrams describe interactions between objects. In UML, you use an underline to distinguish object rectangles from class rectangles. The text inside an object rectangle has one of the following three formats:

- `object_name : ClassName` (full description)
- `object_name` (class not specified)
- `: ClassName` (object not specified)

The dashed vertical line that emanates from the object is called the *lifeline*. The lifeline indicates the lifetime of the object. For local variables the lifetime is the time the surrounding function is active. Heap-allocated variables will have a lifetime that begins when the object is created until the point the memory is recovered.

The rectangles along the lifeline are called *activation bars*. They show when the object has control, executing a member function or waiting for a function to return. When you call a function, start an activation bar at the end of the call arrow. The activation bar ends when the function returns. (Note that the activation bar of a called function should always be smaller than that of the calling function.)

In the most common form, a sequence diagram illustrates the behavior of a single member function. Then the leftmost object has one long activation bar, from which one or more call arrows emanate. For example, the diagram in Figure 8 illustrates the add function of the Mailbox class. A message is added to the message queue that holds the new messages. The diagram corresponds to the statement

```
new_messages.add(...)
```

You cannot tell from the diagram what parameter was passed to the function.

A function can call another member function on the same object. In such a self-call, draw the activation bar of the called function over that of the calling function, as in Figure 9.

If a function dynamically allocates a new object, you can use the notation «create» to indicate the timing of the creation. Arrange the object rectangle of the created object as in Figure 10.

When drawing a sequence diagram, you omit a large amount of detail. Generally, you do not indicate branches or loops. (The UML defines a notation for that purpose, but it is a bit cumbersome and rarely used.) The principal purpose of a sequence diagram is to show the objects that are involved in carrying out a particular scenario and the order of the function calls that are executed.

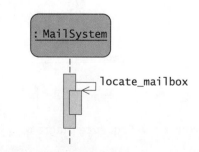

Figure 9
Self-Call

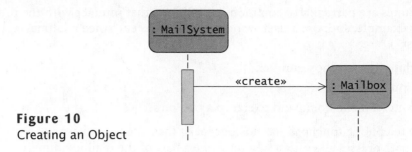

Figure 10
Creating an Object

Sequence diagrams are valuable for documenting complex interactions between objects. These interactions are common in object-oriented programs where any one object tends to have limited responsibilities and requires the collaboration of several other objects. You will see examples in the case study at the end of this chapter.

23.4 State Diagrams

> State diagrams are useful for documenting objects that change their behavior according to their current state during the course of execution.

Some objects have a discrete set of states that affect their behavior. For example, a voice mail system is in a "connected" state when a caller first connects to it. After the caller enters an extension number, the system enters the "recording" state where it records whatever the caller speaks. When the caller enters a passcode, the system is in the "mailbox menu" state. The state diagram in Figure 11 shows these states and the transitions between them.

The system object's state has a noticeable impact on its behavior. If the caller speaks while the system is in the "mailbox menu" state, the spoken words are simply ignored. Voice input is recorded only when the system is in the "recording" state.

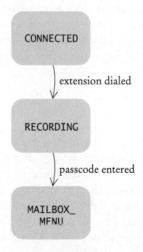

Figure 11   A State Diagram

States are particularly common with objects that interact with the program user. For example, suppose a user wants to retrieve recent voice mail messages. The user must

- Enter the mailbox number.
- Enter the passcode.
- Enter a menu command to start playing messages.

The telephone touchpad has no concept of these steps—it keeps no state. Whenever the user presses a key, that key might be a part of the mailbox number, passcode, or menu command. Some part of the voice mail system must keep track of the current state so that it can process the key correctly. We will discuss this issue further in the case study.

23.5 Case Study: A Voice Mail System

In this section we will continue with the voice mail application to show how the diagrams and use case techniques introduced in previous sections lead to a final completed application.

In a voice mail system, a person dials an extension number and, provided the other party does not pick up the telephone, leaves a message. The other party can later retrieve the messages, keep them, or delete them. Real-world systems have a multitude of fancy features: Messages can be forwarded to one or more mailboxes; distribution lists can be defined, retained, and edited; and authorized persons can send broadcast messages to all users.

We will design and implement a program that simulates a voice mail system, without creating a completely realistic working phone system. We will simply represent voice mail by text that is entered through the keyboard. We need to simulate the three distinct input events that occur in a real telephone system: speaking, pushing a button on the telephone touchpad, and hanging up the telephone. We use the following convention for input: An input line consisting of a single character 1 ... 9 or # denotes a pressed button on the telephone touchpad. For example, to dial extension 13, you enter

```
1
3
#
```

The # symbol is used as a sentinel, a marker to indicate the end of a sequence of digit values. An input line consisting of the single letter H denotes hanging up the telephone. Any other text denotes voice input.

The first formal step in the process that leads us toward the final product (the voice mail system) is the analysis phase. Its role is to crisply define the behavior of the system. In this example, we will define the behavior through a set of use cases. Note that the use cases by themselves are *not* a full specification of a system. The functional specification also needs to define system limitations, performance, and so on.

23.5.1 Use Cases for the Voice Mail System

Reach an Extension

1. The caller dials the main number of the voice mail system.
2. The voice mail system speaks a prompt.

   `Enter mailbox number followed by #.`
3. The caller types in the extension number of the message recipient.
4. The voice mail system speaks.

   `You have reached mailbox xxxx. Please leave a message now.`

Leave a Message

1. The caller carries out Reach an Extension.
2. The caller speaks the message.
3. The caller hangs up.
4. The voice mail system places the recorded message in the recipient's mailbox.

Log in

1. The mailbox owner carries out Reach an Extension.
2. The mailbox owner types the passcode, followed by the # key. (The default passcode is the same as the mailbox number. The mailbox owner can change it—see Change the Passcode.)
3. The voice mail system plays the mailbox menu:

   `Enter 1 to listen to your messages.`

   `Enter 2 to change your passcode.`

   `Enter 3 to change your greeting.`

Retrieve Messages

1. The mailbox owner carries out Log in.
2. The mailbox owner selects the "listen to your messages" menu option.
3. The voice mail system plays the message menu:

   `Enter 1 to listen to the current message.`

   `Enter 2 to save the current message.`

   `Enter 3 to delete the current message.`

   `Enter 4 to return to the main menu.`
4. The mailbox owner selects the "listen to the current message" menu option.
5. The voice mail system plays the current new message, or, if there are no new messages, the current old message. Note that the message is played, not removed from the queue.

6. The voice mail system plays the message menu.
7. The mailbox owner selects "delete the current message". The message is permanently removed.
8. Go back to Step 3.

Variation #1. Saving a message

1.1. Start at Step 6.
1.2. The mailbox owner selects "save the current message". The message is removed from its queue and appended to the queue of old messages.
1.3. Go back to Step 3.

Change the Greeting

1. The mailbox owner carries out Log in.
2. The mailbox owner selects the "change your greeting" menu option.
3. The mailbox owner speaks the greeting.
4. The mailbox owner presses the # key.
5. The voice mail system sets the new greeting.

Variation #1. Hang up before confirmation

1.1. Start at Step 3.
1.2. The mailbox owner hangs up the telephone.
1.3. The voice mail system keeps the old greeting.

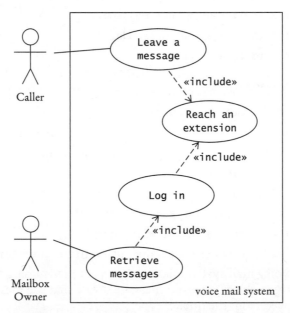

Figure 12   Use Case Diagram for the Voice Mail System

Change the Passcode

1. The mailbox owner carries out Log in.
2. The mailbox owner selects the "change your passcode" menu option.
3. The mailbox owner types the new passcode.
4. The mailbox owner presses the # key.
5. The voice mail system sets the new passcode.

Variation #1. Hang up before confirmation

1.1. Start at Step 3.
1.2. The mailbox owner hangs up the telephone.
1.3. The voice mail system keeps the old passcode.

Figure 12 shows the relationships among the first four use cases. The last two use cases are so simple that a use case diagram would not add meaningful information.

23.5.2 CRC Cards for the Voice Mail System

Let us walk through the process of discovering classes for the voice mail system. Some obvious classes, whose nouns appear in the functional specification, are

- `Mailbox`
- `Message`
- `MailSystem`

Let's start with `Mailbox` because it is both important and easy to understand. The principal job of the mailbox is to keep messages. The mailbox should keep track of which messages are new and which are saved. New messages may be deposited into the mailbox, and users should be able to retrieve, save, and delete their messages.

The messages need to be kept somewhere. Because we retrieve messages in a first-in, first-out (FIFO) fashion, a queue is an appropriate data structure. Because we need to differentiate between new and saved messages, we'll use two queues, one for the new messages and one for the saved messages.

So far, the CRC cards look like this:

Mailbox	
keep new and saved messages	`MessageQueue`

MessageQueue
add and remove messages in FIFO order

Where are the mailboxes kept? There needs to be a class that contains them all. We'll call it `MailSystem`. The responsibility of the mail system is to manage the mailboxes.

MailSystem
manage mailboxes   `Mailbox`

We can't go much further until we resolve how input and output are processed. Because we have been simulating telephone equipment, let's start with a class `Telephone`. A telephone has two responsibilities: to take user input (button presses, voice input, and hangup actions), and to play voice output on the speaker.

Telephone
take user input from touchpad, microphone, hangup
speak output

When the telephone gets user input, it must communicate it to some object. Could it tell the mail system? Superficially, that sounds like a good idea. But it turns out that there is a problem. In a real voice mail system, it is possible for multiple telephones to be connected to the voice mail system. *Each* connection needs to keep track of the current state (recording, retrieving messages, and so on). It is possible that one connection is currently recording a message while another is retrieving messages. It seems a tall order for the mail system to keep multiple states, one for each connection. Instead, let's have a separate Connection class. A connection communicates with a telephone, carries out the user commands, and keeps track of the state of the session.

Connection	
get input from telephone	Telephone
carry out user commands	MailSystem
keep track of state	

The creation of the Telephone, the MailSystem, and the Connection between them is the responsibility of the main driver program.

Now that we have some idea of the components of the system, it is time for a simple scenario walkthrough. Let's start with the Leave a Message use case.

1. The user types an extension. The Telephone sends the extension number to the Connection. (Add Connection as a collaborator of Telephone. Place the two cards next to each other.)

2. The Connection asks the MailSystem to find the Mailbox object with the given extension number. (This is vaguely included in the "manage mailboxes" responsibility. Arrange the MailSystem and Mailbox cards close to the Connection card.)

3. The Connection asks the Mailbox for its greeting. (Add "manage greeting" to the Mailbox responsibilities, and add Mailbox as a collaborator of Connection.)

4. The Connection asks the Telephone to play the greeting on the speaker.

5. The user speaks the message. The Telephone asks the Connection to record it. (Add "record voice input" to the responsibilities of Connection.)

6. The user hangs up. The Telephone notifies the Connection.

7. The Connection constructs a Message object that contains the recorded message. (Add Message as a collaborator of Connection. Make a Message card with a responsibility "manage message contents".)

8. The Connection adds the Message object to the Mailbox.

As a result of this walkthrough, the Telephone, Connection, and Mailbox cards have been updated, and a Message card has been added.

Telephone	
take user input from touchpad,	`Connection`
microphone, hangup	
speak output	

Connection	
get input from telephone	`Telephone`
carry out user commands	`MailSystem`
keep track of state	`Mailbox`
record voice input	`Message`

Mailbox	
keep new and saved messages	`MessageQueue`
manage greeting	

Message	
manage message contents	

Now let's consider the use case **Retrieve Messages**. The first steps of the scenario are the same as that of the preceding scenario. Let's start at the point where the user types in the passcode.

1. The user types in the passcode. The `Telephone` notifies the `Connection`.
2. The `Connection` asks the `Mailbox` to check the passcode. (Add "manage passcode" to the responsibilities of the `Mailbox` class.)
3. Assuming the passcode was correct, the `Connection` sets the `Mailbox` as the current mailbox and asks the `Telephone` to speak the mailbox menu.
4. The user types in the "retrieve messages" menu option. The `Telephone` passes it on to the `Connection`.
5. The `Connection` asks the `Telephone` to speak the message menu.
6. The user types in the "listen to current message" option. The `Telephone` passes it on to the `Connection`.
7. The `Connection` gets the first `Message` from the current `Mailbox` and sends its contents to the `Telephone`. (Add "retrieve messages" to the responsibilities of `Mailbox`.)
8. The `Connection` asks the `Telephone` to speak the message menu.
9. The user types in the "save current message" menu option. The `Telephone` passes it on to the `Connection`.
10. The `Connection` tells the `Mailbox` to save the current message. (Modify the responsibilities of `Mailbox` to "retrieve, save, delete messages".)

11. The Connection asks the Telephone to speak the message menu.

This finishes the scenario. As a result, the Mailbox CRC card has been updated.

Mailbox	
keep new and saved messages	MessageQueue
manage greeting	
manage passcode	
retrieve, save, delete messages	

The remaining use cases do not add any new information, so we omit the scenarios.

23.5.3 UML Class Diagrams for the Voice Mail System

The "collaboration" parts of the CRC cards show the following dependency relationships (shown in Figure 13):

- Mailbox depends on MessageQueue
- MailSystem depends on Mailbox
- Connection depends on Telephone, MailSystem, Message, and Mailbox
- Telephone depends on Connection

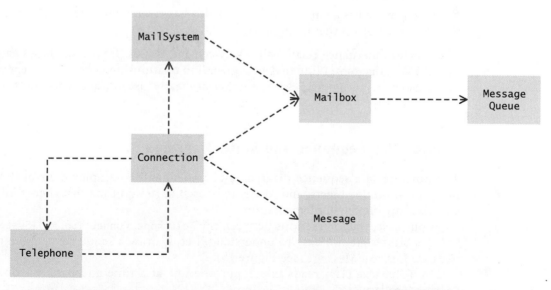

Figure 13 The Voice Mail System Dependencies from the CRC Cards

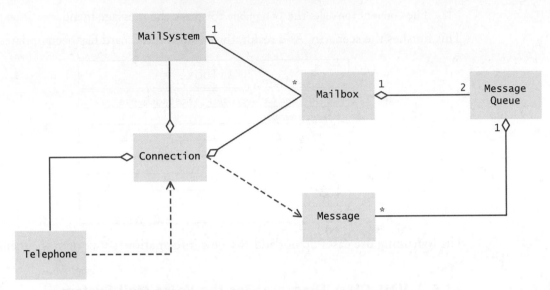

Figure 14   The UML Class Diagram for the Voice Mail System

Next, consider the aggregation relationships. From the previous discussion, we know the following:

- A mail system has mailboxes.
- A mailbox has two message queues.
- A message queue has some number of messages.
- A Connection has a current mailbox. It also has references to the MailSystem and Telephone objects that it connects.

There is no inheritance relationship between the classes. Figure 14 shows the completed UML diagram. Note that an aggregation relationship subsumes a dependency relationship. If a class aggregates another, it clearly uses it, and you don't need to record the latter.

23.5.4 UML Sequence and State Diagrams

The purpose of a sequence diagram is to understand a complex control flow that involves multiple objects, and to assure oneself at design time that there will be no surprises during the implementation.

In our case, the interactions between the Telephone, Connection, MailSystem, and Mailbox classes are not easy to understand. Let us draw a sequence diagram for the use case Leave a Message (see Figure 15).

The Telephone class reads user input one line at a time and passes it on to the Connection class.

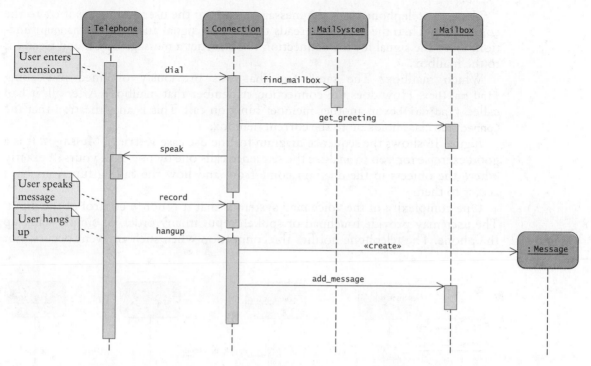

Figure 15 Sequence Diagram for Leaving a Message

Let's postulate three functions for the Connection class:

- dial passes on a button press
- record passes on speech
- hangup tells the connection that the telephone has hung up

First, the caller keys in the extension number, resulting in several calls to dial. We show only one of them—there is no advantage in modeling the repetition.

Once the Connection has the complete mailbox number, it needs to play the greeting. How does it know what greeting to play? It needs to get the mailbox and ask it for the greeting. How does it get the mailbox? It asks the mail system, calling a function that we call find_mailbox.

The find_mailbox function returns a Mailbox object. You don't see parameters and return values in the sequence diagram. You have to keep track of the objects yourself and realize that the Mailbox object to the right of the figure is meant to be the object returned by the find_mailbox call.

Now that the connection has access to the mailbox, it needs the greeting. Thus, it invokes the get_greeting function on the mailbox and gets the greeting, which it then plays on the telephone speaker. Note that the greeting does not show up at all in the sequence diagram because it is entirely passive—no functions are invoked on it.

Next, the telephone reads the message text from the user and passes it on to the connection. Then the telephone reads the hangup signal and calls the `hangup` function; that's the signal for the connection to construct a message object and to add it to the mailbox.

Which mailbox? The same one that was previously obtained by calling `find_mailbox`. How does the connection remember that mailbox? After all, it had called `find_mailbox` in another member function call. This is an indication that the `Connection` class holds on to the current mailbox.

Figure 16 shows the sequence diagram for the use case **Retrieve Messages**. It is a good exercise for you to analyze the sequence calls one by one. Ask yourself exactly where the objects in the diagram come from and how the calling functions have access to them.

One complexity of the voice mail system is that it is not in control of the input. The user may provide touchpad or spoken input in any order, or simply hang up the phone. The telephone notifies the connection when such an event occurs. For

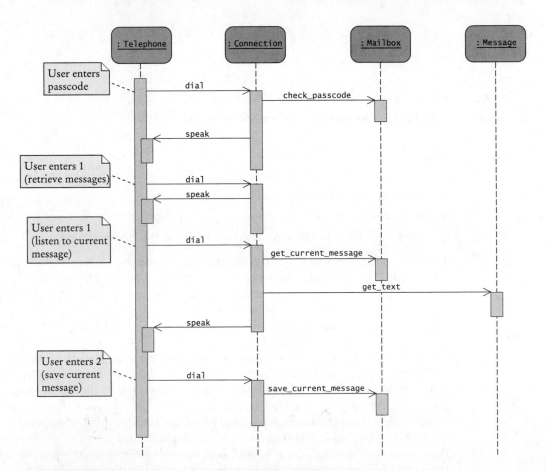

Figure 16   Sequence Diagram for Retrieving a Message

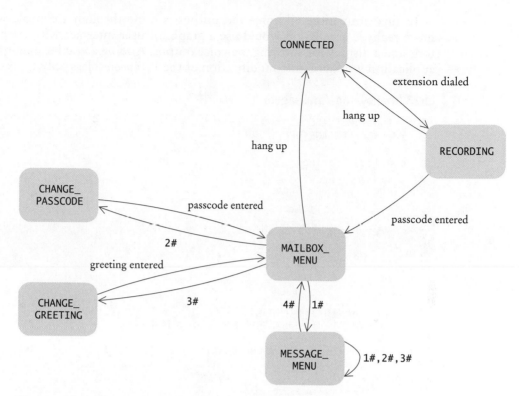

Figure 17 State Diagram for the Connection States

example, notice that the connection is called at least three times in the Leave a Message scenario. (As already mentioned, the dial function is called for each separate key. The connection needs to aggregate keys until the user hits the # key. We didn't show that detail in the sequence diagrams.) The connection needs to keep track of the various states so that it can pick up at the right place when it receives the next user input. Figure 17 shows the state diagram.

23.5.5 Implementation

Now we are ready to implement the system in C++. The files below give the implementation, which at this point is quite straightforward. You can download, compile, and run the program to see the voice mail system in action. When you run the program, type Q to terminate.

After running the program, have a look at each of the classes. Read the documentation comments and compare them with the CRC cards and the UML class diagrams. Look again at the UML sequence diagrams and trace the function calls in the actual code. Find the state transitions of the Connection class.

In this simulation, all input and output is done through a console window. A more realistic simulation would use a graphical user interface with telephone buttons and a display for showing the voice output. Adding a graphical interface to our application would require modification of the Telephone class only.

ch23/mailsystem/message.h

```
1   #ifndef MESSAGE_H
2   #define MESSAGE_H
3
4   #include <string>
5
6   using namespace std;
7
8   /**
9       A message left by a caller.
10  */
11  class Message
12  {
13  public:
14      /**
15          Constructs a message object.
16          @param message_text the message text
17      */
18      Message(string message_text);
19
20      /**
21          Gets the message text.
22          @return message text
23      */
24      string get_text() const;
25  private:
26      string text;
27  };
28
29  inline Message::Message(string message_text)
30      : text(message_text) {}
31
32  inline string Message::get_text() const
33  {
34      return text;
35  }
36
37  #endif
```

ch23/mailsystem/mailbox.h

```
1   #ifndef MAILBOX_H
2   #define MAILBOX_H
3
4   #include <string>
5   #include <queue>
6
7   using namespace std;
```

```
 8
 9   class Message;
10
11   /**
12       A mailbox contains messages that can be listed, kept, or discarded.
13   */
14   class Mailbox
15   {
16   public:
17       /**
18           Creates a mailbox object.
19           @param a_passcode  passcode number
20           @param a_greeting  greeting string
21       */
22       Mailbox(string a_passcode, string a_greeting);
23
24       /**
25           Checks if the passcode is correct.
26           @param a_passcode  a passcode to check
27       */
28       bool check_passcode(string a_passcode) const;
29
30       /**
31           Adds a message to the mailbox.
32           @param a_message  the message to be added
33       */
34       void add_message(Message* a_message);
35
36       /**
37           Gets the current message.
38           @return  the current message
39       */
40       Message* get_current_message() const;
41
42       /**
43           Removes the current message from the mailbox.
44       */
45       void remove_current_message();
46
47       /**
48           Saves the current message.
49       */
50       void save_current_message();
51
52       /**
53           Changes the mailbox's greeting.
54           @param new_greeting  the new greeting string
55       */
56       void set_greeting(string new_greeting);
57
58       /**
59           Changes mailbox's passcode.
60           @param new_passcode  the new passcode
61       */
62       void set_passcode(string new_passcode);
```

```
63
64      /**
65          Gets the mailbox's greeting.
66          @return the greeting
67      */
68      string get_greeting() const;
69   private:
70      queue<Message*> new_messages;
71      queue<Message*> kept_messages;
72      string greeting;
73      string passcode;
74   };
75
76   inline Mailbox::Mailbox(string a_passcode, string a_greeting)
77      : passcode(a_passcode), greeting(a_greeting)
78   {
79   }
80
81   inline bool Mailbox::check_passcode(string a_passcode) const
82   {
83      return passcode == a_passcode;
84   }
85
86   inline void Mailbox::add_message(Message* a_message)
87   {
88      new_messages.push(a_message);
89   }
90
91   inline void Mailbox::set_greeting(string new_greeting)
92   {
93      greeting = new_greeting;
94   }
95
96   inline void Mailbox::set_passcode(string new_passcode)
97   {
98      passcode = new_passcode;
99   }
100
101  inline string Mailbox::get_greeting() const
102  {
103     return greeting;
104  }
105
106  #endif
```

ch23/mailsystem/mailbox.cpp

```
1   #include "message.h"
2   #include "mailbox.h"
3
4   Message* Mailbox::get_current_message() const
5   {
6      if (new_messages.size() > 0)
7         return new_messages.front();
```

```
 8        if (kept_messages.size() > 0)
 9           return kept_messages.front();
10        return NULL;
11     }
12
13     void Mailbox::remove_current_message()
14     {
15        if (new_messages.size() > 0)
16        {
17           Message* m = get_current_message();
18           new_messages.pop();
19           delete m;
20        }
21        else if (kept_messages.size() > 0)
22        {
23           Message* m = get_current_message();
24           kept_messages.pop();
25           delete m;
26        }
27     }
28
29     void Mailbox::save_current_message()
30     {
31        Message* m = get_current_message();
32        if (m != NULL)
33        {
34           kept_messages.push(new Message(*m));
35           remove_current_message();
36        }
37     }
```

ch23/mailsystem/mailsystem.h

```
 1     #ifndef MAILSYSTEM_H
 2     #define MAILSYSTEM_H
 3
 4     #include <vector>
 5     #include <string>
 6
 7     using namespace std;
 8
 9     class Mailbox;
10
11     /**
12         A system of voice mail mailboxes.
13     */
14     class MailSystem
15     {
16     public:
17        /**
18            Constructs a voice mail system with a given number of
19            mailboxes.
20            @param mailbox_count the number of mailboxes
21        */
22        MailSystem(int mailbox_count);
```

```
23
24    /**
25       Locates a mailbox.
26       @param ext  the extension number
27       @return  the mailbox, or NULL if not found
28    */
29    Mailbox* find_mailbox(string ext) const;
30 private:
31    vector<Mailbox*> mailboxes;
32 };
33
34 #endif
```

ch23/mailsystem/mailsystem.cpp

```
1  #include <sstream>
2  #include "mailbox.h"
3  #include "mailsystem.h"
4
5  using namespace std;
6
7  MailSystem::MailSystem(int mailbox_count)
8  {
9     for (int i = 0; i < mailbox_count; i++)
10    {
11       ostringstream passcode;
12       passcode << i;
13       ostringstream greeting;
14       greeting << "You have reached mailbox " << i
15          << ". \nPlease leave a message now.";
16       mailboxes.push_back(new Mailbox(passcode.str(), greeting.str()));
17    }
18 }
19
20 int string_to_int(string s)
21 {
22    istringstream instr(s);
23    int n;
24    instr >> n;
25    return n;
26 }
27
28 Mailbox* MailSystem::find_mailbox(string ext) const
29 {
30    int i = string_to_int(ext);
31    if (1 <= i && i <= mailboxes.size())
32       return mailboxes[i];
33    return NULL;
34 }
```

ch23/mailsystem/telephone.h

```
1  #ifndef TELEPHONE_H
2  #define TELEPHONE_H
```

```
3
4   #include <iostream>
5   #include <string>
6
7   using namespace std;
8
9   class Connection;
10
11  /**
12      A telephone that takes simulated keystrokes and voice input
13      from the user and simulates spoken text.
14  */
15  class Telephone
16  {
17  public:
18      /**
19          Speaks a message to standard output.
20          @param output the text that will be spoken
21      */
22      void speak(string output);
23
24      /**
25          Loops reading user input and passes the input
26          to the Connection object's functions dial, record,
27          or hangup.
28          @param c the connection that connects this phone
29          to the voice mail system
30      */
31      void run(Connection& c);
32  };
33
34  inline void Telephone::speak(string output)
35  {
36      cout << output;
37  }
38
39  #endif
```

ch23/mailsystem/telephone.cpp

```
1   #include "telephone.h"
2   #include "connection.h"
3
4   void Telephone::run(Connection& c)
5   {
6       bool more = true;
7       while (more)
8       {
9           string input;
10          getline(cin, input);
11          if (input == "H")
12              c.hangup();
13          else if (input == "Q")
14              more = false;
```

```
15        else if ((input.length() == 1) &&
16           (isdigit(input[0]) || input[0] == '#'))
17           c.dial(input);
18        else
19           c.record(input);
20     }
21  }
```

ch23/mailsystem/connection.h

```
1   #ifndef CONNECTION_H
2   #define CONNECTION_H
3
4   #include "mailsystem.h"
5   #include "telephone.h"
6   #include "mailbox.h"
7
8   using namespace std;
9
10  /**
11     Connects a phone to the voice mail system.
12     The purpose of this class is to keep track
13     of the state of a connection, because the phone
14     itself is only the source of individual key presses.
15  */
16  class Connection
17  {
18  public:
19     /**
20        Constructs a Connection object.
21        @param s a MailSystem object
22        @param p a Telephone object
23     */
24     Connection(MailSystem& s, Telephone& p);
25
26     /**
27        Responds to the user's pressing a key
28        on the phone touchpad.
29        @param key the phone key pressed by the user
30     */
31     void dial(string key);
32
33     /**
34        Records voice.
35        @param voice voice spoken by the user
36     */
37     void record(string voice);
38
39     /**
40        The user hangs up the phone.
41     */
42     void hangup();
43
```

```
44   private:
45      /**
46         Resets the connection to the initial state
47         and prompts for mailbox number.
48      */
49      void reset_connection();
50
51      /**
52         Tries to connect the user with the specified mailbox.
53         @param key the phone key pressed by the user
54      */
55      void connect(string key);
56
57      /**
58         Tries to log in the user.
59         @param key the phone key pressed by the user
60      */
61      void login(string key);
62
63      /**
64         Changes the passcode.
65         @param key the phone key pressed by the user
66      */
67      void change_passcode(string key);
68
69      /**
70         Changes the greeting.
71         @param key the phone key pressed by the user
72      */
73      void change_greeting(string key);
74
75      /**
76         Responds to the user's selection from mailbox menu.
77         @param key the phone key pressed by the user
78      */
79      void mailbox_menu(string key);
80
81      /**
82         Responds to the user's selection from message menu.
83         @param key the phone key pressed by the user
84      */
85      void message_menu(string key);
86
87      MailSystem& system;
88      Mailbox* current_mailbox;
89      string current_recording;
90      string accumulated_keys;
91      Telephone& phone;
92
93      enum states {DISCONNECTED, CONNECTED, RECORDING,
94         MAILBOX_MENU, MESSAGE_MENU,
95         CHANGE_PASSCODE, CHANGE_GREETING};
96      enum states state;
97
```

```
 98       const string INITIAL_PROMPT;
 99       const string MAILBOX_MENU_TEXT;
100       const string MESSAGE_MENU_TEXT;
101    };
102
103    #endif
```

ch23/mailsystem/connection.cpp

```
 1    #include "message.h"
 2    #include "mailbox.h"
 3    #include "mailsystem.h"
 4    #include "connection.h"
 5    #include "telephone.h"
 6
 7    Connection::Connection(MailSystem& s, Telephone& p)
 8       : system(s), phone(p),
 9       INITIAL_PROMPT("Enter mailbox number followed by #\n"),
10       MAILBOX_MENU_TEXT("Enter 1 to listen to your messages\n"
11       "Enter 2 to change your passcode\n"
12       "Enter 3 to change your greeting\n"),
13       MESSAGE_MENU_TEXT("Enter 1 to listen to the current message\n"
14       "Enter 2 to save the current message\n"
15       "Enter 3 to delete the current message\n"
16       "Enter 4 to return to the main menu\n")
17    {
18       reset_connection();
19    }
20
21    void Connection::dial(string key)
22    {
23       if (state == CONNECTED)
24          connect(key);
25       else if (state == RECORDING)
26          login(key);
27       else if (state == CHANGE_PASSCODE)
28          change_passcode(key);
29       else if (state == CHANGE_GREETING)
30          change_greeting(key);
31       else if (state == MAILBOX_MENU)
32          mailbox_menu(key);
33       else if (state == MESSAGE_MENU)
34          message_menu(key);
35    }
36
37    void Connection::record(string voice)
38    {
39       if (state == RECORDING || state == CHANGE_GREETING)
40          current_recording += voice;
41    }
42
43    void Connection::hangup()
44    {
45       if (state == RECORDING)
46          current_mailbox->add_message(new Message(current_recording));
```

```
47         reset_connection();
48    }
49
50    void Connection::reset_connection()
51    {
52       current_recording = "";
53       accumulated_keys = "";
54       state = CONNECTED;
55       phone.speak(INITIAL_PROMPT);
56    }
57
58    void Connection::connect(string key)
59    {
60       if (key == "#")
61       {
62          current mailbox = system.find_mailbox(accumulated_keys);
63          if (current_mailbox != NULL)
64          {
65             state = RECORDING;
66             phone.speak(current_mailbox->get_greeting());
67          }
68          else
69             phone.speak("Incorrect mailbox number. Try again!");
70          accumulated_keys = "";
71       }
72       else
73          accumulated_keys += key;
74    }
75
76    void Connection::login(string key)
77    {
78       if (key -- "#")
79       {
80          if (current_mailbox->check_passcode(accumulated_keys))
81          {
82             state = MAILBOX_MENU;
83             phone.speak(MAILBOX_MENU_TEXT);
84          }
85          else
86             phone.speak("Incorrect passcode. Try again!");
87          accumulated_keys = "";
88       }
89       else
90          accumulated_keys += key;
91    }
92
93    void Connection::change_passcode(string key)
94    {
95       if (key == "#")
96       {
97          current_mailbox->set_passcode(accumulated_keys);
98          state = MAILBOX_MENU;
99          phone.speak(MAILBOX_MENU_TEXT);
100         accumulated_keys = "";
```

```
101        }
102     else
103        accumulated_keys += key;
104  }
105
106  void Connection::change_greeting(string key)
107  {
108     if (key == "#")
109     {
110        current_mailbox->set_greeting(current_recording);
111        current_recording = "";
112        state = MAILBOX_MENU;
113        phone.speak(MAILBOX_MENU_TEXT);
114     }
115  }
116
117  void Connection::mailbox_menu(string key)
118  {
119     if (key == "1")
120     {
121        state = MESSAGE_MENU;
122        phone.speak(MESSAGE_MENU_TEXT);
123     }
124     else if (key == "2")
125     {
126        state = CHANGE_PASSCODE;
127        phone.speak("Enter new passcode followed by the # key");
128     }
129     else if (key == "3")
130     {
131        state = CHANGE_GREETING;
132        phone.speak("Record your greeting, then press the # key");
133     }
134  }
135
136  void Connection::message_menu(string key)
137  {
138     if (key == "1")
139     {
140        string output = "";
141        Message* m = current_mailbox->get_current_message();
142        if (m == NULL) output += "No messages.\n";
143        else output += m->get_text() + "\n";
144        output += MESSAGE_MENU_TEXT;
145        phone.speak(output);
146     }
147     else if (key == "2")
148     {
149        current_mailbox->save_current_message();
150        phone.speak(MESSAGE_MENU_TEXT);
151     }
152     else if (key == "3")
153     {
```

```
154          current_mailbox->remove_current_message();
155          phone.speak(MESSAGE_MENU_TEXT);
156       }
157       else if (key == "4")
158       {
159          state = MAILBOX_MENU;
160          phone.speak(MAILBOX_MENU_TEXT);
161       }
162    }
```

ch23/mailsystem/mailsystemtest.cpp

```
1   #include "mailsystem.h"
2   #include "telephone.h"
3   #include "connection.h"
4
5   int main()
6   {
7      const int MAILBOX_COUNT = 20;
8      MailSystem system(MAILBOX_COUNT);
9      Telephone p;
10     Connection c(system, p);
11     p.run(c);
12     return 0;
13  }
```

CHAPTER SUMMARY

1. The UML notation is the unification of several notations for object-oriented design diagrams.

2. Use cases assist problem analysis by providing concrete scenarios from which general action can be abstracted.

3. Sequence diagrams record the dynamic interaction between objects.

4. State diagrams are useful for documenting objects that change their behavior according to their current state during the course of execution.

FURTHER READING

1. Ivar Jacobson, Grady Booch, and James Rumbaugh, *The Unified Software Development Process*, Addison-Wesley, 1999.

REVIEW EXERCISES

Exercise R23.1. Draw a UML diagram that describes the relationships between the classes List, Node, and Iterator for the linked list abstraction developed in Chapter 12.

Exercise R23.2. Describe a scenario, with variations, for one round of the clock game described in Chapter 22.

Exercise R23.3. Consider the task of modeling checkout times at a supermarket with multiple cashiers. Customers line up at the cashier with the shortest queue. Identify suitable classes. Draw a sequence diagram that shows the actions taken by a customer when lining up. Draw another sequence diagram that shows the actions taken when a customer has completed checkout and the next waiting customer is served.

Exercise R23.4. Consider the development of an online course registration system that allows students to add and drop classes at a university. Describe the activities that will take place during the analysis, design, and implementation phases. Give specific examples of activities that relate to the registration system.

Exercise R23.5. List at least eight classes that can be used in an online course registration system that allows students to add and drop classes at a university.

Exercise R23.6. What relationship is appropriate between the following classes: aggregation, inheritance, or neither?

   a. University–Student
   b. Student–TeachingAssistant
   c. Student–Freshman
   d. Student–Professor
   e. Car–Door
   f. Truck–Vehicle
   g. Traffic–TrafficSign
   h. TrafficSign–Color

Exercise R23.7. Consider an online course registration system that allows students to add and drop classes at a university. Give the multiplicities of the associations between these class pairs.

   a. Student–Course
   b. Course–Section
   c. Section–Instructor
   d. Section–Room

Exercise R23.8. Consider an airline reservation system with classes Passenger, Itinerary, Flight, and Seat. Consider a scenario in which a passenger adds a flight to an itinerary and selects a seat. What responsibilities and collaborators will you record on the CRC cards as a result?

Exercise R23.9. How does the design of Exercise R23.8 change if you have a group of passengers that fly together?

Exercise R23.10. Consider an online store that enables customers to order items from a catalog and pay for them with a credit card. Draw a UML diagram that shows the relationships between these classes:

```
Customer
Order
RushOrder
Product
Address
CreditCard
```

Exercise R23.11. Consider a program that plays tic-tac-toe with a human user. A class TicTacToeBoard stores the game board. A random number generator is used to choose who begins and to generate random legal moves when it's the computer's turn. When it's the human's turn, the program prompts for the next move and checks that it is legal. After every move, the program checks whether the game is over. Draw a sequence diagram that shows a scenario in which the game starts, the computer gets the first turn, and the human gets the second turn. Stop the diagram after the second turn.

Exercise R23.12. Consider the scenario "A user changes the mailbox passcode" in the voice mail system. Carry out a walkthrough with the mail system's CRC cards. What steps do you list in your walkthrough? What collaborations and responsibilities do you record as a result of the walkthrough?

PROGRAMMING EXERCISES

Exercise P23.1. Design and implement a program that simulates a vending machine. Products can be purchased by inserting the correct number of coins into the machine. A user selects a product from a list of available products, adds coins, and either gets the product or gets the coins returned if insufficient money was supplied or if the product is sold out. Products can be restocked and money removed by an operator. Follow the design process that was described in this chapter.

Exercise P23.2. Design and implement a program that manages an appointment calendar. An appointment includes the description, date, starting time, and ending time; for example,

```
Dentist 2010/10/1 17:30 18:30
CS1 class 2010/10/2 08:30 10:00
```

Supply a user interface to add appointments, remove canceled appointments, and print out a list of appointments for a particular day. Follow the design process that was described in this chapter.

Exercise P23.3. *Airline seating.* Design and implement a program that assigns seats on an airplane. Assume the airplane has 20 seats in first class (5 rows of 4 seats each, separated by an aisle) and 180 seats in economy class (30 rows of 6 seats each, separated by an aisle). Your program should take three commands: add passengers, show seating, and quit. When passengers are added, ask for the class (first or economy), the number of passengers traveling together (1 or 2 in first class; 1 to 3 in economy), and the seating preference (aisle or window in first class; aisle, center, or window in economy). Then try to find a match and assign the seats. If no match exists, print a message. Follow the design process that was described in this chapter.

Exercise P23.4. In the voice mail system, when a message is saved, the instance of class Message is duplicated using a copy constructor. This allows the function remove_current_message to simply delete the message found in the message queue. Replace this simple memory management technique with a reference counting system similar to the one described in Chapter 15.

Exercise P23.5. Add a class EncryptedMessage that derives from Message. An EncryptedMessage is stored in encrypted form, and decrypted when it is retrieved. For simplicity, you can use the Caesar cipher (Section 9.4) for performing the encryption and decryption.

Exercise P23.6. In a real voice mail system, users can have arbitrary extension numbers, such as extension 4753. Reimplement the voice mail system, and rather than storing the mailboxes in a vector indexed by the extension number, use a map<string, Mailbox*>. The key for the map should be the extension number, while the value is the mailbox associated with the extension.

Exercise P23.7. Improve the solution of Exercise P23.6 by adding an administration interface to the voice mail system. Administration commands allow addition and removal of mailboxes with arbitrary extension numbers. To do this, design a class AdminConnection that extends the Connection class and understands the additional commands.

An Introduction to Design Patterns

CHAPTER GOALS

- To review the advantages of iterators

- To learn about the pattern concept

- To study several common design patterns: ITERATOR, ADAPTER, TEMPLATE METHOD, STRATEGY, and COMPOSITE

- To learn where patterns are used in the standard C++ library

- To put patterns to work in a complex program

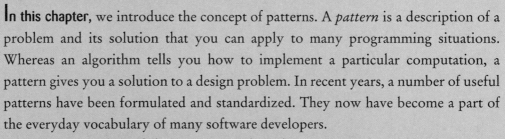

In this chapter, we introduce the concept of patterns. A *pattern* is a description of a problem and its solution that you can apply to many programming situations. Whereas an algorithm tells you how to implement a particular computation, a pattern gives you a solution to a design problem. In recent years, a number of useful patterns have been formulated and standardized. They now have become a part of the everyday vocabulary of many software developers.

A large number of design patterns have been proposed. In this chapter, we introduce five design patterns that are both commonly used and easy to comprehend. We show how the chosen patterns relate to familiar programming situations and to constructs from the C++ standard library.

24.1 Iterators

> Iterators are preferred over cursors because you can attach more than one iterator to a collection.

In order to motivate our first design pattern, let us have another look at the list iterators of the standard C++ library. Here is how you visit all items in a linked list:

```
list<string>::iterator pos;
for (pos = list.begin(); pos != list.end(); ++pos)
{
    string item = *pos;
    ...
}
```

The begin and end functions yield iterators to the beginning position and the position past the end of the list. The ++ operator advances the iterator to the next position. The * operator returns the current element.

Why does the C++ library use iterators to traverse a linked list? The library designers chose iterators because they had learned from past mistakes. If you look at a traditional data structures book, you will find traversal code that manipulates the nodes directly:

```
Node* current = list.head;
while (current != NULL)
{
    string item = current->data;
    current = current->next;
    ...
}
```

This approach has two disadvantages. From a high-level point of view, it is not satisfactory because it exposes the nodes to the user of the list. But the nodes are just an artifact of the implementation that should be hidden from the user. As you may know, there are several variations of list implementations, such as circular lists or

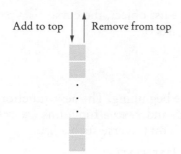

Add to top ↓ ↑ Remove from top

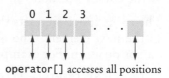

0 1 2 3

operator[] accesses all positions

Figure 1 The Stack Interface   **Figure 2** The Array Interface

lists with a dummy header node. List users certainly should not have to worry about those implementation details.

Furthermore, as anyone who has ever implemented a linked list knows, it is very easy to mess up nodes and corrupt the link structure of a linked list. Thus, survival instinct dictates that list users should be shielded from the raw nodes and links.

Let us return to the high-level point of view. In Chapter 12, we used a stack class and had no problem defining the operations that make up a stack (see Figure 1):

```
void push(const T& t)
T pop()
T top() const
```

Similarly, it is an easy matter to define the operations that make up an array structure with random access (see Figure 2):

```
T& operator[](int i)
void push_back(const T& t)
int size() const
```

But the interface for a linked list is not so simple. We want to be able to add and remove elements in the middle of the linked list, but it would be very inefficient to specify a position in a linked list with an integer index.

One implementation that you sometimes see is a list with a *cursor* (see Figure 3). It has the following interface:

```
T get() const   // Get element at cursor
void set(const T& t)   // Set element at cursor to t
T remove()   // Remove element at cursor
void insert(const T& t)   // Insert t before cursor
void reset()   // Reset cursor to head
void next()   // Advance cursor
bool is_done()   // Check if cursor can be advanced
```

Cursor

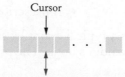

Figure 3 List with a Cursor   get/set/insert/remove access cursor position

Unlike an iterator, which is external to the list object, the cursor is a part of the list itself. The state of a list with a cursor consists of

- the sequence of the stored elements
- the cursor position

The reset function resets the cursor to the beginning. The next function advances it to the next element. The get, set, insert, and remove functions are relative to the cursor position. For example, here is how you traverse such a list.

```
for (list.reset(); !list.is_done(); list.next())
{
   T item = list.get();
   ...
}
```

At first glance, a list with a cursor seems like a good idea. The links are not exposed to the list user. No separate iterator class is required.

However, that design has severe limitations. Since there is only one cursor, you can't implement algorithms that compare different list elements. You can't even print the contents of the list for debugging purposes. Printing the list would have the side effect of moving the cursor to the end!

Thus, the iterator is a superior concept. A list can have any number of iterators attached to it. That means that you should supply iterators, and not a cursor, whenever you implement a collection class.

Furthermore, the iterator concept is useful outside the domain of linked lists. Here are a couple of examples. Conceptually, an istream object is an iterator that yields a sequence of bytes from an input source. If you need to visit the rows of a database table, an iterator can do the job, and it is a better solution than a cursor or low-level pointer. Thus, list iterators are just one instance of a common *pattern*. We will explore the concept of patterns in the next section.

24.2 The Pattern Concept

> A design pattern uses a standard format to give advice about a problem in software design.

The architect Christopher Alexander formulated more than 250 patterns for architectural design. (See [1].) Alexander's patterns lay down rules for building houses and cities. Alexander uses a very distinctive format for these rules. Every pattern has

- A short *name*
- A brief description of the *context*
- A lengthy description of the *problem*
- A prescription for a *solution*

Here is a typical example, showing the context and solution exactly as they appear in Alexander's book. The problem description is long; it is summarized here.

DESIGN PATTERN 24.1

SHORT PASSAGES

Context

1. "… long, sterile corridors set the scene for everything bad about modern architecture."

Problem

This section contains a lengthy description of the problem of long corridors, with a depressing picture of a long, straight, narrow corridor with closed doors, similar to the one below.

Alexander discusses issues of light and furniture. He cites research results about patient anxiety in hospital corridors. According to the research, corridors that are longer than 50 feet are perceived as uncomfortable.

Solution

Keep passages short. Make them as much like rooms as possible, with carpets or wood on the floor, furniture, bookshelves, beautiful windows. Make them generous in shape and always give them plenty of light; the best corridors and passages of all are those that have windows along an entire wall.

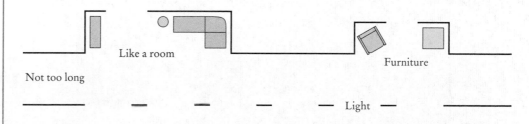

As you can see, this pattern distills a design rule into a simple format. If you have a design problem, you first check whether the pattern is useful to you. If you decide that the pattern applies to your situation, then you follow the recipe for a solution. Because that solution has been successful in the past, there is a good chance that you will benefit from it as well.

Alexander was interested in patterns that solve problems in architecture. Of course, our interest lies in software development. In this chapter, you will see patterns that give you guidance on object-oriented design.

The ITERATOR pattern teaches how to access the elements of an aggregate object.

Let's start by presenting the ITERATOR pattern. As you saw in the preceding section, iterators are useful for traversing the elements of a linked list, but they occur in many programming situations. Input streams are another example of the ITERATOR pattern.

DESIGN PATTERN 24.2

ITERATOR

Context

1. An object (which we'll call the *aggregate*) contains other objects (which we'll call *elements*).
2. *Clients* (that is, functions that use the aggregate) need access to the elements.
3. The aggregate should not expose its internal structure.
4. There may be multiple clients that need simultaneous access.

Solution

1. Define an iterator class that fetches one element at a time.
2. Each iterator object needs to keep track of the position of the next element to fetch.

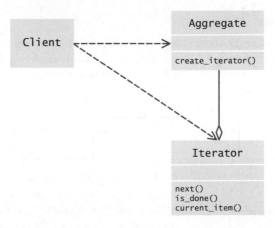

Note that the names of the classes and functions (such as `Aggregate`, `Iterator`, `create_iterator`, `is_done`) are *examples*. In an actual realization of the pattern, the names may be quite different.

For example, in the case of linked list iterators, we have:

Name in Design Pattern	Actual Name (List Iterators)
Aggregate	list<T>
Iterator	list<T>::iterator
create_iterator()	begin(), end()
next()	++ operator
is_done()	Test for equality with end()
current_item()	* operator

The actual names are quite different when considering input streams as a manifestation of the iterator pattern.

Name in Design Pattern	Actual Name (Input Streams)
Aggregate	A source of bytes such as a file
Iterator	istream
create_iterator()	open()
next()	get()
is_done()	!fail()
current_item()	Return value of get()

As you can see, a pattern is more abstract than an algorithm. An algorithm gives you specific instructions how to implement a computation. A pattern gives you advice on solving a design problem. The influential book, *Design Patterns* by Gamma, Helm, Johnson, and Vlissides, contains a description of many patterns for software design, including the ITERATOR pattern. (See [2].) Because the book has four authors, it is sometimes referred to as the "Gang of Four" book. (The original Gang of Four were radical Chinese communists who were advocates of the Cultural Revolution. There is no apparent connection between the two "gangs" beyond the fact that they each have four members.)

In this chapter, we cover five of the patterns in the *Design Patterns* book: ITERATOR, ADAPTER, TEMPLATE METHOD, STRATEGY, and COMPOSITE. We selected these patterns because they are are useful and can be motivated with familiar examples. There are many other important patterns—see Table 1, "Other Common Design Patterns," on page 946 for a brief summary.

ADVANCED TOPIC 24.1

Generic Programming with Inheritance and Templates

If you read the description of the ITERATOR pattern in [2], you will find another recommendation that we omitted from our pattern. The authors suggest using abstract base classes for the iterator and aggregate, so that the client doesn't have to know about the exact types of the iterator and aggregate. A client can then write generic code such as the following:

```
void print_all(AbstractAggregate* items)
{
    AbstractIterator* iter = items->create_iterator();
    while (!iter->is_done())
    {
        cout << iter->current_item() << "\n";
        iter->next();
    }
}
```

This function can be used to print items of any derived class of AbstractAggregate. For example, if there are list and array classes that both inherit from AbstractAggregate, then the virtual create_iterator function returns an appropriate iterator that belongs to some derived class of AbstractIterator. The implementations for list iterators and array iterators will be very different, but the client won't know or care. The virtual functions is_done, current_item, and next automatically invoke the appropriate functionality of the iterator objects.

In some programming languages—in particular Java and Smalltalk—this style of iteration is very common. There are also C++ libraries whose aggregate and iterator classes derive from common base classes. However, the standard C++ library uses templates, not inheritance, to achieve genericity. Using templates is more efficient because it avoids the cost of virtual function calls.

With the standard C++ library, we implement print_all as a function template. A template parameter denotes an arbitrary container.

```
template<typename T>
void print_all(const T& items)
{
    T::iterator iter = items.begin();
    while (iter != items.end())
    {
        cout << *iter << "\n";
        iter++;
    }
}
```

There is no inheritance at work. For the template to compile, T must be a type that has begin() and end() functions and a nested type called iterator. That iterator type must have operators !=, *, and ++. If the function is called with an inappropriate type, then the compiler reports an error.

24.3 The ADAPTER Pattern

> The ADAPTER pattern teaches how to use a class in a context that requires a different interface.

If you have ever tried to hook up a laptop computer in a foreign country, you are probably familiar with the concept of an *adapter*. The power plug of your computer may not fit into the wall outlet, and the foreign telephone plug may not fit into your computer modem. To solve these problems, travelers often carry a set of adapter plugs that convert one kind of plug into another.

In object-oriented programming, you often have similar problems. For example, suppose you want to convert a string containing digits (such as "235") into an integer (such as 235). Unfortunately, the string class has no function to carry out this conversion. If the digits were stored in a stream, the task would be solved easily: You would just use the >> operator of the istream class. What we need is an intermediary that *adapts* a string object to an istream object.

As you saw in Chapter 9, the istringstream class provides just such an adapter. Convert a string to a stream and you can easily extract the integer value:

```
string s = "235";
istringstream istr(s);
int n;
s >> n;   // Now n is the integer 235
```

Stream adapters are just one example of a general design pattern. You use the ADAPTER pattern whenever you would like to use an existing class but its interface doesn't match the one you need.

How does the istringstream class work? The >> operator of the istream base class repeatedly calls the get function to fetch digits, and assembles an integer from their numerical values. The istringstream class defines the get function to obtain characters from the string, by calling the [] operator of the string class. The istringstream class is one instance of the ADAPTER pattern.

DESIGN PATTERN 24.3

ADAPTER

Context

1. You want to use an existing class without modifying it. We'll call this class the *adaptee*.
2. The context in which you want to use the class requires conformance to a *target* interface that is different from that of the adaptee.
3. The target interface and the adaptee interface are conceptually related.

Solution

1. Define an *adapter* class that conforms to the target interface.
2. The adapter class aggregates the adaptee class. It translates target functions to adaptee functions.
3. The client wraps the adaptee into an adapter class object.

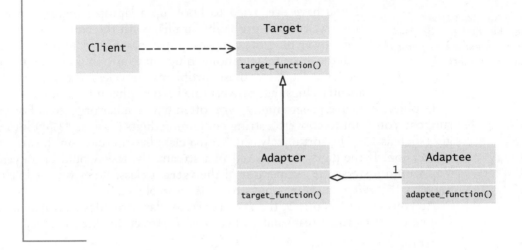

For example, in the case of the string stream adapter, we have:

Name in Design Pattern	Actual Name (String Streams)
Adaptee	string
Target	istream
Adapter	istringstream
Client	The code that wants to use the >> operator to read data from a string
target_function()	get()
adaptee_function()	The [] operator

You find another use of the ADAPTER pattern in the standard C++ library. Consider the standard copy algorithm:

```
template <typename SI, typename TI>
void copy(SI from, SI end, TI to>
{
```

```
    while (from != end)
    {
        *to = *from; from++; to++;
    }
}
```

Here SI is an iterator type for a source of objects, and TI an iterator for the target. You use the copy algorithm whenever you want to copy a source range into a target, for example:

```
vector<string> source(10);
vector<string> target(10);
...
copy(source.begin(), source.end(), target.begin());
```

Recall that the copy algorithm was provided in the standard library because the function call is easier to read than the explicit loop.

Now suppose you want to *print* the values in the vector. Of course, you could program an explicit loop. Or perhaps the standard library could provide a print function. However, the standard library has taken a different approach. As you have seen in Chapter 20, there is an adapter that turns a stream into an iterator. You can print the contents of the vector with the following command:

```
ostream_iterator<string> to(cout, "\n");
copy(source.begin(), source.end(), to);
```

or, more concisely:

```
copy(source.begin(), source.end(), ostream_iterator<string>(cout, "\n"));
```

The ostream_iterator class turns an ostream (such as cout in our example) into an iterator. Whenever a value is "assigned" to the iterator through a statement of the form

```
*to = value;
```

then the value is actually printed to the output stream. This is achieved by cleverly overloading the * and = operators. (The ++ operator is defined as a dummy operation that does nothing.)

The second parameter of the ostream_iterator constructor is a string that is printed after each value, so that the values are separated from each other. In our example, we use a newline character to place the values on separate lines.

Similarly, there is an istream_iterator that adapts an istream to an iterator. You can use it to insert items from an input stream into a container:

```
copy(istream_iterator<string>(cin), istream_iterator<string>(),
    target.begin());
```

The default constructor istream_iterator<string>() constructs an iterator object that signifies the end of the input stream. This adapter overloads the * and != operators to read values and to test for the end of input.

Perhaps you don't find these stream adapters very natural—many programmers have argued that they are a solution in search of a problem. Nevertheless, the stream adapters are a good illustration of the Adapter pattern. The stream adapters translate the interface of iterators (that is, the operators such as * and ++) into the interface of streams (that is, << and >> operations). Thus, they let programmers use streams in algorithms that expect iterator parameters.

Name in Design Pattern	Actual Name (String Streams)
Adaptee	istream, ostream
Target	iterator
Adapter	istream_iterator, ostream_iterator
Client	The code that wants to use a stream in a standard algorithm function
target_function()	<<, >>, fail()
adaptee_function()	The *, =, ++, != operators

24.4 The TEMPLATE METHOD Pattern

> The TEMPLATE METHOD pattern teaches how to supply varying behavior patterns to an algorithm.

In this section, you will learn about an ingenious design pattern that allows a programmer to implement an algorithm in a base class, even though some of the details of the algorithm are not known. These details are supplied in virtual functions of a derived class. The template method in the base class tells how to fit the details into the desired algorithm.

Let us first look at an example, again from the C++ stream library. Each stream has a *buffer* associated with it. When a character is written to the stream, it is first placed in the buffer. Once the buffer is full, the entire buffer contents is sent to its target, for example, a file. Buffering is useful for efficiency. It is much faster to write a chunk of characters to a file than to write each character separately. (Reading from a stream is also buffered, but for simplicity, we will focus on writing.)

The only difference between an ofstream and an ostringstream is the buffer that is attached to the stream. An ofstream class has a filebuf object that saves characters to a file, whereas an ostringstream has a stringbuf object that inserts characters into a string. Similarly, you can define a stream that sends its output to a window in a graphics system, simply by attaching a buffer that draws characters on the window (see Exercise P24.16).

Consider an output operation such as

```
cout << "Hello, World!";
```

The appropriate `operator<<` function converts each value into a sequence of individual characters. It then inserts each character into the stream buffer. Here is one possible implementation:

```
ostream& ostream::operator<<(const char s[])
{
    int i = 0;
    while (s[i] != '\0')
    {
        rdbuf()->sputc(s[i]);
        i++;
    }
    return *this;
}
```

The `rdbuf` function returns a pointer to the stream buffer. The `sputc` function inserts a character into the buffer. Here is the outline of that function:

```
int streambuf::sputc(char c)
{
    if (buffer full)
        return overflow(c);
    else
    {
        add c to the buffer
        return c;
    }
}
```

The `overflow` function writes the buffer content and the character `c` to its destination. Remarkably, the `streambuf` class has no idea where that function places characters. The `overflow` function is a virtual function. The `streambuf` class merely supplies a dummy implementation that discards `c` and returns an "end of file" indicator. Derived classes such as `filebuf` and `streambuf` redefine the `overflow` function to do real work.

Note that the derived classes do not redefine the `sputc` function. That function is defined in the `streambuf` base class, even though a `streambuf` does not know where to send characters! It merely knows that the derived classes will supply a function for this purpose.

The `sputc` function is an example of the TEMPLATE METHOD pattern. In this pattern, a base class defines an algorithm that calls *primitive operations*. These primitive operations are not supplied by the base class. Instead, each derived class supplies the primitive operation that is most appropriate for it. The template method contains the knowledge of how to combine the primitive operations into a more complex algorithm. For example, the `sputc` function calls the primitive operation `overflow` at the appropriate moment. The contribution of the template method is to know *when* to call the primitive operations.

The term "template method" has no connection with the C++ templates that you saw in Chapter 16. Instead, you should view the base class algorithm as a template that defines a method for producing operations for the various derived classes.

DESIGN PATTERN 24.4

TEMPLATE METHOD

Context

1. An algorithm is applicable for multiple types.
2. The algorithm can be broken down into *primitive operations*. The primitive operations can be different for each type.
3. The order in which the *primitive operations* are executed in the algorithm doesn't depend on the type.

Solution

1. Define a base class that has a function for the algorithm and virtual functions for the primitive operations.
2. Implement the algorithm to call the primitive operations in the appropriate order.
3. In the base class, define the primitive operations to have appropriate default behavior, or leave them undefined if there is no suitable default.
4. Each derived class defines the primitive operations but not the algorithm.

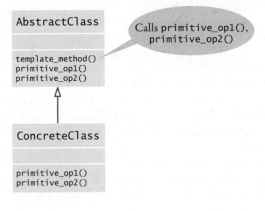

Here is the mapping of the pattern concepts to the integer input algorithm:

Name in Design Pattern	Actual Name (Stream Buffers)
AbstractClass	streambuf
ConcreteClass	filebuf, stringbuf
template_method()	sputc
primitive_op1()	overflow

24.5 Function Objects and the STRATEGY Pattern

24.5.1 Function Objects

The STRATEGY pattern teaches how to supply variants of an algorithm to a client.

The STRATEGY pattern shows how to supply a variety of algorithms to a computation. To motivate this design pattern, let us first review the sort algorithm in the standard C++ library. For example, consider the following function call to sort a vector of strings:

```
vector<string> names;
...
sort(names.begin(), names.end());
```

The sort algorithm can sort vectors holding elements of any type, provided there is a < operator that compares the elements. Recall that the < operator is defined for string objects and that it compares strings in dictionary order.

Now suppose we want to sort a vector of Employee objects.

```
vector<Employee> staff;
sort(staff.begin(), staff.end());
```

This call will only compile if the < operator has been overloaded for Employee objects. Of course, we can define such an operator:

```
bool operator<(const Employee& a, const Employee& b)
{
    return a.get_name() < b.get_name();
}
```

Now the employees will be sorted by name.

However, suppose we want to sort the employees by salary instead of by name. We can't redefine the operator< function every time we want to change the sort order. Instead, there is a second sort function that is more flexible. That function lets you supply *any* sort order. You specify a sort order as a class that overloads the function call operator.

Let's define such a class:

```
class SalaryComparator
{
public:
    bool operator()(const Employee& a, const Employee& b)
    {
        return a.get_salary() < b.get_salary();
    }
};
```

To sort the staff vector, you construct an object of this class and pass it to the sort function:

```
SalaryComparator comp;
sort(staff.begin(), staff.end(), comp);
```

As a shorthand, you can pass an anonymous object, constructed with the default constructor:

```
sort(staff.begin(), staff.end(), SalaryComparator());
```

What goes on behind the scenes? We don't have to know exactly which sorting algorithm the C++ standard library uses. Every sorting algorithm compares objects in various locations in the collection and rearranges them if they are out of order. The code for the sort function contains statements such as the following:

```
if (!comp(x, y))
    rearrange x and y;
```

Here comp is the comparator object that was passed to the sort function. The call comp(x, y) invokes the operator() function. That function is defined in the Salary-Comparator class to compare the objects by their salaries.

Clearly, you can carry out any desired comparison by supplying a class with an appropriate operator() function.

An object such as comp is often called a *function object* because its sole purpose is to execute the comparator function.

The SalaryComparator object has no state—all objects of this class behave in exactly the same way. Indeed, many simple function objects are stateless. However, you can achieve more sophisticated behavior by adding data fields to function objects. Here is an enhancement of the comparator class that can sort in either ascending or descending order.

```
class SalaryComparator
{
public:
    SalaryComparator(bool a)
    {
        ascending = a;
    }
    bool operator()(const Employee& a, const Employee& b)
    {
        if (ascending)
            return a.get_salary() < b.get_salary();
        else
            return a.get_salary() > b.get_salary();
    }
private:
    bool ascending;
};
```

Then an object

```
SalaryComparator reverse_comp(false);
```

can be used to sort Employee objects in decreasing salary order.

COMMON ERROR 24.1

Confusing Function Objects and Classes

Look carefully at the call

```
sort(staff.begin(), staff.end(), SalaryComparator());
```

Note that there is a pair of parentheses after the class name SalaryComparator. These parentheses denote a call to the default constructor of the SalaryComparator class. It would be an error to omit the parentheses.

```
sort(staff.begin(), staff.end(), SalaryComparator);   // Error
```

After all, the parameters of the staff function must be values, not types.

24.5.2 The STRATEGY Pattern

You have seen how the comparator concept gives programmers a great deal of flexibility. If the default ordering is not appropriate, you can change the sort order to any ordering. To produce a particular order, you simply define a class with an overloaded function call operator, make an object of that class, and give it to the sort function. When the sort function needs to compare two values, it calls the operator() function of the comparator object. This is an example of the STRATEGY pattern.

The STRATEGY pattern applies whenever you want to allow a client to supply an algorithm. The pattern tells us to place the essential steps of the algorithm in a strategy interface. (Note that in the case of the sort function, the algorithm in question is not the sorting algorithm, but the algorithm used for comparing objects.)

By supplying objects of different classes that implement the strategy interface functions, the algorithm can be varied.

DESIGN PATTERN 24.5

STRATEGY

Context

1. A class (which we'll call the *context* class) can benefit from different variants of an algorithm.
2. Clients of the context class sometimes want to supply custom versions of the algorithm.

Solution

1. Define an interface that is an abstraction for the algorithm. We'll call this the *strategy interface*.
2. Concrete strategy classes supply the functions of the strategy interface. Each strategy class implements a version of the algorithm.

3. The client supplies a concrete strategy object to the context class.
4. Whenever the algorithm needs to be executed, the context class calls the appropriate functions of the strategy object.

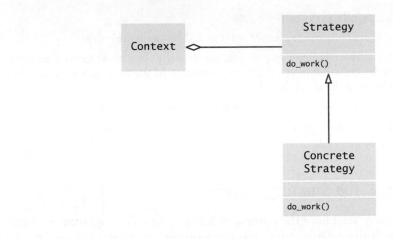

Here is the relationship between the names in the STRATEGY design pattern and the sorting manifestation.

Name in Design Pattern	Actual Name (Sorting)
Context	The sort function
Strategy	The interface that the sort algorithm expects the comparator object to have, i.e., operator()
ConcreteStrategy	The comparator class
do_work()	The operator() comparator function

24.6 The COMPOSITE Pattern

The COMPOSITE pattern teaches how to combine several objects into an object that has the same behavior as its parts.

In Chapter 22, we developed a program to print an invoice. The invoice bills a customer for a set of items. A typical invoice item is a charge for three toasters at $29.95 each.

Now let's consider a more complex situation. Sometimes, stores will sell *bundles* of related items. A bundle might be a stereo system consisting of a tuner, amplifier, CD player, and speakers, or a hammer with 100 nails. It should be possible to add a bundle to an invoice.

There is just one technical issue. You can only add items to an invoice. Can a bundle of items itself be an item?

The solution is to make a `Bundle` class that contains a collection of items, and that inherits from the `Item` class.

```
class Bundle : public Item
{
    ...
private:
    vector<Item*> items;
};
```

This is an example of the COMPOSITE pattern. This pattern addresses situations where primitive objects can be grouped into composite objects, and the composites themselves are considered primitive objects. For example, in an HTML editor, elements can be grouped into a table, and the table is again considered an element.

One characteristic of the COMPOSITE design pattern is how a function of the composite class does its work. It must apply the function to all of its primitive objects and then combine the results.

For example, to compute the price of a bundle, the bundle class computes the prices of each of its items and returns the sum of these values. (A useful enhancement would be to give a discount for the bundle—see Exercise P24.8.)

```
double Bundle::get_unit_price() const
{
    double price = 0;
    for (int i = 0; i < items.size(); i++)
    {
        price = price
            + items[i]->get_unit_price() * items[i]->get_quantity();
    }
    return price;
}
```

Similarly, consider the task of drawing a table in an HTML editor. The table carries out the drawing operation by drawing the elements in all of its cells.

DESIGN PATTERN 24.6

COMPOSITE

Context

1. Primitive objects can be combined into composite objects.
2. Clients treat a composite object as a primitive object.

Solution

1. Define a class that is an abstraction for the primitive objects.
2. Both primitive classes and composite classes inherit from that class.
3. A composite object contains a collection of primitive objects.

4. When implementing an operation in the composite class, apply the operation to the primitive objects and combine the results.

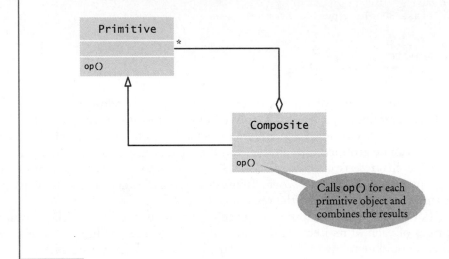

As with the previous patterns, we show how the names in the design pattern map to an example, in this case, a bundle of invoice items.

Name in Design Pattern	Actual Name (Bundle of Items)
Primitive	Item
Composite	Bundle
op()	get_unit_price

COMMON ERROR 24.2

Pattern Recognition

Students of object-oriented design often have trouble recognizing patterns. The patterns have such intuitive names that it is tempting to suspect their usage in many situations where they don't actually apply. Just because something appears to be strategic does not mean that the STRATEGY pattern is at work. Patterns are not vague concepts. They are very specific. The STRATEGY pattern only applies when a specific set of circumstances is fulfilled, as described by the pattern context and solution.

For example, a list iterator might be a good strategy for accessing list elements, but it has nothing to do with the STRATEGY pattern. The first context condition of the STRATEGY pattern doesn't even apply: The user of a list isn't interested in different variants of iteration.

Consider a more subtle scenario. The sort function sorts elements by repeatedly calling a comparison function:

```
while (...)
{
    if (!comp(x, y))
        rearrange x and y;
}
```

Is this an example of the TEMPLATE METHOD pattern? The context seems to match perfectly. We have an algorithm (sorting) that is applicable for multiple types and can be broken down into primitive operations (comparing).

However, the solution of the TEMPLATE METHOD pattern is very different. The pattern suggests defining a base class with a virtual function for the primitive operation:

```
template <typename T>
class Sorter
{
public:
    void sort(vector<T>& v);
    virtual bool compare(const T& a, const T& b);
};
```

To sort employees by salary, form a derived class:

```
class SalarySorter : public Sorter<Employee>
{
    virtual bool compare(const Employee& a, const Employee& b)
    {
        return a.get_salary() < b.get_salary();
    }
};
```

This approach has nothing in common with the approach taken by the sort function in the C++ standard library. Thus, the sort function does *not* use the TEMPLATE METHOD pattern.

As you can see, you must carefully inspect both the context and the solution of a pattern to see whether it applies to a given situation.

24.7 Case Study: Putting Patterns to Work

Design patterns apply in specific situations that are described by the context and solution parts of the pattern.

In this section, we will put several patterns to work in a simple application. We will refine the invoice printing program of Chapter 22. Specifically, we will include the Bundle class of the preceding section and make other changes that show various patterns at work.

An invoice contains a collection of items. Unlike the implementation of Chapter 22, we define a general Item class with pure virtual functions get_unit_price, get_quantity, and get_description.

```
class Item
{
```

```
public:
    virtual double get_unit_price() const = 0;
    virtual int get_quantity() const = 0;
    virtual string get_description() const = 0;
    double get_total_price() const;
    ...
};
```

It is up to derived classes to implement these three functions. For example, the `Bundle` class computes the unit price of the bundle from the unit prices of the collected items. However, the `get_total_price` function is defined in the `Item` class:

```
double Item::get_total_price() const
{
    return get_quantity() * get_unit_price();
}
```

A generic item does not know how to compute the quantity and the unit price, but it knows that their product is the total price. This is the TEMPLATE METHOD pattern at work.

You have seen in the preceding section how the `Bundle` class extends the `Item` class. It produces the unit price and description of a bundle, by combining the unit prices and descriptions of the individual items.

However, we also want to be able to add simple products to the invoice, not just bundles. We now have a problem. The invoice stores items, not products. To solve this problem, we use the ADAPTER pattern and define a class `ProductItem` that turns a product into an item (see Figure 4).

```
class ProductItem : public Item
{
public:
    ProductItem(Product p);
    virtual double get_unit_price() const;
    virtual string get_description() const;
private:
    Product prod;
};
```

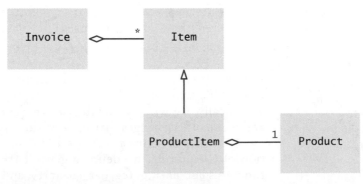

Figure 4   The ProductItem Adapter

The adapter methods call the appropriate methods of the Product class, for example:

```
double ProductItem::get_unit_price() const
{
    return prod.get_price();
}
```

Now let's look at the Invoice class. An invoice holds a collection of items.

```
class Invoice
{
public:
    void add(Item* item)
    {
        items.push_back(item);
    }
    ...
private:
    vector<Item*> items;
};
```

Clients of the Invoice class may need to know the line items inside an invoice. However, we do not want to reveal the structure of the Invoice class. For example, it would be unwise to return the items vector or even a vector<Item*>::iterator. This simple-minded approach causes problems if we later change the internal implementation, storing the items in another data structure or in a relational database table. Instead, we will follow the ITERATOR pattern and design an iterator class.

```
class ItemIterator
{
public:
    ...
    bool is_done() const;
    void next();
    Item* get() const;
private:
    vector<Item*>& items;
    int pos;
};
```

These functions access a reference to the original vector. The member function definitons show how the iterator object traverses the vector elements.

```
Item* ItemIterator::get() const
{
    if (pos < items.size())
        return items[pos];
    else
        return NULL;
}

inline void ItemIterator::next()
{
    pos++;
}
```

```
bool ItemIterator::is_done() const
{
    return pos >= items.size();
}
```

Finally, let's take a closer look at the task of formatting an invoice. Our sample program formats an invoice very simply (see below). As you can see, we have a string "INVOICE" on top, followed by the descriptions and prices of the line items, and the amount due at the bottom.

```
                            INVOICE

        Description        Unit Price   Qty   Total Price
        Toaster                 29.99    3          89.97
        Hammer, Nails           20.95    1          20.95

        AMOUNT DUE: 110.92
```

However, that simple format may not be good enough for all applications. Perhaps we want to show the invoice on a Web page. Then the format should contain HTML tags, and the line items should be rows of a table. Thus, it is apparent that there is a need for multiple algorithms for formatting an invoice.

The STRATEGY pattern addresses this issue. This pattern teaches us to design an interface to abstract the essential steps of the algorithm. The essential steps are:

- Print the header
- Print the footer
- Print a column entry (a string or a number)

Here is the class definition:

```
class InvoicePrinter
{
public:
    virtual void print_header(string s) = 0;
    virtual void print_string(string value, bool pad_right) = 0;
    virtual void print_number(double value, int precision) = 0;
    virtual void print_footer(string s, double total) = 0;
};
```

Then we can design classes such as SimpleInvoicePrinter and HTMLInvoicePrinter that format the invoice in various ways.

We make a strategy object available to the print function of the Invoice class:

```
void Invoice::print(InvoicePrinter& formatter)
{
    print_header("I N V O I C E");
    print_string("Description", true);
    print_string("Unit Price", false);
    print_string("Qty", false);
    print_string("Total Price", false);

    double amount_due = 0;
```

```
    for (ItemIterator iter = inv.create_iterator();
        !iter.is_done(); iter.next())
    {
        Item* it = iter.get();
        print_string(it->get_description(), true);
        print_number(it->get_unit_price(), 2);
        print_number(it->get_quantity(), 0);
        print_number(it->get_total_price(), 2);
        amount_due = amount_due + it->get_total_price();
    }

    print_footer("AMOUNT DUE:", amount_due);
}
```

Figure 5 shows the relationships between the classes used for formatting.

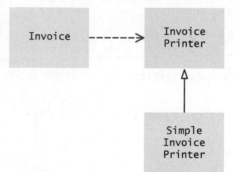

Figure 5
Printing an Invoice

This particular version provides a very simple formatting algorithm. Exercise P24.12 asks you to supply an invoice printer that produces HTML output.

This concludes the design of the invoice program. We have made use of five separate patterns during the design. Here is the code for the complete application.

ch24/invoice/product.h

```
1   #ifndef PRODUCT_H
2   #define PRODUCT_H
3
4   #include <string>
5
6   using namespace std;
7
8   /**
9       Describes a product with a description and a price.
10  */
11  class Product
12  {
13  public:
14      /**
15          Constructs a product with a given description and price.
16          @param d the description
17          @param p the price
18      */
```

```
19    Product(string d, double p);
20
21    /**
22        Gets the product description.
23        @return  the description
24    */
25    string get_description() const;
26
27    /**
28        Gets the product price.
29        @return  the price
30    */
31    double get_price() const;
32 private:
33    string description;
34    double price;
35 };
36
37 inline string Product::get_description() const
38 {
39    return description;
40 }
41
42 inline double Product::get_price() const
43 {
44    return price;
45 }
46
47 #endif
```

ch24/invoice/item.h

```
1  #ifndef ITEM_H
2  #define ITEM_H
3
4  #include <string>
5
6  using namespace std;
7
8  /**
9      Describes an item in an invoice.
10 */
11 class Item
12 {
13 public:
14    /**
15        Gets the unit price of this item.
16        @return  the unit price
17    */
18    virtual double get_unit_price() const = 0;
19
20    /**
21        Gets the description of this item.
22        @return  the description
```

```
23      */
24      virtual string get_description() const = 0;
25
26      /**
27          Gets the quantity of this item.
28          @return the quantity
29      */
30      virtual int get_quantity() const = 0;
31
32      /**
33          Gets the total price of this item.
34          @return the total price
35      */
36      double get_total_price() const;
37
38      virtual ~Item();
39   };
40
41   #endif
```

ch24/invoice/productitem.h

```
1    #ifndef PRODUCTITEM_H
2    #define PRODUCTITEM_H
3
4    #include "product.h"
5    #include "item.h"
6
7    /**
8        An item that results from selling a quantity of a product.
9    */
10   class ProductItem : public Item
11   {
12   public:
13       /**
14           Constructs this item.
15           @param p the product that is being sold
16           @param q the quantity
17       */
18       ProductItem(const Product& p, int q);
19       virtual double get_unit_price() const;
20       virtual string get_description() const;
21       virtual int get_quantity() const;
22   private:
23       Product prod;
24       int quantity;
25   };
26
27   inline int ProductItem::get_quantity() const
28   {
29       return quantity;
30   }
31
32   #endif
```

ch24/invoice/bundle.h

```
1  #ifndef BUNDLE_H
2  #define BUNDLE_H
3
4  #include <vector>
5  #include "item.h"
6
7  /**
8      A bundle of items that is again an item.
9  */
10 class Bundle : public Item
11 {
12 public:
13    /**
14        Adds an item to this bundle.
15        @param it the item to add
16    */
17    void add(Item* it);
18    virtual double get_unit_price() const;
19    virtual string get_description() const;
20    virtual int get_quantity() const;
21 private:
22    vector<Item*> items;
23 };
24
25 #endif
```

ch24/invoice/itemiterator.h

```
1  #ifndef ITEMITERATOR_H
2  #define ITEMITERATOR_H
3
4  #include <vector>
5  #include "item.h"
6
7  /**
8      An iterator through a collection of items.
9  */
10 class ItemIterator
11 {
12 public:
13    /**
14        Constructs the iterator from a vector.
15        @param its a reference to a vector of Item pointers
16    */
17    ItemIterator(vector<Item*>& its);
18
19    /**
20        Gets the current item.
21        @return the current item pointer
22    */
23    Item* get() const;
24
25    /**
```

```
26              Advances to the next item.
27      */
28      void next();
29
30      /**
31          Tests whether there are more items.
32          @return true if no more items are available
33      */
34      bool is_done() const;
35  private:
36      const vector<Item*>& items;
37      int pos;
38  };
39
40  inline void ItemIterator::next()
41  {
42      pos++;
43  }
44
45  #endif
```

ch24/invoice/invoiceprinter.h

```
1   #ifndef INVOICEPRINTER_H
2   #define INVOICEPRINTER_H
3
4   #include <string>
5
6   using namespace std;
7
8   /**
9       Formats an invoice.
10  */
11  class InvoicePrinter
12  {
13  public:
14      /**
15          Prints the invoice header.
16          @param s the header string
17      */
18      virtual void print_header(string s) = 0;
19
20      /**
21          Prints a string in the next table cell.
22          @param value the value to print
23          @param pad_right true if the cell is padded on the right
24              with spaces
25      */
26      virtual void print_string(string value, bool pad_right) = 0;
27
28      /**
29          Prints a number in the next table cell.
30          @param value the value to print
31          @param precision the number of digits after the decimal point
```

```
32      */
33      virtual void print_number(double value, int precision) = 0;
34
35      /**
36          Prints the invoice footer.
37          @param s  the footer string
38          @param total  the total amount due
39      */
40      virtual void print_footer(string s, double total) = 0;
41  };
42
43  #endif
```

ch24/invoice/simpleinvoiceprinter.h

```
1   #ifndef SIMPLEINVOICEPRINTER_H
2   #define SIMPLEINVOICEPRINTER_H
3
4   #include <string>
5   #include <vector>
6
7   using namespace std;
8
9   #include "invoiceprinter.h"
10
11  /**
12      Prints an invoice in a monospaced font, using spaces to
13      align the columns.
14  */
15  class SimpleInvoicePrinter : public InvoicePrinter
16  {
17  public:
18      /**
19          Constructs a simple invoice printer and sets the column widths.
20          @param widths  an array of column widths
21      */
22      SimpleInvoicePrinter(vector<int> widths);
23      virtual void print_header(string s);
24      virtual void print_string(string value, bool pad_right);
25      virtual void print_number(double value, int precision);
26      virtual void print_footer(string s, double total);
27  private:
28      void next_column();
29      int column;
30      vector<int> column_widths;
31  };
32
33  #endif
```

ch24/invoice/invoice.h

```
1   #ifndef INVOICE_H
2   #define INVOICE_H
3
4   #include <vector>
```

```
5
6    #include "item.h"
7    #include "invoiceprinter.h"
8    #include "itemiterator.h"
9
10   using namespace std;
11
12   /**
13       Describes an invoice that bills for a sequence of items.
14   */
15   class Invoice
16   {
17   public:
18       /**
19           Adds an item to this invoice.
20           @param it the item that the customer ordered
21       */
22       void add(Item* it);
23
24       /**
25           Prints the invoice.
26       */
27       void print(InvoicePrinter& printer);
28
29       /**
30           Creates an iterator through the items of this invoice.
31           @return the iterator
32       */
33       ItemIterator create_iterator();
34   private:
35       vector<Item*> items;
36   };
37
38   #endif
```

ch24/invoice/product.cpp

```
1    #include "product.h"
2
3    Product::Product(string d, double p)
4    {
5        description = d;
6        price = p;
7    }
```

ch24/invoice/item.cpp

```
1    #include "item.h"
2
3    double Item::get_total_price() const
4    {
5        return get_quantity() * get_unit_price();
6    }
7
8    Item::~Item() {}
```

ch24/invoice/productitem.cpp

```
1   #include "productitem.h"
2
3   ProductItem::ProductItem(const Product& p, int q)
4      : prod(p)
5   {
6      quantity = q;
7   }
8
9   double ProductItem::get_unit_price() const
10  {
11     return prod.get_price();
12  }
13
14  string ProductItem::get_description() const
15  {
16     return prod.get_description();
17  }
```

ch24/invoice/bundle.cpp

```
1   #include "bundle.h"
2
3   void Bundle::add(Item* it)
4   {
5      items.push_back(it);
6   }
7
8   double Bundle::get_unit_price() const
9   {
10     double price = 0;
11     for (int i = 0; i < items.size(); i++)
12     {
13        price = price
14           + items[i]->get_unit_price() * items[i]->get_quantity();
15     }
16     return price;
17  }
18
19  string Bundle::get_description() const
20  {
21     string description = "";
22     for (int i = 0; i < items.size(); i++)
23     {
24        if (i > 0) description = description + ", ";
25        description = description + items[i]->get_description();
26     }
27     return description;
28  }
29
30  int Bundle::get_quantity() const
31  {
32     return 1;
33  }
```

ch24/invoice/itemiterator.cpp

```cpp
1  #include "itemiterator.h"
2
3  ItemIterator::ItemIterator(vector<Item*>& its)
4     : items(its)
5  {
6     pos = 0;
7  }
8
9  Item* ItemIterator::get() const
10 {
11    if (pos < items.size())
12       return items[pos];
13    else
14       return NULL;
15 }
16
17 bool ItemIterator::is_done() const
18 {
19    return pos >= items.size();
20 }
```

ch24/invoice/simpleinvoiceprinter.cpp

```cpp
1  #include <iostream>
2  #include <iomanip>
3
4  #include "simpleinvoiceprinter.h"
5
6  using namespace std;
7
8  SimpleInvoicePrinter::SimpleInvoicePrinter(vector<int> widths)
9  {
10    column_widths = widths;
11    column = 0;
12 }
13
14 void SimpleInvoicePrinter::print_header(string s)
15 {
16    int width = 0;
17    for (int i = 0; i < column_widths.size(); i++)
18       width = width + column_widths[i];
19    for (int j = 0; j < (width - s.length()) / 2; j++)
20       cout << " ";
21    cout << s << "\n\n";
22 }
23
24 void SimpleInvoicePrinter::next_column()
25 {
26    column++;
27    if (column == column_widths.size())
28    {
29       cout << "\n";
30       column = 0;
```

```
31        }
32   }
33
34   void SimpleInvoicePrinter::print_string(string value, bool pad_right)
35   {
36      if (pad_right) cout << value;
37      // print padding
38      for (int i = value.length(); i < column_widths[column]; i++)
39         cout << " ";
40      if (!pad_right) cout << value;
41      next_column();
42   }
43
44   void SimpleInvoicePrinter::print_number(double value, int precision)
45   {
46      cout << setw(column_widths[column])
47         << fixed << setprecision(precision)
48         << value;
49      next_column();
50   }
51
52   void SimpleInvoicePrinter::print_footer(string s, double total)
53   {
54      cout << "\n" << s << " " << total << "\n";
55   }
```

ch24/invoice/invoice.cpp

```
1   #include "invoice.h"
2   #include "itemiterator.h"
3   #include "invoiceprinter.h"
4
5   void Invoice::add(Item* it)
6   {
7      items.push_back(it);
8   }
9
10  ItemIterator Invoice::create_iterator()
11  {
12     return ItemIterator(items);
13  }
14
15  void Invoice::print(InvoicePrinter& printer)
16  {
17     printer.print_header("I N V O I C E");
18     printer.print_string("Description", true);
19     printer.print_string("Unit Price", false);
20     printer.print_string("Qty", false);
21     printer.print_string("Total Price", false);
22
23     double amount_due = 0;
24     for (ItemIterator iter = create_iterator();
25          !iter.is_done(); iter.next())
26     {
```

```
27        Item* it = iter.get();
28        printer.print_string(it->get_description(), true);
29        printer.print_number(it->get_unit_price(), 2);
30        printer.print_number(it->get_quantity(), 0);
31        printer.print_number(it->get_total_price(), 2);
32        amount_due = amount_due + it->get_total_price();
33     }
34
35     printer.print_footer("AMOUNT DUE:", amount_due);
36 }
```

ch24/invoice/invoicetest.cpp

```
1  #include <vector>
2
3  #include "bundle.h"
4  #include "invoice.h"
5  #include "productitem.h"
6  #include "simpleinvoiceprinter.h"
7
8  using namespace std;
9
10 int main()
11 {
12    Invoice sample_invoice;
13    vector<int> widths;
14    widths.push_back(30);
15    widths.push_back(12);
16    widths.push_back(4);
17    widths.push_back(12);
18    SimpleInvoicePrinter printer(widths);
19    sample_invoice.add(new ProductItem(Product("Toaster", 29.99), 3));
20    Bundle* combo = new Bundle();
21    combo->add(new ProductItem(Product("Hammer", 19.95), 1));
22    combo->add(new ProductItem(Product("Nails", 0.01), 100));
23    sample_invoice.add(combo);
24
25    sample_invoice.print(printer);
26    return 0;
27 }
```

You have seen a number of common design patterns, how they arise in the C++ standard library, and simple code examples that put them to work. Table 1 on pages 946–947 shows the remaining design patterns of the "Gang of Four" book, with brief explanations of their purpose.

Table 1   Other Common Design Patterns

Pattern Name	Description	Example
ABSTRACT FACTORY	An abstract class defines methods that construct related products. Concrete factories create these product sets.	An abstract class specifies methods for constructing buttons, methods, and so on. Each user interface "look and feel" supplies a concrete subclass.
BRIDGE	An abstraction and its implementation have separate inheritance hierarchies.	A hierarchy of window types has separate implementations in various operating systems.
BUILDER	A builder class has methods to build parts of a complex product, and to retrieve the completed product.	A document builder has methods to build paragraphs, tables, and so on.
CHAIN OF RESPONSIBILITY	A request is passed to the first handler in a chain. Each handler acts on the request (or chooses not to act), and passes the request on to the next handler.	An event-handling mechanism passes a mouse or key event to a component, which then passes it to the parent component.
COMMAND	Commands are implemented as objects.	A word processor stores recently issued commands so that they can be undone.
DECORATOR	The behavior of a class is enhanced, keeping its interface.	A user interface component is decorated with scroll bars or borders.
FAÇADE	A complex subsystem is accessed through a single class.	A driver class provides access to the functionality of a database system.
FACTORY METHOD	A "virtual constructor" can be redefined by derived classes.	Collection classes that derive from a common base class redefine the `create_iterator` function.
FLYWEIGHT	Uses shared objects instead of large numbers of separate objects with identical state.	A word processor uses shared objects for styled characters rather than a separate object for each character.
INTERPRETER	A class hierarchy represents grammar rules. The interpreter recursively evaluates a parse tree of rule objects.	A program interactively evaluates mathematical expressions by building and evaluating a parse tree.
MEDIATOR	An object encapsulates the interaction of other objects.	All components in a dialog box notify a mediator of state changes. The mediator updates affected components.
MEMENTO	An object yields an opaque snapshot of a part of its state, and can later return its state from that snapshot.	An "undo" mechanism requests a memento from an object before mutating it. If the operation is undone, the memento is used to roll the object back to its old state.

Table 1 Other Common Design Patterns (continued)

Pattern Name	Description	Example
OBSERVER	An object wants to be notified when another object generates an event.	User interface components generate events, such as button clicks and text changes. A dialog box observes the events and repaints its contents.
PROXY	A service needs to be made more versatile without affecting the service provider or client.	A proxy class sends client requests to a server object on a different computer.
SINGLETON	All clients need access to a single shared object of a class.	A random number singleton gives all clients access to the same generator.
STATE	A separate object is used for each state. State-dependent code is distributed over the various state classes.	An image editor has different drawing states. Each state is handled by a separate "tool" object.
VISITOR	A structure with a fixed set of element classes needs an extensible set of operations.	An XML visitor visits a tree of XML elements, applying arbitrary operations to each node.

CHAPTER SUMMARY

1. Iterators are preferred over cursors because you can attach more than one iterator to a collection.

2. A design pattern uses a standard format to give advice about a problem in software design.

3. The ITERATOR pattern teaches how to access the elements of an aggregate object.

4. The ADAPTER pattern teaches how to use a class in a context that requires a different interface.

5. The TEMPLATE METHOD pattern teaches how to supply varying behavior patterns to an algorithm.

6. The STRATEGY pattern teaches how to supply variants of an algorithm to a client.

7. The COMPOSITE pattern teaches how to combine several objects into an object that has the same behavior as its parts.

8. Design patterns apply in specific situations that are described by the context and solution parts of the pattern.

FURTHER READING

1. Christopher Alexander et al., *A Pattern Language: Towns, Buildings, Construction*, Oxford University Press, 1977.

2. Erich Gamma, Richard Helm, Ralph Johnson, and John Vlissides, *Design Patterns*, Addison-Wesley, 1995.

REVIEW EXERCISES

Exercise R24.1. The ITERATOR pattern suggests that iterators have an operation `is_done`. However, the iterators in the standard C++ library do not have such an operation. Explain how you can test whether such an iterator has reached the end of its collection. Explain the advantages and disadvantages of the approach chosen by C++ designers, compared to the one advocated in the design pattern.

Exercise R24.2. Calling `copy` to insert elements into a vector has a drawback: The vector must already have a size that is sufficient to hold the copied elements. The standard library provides a `back_inserter` class to remedy this problem. Consider the code

```
vector<string> to;
copy(source.begin(), source.end(), back_inserter<string>(to));
```

The `back_inserter` is an iterator that calls `push_back` on the underlying container when storing an element. Discuss whether this is a manifestation of the ADAPTER pattern.

Exercise R24.3. Both the STRATEGY and the TEMPLATE METHOD patterns are concerned with variations in algorithms. Explain the essential difference between these patterns.

Exercise R24.4. Look up the documentation of the `transform` function in the standard C++ library. What design pattern is at work to supply the transformer?

Exercise R24.5. Find a description of the PROXY pattern and discuss whether the `SharedString` class that was discussed in Chapter 15 is an example of this pattern.

Exercise R24.6. Find a description of the DECORATOR pattern and describe the design of a `DiscountedItem` decorator of the `Item` class.

Exercise R24.7. A vector is composed of individual elements. Is this an example of the COMPOSITE pattern? Why or why not?

Exercise R24.8. Make tables for the five patterns of the invoice program that show how the names used in the pattern descriptions map to the actual names in the implementations.

Exercise R24.9. Suppose the responsibility of printing an invoice was shifted from the Invoice class to the InvoicePrinter class. Consider the implementation of

```
void InvoicePrinter::print(Invoice& inv)
```

and show how it is an example of the TEMPLATE METHOD pattern.

Exercise R24.10. Write a new pattern from your own programming experience. Think of a problem that you ended up solving more than once, and describe the problem and solution in the pattern format.

G   **Exercise R24.11.** Consider the wxSizer class of the wxWidgets library that is described in Chapter 25. A sizer can hold user interface components, such as buttons and nested sizers. What design pattern is at work?

PROGRAMMING EXERCISES

Exercise P24.1. Implement an iterator that traverses the fields of a tic-tac-toe board. Sample usage:

```
char board[3][3];
...
BoardIterator iter(board);
while (!iter.is_done())
{
   cout << iter.get();
   iter.next();
}
```

Exercise P24.2. Supply an iterator that enumerates all items of a product bundle. If a bundle contains another bundle, the iterator should traverse it as well.

Exercise P24.3. Provide your own implementations of the ostream_iterator and istream_iterator adapters. You need to define functions for the various operators.

Exercise P24.4. Implement the game of Nim that is described in Exercise P3.22. A player should have one of three strategies: the smart strategy described in this exercise, choosing moves at random, or asking a human for the next move. Use the STRATEGY pattern.

Exercise P24.5. Write a program that uses the standard sort function to sort a vector of Product objects, first by description and then by price (starting with the most expensive one). Supply objects of two comparator classes.

Exercise P24.6. Section 9.5 contains a program that encrypts and decrypts a file. Using a design pattern from this chapter, reorganize the program so that several encryption and decryption algorithms can be plugged in easily. Validate your approach by producing sample programs that use the Caesar cipher and the Playfair cipher (described in Exercise P9.5).

Exercise P24.7. Common Error 24.2 on page 930 outlines a sorter whose comparison operation is specified in a derived class, following the TEMPLATE METHOD pattern. Complete the implementation, using the merge sort algorithm. Provide a test program that sorts a vector of employees by decreasing salary.

Exercise P24.8. Enhance the Bundle class to give a discount for the bundle. The get_unit_price function should compute the price of the bundle items and then apply the discount.

Exercise P24.9. The get_quantity function of the Bundle class always returns 1. Reimplement the class so that bundles can have arbitrary quantities.

Exercise P24.10. Improve the invoice program by computing sales tax. Iterate through the items in the invoice and add a TaxItem that charges sales tax.

Exercise P24.11. Provide a class that derives from the InvoicePrinter class, which saves the invoice in a file.

Exercise P24.12. Provide a class that derives from the InvoicePrinter class, using HTML to format the output prettily.

Exercise P24.13. The program in Section 24.7 prints the invoice to cout. It would be better to format the invoice as a string, which can then be sent to any destination. Define a class InvoiceFormatter and a subclass SimpleInvoiceFormatter whose member functions return the formatted strings instead of printing them to cout.

G   **Exercise P24.14.** Design a base class Shape with virtual functions

```
void draw(GraphicWindow& win) const;
void move(double dx, double dy);
```

The Circle, Line, and Message classes of Chapter 2 are not derived from the Shape class. Supply three adapter classes CircleShape, LineShape, and MessageShape. Supply a test program that populates a vector<Shape*> with adapted objects, and demonstrates the draw and move functions.

G   **Exercise P24.15.** Continue Exercise P24.14 by providing a class CompoundShape. A compound shape consists of multiple individual shapes, and can be drawn or moved as a unit. What design pattern is at work here?

G   **Exercise P24.16.** Implement a class WinStream that writes output to cwin, the graphics object of Chapter 2. For example,

```
WinStream out;
out << setw(10) << setprecision(2) << 10.0 / 3;
```

First, define a class WinBuffer that derives from streambuf. Override the overflow method to send a character to the next available position on the screen. Then define WinStream as a subclass of ostream.

C++ Language Coding Guidelines

Introduction

This coding style guide is a simplified version of one that has been used with good success both in industrial practice and for college courses. It lays down rules that you must follow for your programming assignments.

A style guide is a set of mandatory requirements for layout and formatting. Uniform style makes it easier for you to read code from your instructor and classmates. You will really appreciate the consistency if you do a team project. It is also easier for your instructor and your grader to grasp the essence of your programs quickly.

A style guide makes you a more productive programmer because it *reduces gratuitous choice*. If you don't have to make choices about trivial matters, you can spend your energy on the solution of real problems.

In these guidelines a number of constructs are plainly outlawed. That doesn't mean that programmers using them are evil or incompetent. It does mean that the constructs are of marginal utility and can be expressed just as well or even better with other language constructs.

If you have already programmed in C or C++, you may be initially uncomfortable about giving up some fond habits. However, it is a sign of professionalism to set aside personal preferences in minor matters and to compromise for the benefit of your group.

These guidelines are necessarily somewhat long and dull. They also mention features that you may not yet have seen in class. Here are the most important highlights:

- Tabs are set every three spaces.
- Variable and function names are lowercase.
- Constant names are uppercase. Class names start with an uppercase letter.
- There are spaces after keywords and between binary operators.
- Braces must line up.
- No magic numbers may be used.
- Every function must have a comment.
- At most 30 lines of code may be used per function.
- No goto, continue, or break is allowed.
- At most two global variables may be used per file.

A note to the instructor: Of course, many programmers and organizations have strong feelings about coding style. If this style guide is incompatible with your own preferences or with local custom, please feel free to modify it. For that purpose, this coding style guide is available in electronic form in the WileyPLUS course for this book.

Source Files

Each program is a collection of one or more files or modules. The executable program is obtained by compiling and linking these files. Organize the material in each file as follows:

- Header comments
- #include statements
- Constants
- Classes
- Global variables
- Functions

It is common to start each file with a comment block. Here is a typical format:

```
/**
   @file invoice.cpp
   @author Jenny Koo
   @date 2010-01-24
   @version 3.14
*/
```

You may also want to include a copyright notice, such as

```
/* Copyright 2010 Jenny Koo */
```

A valid copyright notice consists of

- the copyright symbol © or the word "Copyright" or the abbreviation "Copr."
- the year of first publication of the work
- the name of the owner of the copyright

(Note: To save space, this header comment has been omitted from the programs in this book as well as the programs on disk so that the actual line numbers match those that are printed in the book.)

Next, list all included header files.

```
#include <iostream>
#include "ccc_empl.h"
```

Do not embed absolute path names, such as

```
#include "c:\me\my_homework\widgets.h"   // Don't !!!
```

After the header files, list constants that are needed throughout the program file.

```
const int GRID_SIZE = 20;
const double CLOCK_RADIUS = 5;
```

Then supply the definitions of all classes.

```
class Product
{
   ...
};
```

Order the class definitions so that a class is defined before it is used in another class. Very occasionally, you may have mutually dependent classes. To break cycles, you can declare a class, then use it in another class, then define it:

```
class Link; // Class declaration

class List
{
   ...
   Link* first;
};

class Link // Class definition
{
   ...
};
```

Continue with the definitions of global variables.

```
ofstream out; // The stream for the program output
```

Every global variable must have a comment explaining its purpose. Avoid global variables whenever possible. You may use at most two global variables in any one file.

Finally, list all functions, including member functions of classes and nonmember functions. Order the nonmember functions so that a function is defined before it is called. As a consequence, the main function will be the last function in your file.

Functions

Supply a comment of the following form for every function.

```
/**
    Explanation.
    @param argument₁   explanation
    @param argument₂   explanation
    ...
    @return explanation
*/
```

The introductory explanation is required for all functions except `main`. It should start with an uppercase letter and end with a period. Some documentation tools extract the first sentence of the explanation into a summary table. Thus, if you provide an explanation that consists of multiple sentences, formulate the explanation such that the first sentence is a concise explanation of the function's purpose.

Omit the `@param` comment if the function takes no parameters. Omit the `@return` comment for `void` functions. Here is a typical example.

```
/**
    Converts calendar date into Julian day. This algorithm is from Press
    et al., Numerical Recipes in C, 2nd ed., Cambridge University Press, 1992.
    @param year the year of the date to be converted
    @param month the month of the date to be converted
    @param day the day of the date to be converted
    @return the Julian day number that begins at noon of the given
    calendar date
*/
long dat2jul(int year, int month, int day)
{
    ...
}
```

Parameter names must be explicit, especially if they are integers or Boolean.

```
Employee remove(int d, double s); // Huh?
Employee remove(int department, double severance_pay); // OK
```

Of course, for very generic functions, short names may be very appropriate.

Do not write `void` functions that return exactly one answer through a reference. Instead, make the result into a return value.

```
void find(vector<Employee> c, bool& found); // Don't!
bool find(vector<Employee> c); // OK
```

Of course, if the function computes more than one value, some or all results can be returned through reference parameters.

Functions must have at most 30 lines of code. (Comments, blank lines, and lines containing only braces are not included in this count.) Functions that consist of one long `if`/`else`/`else` statement sequence may be longer, provided each branch is 10 lines or less. This rule forces you to break up complex computations into separate functions.

Local Variables

Do not define all local variables at the beginning of a block. Define each variable just before it is used for the first time.

Every variable must be either explicitly initialized when defined or set in the immediately following statement (for example, through a >> instruction).

```
int pennies = 0;
```

or

```
int pennies;
cin >> pennies;
```

Move variables to the innermost block in which they are needed.

```
while (...)
{
   double xnew = (xold + a / xold) / 2;
   ...
}
```

Do not define two variables in one statement:

```
int dimes = 0, nickels = 0; // Don't
```

When defining a pointer variable, place the * with the type, not the variable:

```
Link* p; // OK
```

not

```
Link *p; // Don't
```

Constants

In C++, do not use #define to define constants:

```
#define CLOCK_RADIUS 5 // Don't
```

Use const instead:

```
const double CLOCK_RADIUS = 5; // The radius of the clock face
```

You may not use magic numbers in your code. (A magic number is an integer constant embedded in code without a constant definition.) Any number except 0, 1, or 2 is considered magic:

```
if (p.get_x() < 10) // Don't
```

Use a const variable instead:

```
const double WINDOW_XMAX = 10;
if (p.get_x() < WINDOW_XMAX) // OK
```

Even the most reasonable cosmic constant is going to change one day. You think there are 365 days per year? Your customers on Mars are going to be pretty unhappy about your silly prejudice.

Make a constant

```
const int DAYS_PER_YEAR = 365;
```

so that you can easily produce a Martian version without trying to find all the 365's, 364's, 366's, 367's, and so on in your code.

Classes

Lay out the items of a class as follows:

```
class ClassName
{
public:
    constructors
    mutators
    accessors
private:
    data
};
```

All data fields of classes must be private. Do not use `friend`, except for classes that have no public member functions.

Control Flow

The `if` Statement

Avoid the "if...if...else" trap. The code

```
if (...)
    if (...) ...;
else
{
    ...;
    ...;
}
```

will not do what the indentation level suggests, and it can take hours to find such a bug. Always use an extra pair of {...} when dealing with "if...if...else":

```
if (...)
{
    if (...) ...;
}  // {...} are necessary
else ...;

if (...)
{
    if (...) ...;
    else (...) ...;
}  // {...} not necessary, but they keep you out of trouble
```

The for Statement

Use for loops only when a variable runs from somewhere to somewhere else with some constant increment/decrement.

```
for (int i = 0; i < a.size(); i++)
    print(a[i]);
```

Do not use the for loop for weird constructs such as

```
for (xnew = a / 2; count < ITERATIONS; cout << xnew) // Don't
{
    xold = xnew;
    xnew = xold + a / xold;
    count++;
}
```

Make such a loop into a while loop, so the sequence of instructions is much clearer.

```
xnew = a / 2;
while (count < ITERATIONS) // OK
{
    xold = xnew;
    xnew = xold + a / xold;
    count++;
    cout << xnew;
}
```

A for loop traversing a linked list can be neat and intuitive:

```
for (p = a.begin(); p != a.end(); p++)
    cout << *p << "\n";
```

Nonlinear Control Flow

Don't use the switch statement. Use if/else instead.

Do not use the break, continue, or goto statement. Use a bool variable to control the execution flow.

Lexical Issues

Naming Conventions

The following rules specify when to use upper- and lowercase letters in identifier names.

1. All variable and function names and all data fields of classes are in lowercase, sometimes with an underscore in the middle. For example, first_player.

2. All constants are in uppercase, with an occasional underscore. For example, CLOCK RADIUS.

3. All class names start with uppercase and are followed by lowercase letters, with an occasional uppercase letter in the middle. For example, BankTeller.

4. Template type parameters are in uppercase, usually a single letter.

Names must be reasonably long and descriptive. Use `first_player` instead of `fp`. No drppng f vwls. Local variables that are fairly routine can be short (`ch`, `i`) as long as they are really just boring holders for an input character, a loop counter, and so on. Also, do not use `ctr`, `c`, `cntr`, `cnt`, `c2` for five counter variables in your function. Surely each of these variables has a specific purpose and can be named to remind the reader of it (for example, `ccurrent`, `cnext`, `cprevious`, `cnew`, `cresult`). However, it is customary to use single-letter names such as `T` for template type parameters.

Indentation and White Space

Use tab stops every three columns. Save your file so that it contains no tabs at all. That means you will need to change the tab stop setting in your editor! In the editor, make sure to select "3 spaces per tab stop" and "save all tabs as spaces". Every programming editor has these settings. If yours doesn't, don't use tabs at all but type the correct number of spaces to achieve indentation.

Use blank lines freely to separate logically distinct parts of a function.

Use a blank space around every binary operator:

```
x1 = (-b - sqrt(b * b - 4 * a * c)) / (2 * a); // Good
x1=(-b-sqrt(b*b-4*a*c))/(2*a); // Bad
```

Leave a blank space after (and not before) each comma, semicolon, and keyword, but not after a function name.

```
if (x == 0) ...
f(a, b[i]);
```

Every line must fit in 80 columns. If you must break a statement, add an indentation level for the continuation:

```
a[n] = .................................................
     + ................;
```

Start the indented line with an operator (if possible).

If a line break happens in an `if` or `while` condition, be sure to brace the body in, *even if it consists of only one statement:*

```
if (......................................................
   && ................
   || ..........)
{
   ...
}
```

If it weren't for the braces, it would be hard to distinguish the continuation of the condition visually from the statement to be executed.

Braces

Opening and closing braces must line up, either horizontally or vertically.

```
while (i < n) { print(a[i]); i++; }  // OK
```

```
while (i < n)
{
    print(a[i]);
    i++;
}  // OK
```

Some programmers don't line up vertical braces but place the { *behind* the while:

```
while (i < n) {    // Don't
    print(a[i]);
    i++;
}
```

This style saves a line, but it is difficult to match the braces.

Unstable Layout

Some programmers take great pride in lining up certain columns in their code:

```
class Employee
{
    ...
private:
    string  name;
       int  age;
    double  hourly_wage;
      Time  start_time;
};
```

This is undeniably neat, and we recommend it if your editor does it for you, but *don't* do it manually. The layout is not *stable* under change. A data type that is longer than the preallotted number of columns requires that you move *all* entries around.

Some programmers like to format multiline comments so that every line starts with **:

```
/* This is a comment
** that extends over
** three source lines
*/
```

Again, this is neat if your editor has a command to add and remove the asterisks, and if you know that all programmers who will maintain your code also have such an editor. Otherwise, it can be a powerful method of *discouraging* programmers from editing the comment. If you have to choose between pretty comments and comments that reflect the current facts of the program, facts win over beauty.

Keyword Summary

Keyword	Description	Reference Location
asm	Insert assembly instructions	Not covered
auto	Define a local variable (optional)	Not covered
bool	The Boolean type	Section 3.5
break	Break out of a loop or switch	Advanced Topic 3.4
case	A label in a switch statement	Advanced Topic 3.2
catch	A handler of an exception	Section 17.3
char	The character type	Section 6.5.3
class	Definition of a class	Section 5.2
const	Definition of a constant value, reference, member function, or pointer	Section 2.4, Advanced Topic 4.2, Section 5.4, Section 7.4
const_cast	Cast away const-ness	Not covered
continue	Jump to the next iteration of a loop	Not covered
default	The default case of a switch statement	Advanced Topic 3.2
delete	Return a memory block to the heap	Section 7.2

Keyword	Description	Reference Location
do	A loop that is executed at least once	Section 3.8
double	The double-precision, floating-point type	Section 2.1
dynamic_cast	A cast to a derived class that is checked at run time	Section 19.3
else	The alternative clause in an if statement	Section 3.1
enum	Definition of an enumerated type	Advanced Topic 2.5
explicit	A constructor that is not a type converter	Advanced Topic 14.4
export	Export a template to other modules	Not covered
extern	A global variable or function defined in another module	Section 5.9
false	The false Boolean value	Section 3.5
float	The single-precision, floating-point type	Advanced Topic 2.1
for	A loop that is intended to initialize, test, and update a variable	Section 3.7
friend	Allows another class or function to access the private features of this class	Section 18.4
goto	Jump to another location in a function	Not covered
if	The conditional branch statement	Section 3.1
inline	A function whose body is inserted into the calling code	Advanced Topic 14.6
int	The integer type	Section 2.1
long	A modifier for the int and double types that indicates that the type may have more bytes	Advanced Topic 2.1, Appendix F
mutable	A data field that may be modified by a constant member function	Not covered
namespace	A name space for disambiguating names, or a declaration of an alias	Section 18.7
new	Allocate a memory block from the heap	Section 7.1
operator	An overloaded operator	Section 14.1
private	Features of a class that can only be accessed by this class and its friends	Section 5.2

Keyword	Description	Reference Location
protected	Features that can only be accessed by this class and its friends and subclasses	Advanced Topic 8.1, Section 18.3
public	Features of a class that can be accessed by all functions	Section 5.2
register	A recommendation to place a local variable in a processor register	Not covered
reinterpret_cast	A cast that reinterprets a value in a nonportable way	Not covered
return	Returns a value from a function	Section 4.4
short	A modifier for the int type that indicates that the type may have fewer bytes	Appendix F
signed	A modifier for the int and char types that indicates that values of the type can be negative	Appendix F
sizeof	The size of a value or type, in bytes	Not covered
static	A global variable that is private to a module, or a local variable that persists between function calls, or a class feature that does not vary among instances	Section 18.2
static_cast	Convert from one type to another	Advanced Topic 2.2, Section 19.3
struct	Defines a class type whose features are public by default	Not covered
switch	A statement that selects among multiple branches, depending upon the value of an expression	Advanced Topic 3.2
template	Defines a parameterized type or function	Chapter 16
this	The pointer to the implicit parameter of a member function	Advanced Topic 7.1
throw	Throw an exception	Section 17.3
true	The true value of the Boolean type	Section 3.5
try	Execute a block and catch exceptions	Section 17.3
typedef	Defines a type synonym	Section 7.6
typeid	Gets the type_info object of a value or type	Section 19.3
typename	A type parameter in a template	Section 16.1

Keyword	Description	Reference Location
union	Multiple fields that share the same memory region	Not covered
unsigned	A modifier for the int and char types that indicates that values of the type cannot be negative	Appendix F
using	Importing a name space into a module	Section 18.7
virtual	A member function with dynamic dispatch, or a shared base class	Section 8.4, Section 19.4
void	The empty type of a function or pointer	Section 4.8
volatile	A variable whose value can change through actions that are not defined in a function	Not covered
wchar_t	The 16-bit wide character type	Not covered
while	A loop statement that is controlled by a condition	Section 3.6

Operator Summary

The operators are listed in groups of decreasing precedence in the table on the following pages. The horizontal lines in the table indicate a change in operator precedence. For example,

```
z = x - y;
```

means

```
z = (x - y);
```

because = has a lower precedence than -.

The prefix unary operators and the assignment operators associate right-to-left. All other operators associate left-to-right. For example,

```
x - y - z
```

means

```
(x - y) - z
```

because - associates left-to-right, but

```
x = y = z
```

means

```
x = (y = z)
```

because = associates right-to-left.

Operator	Description	Reference Location
::	Scope resolution	Section 5.4
.	Access member	Section 2.6
->	Dereference and access member	Section 7.1
[]	Vector or array subscript	Section 6.1, Section 14.9
()	Function call	Section 2.5, Section 14.10
++	Increment	Section 2.3
--	Decrement	Section 2.3
!	Boolean NOT	Section 3.5
~	Bitwise NOT	Appendix G
+ (unary)	Positive	Section 14.3
- (unary)	Negative	Section 2.5, Section 14.3
* (unary)	Pointer dereferencing	Section 7.1
& (unary)	Address of variable	Advanced Topic 7.2, Section 14.3
new	Heap allocation	Section 7.1
delete	Heap recycling	Section 7.2
sizeof	Size of variable or type	Not covered
(*type*)	Cast	Advanced Topic 2.2
.*	Access pointer to member	Advanced Topic 14.4
->*	Dereference and access pointer to member	Advanced Topic 14.4
*	Multiplication	Section 2.5
/	Division or integer division	Section 2.5
%	Integer remainder	Section 2.5

Operator	Description	Reference Location
+	Addition	Section 2.5
-	Subtraction	Section 2.5
<<	Output (or bitwise shift)	Section 2.2, Appendix G
>>	Input (or bitwise shift)	Section 2.2, Appendix G
<	Less than	Section 3.2
<=	Less than or equal	Section 3.2
>	Greater than	Section 3.2
>=	Greater than or equal	Section 3.2
==	Equal	Section 3.2
!=	Not equal	Section 3.2
&	Bitwise AND	Appendix G
^	Bitwise XOR	Appendix G
|	Bitwise OR	Appendix G
&&	Boolean AND	Section 3.5, Appendix G
||	Boolean OR	Section 3.5, Appendix G
? :	Selection	Advanced Topic 3.1
=	Assignment	Section 2.3
+= -= *= /= %= &= |= ^= >>= <<=	Combined operator and assignment	Advanced Topic 2.3, Section 14.7
,	Sequencing of expressions	Advanced Topic 14.4

Character Codes

These escape sequences can occur in strings (for example, "\n") and characters for example, '\'').

Escape Sequence	Description
\n	Newline
\r	Carriage return
\t	Tab
\v	Vertical tab
\b	Backspace
\f	Form feed
\a	Alert
\\	Backslash
\"	Double quote
\'	Single quote
\?	Question mark
$\backslash x h_1 h_2$	Code specified in hexadecimal
$\backslash o_1 o_2 o_3$	Code specified in octal

ASCII Code Table

Dec. Code	Hex Code	Char-acter	Dec. Code	Hex Code	Char-acter	Dec. Code	Hex Code	Char-acter	Dec. Code	Hex Code	Char-acter
0	00		32	20	Space	64	40	@	96	60	`
1	01		33	21	!	65	41	A	97	61	a
2	02		34	22	"	66	42	B	98	62	b
3	03		35	23	#	67	43	C	99	63	c
4	04		36	24	$	68	44	D	100	64	d
5	05		37	25	%	69	45	E	101	65	e
6	06		38	26	&	70	46	F	102	66	f
7	07	\a	39	27	'	71	47	G	103	67	g
8	08	\b	40	28	(	72	48	H	104	68	h
9	09	\t	41	29	)	73	49	I	105	69	i
10	0A	\n	42	2A	*	74	4A	J	106	6A	j
11	0B	\v	43	2B	+	75	4B	K	107	6B	k
12	0C	\f	44	2C	,	76	4C	L	108	6C	l
13	0D	\r	45	2D	-	77	4D	M	109	6D	m
14	0E		46	2E	.	78	4E	N	110	6E	n
15	0F		47	2F	/	79	4F	O	111	6F	o
16	10		48	30	0	80	50	P	112	70	p
17	11		49	31	1	81	51	Q	113	71	q
18	12		50	32	2	82	52	R	114	72	r
19	13		51	33	3	83	53	S	115	73	s
20	14		52	34	4	84	54	T	116	74	t
21	15		53	35	5	85	55	U	117	75	u
22	16		54	36	6	86	56	V	118	76	v
23	17		55	37	7	87	57	W	119	77	w
24	18		56	38	8	88	58	X	120	78	x
25	19		57	39	9	89	59	Y	121	79	y
26	1A		58	3A	:	90	5A	Z	122	7A	z
27	1B		59	3B	;	91	5B	[	123	7B	{
28	1C		60	3C	<	92	5C	\	124	7C	|
29	1D		61	3D	=	93	5D	]	125	7D	}
30	1E		62	3E	>	94	5E	^	126	7E	~
31	1F		63	3F	?	95	5F	_	127	7F	

C++ Library Summary

Standard Code Libraries

<cmath>

- double **sqrt**(double x)
  Function: Square root, $\sqrt{x}$
- double **pow**(double x, double y)
  Function: Power, x^y. If $x > 0$, y can be any value. If x is 0, y must be > 0.
  If $x < 0$, y must be an integer.
- double **sin**(double x)
  Function: Sine, $\sin x$ (x in radians)
- double **cos**(double x)
  Function: Cosine, $\cos x$ (x in radians)
- double **tan**(double x)
  Function: Tangent, $\tan x$ (x in radians)
- double **asin**(double x)
  Function: Arc sine, $\sin^{-1} x \in \left[-\pi/2,\ \pi/2\right]$, $x \in \left[-1,1\right]$
- double **acos**(double x)
  Function: Arc cosine, $\cos^{-1} x \in \left[0,\ \pi\right]$, $x \in \left[-1,1\right]$
- double **atan**(double x)
  Function: Arc tangent, $\tan^{-1} x \in \left(-\pi/2,\ \pi/2\right)$
- double **atan2**(double y, double x)
  Function: Arc tangent, $\tan^{-1}\left(y/x\right) \in \left[-\pi/2,\ \pi/2\right]$, x may be 0
- double **exp**(double x)
  Function: Exponential, e^x
- double **log**(double x)
  Function: Natural log, $\ln (x)$, $x > 0$

- double `log10`(double x)
  Function: Decimal log, $\log_{10}(x)$, $x > 0$
- double `sinh`(double x)
  Function: Hyperbolic sine, $\sinh x$
- double `cosh`(double x)
  Function: Hyperbolic cosine, $\cosh x$
- double `tanh`(double x)
  Function: Hyperbolic tangent, $\tanh x$
- double `ceil`(double x)
  Function: Smallest integer $\geq x$
- double `floor`(double x)
  Function: Largest integer $\leq x$
- double `fabs`(double x)
  Function: Absolute value, $|x|$

<cstdlib>

- int `abs`(int x)
  Function: Absolute value, $|x|$
- int `rand`()
  Function: Random integer
- void `srand`(int n)
  Function: Sets the seed of the random number generator to n.
- void `exit`(int n)
  Function: Exits the program with status code n.

<cctype>

- bool `isalpha`(char c)
  Function: Tests whether c is a letter.
- char `isalnum`(char c)
  Function: Test whether c is a letter or a number.
- bool `isdigit`(char c)
  Function: Tests whether c is a digit.
- bool `isspace`(char c)
  Function: Tests whether c is white space.
- bool `islower`(char c)
  Function: Tests whether c is lowercase.
- bool `isupper`(char c)
  Function: Tests whether c is uppercase.
- char `tolower`(char c)
  Function: Returns the lowercase of c.
- char `toupper`(char c)
  Function: Returns the uppercase of c.

`<ctime>`

- `time_t time(time_t* p)`
  Function: Returns the number of seconds since January 1, 1970, 00:00:00 GMT. If p is not NULL, the return value is also stored in the location to which p points.

`<string>`

- `istream& getline(istream& in, string s)`
  Function: Gets the next input line from the input stream in and stores it in the string s.

Class `string`

- `int string::length() const`
  Member function: The length of the string.
- `string string::substr(int i, int n) const`
  Member function: The substring of length n starting at index i.
- `string string::substr(int i) const`
  Member function: The substring from index i to the end of the string.
- `const char* string::c_str() const`
  Member function: A char array with the characters in this string.

`<iostream>`

Class `istream`

- `bool istream::fail() const`
  Function: True if input has failed.
- `istream& istream::get(char& c)`
  Function: Gets the next character and places it into c.
- `istream& istream::unget()`
  Function: Puts the last character read back into the stream, to be read again in the next input operation; only one character can be put back at a time.
- `istream& istream::seekg(long p)`
  Function: Moves the get position to position p.
- `istream& istream::seekg(long n, int f)`
  Function: Moves the get position by n. f is one of ios::beg, ios::cur, ios::end.
- `long istream::tellg()`
  Function: Returns the get position.

Class `ostream`

- `ostream& ostream::seekp(long p)`
  Function: Moves the put position to position p.
- `ostream& ostream::seekp(long n, int f)`
  Function: Moves the put position by n. f is one of ios::beg, ios::cur, ios::end.
- `long ostream::tellp()`
  Function: Returns the put position.

Class ios

- `ios::left`
  Flag: Left alignment.
- `ios::right`
  Flag: Right alignment.
- `ios::internal`
  Flag: Sign left, remainder right.
- `ios::dec`
  Flag: Decimal base.
- `ios::hex`
  Flag: Hexadecimal base.
- `ios::oct`
  Flag: Octal base.
- `ios::showbase`
  Flag: Show base (as 0x or 0 prefix).
- `ios::uppercase`
  Flag: Uppercase E, X, and hex digits A...F.
- `ios::fixed`
  Flag: Fixed floating-point format.
- `ios::scientific`
  Flag: Scientific floating-point format.
- `ios::showpoint`
  Flag: Show trailing decimal point and zeroes.
- `ios::beg`
  Flag: Seek relative to the beginning of the file.
- `ios::cur`
  Flag: Seek relative to the current position.
- `ios::end`
  Flag: Seek relative to the end of the file.

Note: • Use `setfill('0')` in combination with `setw` to show leading zeroes.

`<iomanip>`

- `setw(int n)`
  Manipulator: Sets the width of the next field.
- `setprecision(int n)`
  Manipulator: Sets the precision of floating-point values to n digits after the decimal point.
- `fixed`
  Manipulator: Selects fixed floating-point format, with trailing zeroes.
- `scientific`
  Manipulator: Selects scientific floating-point format, with exponential notation.
- `setiosflags(int flags)`
  Manipulator: Sets one or more flags. Flags are listed below.

- `resetiosflags(int flags)`
  Manipulator: Resets one or more flags. Flags are listed below.
- `setfill(char c)`
  Manipulator: Sets the fill character to the character c.
- `setbase(int n)`
  Manipulator: Sets the number base for integers to base n.
- `hex`
  Manipulator: Sets hexadecimal integer format.
- `oct`
  Manipulator: Sets octal integer format.
- `dec`
  Manipulator: Sets decimal integer format.

`<fstream>`

Class `ifstream`

- `void ifstream::open(const char n[])`
  Function: Opens a file with name n for reading.

Class `ofstream`

- `void ofstream::open(const char n[])`
  Function: Opens a file with name n for writing.

Class `fstream`

- `void fstream::open(const char n[])`
  Function: Opens a file with name n for reading and writing.

Class `fstreambase`

- `void fstreambase::close()`
  Function: Closes the file stream.

Note:
- `fstreambase` is the common base class of `ifstream`, `ofstream`, and `fstream`.
- To open a binary file both for input and output, use `f.open(n, ios::in | ios::out ios::binary)`

`<sstream>`

Class `istringstream`

- `istringstream::istringstream(string s)`
  Constructs a string stream that reads from the string s.

Class `ostringstream`

- `string ostringstream::str() const`
  Function: Returns the string that was collected by the string stream.

Note:
- Call `istringstream(s.c_str())` to construct an `istringstream`.
- Call `s = string(out.str())` to get a string object that contains the characters collected by the `ostringstream` out.

Containers

All STL Containers, *C*

Note: • *C* is any STL container such as vector<T>, list<T>, set<T>, multiset<T>, or map<T>.

• int *C*::**size**() const
Function: The number of elements in the container.

• *C*::iterator *C*::**begin**()
Function: Gets an iterator that points to the first element in the container.

• *C*::iterator *C*::**end**()
Function: Gets an iterator that points past the last element in the container.

• bool *C*::**empty**() const
Function: Tests if the container has any elements.

<vector>

Class vector<T>

• vector<T>::**vector**(int n)
Function: Constructs a vector with n elements.

• void vector<T>::**push_back**(const T& x)
Function: Inserts x after the last element.

• void vector<T>::**pop_back**()
Function: Removes (but does not return) the last element.

• T& vector<T>::**operator**[](int n)
Function: Accesses the element at index n.

• T& vector<T>::**at**(int n)
Function: Accesses the element at index n, checking that the index is in range.

• vector<T>::iterator vector<T>::**insert**(vector<T>::iterator p, const T& x)
Function: Inserts x before p. Returns an iterator that points to the inserted value.

• vector<T>::iterator vector<T>::**erase**(vector<T>::iterator p)
Function: Erases the element to which p points. Returns an iterator that points to the next element.

• vector<T>::iterator vector<T>::**erase**(
    vector<T>::iterator begin, vector<T>::iterator end)
Function: Erases all the elements between the start and the stop iterator. Returns an iterator that points to the next element.

<deque>

Class deque<T>

• void deque<T>::**push_back**(const T& x)
Function: Inserts x after the last element.

- `void deque<T>::`**`pop_back`**`()`
  Function: Removes (but does not return) the last element.
- `void deque<T>::`**`push_front`**`(const T& x)`
  Function: Inserts x before the first element.
- `void deque<T>::`**`pop_front`**`()`
  Function: Removes (but does not return) the first element.
- `T& deque<T>::`**`front`**`()`
  Function: The first element of the container.
- `T& deque<T>::`**`back`**`()`
  Function: The last element of the container.
- `T& deque<T>::`**`operator`**`[](int n)`
  Function: Access the element at index n.
- `T& deque<T>::`**`at`**`(int n)`
  Function: Access the element at index n, checking index.
- `deque<T>::iterator deque<T>::`**`erase`**`(deque<T>::iterator p)`
  Function: Erases the element to which p points. Returns an iterator that points to the next element.
- `deque<T>::iterator deque<T>::`**`erase`**`(`
  `    deque<T>::iterator begin, deque<T>::iterator end)`
  Function: Erases all the elements between the start and the stop iterator. Returns an iterator that points to the next element.

<list>

Class list<T>

- `void list<T>::`**`push_back`**`(const T& x)`
  Function: Inserts x after the last element.
- `void list<T>::`**`pop_back`**`()`
  Function: Removes (but does not return) the last element.
- `void list<T>::`**`push_front`**`(const T& x)`
  Function: Inserts x before the first element.
- `void list<T>::`**`pop_front`**`()`
  Function: Removes (but does not return) the first element.
- `T& list<T>::`**`front`**`()`
  Function: The first element of the container.
- `T& list<T>::`**`back`**`()`
  Function: The last element of the container.
- `list<T>::iterator list<T>::`**`insert`**`(list<T>::iterator p, const T& x)`
  Function: Inserts x before p. Returns an iterator that points to the inserted value.
- `list<T>::iterator list<T>::`**`erase`**`(list<T>::iterator p)`
  Function: Erases the element to which p points. Returns an iterator that points to the next element.

- list<T>::iterator list<T>::**erase**(list<T>::iterator begin, list<T>::iterator end)
Function: Erases all the elements between the start and the stop iterator. Returns an iterator that points to the next element.
- void **sort**()
Function: Sorts the list into ascending order.
- void **merge**(list<T>& x)
Function: Merges elements with the sorted list x.

<set>

Class set<T>

- pair< set<T>::iterator, bool > set<T>::**insert**(const T& x)
Function: If x is not present in the list, inserts it and returns an iterator that points to the newly inserted element and the Boolean value true. If x is present, returns an iterator pointing to the existing set element and the Boolean value false.
- int set<T>::**erase**(const T& x)
Function: Removes x and returns 1 if it occurs in the set; returns 0 otherwise.
- void set<T>::**erase**(set<T>::iterator p)
Function: Erases the element at the given position.
- int set<T>::**count**(const T& x) const
Function: Returns 1 if x occurs in the set; returns 0 otherwise.
- set<T>::iterator set<T>::**find**(const T& x)
Returns an iterator to the element equal to x in the set, or end() if no such element exists.

Note: • The type T must be totally ordered by a < comparison operator.

<multiset>

Class multiset<T>

- multiset<T>::iterator multiset<T>::**insert**(const T& x)
Function: Inserts x into the container. Returns an iterator that points to the inserted value.
- int multiset<T>::**erase**(const T& x)
Function: Removes all occurrences of x. Returns the number of removed elements.
- void multiset<T>::**erase**(multiset<T>::iterator p)
Function: Erases the element at the given position.
- int multiset<T>::**count**(const T& x) const
Function: Counts the elements equal to x.
- multiset<T>::iterator multiset<T>::**find**(const T& x)
Function: Returns an iterator to an element equal to x, or end() if no such element exists.

Note: • The type T must be totally ordered by a < comparison operator.

<map>

Class map<K, V>

- V& map<K, V>::**operator[]**(const K& k)
  Function: Accesses the value with key k.
- int map<K, V>::**erase**(const K& k)
  Function: Removes all occurrences of elements with key k. Returns the number of removed elements.
- void map<K, V>::**erase**(map<K, V>::iterator p)
  Function: Erases the element at the given position.
- int map<K, V>::**count**(const K& k) const
  Function: Counts the elements with key k.
- map<K, V>::iterator map<K, V>::**find**(const K& k)
  Function: Returns an iterator to an element with key k, or end() if no such element exists.

Note:
- The key type K must be totally ordered by a < comparison operator.
- A map iterator points to pair<K, V> entries.

Class multimap<K, V>

- multimap<K, V>::iterator multimap<K, V>::**insert**(const pair<K, V>& kvpair)
  Function: Inserts a key/value pair and returns an iterator pointing to the inserted pair.
- void multimap<K, V>::**erase**(multimap<K, V>::iterator pos)
  Function: Erases the key/value pair at the position pos.
- multimap<K, V>::iterator multimap<K, V>::**lower-bound**(const K& k)
- multimap<K, V>::iterator multimap<K, V>::**upper-bound**(const K& k)
  Function: Returns the position of the first and after the last key/value pair with key k.

<stack>

Class stack<T>

- T& stack<T>::**top**()
  Function: The value at the top of the stack.
- void stack<T>::**push**(const T& x)
  Function: Adds x to the top of the stack.
- void stack<T>::**pop**()
  Function: Removes (but does not return) the top value of the stack.

<queue>

Class queue<T>

- T& queue<T>::**front**()
  Function: The value at the front of the queue.
- T& queue<T>::**back**()
  Function: The value at the back of the queue.
- void queue<T>::**push**(const T& x)
  Function: Adds x to the back of the queue.

- void queue<T>::**pop**()
  Function: Removes (but does not return) the front value of the queue.
- T& priority_queue<T>::**top**()
  Function: The largest value in the container.
- void priority_queue<T>::**push**(const T& x)
  Function: Adds x to the container.
- void priority_queue<T>::**pop**()
  Function: Removes (but does not return) the largest value in the container.

<utility>

Class pair

- pair<F, S>::**pair**(const F& f, const F& s)
  Constructs a pair from a first and second value.
- F pair<F, S>::**first**
  The public field holding the first value of the pair.
- S pair<F, S>::**second**
  The public field holding the second value of the pair.

Algorithms

<algorithm>

- T **min**(T x, T y)
  Function: The minimum of x and y.
- T **max**(T x, T y)
  Function: The maximum of x and y.
- void **swap**(T& a, T& b)
  Function: Swaps the contents of a and b.
- I **min_element**(I begin, I end)
  Function: Returns an iterator pointing to the minimum element in the iterator range [begin, end).
- I **max_element**(I begin, I end)
  Function: Returns an iterator pointing to the maximum element in the iterator range [begin, end).
- F **for_each**(I begin, I end, F f)
  Function: Applies the function f to all elements in the iterator range [begin, end). Returns f.
- I **find**(I begin, I end, T x)
  Function: Returns the iterator pointing to the first occurrence of x in the iterator range [begin, end), or end if there is no match.

- I **find_if**(I begin, I end, F f)

  Function: Returns the iterator pointing to the first element x in the iterator range [begin, end) for which f(x) is true, or end if there is no match.

- int **count**(I begin, I end, T x)

  Function: Counts how many values in the iterator range [begin, end) are equal to x.

- int **count_if**(I begin, I end, F f)

  Function: Counts for how many values x in the iterator range [begin, end) f(x) is true.

- bool **equal**(I1 begin1, I1 end1, I2 begin2)

  Function: Tests whether the range [begin1, end1) equals the range of the same size starting at begin2.

- I2 **copy**(I1 begin1, I1 end1, I2 begin2)

  Function: Copies the range [begin1, end1) to the range of the same size starting at begin2. Returns the iterator past the end of the destination of the copy.

- void **replace**(I begin, I end, T xold, T xnew)

  Function: Replaces all occurrences of xold in the range [begin, end) with xnew.

- void **replace_if**(I begin, I end, F f, T xnew)

  Function: Replaces all values x in the range [begin, end) for which f(x) is true with xnew.

- void **fill**(I begin, I end, T x)

  Function: Fills the range [begin, end) with x.

- void **fill**(I begin, int n, T x)

  Function: Fills n copies of x into the range that starts at begin.

- I **remove**(I begin, I end, T x)

  Function: Removes all occurrences of x in the range [begin, end). Returns the end of the resulting range.

- I **remove_if**(I begin, I end, F f)

  Function: Removes all values x in the range [begin, end) for which f(x) is true. Returns the end of the resulting range.

- I **unique**(I begin, I end)

  Function: Removes adjacent identical values from the range [begin, end). Returns the end of the resulting range.

- void **random_shuffle**(I begin, I end)

  Function: Randomly rearranges the elements in the range [begin, end).

- void **next_permutation**(I begin, I end)

  Function: Rearranges the elements in the range [begin, end). Calling it $n!$ times iterates through all permutations.

- void **sort**(I begin, I end)

  Function: Sorts the elements in the range [begin, end).

- I **nth_element**(I begin, I end, int n)

  Function: Returns an iterator that points to the value that would be the nth element if the range [begin, end) was sorted.

- bool **binary_search**(I begin, I end, T x)

  Function: Checks whether the value x is contained in the sorted range [begin, end).

Exceptions

`<stdexcept>`

Class exception
Base class for all standard exceptions.

Class logic_error
An error that logically results from conditions in the program.

Class domain_error
A value is not in the domain of a function.

Class invalid_argument
A parameter value is invalid.

Class out_of_range
A value is outside the valid range.

Class length_error
A value exceeds the maximum length.

Class runtime_error
An error that occurs as a consequence of conditions beyond the control of the program.

Class range_error
An operation computes a value that is outside the range of a function.

Class overflow_error
An operation yields an arithmetic overflow.

Class underflow_error
An operation yields an arithmetic underflow.

Note:
- All standard exception classes have a constructor:
  ExceptionClass::*ExceptionClass*(`string` *reason*)
- The exception class has a member function to retrieve the reason for the exception: `const char* exception::what() const`

Book Library

`"ccc_time.h"`

Class Time

- `Time::Time()`
  Constructs the current time.
- `Time::Time(int h, int m, int s)`
  Constructs the time with hours h, minutes m, and seconds s.
- `int Time::get_seconds() const`
  Function: Returns the seconds value of this time.

- `int Time::`**`get_minutes`**`() const`
  Function: Returns the minutes value of this time.
- `int Time::`**`get_hours`**`() const`
  Function: Returns the hours value of this time.
- `void Time::`**`add_seconds`**`(int n)`
  Function: Changes this time to move by n seconds.
- `int Time::`**`seconds_from`**`(t) const`
  Function: Computes the number of seconds between this time and t.

"ccc_empl.h"

Class Employee

- `Employee::`**`Employee`**`(string n, double s)`
  Function: Constructs an employee with name n and salary s.
- `string Employee::`**`get_name`**`() const`
  Function: Returns the name of this employee.
- `double Employee::`**`get_salary`**`() const`
  Function: Returns the salary of this employee.
- `void Employee::`**`set_salary`**`(double s)`
  Function: Sets the salary of this employee to s.

"ccc_win.h"

Class GraphicWindow

- `void GraphicWindow::`**`coord`**`(double x1, double y1, double x2, double y2)`
  Function: Sets the coordinate system for subsequent drawing; (x1, y1) is the top-left corner, (x2, y2) is the bottom-right corner.
- `void GraphicWindow::`**`clear`**`()`
  Function: Clears the window (that is, erases its contents).
- `string GraphicWindow::`**`get_string`**`(string p)`
  Function: Displays prompt p and returns the entered string.
- `int GraphicWindow::`**`get_int`**`(string p)`
  Function: Displays prompt p and returns the entered integer.
- `double GraphicWindow::`**`get_double`**`(string p)`
  Function: Displays prompt p and returns the entered value.
- `Point GraphicWindow::`**`get_mouse`**`(string p)`
  Function: Displays prompt p and returns the mouse-click point.

Class Point

- `Point::`**`Point`**`(double x, double y)`
  Constructs a point at location (x, y).
- `double Point::`**`get_x`**`() const`
  Function: Returns the x-coordinate of the point.

- `double Point::`**`get_y`**`() const`
  Function: Returns the y-coordinate of the point.
- `void Point::`**`move`**`(double dx, double dy)`
  Function: Moves the point by (`dx`, `dy`).

Class `Circle`

- `Circle::`**`Circle`**`(Point p, double r)`
  Constructs a circle with center p and radius r.
- `Point Circle::`**`get_center`**`() const`
  Function: Returns the center point of the circle.
- `double Circle::`**`get_radius`**`() const`
  Function: Returns the radius of the circle.
- `void Circle::`**`move`**`(double dx, double dy)`
  Function: Moves the circle by (`dx`, `dy`).

Class `Line`

- `Line::`**`Line`**`(Point p, Point q)`
  Constructs a line joining the points p and q.
- `Point Line::`**`get_start`**`() const`
  Function: Returns the starting point of the line.
- `Point Line::`**`get_end`**`() const`
  Function: Returns the ending point of the line.
- `void Line::`**`move`**`(double dx, double dy)`
  Function: Moves the line by (`dx`, `dy`).

Class `Message`

- `Message::`**`Message`**`(Point p, string s)`
  Constructs a message with starting point p and text string s.
- `Message::`**`Message`**`(Point p, double x)`
  Constructs a message with starting point p and label equal to the number x.
- `Point Message::`**`get_start`**`() const`
  Function: Returns the starting point of the message.
- `string Message::`**`get_text`**`() const`
  Function: Gets the text string of the message.
- `void Message::`**`move`**`(double dx, double dy)`
  Function: Moves the message by (`dx`, `dy`).

wxWidgets Library

<wx/wx.h>

Class wxApp

- bool wxApp::**OnInit**()
  Function: Overrides this function to initialize the application. Returns true to continue, false to terminate.

Class wxFrame

- wxFrame::**wxFrame**(wxWindow* parent,wxWindowID id, const wxString& title)
  Constructs a frame. Use NULL if the frame has no parent and –1 for a default ID.
- void wxFrame::**SetMenuBar**(wxMenuBar* menu_bar)
  Function: Sets the menu bar.

Class wxWindow

- void wxWindow::**Show**(bool b)
  Function: If b is true, shows the window. Otherwise, hides the window.
- wxSize wxWindow::**GetSize**() const
  Function: Gets the size of the window in pixels.
- void wxWindow::**Refresh**()
  Function: Causes the window to be repainted.
- void wxWindow::**SetAutoLayout**(bool b)
  Function: If b is true, the window is automatically laid out whenever it is resized.
- void wxWindow::**setSizer**(wxSizer* sizer)
  Function: Sets a sizer to lay out the controls in this window.
- bool wxWindow::**Destroy**()
  Function: Deletes this window and its children. Returns true if the window is destroyed immediately, false if the window will be destroyed later.

Note: • wxWindow is the common base class of wxFrame, wxPanel, and wxDialog.

Class wxTextCtrl

- wxTextCtrl::**wxTextCtrl**(wxWindow* parent, int id)
  Constructs a single-line text control with the given parent and ID. Use –1 for a default ID.
- wxTextCtrl::**wxTextCtrl**(wxWindow* parent, int id, const wxString& value, const wxPoint& pos, const wxSize& size, long style)
  Constructs a text control. Use –1 for a default ID, wxDefaultPosition and wxDefaultSize for default position and size, and a style of wxTE_MULTILINE to display multiple lines of text.
- void wxTextCtrl::**AppendText**(const wxString& text)
  Function: Appends text to this text control.

Class wxStaticText

- wxStaticText::**wxStaticText**(wxWindow* parent, int id, const wxString& text)

  Constructs a static text control. Use –1 for a default ID.

Class wxMenu

- wxMenu::**wxMenu**()

  Constructs an empty menu.

- void wxMenu::**Append**(int id, const wxString& item)

  Function: Appends a menu item with the given ID.

- void wxMenu::**Append**(int id, const wxString& name, wxMenu* sub_menu)

  Function: Appends a submenu with the given name. You can use –1 for the ID.

Class wxMenuBar

- wxMenuBar::**wxMenuBar**()

  Constructs an empty menu bar.

- void wxMenu::**Append**(wxMenu* menu, const wxString& name)

  Function: Appends a menu with the given name.

Class wxButton

- wxButton::**wxButton**(wxWindow* parent, int id, const wxString& name)

  Constructs a button.

Class wxBoxSizer

- wxBoxSizer::**wxBoxSizer**(int orientation)

  Constructs a box sizer that lays out components in one direction. orientation is wxHORIZONTAL or wxVERTICAL.

Class wxFlexGridSizer

- wxFlexGridSizer::**wxFlexGridSizer**(int columns)

  Constructs a sizer that arranges its children into rows and columns.

Class wxSizer

- void wxSizer::**Add**(wxWindow* window)

  Function: Adds the given window to this sizer.

- void wxSizer::**Add**(wxSizer* item, int option, int flag)

  Function: Adds a control or child sizer to a sizer. The option parameter is relevant for wxBoxSizer only; it is a weight that indicates the growth relative to the other item weights. The flag should be wxGROW, wxALIGN_CENTER, wxALIGN_LEFT, wxALIGN_TOP, wxALIGN_RIGHT, or wxALIGN_BOTTOM.

- void wxSizer::**Fit**(wxWindow* window)

  Function: Fits the window to match the sizer's minimum size.

Class wxPaintDC

- wxPaintDC::**wxPaintDC**(wxWindow* window)

  Constructs a paint device context for the given window.

Class wxDC

- void wxDC::**SetBrush**(const wxBrush& brush)
  Function: Sets the brush that is used for filling areas. Use *wxTRANSPARENT_BRUSH to turn off filling.
- void wxDC::**DrawLine**(int x1, int x2, int y1, int y2)
  Function: Draws a line from (x1, y1) to (x2, y2).
- void wxDC::**DrawEllipse**(int x, int y, int width, int height)
  Function: Draws an ellipse whose bounding box has top-left corner (x, y) and the given width and height.
- void wxDC::**DrawText**(int x, int y, const wxString& text)
  Function: Draws text whose top-left corner is at (x, y).

Class wxMouseEvent

- wxPoint wxMouseEvent::**GetPosition**() const
  Function: Gets the mouse position of this event.
- bool wxMouseEvent::**ButtonDown**()
  Function: Returns true if this is a button down event.
- bool wxMouseEvent::**ButtonUp**()
  Function: Returns true if this is a button up event.
- bool wxMouseEvent::**Moving**()
  Function: Returns true if this is a motion event (no button down).
- bool wxMouseEvent::**Dragging**()
  Function: Returns true if this is a drag event (moving with button down).

Class wxMessageDialog

- wxMessageDialog::**wxMessageDialog**(wxWindow* parent, const wxString& message)
  Constructs a dialog that displays a message.

Class wxTextEntryDialog

- wxTextEntryDialog::**wxTextEntryDialog**(wxWindow* parent, const wxString& prompt)
  Constructs a dialog that prompts the user to enter a text string.
- wxString wxTextEntryDialog::**GetValue**() const
  Function: Gets the value that the user supplied.

Class wxDialog

- wxDialog::**wxDialog**(wxWindow* parent, int id, const wxString& title)
  Constructs a dialog. Use –1 for a default ID.
- bool wxDialog::**ShowModal**()
  Function: Shows the dialog and waits until the user accepts or cancels it. Returns true if the user accepts the dialog.

Class wxString

- wxString::**wxString**(const char* s)
  Constructs a wxString from a character array.
- const char* wxString::**c_str**() const
  Function: Returns the character array contained in this wxString.

Class `wxSize`

- `int wxSize::`**`GetWidth`**`() const`
  Function: Gets the width of this size.
- `int wxSize::`**`GetHeight`**`() const`
  Function: Gets the height of this size.

Class `wxPoint`

- `int wxPoint::`**`x`**
  The public field containing the *x*-value.
- `int wxPoint::`**`y`**
  The public field containing the *y*-value.
- **`DECLARE_APP`**(*AppClass*)
  Macro: Place in header file of *AppClass*. The class must inherit from `wxApp`.
- **`IMPLEMENT_APP`**(*AppClass*)
  Macro: Place in source file of *AppClass*.
- **`DECLARE_EVENT_TABLE`**()
  Macro: Place in class that contains event handler functions.
- **`BEGIN_EVENT_TABLE`**(*Class*, *BaseClass*)
  Macro: Begins defining event handlers.
- **`END_EVENT_TABLE`**()
  Macro: Ends defining event handlers.
- **`EVT_MENU`**(id, *Class::function*)
  Macro: Declares a menu event handler. The function must have the form
  `void` *Class::function*(`wxCommandEvent& event`).
- **`EVT_BUTTON`**(id, *Class::function*)
  Macro: Declares a button event handler. The function must have the form
  `void` *Class::function*(`wxCommandEvent& event`).
- **`EVT_PAINT`**(*Class::function*)
  Macro: Declares a paint event handler. The function must have the form
  `void` *Class::function*(`wxPaintEvent& event`).
- **`EVT_MOUSE_EVENTS`**(*Class::function*)
  Macro: Declares a mouse event handler. The function must have the form
  `void` *Class::function*(`wxMouseEvent& event`).

MySQL Library

<mysql.h>

- MYSQL* **mysql_init**(MYSQL* conn)

  Function: Initializes a connection object. If conn is NULL, the object is allocated.

- MYSQL* **mysql_real_connect**(MYSQL* conn, const char host[], const char user[], const char passwd[], const char database[], unsigned int port, const char unix_socket[], unsigned long client_flag)

  Function: Connects to a database. To connect to a local server, the host, user, passwd, and unix_socket parameters can be NULL. The port and client_flag parameters can be 0.

- void **mysql_close**(MYSQL* conn)

  Function: Closes the connection and deallocates the connection object.

- int **mysql_query**(MYSQL* conn, const char query[])

  Function: Executes a query. Returns 0 on success.

- MYSQL_RES* **mysql_store_result**(MYSQL * conn)

  Function: Stores the result of the last query and returns a pointer to the result set.

- long **mysql_num_rows**(MYSQL_RES* result)

  Function: Returns the number of rows in the result set.

- int **mysql_num_fields**(MYSQL_RES* result)

  Function: Returns the number of fields in the result set.

- MYSQL_ROW **mysql_fetch_row**(MYSQL_RES* result)

  Function: Fetches the next row from the result set. Returns an array of C strings, or NULL at the end of the result set. Use the expression string(row[i]) to get the ith field as a C++ string.

- void **mysql_free_result**(MYSQL_RES* result)

  Function: Deallocates the memory for a result set.

Number Systems

Binary Numbers

Decimal notation represents numbers as powers of 10, for example

$$1729_{\text{decimal}} = 1 \times 10^3 + 7 \times 10^2 + 2 \times 10^1 + 9 \times 10^0$$

There is no particular reason for the choice of 10, except that several historical number systems were derived from people's counting with their fingers. Other number systems, using a base of 12, 20, or 60, have been used by various cultures throughout human history. However, computers use a number system with base 2 because it is far easier to build electronic components that work with two values, which can be represented by a current being either off or on, than it would be to represent 10 different values of electrical signals. A number written in base 2 is also called a *binary* number.

For example,

$$1101_{\text{binary}} = 1 \times 2^3 + 1 \times 2^2 + 0 \times 2^1 + 1 \times 2^0 = 8 + 4 + 1 = 13$$

For digits after the "decimal" point, use negative powers of 2.

$$1.101_{binary} = 1 \times 2^0 + 1 \times 2^{-1} + 0 \times 2^{-2} + 1 \times 2^{-3}$$

$$= 1 + \frac{1}{2} + \frac{1}{8}$$

$$= 1 + 0.5 + 0.125 = 1.625$$

In general, to convert a binary number into its decimal equivalent, simply evaluate the powers of 2 corresponding to digits with value 1, and add them up. Table 1 shows the first powers of 2.

Table 1 Powers of Two	
Power	Decimal Value
2^0	1
2^1	2
2^2	4
2^3	8
2^4	16
2^5	32
2^6	64
2^7	128
2^8	256
2^9	512
2^{10}	1,024
2^{11}	2,048
2^{12}	4,096
2^{13}	8,192
2^{14}	16,384
2^{15}	32,768
2^{16}	65,536

To convert a decimal integer into its binary equivalent, keep dividing the integer by 2, keeping track of the remainders. Stop when the number is 0. Then write the remainders as a binary number, starting with the *last* one. For example,

$$100 \div 2 = 50 \text{ remainder } 0$$
$$50 \div 2 = 25 \text{ remainder } 0$$
$$25 \div 2 = 12 \text{ remainder } 1$$
$$12 \div 2 = 6 \text{ remainder } 0$$
$$6 \div 2 = 3 \text{ remainder } 0$$
$$3 \div 2 = 1 \text{ remainder } 1$$
$$1 \div 2 = 0 \text{ remainder } 1$$

Therefore, $100_{\text{decimal}} = 1100100_{\text{binary}}$.

Conversely, to convert a fractional number less than 1 to its binary format, keep multiplying by 2. If the result is greater than 1, subtract 1. Stop when the number is 0. Then use the digits before the decimal points as the binary digits of the fractional part, starting with the *first* one. For example,

$$0.35 \cdot 2 = 0.7$$
$$0.7 \cdot 2 = 1.4$$
$$0.4 \cdot 2 = 0.8$$
$$0.8 \cdot 2 = 1.6$$
$$0.6 \cdot 2 = 1.2$$
$$0.2 \cdot 2 = 0.4$$

Here the pattern repeats. That is, the binary representation of 0.35 is 0.01 0110 0110 0110 . . .

To convert any floating-point number into binary, convert the whole part and the fractional part separately.

Long, Short, Signed, and Unsigned Integers

There are two important properties that characterize integer values in computers. These are the number of bits used in the representation, and whether the integers are considered to be signed or unsigned.

Most computers you are likely to encounter use a 32-bit integer. However, the C++ language does not require this, and there have been machines that used 16-, 20-, 36-, or even 64-bit integers. There are times when it is useful to have integers of different sizes. The C++ language provides two modifiers that are used to declare such integers. A short int (or simply a short) is an integer that, on most implementations, has fewer bits than an int. (The phrase "on most implementa-tions" is necessary because the language definition only requires that a short integer have no more bits than a standard integer.) On most platforms that use a 32-bit inte-ger, a short is 16 bits. At the other extreme are long integers. As you might expect, a long int (or simply a long) contains no fewer bits than a standard integer. At the present time most personal computers still use a 32-bit long, but processors that provide 64-bit longs have started to appear and will likely be more common in the future. A character (or char) is sometimes used as a very short (8-bit) integer. The C++ programmer therefore has the following hierarchy of integer sizes:

Type	Typical Size
char	8-bit
short	16-bit
int	32-bit
long	32- or 64-bit

The sizeof operator can be used to tell how many bits your compiler assigns to each type. This operator takes a type as argument and returns the number of bytes each type requires. Multiplying the number of bytes by 8 will tell you the number of bits:

```
cout << "Number of bytes for char " << sizeof(char)
    << " number of bits " << 8 * sizeof(char) << "\n";
cout << "Number of bytes for short " << sizeof(short)
    << " number of bits " << 8 * sizeof(short) << "\n";
cout << "Number of bytes for int " << sizeof(int)
    << " number of bits "   << 8 * sizeof(int) << "\n";
cout << "Number of bytes for long " << sizeof(long)
    << " number of bits " << 8 * sizeof(long) << "\n";
```

If the only numbers you needed were positive, then the preceding discussion would be everything you needed to know. However, in most applications it is more useful to allow both positive and negative values, and so a more complicated encoding is necessary. This characteristic of an integer is declared using the modifiers signed and unsigned.

An unsigned integer holds only positive values. An unsigned short int that is represented using 16 bits can maintain the values between 0 and 65,535 (that is, between zero and $2^{16}-1$). A 32-bit unsigned int can represent values between 0 and 4,294,967,295. If no modifier is provided, an integer is assumed to be signed.

Allowing both positive and negative values requires changing the representation of an integer value. The details of this representation are described in the next sec-tion. However, an important feature is that allowing both positive and negative numbers requires setting aside one bit (the so-called sign bit) to indicate whether the number is positive or negative. This reduces the largest value that can be represented. The following table shows the range of values that can be represented using signed and unsigned integers of 8, 16, 32, and 64 bits.

Integer Type	Range of Values
8-bit signed	−128 to 127
8-bit unsigned	0 to 255
16-bit signed	−32,768 to 32,767
16-bit unsigned	0 to 65,535
32-bit signed	−2,147,483,648 to 2,147,483,647
32-bit unsigned	0 to 4,294,967,295
64-bit signed	−9,223,372,036,854,775,808 to 9,223,372,036,854,775,807
64-bit unsigned	0 to 18,446,744,073,709,551,615

Two's Complement Integers

To represent negative integers, there are two common representations, called "signed magnitude" and "two's complement". Signed magnitude notation is simple: use the leftmost bit for the sign (0 = positive, 1 = negative). For example, when using 8-bit numbers,

$$-13 = 10001101_{\text{signed magnitude}}$$

However, building circuitry for adding numbers gets a bit more complicated when one has to take a sign bit into account. The two's complement representation solves this problem. To form the two's complement of a number,

- Flip all bits.
- Then add 1.

For example, to compute −13 as an 8-bit value, first flip all bits of 00001101 to get 11110010. Then add 1:

$$-13 = 11110011_{\text{two's complement}}$$

Now no special circuitry is required for adding two numbers. Just follow the normal rule for addition, with a carry to the next position if the sum of the digits and the prior carry is 2 or 3.

For example,

```
            1 1111 111
+13           0000 1101
-13           1111 0011
            1 0000 0000
```

But only the last 8 bits count, so +13 and –13 add up to 0, as they should.

In particular, –1 has two's complement representation 1111 . . . 1111, with all bits set.

The leftmost bit of a two's complement number is 0 if the number is positive or zero, 1 if it is negative.

Two's complement notation with a given number of bits can represent one more negative number than positive numbers. For example, the 8-bit two's complement numbers range from –128 to +127.

This phenomenon is an occasional cause for a programming error. For example, consider the following code:

```
short b = ...;
if (b < 0) b = -b;
```

This code does not guarantee that b is nonnegative afterwards. If short values are 16 bits and b happens to be –32,768, then computing its negative again yields –32,768. (Try it out—take 100 . . . 00 (15 zeros), flip all bits, and add 1.)

IEEE Floating-Point Numbers

The Institute for Electrical and Electronics Engineering (IEEE) defines standards for floating-point representations in the IEEE-754 standard. Figure 1 shows how single-precision (float) and double-precision (double) values are decomposed into

- A sign bit
- An exponent
- A mantissa

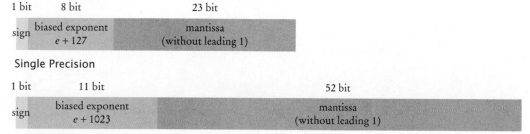

Single Precision

Double Precision

Figure 1 IEEE Floating-Point Representation

Floating-point numbers use scientific notation, in which a number is represented as

$$b_0.b_1 b_2 b_3 \ldots \times 2^e$$

In this representation, e is the exponent, and the digits $b_0.b_1 b_2 b_3 \ldots$ form the mantissa. The normalized representation is the one where $b_0 \neq 0$. For example,

$$100_{decimal} = 1100100_{binary} = 1.100100_{binary} \times 2^6$$

Because in the binary number system the first bit of a normalized representation must be 1, it is not actually stored in the mantissa. Therefore, you always need to add it on to represent the actual value. For example, the mantissa 1.100100 is stored as 100100.

The exponent part of the IEEE representation uses neither signed magnitude nor two's complement representation. Instead, a *bias* is added to the actual exponent. The bias is 127 for single-precision numbers and 1023 for double-precision numbers. For example, the exponent $e = 6$ would be stored as 133 in a single-precision number.

Thus,

$$100_{decimal} = \text{0 10000101 10010000000000000000000}_{\text{single-precision IEEE}}$$

In addition, there are several special values. Among them are:

- *Zero:* biased exponent = 0, mantissa = 0.
- *Infinity:* biased exponent = 11. . .1, mantissa = ±0.
- *NaN* (not a number): biased exponent = 11. . .1, mantissa ≠ ±0.

Hexadecimal Numbers

Because binary numbers can be hard to read for humans, programmers often use the hexadecimal number system, with base 16. The digits are denoted as 0, 1, ..., 9, A, B, C, D, E, F. (See Table 2.)

Four binary digits correspond to one hexadecimal digit. That makes it easy to convert between binary and hexadecimal values. For example,

$$11|1011|0001_{binary} = 3B1_{hexadecimal}$$

In C++, hexadecimal integers are denoted with a 0x prefix, such as 0x3B1.

Table 2	Hexadecimal Digits	
Hexadecimal	**Decimal**	**Binary**
0	0	0000
1	1	0001
2	2	0010
3	3	0011
4	4	0100
5	5	0101
6	6	0110
7	7	0111
8	8	1000
9	9	1001
A	10	1010
B	11	1011
C	12	1100
D	13	1101
E	14	1110
F	15	1111

Bit and Shift Operations

There are four bit operations in C++: the unary negation (~) and the binary *and* (&), *or* (|), and *exclusive or* (^), often called *xor*.

Tables 1 and Table 2 show the truth tables for the bit operations in C++. When a bit operation is applied to integer values, the operation is carried out on corresponding bits.

Table 1 The Unary Negation Operation

a	~a
0	1
1	0

Table 2 The Binary And, Or, and Xor Operations

a	b	a & b	a | b	a ^ b
0	0	0	0	0
0	1	0	1	1
1	0	0	1	1
1	1	1	1	0

For example, suppose you want to compute 46 & 13. First convert both values to binary. $46_{decimal} = 101110_{binary}$ (actually 00000000000000000000000000101110 as a 32-bit integer), and $13_{decimal} = 1101_{binary}$. Now combine corresponding bits:

```
  0.....0101110
& 0.....0001101
  ─────────────
  0.....0001100
```

The answer is $1100_{binary} = 12_{decimal}$.

You sometimes see the | operator being used to combine two bit patterns. For example, the symbolic constant BOLD is the value 1, and the symbolic constant ITALIC is 2. The binary *or* combination BOLD | ITALIC has both the bold and the italic bit set:

```
  0.....0000001
| 0.....0000010
  ─────────────
  0.....0000011
```

Don't confuse the & and | bit operators with the && and || operators. The latter should be thought of as operating only on bool values, not on bits of numbers. However, through the accident of history (C++ did not originally have Boolean values), these operators also work with integer values. To see the difference yourself, try assigning the value of 1 & 2 to an integer variable and printing the result. Then try the same with 1 && 2. Whether they are working with integers or Booleans, another important difference is that the && and || operators evaluate their result using lazy evaluation. This means that if the result can be determined using the left operand by itself, then the right operand is not even considered.

In addition to the operators that work on individual bits, there are shift operators that take the bit pattern of a number and shift it to the left or right by a given number of positions.

The left shift (<<) moves all bits to the left, filling in zeroes in the least significant bits (see Figure 1). Shifting to the left by n bits yields the same result as multiplication by 2^n. The expression

```
1 << n
```

yields a bit pattern in which the nth bit is set (where the 0 bit is the least significant bit).

To set the nth bit of a number, carry out the operation

```
x = x | 1 << n
```

To check whether the nth bit is set, execute the test

```
if ((x & 1 << n) != 0) . . .
```

Note that the parentheses around the & are required—the & operator has a lower precedence than the relational operators.

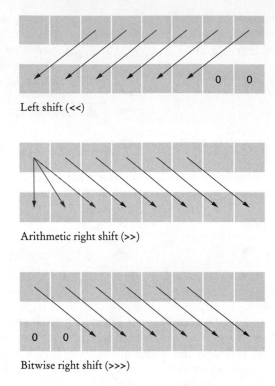

Left shift (<<)

Arithmetic right shift (>>)

Bitwise right shift (>>>)

Figure 1   The Shift Operations

The right shift (>>) moves bits to the right. An important question for right shifts is the bit value that is assigned to the high-order positions as the bits are shifted. For unsigned integers (see Appendix F) zero bits are used. Therefore, the result is the same as integer division by 2^n. For signed integers the language specification does not specify which bit values should be used. Many platforms will duplicate the sign bit, however this behavior is not guaranteed, and so right shifts using anything other than unsigned integers should not be used. Figure 1 shows both variations of the right shift operator.

UML Summary

In this book, we use a very restricted subset of the UML notation. This appendix lists the components of the subset. For a complete discussion of the UML notation, see [1].

CRC Cards

CRC cards are used to describe in an informal fashion the responsibilities and collaborators for a class. Figure 1 shows a typical CRC card.

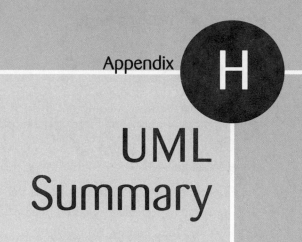

Figure 1   Typical CRC Card

Use Cases

Use cases describe how a computer system should work by describing a scenario from a typical application. Here is a sample use case for the voice mail system described in Chapter 23.

Leave a Message

1. The caller dials the main number of the voice mail system.
2. The voice mail system speaks a prompt.

   ```
   Enter mailbox number followed by #.
   ```
3. The user types in the extension number of the message recipient.
4. The voice mail system speaks.

   ```
   You have reached mailbox xxxx. Please leave a message now.
   ```
5. The caller speaks the message.
6. The caller hangs up.
7. The voice mail system places the recorded message in the recipient's mailbox.

Variation #1

1.1. In Step 3, the user enters an invalid extension number.
1.2. The voice mail system speaks.

   ```
   You have typed an invalid mailbox number.
   ```
1.3. Continue with Step 2.

Variation #2

2.1. After Step 4, the caller hangs up instead of speaking a message.
2.2. The voice mail system discards the empty message.

Figure 2 shows the UML notation for use case diagrams. Actors are drawn as stick figures, use cases as ellipses, and system boundaries as rectangles.

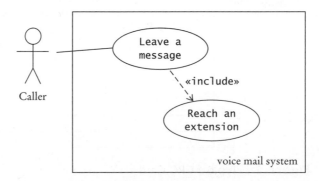

Figure 2   Use Case Diagram

UML Diagrams

Figure 3 shows the UML notation for class diagrams. Table 1 shows the arrows that indicate relationships between them.

Table 1 UML Symbols for Relationships Between Classes

Relationship	Symbol	Line Style	Arrow Tip
Dependency	- - - - - - - ->	Dotted	Open
Aggregation	◇—————	Solid	Open, Diamond
Inheritance	————▷	Solid	Closed
Composition	◆—————	Solid	Solid, Diamond
Association	—————	Solid	None
Directed Association	————→	Solid	Open

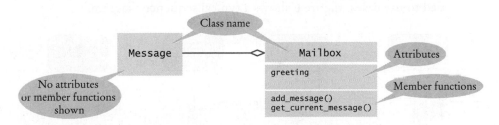

Figure 3 UML Symbols for Classes

Multiplicity can be indicated in a diagram, as in Figure 4, using the symbols described in Table 2. Dependencies between objects are described by a dependency diagram. Figure 5 is a typical example.

Table 2 Multiplicity

*	any number (zero or more)
1..*	one or more
0..1	zero or one
1	exactly one

Figure 4
Multiplicities of an Aggregation Relationship

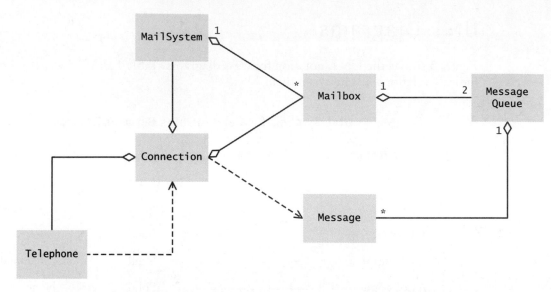

Figure 5   The UML Class Diagram for the Voice Mail System

Sequence diagrams describe the relationships among the classes as they interact at run time during the execution of the application. Sequence diagrams are frequently tied to use cases. Figure 6 shows a typical sequence diagram.

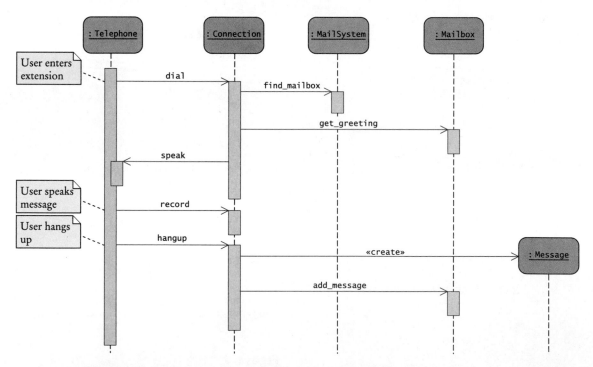

Figure 6   UML Sequence Diagram for Leaving a Message

State diagrams are used when an object goes through a discrete set of states that affects their behavior (see Figure 7).

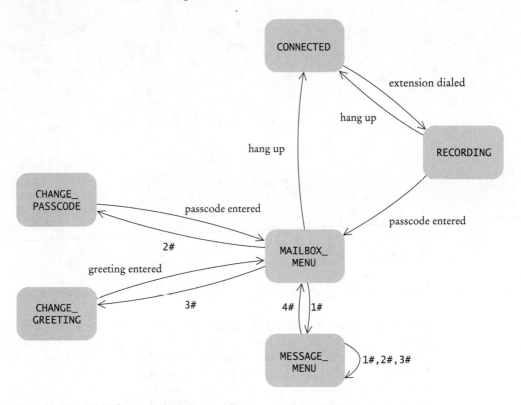

Figure 7 UML Sequence Diagram for Leaving a Message

FURTHER READING

1. Grady Booch, James Rumbaugh, and Ivar Jacobson, *The Unified Modeling Language User Guide*, Addison-Wesley, 2005, 1999.

A C++/Java Comparison

New Languages

Learning to move from one language to another is a fact of life for today's software professionals. Whether or not C++ is your first programming language, it will undoubtedly not be your last. It is not uncommon for a software professional to be fluent in at least a half dozen or more programming languages of various types. Categories of languages include general purpose languages (C++, Java, C#, Smalltalk), scripting languages (Perl, Python), Web-based languages (Javascript, PHP, Curl), functional languages (ML, Haskell), AI languages (Common Lisp, Prolog), and many others.

Java and C++ are currently the two most commonly used general purpose programming languages. For this reason many programmers find it useful to have at least a passing familiarity with both languages. Fortunately, Java was inspired by C++ and many features, such as the control flow statements if, while, and for, were adopted almost without change.

In this appendix we will describe the most basic differences between the two languages. Further information on the Java language can be found in [1]. Information on moving to C++ if Java is your first programming language can be found in [2].

Data Types and Variables

In C++ the number of bits used by an integer is implementation dependent. While many compilers use 32-bit integers, there are some machines that use 16-, 20-, 36-, or even 64-bit integers. In Java the language specifies that an integer must be exactly 32 bits.

The Boolean type is called `boolean` in Java, not `bool` as in C++.

The Java string type is called `String`. It is similar to the C++ `string` type, but note the following differences.

- Java strings cannot be modified (they are implicitly const, in C++ terms).

- Java strings store 16-bit Unicode characters, not 8-bit ASCII characters.

- You can concatenate strings with any type of object in Java, while in C++ strings can only be combined with strings.

- To compare strings in Java, use the member functions `equals` or `compareTo`. Both take an argument string. The function `equals` returns a Boolean, while `compareTo` returns an integer value that is less than zero if the first string is smaller than the second, zero if they are equal, and greater than zero if the first is larger than the second.

```
String p = "abc";
String q = "pqr";
if (p.compareTo(q) < 0) . . .
```

- Many member functions in the Java string class have functionality (substrings, indexing) similar to, but names different from their C++ counterparts.

Java does not have explicit pointer values or references, although internally pointers are used extensively (see the section on Objects, below).

Variables, Constants, and Functions

The Java compiler is obligated to check that local variables and data fields are initialized before they are used. This eliminates a common error in C++ programs.

It is not possible to create global variables or functions in Java that are not associated with a class. That is, the only functions in Java are member functions. Member functions in Java are often called *methods*.

Java does not have the const reserved word. An analogous reserved word, `final`, means that a value can not be reassigned. While not exactly the same (a `final` value can change its internal state, while a const in C++ cannot change in any way), the two are frequently used in the same fashion.

Classes

Although classes in C++ and Java are similar in intent, there are a number of superficial differences between them:

- In Java inheritance is signaled by the reserved word extends, rather than a colon.
- In Java the visibility modifiers public, protected, and private are attached to each data field and member function independently, rather than dividing the class definition into sections.
- All classes inherit from a base class in Java. If no explicit base class is specified, the class Object is used as a base class. Therefore, all classes ultimately inherit from a single base class named Object.
- The member function bodies are placed directly in the class definition, rather than being written separately.
- There is no semicolon at the end of a class.
- There is no virtual reserved word. All member functions are implicitly virtual (and thereby potentially subject to being overridden).
- There is no field initializer list. Data fields are initialized by an assignment statement in the body of a constructor. To pass data values to the constructor for a base class, the reserved word super is used.
- The reserved word super is also used to refer to a base class when a derived class wishes to invoke an overridden member function. This replaces the use of qualified names in C++ programs. The member function changeSalary in the example below illustrates this use.

The following is an example Java class definition:

```java
public class Manager extends Employee
{
    public Manager(String name, int salary, double bp)
    {
        super(name, salary); // Invoke constructor for Employee base class
        bonus_percent = bp;
        bonus = bp * salary;
    }

    void changeBonus(double new_bp)
    {
        bonus_percent = new_bp;
        bonus = bonus_percent * salary;
    }

    void changeSalary(int new_salary)
    {
        super.changeSalary(new_salary); // Invoke function from base class
        bonus = bonus_percent * new_salary;
    }

    private int bonus;
    private double bonus_percent;
}
```

Interfaces

Java supports a concept called an *interface*. An interface looks superficially like a class, but uses the reserved word `interface` rather than `class`. An interface cannot include variable data fields (although it can include constants—that is, data fields declared using the modifier `final`), and does not provide implementations for member functions. In C++ terms, it is as if each member function were a pure virtual. An interface is therefore a description of a set of desired behaviors, with no implementation. The following illustrates the syntax:

```
/**
    Interface for collections that can be searched.
*/
interface LookUp
{
    /**
        @param name the name being examined
        @return true if the name is part of the collection
    */
    public boolean contains(String name);

    /**
        @param name the name of the value desired
        @return object associated with a given name
    */
    public Object find(String name);
}
```

A class indicates that it supports the interface with the `implements` reserved word. It must then provide an implementation of each method defined by the interface.

```
class SearchableContainer implements LookUp
{
    . . .
    public boolean contains(String name)
    {
       Implementation here
    }
}
```

Java does not support multiple inheritance of classes. However, it does allow a class to implement multiple interfaces.

Objects

The most notable difference between Java and C++ is the treatment of objects. In Java object variables are treated internally as pointers. The Java literature refers to object variables as references, although they are not exactly the same as C++ references. (For example, Java object variables can be reassigned, whereas C++ references cannot. Java object variables can be null, but C++ references can never be

NULL.) This means that all Java objects must be created using the new reserved word, as in the following:

```
Employee sarah = new Employee("Sarah Smith", 67000);
```

Parentheses are required even if there are no arguments being passed to the constructor. Note carefully that the variable is declared as a simple name, not as a pointer. Java does not have the pointer/non-pointer distinction. Even arrays must be created using the new operator. The size is not included as part of the declaration, but instead as part of the new operation:

```
Employee[] department = new Employee[10]; // Create 10 new Employee values
```

The number of elements in an array can be determined using a data field named length, as in department.length. Assignment in Java is equivalent to the assignment of pointers in C++. That is, assignment establishes the two values as referring to the same object, instead of making a true copy as in C++:

```
Manager fred = new Manager("Fred Smith", 47000, 120);
Manager james = fred; // Now they refer to the same object.
james.changeBonus(200); // Now fred's bonus is also changed.
```

To make a true copy in Java you must explicitly define a member function that returns a clone.

Functions

In Java every function is associated with a class. There are no global variables, nor ordinary (that is, nonmember) functions. To execute a Java program you specify the starting class, and the function named main in that class is invoked. The function main does not return a value in Java.

Function invocations pass object references by value. There is no equivalent to the C++ pass by value or pass by reference. This is illustrated by the following:

```
class RewardSystem
{
    // Functions can only be found in classes
    public void yearEndUpdate(Manager man)
    {
        man.changeBonus(0.35); // Update bonus to 35%
        man = new Manager("Sally Jones", 47000, 23);
            // Unlike C++ pass by reference, will NOT change the value of the
            // actual argument.
    }
}

RewardSystem man_class = new RewardSystem();
Manager fred = new Manager("Fred Smith", 47000, 120);
man_class.yearEndUpdate(fred); // Will have the effect of changing
                               // the value fred.bonus
```

Arrays and Array Lists

All Java arrays are allocated on the heap:

```
String[] names = new String[100];
```

Note that the [] is placed with the type, not the variable name.

The analog to the C++ vector is the ArrayList. You use the get and set methods, not the [] operator, to access the elements:

```
ArrayList<String> names;
names.add("Harry"); // The analog of push_back
names.add("Lisa");
for (int i = 0; i < names.size(); i++)
{
    String name = names.get(i);
    names.set(i, "***");
}
```

Memory Management

In C++ the programmer is explicitly required to manage dynamic memory using the new and delete operators. Java includes a garbage collection system as part of its run-time library. The garbage collector monitors a running program and automatically recovers memory when it can no longer be used. This eliminates many memory leaks that can plague C++ programs.

Exception Handling

Exception handling is much more tightly integrated in Java than it is in C++. There are two categories of exceptions: *checked* exceptions (similar to runtime_error in C++), and *unchecked* exceptions (similar to logic_error in C++). Member functions that potentially can throw a checked exception must declare this using the throws reserved word. The compiler ensures that an invocation of such a function occurs in the context of a try/catch statement that will handle the exception. Values thrown must be objects from a class that is derived from a system class named Throwable. There are other small differences in the various forms the catch statement; these are described in [2].

```
public class Employee
{
    . . .
    void initializeFromFile(File f) throws IOException
    {
        . . .
        if (. . .)
            throw new IOException("Cannot Initialize");
    }
```

```
}

Employee fred = new Employee();
File fin = new File("fred.data");
try
{
    fred.initializeFromFile(fin);
}
catch (IOException e)
{
    System.out.println("Received I/O Exception " + e);
}
catch (Exception e) // Catch any other type of exception
{
    System.out.println("Received other exception " + e);
}
```

Standard Library

While the Java language is arguably smaller and simpler than C++, the same cannot be said for the standard library. The Java standard library is enormous, covering such features as internationalization, networking, mathematics, sound, Web applications and services, databases, and much more. Because the library is continually being added to, no reference can be entirely comprehensive. Most programmers are familiar with only a tiny fraction of this library. The most up-to-date information can be found at Sun's official Java Web site, http://java.sun.com.

FURTHER READING

1. Cay Horstmann, *Big Java*, 3rd ed., John Wiley & Sons, Inc., 2008.

2. Timothy Budd, *C++ for Java Programmers*, Addison-Wesley, 1999.

Glossary

Abstract class A class that cannot be instantiated, because it contains at least one pure virtual member function.

Abstraction The process of finding the essential feature set for a building block of a program such as a class.

Accessor function A function that accesses an object but does not change it.

Actual parameter The expression supplied by the caller for a formal parameter of a function.

Activation bars The bars in a sequence diagram that indicate when a function is called.

Activation record The section of memory set aside when a function in invoked and used to hold local variables, parameters, and the return address to the calling function.

Address A value that specifies the location of a variable in memory.

ADAPTER pattern A design pattern that allows you to use an existing class even when its interface doesn't match the one you need.

ADT (Abstract data type) A specification of the fundamental operations that characterize a data type, without supplying an implementation.

Aggregation relationship The "has-a" relationship between classes.

Algorithm An unambiguous, executable, and terminating specification to solve a problem.

Analysis phase The phase of a software project that concerns itself solely with an understanding of the problem domain and the problem to be solved, not with any design or implementation strategy.

ANSI/ISO C++ Standard The standard for the C++ language that was developed by the American National Standards Institute and the International Standards Organization.

Application framework A framework for building application programs.

Argument A parameter value in a function call, or one of the values combined by an operator.

Array A collection of values of the same type, each of which can be accessed by an integer index.

Arrow operator The -> operator. p->m is the same as (*p).m.

ASCII code The American Standard Code for Information Interchange, which associates code values between 0 and 127 to letters, digits, punctuation marks, and control characters.

Assertion A claim that a certain condition holds in a particular program location; often tested with the assert macro.

Assignment Placing a new value into a variable.

Association A relationship between classes in which one can navigate from objects of one class to objects of the other class, usually by following object references.

Attribute A named property that an object is responsible for maintaining.

Balanced tree A tree in which each subtree has the property that the number of descendants to the left is approximately the same as the number of descendants to the right.

Base class A class from which another class is derived.

Big-Oh notation The notation $g(n) = O(f(n))$, which denotes that the function g grows at a rate that is bounded by the growth rate of the function f with respect to n. For example, $10n^2 + 100n - 1000 = O(n^2)$.

"Big three" management functions The three management functions that are essential for classes that manage heap memory or other resources: copy constructor, destructor, and assignment operator.

Binary file A file in which values are stored in their binary representation and cannot be read as text.

Binary operator An operator that takes two arguments, for example, + in $x + y$.

Binary search A fast algorithm to find a value in a sorted array. It narrows the search down to half of the array in every step.

Binary search tree A binary tree in which each subtree has the property that all left descendants are smaller than the value stored in the root, and all right descendants are larger.

Binary tree A tree in which each node has at most two child nodes.

Bit Binary digit; the smallest unit of information, having two possible values, 0 and 1. A data element consisting of n bits has 2^n possible values.

Black-box testing Testing functions without knowing their implementation.

Block A group of statements bracketed by {}.

Boolean operator See **Logical operator**.

Boolean type A type with two values, true and false.

Boundary test case A test case involving values that are at the outer boundary of the set of legal values. For example, if a function is expected to work for all nonnegative integers, then 0 is a boundary test case.

Bounds error Trying to access an array element that is outside the legal range.

break **statement** A statement that terminates a loop or switch statement.

Breakpoint A point in a program, specified in a debugger, at which the debugger stops executing the program and lets the user inspect the program state.

Buffer A temporary storage location for holding values that have been produced (for example, characters typed by the user) and are waiting to be consumed (for example, read a line at a time).

Buffered input Input that is gathered in batches, for example, one line at a time.

Byte A number between 0 and 255 (eight bits). Essentially all currently manufactured computers use a byte as the smallest unit of storage in memory.

Call stack The set of all functions that currently have been called but not terminated, starting with the current function and ending with main.

Capacity The number of values that a data structure such as a vector or deque can potentially hold, in contrast to the size (the number of elements it currently holds).

Case-sensitive Distinguishing upper- and lowercase characters.

Cast Converting a value from one type to a different type. For example, the cast from a floating-point number x to an integer is expressed in C++ by the static cast notation, static_cast<int>(x). See also **Dynamic cast**.

Catch clause The part of a try block that is executed when a matching exception is thrown by any statement in the try block.

Child class A synonym for derived class. The term *derived class* is preferred in C++; the term *child class* is common in other object-oriented languages.

Class A programmer-defined data type.

Class diagram A diagram that depicts classes and their relationships.

Class template A specification describing how a class will be constructed once template parameters are provided.

Coercion A conversion from one type to another.

Cohesion The quality a class has if its features support a single abstraction.

Collaborator A class on which another class depends.

Command line The line you type when you start a program in a command window. It consists of the program name and the command line arguments.

Comment An explanation to make the human reader understand a section of a program; ignored by the compiler.

Compiler A program that translates code in a high-level language such as C++ to machine instructions.

Compile-time error See **Syntax error**.

Composite pattern A design pattern that teaches how to combine several objects into an object that has the same behavior as its parts.

Composition A stronger form of aggregation in which the contained objects do not have an existence independent of their container.

Compound statement A statement such as if or for that is made up of several parts (for example, condition, body).

Concatenation Placing one string after another.

Constant A value that cannot be changed by the program. In C++ constants are marked with the keyword const.

Construction Setting a newly allocated object to an initial value.

Constructor A function that initializes a newly allocated object.

Container A data structure, such as a list, that can hold a collection of objects and present them individually to a program.

Conversion operator A member function operator used to convert from one type to another.

Copy constructor A function that initializes an object as a copy of another.

Coupling The degree to which classes are related to each other by dependency.

CPU (Central Processing Unit) The part of a computer that executes the machine instructions.

CRC card An index card representing a class, listing its responsibilities and its collaborating classes.

Curry A function constructed from another function by binding one or more arguments to a constant. For example, changing the plus function by binding an argument to 2, creating a one-argument "add two" function.

Dangling pointer A pointer that does not point to a valid location.

Database A collection of data that is organized for efficient retrieval and update.

Database Management System (DBMS) A software system for the management of databases.

Database query A request for retrieving or updating database information.

Data field A variable that is present in every object of a class.

Debugger A program that lets a user run another program one or a few steps at a time, stop execution, and inspect the variables in order to analyze it for bugs.

Declaration A statement that announces the existence of a variable, function, or class but does not define it.

Default constructor A constructor that can be invoked with no parameters.

#define directive A directive that defines constant values and macros for the preprocessor. Values can be queried during the preprocessing phase with the #if and #ifndef directives. Macros are replaced by the preprocessor when they are encountered in the program file.

Definition A statement or series of statements that fully describes a variable, a function and its implementation, a type, or a class and its properties.

delete operator The operator that recycles memory to the heap.

Dependency The "uses" relationship between classes, in which one class needs services provided by another class.

Deque A sequential container that permits efficient insertion and removal of elements from either end. Contrast with **Stack** and **Queue**.

Dereferencing Locating an object when a pointer to the object is given.

Derived class A class that modifies a base class by adding data fields or member functions or by redefining member functions.

Design pattern A description of a design problem and a proven solution.

Design phase The phase of a software project that concerns itself with the discovery of the structural components of the software system to be built, not with implementation details.

Destructor A function that is executed whenever an object goes out of scope.

Directory A structure on a disk that can hold files or other directories; also called a folder.

Dot notation The notation *object.function(parameters)* used to invoke a member function on an object.

Doubly-linked list A linked list in which each node has a pointer to both its predecessor and successor nodes.

Downcast A cast of a polymorphic variable that converts from a base class type to a derived class type.

Dynamic binding Selecting a particular function to be called, depending on the exact type of the object invoking the function when the program executes.

Dynamic cast A cast operator that performs a downcast, checking that the run-time types are appropriate before completing the operation.

Dynamic memory allocation Allocating memory as a program runs as required by the program's needs.

Dynamic type The type associated with the value an object pointer currently references. Contrast to **Static type.**

Encapsulation The hiding of implementation details.

End of file Condition that is true when all characters of a file have been read. Note that there is no special "end-of-file character". When composing a file on the keyboard, you may need to type a special character to tell the operating system to end the file, but that character is not part of the file.

Enumerated type A type with a finite number of values, each of which has its own symbolic name.

Escape character A character in text that is not taken literally but has a special meaning when combined with the character or characters that follow it. The \ character is an escape character in C++ strings.

Exception A class that signals a condition that prevents the program from continuing normally. When such a condition occurs, an exception object is thrown.

Exception handler A sequence of statements that is given control when an exception of a particular type has been thrown and caught.

Executable file The file that contains a program's machine instructions.

Explicit parameter A parameter of a member function other than the object on which the function in invoked.

Expression A syntactical construct that is made up of constants, variables, and/or function calls, and the operators combining them.

Extension The last part of a file name, which specifies the file type. For example, the extension .cpp denotes a C++ file.

Failed stream state The state of a stream after an invalid operation has been attempted, such as reading a number when the next stream position yielded a nondigit, or reading after the end of file was reached.

Fibonacci numbers The sequence of numbers 1, 1, 2, 3, 5, 8, 13, . . ., in which every term is the sum of its two predecessors.

File A sequence of bytes that is stored on disk.

File pointer The position within a file of the next byte to be read or written. It can be moved so as to access any byte in the file.

Floating-point number A number with a fractional part.

Folder Directory.

Forward reference The introduction of a name for a class or a function before the complete definition has been given.

Foreign key A reference to a primary key in a linked list.

Formal parameter A variable in a function definition; it is initialized with an actual parameter value when the function is called.

Framework A collection of classes that provides mechanisms for a particular problem domain.

Function A sequence of statements that can be invoked multiple times, with different values for its parameters.

Function call operator An operator that is invoked using the same syntax as a function call. Defining this operator in a class produces a function object.

Function object An instance of a class that includes a definition for the function call operator. Such an object can be invoked using the same syntax as a function call.

Function signature The name of a function and the types of its parameters.

Functional specification A detailed specification of the externally observable behavior of a software system.

Function template A definition for a set of functions, formed using the `template` keyword.

Garbage collection Automatic reclamation of heap memory that is no longer needed; C++ does not have garbage collection.

Generator A function that potentially produces a different value each time it is invoked. Generally used to initialize each element in a collection, such as a vector or list.

Global variable A variable whose scope is not restricted to a single function.

`goto` **statement** A statement that transfers control to a different statement that is tagged with a label.

Grammar A set of rules that specifies which sequences of tokens are legal for a particular language.

grep The "global regular expression print" search program, useful for finding all strings matching a pattern in a set of files.

GUI (Graphical User Interface) A user interface in which the user supplies inputs through graphical components such as buttons, menus, and text fields.

Header file A file that informs the compiler of features that are available in another module or library.

Heap A reservoir of storage from which memory can be allocated when a program runs.

Heap Manager The part of the run-time system that responds to dynamic requests for heap memory.

Heterogeneous Having different types. A heterogeneous collection consists of elements that are not all the same type. Compare to **Homogeneous**.

Higher-order function A function that takes another function as argument, or that returns a function as a result.

Homogeneous Having the same type. A homogeneous collection consists of elements that all have the same type. Compare to **Heterogeneous**.

IDE (Integrated Development Environment) A programming environment that includes an editor, compiler, and debugger.

#if directive A directive to the preprocessor to include the code contained between the #if and the matching #endif if a condition is true.

Implementation phase The phase of software development that concerns itself with realizing the design in a programming environment.

Implicit parameter The object on which a member function is called. For example, in the call x.f(y), the object x is the implicit parameter of f.

#include directive An instruction to the preprocessor to include a header file.

Inheritance The "is-a" relationship between a general base class and a specialized derived class.

Initialization Setting a variable to a well-defined value when it is created.

Inserter An object that inserts a value into a container each time it is assigned. Inserters are used to change certain generic algorithms that assign elements so that they can be used to insert new elements into a container.

Instantiation of a class Constructing an object of that class.

Integer A number without a fractional part.

Integer division Taking the quotient of two integers and discarding the remainder. In C++, the / symbol denotes integer division if both arguments are integers. For example, 11 / 4 is 2, not 2.75.

Interface The set of functions that can be applied to objects of a given type.

Iterator An object that can inspect all elements in a container such as a linked list.

ITERATOR pattern A design pattern that teaches how to access the elements of an aggregate object.

Join A database query that involves multiple tables.

Late binding Choosing at run time among several member functions with the same name invoked on objects belonging to derived classes of the same base class.

Lexicographic ordering Ordering strings in the same order as in a dictionary, by skipping all matching characters and comparing the first nonmatching characters of both strings. For example, "orbit" comes before "orchid" in the lexicographic ordering. Note that in C++, unlike a dictionary, the ordering is case-sensitive: Z comes before a.

Library A set of precompiled functions that can be included in programs.

Lifeline The vertical line below an object in a sequence diagram that indicates the time during which the object is alive.

Lifetime The portion of execution during which a variable is potentially active.

Linear search Searching a container (such as an array, list, or vector) for an object by inspecting each element in turn.

Linked list A data structure that can hold an arbitrary number of objects, each of which is stored in a node object that contains a pointer to the next node.

Linker The program that combines object and library files into an executable file.

Liskov substitution principle The rule that states that you can use a derived-class object whenever a base-class object is expected.

Local variable A variable whose scope is a single block.

Logic error An error in a syntactically correct program that causes it to act differently from its specification.

Logical operator An operator that can be applied to Boolean values. C++ has three logical operators: &&, ||, and !.

Loop A sequence of instructions that is executed repeatedly.

Loop and a half A loop whose termination decision is neither at the beginning nor at the end.

Loop invariant A statement about the program state that is preserved when the statements in the loop are executed once.

Machine code Instructions that can be executed directly by the CPU.

Macro A mechanism to replace a command with a predefined sequence of other commands.

Magic number A number that appears in a program without explanation.

main **function** The function that is called first when a program executes.

make **file** A file that contains directives for how to build a program by compiling and linking the constituent files. When the make program is run, only those source files that are newer than their corresponding object files are rebuilt.

Map A data structure that keeps associations between key and value objects.

Member function A function that is defined by a class and operates on objects of that class.

Memberwise copy A copy of an object that is formed by recursively copying each data member.

Memory allocator An object used as a template parameter in a container class whose primary purpose is to allocate blocks of memory.

Memory leak Memory that is dynamically allocated but never returned to the heap manager. A succession of memory leaks can cause the heap manager to run out of memory.

Merge sort A sorting algorithm that first sorts two halves of an array and then merges the sorted subarrays together.

Method A synonym for member function. The term member function is preferred in C++, while the term method is common in other object-oriented languages.

Module A program unit that contains related classes and functions. C++ has no explicit support for modules. By convention, each module is stored in a separate source file.

Modulus operator The % operator that yields the remainder of an integer division.

Multiple inheritance Inheriting from two or more base classes.

Mutator function A member function that changes the state of an object.

Name clash Accidentally using the same name to denote two program features in a way that cannot be resolved by the compiler.

Name collision The process of creating a name clash.

Name spaces A way of organizing classes and functions so as to avoid name clashes.

Negative test case A test case that is expected to fail. For example, when testing a root-finding program, an attempt to compute the fourth root of 1 is a negative test case.

Nested block A block that is contained inside another block.

Nested class A class that is contained inside another class.

new operator The operator that allocates new memory from the heap.

Newline The '\n' character, which indicates the end of a line.

NULL pointer The value that indicates that a pointer does not point to any object.

Object A value of a user-defined type.

Object file A file that contains machine instructions from a module. Object files must be combined with library files by the linker to form an executable file.

Object-oriented design Designing a program by discovering objects, their properties, and their relationships.

Object-oriented programming A programming style in which tasks are solved by collaborating objects.

Off-by-one error A common programming error in which a value is one larger or smaller than it should be.

Opening a file Preparing a file for reading or writing.

Operating system The software that launches application programs and provides services (such as a file system) for those programs.

Operator A symbol denoting a mathematical or logical operation, such as + or &&.

Operator associativity The rule that governs in which order operators of the same precedence are executed. For example, in C++ the - operator is left-associative, since a - b - c is interpreted as (a - b) - c, and = is right-associative, since a = b = c is interpreted as a = (b = c).

Operator overloading Assigning a new function to an operator that will be selected if the operator has arguments of a specific type.

Operator precedence The rule that governs which operator is evaluated first. For example, in C++ the && operator has a higher precedence than the || operator. Hence a || b && c is interpreted as a || (b && c).

Oracle A program that predicts how another program should behave.

Overloading Giving more than one meaning to a function name or operator.

Overriding Redefining a function from a base class in a derived class.

Parallel vectors Vectors of the same length, in which corresponding elements are logically related.

Parameter A value in the execution of a function that is set when the function is called. For example, in the function double root(int n, float x), n and x are parameters.

Parameter passing Using expressions to initialize the parameter variables of a function when it is called.

Parameter value The expression supplied for a parameter by the caller of a function.

Parameter variable A variable in a function that is initialized with the parameter value when the function is called.

Parent class A synonym for base class. The term *base class* is preferred in C++, the term *parent class* is common in other object-oriented programming languages.

Pattern See **Design pattern**.

Pointer A value that denotes the memory location of an object.

Polymorphic variable An object pointer or reference that is declared as a base class type (the static type) but that can potentially hold values from derived classes (the dynamic type).

Polymorphism Selecting a function among several functions with the same name, by comparing the actual types of the parameters.

Popping a value Removing a value from the top of a stack.

Positive test case A test case that a function is expected to handle correctly.

Postfix operator A unary operator that is written behind its argument.

Precondition A condition that must be true when a function is called.

Predicate function A function that returns a Boolean value.

Prefix operator A unary operator that is written before its argument.

Preprocessor A program that processes a source file before the compiler. The preprocessor includes files, conditionally includes code sections, and performs macro replacement.

Primary key A column (or combination of columns) whose value uniquely specifies a table record.

Principle of least astonishment The principle that functions should be defined in a fashion that is consistent with prior use in order to avoid confusing the programmer.

Priority queue An abstract data type that enables efficient insertion of elements and efficient removal of the smallest element.

Private feature A feature that is accessible only by functions of the same class, its friends, and its nested classes.

Private inheritance Inheritance in which only the member functions can use the base-class functions.

Procedure A function that does not return a value.

Project A collection of source files and their dependencies.

Prompt A string that prompts the program user to provide input.

Prototype See **Declaration**.

Pseudocode A mixture of English and C++ that is used when developing the code for a program.

Pure virtual member function A member function with a name, parameter types, and a return type but without an implementation.

Pushing a value Adding a value to the top of a stack.

Query See **Database query**.

Queue A container that supports "first in, first out" retrieval.

RAM (random-access memory) The computer memory that stores code and data of running programs.

Random access The ability to access any value directly without having to read the values preceding it.

Recursive function A function that can call itself with simpler values. It must handle the simplest values without calling itself.

Redirection Linking input or output of a program to a file instead of the keyboard or display.

Reference counting A memory management technique that involves keeping track of the number of references (pointers) to a block of memory. When the reference count reaches zero, the memory can be recovered.

Reference parameter A parameter that is bound to a variable supplied in the call. Changes made to the parameter within the function affect the variable outside the function.

Referential transparency The principle that asserts that a function should produce the same result every time it is invoked with the same arguments. Functions that support this principle are said to be referentially transparent.

Regression testing Keeping old test cases and testing every revision of a program against them.

Regular expression An expression denoting a set of strings. A regular expression can consist of individual characters, sets of characters such as abc; ranges such as a-z; sets of all characters outside a range, such as 94 0-9; repetitions of other expressions, such as 0-9*; alternative choices such as +-; and concatenations of other expressions.

Relational database A data repository that stores information in tables and retrieves data as the result of queries that are formulated in terms of table relationships.

Reverse Polish notation A style of writing expressions in which the operators are written following the operands, such as 2 3 4 * + for 2 + 3 * 4.

Reserved word A word that has a special meaning in a programming language and therefore cannot be used as a name by the programmer.

Responsibility A high level task that a class is expected to carry out.

Return value The value returned by a function through a return statement.

Roundoff error An error introduced by the fact that the computer can store only a finite number of digits of a floating-point number.

Run-time error See **Logic error**.

Run-time stack The data structure that stores the local variables and return addresses of functions when a program runs.

Scope The part of a program in which a variable is defined.

Sequence diagram A diagram that depicts a sequence of function calls between objects in a program.

Selection sort A sorting algorithm in which the smallest element is repeatedly found and removed until no elements remain.

Sentinel A value in input that is not to be used as an actual input value but to signal the end of input.

Separate compilation Compiling each source file separately and combining the object files later into an executable program.

Sequential access Accessing values one after another without skipping over any of them.

Sequential containers Containers in which values are generally accessed one after another. The sequential containers in the STL are the vector, list, and deque.

Set An unordered collection that allows efficient addition, location, and removal of elements.

Shadowing Hiding a variable by defining another one with the same name in a nested block.

Shell A part of an operating system in which the user types commands to execute programs and manipulate files.

Shell script A file that contains commands for running programs and manipulating files. Typing the name of the shell script file on the command line causes those commands to be executed.

Side effect An effect of a function other than returning a value.

Simple statement A statement consisting of a single expression.

Single-stepping Executing a program in the debugger one statement at a time.

Size The number of elements a container currently holds. For the vector and deque classes this can be contrasted to the capacity, which is the number of elements it can potentially maintain.

Slicing an object Copying an object of a derived class into a variable of the base class, thereby losing the derived-class data.

Smart pointers Objects that are instances of a class that defines pointer operations as member functions.

Software life cycle All activities related to the creation and maintenance of the software from initial analysis until obsolescence.

Software reuse The reuse of software components across many different applications.

Source file A file containing instructions in a programming language.

Specialization The process of refining a general purpose software component by inheritance or the use of template arguments to make it applicable to a specific problem.

Stack A data structure in which elements can only be added and removed at one location, called the top of the stack. A stack supports "last in, first out" retrieval.

Statement A syntactical unit in a program. In C++ a statement is either a simple statement, a compound statement, or a block.

Static binding Selecting at compile time which function is to be called, based on the type of the object on which it is invoked.

static **keyword** A C++ keyword with several unrelated meanings: It denotes local variables that are not allocated on the stack; global variables or functions that are private to a module; class variables that are shared among all objects of a class; and member functions that do not have an implicit parameter.

Static type The type associated with the declaration of an object pointer. May differ from the type it holds (see **Dynamic type**).

STRATEGY pattern A design pattern that teaches how to supply variants of an algorithm.

Stepwise refinement Solving a problem by breaking it into smaller problems and then further decomposing those smaller problems.

Stream An abstraction for a sequence of bytes from which data can be read or to which data can be written.

String A sequence of characters.

Structured Query Language (SQL) A command language for interacting with a database.

Stub A function with no or minimal functionality.

Subclass A synonym for derived class. The term *derived class* is preferred in C++; the term *subclass* is common in other object-oriented programming languages.

Subscript operator The operator that mimics element access in an array. Typically used to provide access to individual elements in a container.

Substitution principle See **Liskov substitution principle**.

Superclass A synonym for base class. The term *base class* is preferred in C++; the term *superclass* is common in other object-oriented programming languages.

Syntax Rules that define how to form instructions in a particular programming language.

Syntax error An instruction that does not follow the programming language rules and is rejected by the compiler.

Tab character The '\t' character, which advances the next character on the line to the next one of a set of fixed screen positions known as tab stops.

Template A definition for a set of classes. For example, the vector template defines a class vector<T> (a vector of T objects) for any type T.

Template arguments Arguments used in the creation of a function template or a class template. Template arguments are usually types.

Template class A class formed by instantiating a class template by providing specific values for the template arguments.

Template function A function formed by instantiating a function template by providing specific values for the template arguments.

TEMPLATE METHOD pattern A design pattern that teaches how to supply an algorithm for multiple types, provided that the sequence of steps does not depend on the type.

Ternary operator An operator with three arguments. C++ has one ternary operator, a ? b : c.

Test coverage The instructions of a program that are executed when a set of test cases are run.

Test harness A program that calls a function that needs to be tested, supplying parameters and analyzing the function's return value.

Test suite A set of test cases for a program.

Text file A file in which values are stored in their text representation.

Throwing an exception Indicating an abnormal condition by terminating the normal control flow of a program and transferring control to a matching catch clause.

Trace message A message that is printed during a program run for debugging purposes.

Transaction A set of database operations that should either succeed in their entirety, or not happen at all.

Transformation The process of systematically changing each element in a container.

Turing machine A very simple model of computation that is used in theoretical computer science to explore the computability of problems.

Type parameters Parameters used with a template to create a specific instance from a set of classes.

UML (Unified Modeling Language) A notation for specify, visualizing, constructing, and documenting the artifacts of software systems.

Unary operator An operator with one argument.

Unicode A standard code that assigns values consisting of two bytes to characters used in scripts around the world.

Uninitialized variable A variable that has not been set to a particular value. It is filled with whatever "random" bytes happen to be present in the memory location that the variable occupies.

Unit test A test of a function by itself, isolated from the remainder of the program.

Upcast A cast that changes the type of a value from a derived type to a base type. Generally upcasts do not require any special notation. Contrast with downcast.

Use case A sequence of actions that yields a result that is of value to an actor.

Value parameter A function parameter whose value is copied into a parameter variable of a function. If a variable is passed as a value parameter, changes made to the parameter inside the function do not affect the original variable outside the program.

Variable A storage location that can hold different values.

Vector The standard C++ template for a dynamically-growing array.

Virtual base class A class whose fields are not replicated when they are repeatedly inherited.

Virtual function A function that can be redefined in a derived class. The actual function being called depends on the type of the object on which it is invoked at run time.

Visual programming Programming by arranging graphical elements on a form, setting program behavior by selecting properties for these elements, and writing only a small amount of "glue" code linking them.

void **keyword** A keyword indicating no type or an unknown type.

vtable An internal table constructed by the compiler in order to help determine which overridden member function to execute in an expression involving an object pointer.

vtable function A member function pointer stored in a vtable.

Walkthrough Simulating a program or a part of a program by hand to test for correct behavior.

Watch window A window in a debugger that shows the current values of selected variables.

Waterfall model A sequential model of the software development process, consisting of a sequence of analysis, design, implementation, testing, and deployment.

White-box testing Testing functions taking their implementation into account; for example, by selecting boundary test cases and ensuring that all branches of the code are covered by some test case.

White space A sequence consisting of space, tab, and/or newline characters.

Index

Page numbers followed by *t* indicate material in tables.